Children
of
Bondage

The Dutch mode of punishing the Hottentot Slaves, by flogging them till he has smoaked as many pipes of tobacco as he may judge the magnitude of the crime to deserve. Vide page

Pub.ᵈ by J. Lee May 1.ˢᵗ 1802.

CHILDREN

OF

BONDAGE

A *Social History of the*
Slave Society at the Cape of Good Hope,
1652–1838

ROBERT C.-H. SHELL

Wesleyan University Press
Published by University Press of New England
Hanover and London

UNIVERSITY PRESS OF NEW ENGLAND
publishes books under its own imprint and is the publisher for Brandeis
University Press, Brown University Press, University of Connecticut,
Dartmouth College, Middlebury College Press, University of New Hampshire,
University of Rhode Island, Tufts University, University of Vermont,
Wesleyan University Press, and Salzburg Seminar.

Wesleyan University Press
Published by University Press of New England,
Hanover, NH 03755

Published in the Republic of South Africa by Witwatersrand University Press,
1 Jan Smuts Avenue, Johannesburg, 2001, South Africa

Library of Congress Cataloging-in-Publication Data
Shell, Robert Carl-Heinz.
    Children of bondage : a social history of the slave society at the Cape of
Good Hope, 1652–1838 / Robert C.-H. Shell.
        p.   cm.
    Includes bibliographical references and index.
    ISBN 0-8195-5273-9
    1. Slavery — South Africa — Cape of Good Hope — History.   2.
Blacks — South Africa — Cape of Good Hope — History.   I. Title.
    HT1394.S6S48   1994
    305.5'67'09687 — dc20   94-2194
                                                             CIP

South African ISBN 1–86814–275–2

For my daughter, Elisabeth Rozalette Shell

The acquisition of a male slave is a life interest; that of a female is considered to be a perpetual heritage.
—W. W. Bird, *State of the Cape of Good Hope in 1822*

Contents

Conclusions   395

Slavery, the Authoritarian Cape Family and Recursive Identities

A Chronology of Slavery and Serfdom at the Cape   417

Abbreviations   419

Glossary   421

A Note on Terminology and Currency   423

Appendix 1: Archival Sources and a Note on the Data Sets   426

Appendix 2: The Records of the Slave Trade   427

FIGURES

Preface
On the Moral Question of Writing about Slavery

A SIGNIFICANT PROBLEM in writing about slavery lies in the anxiety and moral apprehension every historian of slavery feels toward the institution. This anxiety has imbued the study of slavery with a complex intellectual fever in which shame and guilt each play a large part. This is a painful process that will never end, and my own anxiety certainly affected the writing of this book.

I have learned that some people do not want to admit that slavery has been central to much human economic and social "development." Slavery is at the heart of many "civilizations," from the ancient African, American, Egyptian, European, Islamic, Judaic, Greek, Roman, and Sumerian civilizations to the present era. I have learned that some shy away from any reminders of a slave past while others embrace the guilt of slavery. While I have sought to put such moral anxiety in the background in the writing of this book, it nevertheless informs every sentence. The truth is, we are all the descendants of slavery. Because slavery is so universal, so shameful, so damaging, and also so recent, it remains perhaps the most suppressed and least understood part of our human heritage.

My own position on slavery should perhaps be considered especially idiosyncratic. My interpretations are fashioned, in part, by having lived in South Africa for the first twenty-five years of the apartheid era. As an undergraduate I was struck by the similarities between the system of apartheid and the slave societies of the past. This interpretation was denied by historians, including revisionists, but I am not sure that my early intuition was wrong after all. There are compelling legal and demographic similarities. Violence and coercion undergirded both systems. Cape slaves and twentieth-century black South African workers were both denied a broad and suspiciously similar range of basic human rights. They could not move freely. They could not own land. Under both apartheid and slavery, workers were carefully selected by age and sex and were brought in from outside the core area of the economy. Both groups were natally alienated, that is, their condition at birth limited their future rights, neither could have an independent family life.[1] The systematic natal alienation of black men and the informal incorporation of black women in the white domestic arena are profoundly similar in both societies. With both groups, their mother tongues were stilled. Their political identities were effectively, even ruthlessly, eliminated. Both slaves and modern workers in South Africa were, in Orlando Patterson's striking phrase, "socially dead." I determined to find out why the demographic and social structures of the two different economic systems were so similar. After all, slavery was abolished in South Africa in 1838, and mining and industrial "revolutions" followed closely on the heels of abolition. How could these demographic structures endure so stubbornly through such fundamental and "modernizing" transformations of the economy and society? I trust this work will answer some of these questions and possibly raise others.

Robert C.-H. Shell
Princeton, 1994

---

[1] However, the present day "African" population of South Africa is not the same group as the descendants of slaves, whom past governments termed the "coloured people." They enjoyed a higher status, and fewer, less-restrictive laws; indeed, some have their own "African" servants. The language of racial identity was designed to be demeaning and is avoided in this book except to discuss its evolution.

Acknowledgments

In a project conducted over a period of 15 years, one incurs obligations to both institutions and individuals. It is a pleasure to acknowledge these debts, even so belatedly. First, I would like to thank Yale University and the South African Research Project (SARP) for providing both a critical forum for drafts and an associate fellowship in 1991. The National Endowment for the Humanities also provided funding that enabled me to attend the Newbery Library Summer Institute for Quantitative Research. A Fulbright-Hayes Scholarship allowed me to travel to archives in Europe and Africa. The Social Science Research Council of Canada provided funds to do computer-aided cartographic work at Waterloo University in 1980. Thanks are also due to the Cape Tercentenary Foundation in South Africa for a grant that allowed me to travel to Yale in 1979. The University of Cape Town awarded me a Robert Kotze Scholarship which supported me for one year. The University of Rochester gave much financial assistance. Princeton University provided both generous leave and financial assistance. The Center for International Studies at Princeton provided a generous travel grant to do research in England and South Africa. I am indebted to the Peter B. Lewis Fund for a grant in 1989. The Office of the President at Princeton was generous, too. The South African Library staff always helped with my extensive research enquiries. Arlene Fanarof, the senior research librarian, has often changed the course of my enquiries through her diligent research and prompt and detailed responses to my (faxed) queries. This project owes much to her unflagging professionalism and enthusiasm. No historian, based so far away, could wish for more help. Lalou Melzer at the William Fehr Collection in Cape Town, the staff at the Africana Museum in Johannesburg, and the staff at the University of the Witwatersrand Gibbon Library provided illustrations. The Delft Topografische Dienst acceded to my unusual request for full-size negatives of E. V. Stade's 1710 large pen and wash drawings of the old Cape. The Rijksarchief proved to be a fine environment for research. The late Marius P. H. Roessingh proved to be an indispensable resource, and he is sorely missed. Robert Ross helped me find my feet in Leiden in 1981, and also provided data, stimulation, and commentary. The staff of the Cape Archives Depot also provided pictorial material and invaluable assistance in all areas of research; David McCellan was particularly helpful. The archivists of the Dutch Reformed Church, especially Dominee Strydom, gave me full support. They allowed me complete access to their invaluable seventeenth- and eighteenth-century baptismal registers. Moore Crossey at Yale was most helpful.

Many individuals helped me in numerous ways. Leonard Guelke, in particular, unstintingly shared his legendary Cape data. He also provided unflagging support for my work. My six-month research post in his department was a most rewarding period. Many persons devoted their time, skills, and energy to the compilation and computer coding of the thousands of cases and documents on which this study is based: Gillian Friedlander, Lesley Eddy, Susan Ladd, Neil Lazarus, Susan Schneier, Tessa Lever, Anthony Whyte and Mary Caroline Cravens. The late Robin Whiteford, my former headmaster, helped with translations of the difficult seventeenth- and eighteenth-century Latin. Christopher Saunders, my former adviser at the University of Cape Town, provided encouragement and a forum for my papers. He also provided much useful data on the "prize negroes." Kenneth Hughes provided lengthy and most valuable commentaries on initial drafts of most chapters; many ideas in this book derive from Ken. John Mason provided me with some unique population data on Cape slaves, and always camaraderie. James Armstrong generously shared primary material. Both he and Helen Armstrong devoted many hours to a careful annotation of an initial reading of the manuscript. His correspondence over the years has amounted to a bulging file. Many specialists provided extra resonance on topics with which I was unfamiliar. These scholars include Lyn Berat, Anna Böeseken, Margaret Cairns, David Brion Davis, Rodney Davenport, Leonard Dube, J. H. Elliot, Harvey Feinberg, Eugene D. Genovese, Anthony Grafton, Leon Hattingh, Hans Heese, Candy Malherbe, Shula Marks, Joseph C. Miller, E. S. Morgan, Robert Ross, Carmel Schrire, Stanley Trapido, and Michael Whisson. Students at Santa Barbara, Oswego, and Princeton worked hard on many of my primary documents and often changed the course of my interpretations. I am especially in debt to Mary Caroline Cravens, Eric Dobmeier, Patrick Furlong, Robert Garret, and Colin and Vaughn Masthoff. Anthony Whyte and Shāmil Jeppie challenged each point of my argument and thereby strengthened it. Both provided fresh references from their own research on the Cape. The manuscript would be immeasurably weaker without all their help.

Richard and Ester Elphick provided assistance in many more ways than I dare to dwell on; their inspiration and warm friendship extend back 16 years. David Brion Davis and Edmund Morgan provided encouragement, constructive criticism, and stimulation throughout the long incubation period and went far beyond the professional call of duty. Those who know the literature on slavery are aware of the enormous influence Stanley Engerman has had on the field. Stan has painstakingly read every chapter, some more than once. He has tirelessly corrected errors and interpretations and suggested new ways of looking at the data. He, more than anyone, has directed my reading in the field of comparative slavery. My enormous debt to his teaching and inspiration go back to my early days at the University of Rochester in 1976. Robert Tignor at Princeton has devoted many painstaking hours to making my arguments and style clearer. He often took time from a busy chairman's schedule, at short notice, to improve the basic text. Leonard Thompson's guidance, help, gentle criticism, patience, and inspiration were present throughout the creation of this book. I will always remain one of the most grateful students of this great scholar. Thanks to Pamela Long and Mary Caroline Cravens who suffered through my handwriting to retype parts of this manuscript. Julie Eriksen Hagen, Susan Hayes and Jeanette Hopkins had an enormous influence on the manuscript. Susan Shell, herself a historian, has my gratitude for many hours of careful editing and much constructive yet always gracious criticism. While I have been deeply influenced by my colleagues' criticism and commentary, any faults in the manuscript are mine alone.

Introduction

IN 1652 THE BEDRAGGLED CREWS of three Dutch East India Company ships splashed ashore in Table Bay to confront the area's original inhabitants, the Khoikhoi (the Dutch called them Hottentots). Although Europeans had visited the Cape earlier, 1652 was the year in which they took permanent possession of the Cape peninsula and, in doing so, closed one arc of a primordial population movement that had begun in Africa nearly one hundred millennia before. A few years later, when the Dutch imported slaves from the eastern side of the Indian Ocean, another population arc closed.[1] By 1660, all the major language groups of the world, African (Bantu and Khoisan), Indo-European, and Malayo-Polynesian were represented in the windswept peninsula near the southernmost tip of Africa. South Africans began their colonial era with one of the most polyglot populations in the world, a dramatic reunion of all the main branches of humankind. In the following 186 years a unique slave society evolved out of this diversity within a geographical cocoon of isolation and obscurity. By the time of full emancipation in 1838, a distinctive, complex, highly segmented and stratified society had emerged.[2] This book is directed toward building an understanding of the development of that society, from the level of the slave-owning household. This is history not only from the bottom up, but from the inside out. It is a history of the alienation of male slaves and serfs from birth, and also a history of the domestic incorporation of female slaves and free native women into the family and household. This book is the story of all the social, cultural, and biological progeny of that slave society, white, black, and mixed. Not only slaves were in bondage; in a profound sense, the owners were as well, hence the omnibus title, *Children of Bondage.*

---

[1] Many hundreds of slaves had been shipwrecked on the South African coastline in the century preceding 1652.

[2] The emancipation decree was passed in 1833, to be effective in 1838, after a four-year period of "apprenticeship."

The Family as Central Motif

The principal assumptions of this book are that frontier, class, and settler-autochthonous relations have been overemphasized in the formative centuries of South Africa. A more fruitful way to explore these early years of the South African colonial past is to look at the domestic household. It is there that a set of intimate and far-reaching relationships developed, and it is these relationships that most profoundly shaped South African colonial society. The frontier and class interests were vital forces in this period; I do not downplay them. However, they were secondary manifestations of more universal human drives. I do not intend to "naturalize" the historical process, but rather to historicize those drives. The propensity to create domestic hierarchies lies at the heart of this book. I do not attempt to answer why these hierarchies arose. I am interested in how they evolved.

Anthropologists have fruitfully studied the complex kin networks and chain reactions to which the incorporation of slaves into households in other (especially African) societies gave rise. Such slave societies, based on family incorporation, have been judged mild.[3] Few anthropologists have paid any attention to the same process within premodern European slave-holding societies. On the other hand, historians have critiqued the family-oriented paternalistic ethos of slave societies (especially American) — without, however, detailing whether paternalism was ever more than a figure of speech. There are thus two distinct traditions of looking at the family and slavery. One is anthropological, apologist, and concerns African societies; the other is historical, abolitionist, and concerns slave societies run by people of European descent. This book attempts to blend these two traditions.

The family was the source of all concepts and patterns of subordination in all metropolitan and colonial areas. David Brion Davis aptly captures the importance of the family as the most formative social institution in seventeenth- and eighteenth-century Europe: "the family, whether nuclear or extended, [was] the prime agent of socialization and the source for later concepts of authority, subordination, security, rebellion, and identity."[4] As Jonathan Glassman, an African historian, has observed: "The domination of the master over the slave was an historically evolved variant of the domination of a man over a woman, of a senior householder over his junior and female dependents, of a patron over his clients."[5] He might have added "of parents over their children." The metaphor of family

---

[3] Suzanne Miers and Igor Kopytoff (eds.), *Slavery in Africa: Historical and Anthropological Perspectives* (Madison: University of Wisconsin Press, 1977); see especially "The 'Slavery'-to-Kinship Continuum," pp. 22–24.

[4] David Brion Davis, *Slavery and Human Progress* (New York: Oxford University Press, 1984), p. 16.

[5] Jonathan Glassman, "The Bondsman's New Clothes: The Contradictory Consciousness of Slave Resistance on the Swahili Coast," *Journal of African History* 32 (1991): 286.

control was projected over all members of the Cape household. Consequently, all members of the household, free and unfree, male and female, young and old, native, creole (locally born), mulatto (creole of mixed descent), and imported, are the subjects of this study.

*P*atriarchal, Paternalistic, and Patrician Family Forms

At the Cape there were distinctions in family management between patriarchal, paternalistic, and patrician family forms. As Philip Morgan, a historian of the American South has stressed, the distinction between patriarchalism and paternalism is a fine one. Nevertheless, there are at least four differences between them. First, patriarchy is a more severe code than paternalism. Patriarchal slave owners stressed order, authority, unswerving obedience; they were quick to resort to violence when their authority was questioned. Paternalistic owners, on the other hand, while not against violence, were more inclined to stress their solicitude and their generous treatment of their dependents. Second, patriarchy was a less sentimental code. Paternalists expected gratitude, even love, from their slaves. Patriarchs never underestimated their slaves' capacity to rebel or to run away. Consequently, patriarchal punishments were vicious, sometimes involving the death of the slave or dependent serf. Human life was cheap to the patriarchal owner, while the paternalist owners created the fictional ideal of the humble, contented, and docile slave.[6] Third, and perhaps most important, patriarchal society was more chauvinistic, more starkly based on sexual difference. Women and children in slave owning families were on almost the same low level as the slaves and servants. The social distance between men and women was far greater in patriarchal families than in paternalistic families. In paternalistic families control was also centered on the father, but the mother could more easily assume some spousal authority. Fourth, the patriarchal family was more respectful of age as constituting authority; after gender, age was the classic criterion for power in a patriarchy. In the paternalist family, these coordinates of authority were not so crisp.

The third family form — the patricians — introduced chattel slavery to South Africa, and the patricians managed the slave trade until 1795. Hermanus Hoetink, a historian of the Dutch Caribbean, titled his fine book on the Dutch slave society of Curaçao *Het Patroon*. The closest (and by no means entirely satisfactory) English translation of *patroon* is patrician. The implied parallel with the Roman patricians is deliberate. "Patrician" connotes dynastic family behavior. The word implies aloofness, coupled with ruthlessness. In Africa, the patrician

---

6 Philip Morgan, "Three Planters and Their Slaves . . . ," in Winthrop Jordan and Sheila L. Skemp (eds.), *Race and Family in the Colonial South* (Jackson: University Press of Mississippi, 1987), pp. 39–40.

"golden age" was symbolized by the Van der Stel dynasty, the families that ruled the Cape from 1680 until 1706, in a consecutive father-and-son governorship that ended in ignominy for the family and expulsion from the colony for the son.

Up until the burgher rebellion of 1706, the patricians had the largest slave holdings. They established the first slave plantations of more than two hundred slaves. Although weakened by the settler revolt of 1706, the patricians remained in control of the slave trade for the whole colony from 1652 to 1795. After the demise of the Dutch East India Company in 1795, the power of the patricians was reduced to commercial activities in the port.

The patricians' main functions were administering the colony, overseeing the Company's large holding of slaves, known as the Lodge, and managing the oceanic slave trade — activities that were by no means dissimilar. Initially the patricians were drawn solely from the upper echelons of local officials. They also came to incorporate, by intermarriage, some of the richest urban Cape Town burghers, the settler families. Through such intergenerational dynastic alliances, many patricians came to own, in addition to town properties, multiple rural estates. Since plantation owning was illegal for Company employees after 1706, the acquisition of a plantation by marriage was followed by retirement from the Company service. This continued until 1795 when the patricians were virtually displaced by the new British administration and new British officials, and some English freebooters who took over the slave trade. For the purpose of this book, the word *patrician* describes all wealthy urban slave owners at the Cape.

The year 1795 was a critical moment in the political economy of South Africa. Patrician slave-trading families who had run the colony surrendered their political power to the British imperial state and simultaneously surrendered part of their monopoly of the slave trade to private enterprise. The purely mercantilist and prebendal slave-owning dynasties were at an end at the Cape.

Of course, no such taxonomy of families can be perfect. The coordinates of authority within a single family might change both suddenly and dramatically. Widowhood, for example, could transform a patriarchal family into a paternalistic family. A wealthy, urban, footloose son of a patrician could became a patriarchal farmer in the far interior. I have not attempted to delineate these family types in quantitative terms, since there was considerable overlap. Yet some rough patterns in geographical distribution and over time do emerge. Patriarchs were found in the ranching areas. Paternalists lived in the arable areas, but mostly they were found in the port environment of Cape Town and to a much lesser extent in the urban milieus of nearby Stellenbosch and later Graaff Reinet. Patricians were always found in the port, were always wealthy, and all had connections to the Company. Thus, the types of families varied according to place.

The families also varied in terms of time. Early arrivals on the frontier tended to become patriarchal. The hard tasks of clearing land, running cattle, and eking out an existence on slender resources took their toll on all family forms among new frontier arrivals. Survivors passed on their skills and family expectations to the next generation. The abolition of the slave trade ushered in a new era of paternalism, as slave owners realized that the slaves they owned in 1807 were going to be the only stock for the future. Even the sternest patriarch had to become more solicitous under the new regime.

The spice in much of our current culture derives from comparing the banality of a particular family form with a cherished, or approved, family form. We are intrigued by a movie of an "organized crime" family, for example, not because family values have been perverted, but because so many have been preserved amidst the mayhem. In the same way, we are comforted by a Jane Austen novel about improving family manners and sensibilities. Persistent sentimentality prompts us to view the family per se as benign, but what should be stressed above all is that the family must be uncoupled from associations with benevolence. The family institution is quite neutral in value. In fact, channels of familial authority may too easily go awry. I believe this occurs on a societal level when slaves are introduced into the household. Immanuel Kant put it well: "Paternalism is the cruelest tyranny of all."

Some have argued that by concentrating on the family I am denying the use of violence on slaves, but violence was primarily part of family governance. I am therefore not denying the use of violence on slaves in the paternalist — let alone patriarchal — families in the Cape. Members of all the Cape families were beaten at some time in their lives, although domestic violence, too, had pronounced regional and chronological aspects. Generally, the further from the port the family was, the more violence there was. The paternalistic-patriarchal spectrum stretched from the town to the country. In an expanding frontier-bound population, violence became more pronounced and, over time, easier to justify.

The family mode of control achieved a managerial efficiency, but at great cost to the humanity of all its members. The slave-owning family cynically promised incorporation, but nearly always reneged. This intimate offer of incorporation gradually perverted the settlers' family values just as profoundly as it cheated the slaves. The process resulted in a new creole system of domestic family values. As these values became increasingly hypocritical, the families became increasingly authoritarian.

Only by looking inside the household can one obtain a picture of the evolving authoritarian and hierarchical nature of the society. In the public sphere many of those hierarchies disappear, because they have been written out of traditional histories by traditional historians intent on inventing a *herrenvolk* democracy, a golden age of equality for all of European descent. For the Cape slave society, because of the especially small individual family distributions of slaves, the slave-holding family became a natural theater for paternalism and patriarchies. One must therefore shift from looking at intergroup or interclass relations to examining interpersonal relations in the household.

Historicizing Slavery

Many studies of slave societies still present a static picture of the institution. While scholars such as Eugene Genovese have produced accurate delineations of the fully fledged paternalistic planter society of the nineteenth-century American South, the picture is static.[7] The historical evolution of the slave-holding family over three centuries remains a mystery. Willie Lee Rose, a commentator of the antebellum South, noted in an unpublished fragment: "Almost never has the institution of slavery been treated as an evolving institution, very different in the seventeenth century from what it became in the eighteenth, and eventually in the nineteenth. In fact most studies of slavery are static in their conception. . . . Somehow the idea of the passage of time and the sense of change must be interjected into this history if it is to become meaningful history, as opposed to sociology."[8] It is still rare to find a historical analysis of change within a slave society, although the literature is full of studies considering the introduction or termination of the institution. For these reasons, slavery remains, as Herbert Gutman first pointed out in a judgment shared by two historians of African slavery, Frederick Cooper and Joseph Miller, "frozen in time."[9]

Such considerations led me to attempt a comprehensive overview of the changes Cape slavery underwent from 1652 to the general emancipation in 1838, a time frame that allows for a coherent historical overview of the development of the slave society from its inception to the day of emancipation. The beginning date needs a slight justification. Abraham van Batavia, the first imported slave, arrived at the Cape in 1653. There seems little point in dating the history of the slave society from that year, however, since the Dutch East India Company had supported slave societies in their possessions in the East from at least 1609. When the Dutch landed at the Cape, they introduced a legal system partly based on slave holding. Thus 1652, the date of initial occupation, seems appropriate for the date when slavery began there, for from the outset of Dutch occupation the Cape was a slave society. Within a month of his arrival the commander, Jan van Riebeeck was pleading with the directors to be allowed to import slaves, and he also requested permission to export the native Khoi as slaves to the East.

The long time frame also allows one to trace changes through the cessation of the oceanic slave trade in 1808 (the legislation was passed in 1807 but only became effective in 1808). The character of all slave societies in the British sphere of

---

[7] Eugene D. Genovese, *Roll, Jordan, Roll: The World the Slaves Made* (New York: Vintage Books, 1976), pp. 3–7.

[8] As quoted in William W. Freehling (ed.), Willie Lee Rose, *Slavery and Freedom* (New York: Oxford University Press, 1982), pp. viii–ix.

[9] Frederick Cooper, "The Problem of Slavery in African Societies," *Journal of African History* 20, 1 (1979): 110. Private communication with Joseph Miller, 1989.

influence changed because of this watershed legislation, and the Cape was no exception. Slavery changed and in changing reshaped the whole society. Slavery at the Cape was not what the neoabolitionists termed a "peculiar institution" but was a dynamic, ever-changing aspect of the South African society.

The Cape Slave Populations

The Lodge

In the beginning of the colony, the Dutch East India Company purchased slaves for its own purposes — building massive fortifications for the strategic harbor town. By 1770, the Company's slave force in the Lodge had grown to 1,000, most of whom worked in Cape Town. Slavery in South Africa thus began in an urban context. The Lodge slaves were nearly all (90 percent) urban. There are no clearly analogous comparative models for these Lodge slaves. Lodge slaves never held high administrative offices, as the slaves of the *Familiae Caesaris* did (the slaves belonging to the Roman Emperor and probably the origin of the Lodge concept), nor were they an undifferentiated mass of "outsiders" like the slaves on large plantations in the Caribbean or the antebellum American South. Local patrician Company officials monitored every detail of their lives. They were protected in some measure by the Dutch East India Company commissioners' visits and also by periodic inspections of the Lodge.

Lodge slaves were supposed to represent to the free population the "model" treatment of slaves. Cape slave statutes affected the Lodge slaves first, and most documentation on Cape slavery in the first hundred years concerns the Lodge. Because of this documentary artifact, historians who wrote about Cape slavery were really writing about the Lodge slaves only, yet those slaves were atypical. The predominance of primary sources on the Lodge might have helped create the myth of the "mildness" of Cape slavery. All Lodge slaves born in that "household" of the Company, for example, were baptized, and those few who survived to their twenty-fifth year were routinely manumitted. They were well fed and clothed for every season. Regulations stipulated certain safeguards for both their physical and their spiritual well-being, and there was a school for those slaves born in the Lodge.

The Lodge survived until 1828, when all the Lodge slaves were manumitted en bloc. Even then, their emancipation was an example the government set to prepare all Cape slave owners for universal emancipation, which was, indeed, around the corner.

Patricians' Slaves

The second slave population belonged to the locally based Dutch East India Company officials, the same people who had oversight of the Lodge. Their personal slaves have never been discussed in the literature of Cape slavery. This is because ownership of large numbers of slaves by officials was not allowed by the Company. Consequently local officials, who were responsible for the Cape records, never mentioned their own slaves in documents forwarded to Holland. Such slaves, for example, were not included in the burgher censuses, from which historians have made their estimates of the Cape slave population. I have termed this group the patricians' slaves.

Burghers' Slaves

The third group of slaves represented the overwhelming majority. These slaves belonged to the burghers — free, settled, and semi-nomadic patriarchal farmers, who came to have a quite distinctive household structure and pattern of behavior. By the sheer weight of their numbers, their horses and guns, the burghers first dispossessed, then enserfed and absorbed the Khoikhoi people into their households. South Africa was one of a handful of societies to develop parallel and discrete systems of slavery and serfdom.[10] These systems fused into what I have termed cadastral slavery, in which rights to a person's labor were informally passed along when land changed hands. Far from being unique, South Africa represents a perfect model for colonial slavery and colonial serfdom.

The power of the burghers grew slowly, since the patrician officials jealously guarded their own mercantile privileges and political power. The burghers made some headway in 1706, when they succeeded in having one entire patrician administration recalled. Although they won that struggle, the burghers continued to have little political voice for almost 90 years — for instance, they did not win the right to trade on their own behalf for slaves until 1792. Their latent political power was finally inadvertently unleashed by the first British administration, which abolished all mercantilist restrictions and provided a greatly enlarged garrison presence that stimulated all burgher sectors of the Cape economy. The burghers' "golden age" was from 1791 until 1808, when they suffered their first real challenge when the British put an end to the oceanic slave trade. The bulk of the slave population at the Cape was owned by burghers for the longest period of time.

The Free Blacks' Slaves

A fourth and very minor group of slaves was owned by the free blacks. The free blacks were a subgroup of the burghers; both were included in the annual census. But the blacks originated from the slave population, from a handful of political exiles, and from several hundred Chinese convicts. Their exact legal status is disputed by historians. What one can say is that they were the most urbanized and

---

[10] The distinctions between the two systems will be delineated in chapter 1.

also the poorest group of all the slave owners.[11] Consequently, their family structure and slave-owning behavior were substantially different from the other groups.

Definitions

Central to any study of slavery is a definition of slaves and what constitutes a slave society. A definition of slavery must allow for historical change. Slavery in South Africa may be defined as the system in which a person was freely disposed of to another free person in a legally sanctioned sale, rite, transfer, or will, or hired out for work, without any consultation of, but not necessarily without compensation to, the enslaved person. Slaves at the Cape did have rights: slaves could inherit, bear witness, earn money, and initiate legal cases. But they were denied important family-centered rights, a deprivation of rights peculiar to South Africa. Until 1823, female slaves could not marry in established Christian churches (mission marriages were challenged), and Cape slave women never could have free offspring (unless those children were bought to be freed). Male slaves also could not marry in the Christian church until 1823, but they could and did have free offspring from free females. Offspring of free men and slave women remained slaves. Offspring of slave men and free women were free but termed "bastards," that is persons without a religious or civic identity. Many bastards were enserfed. Unable to marry in the Christian church for many generations, many slaves were married in Muslim rites, although Islam was not recognized by the Cape authorities. People who identified themselves as Muslims had no colonial civic status. South African law still does not recognize the Muslim marital rite.

There have been many different types of slave societies. Since the metaphors of slavery are part of everyday speech, the concept of slavery has broadened to encompass many meanings. Some have defined a slave society as one in which the main products of the society are produced by slave labor. In the United States, popular familiarity with the slave system of the antebellum South has comfortably defined for most Americans what slavery was. Slaves in America were all from Africa, they were all "black." American slaves had few if any legal rights; they could be freely sold and punished by the owner. Considered in a global, comparative context, however, American slavery was atypical in several respects. One compelling difference was that both male and female slaves imported into America were, with some regional variations, put to work in the fields.[12] In America little gender deference was shown to African women. Indentured female European servants on the other hand, imported at the same time, rarely worked in the fields. In South Africa, in contrast, all women — free and slave — were kept in the household until near the end of slavery.

---

[11] They are currently the subject of a dissertation by Anthony Whyte at Princeton University.
[12] I am grateful to Kathleen Brown and E. S. Morgan for this point.

After the abolition of the oceanic slave trade in 1808, American slaves were among the few bonded populations that reproduced themselves. They also encountered very high barriers to manumission. American slavery gave rise to what anthropologists have termed "hyperdescent," meaning that any African descent whatsoever meant a person was unambiguously "black." This has proved to be a persistent and idiosyncratic American legacy. Also, freed slaves had particular difficulty assimilating into the dominant sectors of the population. Another profound difference in American slavery was that the United States, after the devastating Civil War, abolished slavery on its own. This achievement is a solitary one in the chronicle of slave societies. The Civil War defined America. Elsewhere slavery was abolished without force, but only with help or prodding from external powers. Slavery in the Cape resembled Caribbean and South American slave history mainly in their respective emancipation processes. All slaves in those areas were freed from outside the host regions. Emancipation was forced.

The Hierarchical Structure of the Slave Populations

Race and Slavery

North American slavery, like Caribbean and South American slavery, was biracial. South African slavery was really quite different. Studies of other slave societies from antiquity to modern times have shown that slavery was not always biracial as it was in the United States and elsewhere in the Americas. Autochthonous African slavery, for example, was not racially based. Slaves at the Cape, in clear contrast to those of the American South or of the rest of the African continent, were not all African. A large proportion of Cape slaves in the first century of occupation came from the entire perimeter of the Indian Ocean basin, one of the oldest slave trading areas in the world, dating back to 1580 B.C.[13] Enslaved persons imported to the Cape came from ancient slave societies. The slave society at the Cape was multi-racial, by which I mean that many "races" were represented among both slaves and owners. Moreover, many creole mulatto Cape slaves (slaves born at the Cape, of partial European descent) were indistinguishable in appearance from their owners. European visitors to Cape Town were invariably shocked to see some green- and blue-eyed slaves around the port.

In South Africa, that slaves were drawn from outside the regions of the slave society, or had some somatic features that distinguished them from the owner class made the management of the colony's slaves more efficient. It made apprehension of runaways easier. Such differentiation also made slavery psychologically easier for slave owners to justify. However, the identity of the owners in South Africa was

---

[13] Orlando Patterson, *Slavery and Social Death: A Comparative Study* (Cambridge, Mass.: Harvard University Press, 1982), p. 150.

only partly construed from racial or ethnic differentiations. Religion was also used to create identities. Pagan, Christian, and Muslim identities predominated in colonial South Africa.

In nonracial slave societies, where there was little difference between owner and slave, often owners created a distinguishing appearance by disfiguring the slaves through branding. Roman hortators, for example, branded "GAL" on the shoulders of galley slaves. Owners in other societies cropped the hair of their slaves; some clipped the slaves' ears. The Dammarra of southern Africa pulled the incisor teeth and circumcised male slaves.[14] In South Africa religion, clothing, geographic origin, and civic identities also were used to create a sense of difference. By the nineteenth century, race was decisively folded into the social order when the word *colored* was applied by self-styled whites to the descendants of slaves.

The importation of many groups of slaves from many different societies, coupled with the process of creolization and intermixture, made Cape slavery based solely on the biracial system or physical disfigurement increasingly impossible to justify. The Cape owners stopped short of branding their slaves, although Dutch owners in the Dutch Antilles did brand theirs. At the Cape, differentiation was accomplished through a wide variety of coordinates of age, gender, wardrobe, ethnicity, and geographic origin. All of these had their source in the household.

From the Cape slave owners' viewpoint, slavery seemed to work most efficiently when there *was* some physical difference between owner and slave. This was a factor of profound anthropological and psychological significance when considering the legacy of the Cape slave society.[15] Race was not a constant part of Cape slavery, or of many other slave systems, but race did become a convenience for Cape slave owners. Race played a large but *changing* role in that slave society, in a variety of ways. One must speak of race in the seventeenth, eighteenth and early nineteenth centuries in ways different from its late twentieth-century meaning.

When discussing the interconnections of slavery and race, one should also remember the effect of race on slavery. The classical historian William Westerman pointed out that once slavery became associated with a single race, the institution itself was doomed. Slavery, which had never been a serious moral issue in the multiracial slave societies of antiquity, became one once the institution became biracial in modern times. This new development prompted intellectuals to ask why people of only one "race" were enslaved. This new injustice within slavery was the principal point of a dissertation written by Jacobus Elisa Joannes Capiteijn, a West African ex-slave at Leiden University in 1742, who was persuaded that

---

[14] Robert C.-H. Shell, "Reader's Comment," in *Quarterly Bulletin of the South African Library* 43, 2 (December 1988): pp. 91–92.

[15] Hermanus Hoetink, *Slavery and Race Relations in the Americas* (New York: Harper Torchbooks, 1973), pp. 192 ff.

slavery and Christianity were not incompatible, but thought that slavery — if it were to be "fair" — should encompass Europeans as well.[16] The important distinction between biracial and multiracial slavery seems to offer the best explanation for why antislavery movements did not develop earlier in the Netherlands, which presided over the most extremely diverse colonial slave populations.[17] Similarly, one possible reason that South Africa never developed a convincing local abolitionist movement was that no single race was systematically enslaved. When considering the unimpressive abolition movement within the colony, it seems that the Enlightenment passed South Africa by.

The Cape Household Descent Rules

Identity at the Cape was based not on race as such — at least not to begin with — but on descent. And notions of descent derived, increasingly, from the family. Cape slave owners were not all of European descent, but Europeans represented the majority of slave owners. There were also African, Indian, Indonesian, and mulatto slave owners. The only group that did not aspire to slave ownership was the native people. There was no law forbidding them from owning slaves, but only one native woman, Eva, the first Khoi *assimilée* at the Cape, owned slaves. She inherited them when her European husband was killed on a slaving expedition to Madagascar.

No person of purely European descent (of two European parents) was ever enslaved. This circumstance arose by the coincidence of colonialism and the principles of Roman-Dutch law. From 1652 through 1819, the legal line of descent for both slaves and free citizens was matrilineal, or uterine. If the mother was a slave and the father free, the child was a slave. If the father was a slave and the mother free, the child was free. The colonial authorities conceded in 1819 that slave children had the right to petition for their freedom on grounds of free paternity. Up until 1819, slaves with free fathers could only claim freedom through the prior and proper manumission of their mother. All slave-owning societies had to deny patrilineal descent, for if patrilineal descent were recognized, slave mothers could theoretically petition for their children's freedom on grounds of free paternity, putting an intolerable burden on any court's ability to establish the identity of the father.

Attitudes toward racial difference in the context of the Cape slave society had a particular history based partly on descent, but racial attitudes were initially different and distinct from descent. Descent at the Cape was quite unlike other biracial slave societies, such as those in the American South, the Caribbean, or

---

[16] Jacobus Elisa Joannes Capitein, *De Slaverny, als niet Strydig tegen de Christelyke Vryheid* (Leiden: Philipus Bonk, 1742).

[17] Frank Tannenbaum, *Slave and Citizen*, pp. 110–112; Edgar Thompson and Everett C. Hughes (eds.), *Race and Collective Behavior* (New York: The Free Press, 1958), pp. 293–294.

South America. The Cape descent rules properly characterize that slave system as more of an African than an Atlantic slave society. Cape slavery approached, but stopped just short of, what anthropologists call "lineage slavery." Cape slaves were brought into the slave-owning family, but unlike in lineage systems elsewhere on the continent, only rarely became full members of the slave-owning group.

At the beginning of the slave society at the Cape, there were two overriding rules: neither a European nor a native person could be enslaved. The former was custom, the latter law. While the law was not observed, allowing for the gradual and yet almost total enserfment of the Khoi by 1828, the custom of not enslaving people of European descent became more powerful than any law. Moreover, the descent systems for both slavery and freedom at the Cape were based on uterine descent. In the interstices of the two descent rules there was only a limited opportunity for miscegenated persons born of slave or bonded mothers to acquire their freedom. The unbalanced sex ratios — more men than women — remained high until well into the late nineteenth century in both slave and free populations. This superfluity of men, combined with the matrilineal legal descent systems, set in motion a process favoring the emergence of an entitled patriarchy and an elaborate hierarchical system of incorporation of females and alienation of males.

Outsiders and Insiders

One widespread definition of a slave is as an "outsider." In this view slaves are, again to use a phrase of Orlando Patterson's, "natally alienated." By this Patterson means that slaves are brought into the dominant society from outside that society and are deliberately deprived of all kinship ties. Slaves have no right to or even possibility of having an independent family life. For Patterson, the archetypal slave outsider was the foreign-born eunuch in the elaborate slave households of the late Roman Empire.[18]

For two reasons, this definition does not work satisfactorily at the Cape. First, the outsiders in the society (in a legal sense) were not the slaves but the native people. The Khoi were not tried by the Dutch colonials, for example, but by their own leaders and courts. Reasons of cost probably prompted the Company's system of "indirect" rule.[19] The Khoi outsider status is clearly evident in the Europeans' linguistic constructions for the Khoisan peoples. Administrators, colonists, and travelers not only created an ethnic alterity for the native people (Hottentot), but also a differentiation of species: European naturalists did not consider them part of humankind. At first the contemporary European characterizations of the Khoisan

---

[18] Eunuchs were expensive for two reasons: (1) some slaves died during the operation, raising the costs of the survivors, and (2) the operation itself was forbidden in Roman territory, forcing expensive importation from outside the empire. Phillips, *Slavery from Roman Times*, p. 24.

[19] This concept was popularized by Lord Lugard in the late nineteenth century in Nigeria.

people were more extreme than their depictions of slaves. As the native people were incorporated into colonists' households however, this characterization changed.

The second objection to defining Cape slaves as outsiders is that "outsider" status does not explain the gradual preference shown by all Cape owners for mulatto, house-born, or creole (locally born) slaves. Nor does outsider status explain the preferential treatment slave women received at the Cape. Were Cape slave women deracinated, natally alienated, or stopped from having families? A few were. Were they considered outsiders? No. Many female slaves became free. Moreover, many slave women married Europeans after their manumission. Slave women, married or not, often became the mothers of settlers and slave owners. In the Cape, where there was the heaviest reliance on the slave trade until 1808, the most prized slaves were not foreign-born slaves, but the house-born, Dutch patois-speaking, creole slaves. A chasm separated the foreign-born slave from one born into the slave society, and the latter was preferred in all cases. Outsider status does not address, nor can ever explain, the preference of Cape slave owners for different categories of slaves. Lumping all Cape slaves into one gross "outsider" category flattens the elaborate hierarchical nature of the slave-owning household. Outsider status quite obscures the gender dynamics in the creation of those social hierarchies. Outsider status also obscures the reproductive behavior of both slaves and the owners.

Marginality

A key to my modified use of marginality in this study is the realization that the marginality of the slave existed in several social spheres. There was residential or "architectural" marginality in whether slaves lived in the house of the owner, and where they lived. There was religious marginality in the degree to which the slave was included in the owner's religion (at the Cape there were Christian and Muslim slave owners). Familial marginality refers to the degree of incorporation into the family. Civic marginality implies the difficulty or ease with which a slave was protected in the legal system. Notions of marginality must also incorporate gender. An important point that I will make in this book is that in South Africa, the best prospect of freedom existed for a slave when owner and slave were sexually involved. Thus for a slave woman the best prospect for technical, civic freedom might be through the process of fullest (biological) incorporation into the family — that is, through marriage to a slave owner. Only by examining all aspects of marginality can the complex hierarchy within each household type be perceived.

Reduction and Restitution

In this study two dynamic elements are seen as influencing and changing the nature of the slave society over several generations. These are the opposing processes of what one scholar, Agnes Wergeland, called the forces of reduction and restitution within slave societies.[20] These forces are first and most forcefully expressed at the household level. The social reduction of the person to servile status and the maintenance of that position is the cohesive, driving force that keeps the society a slave or serf society. The opposing force of restitution is that which weakly but constantly works in the opposite direction, to restore the slave to a free condition. In this domestic counterstruggle, the slaves and serfs are the only agents. In this view, slaves work in their own interest to devote their whole being to obtaining the restitution of what they do not possess, their freedom and identity. The owners, for their part, have to maintain the reduction of their bondsmen and women to servile status on a daily basis. Both slave and owner work in not one dimension of reduction and restitution, but in many, often simultaneously. Thus a slave might become a Christian because of perceived civic advantages, while the owner works to obtain some legal means to nullify the Christian status of the slave. Neither process is certain, although in most slave societies the social power in the short run has been on the side of the owners. External forces, such as international opinion, religious movements, and legal systems, have their effects on both processes, but not always, it may be noted, with predictable results.

Similar principles of human aspiration apply in many social situations. They appear in the clear contrast between the self-interest of dominant elite or individuals in contemporary society and the weak but persistent individual efforts, altruistic visions, and sporadic impulses toward a more "just" society. They apply most cogently in family life. Parents attempt to bring up their children as children, and they instill duties, dependencies, and obligations. Children, for their part, attempt to assume adult status and independence. In South Africa, owners scheduled the serfs and slaves for perpetual childhood. In this constant, everyday waxing and waning of domination and independence, the heaving of opposing wills within the domestic confines of the slave-holding unit, one may perceive the respiration of Cape slave society.

Outline

The main mechanisms for the reduction of humans to slavery in the Cape were the slave trade, slavery by birth, and plagium (the kidnapping of native people). This volume opens with these topics. Chapter 1 explains why South Africa became a slave society. The availability of land resulted in labor becoming the scarce factor in both rural and urban production. This scarcity was felt and resolved at the household level. Free labor all but disappeared, and individual burgher farmers

---

[20] Agnes M. Wergeland, *Slavery in Germanic Society during the Middle Ages* (Chicago: University of Chicago Press, 1916), pp. 3–5.

gradually reduced the native people to serfdom. The chapter analyzes the life cycle of the Cape family over time. It shows at what points it was more convenient to buy than to hire labor. Over time, more and more Cape householders, like their counterparts elsewhere in the colonial world, found it more expedient to own labor. This realization set in motion a demographic and economic process that led to the slow but certain demise of free wage labor. Among other side effects, the process quite quickly led to the colonial European *mentalité* that considered menial labor for Europeans unthinkable. That *mentalité*, I argue, arose in the home.

Chapter 2 charts the history of the oceanic slave trade to the Cape, from the first imported slaves in the 1650s to the last recorded illegal imports in 1822. Without the prior existence of the Indian Ocean slave trade, Cape slavery could not have developed as easily or as quickly. Initially the Dutch East India Company declared that enslaving the native people was illegal. The importation of so many different people from so many areas had long-term cultural and demographic consequences within the household, and the slave trade transformed individual household management. As the slave populations increased, a process of creolization occurred. More slaves were locally born, more slaves were born in the houses of the owners, and more slaves were born whose fathers were also their owners. By the nineteenth century, there is clear evidence that some owners deliberately fathered their own slaves. As a result of the slave trade and creolization, the language and culture of each slave-holding family was transformed. Identities within the household had to be changed or maintained, but above all, managed.

The third chapter explores the role of gender and the slave trade. The particular sex composition of the slave trade was quite different from those in other slave societies. There were consequently even fewer opportunities for stable or independent family life among the Cape slave population. Imported female slaves originated from different points of the compass than their male counterparts. This also had long-term consequences for family formation and social relations among both slave groups and free.

The fourth chapter explains how the domestic trade in slaves worked at the family level. An important question is how owners up to 1808 struggled to maintain the slave-owning household unit. Slaves and ex-slaves used the domestic trade to free themselves and their kin. After 1808 the internal market took on a new importance, becoming the only legal means of acquiring any more slaves. The character of the slave market changed as the slave-owning society turned inward for its own replenishment.

Chapter 5 describes and explains the changing geographical and statistical distributions of the slaves in the colony. These include the small holdings and the domestic nature of nearly all holdings with the exception of the Lodge. The chapter deals with the types of changes in domestic holdings that came about because of the inheritance system and the changing demography and geography of settlement, and concludes by emphasizing the shifts in the regional patterns of distribution as the colony expanded beyond its original boundaries during the British occupations in the late eighteenth and early nineteenth centuries.

The sixth chapter deals with the largest single distribution of slaves in the colony, the Company Lodge. The Lodge allows one to look at a single group of slaves not incorporated into a family. The well-documented building and the very large number of the slaves in the Lodge also allow for a detailed analysis of its management. The patrician local officials had oversight of the Lodge, but their initial "army-style" organization of the Lodge (used for both male and female slaves) was transformed over time into a familial model by the slaves themselves. The main (and astonishing) characteristic of the Lodge was its complex internal hierarchy, based on gender, age, occupation, creole status, and descent.

The family was the primary means of incorporating slaves into the characteristically small distributions of the Cape slave society. Chapter 7 shows how the different slave-owning family forms, paternalistic, patriarchal, and patrician, operated at the household level. These forms overlapped in space and time and sometimes were found within one family. There were, however, discernible differences in household behavior. Paternalists were generally immigrants from Europe who arrived with ideas of paternalism freshly derived from their mother countries. Such owners often intended to return "home" to Europe. Patriarchs were second-, third-, fourth-, and even fifth-generation settlers who had no intention of ever leaving the colony. Patricians were the urbane — and also ·urban — Company officials (increasingly intermarried with wealthy urban burghers), often with a lifetime of colonial experience in the East. They were usually wealthy and worked in an executive capacity in the Company hierarchy. They were a shifting population and often retired to the East rather than to Europe. Family structure, behavior, and slave-holding patterns were by no means uniform, and the chapter explores the range and extraordinary degree of family incorporation of slaves.

Chapter 8 addresses the changing language of the household. If the household was the theater of subordination, the language in the home was the script. The chapter uses slave names and crime records to explore the everyday language and the conventions of domestic hierarchies.

Chapter 9 details how slavery molded both public and vernacular architecture at the Cape. First, the floor plans of houses and the layout of plantations were affected by the distribution of male and female slaves in the family's holding. Generally, women and children were housed in the kitchen of the main house, male slaves outside in separate quarters. Also, urban architecture, even the layout of the streets, was based on a defense against slave arson. Rural architecture, on the other hand, was fashioned as a celebration of the Cape's patriarchal ideal. There was much less risk of arson in the isolated rural areas, where the bonds of dependence were stronger and violent punishment was more prevalent. In short, the development of Cape architecture can be better appreciated in terms of colonial domestic slavery than in terms of transplanted metropolitan architectural patterns.

Chapter 10 explores changing sexual and gender relations within the slave society. The choices women made and the constraints they lived under transformed both slave-owning women and the slave women. Slave women in the household had multiple and changing tasks within the household. These ranged from domestic work to the reproductive functions of being a wet nurse, a nanny, a mistress, and sometimes a wife. In strong contrast to colonial America and other slave societies, where slave women were expected to do the same work as slave men, this pattern emerged only in the final years of slavery at the Cape. Full civic assimilation into the free community (the rare fulfillment of the promise of incorporation into the family) was always much higher for slave women than for slave men. While it was always higher, however, the rate of assimilation dropped slowly throughout the period. As a result of their quite different expectations, male and female slaves had quite different outlooks on their condition. By 1838 this process had resulted in a complex, vertical segmentation of the society by gender. The roles of women, both slave and free, were quite transformed.

Chapter 11 deals with religion, political identity, and Cape slavery. The chapter traces how the Dutch Reformed Church promised not only incorporation but also assimilation and even freedom to *all* members of the household. Colonial free parishioners, however, acting in their economic best interest, excluded slaves from their congregations. From 1618, the Dutch Reformed Synod of Dordt had proclaimed that Christians had evangelical obligations to all persons within the household, whether servile or free. Most Cape owners moved away from the Reformed Church's precepts of incorporating all members of the household into the Christian fold. Far from being pious Calvinists, Cape slave owners eventually corrupted their own idealistic religion, becoming Christians in name but not in deed. They chose not to include their male slaves at all in the domestic and civic spheres of Christendom. Female slaves, on the other hand, being closer to their owners in a number of ways, were more likely to convert to Christianity. Based on their perceptions of religion in the Cape setting, slaves made their own choices. Many male slaves turned to Islam and other religions — in fact, by the nineteenth century, Islam was the religion of choice for Cape male slaves. The Christian identity became exclusionary and highly gendered.

Chapter 12 deals with the process of manumission, the most profound (although rare) event in a slave's life. All individual slaves struggled from within the confines of the holding to obtain their freedom, and many owners attempted to stop that process. Manumissions occurred in lockstep with certain events in the life cycle of the slave-holding family. The process of manumission favored adult female slaves and their children.

The concluding chapter synthesizes the findings of this study and places the topic of Cape slavery within an overall comparative perspective.

Children
of
Bondage

An Unthinking Decision
The Introduction of Slavery and Serfdom

A CURIOUS RELATIONSHIP between land and labor shaped South Africa before the discovery of diamonds in the 1860s, and in the evolution of that relationship, South Africa became a highly stratified society based on a system of family labor, slavery, and native serfdom. Evsey Domar, an economist, argued in 1970 that slavery or serfdom arose where abundant land resources allowed all "free" people to avoid working for others.[1] In his view, the scarce factor of production was not land but labor. Those who acquired land, in turn, became independent bosses in search of labor. In such a society, a class of laborers had to be introduced who would not be able or permitted to own land, but who could only work.[2] In this special sense, Domar uses serfdom and slavery as interchangeable

---

[1] Evsey Domar, "The Causes of Slavery or Serfdom," *Journal of Economic History* 30, 1 (1970): 18–32. In this study, the term *slaves* refers to imported persons or those born into slavery who could be legally sold on their own, or legally passed on to heirs. Serfs, on the other hand, were locally born native people who were bonded to their owners for 25 years (in practice the bonded period was exceeded). Such people were unable to move freely and were passed on to the next owner of the property de facto, if not de jure.

The word *free* requires definition, since it had multiple definitions and consequences in early South Africa. I use it here only in the broadest, nonjuridical sense of "unattached." Although the Dutch East India Company declared that the native were a "free people" (*vrijvolk*) in the seventeenth century, nobody argued that this meant they were to be treated in the same privileged way as the free burghers (*vriburghers*) or even the free blacks (*vrijzwarten*). I will argue in this chapter that they are more appropriately considered as bonded labor, or serfs. So long as there was available land, all free (unattached) individuals would have preferred to be independent. In this sense the Company's employees and slaves were in the same "nonfree" group. The difference was that Company employees, who could not own land while they worked for the Company, could choose to leave the service of the Company and *then* become free landowners. Slaves theoretically could become free and then own land, but their manumission cost money. For practical purposes, all manumitted slaves started their lives as free blacks in penury, quite unable to afford land.

[2] The concept of class was first used by European colonial theorists of the 1820s and 1830s, such as Edward Gibbon Wakefield, and then later elaborated by Karl Marx and others. Marx,

terms. Another way of putting this ironic and dismal formulation is that "free" land and a universally "free" population would be unlikely to coexist. Nobody would willingly work for another person as long as land resources were freely available. Domar put this in the form of an hypothesis. When an intensive agricultural system is begun (as at the outset of all colonization processes), of all three elements of the system (free land, free peasants, and nonworking land-owners), any two elements, but *never all three can exist simultaneously.*[3]

In a society where there was available land and a group of armed or similarly empowered free persons, it would be extremely unlikely for slavery or serfdom *not* to arise. In 1652 and 1653, the Europeans introduced two technologies into the southern continent that made the development of slavery likely: guns and horses were unloaded from the Dutch East India Company ships. In the Western Sudan, these revolutionary technologies (Jack Goody terms them "the means of destruc-tion") introduced great changes in the way in which all Sahelian cultures evolved. Cavalry states (based on knights and horses) and slavery arose simultaneously.[4] These same technologies enabled the first permanent Europeans in South Africa to perceive all land as being "free." Since available land and a group of powerful persons were present in early South Africa, we should not be surprised that Domar's predicted results — slavery and serfdom — also quickly came about.[5] Effective religious, moral, or legal sanctions would have been needed to *prevent* slavery or coerced labor forms. No such sanctions existed in South Africa.[6] Slavery or serfdom was simply the most efficient labor system in such a situation.

• In addition, once slavery was established the institution seemed impossible to eradicate. Even after formal emancipation in 1838, new forms of legislation, such as the Masters and Servants Ordinance (passed 1841, strengthened 1856, repealed 1974 [*sic*]) made for similar and enduring forms of bondage that harked back to the seventeenth century.[7] Slavery had, moreover, a recursive effect. In itself, and in

---

although disapproving of Wakefield, read his works closely. Marx considered Wakefield "the most notable political economist of the thirties." See Edward Gibbon Wakefield, *The Collected Works of Edward Gibbon Wakefield* (London: Collins, 1968), pp. 21, 24; Wakefield, *A Letter from Sydney, the Principal Town of Australasia and Other Writings on Colonization* (London: J. M. Dent, 1929), 9.

[3] Domar, "The Causes of Slavery or Serfdom," 21.

[4] Jack Goody, *Technology, Tradition and the State in Africa* (Cambridge: Cambridge University Press, 1971), p. 72.

[5] Leonard Guelke and Robert C.-H. Shell, "An Early Colonial Landed Gentry: Land and Wealth in the Cape Colony 1682–1731," *Journal of Historical Geography* 9, 3 (1983): 265–286; Leonard Guelke, "A Computer Approach to Mapping the *Opgaaf*: The Population of the Cape in 1731," *South African Journal of Photogrammetry, Remote Sensing and Cartography* 13, 4 (1983): 227–237.

[6] See Chapter 11.

[7] "The Cape legislation was designed to tie the ex-slaves to their masters, especially on the farms. Oral contracts were made binding, and stringent penalties laid down for desertion." Christopher Saunders, *Historical Dictionary of South Africa* (Metuchen, N.J.: Scarecrow Press, 1983), p. 106.

combination with slave hiring, it always curtailed the potential of existing free wage labor, and once established, slavery and serfdom could exist long after their initial causes had disappeared.

This formulation is not new. Adam Smith, Edward Gibbon Wakefield, V. Kliuchevsky, Achille Loria, Ester Boserup, and H. J. Nieboer have long argued that where land was abundant and rents low — as in colonial America, medieval Italy and Russia, colonial and precolonial Africa and Australia — entrepreneurial classes developed some form of slavery or serfdom.[8] This is also, in part, E. S. Morgan's explanation for the introduction of slavery in Virginia and the replacement of indentured servants with slave labor there. He emphasizes that slaves were easier to coerce than servants and, moreover, could be inherited.[9] His analysis also adds what Domar called "the exogenous variable," the political factor.

In early South Africa, only when free land ceased to exist were many individuals obliged to work for others and to pay rent in some form. This occurred in the late nineteenth century, long after the formal abolition of slavery in 1838. The settlers, by then, as far north as the Zambezi River, had appropriated as much land and labor as they were able from the African majority. In the formative early period, neither the original inhabitants nor freed slaves were financially able to compete in the race for land and resources. The first native people whom the Dutch encountered — the Khoi — were not forbidden to own land; they were simply told by the Dutch East India Company officials that they had lost their land in war. In the seventeenth and eighteenth centuries, only one Griqua, Adam Kok, ever registered land with the Company authorities in Cape Town.[10] The other original inhabitants of South Africa — the Nguni speakers and the bulk of the population — were also persistently denied the right to own land by law and military might. This process culminated in the Natives Land Act of 1913, in which 87 percent of the land was reserved for exclusive white settlement.

A most important question is who in the colonial society decided whether

---

[8] Domar, "The Causes of Slavery or Serfdom," 18–32; Domar traces the genealogy of the principle from Adam Smith onwards, see p. 31; Wakefield, *A Letter from Sydney;* Wakefield, *The Collected Works;* H. J. Nieboer, *Slavery as an Industrial System: Ethnological Researches* (The Hague: Martinus Nijhoff, 1900; 2nd rev. ed., 1910); Ester Boserup, *The Conditions of Agricultural Growth: The Economics of Agrarian Change* (New York: Aldine, 1965), p. 73; Using examples from a broad range of slave societies where these variables did not obtain, Orlando Patterson refuted the pure form of the Domar-Nieboer hypothesis; see Orlando Patterson, "The Structural Origins of Slavery: A Critique of the Nieboer-Domar Hypothesis from a Comparative Perspective," in Vera Rubin and Arthur Tuden (eds.), *Comparative Perspectives on Slavery in New World Plantation Societies,* Annals of the New York Academy of Sciences, vol. 292 (New York: New York Academy of Sciences, 1977), pp. 12–34.

[9] For early Virginia, see Edmund S. Morgan, *American Slavery, American Freedom* (New York: W. W. Norton, 1975), p. 218 note 11, pp. 295-297.

[10] CAD: Receiver of Land Revenue books, vol. 1–7.

slave or wage labor should be used? The state, in the form of the Dutch East India Company administration, had only a secondary function. Early "nation-building" or "settler" historians of South Africa wished to emphasize and celebrate the freedom of the first "free burghers." But how could the colony be seen as free if there was slavery? Historians ignored the institution. This initial false image of freedom led to the construction of another equally false situation in 1717, when the Dutch East India Company formed a commission to reformulate ideas for the future of the colony.

The 1717 Company commission advised its directors to stop assisted European family emigration to South Africa on the grounds that free wage labor had failed. But of course by 1717 slavery was a fait accompli. At that time, 8,589 persons had already been enslaved or born into slavery: 2,759 slaves had already been imported into the Lodge (the building that housed the Company's own slaves); 582 creole slaves had been born in the Lodge; free burghers and local officials had imported 3,997 slaves; and 1,251 slaves had been born in their households. In fact, by 1717 slaves outnumbered the settlers. One dissenting commissioner still urged free labor, but an impatient local official, H. van de Meer Pietersoon, secretary of the Council of Policy, an auction master, and a slave trader, shut out all dissension by arguing that slavery had flourished in all other colonial areas primarily because slaves were more easily coerced than free labor:

We need not even mention the great difference in obedience and subjection in the relations between slave and master and between free-born servant and master. . . . [W]ould there not be reason to fear that these [free-wage] laborers would always be the master. . . . Whether these servants, knowing who they are, would not always act together, and having little respect for their masters, lay down the law for him. . . . I cannot, however, understand who has dared to trouble our masters [the directors] with such useless suggestions [free labor]. For the benefit of those who may doubt my statements, I may add to the above, that they should carefully consider in what way the work is done, throughout the whole of India, all the Colonies, the West Indies, [and] Surinam[e].[11]

Historians interpreted the Dutch East India Company Commission's advice in 1717 with such phrases as "the colony was condemned to slave labor."[12] Slavery, such authorities imply, was imposed on South Africa by the Dutch East India Company. Yet no one forced Cape householders to buy slaves, and, indeed, the same commission denied free burghers permission to send slave ships to the east coast of Africa. As the historian Winthrop D. Jordan wrote of the introduction of slavery into the Americas, slavery was a local "unthinking decision."[13] The truth is

[11] M. P. de Chavonnes and G. W. van Imhoff, *The Reports of Chavonnes and His Council, and of Van Imhoff, on the Cape* (Cape Town: Van Riebeeck Society, 1918), p. 126.

[12] Eric Walker, *A History of Southern Africa* (London: Longmans, Green, 1968), p. 76.

[13] Winthrop D. Jordan, *White over Black: American Attitudes towards the Negro, 1550–1812* (Baltimore: Pelican, 1969), pp. 44-98.

that the colony had been "based on slavery" from the initial grant of land to the free burghers in 1657. Moreover, it was never one decision, but a series of thousands of decisions made at the individual household level.

The Company was not responsible for slavery. Labor proposals by the Company directors in Holland had always stressed free labor, not because of any distaste for slavery, but as a mercantilist cost-cutting venture: slaves required capital expenditure. For example, the Dutch East India Company commissioner Jan Pieterzoon Coen had dreams of a Dutch "free burgher" middle class in Indonesia as early as 1619, to reduce costs.[14] Later Company solutions continued to stress free labor for the same reason. The Company considered importing freed slaves (sometimes termed *Mardijkers*), and suggested enticing "free" Chinese persons from Formosa to settle at the Cape. They also persuaded and assisted persecuted French Huguenots to emigrate to South Africa as "free" settlers.[15]

When the Dutch occupation began in 1652, for the first five years the local Dutch officials used the contracted wage labor of their own employees. By 1657, the Dutch East India Company released their own employees to become "free burghers." But colonial freedom was not equivalent to metropolitan freedom. The company was quite prepared to sacrifice the colonial citizenry, as they had earlier noted in a letter of 1651: "We must remain the masters of the enterprize, even if that means the disposal of the . . . citizenry."[16] Free burghers' political rights were vulnerable, and they were *not* wage laborers; along with their freedom, they received plots of land, credit, and slaves.

The modest production of the early Cape farms did not generate wages high enough to attract wage labor. The hard work and low pay of primary colonization was plainly distasteful both to the first free Europeans and to the early original inhabitants (see Figure 1-1).[17] When some of the first farmers returned to the Netherlands, local officials were quick to urge the Company directors to allow slave labor. Within months it was apparent that the early free burghers could only

---

[14] Leonard Blussé, *Strange Company: Chinese Settlers, Mestizo Women and the Dutch in VOC Batavia* (Providence: Foris, 1988), pp. 24–25.

[15] James C. Armstrong, "The Slaves," and Leonard Guelke, "The White Settlers, 1652–1780" in R. Elphick and H. Giliomee (eds.), *The Shaping of South African Society, 1652–1820* (Cape Town: Longmans, 1979); C. Graham Botha, *The French Refugees at the Cape* (Cape Town: Struik, 1970); AR VOC 4032: "Rolle der vrijluiden die bij anderen in dienst, als mede die voor de kost en ook buijten dienst gehuijsvest zijn te weeten" (31 December 1693), folios 233–236.

[16] Blussé, *Strange Company*, 25. The word *disposal* was no euphemism. In 1742, in "the Chinese massacre" in Batavia, the Dutch did dispose of 12,000 of their citizens.

[17] This seventeenth century picture ably shows the sort of activity on early Cape farms. The enormous hay ricks emphasize the industry of the farm while the foreground inactivity is in contrast. A Khoi laborer is asking for tobacco from a running knecht. One notices the evidence of land clearing — the tree stump in the right hand corner. Source: INIL 6259, Courtesy of South African Library.

Figure 1–1. Khoi with ox wagons transporting and stacking hay, c. 1710.

succeed if they had considerable slave labor in their fledgling households. Slavery and freedom were thus combined within the Cape household from the outset of occupation. A letter from the Cape commandant to the Company directors, dated 5 March 1657, referred to the supplementation of the labor of free burghers and their families with slave labor:

Now that we observe that your honors are in earnest, and have equipped a vessel for Angola to fetch us slaves, we shall prosecute the further cultivation through further free persons (who may volunteer) [a reference to Company servants] under such conditions, until approved, there being land enough at the Cape to grow food for all the possessions of the Company in India that require it, had we but people, horses and slaves, *without which very little is to be done*. . . . [B]ut as your honors are pleased to supply us with slaves . . . for there are no servants to be had for hire . . . so that slaves will be quite indispensable here . . . particularly in the cultivation of the ground . . . free inhabitants could do little in farming without slaves.[18]

By 1717, the elite local officials, whom I term the patrician slave owners, had become the main beneficiaries of the oceanic slave trade to the Cape. The relationship between the occupation of land and the recruitment of labor at the Cape had already became a complex operation with multiple vested interests. From the start, decisions about the economy and the forms of labor at the Cape were directly in the hands of both the individual settler householders and local officials. This proved a powerful partnership.

---

[18] [Emphasis added] Donald Moodie, comp., *The Record or a Series of Official Papers . . .* (Cape Town: Balkema, 1960), p. 95.

T*he Cape Tenure Systems*

With available land beckoning from the frontier, no free person wanted to work for someone else. From 1652 to 1701, small freehold portions ranging from small plots to 135 acre tracts were allotted to individual settlers. By the turn of the century, the Cape peninsula was settled. A new "loan" farm system, inaugurated in 1702, allowed even more Cape land to be appropriated, and the average farm size jumped to 6,000 acres. Loan farms were applied for on a temporary basis. If the farm proved to be unworkable, a farmer could abandon it without loss of capital. A modest annual "recognition fee" of only 24 Rixdollars was imposed after the "ordination" of the farm, and if successful, a loan farm could be converted to freehold ownership. Between 1702 and 1743, farmers applied for more than 100 million acres.[19] A Dutch official, G. W. van Imhoff, regretfully noted in that year:

I believe it would have been far better had we, when this colony was founded, commenced with Europeans and brought them hither in such numbers that hunger and want would have forced them to work. But having imported slaves, every common or ordinary European becomes a gentleman and prefers to be served than to serve. We have in addition the fact that the majority of the farmers in this Colony are not farmers in the real sense of the word, but owners of plantations, and that many of them consider it a shame to work with their hands. Such a bad example makes the farm-hands worse. . . . There is to my mind little doubt that to give out farms on the loan system is a drawback. . . . In addition the system may have other bad features caused by the covetousness of human nature to which this form of tenure gives every opportunity.[20]

The Cape system, far from being unique, was a pro forma model for European colonization everywhere. If there was any uniqueness, it lay in the territorial extravagance of the system. Edward Gibbon Wakefield, a colonial theoretician of the early nineteenth century, believed that the Cape tenure system was responsible for changing the free wage labor system and culture of the Dutch. He compared the tenure systems of colonial New York (also settled by the Dutch) and the Cape colony to make his point:

The most striking instance . . . has occurred in the Dutch colony of South Africa. Here . . . the colonial government, having absolute control over all the land in the country, disposed of that land in the following way. They first declared that anyone desirous to obtain land should be at liberty to do so on one condition; namely that of taking a hundred times, at least, more land than he could possibly cultivate. The whole district to be granted was marked out in circles, the diameter of each circle

---

[19] Leonard Guelke and Robert Shell, "Landscape of Conquest: Frontier Water Alienation and Khoikhoi Strategies of Survival, 1652–1770," *Journal of South African Studies* 18, 4 (December 1992): 1–22.

[20] De Chavonnes and van Imhoff, *The Reports of Chavonnes*, 137–138.

being some miles; and anyone who undertook to live in the center of one of the circles obtained a title to all the land within the circle. . . . The object of the system was to separate those who should become proprietors; to separate them, all from each other, by a distance equal to the diameter of the circles; and the motive for this object was fear lest, if the colonists were not separated, they might, as union is force, be strong enough to think of self government. The object was fully accomplished, and the colony was effectively ruined. . . . If they had not obtained some slaves, that is, some combination of labor in the particular works of their farms, they would, being so scattered and prevented from combining their own labor, have degenerated into the state of those savage descendants of Spaniards who inhabit the plains of Buenos Ayres. . . . If the Dutch governor of New York had been able, he would probably have been willing enough to ruin that colony by planting each of the first settlers in the center of a circle nine or twelve miles around . . . [however] the first [New York] settlers were allowed to settle whereabouts they pleased . . . to assist each other in some degree, to accumulate some capital, to preserve in some degree the arts and civilization of their mother country. . . . This case is not therefore, an example of attention in a government to the first rule in the art of colonization: it is mentioned by way of contrast with the preceding case; a contrast the more remarkable, since the miserable colony of South Africa, and the prosperous colony of New York, were founded by the same industrious, skilful and thrifty nation.[21]

Although there were slaves in early Dutch New York, the differences in land tenure led to vastly different land holdings, slave holdings, economic systems, and culture.

The Cape Settler Diaspora

Many company employees completed their contracts and left the employment of the Company to start farming. As Otto Mentzel, a German-speaking immigrant explained, this process had begun in the seventeenth century: "Since the Company had given express orders that all servants, soldiers and sailors who desired to leave the Company's service and set up as burghers and carry on private vocations or to become agricultural, or livestock farmers, should not be prevented, but should be given the same faculties as free immigrants, i.e. they were to receive a grant of land and other assistance upon credit. Consequently, there were many such Company servants who believed . . . they would make much more by employing their talents in a private capacity, than by working for a fixed monthly wage." (see Figure 1-2).[22]

---

[21] Wakefield, *A Letter from Sydney*, pp. 134–135.

[22] Otto Friederich Mentzel, *A Complete and Authentic Geographical and Topographical Description. . .*, trans. G. V. Marais and J. Hoge, rev. ed. (Cape Town: Van Riebeeck Society, 1921–1944) vol. 1, p. 64, cf. vol. 2, 100; Moodie, *The Record*, vol. 1, 293–294.

Figure 1–2. Boere knecht (farmer's laborer), c. 1710.

The Company monitored this process carefully, recording each request to leave the service of the Company, such as that of sailor Jurian Adelaar, who arrived from Dresden in 1705, was first "loaned" as a farm laborer by the Company in 1713, and who in 1724 requested burgher papers, convinced "that he will be able to support himself as an agriculturist." Three years later he was listed not as a hired worker but as a farm owner on the Berg River in the frontier district of Drak-ensteijn. By 1731, he owned two male slaves, one horse, 12 oxen, and 300 sheep in the Drakensteijn district.[23] Another, David Bonk, a soldier, arrived in the colony in 1703. According to his 1718 request for burgher papers, he noted he "had been *knecht* [a contracted wage laborer, see Figure 1-2.][24] to various agriculturists and obtained a knowledge of farming."[25] Jan Blignault, who arrived as an ensign in 1723, chose a path that Mentzel always advised: marriage. His 1726 request said that "by his marriage here, he has come into possession of some land on which he thinks he can support himself as a freeman, [and now] asks for burgher papers."[26] Hundreds of other Company knechts wrote similar petitions. Most served an

---

[23] LR 1 (1724): 2; J. Hoge, "Personalia of Germans at the Cape, 1652–1806," *Archives Year Book* 9 (1946): 2; AR Rademacher Collection *The De la Fontaine Report (30 January 1732) Inventory no. 507*, comps. Leonard Guelke, Robert Shell, Anthony Whyte, (Opgaaf Project, 1990), no. 35; VOC Opgaaf, AR KA 4095 (30 April, 1 and 2 May 1731).

[24] This is a newly discovered picture of a seventeenth century "knecht." One notices the "veldskoens," faithfully copied from the Khoisan. The knecht in this phase appears as a medieval laborer. Source: INIL 6261v [S.A. Computerized Index to Illustrations], Courtesy of South African Library.

[25] LR 1 (1718): 47; Hoge, "Personalia of Germans," 38.

[26] LR 1 (1726): 60.

average of five years as a knecht before petitioning for their release from the
Company, their burgher papers, and land.[27] However, the majority of frontier-
bound farmers were not knechts, but the maturing male children of the burgeoning settler population. Free land was the principal stimulus luring both wage
laborers and settlers' sons to become independent farmers.

The Rise of Unpaid Family Labor and the Decline of Wage Labor

There was also a major push factor behind this process. For the most revealing
explanation of the complex failure of wage labor and the introduction of slavery
one must look at the basic unit of the colonial society, the household. The male
youths (13 to 17 years of age) of Cape settler families provided temporary unpaid
labor for their parents' farm enterprises, but as soon as they were adults (18 and
over years of age) they sought their independence, left the family farm, and became
employers themselves in search of labor for their new farms. If prosperous, such
households became increasingly dependent on the acquisition of slaves or serfs.
The shortage of free wage labor at the Cape was always accompanied by the
expansion of the settlement, and that shortage of labor was always first felt in the
individual household.

   In 1717, contemporaries referred to family labor among frontier farmers,
"whose children help in their work," but such labor patterns probably started with
the Huguenot family migrations of 1688 to 1701.[28] By 1731 there was substantial
competition for free wage labor from farmers' grown children. The second and
third generations of highly interrelated creole colonists in the colony were much
more likely to be employed by close family members even after they were recorded
as independent heads of households. Governor Jan de la Fontaine's annotated
1731 list of all householders shows the extent of unpaid family labor and free
knecht labor. He noted that a Theunis van Aart, for example, was "living on his
father's farm from which he sustained himself"; a Samuel de Beer was "living with
his mother"; a Martinus Becker "worked at his mother's"; Isaq van der Merwe
worked "at his father's"; and Gerrit, Lammert, and Pieter van der Bijl all lived with
their mother. So, too, Johannes Marais "worked at his parents"; Cornelis Be-
zuidenhout "lived with his brothers"; and Daniel Bockelenberg "lived with his
step-father." Fully 15 percent of the 801 heads of households were still living with
their parents or other, lateral family members. Five percent of these had already

---

   [27] The five volumes of Leibbrandt's *Requesten* contain translations of hundreds of such
petitions; Hoge's "Personalia of Germans" contains even more biographical information on the
German knechts. There is no equivalent published list of Dutch knechts in South Africa.
   [28] De Chavonnes and van Imhoff, *Reports of Chavonnes,* 104.

started their own families. Moreover, 1,623 children of these householders would later be listed as heads of households when they reached their census maturity at 16 years. These young people were the free knechts' unbeatable competition. Each year more and more settlers' children were listed in the census. Moreover, the proportion of free children in free households increased steadily until it stabilized at about 50 percent, circa 1740 (see Figure 1-3).[29]

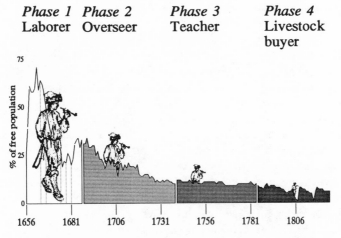

| *Phase 1* | *Phase 2* | *Phase 3* | *Phase 4* |
| Laborer | Overseer | Teacher | Livestock buyer |

Figure 1–3. Percentage of free population who were contracted labor (knechts), 1656 to 1824.

The Knecht: An Adjunct of the Household

The primary seventeenth-century auxiliary to free burgher labor, the knecht, was either a Company knecht — subcontracted wage labor "on loan" from the Company — or a free knecht who worked without a contract.[30] The knechts are important because their decline in the Cape labor spectrum presaged the failure of *all* free wage labor in South Africa until 1838.[31] Both knechts and wage laborers

---

[29] This excludes the free Khoisan peoples and all those working directly for the Company. Both free and company knechts are included. Free knechts were estimated from the number of *eenlopendes* (male singletons); Shell, "Popucape," see appendices for full details of data set.

[30] The literal translation of knecht, "retainer" or "manservant" does not adequately encompass all the duties of this jack-of-all-trades, nor does the translation do justice to his ambiguous social position, sandwiched between the owners and the slaves. "Indentured servant" is also an inadequate translation, since there were no female knechts at the Cape, while between 10 and 20 percent of indentured servants in colonial America were women. Therefore, I prefer to use the original Dutch word.

[31] The word *knecht* survives in the Afrikaans language, however, and has a derogatory connotation; see P. C. Schonees et al. (eds.), *Woordeboek van die Afrikaanse Taal* (Pretoria: Government Printer, 1950-), vol. 6, pp. 429–431.

were similar to earlier North American colonial indentured servants,[32] but the Cape term of indenture was shorter than the equivalent contract in, say, Virginia, where the period of indenture varied between two and seven years.[33] At the Cape, the knecht signed a renewable one-year contract with the head of household and received a cash wage of between seven and nine guilders a month,[34] thus the Cape knecht was closer to a real wage laborer than was the Virginian indentured servant. Unlike his Virginian counterpart, the Cape knecht received no assisted passage in return for his contract. There was no headright system at the Cape, whereby plantation owners received grants of land in return for paying the passage of a servant. At the Cape, unlike in Virginia, there was no provision for female knechts or female partners for the male knechts. As one Company official put it, such people "should not be encumbered with families, but should be unmarried farm laborers from Europe." The officials even proposed single-sex hostel accommodation for the urban knechts.[35]

Contracted European wage labor was the Company's first choice for labor. The Company knecht, a soldier or sailor in the Company's employ, was hired out to a settler for a year. The knecht did not have the right to refuse his "secondment," nor was he a party to the terms of his own employment to a farmer. Such company knechts were listed as part of the settler's household in the Cape census, occupying the same position in the census as they did in real life, sandwiched between the offspring of the householder and his slaves.[36] The use of company knechts declined dramatically from the seventeenth century, when they made up not quite half of the household (excluding slaves), to the eighteenth, when from 1700 to 1765 they constituted 5 percent, and from 1765 to 1824, less than 1 percent of households. In the early nineteenth century, only nine knechts were listed, for example, in the populous Swellendam frontier region.[37] As Cape settler families grew, and more family and slave labor became available to successful plantation owners, the proportion of company knechts in households diminished.

To protect its own servants, the Company insisted that after 1692 all contracts between Company knechts and colonists should be in written form and have a fixed wage. Such Company solicitousness ensured, until 1795, that the company

---

[32] There was also collective farming: two individuals could be listed *in companje* on the local censuses as joint householders. No more than 1 percent of all householders were listed in this way.

[33] Morgan, *American Slavery, American Freedom*, 174–175.

[34] Mentzel, *Description*, vol. 1, 164–166.

[35] De Chavonnes and van Imhoff, *The Reports of Chavonnes*, 104, 106.

[36] No other company employees appeared on the burgher census. After 1668 there was a real distinction between free burghers and all Company employees, who until 1795 were listed on separate censuses called *Monsterrollen*.

[37] CAD 1/5/J 318: "Opgaaf Rolle van Swellendam," 1805. There were: 1,193 male settlers, 807 female settlers, 1,296 settler boys, 1,339 settler girls, 9 knechts, 1,405 adult male slaves, 263 slave boys, 777 adult female slaves, 147 slave girls.

knecht had a protected and fixed wage.[38] With all Company knechts coming from Europe, this also had the consequence of protecting the wages of all *European* Company knechts. This protection was double-edged, however. Company knechts' wages (fixed by contract) did not move up with the other inflationary trends of the colony. This wage stagnation further fueled the dissatisfaction of the European Company knechts.

Free knechts, on the other hand, among whom there were free blacks, enjoyed no such institutional or contractual protection; they were single men who owned no landed property but were not employed by the Company. They could negotiate their own wage. Although they had no full year's contract, they were paid much higher wages than were paid to Company knechts. In 1666, for example, they were paid twice as much.[39] In 1692, they were the largest labor pool in the Cape population (excluding the native population).[40] The Cape archivist G. C. de Wet has estimated that there were 424 free knechts between 1658 and 1707, more than a quarter of all free adult men who came to the Cape in that period.[41] Not all Cape freehold farmers could afford to hire a free knecht, nor was such employment anything more than seasonal. One official scornfully noted that poor farmers "are also to be seen active enough, and grubbing in the ground like moles, late and early — but alas poor men! They can make very little of it, because they are too poor to keep one or two Dutch knechts in pay for the whole year (and such knechts are absolutely necessary for that hard work)."[42]

Both types of knechts were hired at different stages in the life cycle of the employer's family.[43] Shortly after the arrival of the Huguenot families (1688), the knecht began to be displaced from Cape households by a surfeit of family members. Many of the Company and free knechts in 1692 were hired instead by farmers just beginning their enterprises and their families. With no spare capital to buy slaves and too few family members to maintain the farm, novice farmers were often obliged to hire such wage laborers for a short term, especially on farms that

---

[38] Kathleen M. Jeffreys and S. D. Naude (eds.), *Kaapse Plakkaatboek, 1652–1806*, vol. 1 (Cape Town: Kaapse Argiefstukke, 1944–1949), pp. 115, 276; J. Hoge, "Privaatskoolmeesters aan die Kaap in die 18de eeu," *Annals of the University of Stellenbosch* (1933): 10.

[39] Moodie, *The Record*, 293.

[40] See, for example, AR VOC 4032: "Rolle der vrijluiden die bij anderen in dienst, als mede die voor de kost en ook buijten dienst gehuijsvest zijn te weeten" (31 December 1693), folios 233–236.

[41] G. C. de Wet, *Die Vryliede en Vryswartes in die Kaapse Nedersetting, 1657–1707* (Cape Town: Historiese Publikasie-Vereniging, 1981), Bylae 2, "Naamlys van Vryknegte in die Kaapse Nedersetting," pp. 224–228.

[42] Moodie, *The Record*, 293.

[43] Lutz K. Berkner, "The Stem Family and the Developmental Cycle of the Peasant Household: an Eighteenth Century Austrian Example," *American Historical Review* 77, 2 (April 1972): 398-418; and also Berkner, "The Use and Misuse of Census Data for the Historical Analysis of Family Structure," *Journal of Interdisciplinary History* 4 (Spring 1975): 721-738.

required much clearing of land and building. Matthijs Greef appeared on the 1692 census in the Stellenbosch district with no adult children and no slaves and as cultivating a few vines and running a few sheep: this was a farm in the making. He had a Company knecht, and hired two free knechts, Pieter Andriesz and Pieter Meijer.[44] Nine years later, the family reported 8 of their own children, 13 male slaves, 2 female slaves, 1 male slave child and 2 female slave children. The husband and wife were now presiding over an established and extremely productive farm; with the eldest son now 14 years old, and with a number of slaves, Greef could dispense with his Company and free knechts. By 1706, his eldest son, 19, was listed in a separate household, and Greef senior once again hired a Company knecht, this time keeping him on for a year before letting him go.[45]

On a Cape farm, the knecht's labor was the most expendable and therefore the most flexible. Of the three sources of labor — the family, slave labor, and knechts — only the knechts' labor could be terminated at will without repercussions. Another settler, Baerend Burgert, hired knechts for different purposes at different stages of the life of his household. Burgert married in 1690; in 1692 he was listed in the Drakensteijn district as a blacksmith, with an infant son, one free knecht, two slaves, and no crops. By 1701, he had purchased a freehold farm, and he reported owning six slaves and employing two Company knechts. When he died four years later, he left four children, all of whom went on to farm their own land and establish dynasties of their own. After his death, the knechts disappeared.[46]

The hiring of knechts was, therefore, a flexible and temporary convenience for a poor, novice, or struggling farmer, but mainly in the seventeenth century, when the few immigrant colonists had small families. The use of knechts in the eighteenth century declined for several reasons. Family labor became common as the original colonists established large families. Younger members worked on the family farm for expectations — but no wages — and on reaching maturity, established a new farm and a new family. If the new farm enterprise was successful, family labor was supplemented by "borrowing" slave labor from the parental farm (termed an inter vivos transfer), or by slave hiring from older areas, including Cape Town.

---

[44] AR VOC 4030: "Rolle der Vrijeluijden, " folios 52–64; VOC 4032: "Rolle . . . die bij anderen in dienst" (31 December 1693), folios 233–236.

[45] AR VOC 4045: "Opneem der Vrije luijden deselver gedoente en effecten aen de Caap op primo January 1701," folios 972 ff.; AR VOC 4052: "Generale Opneem der Vrijeluijden, derselver bezitting enz. aen de Caeb," folios 454 ff.

[46] C. Pama, comp., and C. C. de Villiers, *Geslagsregisters van die ou Kaapse Families* (Cape Town: Balkema, 1981); VOC 4030, "Rolle der Vrijeluijden," folios 52–64; AR VOC 4045: "Opneem der Vrije luijden," folio 972 ff.

The Effect of Slave Hiring on Wage Labor

The hiring of a slave was always cheaper than hiring a knecht. Poorer or younger farmers always found it easier to hire or borrow the labor of slaves than to pay the high wages of the knecht in cash. Once slavery was widespread, slave hiring competed with the limited free wage labor. The hiring out of slaves was most common in the service sector, but it occurred in all areas, even in agriculture. According to Mentzel, the hirer paid the slave's owner 4 Rixdollars a month, and provided the slave with food and tobacco, though not clothes. This compared with monthly wages for free men of between 10 and 12 Rixdollars, without food. Some privileged slaves were allowed to hire themselves out for their own negotiable wage. In such cases the slave paid the owner a flat 6 *stuivers* a day, but the slave had to find his own food.[47]

The practice of slave hiring explains why a few slaves had money in their possession and how some could gamble and others could save up their *peculium*[48] and eventually free their slave kin.[49] In one early case in 1704, Jacob of Macassar, a rural slave, took his boss, Louis le Riche, a settler farmer, to court over a dispute about his slave wage. The legitimacy and positive outcome of the case reveal that slaves were a recognized part of the wage economy from early in the colony's history. Moreover, the case reveals that the slave's *peculium* was protected in law just as it was in Roman times.[50] Piet Retief, the Afrikaner *Voortrekker* martyr,

---

[47] Mentzel, *Description*, vol. 2, 89–90; aside from hiring, the Company occasionally imposed a slave corvée on the burghers of the town, in which each burgher had to lend a slave to the Company to work on the fortifications for an unspecified time; see G. C. de Wet et al. (eds.) *Resolusies van die Politieke Raad* (Pretoria: Government Printer, 1958- hereafter *Resolutions*) vol. 3, p. 203 (23 February 1689).

[48] The wage paid to a slave.

[49] Even in the seventeenth century, Cape slaves obtained money. The first hint of the power of the consumerism of Cape slaves are reports that they had a special passion for fish and whale oil (*traan*), and bought this product in such quantities for ready cash (*voor gelt*) that the Political Council specifically forbade its purchase by slaves; see Jeffreys and Naude, *Kaapse Plakkaatboek* (31 October 1661), vol. 1, 69. For an example of a slave who loved gambling, see the will of the ex-slave Rangton of Bali, whose estate was worth 400 Rixdollars, among the possessions — one new blanket, two tobacco pouches, two chisels, 6 planes and a box of rubbish (*een partij Rommeling*) — were no fewer than 8 decks of playing cards in good order, CAD MOOC 10/2/14 (4 May 1720). Cf. Robert C.-H. Shell, "Rangton of Bali: The Short Life and Material Possessions of a Cape Slave," *Kronos* 18 (1991): 1–6; also Jeffreys and Naude, *Kaapse Plakkaatboek*, vol. 1, 227, 265, 297, and passim throughout the remainder of the Dutch East India Company period 1705–1795; see also chapters 4 and 12 in this volume, on the domestic slave trade and manumission, for examples of slaves paying for manumission of their kin.

[50] As quoted in Anna J. Böeseken, "The First Fifteen Farmers in the Wagenmakersvalleij," in J. G. Kesting et al. (eds.), *Libraries and People: Essays Offered to R. F. Immelman* (Cape Town: 1970), 109; Slaves indeed could also become their masters' creditors. In such cases, the slave's position was also protected in Cape law, cf. *RCC*, D. Denyssen, "Statement of the Laws of the Colony of the Cape of Good Hope Regarding Slavery" (16 March 1813), 9: 146–161; Article 35.

borrowed considerable money from a slave woman and then reneged on the debt. The woman claimed that Retief had promised to pay within a week and had since "put her off from time to time with promises of payment." The slave's owner (not Retief) eventually produced an acknowledgment of the *Voortrekker's* debt with no fewer than four witnesses.[51]

The hiring out of slaves increased throughout the eighteenth century. By 1806, according to Samuel Hudson, a group of urban slave owners had emerged who inherited slaves themselves and who lived entirely off the proceeds of their hired-out slaves. No passage better exemplifies not only how free wage labor had failed but also how the family slave holdings had become the linchpin of the dynastic fortunes of Cape families:

'Tis a very common custom with the inhabitants of this colony when a child is born, to give them a slave which is ever considered their own property and generally waits upon them and the[y] acknowledge no other master or mistress. By this means many of them who have a couple of these slaves let them out for so much per month, particularly those [slaves] who have learnt trades. By which means they [the owners] are in the receipt of sufficient cash to support them in the usual amusements and extravagances of the place. Others who are prudent, soon acquire money enough to increase their stock of human property so that it enables them by the time they arrive at a marriageable state they are provided with the means of forming a decent establishment without the assistance of their parents. One man, who is now considered very rich, informed me his beginning was from this source. He had two boys [i.e., slaves]. They were both put to trades and became very good workmen which at the time he was sixteen brought him in regularly 80 rix dollars per month. Before he was twenty he had saved sufficient from the proceeds of these two boys to purchase three more. At five and twenty he married and at that time was in possession of eight slaves, a house, and a well furnished store of different kind of merchandise and at the same time [was] considered a good master, husband and punctual tradesman. From this way of proceeding, aided with prudence, man must grow rich.[52]

James Ewart, who had never read Hudson's then unpublished manuscript, wrote almost a decade later to confirm Hudson's point: "Nothing is more common than to see at all hours of the day, numbers of young men whose parents derive the whole income from the wages of two or three slaves, dressed in the first style and loitering away their time."[53] One British official estimated that 2,000 slaves were on hand for hire in Cape Town in the 1820s.[54] As late as 1827, the governor, Lord

---

[51] Johannes Stephanus Marais, *The Cape Coloured People, 1652–1937* (Johannesburg: Witwatersrand University Press, 1968; first published 1939), 167 and note 4.

[52] Robert C.-H. Shell, (ed.), " 'Slaves,' an Essay by Samuel Eusebius Hudson," *Kronos* 9 (1984): 67.

[53] *James Ewart's Journal* (Cape Town: C. Struik, 1970), 27.

[54] George McCall Theal, *Records of the Cape Colony* (Cape Town: C. Struik, 1967 reprint; hereafter *RCC*), "Bourke to Commissioners of Enquiry" (1826), 27: 81-83.

Charles Somerset, complained that "free servants are only to be obtained at the Cape at exorbitant rates of wages and that the ordinary price [i.e., wage] of the best slave laborers does not exceed from 18 to 20 Rixdollars a month."[55] Even "prize negroes" (those slaves captured at sea after 1808 and "liberated" at the Cape) and their children were hired out.[56] Once introduced, slavery had a pernicious effect on wage labor, since established slave owners interpolated their "for hire" bondsmen into every part of the economy where wage labor could operate.

The final and most costly commitment for those seeking labor was the purchase of a slave. Only successful farmers paid the purchase price and they then offset their original cash outlay by renting out their slaves. Consequently, slaves became common both *behind* the frontier in the hinterlands and in the towns and villages. The principal advantage of slaves over expensive free labor was that slaves were negotiable assets who, after the original cost of purchase, could be passed on, with their offspring, to family members, or hired out, or borrowed from parents.[57] With each subsequent generation of settlers there was less and less room for the wage-earning career knecht in the Cape household economy. That is not to say that there were no opportunities for a knecht — he could always apply for a land grant. All the eighteenth-century knecht needed was a grubstake, and for that he had only to be a temporary laborer, overseer, or teacher within some established family.

The Evolution of the Knecht's Status

A crucially important consideration in the Cape household was status.[58] Every Cape household had its own domestic atmosphere thick with status considerations. Despite their short contracts, knechts were discontented with their indeterminate status — neither boss nor free — and householders were discontented with their knechts. Complaints about the high wages of the knechts and about their rowdiness, drunkenness, unreliability, and propensity to run away at harvest time clog the seventeenth- and early eighteenth-century petitions from the settlers.[59]

After the arrival of hundreds of Huguenot families, the proportion of knechts in established households dropped precipitously. One can only surmise that the children who had accompanied their parents in the migration were put to work

---

55 Theal, *RCC*, "Colebrooke to Earl Bathurst" (18 January 1827), 30: 109.

56 Theal, *RCC*, "Return of the Finances" (6 September 1826), 27: 493.

57 Mentzel, *Description*, vol. 3, 165–166.

58 Nigel Worden, *Slavery in Dutch South Africa* (Cambridge: Cambridge University Press, 1985), pp. 64–85.

59 De Chavonnes and van Imhoff, *Reports of Chavonnes*, 87, 126, 137; Moodie, *The Record*, 293–294; Mentzel, *Description*, vol. 1, 166; Jeffreys and Naude, *Kaapse Plakkaatboek*, vol. 1, 183, 286.

tout de suite. As the knecht was edged out of the laboring role, he merged into another: the overseer of slaves on successful, established plantations. If the owner had multiple estates, and no children of a working age, he or she might well need an overseer. The use of an overseer was a vital consideration in the management of large estates and multiple slave-holdings, well into the nineteenth century.

Company knecht overseers, always under the ultimate control of the Company, were also disciplined by their temporary bosses when they proved refractory. One Stellenbosch owner told another colonist in 1775 that he could treat his schoolmaster knecht, "and all others who were in his service in his own fashion and even beat them."[60] Slaves on farms with absentee owners, too, were under two masters: Mentzel provides an example of the multitiered control of a single Cape plantation:

No master will listen with patience to complaints [of his slaves] about ill-treatment and blows [at the hands of the overseer knecht], but would rebuke the slaves and even command the knecht in their hearing, to give them a good thrashing if they refuse to obey him; but at the same time he would in private reprimand the *knecht* for such brutality, and point out to him that the slaves were human beings and that he had to pay a high price for them. I myself knew a knecht, who on account of his too drastic actions, was not only taken back into the Company's rule, before the end of the year, but was sent back as a sailor to Europe . . . this may be considered as little short of banishment.[61]

Company knechts then had two masters, one within the household and one without: the head of household and the Company, a double tyranny. For that reason the Company knecht was more tractable than the free knecht, sometimes called an *eenlopende* (a singleton), who owed allegiance only to his pocket and was often accused of abandoning the farmer at harvest time. The free knecht always had the option of becoming really "free" and supporting himself on a smallholding of his own.

The conversion of the knecht from laborer to overseer can be dated by comparing a census of 1692, which listed the property owners, their knechts, and their slaves, with a contemporary Company list of such knechts.[62] Of all free knechts listed in 1692, one-third were on farms with two or more male slaves, which may be regarded as the minimum holding for having an overseer, while in the same year, fewer than one-fourth of the Company knechts were on estates with

---

60 Wayne Dooling, "Law and Community in a Slave Society: Stellenbosch District, c. 1760–1820," M.A. thesis, University of Cape Town, 1991, p. 64.

61 Mentzel, *Description* vol. 3, 100 ff.

62 AR VOC 4030: "Rolle der Vrijeluijden onder de Cabo, Stellenbosch en Drakensteijn gehorende," folios 52–64; AR VOC 4032: "Rolle . . . die bij anderen in dienst" (31 December 1693), folios 233–236.

two or more slaves. By 1692, between a quarter and a third of all knechts could have been employed as overseers.

Over a generation later, there is concrete evidence of free knechts' being squeezed out — not only out of the manual labor pool but also out of the overseeing pool — and becoming "poor whites." De la Fontaine, who had married into a Cape family and knew the colonists well, invariably described the 1731 free knechts as poor men like Carl Frederick Boetendag, a monopolist's (*pagter's*) knecht, "richly endowed with debt"; "Jan Brouwer, a farmer's knecht, an old poor man"; Steven van den Burg, as "a tapster's knecht, who was church poor, and has debts"; Franz Hendrik Mare, "a poor man [who] worked for his food."[63] By 1731, a sizeable "poor white" population was emerging, with the free knechts heading the list, a population nudged into a marginal state of existence by the unbeatable combination of burgeoning younger generations of the families of the original settlers and these families' slaves.[64]

After 1731, Company knechts still had one skill to offer the colonists: their literacy. The next-to-the-last option for the European-born and European-educated knechts was the teaching profession; burghers hired Company knechts to give their children the rudiments of an education based on what the knechts remembered from their youth (if somewhat imperfectly, judging from the complaints from the burghers and various officials).[65] The Company knechts were more literate than the children of the rustic patriarchal settlers, and for that solitary reason they became the teachers of the settlers' children. The free knechts (who were born in the colony) had little or nothing to offer in the way of teaching skills. Hoge's and de la Fontaine's lists show that not one locally born burgher and not one free black was a teacher.[66]

Teaching was done cooperatively. Neighboring farmers sent their children to the European-born teacher knecht and paid him. Teacher knechts were paid two guilders *less* than farm knechts. Mentzel, who had been a teacher knecht himself, had some advice for such people: "The schoolmaster who does not succumb to the temptation of habitually drinking more of the abundant wine of the Cape than is good for him can secure his position," but evidently there was no lifetime career for teachers, since he added, "and make a good marriage."[67] The knecht either stayed sober or married into a Cape family. There were only 130 teacher knechts up to

---

[63] AR: Radermacher Collection, no. 507, "Letters of Jan de la Fontaine" (30 January 1732) and Appendices.

[64] The biggest portion of the free poor population, however, was the urban freed blacks, who were generically described as "fishermen."

[65] P. J. Idenburg, *The Cape of Good Hope at the Turn of the Eighteenth Century* (Leiden: University Press, 1963), pp. 106–108.

[66] J. Hoge, "Privaatskoolmeesters," 7-43; AR: Radermacher Collection, no. 507, "Letters of Jan de la Fontaine."

[67] Mentzel, *Description*, vol. 1, 165–166.

1795.[68] The profession of elementary teaching in early South Africa was a low-status job, as it also was in seventeenth-century New England, where sometimes widows, marginalized by disinheritance, took up teaching. Although the population of settler children continued to grow, the proportion of Company knechts (teachers and others) continued to decline.

There was a limited demand for teachers in the early Cape. The final transformation of the knecht was into an itinerant buyer of sheep and cattle. Again, literacy was the principal skill. Petrus Borcherds, himself a farm owner, provides a nineteenth-century description of such a person:

Most of [the farmers'] sheep were disposed of on their farm to butchers' itinerant servants, who travelled amongst them for that purpose, these persons generally Germans, or other foreigners and commonly known as *slagters' knechts*, received previous to their departure from Cape Town certain printed instructions and were obliged to attend at the Fiscal's office to swear that they would abide by them. This was deemed necessary to prevent fraud and deception being practised on the ignorant farmers. The knechts had extensive power to purchase cattle and sheep, and they carried with them a number of blank promissory notes ready signed by the butchers, intended to be filled up with the amount of purchase price of the cattle or sheep. These notes thus secured, had such credit that they circulated as a paper currency from hand to hand until presented for payment to the issuer.[69]

Knechts thus came to be associated with four functions. In the first phase, from 1658 to 1687, they were wage laborers and comprised as much as 50 percent of the entire free population. In the next phase, 1688 to 1739, they were mainly overseers, but they dropped to 5 percent of the free population. In the third stage, 1740 to 1795, they served as teachers of the children of the household, representing less than 1 percent of the free population; and in the fourth stage, from 1795 onward, they were either teachers or itinerant buyers for butchers, making up considerably less than 1 percent of the population. As a result of their displacement from agricultural labor by the younger creole settlers and their slaves, the Cape knechts underwent four changes of occupation and status before disappearing into statistical obscurity. The main difference in status between knechts and slaves was that knechts were allowed to carry arms and ride horses (see Figure 1-4).[70]

The Changing Social and Racial Origins of the Knecht
Changing status was mirrored in the knechts' changing social and racial origins. In the seventeenth century, the free knecht was drawn from several layers of Cape

---

[68] Hoge, "Privaatskoolmeesters," 36-43.

[69] Petrus Borcherds, *An Autobiographical Memoir* (Cape Town: Robertson, 1861), pp. 56-57.

[70] The picture shows the final status evolution of the knecht. He is now mounted. The word "knecht" has the same etymology as the English word "knight." Source: Charles Davidson Bell, ART 179, Courtesy of Brenthurst Library.

Figure 1–4. Untitled: Author's title: "The knecht rides again" [1833].

society: origin or descent did not matter. A minor source of free knechts was the free black population, in one isolated but revealing instance, coming directly from slavery. As the following documents from, July 17 and 18, 1692, indicate, it was possible, though unusual, to move from slave to free knecht in a single day. Although slaves received a *peculium*, a monetary wage was expressly avoided in the second document, "Henning Hussing, settler councilor here . . . declares with the permission of the Governor, to have set his slave, Isaq of Ternate, on free feet [*op vrije voeten*] and outside all the servile status of slavery."[71] And the following day: "Isaq of Ternate, freed slave of Henning Husing and now freeman at Stellenbosch agrees to work for his above-mention boss [*Patroon*] as a loyal and honest free knecht, in return for two years labor, he would receive in lieu of payment sixty breeding ewes and a heifer, and in addition, clothing and food."[72]

Such freed slaves became the first class of "renters" in South Africa, and their masters became *patroons* (*patronus* means someone who has freed a slave). Possibly they can also be called the first representatives of a preindustrial working class — in my meaning, a group of people who could not afford to buy property (or indeed to move off of their *patroon's* property), but survived only on extremely meager handouts. As early as 1714 there was a case in civil court of a free black,

[71] Deeds Office, Cape Town, *Transporten en Schepenkennis* T 1691/1692 (17 July 1692) pp. 126–127.

[72] Deeds Office, Cape Town, *Transporten en Schepenkennis* T 1691/1692 (18 July 1692), 128–129.

Rangton of Bali, who was struggling to pay rent. Probably there were earlier cases.[73] In the change from slave to knecht, we see Cape vassalage changing from a personal to a manorial servitude.

In the upside-down world of the seventeenth-century knecht, there were also several early instances of European free knechts working for free blacks, but they, unlike Isaq of Ternate, the freed slave, *did* work for a monetary wage. For example, Willem Teerling, a free knecht, was first in the service of Louis of Bengal, his free black boss, who owned the Lanzerac farm; then he was fired.[74] Teerling promptly went into the service of Anthonij of Angola, another free black.[75] Anthonij of Angola was so impressed with European labor that he hired a settler bachelor, Hans Jes from Holstein, and an ex-soldier, Christian Martenz from Hamburg.[76] But these instances of Europeans working for wages for people of African or Asian descent were few, and the practice declined at the Cape.

As the combination of European settlers' children's labor and the purchase of slaves on established plantations rendered both wage labor and the free knecht superfluous on Cape farms, they also thus excluded all free black free knechts from the agricultural wage labor pool. On any given farm there might be several labor forms: family labor, knechts, slaves, and native serfs working together in a well-defined social hierarchy in which free blacks were neither welcomed nor hired. Consequently, most male free blacks turned to making an independent livelihood as fishermen in Cape Town and in spots around Table Bay and False Bay, an occupation they held for three centuries, until removed from job and home by the Group Areas Act of 1950. The pool of people from which all knechts were drawn in the seventeenth century became smaller in the eighteenth century and was increasingly limited to Company employees born in Germany and recruited in Holland, and settler children. Many of these knechts married into other settler families, thus reinforcing the near-perfect European hegemony in intensive agriculture.[77]

The Company or free knecht in his laborer or his overseer role, like his counterpart in the American South, was a man of divided loyalties.[78] On the one

---

[73] Rangton was also unmarried and left no heirs; Robert C.-H. Shell, "Rangton of Bali," *Kronos* 19 (November 1992), 88.

[74] J. L. Hattingh, "Die Blanke nageslag van Louis van Bengal en Lijsbeth van die Kaap," *Kronos* 3 (1980): 8.

[75] De Wet, *Die Vryliede*, 102.

[76] De Wet, *Die Vryliede*, 124; AR VOC 4032: "Rolle . . . die bij anderen in dienst" (31 December 1693), folio 233.

[77] Anon., *Gleanings in Africa* . . . (London: James Cundee, 1806), p. 226.

[78] William L. van Deburg, *The Slave Drivers: Black Agricultural Labor Supervisors in the Antebellum South* (Westport, Conn: Greenwood Press, 1979), 124 where he compares white overseers with drivers; Eugene D. Genovese, *Roll, Jordan, Roll: The World the Slaves Made* (New York: Vintage Books, 1976), pp. 13–15.

hand, in the small slave distributions of the typical Cape farmstead, he had to establish a modus vivendi with the slaves. On the other hand, he had to drive them to produce a good yield for the owner. It is not surprising, therefore, that in the Cape, as in the American South, overseers were dismissed as often for leniency as for cruelty. Ostracized from above and forbidden by convention from associating with those below, the Cape knecht lived in a confusing social universe.

Illustrating the point that the European knechts perceived their status as insecure is the 1721 case of Coert Roelofsz van Christiana, a Swedish knecht on the farm of Rudolf Steenbok. After a hard day's work with another European knecht, Paul, and a slave, Andries, he and the others relaxed together in the malt house with pipes of Virginian tobacco and a flask of Cape wine, in an atmosphere of cordiality. Socially excluded from the farmhouse, the knecht was sometimes drawn to the slaves for companionship, but could be thwarted by emerging status considerations among the knechts themselves.[79] The two knechts fell out over a seemingly minor, but evidently crucial, breach of colonial etiquette. Paul, who had arrived in the colony in 1696, and was, at 57, somewhat senior in the hierarchy of the colony, told Coert:

Paul: You must give this boy [slave] a glass of wine; he is doing a European's work!

Coert: Why? This is just a slave, like any other.[80]

Paul's gesture of socializing with the slave offended Coert. Coert's retort, in turn, offended Paul. Paul picked up Coert's toolbox and hurled the tools around the malt house. In the melee that followed, Paul stabbed Coert.[81]

Pieter Holbroek, a Cape knecht, ran away from, in his own words, "the cruelty of his master" in the Drakensteijn district in the 1720s. He lived for months in the mountains, provided for by a network of sympathetic slaves. One slave, Catrijn of Madagascar, eventually joined him in his mountain fastness, where they lived a Bonnie and Clyde-style existence for nearly a year, raiding the nearby farms for food, until they were hunted down and captured by a commando (a group of armed burghers) in 1729.[82] In this case, the knecht had sympathized with the slaves of the household, and the slaves had reciprocated. Will Teerling, the European free knecht who worked for two different free black masters, sought companionship and even love from a slave: he was accused of

---

79 Otto Mentzel, *Life at the Cape* . . . , trans. Margaret Greenlees (Cape Town: Van Riebeeck Society, 1919), p. 40.

80 [Paul: "*Die Jongen moog je wel een glas wijn geeven, dis doet Europeaans werk.*" Coert: "*Dese is soo wel een slaaf als die anderen.*"] AR VOC 4091: "Justitieele papiere van Ao. 1722: Interogatie: Paul" (8 July 1722), folios 1255, 1256.

81 AR VOC 4091: "Interogatie . . . ," (8 July 1722), folios 1255, 1256.

82 AR VOC 4117: "Processtukken: Interogatie: Catrijn van Madagascar" (16 November 1725), folio 933 verso.

"fornication" with his master's household slave, Elizabeth of the Cape, and was tried.[83] At the trial his pregnant mistress "confessed," and Teerling was fired for his domestic indiscretions.

Adam van Claaten, a free knecht in the Picquetberg region, represents a more typical pattern of knecht behavior. Adam was so vicious to the slaves he oversaw that they were inspired to murder him and run away. On a fall night in 1726, Amaai van Mozambique was awakened by Adam van Claaten's gang of slaves, he asked what they were doing there, and Aaron van Bengal, the leader, replied: "This knecht has drawn my blood, I want to suck his blood in return."[84]

The knecht was a wild card on the Cape homestead. For that reason, each knecht was carefully monitored by Company clerks, who kept copious annotated lists of such "singleton" knechts until they were safely married.[85] The knecht had no stable place in society, nor did he have a home.

Not all knechts were insecure in their status, however. Mentzel, as noted, a former knecht himself, stated: "I have known men who have been in this service for 20 years. They have passed from farm to farm, led a comfortable life, and saved a small fortune." He reiterated again the temporary stage of knechthood: "This form of employment was a stepping stone to wealth for competent men. Such men frequently married their master's daughter or widow. In fact I have known cases where widows engaged knechts with a view to matrimony."[86] For the poorly paid Company knecht, there was only a very limited possibility of real economic independence (and freedom) from wage labor alone, and his great expectations increasingly derived from the probability of a judicious marriage into a settler family.[87] In a sample of 202 free men in 1731 traced back to their birth or arrival, 23 percent had neither married nor acquired property in freehold or on loan.[88] The majority, therefore, did succeed in the colonial terms of achieving marriage and owning property. Mentzel always recommended marriage for knechts and noted that "every girl without exception prefers as her husband a man who has been born in Europe to one who is of colonial birth."[89] He himself never married.

As has been noted, in the initial period of settlement, knechts were the main wage laborers — temporary substitutes for family and slave labor. All knechts aspired to be farmers and slave owners in their own right. The only true example of negotiated and contracted wage labor at the Cape, the knecht system failed for

---

[83] Hattingh, "Die Blanke nageslag van Louis van Bengal en Lijsbeth van die Kaap," 8.

[84] *"Des knecht heeft mijn bloed gesoogen, ik wil zijn bloed ook weder zuigen"* in VOC 4102: "Processtukken: Relaas, Amaai van Mocambique (23 May 1726), 1250–1251.

[85] AR: Radermacher Collection, no. 507, "Letters of Jan de la Fontaine."

[86] Mentzel, *Description,* vol. 1, 165–166.

[87] Mentzel, *Description,* vol. 1, 164–165.

[88] Guelke and Shell, "An Early Colonial Landed Gentry," 283, note 37; the sample was generated by numbering the census householders and using a random number generator.

[89] Mentzel, *Description,* vol. 2, 114.

reasons probably similar to the reasons that indentured labor failed in colonial Virginia. As the children of the early settlers matured, they became the obvious and clearly preferred (and unpaid) choice for the higher positions in the farm's labor hierarchy. Knechts withdrew from their roles as paid laborers and overseers of the slave labor force because of both their peculiar indeterminate social and racial status and the ever present attraction of working for themselves on their own land. If they were successful, they, too, could become slave owners and enjoy the benefits of that way of life.

Settler youth with secure expectations of land ownership, working without remuneration, undermined the wage structure of the Cape. When as prosperous adults they opted for extending their property's worth through the purchase of slaves, any remaining wage-earning labor was squeezed out. It was a self-reinforcing cycle. With ever fewer reliable and inexpensive free wage laborers, successful farmers turned increasingly to the purchase of slaves. Except in the first 30 years of settlement, wage labor was not important in the economy of the Cape households. Families relied, at first, on their own labor, then supplemented that with slaves and, later, serfs; by the nineteenth century, slaves and serfs were the primary labor force. Family labor, while it never died out, remained a temporary phase in an individual free person's life and was nearly always rewarded with expectations of inheritance of not only a farm but also a way of life.

The history of one European wage-labor settlement scheme before the abolition of the slave trade in 1808 is instructive. Gijsbert Karel, Graaf van Hogendorp, at his own expense, attempted to import several thousand Dutch artisans into South Africa during the revolutionary Batavian administration (1803 to 1806) on the condition that there should be no slaves, or even free native labor, on his plantations.[90] His father had been an early Dutch abolitionist deeply concerned about the slave systems that had arisen in all the Dutch colonial possessions, and he wanted to do something practical to follow in his father's footsteps.[91] Van Hogendorp is regarded as one of the early theoreticians of colonialism and one of the founders of the Dutch Republic. General Janssens and Commissary de Mist, fired by the ideals of the French revolution, agreed enthusiastically with this philanthropic nobleman: "They could not sufficiently express their regret that the mistake had been made of introducing Negro [*sic*] slaves into the country, but were of the opinion that it was not too late to repair that error. If Europeans in considerable numbers could be obtained as immigrants and further importations of blacks prevented, in course of time the negroes already in the

90 Idenburg, *The Cape of Good Hope at the Turn of the Eighteenth Century*, 70–73; there was another smaller scheme by Baron Friedreich von Buchenröder at the same time, cf. Hoge, "Personalia of Germans," 52–53.

91 M. C. van Vollenhoven, *Verspreide Geschriften* ('s Gravenhage: H. D. Tjeenk Willinck & Zoon, 1985), pp. 306–309.

country might have a tract of land assigned to them where they could live by themselves."[92]

The ambitious project did not work out: most of the industrious Dutchmen left van Hogendorp's plantations before 1810 and settled in Cape Town, whereupon Cape officials, forgetting their former enthusiasm for the scheme, urged him to purchase slaves for the abandoned settlements in Hout Bay. Worse was to come: under the second British occupation in 1806, General David Baird seized the nobleman's property and turned off the land the remaining few Dutch artisans who had managed to settle there. Subsequently, the inspector of lands and woods visited the property and scathingly observed the activities of the last European wage laborer in the scheme: "[he] had not cultivated one square yard of soil and was scraping a living by transporting brushwood, *the property of the government,* into Cape Town." Van Hogendorp's other colonists who were en route to the Cape via America, perhaps receiving news of the debacle, decided to stay in the New World.[93]

Enserfment and the Decline of Native Wage Labor

There were always other sources of labor to serve as auxiliary labor to the knecht and slave populations, especially at times of sharp fluctuations in the international supply of slaves or local epidemics. A shortage of imported slaves would always result in settlers' turning to other sources of free and coerced labor. Whenever this happened, there was a disruption of the native populations who were clinging to increasingly fragile economies and ecosystems.[94] One obvious and ever present option was to hire, coerce, and even enslave the native Khoisan or Xhosa, proposals all actively considered in the seventeenth century. The commandant during the first decade, Jan van Riebeeck, even proposed exporting the Khoi to the East Indies.[95] By the 1680s, local officials were sending ships to explore the possibility of slaving among the Xhosa: a Cape official wrote to the Company Directors on April 16, 1689, denying this possibility: "Here it would be impossible to trade for slaves, as they [the Xhosa] would not be parted from their children for whom they have an outstanding love and affection."[96] The Khoi and Xhosa were not consid-

---

[92] Patricia Storrar, "Count Gijsbert Karel van Hogendorp and His Unfulfilled Dream," *Quarterly Bulletin of the South African Library* 44, 3 (March 1990): 101.

[93] Storrar, "Count Gijsbert Karel van Hogendorp," 102 (emphasis in original).

[94] Guelke and Shell, "Landscape of Conquest: Frontier Water Alienation and Khoikhoi Strategies of Survival," 1–22.

[95] *Report from the Select Committee on Aborigines (British Settlements) with the Minutes of Evidence, Appendix and Index* (London: House of Commons, 26 June 1837), pp. 25–26; Moodie, *The Record,* 23.

[96] "*Hier soude het onmogelijk wesen slaven te verhandelen also sij haar kinderen, noch jemand*

ered as candidates for contract labor (that is, with each party and the state having a copy of the written contract) until the nineteenth-century and the second British occupation.[97] In 1706, Khoi wage laborers were reported as working (briefly) in gangs for monetary wages, moving from farm to farm, but they were not termed knechts at that time. The existing contracts were entirely casual, usually oral, and predominantly seasonal. As Adam Tas, a Christian colonist, noted on his sabbath diary entry of January 20, 1705: "In the afternoon I paid off eleven Hottentots for the corn cutting. They were about to go on from here to Mr. Rochefort."[98] But such roving bands of independent paid Khoi laborers declined. A Cape historian, Richard Elphick, goes so far as to say that, by 1713, "most of the men of some *kraals* [villages] were either in Cape Town or on colonial farms."[99]

The smallpox epidemic of 1713 killed or frightened away so many Khoi that a sharp labor shortage resulted on the peninsula and in the hinterland, as François Valentijn, the peripatetic *predikant* noted:

As to the Hottentots, they died as if by hundreds, so that they lay everywhere along the roads as if massacred as they fled inland with kraals, huts and cattle, all cursing the Dutch, who they said had bewitched them, hoping to be free in the hinterland from this evil sickness. Afterwards as a result (as I found in 1714) very few Hottentots were to be seen here compared with previously, this causing very great inconvenience to the burghers and other inhabitants who now lacked their services, both for cleaning and scouring almost everything in the house *at low pay,* but especially in the cutting and gathering of corn and grapes.[100]

The smallpox epidemic that decimated the Khoi and frightened away the survivors, left their legal position in some doubt. The Company directors did not exclude the Khoi as a coercible laboring force. It is significant that they never reissued the statute forbidding enslavement of the native people, although other ignored statutes were often reissued, nor was any legal protection offered to Khoi wage laborers, although Company knechts' rights were protected by contract and statute. What can be said with certainty is that wages for Khoi labor become less frequently mentioned in all sources after 1713.

---

van de haare voor enigh ding ter wereld souden willen afstaan beminnende hun onderlingh met een uijtstekende liefde en toegenegenheijt," in CAD C.502: "Letters despatched, Cape to Patria" (16 April 1689) pp. 308–309.

[97] Lord Caledon's Proclamation (1809) as quoted in W. W. Bird, *State of the Cape of Good Hope in 1822* (Cape Town: Struik, 1966), pp. 244–248; some Khoi are listed as knechts in CAD: Verbatim Copies, "Opgaaf for Cape Town, 1806."

[98] Adam Tas, *The Diary of Adam Tas,* ed. Leo Fouché et al., trans. J. Smuts (Cape Town: Van Riebeeck Society, 1969–1970) p. 127, cf. 117.

[99] Richard Elphick, *Kraal and Castle: Khoikhoi and the Founding of South Africa* (New Haven, Conn: Yale University Press) p. 178.

[100] François Valentijn, *Description of the Cape of Good Hope . . . ,* ed. E. H. Raidt, trans. Maj. R. Raven-Hart (Cape Town: Van Riebeeck Society, 1973), vol. 1, p. 219, (emphasis added).

In their quest for cheap coercible labor after 1713, the colonists turned their attentions to the native women first. Khoi women were the first native people to be brought into the households of the colonists and were the first to appear, according to a newly discovered sketch and Richard Elphick, "in their own huts on colonial farms, without their men" (see Figure 1-5).[101]

Figure 1–5. "Khoi women with buildings behind," c. 1710.

The ostensible reason was that Khoi men did not want to work the ground.[102] The first formal mention of literally grafting native labor onto slave labor was made in a 1721 request by eight of the wealthiest farmers in the interior districts of Stellenbosch and Drakensteijn:

---

[101] The Khoi women are firmly ensconced on the farm and are already dependent on tobacco. Source: INIL 6260 [S.A. Computerized Index to Illustrations], Courtesy of South African Library.

[102] Elphick, *Kraal and Castle*, 176–177, 179.

We would like to mention how by the present conjuncture of time, which has resulted in the Hottentots, in securing their own sustenance, have come to seek shelter among the free burghers. It transpired that some of the slave men belonging to the undersigned mixed in with the women of this nation, and have bred children from these unions. The costs of the consequent child-rearing have been born by us . . . so that we ask if you could decree that a certain number of years may be stipulated during which these offspring might be bonded [*verbonden*] to serve their foster bosses [*voetserbasen*] otherwise we would have no further recompense for our trouble and expense.[103]

Since the Council of Policy passed this request to the jurisdiction of local magistrates (*Heemraaden en Landdrosten*) of Stellenbosch and Drakensteijn with obvious approval, one cannot assume that the matter was "left in abeyance for fifty years" as Anna Böeseken and Candy Malherbe have argued.[104] Indeed, since one of the signatories had worked in the *Landdrost*'s office in Stellenbosch and two others, Hermanus van Brakel and Matthijs Krugel, had been nominated and served as *Heemraden* of Stellenbosch and Drakensteijn, one can assume complete approval of the request. Richard Elphick, although writing of a slightly earlier period, provides some support for this supposition. He has said that the Company studiously avoided all disputes over local labor contracts.[105] Mentzel, writing of the period 1732 to 1741, confirms that the enserfment of the native population was inaugurated long before 1775: "Hottentot women, in the service of the colonists, do not dislike the slaves, and easily let themselves be persuaded to live with them. Children, born of such a union are always free, although their father is a slave, but they have to stay for 25 years with their mother's employer, unless the mother immediately returns to her kraal with her new born child."[106] Historians have dated the beginnings of this *inboekstelsel* (registration system) from 1775, but

---

103 CAD C.228: "Requesten en Nominatien" (9 September 1721); C.1086, p. 292; cf. *Resolutions* (2 September 1721) 6: 128–129. Leibbrandt has copied the names incorrectly and has a careless translation; see Leibbrandt, *Requesten* (no. 73 of 1721), vol. 2, 518. [*Conjunture* = Dutch word in original].

104 Anna Böeseken and Margaret Cairns, *The Secluded Valley: Tulbagh: 't Land van Waveren, 1700–1804* (Cape Town: Perskor, 1989) p. 74, note 35; this delay came about as one of the members of the political council was "absent"; see also V. C. Malherbe, "Indentured and Unfree Labor in South Africa: Towards an Understanding," *South African Historical Journal* 24 (1991): 15–16.

105 *Resolutions* (9 September 1721) 6: 129 and note 143; Hermanus van Brakel was nominated as *Heemraad* in Leibbrandt, *Requesten* (no. 156 of 14 December 1716), vol. 5, 1231 and confirmed (No 98 of 1 November 1718) vol. 5, 1238; Elphick, *Kraal and Castle*, 182; the historian of the office of *Landdrosten en Heemraaden* does not mention this topic in his book at all, cf. P. J. Venter, "Landdros en Heemrade (1682–1827)" *Archives Year Book* (1940) vol. 2, 1-242.

106 Mentzel, *Description*, vol. 3, 300; cf. 119.

there seems to be every reason to assume that local magistrates oversaw an informal enserfment of the Khoi after 1721 *without* registration.

I believe that this process was not akin to "apprenticeship," as Donald Moodie, the Cape pamphleteer, first euphemistically termed the system, though he admitted that he named the earlier system after the *later* British system.[107] The new process was a specific form of bonded labor that requires some special terminology. First, the rights to a native person's bonded labor period could be passed on either de facto by inheritance or incidentally by (inter vivos) transfer of the property on which the bonded person resided. This tenurial bondage is what I mean by Cape serfdom. The serfs, tied to their workplace by poverty and unable to move from it, could be passed on — only informally — when the property changed hands. This system had no basis in Cape law, but it became an important custom. It is important to appreciate that slaves, on the other hand, could be legally sold, apart from the land, or passed on to heirs, or change owners when the property changed hands. When slaves, in contrast to serfs, were legally sold along with the property, I refer to such transactions as cadastral transfers. Cadastral slavery and serfdom had one thing in common: bonded labor was sold along with the property. This meeting point of the two systems would later form the basis for postemancipation agricultural labor forms.

One should also note that the descent rules for bonded Khoi labor followed the descent rules of Cape slavery. Both systems were based on uterine descent.[108] Children born to bonded women or slave women were, respectively, bonded or enslaved.[109] For Khoi, the bonded labor period was from 12 to 25 years. Children born to such bonded women were also attached to the individual farmers to whom their mothers were bonded. One may even speculate as to whether some children of such unions between Khoi women and slave men were registered as part of the slave population in the census; although this may never be known since the Khoi population itself was not enumerated during the Dutch period. Such speculation is supported by the fact that in every year after 1721, the regional censuses in Stellenbosch (the source of the original request by the eight farmers) reported higher slave child /slave woman ratios than in the Cape district closest to the town, though other variables could also explain such a discrepancy.[110]

Cape historian Nigel Penn has found the first recorded instance of a Khoi

---

[107] Moodie, *The Record,* vol. 3, 77, note 2.

[108] For a discussion of descent systems in slavery, see Orlando Patterson, *Slavery and Social Death: A Comparative Study* (Cambridge, Mass.: Harvard University Press, 1982), pp. 135–147.

[109] See George McCall Theal, *Records of the Cape Colony* (London: William Clowes, 1901) vol. 9, p. 146 (Article 3); Worden, *Slavery in Dutch South Africa,* 36, 80; Böeseken and Cairns, *The Secluded Valley,* 74-75, 141, note 37.

[110] Coenraad Beyers, *Die Kaapse Patriotte, 1779–1791* (Cape Town: Juta, 1929), pp. 242–249.

woman and her three children being captured by commandos and placed into serfdom in another part of the colony, an incident that occurred in 1731. The new governor informed the perpetrators that they should "not write about such incidents, but report them in person."[111] By 1767, there is some evidence from a Cape intellectual that Gunjeman Khoi around Cape Town "furnish slaves for the service of the Honorable Company or for private citizens."[112] We do know that farmers used restraint to keep such Khoi women on their farms, because we have reports of "runaway" Khoi women from such farms. One plantation, whose European owner became "simple in the head," in 1772 became the "happy resort of Hottentot women *who have run away from their masters,* and who already form a considerable number, remaining there, in spite of everyone."[113]

By 1785 Colonel Dalrymple, an Englishman sent out to spy on the possibility of a British invasion, could confidently report on the typical Cape domestic situation, in a passage that exactly describes the enserfed position of the Khoi:

At most of the Farm houses in the province there resides from 10 to 20 Hottentots. The Dutch have made slaves of them all, and they understand a little of the Dutch language. *They are called free because the master cannot sell them [individually], as they do the negroes [sic],* but the Hottentot cannot go from one master to another and is obliged to work *without payment.* [T]he Dutch farmers give some of the most faithful and intelligent a cloth coat once in two years which is to them a most magnificent present. . . . [I]f a British Army acts in that country they should make them presents of clothing according to their services, and feed them with meats which attracts them, as they seldom get anything from their masters but Bread, Milk, Roots and Vegetables.[114]

Wages for native labor had all but stopped in this frontier region, and also elsewhere in the colony.[115] For example, the "revolutionary" hinterland patriarchs of the district of Swellendam presented ten "articles of demand" to the Cape authorities in 1795, among them:

Articul 5 that any Bushmen or Hottentot women caught singly or on commando either previously or now, shall henceforth be the *property* of the farmer employing

---

111 Nigel Penn, "The Frontier in the Western Cape," in John Parkington and Martin Hall (eds.), *Papers in the Prehistory of the Western Cape* (Oxford: BAR International Series 332, 1987), pp. 475-476.

112 Gijsbert Hemmy, *De Promontorio Bonae Spei, The Cape of Good Hope: A Latin Oration Delivered in Hamburg Academy, 10 April 1767* (Cape Town: South African Public Library, 1959) p. 29 (Gijsbert Hemmy's own background was apposite: he was the son of Theodor Hemmy, a successful slaving captain and one of the Cape's wealthiest men.)

113 Leibbrandt, *Requesten* (18 September 1772) vol. 2, 772, (emphasis added).

114 CAD A455 no. 14, "Information respecting Cape Good Hope given by Col. Dalrymple, 1784, 1785" (emphasis added).

115 Anders Sparrman, *A Voyage to the Cape of Good Hope . . .* (Cape Town: Van Riebeeck Society Second Series, No. 7, 1977), vol. 1, p. 181.

them, and *serve him for life*. Should they run away, their master shall be entitled to pursue them and punish them *na merites*.

Articul 6 concerning the ordinary Hottentot farm retainers brought up by Christians, they shall serve their masters up to the age of 25 and not enter another's employ without his consent. No runaway Hottentot shall be allowed sanctuary in any *colonie* (kraal) but shall be accosted and warned by the District Officers and despatched directly back to their *Lord and Master*, or else taken in custody by the messenger.[116]

Honoratus Christiaan Maynier, the *Landdrost* of Graaf Reinet, confirmed that such actions were being perpetrated against the San (Bushman) as well: "I was also made acquainted with the most horrible atrocities committed on those occasions [commando raids] such as ordering the Hottentot [retainers] to dash out against the rocks the brains of infants (*too young to be carried by the farmers for the purpose to use them as bondsmen*), in order to save powder and shot."[117]

This process of capture and enserfment of the Khoi and also the San continued throughout the remainder of the eighteenth century, but became most apparent after the abolition of the slave trade in 1808, during a period of intense missionary activity and also imperial scrutiny. Lord Caledon's proclamation to regularize and, in a certain qualified measure, protect the Khoisan laborers, contained clauses that were quite revealing of the prior domestic practices of the employers:

10. That the master shall in no case be allowed to detain, or prevent from departing, the wife or children of any Hottentot that has been in his service, after the expiration of the term of contract of their husband or father, under pretence of a security for what may be indebted to him . . . and not be allowed by his own authority to attempt the repayment of himself, by the personal services of these natives.

11. That likewise in case of the Hottentot's dying, through which the effect of his personal contract of hire ceases, the wife and children shall be at liberty to depart.[118]

John Philip, the Scottish missionary, clearly saw that the abolition of the oceanic slave trade and the consequent rise of slave prices had resulted in an *increased* enserfment of the Khoisan peoples. In 1826 he wrote to the London Missionary Society a letter that nicely encapsulates the economic and demographic consequences of 1808: "The price of slaves is so high in consequence of the abolition of the slave trade that the farmers are in few instances able to purchase them. In the course of twenty-one or thirty years the colonial population has nearly doubled, consequently to supply that population with substitutes for the slaves, double the

---

[116] As quoted in Edmund H. Burrows, *Overberg Outspan: A Chronicle of People and Places in the South Western Districts of the Cape* (Swellendam: Swellendam Trust, 1988), p. 43.

[117] *Report from the Select Committee on Aborigines (British Settlements) with the Minutes of Evidence, Appendix and Index* (London: House of Commons, 26 June 1837), p. 28.

[118] As reproduced in Bird, *State of the Cape of Good Hope*, 247.

number is wanted; slaves cannot be got and the Hottentots are seized and reduced to a state of slavery."[119] What underlay this enserfdom was the fourfold increase in slave prices following abolition (see Figure 1-6).[120]

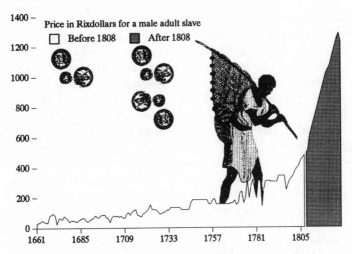

Figure 1–6. Slave prices and the effect of the abolition of the oceanic slave trade, 1661 to 1830.

One farmer living in the Zuurbrak area commented to John Philip about the acquisition of ten of his Khoi laborers, who had been driven off a mission station: "These children are my treasure, they will cultivate my farm, they will serve me instead of slaves, I shall have them all bound to me, until they are twenty five, and perhaps until they are twenty nine years of age."[121] In the same year, John Thomas Bigge, the incorruptible utilitarian royal commissioner, and William Colebroke wrote a joint letter to Earl Bathurst, the colonial secretary, claiming that they knew that Khoi women and children were being "enslaved" in the new frontier districts on the pretext of retaliation raids for cattle rustling.[122] In South African social and

---

119 Theal, *RCC,* "To the Directors of the London Missionary Society" (Layton: November 1826), 30: 157.

120 Prices: DO Transporten; CJ Notarial protocols; CAD Slave Office 10/18; CAD Accessions 45 (N = 7,610); J. S. Marais, *The Cape Coloured People,* p. 163; N. Worden, *Slavery in Dutch South Africa,* p.74. The pictogram of the male slave is based on A. Rodriguez, "Esclavo de Cabo de buena Esperanza", Africana Museum 73/720 from an "unknown" Spanish work. The coins pictured here were in use at the Cape, but the denomination (Y scale) of Rixdollars was the unit of account in both the Dutch and British periods and was issued in paper. See appendix on currency.

121 Theal, *RCC,* "Philip to Directors of L.M.S." (November 1826) 30: 157–158.

122 Theal, *RCC,* "Letter from the Commissioners of Enquiry to Earl Bathurst" (Cape Town: 25 September 1823), 16: 305.

labor history, 1721, 1775, and 1808 become watershed years, for each ushered in new attempts to attach and bond native labor. Ordinance 50, passed in 1828 (also the beginning of settler "grievances" leading to the Great Trek) was locally known as the "emancipation of the Hottentots."

Plagium and "Zombie" Slaves on the Eastern Frontier
The Eastern frontier was little different from the Western Cape frontiers, although earlier generations of historians have averred that there was no slavery in the Eastern districts.[123] The confusion arose because, while there was a prohibition against "predial" (field) slaves, there was none against domestic slaves.[124] Julian Cobbing, the South African historian, and his students have recently argued that events in Natal termed the Zulu Revolution (the Mfecane) might not have been caused by ecological factors as Martin Hall, the historical archeologist, and others have argued. The new school interprets the events as a result of vice-like pressures from northern slave raiding by the Portuguese in Mozambique and also pressures of labor coercion and slave raiding from the south by Dutch, British, Griqua, and Korana slave raiders and traders.[125] Susan Newton-King has shown clearly how the commando raids of the late eighteenth and early nineteenth centuries led to thousands of cases of slave capture in the Graaff Reinet district. This process of person stealing, technically called plagium in the slave literature, also became prevalent in the Eastern frontier.[126] Clifton Crais has pointed out the phenomenon of "zombie" slaves on the Eastern frontier — native people who were enslaved and subsequently registered under dead slaves' names. Slaves who died were never struck off the formal registers. The dead slaves' names became "placeholders," and newly captured slaves were simply registered in place of the dead slaves, with the zombie slave taking on the deceased slave's name.[127] Zombie slaves could be sold like other slaves.

These new directions in South African historiography suggest that the old established versions of not only the Mfecane but also the Great Trek (the diaspora of settlers, following emancipation in 1838) might have to be reassessed. Is it

---

[123] Eric Walker, *A History of Southern Africa* (London: Longmans, 1957) p. 157.

[124] Theal, *RCC,* "Bathurst to Donkin" (20 May 1820), 13: 135; cf. ibid., 13: 478.

[125] Julian Cobbing, "The Mfecane as Alibi," *Journal of African History* 29 (1988): 489–519; Portia Maurice, "Putting the Lid on the Mfecane Myth," *Weekly Mail* (19 September 1991), 11. In an unpublished essay, Alan Webster has argued that even Fingo historiography may be poorly understood. Instead of the traditional and picturesque version in which the missionary John Ayliff leads the Fingo out of Xhosa servitude, the Fingo, Webster argues, were being recruited into a form of coerced labor for Eastern Cape settlers; see Alan Webster, "Ayliff, Whiteside, and the 'Fingo Emancipation' of 1835," History honors thesis, Rhodes University, 1988.

[126] Susan Newton-King, "The Enemy Within," paper presented at the conference on Cape Slavery — and After, Cape Town, August 1991, pp. 1–52.

[127] Clifton Crais, "Slavery and Freedom along a Frontier: The Eastern Cape, South Africa, 1770–1838," *Slavery and Abolition* 11, 2 (September 1990): 190–210.

possible, as Stanley Trapido had earlier suggested, that the *Voortrekkers* were leaving the Cape to reestablish their freedom to coerce labor beyond the view of the enlightened imperial authorities?[128] Certainly one of the results of the demand for labor after 1808 was to place the thousands of 1820 settler households in a quandary similar to that faced by the earliest settler households in the seventeenth century. The similarities lay in the reluctance of the newly arrived European settlers to work as wage laborers and also in the ineffective sanctions against slavery in the newly settled regions.[129] According to British officials, numerous ambitious settlers exposed yet another group of original inhabitants of this region — the Xhosa — to coerced labor and enslavement.[130]

In 1825, British officials noted that "Mantatee and Goe" refugees "in a state of dreadful want and emaciation, in some cases too revolting to humanity to describe" were streaming into the Graaff Reinet and Somerset frontier districts. The Cape government, after a short deliberation, allowed their "apprenticeship,"[131] which in turn gave rise to jealousies among the newly arrived British settlers on the eastern frontier, who were also experiencing labor difficulties at the household level. After some thoughtful diplomatic traffic of letters, the English settlers were also allowed to "apprentice" these refugees.[132]

The so-called apprenticeship of such refugees was not sufficient for some farmers, however, and some slave trading emerged between them and the Xhosa. In providing evidence to the Commissioners of Enquiry as early as 1823, the colonial secretary noted that Gaika (Ngqika), the Xhosa leader, "was enjoined to guard against any future attempt to traffic in slaves with the British Settlers, a caution that was expressly stated to have proceeded from the occurrences and trials which had already reflected disgrace upon the settlers in the encouragement given to the Caffres to barter their people, or those of other tribes, for certain articles in request among them."[133] After the commission finished its hearings and deliberations, Major William Colebrooke and J. T. Bigge firmly concluded: "It is an object of importance to the British Government to extinguish the evil of Slavery in the

128 Stanley Trapido, "Aspects in the Transition from Slavery to Serfdom: The South African Republic, 1842–1902," *The Societies of Southern Africa in the 19th and 20th Centuries*, in University of London: Institute of Commonwealth Studies Seminar Papers, 6 (1975): 24–31.

129 John Barrow, *Travels into the Interior of Southern Africa . . .* , 2nd ed. (London: Cadell, 1806), vol. 2, p. 91.

130 Theal, *RCC,* "Bigge to Bathurst" (25 September 1823), 16: 305.

131 Theal, *RCC,* "Regulations to which Masters of Apprentices Indentured by his Majesty's Fiscal Shall in Future be Bound" (Fiscal's office: [no date, but 30 July 1825, cf. enclosure]), 22: 420–422.

132 Theal, *RCC,* "Letter from Lord Charles Somerset to Earl Bathurst" (Cape of Good Hope: 30 July 1825), 22: 419.

133 Theal, *RCC,* "Extracts from the Minute Book of the Commission of Enquiry" (20 August 1823), 16: 207.

newly planted Settlement of Albany, and to take away the many temptations to it that exist in that quarter from the vicinity of the Savage Tribes on the Frontier." Perhaps there was more than a little irony in the deliberate vague identification of those "Tribes."[134]

There is also some evidence for these developments in the statistical data of the slave population throughout the Cape colony. As one can appreciate from a study of the distribution of slave labor after 1808, the big expansion of slavery at the Cape was into the Eastern districts. In 1833, fully one-sixth of all 38,257 slaves were in the Eastern Cape.[135] A table of the population age and sex structure of the registered slave population in 1833 reveals several anomalies. The high sex ratio (the number of men per 100 women) in the cohorts born before 1807 reveals the colony's dependence on the highly sex-skewed slave cargoes to the Cape. But the low sex ratios (a significant surplus of girls) in the youngest cohort (0 to 5 years old) are beyond explanation by the normal parameters of natural reproduction of any known population. In nearly all societies, a sex ratio of 104 (a slight surplus of males) is normal at birth. The districts of Somerset, Uitenhage, Worcester, Beaufort (with the exception of Worcester, all Eastern districts) all had lower than normal sex ratios in these two age groups (see Figure 1-7).[136]

Were native infant female children being captured and added to the registered slave population? That could be one explanation. Studies of plagium in all other societies do demonstrate that female slaves were captured, possibly because they could become breeding mothers and also could more easily be absorbed into the household.[137] However, too large an incidence of slave raids would result in retribution.[138] Since such plagium was officially considered illegal, documentary evidence of this activity is bound to be difficult to unearth. Philanthropic commissioners, aware of this possibility, noted:

From the loose and hasty manner in which the Opgaaf [census] returns were executed, errors may easily occur, but the accuracy of the Slave Registry depends very much upon the correctness of the original enumeration, which it must be observed has never been tried by any identification of the slaves themselves. The circumstances and position of the Colony are such as to require some Periodical test of the Powers of the Slave Registry, for although experience has proved that

---

[134] Theal, *RCC*, "Report of the Commissioners of Enquiry to the Under Secretary of State, Colonial Department" (Cape Town: 1 June 1825), 21: 440.

[135] PRO CO 53/57 (31 August 1833), 149–150. I am indebted to John Mason for this reference.

[136] CO 53/57 (31 August 1833), folios 149-150. Note the imbalance of sexes in the youngest cohort: more young girls than boys (N = 38,257). A normal ratio at birth is approximately 104 boys to 100 girls.

[137] Orlando Patterson, *Slavery and Social Death: A Comparative Study* (Cambridge: Harvard University Press, 1982), p. 120.

[138] Peter Wood, *Black Majority: Negroes in South Carolina, from 1670 through the Stono Rebellion* (New York: Norton, 1975), pp. 38–39 and Table 1, p. 144.

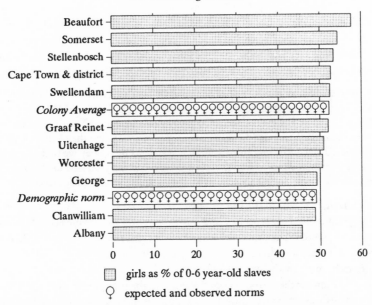

Figure 1–7. Evidence of enslavement of young native girls, 1833.

little is to be apprehended from illicit importation of Slaves by sea into the Colony, yet the variety of feature and complexion of which its Slave Population and that of the Border Tribes is composed, affords opportunities of fraudulent and illicit increase which it would not be easy to detect.[139]

Jason, an enslaved Tswana man who complained to the Guardian that he was illegally held in slavery, may be regarded as the classic case of plagium. Jason's complaint resulted in his being sent to jail for four years, which explains why there were not many more such complaints. The terse wording of the official indicates little discomfort with Jason's case, and there was no redress: "Complains that he is illegally detained as a slave and stated that he is by birth a Briqua (Bechuan[a]) and was bought to this colony when a child, by his parents, who left him with a certain Willem Steenkamp, on whose account he was ultimately sold as a slave."[140] Although strenuously denied by earlier generations of historians, it would appear that the virtually unrestrained ability of the seventeenth-, eighteenth-, and early nineteenth-century settlers to attach "available" land through the relatively cheap domination of water and land resources and through their possession of firearms also underlay their ability to force the native populations into a wide range of coerced forms of labor.

---

[139] Theal, *RCC,* "Report upon the Slaves and State of Slavery at the Cape of Good Hope, London" (5 April 1831), 35: 359.

[140] William Wright, *Slavery at the Cape of Good Hope* (New York: Negro Universities Press, 1969), p. 13.

That the colony came to be "based" on slavery was a result of tens of thousands of decisions at the individual household level. The thought process must have been very much the same as Johanna Margaretha Duminy's account of such a household decision taken in the *Bokkeveld* (an inland region) in 1797:

Our hostess told us that she had been living on this farm for seventeen years, fifteen years of which had been spent in a miserable little *pondok* [Malayan word for house]. She had had no slaves. She had been all by herself with her husband. Until last year she had helped cut the corn. . . . Two years ago they had bought two little slaves, a girl and a boy from a French vessel. "The money we had, Mistress," she said, "was made out of our sheep, and God has truly blessed us, for not only have I a little house to live in now at long last, but also two little slaves."[141]

Mrs. Duminy, the wife of the Cape's most experienced slaver and herself the owner of a large household of slaves in Cape Town, felt sorry for the poverty of her rural hostess's household. She pitied the woman, "for until now she has carried her own wood and water, and likewise . . . [did] her all her own work." Although all historians have claimed that the Company condemned South Africa to slave labor, the explanation for the introduction of slaves and the interpolation of serfs into the Cape domestic environment must be laid squarely at the doorstep of the individual householder. Slaves were purchased and serfs acquired by individual families whenever they needed them.

This chapter provides an economic and also a social and domestic explanation for the decline of all free wage labor and the subsequent introduction and maintenance of both slavery and serfdom. The slave-owning family itself was a push factor. Younger sons, approaching maturity, had secure expectations of inheritance. They worked for their fathers or mothers in a temporary capacity. There was less and less need for wage labor, since the burgeoning settler families provided sufficient internal domestic incentives and expectations, while successful plantation owners bought imported slaves. The younger generations of settlers took over first the traditional labor role and then also the overseer role of the knecht. Both were good training grounds for future slave owners. The native people, ostensibly free, lost their freedom and became an important source of bonded labor from 1721 on. Both slavery and serfdom were instituted and, more important, maintained by Cape households; slavery and serfdom were never mandated by the Company. Slavery and serfdom became the most convenient labor systems at the Cape, since both slaves and serfs were cheaper and more coercible than free wage labor. Both forms of labor produced offspring, that were also property. Both parent slaves and slave children could be passed on to heirs of the free owners. This allowed for the maintenance of settlers' dynastic ambition.

---

[141] J. L. M. Franken, (ed.), *Duminy Dagboek* (Cape Town: Van Riebeeck Society, 1938), "Journal, 1797," pp. 123–124.

Freed slaves, who could own property legally in practice were mostly too impoverished to buy any. Such freed slaves simply became renters and modest wage laborers (mostly as fishermen) struggling to find a niche in the interstices of the growing slave economy, and they did not compete for land on strictly economic grounds. This economic process had racial consequences for the colony. People of European descent came to own most of the land. Slaves and serfs worked the land, while the few freed slaves worked the sea (see Figure 1-8).[142]

Figure 1–8. Free black fishermen, 1833.

Once legally sanctioned slavery was at an end, in 1838, coerced agricultural labor nevertheless continued in one form or another in the "emancipated" Cape colony, a topic that is beyond the scope of this study. Coerced servitude from the native population was the second choice for those acquiring labor for their households from 1652 to 1808. Before the abolition of the oceanic trade the principal sources of enslaved labor at the Cape were importing humans through the slave trade and classifying their descendants as slaves.

---

[142] Free blacks in Cape Town were driven to making their living in the sea because they were financially unable to buy land. There was also some legal problem about their right to own land; while they could and did own land in the seventeenth century, by the 1820s they could only own land "with the express permission of the Governor." RCC 28: 36–37. Artist: Charles Davidson Bell Source: ART 179, Courtesy of the Brenthurst Library.

*T*w o

The Tower of Babel
The Cape Slave Trade and Creolization

TODAY'S DESCENDANTS of the early immigrant settler members of Cape households still celebrate their Dutch, English, French, and German ancestors.[1] This is not so with persons who were imported to the Cape as slaves. With the Cape community's loss of memory of slaves' origins, there was a corresponding loss of identity among the slaves' descendants. Part of this loss of identity may be attributed to our ignorance of two complex processes: the oceanic slave trade and creolization. The oceanic slave trade that supplied slave owners changed dramatically between 1652 and 1822, the date of the last (illegally) imported slaves. In addition, a growing number of slaves were born into slavery at the Cape, the process that I have termed creolization. From these imported and local cultures arose the imperfectly understood but richly textured, syncretistic, domestic creole culture of the Cape. Without knowledge of the slaves' origins, we cannot make meaningful assumptions about the social, cultural, linguistic, and religious behavior of *any* Cape slaveholding households.

Changing shipping patterns, the rise and fall of trading companies, and shifting commercial alliances between urban slave traders and transient maritime personnel all shaped the composition of households at the Cape. The Cape became an increasingly polyglot colony. Between 1652 to 1808, approximately 63,000 slaves were imported to the Cape from four main areas (see Figure 2-1).[2]

---

[1] I would like to thank Stanley Engerman, Kathleen Hasselblad, Shamil Jeppie, Robert Tignor, and Anthony Whyte for reading earlier versions of this chapter.

[2] Shell, "Popucape." Total number of slaves imported, including Lodge slaves: 62,964. This figure was arrived at by an iterative calculation on the population of all Cape slaves (burgher, Lodge and officials) of each census year.

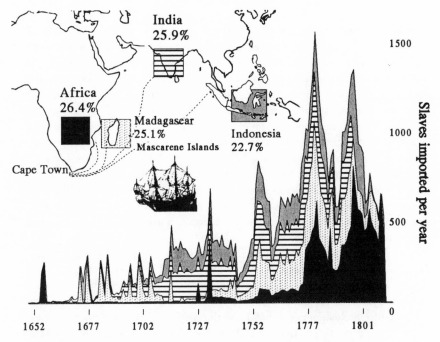

Figure 2–1. Origins of slaves imported to the Cape, 1652 to 1808.

Mercantile Competition

Mercantile rivalries, which often led to maritime conflict, explain the basic vectors of the Cape slave trade until 1792. The Dutch West India Company, for example, would not allow the Dutch East India Company to slave on the coasts of West Africa. Consequently the Company, the patrician officials, and the Cape burghers turned to territories east of Cape Town for all imported slave labor during the first century of Dutch occupation. Victor de Kock, an early South African historian, said that the Dutch West India Company had even claimed the Cape colony itself (technically on the West Coast of Africa) although the Dutch Estates General, who oversaw both companies, did not recognize the claim.[3] Because of this eastern orientation, West African and Central African enslaved persons, who constituted most of the New World's slaves, came to early colonial South Africa only through smuggling, shipwrecks, or as naval "prizes."

Several hundred Bantu-speaking slaves from west and Central Africa were nevertheless imported in the first decades of the colony's occupation. One secret

---

[3] James C. Armstrong and Nigel Worden, "The Slaves," in Richard Elphick and Herman Giliomee (eds.), *The Shaping of South Africa* (Middletown, Conn.: Wesleyan University Press, 1991), p. 77; Victor De Kock, *Those in Bondage: An Account of the Life of the Slave at the Cape in the Days of the Dutch East India Company* (London: Allen & Unwin, 1950), pp. 30–31.

expedition to Dahomey in 1658 returned with a few slaves. In the same year, when a Dutch ship captured a Portuguese slaver bound for Brazil with approximately 500 Angolan slaves, 174 of those slaves were landed at the Cape.[4] West African slaves were also clandestinely shipped from Cape Verde on outward-bound Dutch East India Company ships. After the first decades of colonial rule few slaves were imported from West or Central Africa; the descendants of West and Central Africans were at the Cape for the entire period of formal slavery. One cannot assert, as South African historians still do, that settler contact with Bantu speakers began on the Eastern frontier in the 1770s. There were Bantu-speaking slaves and free blacks in Cape Town from the beginning. Most imported Cape slaves were drawn from the Indian Ocean Basin, from the east coast of Africa to the outer reaches of Borneo and the shores of China; these slaves included persons of (in alphabetical order) Abyssinian, Arabian, Bengali, Borneose, Brazilian, Burmese, Chinese, Iranian, Japanese, and Sri Lankan origin.[5]

Slaving on the east coast of Africa itself proved unreliable and dangerous in the seventeenth and early eighteenth century, and by 1731 slaves from the Eastern possessions of the Dutch East India Company had come to outnumber all other imported slaves at the Cape. The East proved a stable source of slaves until the collapse of Dutch shipping in 1780 and the rise of international maritime commerce around the Cape after 1784. After that, the African mainland and Madagascar became the prime sources of slaves. During the next 24 years, from 1784 to 1808, most of these imported slaves were landed at the Cape. Thus the first slaves imported to the Cape were African, and so were the last.

The Cape officially faced east for its main commercial business until the Commissioners-General issued a statute on the November 21, 1792, allowing

---

4 Armstrong and Worden, "The Slaves," 111.

5 For example, the first commandant of the colony, Jan van Riebeeck, owned two "Arabian slave girls from Abyssinia" Cornelia (10) and Lijsbeth (12); see Willem Blommaert, "Het invoeren van de slavernij aan de Kaap," *Archives Year Book* 1, 1 (1938): 6; for Achmet van Arabia, see African Court Calender, 1819 (Cape Town: SAL, 1986, 94); see also DO: "Transporten en Scheepenkennis" (hereafter Transporten): "Fabia from Brazil" (8 March 1712), "Soutanij from Burma" (24 June 1706), "David Casta from China" (15 March 1685), "Anthony, Moor van Japan" was owned by Jan Dirckz de Beer on their farm Ecklenberg, see MOOC 8/1/63 (1 March 1701); cf. Anna J. Böeseken, *Slaves and Free Blacks at the Cape, 1658–1700* (Cape Town: Tafelberg, 1977), pp. 93, 95–96, 101; conceivably Anthony was owned and imported by the Dutch commandant at the Japanese station at Nagasaki, who sold him at the Cape when he retired; Anthony Whyte has informed me there were four Japanese persons classified as "free blacks" in the nineteenth century (personal communication, 15 May 1992); see "Werf van Persien" in CJ 3047 (11 February 1767), pp. 23–24; "Lacqui van Persie," in Hendrik Carel Vos Leibbrandt, *Requesten (Memorials) 1715–1806,* (Cape Town: Cape Times, 1905), vol. 2 (1790), p. 726; the Company had a post in Gamron in Persia, see Leibbrandt, *Journaal, 1699–1732* (Cape Town: W. A. Richards & Sons, Government Printers, 1896, p.46 (5 January, 1702); Leibbrandt, *Requesten*, "Leonara van Siam vol. 1 (1790), 191; "Achilles van Siam," ibid., vol. 2 (1759), 1086; "Silvia van Borneo," ibid., vol. 1 (1776), 266.

Cape colonists to trade on the West Coast of Africa and in all of the former possessions of the Company in the East.[6] Up until this establishment of free trade in 1792, then, official mercantilist rivalries were the primary cause of the significant changes in the origins of Cape slaves.

Shipping Patterns

Changes in shipping patterns were also responsible for changes in the continental origins of slaves imported to the Cape. In the early decades of the eighteenth century, nearly 80 percent of all slaves imported came from the Indian subcontinent. In the second half of the eighteenth century, the smaller numbers of Ceylon fleets and ships within fleets from both Sri Lanka and India led to a decline in the proportion of slaves imported from the Indian subcontinent.[7] It steadily dropped to a little more than 15 percent in the last decades of the legal oceanic slave trade. If Danish company ships had not continued to bring in slaves from Tranquebar, the proportion imported from the Indian subcontinent would have declined even more rapidly.[8]

---

[6] J. A. De Mist, *Memorandum on the Cape* (Cape Town: Van Riebeeck Society, no. 3, 1920), p. 247.

[7] This was established by counting departure ports of "homeward voyages" of Indiamen from 1652 to 1795; J. R. Bruijn et al. (eds.), *Dutch-Asiatic Shipping in the 17th and 18th Centuries* (The Hague: Martinus Nijhoff, 1979), vol. 1, pp. 60-573.

[8] In the literature since 1825 on the Cape slave trade, much emphasis has been given to the year 1767, during which officials in Batavia resolved that no further male slaves would be brought to the Cape from the East on Dutch ships. James Armstrong, Robert Ross, and Nigel Worden have all opined that this legislation was prompted "by violent crimes by Indonesian slaves" at the Cape, but this set of statutes originating from Batavia should rather be seen in an earlier context of the Dutch East India Company's attempts to stop their homeward-bound captains from transporting Eastern male slaves to the Cape free of charge. A continuous sequence of Batavian legislation from the seventeenth through the eighteenth century supports this line of argument. Any drop in the number of imported Eastern slaves after 1767 may be more persuasively attributed to the precipitous decline in Company shipping past the Cape, as one can see Figure 2-2. In this light, the legislation of 1767 should *not* be regarded as a watershed date in the Cape slave trade; Armstrong and Worden, "The Slaves," 117. See J. A. van der Chijs (comp.), *Nederlandsch-Indisch Plakkaatboek, 1602–1811* ('s-Gravenhage: M. Nijhoff, 1885), 1: 600; 4: 37, 69, 80, 84; 5: 3; 7: 291; 10: 592, 692, 726; 11: 629; 13: 618; 15: 1053; 16: 181 and *passim* throughout the remainder of the series. The slave trade in the East carried on by Dutch officers was probably responsible for this outpouring of legislation. Similar legislation forbade Dutch officers from taking Eastern slaves on board to Sri Lanka, Ibid., 8:673. For the older view, see Izaak David du Plessis, *The Cape Malays: History, Religion, Traditions, Folk Tales, the Malay Quarter* (Cape Town: Balkema, 1972), p. 3, quoting "Realia," Landsarchief, Batavia, 28 September 1867. More compelling evidence for the unimportance of this statute was that it was reissued many times (1784, 1787), an almost certain indication that the clandestine importation of Eastern male slaves continued; Kathleen Jeffreys and S. D. Naude, (eds.), *Kaapse Plakkaatboek, 1652–1806* (Cape Town: Kaapse Argiefstukke, 1944–1949), vol. 3, p. 164. Moreover, only one slaving skipper was ever arrested for importing Eastern male slaves, and only two slaves were ever returned to Batavia. These confiscations occurred under the unrepresentative regime of Fiscal Boers; Armstrong and Worden, "The Slaves," 171, note 42.

Between 1731 and 1765, slaves were increasingly imported from the Indonesian Archipelago and from Madagascar.

The port patricians' traditional trading connections with the slave-trading skippers of Dutch Company ships became less significant with the rise in international shipping after 1765. Cape Town slave traders had to broaden their sources of supply to keep up with the increasing demand for slaves from the hinterland. The broadening of slave-trading contacts broke up the former monopoly of the port's patriciate. New ships based in American, Austrian, French, Hanseatic, Portuguese, Prussian, and Russian ports, arrived at the Cape in larger numbers, and this new shipping overshadowed Company shipping which had predominated in the first 125 years of occupation.

The second major shift in shipping patterns was a consequence of a maritime conflict, the Anglo-Dutch War of 1780 to 1784, in which the Dutch East India Company suffered crippling shipping losses. The English, for their part, obtained freedom of navigation in and around the Indonesian Archipelago with the 1784 Anglo-Dutch treaty. The bulk of the slaves imported to the Cape earlier had come in Dutch ships from Dutch Indonesian possessions. After the treaty, few Dutch ships brought slaves to the Cape. Other shipping nations not only took up the slack, but also acquired by default the Cape's expanding market for imported slaves (see Figure 2-2).[9]

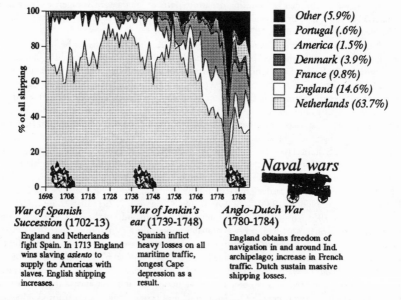

Figure 2–2. Shipping patterns to the Cape, 1698 to 1795.

[9] Coenraad Beyers, *Die Kaapse Patriotte, 1779-1791* (Cape Town: Juta, 1929). Shipping appendix, pp. 237–239; J.R. de Bruijn, et al. (eds.), *Dutch-Asiatic Shipping in the 17th and 18th centuries* (The Hague: Martinus Nijhoff, 1979) vols. 2, 3.

The decline of Dutch East India Company shipping around the Cape after the war was most noticeable after 1784. The Anglo-Dutch War proved to be the true watershed date for the origin of Cape slaves. The Company, which had aligned itself militarily with the French state, invited French garrisons to station themselves at the Cape, ushering in a period of unparalleled prosperity, new investment in slaves, and fiercer competition in the port's slave marketplace. After 1780, Cape farmers and the port's patriciate publicly competed for East African slave cargoes brought in by the French company and French private traders. The French were aggressively building a sugar plantation complex in the Mascarene Islands, and a slave trade came into being to supply those huge plantations. Consequently, slave trading in the southeastern Atlantic increased markedly, and independently of the Cape demand. Cape slave owners benefited from all these developments. The most important consequence was the dissolution of the informal monopoly the local Dutch officials held in the limited Cape slave trade. The new French connection also led to significant slave supplies from mainland Africa, especially from Mozambique, and also from Madagascar and the Mascarenes.[10]

After the first British occupation of the Cape in 1795, the east coast of Africa became the major source of Cape slaves. Portuguese slavers temporarily replaced the French shipping contacts, which were interrupted by the French Revolution and the ensuing Napoleonic wars. Mozambique became the single most important source of slave labor in the late eighteenth and early nineteenth centuries. This was accelerated by the proclamation of the free trade statutes of 1792 and the later licensed slave trade of the first British occupation (1795 to 1803). Slaves from Mozambique became known as *Mozbiekers* by Cape slave owners. French shipping eventually increased again, well after the French Revolution, and Commissioner J. de Mist estimated in 1803 that "slaves are also brought in large numbers from Madagascar, Mozambique by the French for purposes of trade."[11] William Freund, the historian of the Batavian administration who identified and tallied individual imported-slave advertisements, found that of the approximately 1,039 slaves who arrived in Cape Town during the three-year Batavian administration, at least 790 came from Mozambique. This illustrates dramatically the Africanization of the slave force under the post-1795 administrations.[12] Samuel Hudson, who had been the customs officer and who noted all slave ships in his journal, noted that by 1806: "The slaves at the Cape principally consist of Mosambiques, Malays and Bouganeese. Some few from other countries, but these compose the general mass."[13] Mozambique was the principal source of slaves from 1795. After 1808

---

[10] Robert Ross, "The Last Years of the Slave Trade to the Cape Colony, *Slavery and Abolition* 9, 3 (December 1988): 209–219.

[11] De Mist, *Memorandum on the Cape*, 252.

[12] William Freund, "Society and Government in Dutch South Africa: The Cape and the Batavians, 1803–1806," Ph.D. thesis, Yale University, 1971, Table 4, p. 249.

[13] Robert C.-H. Shell, (ed.), "'Slaves,' An Essay by Samuel Eusebius Hudson," *Kronos* 9 (1984): 46 ff.

those slaves captured at sea by the British navy and "liberated" at the Cape as "prize negroes" were also from Mozambique.

Tabulation of individual slave origins confirms that Mozambiquan slaves were imported in increasing numbers from about 1770. The Cape's role in Mozambique was small compared with the other slaving nations. Philip Curtin points out that about 40 percent of all slaves imported to Brazil in the same period came from Mozambique, and that this massive surge in slaving took place over a brief period.[14] The origins of *all* slaves imported to the Cape from 1652 to 1808 comprise a broad palette unparalleled in any other recorded slave population anywhere in the world (see Figure 2-1).

Creolization: The Household as a Source of Slaves

To what extent did Cape slave-owning households depend on the slave trade? Were most Cape slaves imported? The study of slave acculturation, rebellion, runaways, and the formation of a creole culture and language all hinge on establishing the rate of creolization. Most who have written on this topic have claimed that the Cape slave force did not reproduce itself before 1808.[15] Their judgment contradicts Otto Mentzel, a German colonist who, writing of the 1740s, first hinted at the creole origins of the Cape slaves: "On the farms there is always room for more slaves. It therefore pays farmers to keep an equal number of male and female slaves and by their natural increase to cope with the growing needs of the farm and avoid the necessity of buying additional slaves. . . . The majority of privately owned slaves have been born in the country [i.e., the region, not the rural "country"]."[16] To obtain the rate of creolization, the proportion of creole slaves has been calculated for consecutive periods (see Figure 2-3).[17]

---

[14] Philip D. Curtin, *The Atlantic Slave Trade: A Census* (Madison: University of Wisconsin Press, 1969), pp. 229–230.

[15] Andrew Bank, *The Decline of Urban Slavery at the Cape, 1806 to 1843* (Cape Town: Centre for African Studies, 1991), p. 6.

[16] Otto Friedereich Mentzel, *A Complete and Authentic Geographical and Topographical Description of the Famous and All Things Considered Remarkable African Cape of Good Hope . . .*, trans. G. V. Marais and J. Hoge, rev. ed. (Cape Town: Van Riebeeck Society, 1944), vol. 2, pp. 90, 126.

[17] 1652-1731, R. Shell, "Saledeed"; DO; MOOC; Vendu lists; SO 17/1; CO = PRO CO 53/57. Bradlow and M. Cairns, *The Early Cape Muslims* (Cape Town: Balkema, 1978); N. Worden, *Slavery in Dutch South Africa*, Table 4.1. The intervals in the chart are similar to the intervals used in the calculations concerning the geographic origins of slaves, except that two further important sources that reveal creole, but not geographical, origins have been drawn upon. These are a tabulation of all domestic sales between 1823 and 1830 and data for a population pyramid, which British officials tabulated from the slave population of August of 1833. Since this latter document agrees with both the independent Slave Registration Office and the census returns of that year, one can assume these data are accurate.

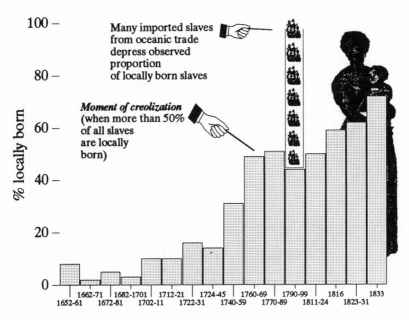

Figure 2–3. Percentage of Cape slave population that was locally born, 1652 to 1833.

The Lodge slaves, those slaves belonging to the Dutch East Company, suffered high mortality and left few survivors who could propagate a locally born generation. Even in 1826, well after the abolition of the slave trade in 1808, there were more imported than creole slaves in the Lodge. However, those few creole Lodge slaves who did survive infancy lived longer than imported slaves. According to the inventories and wills, most of the slaves who belonged to non-Company owners were creole by 1770. Although there was no perceptible change in slave fertility, the surge in slave imports after the arrival of French garrisons was so massive as to outweigh the number of slaves locally born in the following decade. This is simply an artifact. The figures reflect a greater overall percentage of imported slaves in the total slave population with no diminution of the rate of creolization.

Moreover, this surge in imports had an echo effect for later creolization. Because of French slaving practice, slaves imported after 1770 were both younger and more often female than those in earlier cargoes. By the time these younger imported female slaves reached maturity in the 1800s, the entire slave population (imported and creole) was younger and included many more young women than before. After the abolition of the slave trade in 1808, the Cape slave population creolized at an increasing pace, consistent with a "slave-breeding" hypothesis, though the more probable explanation lies in the increasingly favorable age and sex composition of the population from around 1770 (see Figure 2-4).[18]

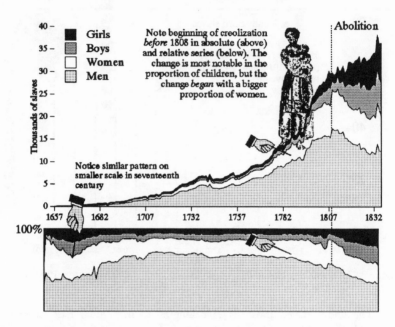

Figure 2–4. Age and sex composition of the slave population, 1652 to 1833.

Most historians regard 1808 as the date around which the slave populations in the English-speaking colonial world started to creolize. The presumption is that slave owners, aware of the shortfall in supply, turned to natural increase and "slave breeding" after this date. This might have been true elsewhere, but it was not so at the Cape. The Cape slave population had several earlier "moments of creolization" (when the slave population was more than 50 percent locally born). Mentzel was partly right, but so too were his detractors. The slave population was reproducing itself; it simply was not reproducing fast enough to meet the demands of the expanding population of slave owners. The population of slave owners was expanding on three fronts: through immigration, natural increase, and personal choice — that is, more free people at the Cape were choosing to become slave owners. All these increases in demand led to a growing slave trade.

---

[18] Shell, "Popucape." All three slave groups are tabulated here, i.e. Lodge slaves, those belonging to the officials and also those belonging to the burghers.

Cultural Consequences of Changing Origins and Creolization

Of all the slaves imported to the Cape, only the slaves who belonged to the Company can be said to have shared a common culture. One incident dramatically illustrates the cultural propinquity of the Company's early slaves from Madagascar. When the Company's Malagasy interpreter — bought on an earlier voyage — was shocked to see "his aunt" being offered for sale, the Company accommodated him buying her too, and bringing her back to the Cape.[19] Of all the slave groups, only the Company slaves were from the same language group, the same religious background, the same geographical areas, and, in at least this one case, the same kin network.

That the first glimmerings of an imported slave culture emanated from the Lodge is, therefore, not surprising. A play about a Cape slave woman who had been ravished, written around 1713 by the son of an exile "was regularly performed at night by firelight in the lodge."[20] According to oral sources, in the 1740s religious meetings, led by a Muslim slave overseer, were also first reported in the Lodge.[21] After that, however, there is little mention of such cultural occurrences. After 1744, the Company's constantly changing slaving areas turned this large household of almost 1,000 slaves into a potpourri of subcultures. Chinese convicts, slaves from Bengal, Sri Lanka, and, finally, large numbers of slaves from Zanzibar changed the cultural makeup of the Lodge. The same process occurred among the bulk of the slave force, but from the start the burghers' slaves had been much more culturally heterogeneous.

Stereotyping by Origin

The primary consequence of the changing origins of imported slaves was the colonial construction of stereotypes by origin. These stereotypes were partly reflected in the price history of all imported and creole slaves. It is important to emphasize that these stereotypes arose in individual households and were not imposed by any agency. These stereotypes were best expressed by slave owners acting in concert at slave auctions. Sources from other colonial areas of the time suggest that premiums based on origin were not unique to the Cape. Jan van Laet, a seventeenth-century historian, said that Political Counselor Servaicus Carpentier

---

[19] AR VOC 4034: "Rapport . . ." (January 1695), no pagination.

[20] Personal communication, Stephen Gray; see also Gray, "Our Forgotten Drama," *Speak* (March/April 1978): 14–15. According to Gray, the manuscript is owned by a person "who does not wish his name revealed for political reasons." A few scholarly doubts have arisen as to its existence.

[21] I. D. du Plessis and C. A. Lückhoff, *The Malay Quarter and Its People* (Cape Town: Balkema, 1983), p. 34; see also Robert C.-H. Shell, "The Establishment and Spread of Islam at the Cape from the beginning of Company Rule to 1838," Honors thesis, University of Cape Town, 1974, p. 32.

claimed that, in Brazil, "The Angolan Negroes were largely employed in agricultural labour but had to be kept at it always with many lashes. The Guinea Negroes are excellent, so that the majority are used for domestic service, for waiting on table, and the like. Those [slaves] of Cape Verde are the best and most robust of all and they are the ones that cost the most here."[22] This is a feature of all New World slave societies, as noted by Philip Curtin and a broad range of scholars: "Slave buyers distinguished between African cultures following a set of stereotyped 'national characters' highlighting traits that seemed important to slave-owners — industry, proneness to rebellion, faithfulness, honesty, or physical suitability for field work. Such stereotypes differed through time and from one colony to another, but they could have a marked influence on the price offered in particular American markets."[23] Curtin puts national character in quotation marks correctly, since geographic origin, not national character, was the target subject of all such stereotypes. But it is not difficult to see how one could become the other, and since the Cape slave population was more heterogeneous than any other slave society, it is not surprising that stereotyping rose to unprecedented — even fantastic — levels.

At the Cape there was a system of premiums based on the geographic origin and creole status of slaves. Indeed, the exact premium Cape slave buyers were willing to pay for a slave from a specific region may be calculated — a useful, if hardly conclusive, measure of criteria based on origin in the division of labor. Male slaves from Indonesia fetched the largest premium based on origin (7.2 percent), their high price confirming the travelers' stereotype of the skilled Malay or Asian craftsperson. Creole slaves were on the top, slaves from the Eastern colonial possessions were next, Malagasy slaves were on the bottom (see Figure 2-5).[24]

---

[22] As quoted in Gilberto Freyre, *The Masters and the Slaves: A Study in the Development of Brazilian Civilization* (New York: Knopf, 1971), p. 303; Cape Verde (sometimes St. Iago in written slave transfers) meant neither the actual cape where Dakar now stands nor the Cape Verde islands, sometimes called the salt islands (cf. François Valentijn, *Description of the Cape of Good Hope. . . .* ed. E. H. Raidt, trans. Maj. R. Raven-Hart (Cape Town: Van Riebeeck Society, 1973) vol. 1, p. 170, but the hinterland of "the Guineau of Cape Verde," stretching roughly from the Cape Verde peninsula to the Sierra Leone River. Slaves from Cape Verde were so expensive at the Cape that the only person who could afford them was the wealthiest slave trader in the colony, the governor himself.

[23] Curtin, *The Atlantic Slave Trade*, 155; see also Peter H. Wood, "More Like a Negro Country: Demographic Patterns in Colonial South Carolina, 1700–1740," in Stanley L. Engerman and Eugene D. Genovese, *Race and Slavery in the Western Hemisphere: Quantitative Studies* (Princeton: Princeton University Press, 1975), p. 152 and notes 64, 65; Daniel Littlefield, the American historian of South Carolina, has also convincingly shown how stereotypes by origin developed momentum in the seventeenth and eighteenth centuries and resulted in different price structures for slaves from different points in Africa. Daniel C. Littlefield, *Rice and Slaves: Ethnicity and the Slave Trade in Colonial South Carolina* (Baton Rouge: Louisiana State University Press, 1981), pp. 8–32.

[24] Robert C.-H. Shell, "Slavery at the Cape of Good Hope, 1680-1731," Ph.D. dissertation,

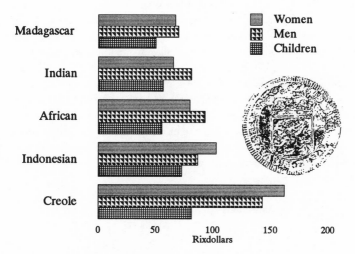

Figure 2–5. Price differentiation by slaves' origin, sex, and age.

Stereotypes and the Division of Labor

Other factors can also affect the different prices. Expectations of high mortality could explain the lower prices for African and Malagasy slaves. Shortages of slaves from one area could lead to a complicated system of arbitrage. Far more convincing, however, are the words of the participants in Cape slave society. From the outset of colonial occupation, settlers and officials definitely perceived each group of slaves differently, and these stereotypes had significant consequences for the Cape household, influencing the choice of a slave's occupation. The skill of slaves was directly attributed to origin in one document that mentions the settlers' geographic preferences in women slaves: "Female slaves from Bengal or the Coast of Coromandel, from Surat and Macassar, are in great demand, because they have a reputation as skillful needlewomen." Mentzel spoke with personal authority on this issue, since he earned some pocket money producing embroidery designs for the settler wives, who passed them on to their slave seamstresses.[25] Imported slave women from these areas were never used in agricultural work, but were always assigned to needle craft within the house. The first sight one encountered on entering a typical eighteenth-century Cape house was "a long, broad gallery where four or six slave women sat on small wooden benches, sewing or knitting."[26]

Yale University, 1986, vol. 2, pp. 451-473. Shell, "Saledeed"; Shell, "Popucape." (N = 4,122 slaves; 566 slave sales, or 13.7 percent, had missing values.)

[25] Mentzel, *Description*, vol. 2, pp. 127–128.

[26] F. C. Dominicus, *Het Huiselik en Maatschappelik Leven van de Zuid-Afrikaner* ('s-Gravenhage: Martinus Nijhoff, 1919), pp. 36–37. Placing the women slave workers in the hall, or *voorkamer*, was evidently an inexpensive way of supervising them, since friends and visitors of the slave owner would always go through the hall.

The skills such women had learned in their Eastern areas of origin not only earned them the right to stay out of agricultural work, but also brought them into closer, more intimate domestic contact with their owners which had important long-term consequences for the role of *all* slave women in later Cape households. How else can one explain that African slave women continued to be employed within the Cape household in the early nineteenth century? The Cape was in striking contrast to the whole of the New World, where African slave women, from the outset of colonization, were immediately put to work in the fields, although a few favored female slaves were also brought into the house.[27] Early stereotyping of female slaves by origin at the Cape resulted in longterm occupational stereotyping by gender, which overrode notions of origin, creole status, and descent (see Figure 2-6).[28]

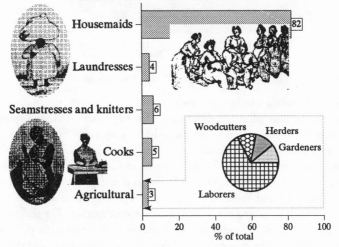

Figure 2–6. Cape slave women's occupations, 1823 to 1830.

Anders Sparrman, a trained botanist, wrote in the 1770s that Malagasy slaves "had a particular knack at finding wild bees and honey."[29] Possibly some aspects of this type of petty stereotyping had some original validity due to domestic customs

[27] E.S. Morgan, *American Slavery, American Freedom* (New York: Norton, 1975), p. 235; Robert C.-H. Shell, "Tender Ties: The Women of the Cape Slave Society," Institute of Commonwealth Studies: Collected Seminar Papers, *The Societies of Southern Africa* 17, 42 (1992): 1, 15, 24; Petrus Borchardus Borcherds, *An Auto-biographical Memoir . . . Being a Plain Narrative of Occurrences from Early Life to Advanced Age Chiefly Intended for His Children and Descendants Countrymen and Friends* (Cape Town: A. S. Robertson, 1861), p. 204.

[28] CAD SO 17/1 (N = 347).

[29] Anders Sparrman, *A Voyage to the Cape of Good Hope towards the Antarctic Polar Circle around the World and to the Country of the Hottentots and the Caffres from the Year 1772–1776* (Cape Town: Van Riebeeck Society Second Series, no. 7, 1977, vol. 2, p. 152.

in the slave's place of origin. Stereotypes based on origin reached their apex just before the abolition of the oceanic slave trade. Stereotyping was both positive and negative.[30] Hudson, a Cape slave owner of some eight years standing, noted on the eve of abolition:

The Mosambiques are mild, peaceable and patient under this slavery. It seldom happens that they are guilty of those crimes so frequent among the Malays and Bouganeese. These [Mozambique] slaves are therefore more useful in the colony for hard labour and all agricultural concerns. Some of them are very ingenious and make excellent workmen. They are capable of conveying heavy burthens which they do without murmuring [and they] are affectionate and faithful to those who treat them well. . . . Each slave is put to a particular employment: the Mosambiques carry water, fetch wood, serve as masons, labourers, coolies and indeed, are generally set to the common drudgery of outdoor work though many of them are extremely serviceable. I have seen good carpenters, masons, markers at billiard tables, cooks, stable boys, in short, every kind of tradesmen from this race of poor despised patient beings. Prejudice has stamped them a dull, stupid link in the great chain and 'tis hard to do away [with] these errors which long custom has rendered sacred. Was I permitted to make choice of slaves for a continuance in the colony, I would certainly make choice of Mosambiques for fidelity & a mild disposition. The Malays certainly are much superior in all kinds of works where a ready imagination and genius is required, but they are a treacherous, shrewd, deceitful race. Scarce one but what has his *creese* [long twisted dagger] and his drugs, and woe betide the man who offends them. They may pass over an injury for a time, but let years roll on, it lives in their remembrance and they will watch the unguarded moment to revenge it. Punishment deters them not: they are fearless of danger, regardless of the consequences, and many of them look upon death as a release from misery and the immediate passport to their own . . . country. . . . Such are the Malay slaves [illegible . . . For] this readyness in all kinds of business they are preferred by the Dutch inhabitants to all others. They bring very great prices when exposed to sale: two, and sometimes three, thousand Rix Dollars has been given for these slaves. The Bouganese are likewise a treacherous set of slaves. These are by no means numerous. They are employed by the butchers and for the most disagreeable offices of slavery.[31]

Hudson draws our attention to a Cape division of labor based on geographical-ethnic stereotypes. Ironically, different societies were to develop different stereotypes for the same people. Stereotypes were constantly updated within the host society; each came to have an arbitrary history of its own. By the nineteenth

---

[30] Some examples are found in Captain Robert Percival, *An Account of the Cape of Good Hope* (London: Baldwin, 1804; reprint ed. New York: Negro Universities Press, 1969), pp. 286–291; James Ewart, *James Ewart's Journal* (Cape Town: Struik, 1970), pp. 27–30; Robert Semple, *Walks and Sketches at the Cape of Good Hope* (London: Baldwin, 1805; reprint Cape Town: Balkema, 1968), pp. 43–54.

[31] Shell, ed., Samuel Hudson, " 'Slaves,' " 46 ff.

century, Cape householders considered that it was natural for Malagasy and African slaves to work the fields, Indonesian slaves to be the artisans, and Indian slaves to be the service workers of the colony.

William Wilburforce Bird, the British colonial comptroller of customs and author of an influential book on the Cape, embellished his own description of slaves' occupational differences with some biblical phrases: "The Negro, who is the least valuable, was brought from Madagascar and Mozambique. These slaves are chiefly *hewers* and carriers *of wood, and drawers of water*, coolies, or public porters for hire, and also employed by the boers and others as the hardiest labourers of the field. . . . The Malay slaves are coachmen, tailors, painters, shoemakers, carpenters, and fishermen. In fact, they are usually engaged in every thing where what is called cleverness is required."[32]

By the 1820s, the origin of the slave was no longer recorded in the official slave transfers. The system based on individual origins changed to one based on descent *and* race. Whether this was a result of new thinking in the post-revolutionary period, or of the new British occupation, or of the now greater number of creole slaves, or whether it was simply a reflection of the cessation of all sectors of the slave trade, is not clear. Nevertheless, the household construction of hierarchies came to be based on ethnicity, not origin alone. The former elaborate system of stereotyping by origin was changed to fit the later, predominantly locally born slave population into a new classification based on descent and race. After the abolition of the slave trade, the convenient word *coloured* was introduced into the South African vocabulary where it stubbornly persists.

The Cape's Eurocentric hierarchical classification and attribution scheme was especially attractive to colonial immigrants from the metropole, who were dealing with a new and uncertain colonial social universe. The solipsistic belief in such character traits based on origin made the world seem a much more predictable, and hence comfortable, place.[33] In the process of positive and negative stereotyping, the identities of all people not from Europe were greatly diminished and hierarchies were established. This way of thinking was more pronounced at the Cape than anywhere in the New World. I refer to it as a naïve household anthropology.

Geographic Origins, Creolization, and Household Security
The cultural and linguistic mixture within the household posed problems of communication for owners and slaves alike, but it also proved to be a security boon for the owner. Individual owners soon learned that it paid to have a diversity of

---

[32] W. W. Bird, *State of the Cape of Good Hope in 1822* (London: John Murray, 1823), p. 73, (emphasis added).

[33] Fritz Heider, *The Psychology of Interpersonal Relations* (New York: John Wiley & Sons, 1958).

slaves on their holdings. The Lodge officials, who imported slaves in boat loads, could not afford this refinement. Consequently newly arrived Lodge slaves, or *baaren* (greenhorns), tended to run away in groups — to try to return home together — whether to Angola, Madagascar, or wherever. Even an impossible geography posed few obstacles to the newly arrived ethnically homogeneous Lodge slaves' escape plans.[34] It was different with the privately owned slaves. Newly imported slaves, purchased singly and brought one at a time into the small Cape slaveholding, shared no common origin or culture with the household's already acculturated slaves (some creole), who were far less likely to seek escape. A household division of labor, based on stereotyping by origin, was reinforced by the quite different notion of not allowing — by default — ethnic solidarity among the slaves on the individual holding.

The wide range of origins of Cape slaves made sense of the ancient Greek slaveholder's maxim: "Mix the nationalities of the slaves, both within the individual holding and within the city."[35] Because the cultural mix in individual households made (at least) slave ethnic solidarity unfeasible, slave rebellion at the Cape was usually a matter of imported slaves acting alone. Imported slaves were nearly always the ones who engaged in arson and "running amok," the most widely feared expressions of slave rebellion at the Cape.[36] Buying slaves of different origins undermined not only any colonywide slave solidarity, but it also undercut household slave rebellion. Slaves were used to hunt down runaway slaves, and a surprising number of slaves informed on one another for comparatively minor crimes. Slave conspiracies were often revealed to the owner by a fellow slave.[37] To the slave owner, therefore, a mixture of slaves was important; too many slaves of the same origin in one holding increased the risk of runaways and rebellion.

The Creole Slave as Supervisor

To Cape slave owners, the creole slaves, born in the colony, were the elite of the Cape slave population, the most valuable and the most "trustworthy." They were often entrusted with the supervisory duties on a plantation, as Anders Sparrman noted in the 1770s: "In the course of our conversation on rural oeconomy I took notice, that a slave born in the country . . . who can drive a wagon well and who can be trusted to inspect the other slaves, or is looked upon as a clever and faithful servant, bears the price of five hundred Rix dollars. One that is newly bought from

---

[34] Gerald W. Mullin, *Flight and Rebellion: Slave Resistance in Eighteenth-Century Virginia* (London: Oxford University Press, 1972), pp. 34–35.

[35] Moses I. Finley, *Economy and Society in Ancient Greece* (New York: Penguin, 1983), p. 171.

[36] Percival, *An Account of the Cape of Good Hope*, 288–290.

[37] Robert Ross, *Cape of Torments: Slavery and Resistance in South Africa* (London: Routledge and Kegan Paul, 1983), p. 20. Slave conspiracies at the Cape were often betrayed at the last minute by fellow slaves, usually women.

Madagascar, or is in other respects not so skilful, nor so much depended upon, costs from a hundred to an hundred and fifty Rixdollars."[38] George Barrington, a British official who visited the Cape in 1791, confirmed these high premiums: "The creole Slaves are the most esteemed at the Cape, and fetch double the price of any other; if they are initiated in any business, their price is exorbitant."[39] Sparrman and Barrington exaggerated only a little. The Cape slave purchaser was willing to pay, on average, a 43 percent premium for a male creole slave, almost half again as much as the mean price for all slaves sold at the Cape. In defense of the travellers though, my analysis of creole premiums is based on all *creole* slaves sold on the Cape market, which was a much younger group (average age under 11) than the other slave groups, and despite being well below the "prime" age of 25, they were nevertheless the most expensive. Perhaps Sparmann and Barrington were talking about adult creoles, who very rarely came on the market, but when they did, they fetched truly high prices.

The Mulatto Slave

There was a hierarchy among creole slaves as well. According to Mentzel, if the creole slave was the product of a European-slave union, even the rearing costs could be offset: "Female slaves sometimes live with Europeans as husband and wife with the permission of their masters who benefit in two ways: the cost of upkeep of the slave is reduced through the presents she receives from the man, and her children are the property of her master."[40] Mentzel said of the preference for creole mulattoes in the household and the creole premium: "These slave children are found useful at a very tender age and cost little to bring up. They are likewise better mannered and better educated than imported slaves."[41] Bird described the three classes of slaves in 1822: "the Negro, The Malay, and the Afrikander."[42] He said that "Afrikanders," whom he also termed creole, were the most valuable. By Bird's time "creole" had become synonymous with "mulatto." By the nineteenth century, color and race had become the predominant stereotypes:

The last and most valuable class of the slaves is the African born slave, — the produce [*sic*] of an European, or of a Cape Dutchman, and of a slave girl. So many years have passed away since the Cape has been in the uninterrupted possession of the Dutch or English, that from black, this class has graduated into brown or yellow, not much darker than a southern European and many have progressed nearly to white. Of this race, both male and female, are the slaves preferred by the inhabitants. The men are active and subtle in mind, slender and of good appear-

---

[38] Sparrman, *A Voyage to the Cape of Good Hope,* vol. 1, 102–103.

[39] George Barrington, *A Voyage to Botany Bay, with a Description of the Country, & c.* (London: H. D. Symonds, 1794), p. 34.

[40] Mentzel, *Description,* vol. 2, 130.

[41] Mentzel, *Description,* vol. 2, 130.

[42] Bird, *State of the Cape,* 73.

ance in body. The females are rather under the middle size, with a bust inclined to fullness . . . Both sexes have much of the character of the Creole. These slaves are engaged in the domestic and most confidential services of the house, and frequently in a store or warehouse where goods are sold.[43]

The work of Laurence Kotlikoff, an economic historian, on the nineteenth-century New Orleans slave market, although in a different economy and time, shows that American slave buyers also were willing to pay a premium for mulatto women, of 10 percent (Kotlikoff makes no mention of mulatto men).[44] Cape slave owners were willing to pay a substantial premium (7 percent) based on the origin of a slave, regardless of age, transportation costs, or any other known influence on price, and a high premium (43 percent) to obtain a locally born slave who was possibly of European descent.

Why were creole slaves more expensive? First, because creole slaves lived longer than imported slaves. Second, the price of specially favored mulatto slaves pushed up all creole prices.[45] Third, according to the court records, including testimony of slave witnesses and accused slaves, the creole slaves' first language tended to be Dutch and hence communication problems were reduced.[46] Fourth, the crime records of accused slaves in this early period indicate that creole slaves were the least likely to run away, to be accused and convicted of crimes, or to rebel.[47] In this respect, the Cape was different from early Virginia. Gerald Mullin, an American colonial historian, has shown that as slaves in Virginia became more assimilated, and more creole slaves were born, the degree of rebelliousness increased. The Cape slave force was only 33 percent locally born by 1740. That mass slave rebellions occurred only late in the Cape's colonial history — 1808 and

---

[43] Bird, *State of the Cape*, 73.

[44] Laurence Kotlikoff, "Towards a Quantitative Description of the New Orleans Slave Market," paper presented to the University of Chicago Workshop in History, 1975, p. 9. Kotlikoff could not investigate regional premiums in the nineteenth-century American South, since such distinctions of slave origin had long since disappeared in the American slave population. By 1850 the percentage of slaves in the American South who had been born in a foreign country was minimal. There were therefore few, if any, distinctions based on region of origin, since the overwhelming majority of American slaves were creole, that is locally born.

[45] The only way to distinguish "pure" creole slaves from "half-breed" creole slaves is to trace these slaves back to their baptismal records, where the deacons labeled them as *casties* and *heelslag*, respectively. This classification scheme was not used throughout the period, however, and since few burghers baptized their slaves, it is only possible to prove this point with the slaves who belonged to officials. Furthermore, most half-breed slaves were kept in the estate of the family of the deceased and were not sold for speculation. Therefore, this point rests on a few cases only.

[46] AR VOC 4019: "Criminele Rolle, Process Stukken en Justiele Papieren," 1680–1731 (civil cases excluded).

[47] CAD CJ 278: "Register van Sententien," 1652–1717, and ibid., "Criminele Rechts Rollen," 1717–1741.

1823 — may support Mullin's analysis of the gradual development of an attitude leading to creole rebellion.[48] But Cape owners always preferred creole slaves.

The Africanization of the Cape slave trade, the creolization of the Cape slave population, increasing numbers of slave women, and a more youthful age composition of the household slaves all came about simultaneously in the decade of the 1770s. (Creolization, as noted earlier, was momentarily retarded by the surge of imports in the 1780s, but there was no regime of lower fertility in that decade; the increase in the number of newly imported male slaves made natural increase less important only in a purely arithmetical sense.) African slave cargoes of the period 1780 to 1808 included more women and children than the earlier, record-breaking Asian male slave cargoes, as I have said, but they still had twice as many men as women. Such cargoes, while they lowered the excessively high sex ratios, could never on their own normalize the slave population. However, while the slave trade fluctuated, creolization worked in a steady, linear fashion. This explains why creolization could supersede the slave trade *at several moments* before 1808. After 1770 more slaves were born into slavery than were imported. After 1808 creolization was all important.

Expectations of an increasing slave force were thwarted by the abolition of the oceanic slave trade. The effect that the slave trade had on the slave population may be seen in the accompanying graphic. The population pyramid for 1833, which summarizes the age and sex of a population, encapsulates both the history of the slave trade and the progress of creolization in the Cape slave population (see Figure 2-7).[49]

The Slave Trade, Creolization, and the Language of the Household

The diversity of geographic origins was of immediate practical significance for the slaves' adjustment and acculturation in their new households. Arriving in the typical small, often quite isolated, Cape slave-holding homestead, the uprooted slave was abruptly thrust into a foreign domestic milieu. There was a less than negligible chance of encountering someone of the same kin group, and a slender chance of encountering persons who spoke the same language, ate familiar food, or even who looked familiar. Some African slaves in the larger Brazilian, Caribbean, and North American slave plantations enjoyed these minor consolations. The Cape homesteads and plantations were nearly always inhabited by somatic and linguistic strangers.

---

[48] Mullin, *Flight and Rebellion*, pp. 161–163.

[49] PRO CO 53/57 (31 August 1833), pp. 149–150. I am grateful to John Mason for this reference.

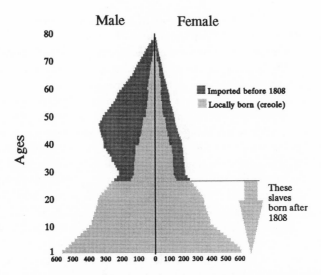

Figure 2–7. Population pyramid of Cape slaves, showing creole status in 1833.

Pieter van der Bijl, a farmer in the Drakenstein district in the 1690s, bought individual slaves from Macassar, Bengal, Malabar, Ternate, and Malacca, and also hired local Khoi to provide seasonal farm labor.[50] The confusion of languages (Dutch, French, Hindi, Khoi, Malay, and Portuguese) undoubtedly led Van der Bijl, a pious man who had built a church on his farm, to name his property *Babijlonsche Tooren,* the Tower of Babel.[51] The farm name has survived. (Besides their own language, many Khoi, according to J. L. M. Franken, the Stellenbosch historian of the topic, had to learn to speak French in this period.[52])

The most common languages of imported slaves were Bouginese, Chinese, Dutch, Javanese, Malagasy, Malay, and Portuguese. No purely African languages were ever translated in the Cape during this period.[53] This confusion of languages could be a major problem for the courts. When all the slaves on the Klapmuts farm of Daniel Pheijl, a settler councilor, were interrogated in 1726 on behalf of the Company authorities, they gave depositions in diverse tongues: Hercules van Bougies and Cupido van Padang, both from the Indonesian Archipelago, spoke

[50] DO: "*Transporten,*" 1680–1731, (19 May 1694, twice; 8 June 1695; 31 May 1697, twice; 8 August 1709); CAD CJ 3074: "Obligatien, Transporten van Slaven, ens.," 1715–1719, (11 October 1719; 22 July 1722, twice).

[51] Adam Tas, *The Diary of Adam Tas,* ed. Leo Fouché et al., trans. J. Smuts (Cape Town: Van Riebeeck Society, 1969–1970), p. 165, note 165 [*sic*].

[52] J. L. M. Franken, "Die Franse Vlugtelinge," *Die Huisgenoot* (16 July, 1926), pp. 35–41; ibid., "Vertolking aan de Kaap in Maleis en Portugees," *Die Huisgenoot* (18 July 1930): 41, 67.

[53] This is based on a compilation of languages mentioned in AR VOC: "*Proccestukken,*" (1680–1731 all criminal cases, every five years). Dutch was spoken mostly by creole slaves.

Malay to their interpreter; Scipio of Bengal gave his answers in Portuguese; only one slave, Jacob of Cochin, gave evidence in Dutch.[54] A battery of court interpreters had to be called in to deal with slaves' depositions in the event of some crime, since, for reasons of juridical efficiency and accuracy, Cape courts always took testimony in the language with which the slave felt most comfortable. Thanks to this courtesy, a clear idea of the linguistic diversity of the early Cape slaves may be obtained.

François Valentijn, the peripatetic multilingual minister writing in 1728, draws our attention to the staggering variety of people and languages at the Cape and rank-orders both in a strictly Eurocentric hierarchy. He conflates "nation" and origin: "All nations [*Natien*] are found here, Dutch, English, French, Germans from all parts, Savoyards, Italians, Hungarians, Malays, Malabaris, Sinhalese, Macassar-folk, Banians, Amboinese, Bandanese, Buginese, Chinese, men of Madagascar, Angolese, inhabitants of Guinea and the salt islands [Cape Verde], with whom one can get along in Dutch, Malay and Portuguese."[55] One Indian observer claimed it was not uncommon even as late as the 1760s for slaves to communicate in sign language and "peculiar noises," since they could not communicate with each other otherwise.[56] Some sought to communicate with other slaves in their own alphabets (see Figure 2-8).[57]

A letter from a slave, written in Bouginese, reveals (in translation) that imported slaves had clear notions of identity, ethnicity, nationality, and even fraternity:

This letter comes as a message from Stellenbosch, you sent me. Brother September, I announce that I have been sick for two months and that no human medicine [can cure me]. Brother September, I seek encouragement from you because I know you care about our Buganese people. I request from you, brother, if you have compassion, actually for your Buganese race, because I know from the time we spoke with our fellow Buganese people, you said we were suffering and that this concerned you, for we are a broken, suffering people in miserable conditions, thus my request to you, Brother September, if you are compassionate for your suffering Buganese compatriots, will you lead the children who came from the places of Boeloe Boloe and Sanja-c.[58]

The conglomeration of such diverse cultures at the household level was overcome to a certain extent by the slaves themselves. They fashioned the primary

---

[54] AR VOC 4102: "Criminele Process Stukken," Appendices.

[55] Valentijn, *Description of the Cape*, vol. 1, 170–171.

[56] De Kock, *Those in Bondage*, 52.

[57] This is an example of a letter written in the Bouginese alphabet by a slave at the Cape. It illustrates the wide range of literate slave cultures at the Cape. The letter written by a fifty year old slave, September of Bougies, talks of "our Bouginese nation," of "the terrible treatment the people from this area receive at the Cape." *Die Huisgenoot* (18 July 1930), page 41. Courtesy of *Die Huisgenoot* and South African Library.

[58] Achmat Davids, "The Afrikaans of the Cape Muslims from 1815 to 1915," M.A. thesis, University of Natal, Durban, 1991, p. 74.

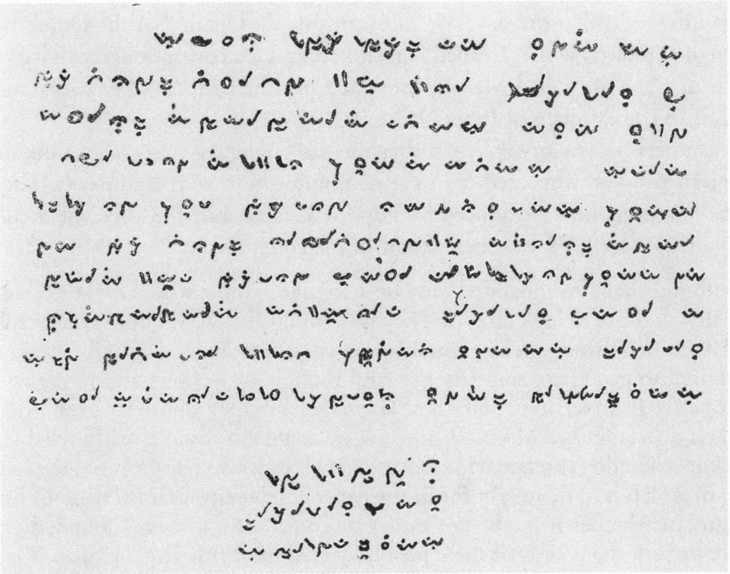

Figure 2–8. A letter from a slave in Bouginese script.

instrument of culture, their own language. A slave lingua franca had, indeed, emerged early on in the Cape, before the late nineteenth century (the currently accepted period). Research into its genesis and extent has been neglected by Afrikaans-speaking linguists, uncomfortable with the idea that Afrikaans' origin lay in the colonial creolization of the Dutch language. Other Dutch colonial societies, for example Suriname and Curaçao, developed similar creole languages, such as the "Neger Hollands" or *Papiament.* The simplification and creolization of Dutch in early South Africa not only resulted from the spontaneous development of new Dutch dialects, it also emerged from domestic interaction among imported and creole slaves, Khoisan serfs, and people of European descent.

There were two stages in the development of the creole language. First came the Malayo-Portuguese phase (1652 to 1770), which might be regarded as the forerunner of UrAfrikaans. This stage was characterized by a large number of "loan words" and new and sporadic grammatical intrusions. The first published words of a Cape slave, who was about to be executed in 1713, offer an example of this Malayo-Portuguese: *"Dios, mio Pay* [God, my father]."[59] This purely slave language was not clearly understood by the master class. An English visitor, Mrs.

[59] Peter Kolbe, *The Present State of the Cape of Good Hope: Containing, the Natural History of the Cape . . .* (1731; reprint ed. London: Johnson Reprint Company, 1968), vol. 1, p. 363.

Kindersley, writing a personal letter from the Cape in 1765, a few years before half
of the slave population was locally born, took pains to point out that the owners
were obliged to learn the slaves' language, not the other way around: "What seems
extraordinary is that the slaves do not learn to talk Dutch, but the Dutch people
learn their dialect, which is called Portuguese, and is a corruption of that language,
some of them are called Malays, brought from the country of Malacca and the
islands to the eastward of India."[60]

Anders Sparrman explained that this slave language also caught on among
Khoisan peoples, who used it to bar communication with Europeans. The new
Cape language, first introduced by imported slaves, had thus become a cultural
mask, which by 1770 was transparent to the colonists:

We found the farm inhabited only by some Hottentots who were left there by a
colonist in order to look after it. They were so ill-disposed as not to answer either
in Dutch or Portuguese Mr. Immelman's enquiries about the road, although he
promised to give them some money, and though, as we were afterwards assured,
they perfectly understood both these languages; but they jabbered a great deal to us
in their own language, of which, however we could not comprehend a syllable. I do
not know whether this behavior proceeded from a wicked disposition, the foundation of which is to be sought for in the general depravity, as it is called, of human
nature, or whether it might not rather be considered, as a well-founded grudge
harboured in the breasts of these people against the Christian colonists. We since
heard of many instances, in which the same thing had happened elsewhere to other
Christians, who by way of putting a trick on these poor fellows, pretended to be
ignorant of the Hottentot language; and by this means heard unsuspected the
answers of the Hottentots, consisting in mere impertinence and scoffing jests,
which they threw out against the Christians with the highest glee, and as they
thought with impunity, till the latter pulled off the mask in order to avenge
themselves.[61]

So as long as the slave trade continued, linguistic borrowings continued in a
chaotic and dynamic process. Mirzu Abū Ṭāleb Khān, a Persian visitor, wrote later
in the century: "Besides the Dutch, there are to be found at the Cape people of
many other nations, and at least seven or eight languages are spoken here."[62] The
mix of languages, including Malayu, Urdu, Malagasy, Portuguese, and Arabic,
influenced the emerging Cape lingua franca. This mix derived from the polyglot
composition of the slave-owning households. Sparrman's is the most fitting

[60] Mrs. Kindersley, *Letters from the Island of Teneriffe, Brazil, the Cape of Good Hope, and the
East Indies* (London: J. Nourse, 1777), pp. 66–67.

[61] Sparrman, *A Voyage to the Cape of Good Hope*, vol. 1, 280 and note 40.

[62] Mirza Abū Ṭālib Ibn Muhammed Khān, *The Voyages of Mirza Abu Taleb Khan in Asia,
Africa and Europe in the Years 1799, 1800, 1801, 1802 and 1803, Written by Himself . . . and
Translated by Charles Stewart* (London: Longman, Hurst Rees and Orme, 1810), vol. 1,
72–73.

description of how the slave trade continued to affect communication in an urban Cape household. His account echoed the sentiments that had been expressed by the Drakenstein farmer Van der Bijl 80 years before: "At mealtimes, various European dialects, together with the languages used in commerce with the Indians, viz. the Malay, and a very bad kind of Portuguese, were spoken at one time, so that the confusion was almost equal to that of the Tower of Babel."[63]

Malayo-Portuguese went through a transformation to Malay, which became the religious language for Cape Muslim slaves, or at any rate that was the assumption of the Anglican Church in the early nineteenth century when it began a pamphlet campaign to convert the Cape Muslims. Malay was last heard in Cape Town in 1923, dying out under the massive pressures of creolization, but it did leave traces in many Afrikaans words and constructions.

The second and more profound phase of the formation of a creole language came with the biological creolization of the Cape slaves and the increasing domestic incorporation and enserfment of the Khoi. The new creole language can be glimpsed from Mentzel's comment on the Cape of the 1740s: "It was no easy task to instruct the Madagascar slaves, for they spoke no language but their own. East Indian officers brought slaves from Java, Mallebar, Bengal, Banda and many other islands and sold them to the inhabitants of the Cape. They [the Eastern slaves] introduced a common slave language, or *lingua franca*, which they had acquired from the Portuguese and which could easily be picked up. This language has now been spoken for many years by slaves, Christian inhabitants and even by half-breed Hottentots."[64]

This second language was intelligible to all in the household and accessible to all in the colony. The creolization of the language has been associated — in time at least — with the creolization of the slave population, but women, both slave and free, were actually its creators. It emerged from the household and from a special place within the home — the kitchen. This explains the derogatory nineteenth-century term for Afrikaans: "kitchen Dutch." There are many Malay and Indian words in today's Afrikaans culinary lexicon, and in the words of C. Louis Leipoldt, the Afrikaans poet and sometime chef, "The most potent influence on Cape cuisine has been the methods, tastes, and culinary customs of the Malay cooks brought directly from Java in the early eighteenth century."[65] Their exotic cuisine overshadowed all the European culinary traditions; there is not a single "Dutch" restaurant in contemporary Cape Town. And from the food came the new kitchen language.

---

[63] Sparrman, *A Voyage to the Cape of Good Hope*, vol. 1, 58.

[64] Mentzel, *Description*, vol. 1, 56.

[65] C. Louis Leipoldt, *Leipoldt's Cape Cookery* (Cape Town: W. J. Flesch, 1976), p. 17; Robert C.-H. Shell, "Historical Background," in Sue Ross, *Fish Cook Book for South Africa* (Cape Town: Southpoint Publishing, 1978), pp. 12–16.

It was only much later that men introduced the creole language into the public sphere. The first book in Afrikaans was written by an *imam,* a slave descendant,[66] and only later in the 1860s did patriotic male European colonists take up the language for themselves. European men were the last to use the Afrikaans language, and some, like Jan Christiaan Smuts, disdained Afrikaans throughout their lives. Breyten Breytenbach, the Afrikaans poet, wittily explained from his own perspective: "We are a bastard people with a bastard language. And like all bastards, we have begun to cling to the concept of purity."[67]

The little-explored issue of language in the early Cape households was, according to a wide range of primary sources, the result of slaves' attempts to forge a means of communication with each other and, later, with their owners. The owners would later adopt this "mighty language," as I.D. du Plessis, the Afrikaans poet once termed it, and call it their own. As the changing slave trade brought many new languages and cultures to the Cape, slaves and the creolization of their descendants transformed each slave-owning household and, ultimately, the whole colony.

Considering the emphasis on "ethnicity" and "race" in South Africa today, it is quite astonishing to realize that these descendants of the premodern South African population do not, in fact, know where they came from. This would be a pedantic, even antiquarian point, except that people in South Africa were legally, and are socially, classified according to origin. A plethora of odd and exotic identities was the result. Some were legally imposed, such as the "coloured" identity, and some were created, such as the "Malay" or the "Afrikaner."

The Cape experience indicates that Africans were by no means the only enslaved, or enslaveable, group in colonial times. At the Cape during the first century of slavery, the overwhelming majority of imported slaves were Asian. The origin of slaves was a function of the shifting arrangements among slaving powers: where they allowed others to slave and were allowed to slave themselves. For example, only one Japanese slave was imported into the Cape, although the Dutch did have a trading station in Nagasaki. Mercantile rivalries, slave trading traditions, and the distribution of firearms were the overarching reasons behind the geographic sources of slaves. Preconceived ideas about the enslaveability of African populations had little to do with slave society at the Cape. The Cape owners

---

66 Adrianus van Selms, "Die Oudste Boek in Afrikaans: Isjmoeni se 'Bertroubare Woord,' " *Herzog Annale* (1953): 61-103.

67 For a survey of some recent literature, and a minor example of this never-ending dispute, see *The Cape Argus* (20–26 December 1977); see also K. Jordaan, "The Origins of the Afrikaners and Their Language, 1652–1720: A Study in Miscegenation and Creole," *Race* 15, 4 (1974): 461–495. For a fuller discussion of the language problem and the debate over the origin of Afrikaans, see Marius Valkhoff, *Studies in Portuguese and Creole, with Special Reference to South Africa* (Johannesburg: Witwatersrand University Press, 1966), and Valkhoff, *New Light on Afrikaans and "Malayo-Portuguese"* (Louvain: Peeters, 1972).

enslaved anybody they could. After the abolition of the slave trade in 1808, this sometimes included people of partial European ancestry and their children.

The popular notion that *most* Cape slaves were imported from the East also has to be modified. The slave trade to the Cape started in West Africa, turned east after 1706, and finally became re-Africanized after 1780. A slim majority of slaves imported to the Cape were African. Hence the origins of Cape slaves were quite diverse, and consequently Cape slaveowning households, for almost two centuries of colonial occupation and slavery, were somatically, ethnically, culturally, and linguistically heterogeneous. This situation prompted the settlers to invent and maintain exotic slave stereotypes based on origin; within the Cape slave-owning households, these stereotypes, although incidental, also proved to have an enduring legacy.

By 1808 and the abolition of the slave trade, the new generation of younger, Cape-born slaves and a similar group of younger imported slaves with a higher proportion of women, were poised for a dramatic demographic expansion. Owners might have contemplated slave breeding far more seriously at this juncture than at any other time, but the underlying conditions for the demographic expansion of the slave population were already there: larger proportions of children and women were present in the slave population than ever before. Still, the unprecedented growth of the slave population in the following quarter century was never sufficient to meet the growing demands of the slave owners. The slave-owning population was growing faster than the slave population.

The fundamental difference between Cape slavery and Caribbean and North and South American colonial slave regimes was that the Cape slaves were drawn from a multitude of starkly different cultures, a greater diversity than in other recorded slave societies. Because of the Cape's geographical position, because of mercantilism, wars, and revolution, a slave-holding society arose that developed an unparalleled set of stereotypes based on slave origins — stereotypes that were constantly elaborated as different hierarchies were constructed within the Cape household. During the operation of the oceanic trade, slave stereotypes were based on discrete notions of descent, creole status, and origin, and after the abolition, they became based on simpler, but more pernicious, notions of descent and color, and, finally, race.

THREE

Capons and Orphan Masters
The Effects of the Oceanic Slave Trade

CAPTAINS OF CAPE SLAVERS, tutored by the English and French, enslaved males rather than females. At the Cape, the crude selection of more men than women and more boys than girls from the oceanic trade was double-edged. On the one hand, the selection of male slaves ensured by default that the slaves would not reproduce (slaves were always cheaper to buy from the Cape's oceanic trade than to raise in the colony); on the other hand, the persistent selection of males had disturbing emotional implications for the slaves. Enslaved persons not only lost their families in the process of the trade (only two entire enslaved families were brought to the Cape), but they were also doomed never to enjoy an independent family life thereafter. The slave trade to the Cape was a factory of both orphans and perpetual bachelors.

As David Galenson, an economic historian of the slave trade, has observed, "in spite of the recognition of its [the sex composition's] significance, the demographic composition of the slave trade has received little systematic analysis."[1] J. E. Inkori, another historian of the slave trade, has pointed out that the sex and age composition of slaves in the slave trade has generally been "a matter of guesswork," while Philip Curtin has noted that the ratios are "rarely known."[2] The persistent selection of male over female slaves from the oceanic slave trade was at the psychological heart of the Cape family system and transformed the Cape slave populations in different ways (see Figure 3-1).[3]

---

[1] David W. Galenson, *Traders, Planters and Slaves: Market Behavior in Early English America* (Cambridge: Cambridge University Press, 1986), p. 93.

[2] G. E. Inkori, *Forced Migration: The Impact of the Export Slave Trade on African Societies* (London: Hutchinson University Library, 1982), p. 22; Philip D. Curtin, *The Atlantic Slave Trade: A Census* (Madison: University of Wisconsin Press, 1969), pp. 19, 28, 41.

[3] Shell, "Popucape." The top of the shaded, rectangular area is the normal ratio (100), as many men as women.

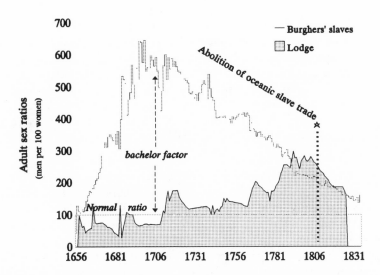

Figure 3–1. Adult sex ratios in two Cape slave populations, 1656 to 1831.

Sex Composition

Perhaps because societies in the modern world generally have a balanced sex composition, with the exception of the work of the French anthropologist, Claude Meillasoux, little scholarship has been directed to the historical phenomenon of enforced unbalanced sex ratios, or even to their obvious behavioral consequences, such as an altered potential for family life, expressions of violence, sexual loneliness and misery, gambling, drinking, a low regard for human life, and low self-esteem.[4] Scholarship on American slavery (the most intensively studied slave society) has concentrated on the antebellum period, when the slave population was no longer affected by the imbalanced cargoes of the Atlantic slave trade, and perhaps,

---

[4] A prevalent notion about the African slave trade, that European traders bought principally male slaves for agricultural labor and Arab traders bought female slaves for concubinage, is thrown into question both by the Cape trading experience and by the detailed Cape slave records; Claude Meillassoux, "The Role of Slavery in the Economic and Social History of the Sahelo-Sudanic Africa" in Inkori, *Forced Migration*, 89–90; Galenson, *Traders, Planters and Slaves*, 105-6; Paul Lovejoy, *Transformations in Slavery: A History of Slavery in Africa* (Cambridge: Cambridge University Press, 1983), 62; There is no evidence to support such a conclusion in Malagasy trading practice — indeed, some evidence clearly contradicts the notion. When, on one voyage, Cape ships met an Arab trader in Malagasy waters and they traded cash for the entire cargo of slaves, the ratio was 450 males to 100 females; James C. Armstrong, "Malagasy Slave Names in the Seventeenth Century," paper presented at the University of Madagascar, Colloque d'Histoire Malagache, Mahajanga, April 13–18, 1981 (voyage of the *Peter and Paul*).

therefore, the effects of the slave trade on the sex composition of other slave societies have been underestimated or ignored. Certainly, few contemporary scholars have studied artificially unbalanced sex compositions, though the populations of armies, some boarding schools, colleges, prisons, and the African populations of contemporary urban South Africa offer clear examples of groups that experience these problems. Contemporary demographers do agree that even minor imbalances, for instance, 120 men to 100 women, or a preponderance of women in a population, are associated with behavioral consequences.[5] If minor imbalances result in alteration of behavior in contemporary societies, one must conclude that historical societies with really high sex ratios were even more severely affected.

The Sex Composition of the Lodge

In strong contrast to the predominance of men in the slave populations belonging to the settlers and officials, in the Company Lodge, until 1715, there were more adult women than adult men. The average Lodge adult sex composition (excluding the all male convicts) was 113.8 men to 100 women over the whole Lodge period (1655 to 1828), the closest to "normal" of the three slave populations (see Figure 3-1).[6] The relatively higher proportion of women was partly a result of the high mortality rate among the Lodge adult male slaves (see Figure 3-2).[7]

The Company's Slave Trade to Madagascar The greater proportion of women in the Lodge was also a result of the nature of the Company slave trade to Madagascar. A specially sponsored and dedicated Company slave trade supplied most of the Lodge slave force until the British took over the Cape in 1795. So far as I know, the Lodge was the only slave holding in one building that had its own slaving ships. More than 5,400 slaves were brought to the Lodge between 1655 and 1795. The detailed accounts of the Company-sponsored slave trade to Madagascar show that the Malagasy sellers' imperatives for selling women often overshadowed Dutch buyers' preferences for buying men in nearly all Lodge cargoes in the seventeenth century and in the first decades of the eighteenth. Malagasy rulers often took advantage of the Company slaving crews' inexperience (and fear) to rid the Malagasy society of unneeded or "troublesome" women. In

---

[5] Hans van Hentig, "The Sex Ratio: A Brief Discussion Based on the United States Census Figures," *Social Forces* 30, 4 (May 1952): 443–449.

[6] The Lodge slave population may be fully reconstituted from detailed censuses such AR VOC 4030: "Generale opneming en monster rolle van ' S Comp. Soo slaven." (1 January, 1693), folios 359 to 367; AR VOC 4032: "Opnemingh van Compagnies groot en kleen vee, mitsgaders der materialen, bouw gereedschapppen en andere goederen in 1693 bevonden" (31 December 1693), folios 65–73; CAD: Attestaties C.336: ". . . verklaring na gedane monsteringe bevonden te hebben onder te naeme 's Comp: leijfeijgenen" (*Ultimo*, August 1714), folios 457–475; CAD: Attestatiën C.336: ". . . tot 't opneemen der slaven en verdere Effecten berustende onder den Baas Tuineer, Jan Hartog verklaren deselve Sodanig bevonden . . . (25 January 1715), folios 323 et seq.

[7] CAD C.338: 525–526, 597–598, 779; C.339: 55, 171–172, 247, 335, 663, 777 (N = 150).

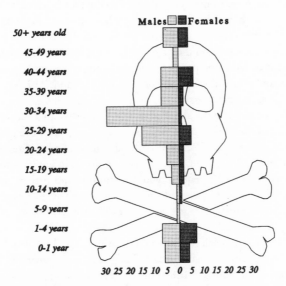

Figure 3–2. Death pyramid of slaves in the Lodge, 1719 to 1721.

early Company-sponsored voyages to Madagascar, therefore, slave traders bought women and children, first because they were obliged to.[8]

In one incident in 1695, the Malagasy ruler King Andian Xiamante, the ruler of Magelagie and Maringar, offered the Dutch the same unwanted slave woman three times; the Dutch refused three times. Consequently, in the words of the Dutch trader Jeremias Brons, the indignant king, "seized a double-barrelled pistol which he always had on his lap, threatened us, grabbed the valuable Cape-based Malagasy slave translator, and said: "You! Translate this! If you [gesticulating to the Dutch] do not take this women for this money I will keep both of these [gesticulating to translator and slave woman], or perhaps just shoot both here and now. . . ." The cool-headed Captain continued to barter, but aware of the two hundred armed royal retainers, eventually gave in — and bought several other slave women for good measure. Jeremias Brons grimly concluded, "so it was not barter but compulsion."[9] On the same voyage, Itsemveha, the king's eldest son, sold the Dutch his unwanted wife, the princess Sara No Moya; on another occasion, a Malagasy queen was sold.[10] Royalty was often sold into Cape slavery.

---

[8] I am grateful to James Armstrong for this information.

[9] AR VOC 4034: "Rapport van den Slavenhandel tot Madagascar" (14 January 1695): folio 106.

[10] AR VOC 4034: "Rapport . . ." (14 January 1695) folio 104 verso ff. The number of the "Andi-" pronyms in the Lodge slave cargo lists are a rough guide to the number of persons of noble descent brought to the Cape as slaves. These sources promise to shed new light on the *social* origins of imported Malagasy people.

Such expelled royal women proved useful to the Dutch slave trading skippers. In revenge against those who had sold them into slavery, they became willing sources of information about slaving conditions on the island. As one captain gleefully wrote in his report on the night of January 14, 1695: "As soon as the ship was out of sight of land, the princess told the interpreter and several others the entire background of the king's operation in the hinterland."[11] However, officials back at the Cape believed that a "superfluity of slave women" (*overschot van vrouwluijden*) was arriving at the Lodge and requested that subsequent slave cargoes be all male (*alle manspersoonen*).[12] Immediately after the pistol incident with Jeremias Brons, the Company officials dispatched polite, businesslike letters — not only in Dutch but also, for good measure, in Latin — to the slaving kings of Madagascar: "We request you, when this ship arrives, to assist the merchant and skipper with good advice, and permit them to buy a number of slaves; also to see that their strength, age and sex be properly notified, that we may not, as has often happened, receive women instead of men."[13] Other similar letters suggest that unwanted Malagasy women continued to be fobbed off on the Dutch.[14] The sex composition of the early Lodge cargoes confirm this impression. The first voyage of the *Sillida* in 1680 bought a cargo of whom "most were female, despite instructions to the contrary."[15] The 1681 voyage of the *Eemlandt* brought back 156 female slaves and only 86 males; the *Jambij*, sailing in 1687, brought 109 slave women and only 100 men.[16]

There was a further, anthropological, explanation that Hendrik Frappé, the commissioner of the slave trade, offered for the early Lodge cargoes of women. In 1715 he reported back to the directors of the Company: "Every [Malagasy] man takes as many women as he can provide for, and pays her closest kin in kind: they deal in wives much as they deal in slaves. When they think it suitable [*goeddunckt*] they trade them again, or chase them away."[17] Possibly the favorable male cargo of Frappé's voyage was one reason for the commissioning of a painting of the slave

---

[11] AR VOC 4034: "Rapport . . ." (14 January 1695) folios 107 ff.

[12] *Resolutions* (10 July 1706) 3: 441–2.

[13] Hendrick Carel Vos Leibbrandt, *Letters despatched* (31 October 1696), in *Precis of the Archives of the Cape of Good Hope* (Cape Town: W. A. Richards & Sons, 1896) pp. 31–32.

[14] AR VOC 4022: "Authentique Copie Latijnse Missive van de tweede persoon Andries de Man ann Cabo aan den Vorst van Magelagie op't eijland Madagascar van 29 October 1685," folios 410 verso and 411; published copies are in Leibbrandt, *Letters Despatched,* 122–123 and *passim.*

[15] AR VOC 4017: "Copia Daghregister gehouden bij den Schipper van't jacht Sillida op sijne reijse nae Madagascar," folios 95–98.

[16] *Eemlandt:* AR VOC 4029 (13 May 1687), no pagination (folio 1); *Jambij:* CAD C.501, "Letters despatched [Cape to Patria]," p. 630 ff.

[17] South African Library Dessinian Collection no. 138, Hendrik Frappé, "Korte Beschrijving," "haere manier in't verkiesen van vrouwen" (1715), folio 1 verso.

ship, *Leidsman,* and of a lengthy celebratory essay about the voyage.[18] The voyage of the *Leidsman* was regarded as especially successful, because it brought back 136 men and 43 women.[19] The Cape officials, having successfully established their desired trading protocol for male slaves, thereafter always received male slaves from the Malagasy rulers.

Despite having included many women in the early period, the Lodge slave population failed to reproduce, primarily because of the high mortality rate. In 1702 and 1713 the Lodge population lost more than 500 slaves to epidemics that raged through the building. Because of low creolization rates in the Lodge, the ratio of men to women continued to climb between 1755 and 1795, while the other Cape slave populations had started their creolization and their ratios began to decline (see Figure 3-1).

Beginning in the seventeenth century with a superfluity of women, sex ratios in the Lodge normalized — there were as many men as women — three times in the eighteenth century, but then gradually climbed after 1745 to an imbalance of men over women. This reflected an increasing reliance on a slave trade that targeted adolescent boys and young men. By the 1780s, the Cape Lodge slaving captains had been instructed that the ideal sex cargo was 250 to 300 slaves, with only a few women among them (*enige vrouwlieden*).[20] The ratio of men to women continued to rise shortly after the British occupation in 1795, suggestive evidence that the Lodge trade continued in the period 1795 to 1803, although there are no records of any such voyages. By 1795, the Dutch East India Company had collapsed, and with its demise went its record keeping. After 1803 and the surrender of the Cape to the Batavian government, the Lodge male-female ratio started to drop sharply until it resembled the ratio of the much larger slave population that belonged to private slave owners.

Domestic Implications As a result of the largely female cargoes of the seventeenth century, the Company Lodge had many times more adult women than the other slave populations at the Cape. Also from 1655 through 1714 the Lodge housed the largest number of unattached women in the male-dominated Cape. If a Cape Town bachelor (free or slave) or a visiting seaman were sexually lonely, the Lodge was the place to visit. Although visiting Company commissioners professed shock at the practice, local officials turned the Lodge into a brothel for an hour every night, with female slaves compelled to act as prostitutes, at the very time that the male slaves (among whom were the spouses of these women) were set to the demeaning and melancholy chore of carrying the town's slurry to the beaches and

---

[18] The documents of this voyage are currently being edited by the director of the South African Library, P. Westra (personal communication, August 1992).

[19] C.336 Attestatie "Verklaring v.d. aangekome slaaven van Madagascar" (23 November 1715), folio 593.

[20] J. L. M. Franken, (ed.), *Duminy Diaries* (Cape Town: Van Riebeeck Society, 1933), p. 14.

hence were not around to object. The operations of the slave trade had, over time, transformed the lodge household both in demographic content and in behavior. From serving as the colony's first school and then its most famous brothel, it would become by the nineteenth century a respectable and even charitable institution for the aged — in short, an old-age home.

The Sex Composition of the Privately Owned Slaves

Unlike the Lodge, the Cape's privately imported slaves were predominantly male from the outset. There were also more males among the burghers' slaves than among the slaves belonging to the wealthy members of the port's community (the patricians). The patrician Company officials did purchase more male slaves than females, but not in the excessively high proportions of the burghers' slave populations. Nearly all the Company employees were housed in or near the town, and all the contemporary estate and house inventories show that there was a relatively higher proportion of female slaves in the town than in the rural areas. In this way, the port became a repository for female slaves.

The increasingly patriarchal burgher farmers principally wanted male slaves. The much higher rural household ratios of slave men to women was the result of explicit burgher demands. W. S. Ryneveld, explaining burgher requests to the new British administration in 1797, described the ideal ratio of slaves to be imported annually for the Cape burghers as "500 men and 100 women," which was twice as high as the ideal Lodge cargo ratios.[21] The burgher preference for males was related to the low cost of importing slaves relative to the costs of rearing them. Every householder knew that it cost three times more to bring up a slave than to purchase one; therefore to have as few female slaves in the holding as possible was a desideratum of the rural Cape slave-owning household until the abolition of the slave trade in 1808. In the boom-and-bust maritime economy of the Cape, it was economically more prudent for the farmers to allow other countries to bear all the costs of rearing the labor force.

Despite both the wide distribution of the slaves' points of origin and the vagaries of the Cape slave trade, the sex ratios of slaves brought back by British ships were exactly the same as the Danish traders' and approximately the same as those of Portuguese and Dutch, which strongly suggests either that there was a standard Indian Ocean slave cargo to the Cape, one that had a much higher ratio of men to women than the Atlantic trade, or (more likely) that patrician and burgher buyers deliberately selected slaves in these proportions. The Cape, it must be remembered, was only a refreshment station, not a terminus of the Atlantic slave trade. Cape buyers, unlike their counterparts in the New World, could pick slaves off cargoes en route to the Americas; they were not obliged to buy the whole

---

[21] W. S. van Ryneveld, "Memorandum . . ." (29 November 1797), Witwatersrand University Library, n.p.; Franken, *Duminy Dagboek,* 14.

cargo. The household sex ratio of these adult slaves, varying between a staggering high of 650 males to every 100 females in 1713, to a low of 180 to 100 as late as 1833, indicate that, for the entire period, farmers persisted in purchasing male slaves. By persistently *not* buying female slaves in the same proportion as male slaves, the burghers obviated or at least reduced nurturing and rearing costs of the slave force, but at massive emotional cost to their male slaves.

After the abolition of the oceanic trade in 1808, the male slave population declined both in absolute terms and in proportion to the females. The main reason was mortality. Slave women were now clearly sought, since they were the only legal source of future slaves. While Cape owners avoided buying women until 1808, after that they became a highly prized commodity.

Comparative Perspectives

Colonial American sex ratios of male slaves to female have long been considered high. One well-known article, written in 1945 by Herbert Moller, a German demographer, made much of the effect of the "high" ratios on the cultural, social, and even sexual behavior of the New World populations.[22] Cape slave cargo sex ratios were higher than cargoes on contemporary Atlantic voyages, however.[23] For the first century, the burgher slave household sex ratios were three times as high as those in South Carolina in 1731, the mainland American colony with the densest slave population.[24]

The abnormally male-dominated sex composition of the Cape household's slave population was consistent throughout the Dutch occupation, with a ratio as high or higher than the most densely slave-populated Caribbean plantations, which were societies traditionally associated with the most severe exploitation of male slave labor. In this respect plantation slavery was no different from Cape household slavery. If one accepts the notion that a superfluity of men in a society has deleterious social effects, then Cape slaves must have suffered greatly, since the Cape ratios were among the most imbalanced slave sex compositions in the colonial world (see Figure 3-3).[25]

---

[22] For the American colonial period, see Herbert Moller, "Sex Compositions and Correlated Culture Patterns of Colonial America," *William and Mary Quarterly* Second Series, 2 (1945): 113–153; and R. Thompson, "Seventeenth Century English and Colonial Sex Ratios: A Postscript," *Population Studies* 1 (28): 150 ff.

[23] Colin Palmer, *Human Cargoes,* 122.

[24] Peter Wood, *Black Majority: Negroes in Colonial South Carolina from 1670 through the Stono Rebellion,* (New York: W. W. Norton and Company, 1974), p. 146, Table 11; pp. 154–155.

[25] Data for Cape from DO: "Tranporten"; comparative data from G. Galenson, *Traders, Planters and Slaves* (Cambridge: Cambridge University Press, 1986), Table 5.1, pp. 94–96. See section on creolization in Chapter 2. In Figure 3-3, I have used only adults in the sex composition, both for the comparative data and for the Cape, since variations in the *general sex ratio,* that is the ratio including children, are inversely correlated with creolization (natural increase). Variations in the adult sex composition are mostly explained by variations in the sex composition of slave cargoes.

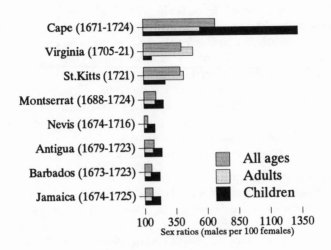

Figure 3–3. Slave sex ratios in comparative perspective.

Effects on Opportunities for Independent Family Life

Rising slave imports in the periods 1670 to 1732, 1780 to 1789, 1795 to 1803 reflect a persistent preference for male over female slaves, perpetuating the imbalance of earlier years. So long as the male numerical dominance of the trade remained high, there were fewer slave women in the general household population and, consequently, less chance of their reproducing enough offspring to meet the high demand of the rapidly expanding Cape slave society, which therefore became even more strongly tied to the slave trade. Every numerical expansion of the slave-owning population, whether by immigration, or choice (as more colonists became slave owners), or by their own natural increase, deepened that dependence. Only creolization and changes in the sex ratios of slave cargoes ushered in by the French slave traders in the 1770s and 1780s modulated this pattern. The sex ratio began to decline after an all-time high of 650 males to 100 females in 1706, but it did not completely normalize (reach 100) until after 1875.[26] Thus, even at emancipation many "elderly" (35 and older) male bachelor slaves faced their new freedom without a spouse (see Figure 3-4).[27] By persisting with the market purchase of men, the patriarchal householders (who came to own most of the slaves and therefore were responsible for shaping the Cape slave population) cut off the opportunities for their male slaves to form stable families.

---

26 *Census of the Cape of Good Hope, 1875* (Cape Town: Government Printer, 1875), "Population: General Summary," p. 1.

27 This photograph appeared in the *Cape Times,* 21 April 1916. The man, an ex-slave, pictured here at Elgin, was believed to be 120 years old. Courtesy of the South African Library.

Figure 3–4. Jan Persent, ex-slave from Mozambique, 1916.

Other Sociological Implications

The violence, gambling, and low regard for life reputed to be characteristic of many Cape slaves, were indirect consequences of the unbalanced sex compositions, and probably of the high mortality rate, too. Overwhelmingly negative stereotypical "racial" explanations for slave behavior were the result. This important point is, though, almost impossible to prove. One traveler commented on such a causal link. Anders Sparrman, the Swedish botanist who was visiting the Cape in the 1770s, recorded the words of an overseer on a frontier farm that had 12 single male slaves. In every way — lack of corporal punishment, good food — he had treated his slaves most "kindly," but, as the overseer explained, "In order to avoid jealousy, quarrels and murder, my master does not permit any female slaves to be kept here, but I could wish it were otherwise, as well as in other places [in this colony], where I was formerly a servant. Now they [the slaves] are lonesome and solitary, and consequently slow and sluggish enough."[28] Sparrman reflected in his journal on the effects of an unbalanced sex composition within this particular, and entirely typical, rural Cape household:

Slaves, even under the mildest tyrant, are bereaved of the rights of nature. The melancholy remembrance of so painful a loss is most apt to arise during the silence

---

[28] Anders Sparrman, *A Voyage to the Cape of Good Hope . . .* , ed. Vernon S. Forbes (Cape Town: Van Riebeeck Society Second Series, no. 7, 1977) vol. 1, pp. 102–103.

of the night . . . what wonder then, if those who commit outrages on their liberties, should sometimes be forced to sign and seal with their blood the violated rights of mankind? Ought not my host, gentle as he was, to fear the effects of despair on twelve stout fellows forcibly taken from their native country, their kindred, and their freedom? Is it not likewise to be dreaded, that thus shut out from the commerce of the fair sex, which sweetens life, and renders its cares supportable, their inclinations, which are extremely warm, should trespass against manhood.[29]

The extreme violence, murder, rape, gambling, homosexuality, and bestiality that characterized the behavior of some of the burgher slaves described by Robert Ross in his survey of the Cape crime records may be principally the result of the unbalanced sex composition.[30] In the Cape crime records, all the lower male echelons of the European society — the soldiers, sailors, knechts, "poor whites," and so on — show similar patterns of social unrest, but these groups have not yet been the subject of systematic historical enquiry, as they should be. Their existence compromised the enduring myth of the *herrenvolk*, so their existence and behavior were denied.

The majority of slave women were imported one by one. They did not arrive in boat loads until the late eighteenth century and even then, the majority still came in singly. This did not mean they were better treated. I suspect that their isolation on the ships placed them in peril. By what must be considered a fantastic coincidence, a complete series of transfers has survived covering the entire pre-Cape life of one slave woman imported from India by a Cape official. Her story contrasts sharply with the captivity experiences of Malagasy slave women brought to the Lodge. But although unparalleled in the sources, her story was more typical of the experience of the majority of women imported to the Cape as slaves. China of Singaracolla had been sold into slavery by her mother long before her embarkation to the Cape, as her transfer deed claims: "On 24 January 1768, in the Company office at Bimilipatnam, Silidana of the Coast, living at Singaracolla, declared that by reason of poverty and lack of a means of livelihood [*gebrek van levens-middelen*], she sold, ceded and in full ownership, transferred her small daughter named China, aged nine or ten, to Jan Christian Lijst, the Company trumpeter at Nagapatnam, for the sum of fifteen silver Rupis."[31] Six years later, on February 15, 1774, "China, renamed Rosa" was resold, for 18 pagodas, to a Dutch East India Company crew member, Hendrik Hillman, who quickly sold her again, on the 26 July, to another crew member, for a profit of 7 pagodas. One month later, the slave, now "Roosa," was sold at a 100 percent profit to a Dutch ship's captain,

---

[29] Sparrman, *Travels*, vol. 1, pp. 102–103.

[30] AR VOC: "Criminele Rechtsrollen" (1680–1730); although Robert Ross does not link the sex ratios with such behavior, see his article "Oppression, Sexuality and Slavery at the Cape of Good Hope," *Historical Reflections* 6, 2 (1979): 421–433.

[31] CAD: M49 (N): "Transfer Deeds of Slaves (1763 [*sic*])," no pagination, (pp. 2–7).

Cornelis Bosch, who kept her for some five months before setting sail on the Company ship *Bovenkerker Polder*, arriving in Cape Town on 24 March 1775.[32] There he sold "Roosa" to the popular Cape Town Company *predikant* (pastor), Johannes Petrus Serrurier, in whose patrician Cape Town home she stayed until her death.[33] Her case, rather than the well-documented Company Lodge slave voyages, represents the typical experience of an imported Cape slave woman. The majority of slave women, according to thousands of deeds of transfer and notarial protocols, were imported in this way, alone and *after* a convoluted middle passage.

Age Composition

The age structure of any population is fundamentally altered by immigration, and age, in turn, has reciprocal effects: according to demographers, age is the most important variable in the determination of all vital rates.[34] Labor supply and economic dependency are also linked to age composition.[35] In the case of the patricians' and burghers' slaves, the individual slave transfers allow for exact measurement of these phenomena. The household population was recorded in the census only in four sex-specific cohorts: men over 16, "boys" under 16, women over 14, "maidens" under 14. The lodge censuses were even more detailed. I have combined all the populations for the following graph (see Figure 3-5).[36]

---

[32] J. R. Bruijn et al. (eds.), *Dutch Asiatic Shipping in the 17th And 18th Centuries* (The Hague: Martinus Nijhoff, 1979) vol. 2, p. 494, (Voyage 7932.2).

[33] CAD M 49 (N): "Transfer Deeds of Slaves (1763)," n.p. (pp. 2-5); see *Dictionary of South Africa Biography*, 2:654-5 for Serrurier's biography.

[34] Henry Shryock et al., *The Methods and Materials of Demography* (Washington: U.S. Department of Commerce, 1975), vol. 1, p. 201.

[35] Several measures of the age composition of Cape slaves are available to demographers. For historians, the type of record narrows the choice. The Lodge officials divided the age composition of the Lodge slave cargoes and the lodge population quite differently. Slaving captains used the terms "suckling (*suijgelinge*, infants to 1 year), boy, (*jongen*), adolescent (*halfwassene*, literally "half adult," ages 11–16) and for adults, the gendered words for slave (*slaaf* and *slavin*), but they were not consistent. Cf. James Armstrong, "Malagasy Slave Names in the Seventeenth Century," *Omaly Sy Anio* 17-20 (1983-4): 43-59; Lodge officials, on the other hand, used five age cohorts within the Lodge household: sucklings (*suijgelingen*, 0–3 years), schoolchildren (*skoolkinderen*) and boys and girls (*jongens en meijsies*, 4-16 and 4-14), maids (*meijdens*, 14 and up), boys (*jongens*, 16 and up); see AR VOC 4030: "Generale Opneming en Monster rolle van 'S Comp: Soo slaven en Bandieten . . ." (1 January 1693), folios 365–367; since the lactation period changed over time, the suckling category is more appropriately collapsed into the next oldest cohorts. In the comprehensive census of Company slaves in 1693, sucklings are divided into one-year cohorts, viz. "suijgelingen, d' Anno, 1692, 1691, 1690," while in the nineteenth century, *suijgelingen* are all considered to be under one year of age; cf. Theal, *RCC*, "Return of Government slaves," 19: 267.

[36] Shell, "Popucape." The most suitable measure for *all* the Cape slave populations is the

The Lodge Slaves

In the first large Cape oceanic slave trade transaction, in 1658, the Dutch slavers chose children. From the beginning of the colony, an important new justification made for the slave trade was that the slave traders were "saving" the children from worse fates. Capturing a Portuguese Angola slaver off the Brazilian coast holding approximately 500 slaves of all ages, the Dutch took 250 children ("mostly boys and girls"). The "Portuguese ship was a [dangerous] hulk," was the Dutch captain's justification. Of these, only 174 survived the passage to the Cape. They were landed at the Cape by the *Amersvoort* in late March of 1658 (see Figure 3-5). The commandant, Jan van Riebeeck, claimed that some were so young that they "would not be able to be in service for four or five years and would have to be matured [*opgequeeckt*]."[37] Outnumbering all the Dutch employees and their

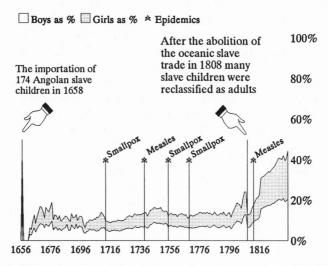

Figure 3–5. Age composition of the combined Cape slave populations, 1656 to 1833.

proportion of children under 15, and the most suitable way to display these data is termed a 100 percent surface chart. The elegance of the technique lies in that only a single line is required to describe the age composition of each population. I have used two lines in Figure 3-4 to show the boys and the girls. In this way one can make determinations of each populations' progress and compare them to see whether they were aging, or as the demographers would have it, "younging." This occurred at the Cape after 1808. For a discussion of this and other measures see Shryock, *The Methods and Materials of Demography*, 1:234.

[37] Jan Anthonisz van Riebeeck, *Daghregister . . .* , ed. D. B. Bosman and H. B. Thom (Cape Town: Balkema, 1952–1957), vol. 2, p. 269 (March 1658).

families at the Cape at the time, the Angolan children transformed the colony.[38] The commandant wrote in his log:

17April [1658] This morning beautiful, clear weather. We have begun to make preparations for the establishment of a school for the Company's Angolan slave children from the *Amersvoort* . . . which school will be held in the morning and afternoon by the sick comforter and sick visitors teaching them the correct Dutch language. To animate their lessons and to make them really hear the Christian prayeɪ₃ ɘᴀch slave should be given a small glass [*croesjen* or *kroesje,* a mug or cup] of brandy and two inches of tobacco, etc. A register must be established and names should be given to those who do not have any names. All slaves, couples or singletons, young or old, will be under the personal aegis of the Commander. Within a few days, these slaves will be brought under a proper sense of discipline and become decent people.[39]

In one passage, Van Riebeeck introduced education, paternalism, and the *dop* system (providing alcohol on a daily basis to servants and slaves) into the infant colony.

On-the-spot Dutch slaving officials later seemed reluctant to take young children, perhaps because most of the surviving young *Amersvoort* cargo had died at the Cape. In 1677, a squeamish Dutch official on the slave ship *Voorhout* told a hopeful Malagasy trader of slave children that "we were old hands [*Orang Baren*] and anyway were not authorized to accept such small children [*sulx kleingoet*]."[40] Nevertheless, the captain did select about 77 children, and as it was, his reluctance was out of place, for when the ship arrived at the Cape, the cargo was applauded by the governor and the council: "All the said slaves were under 16 years of age, a time of life which experience and the English have taught us to be the best; for those who are older take to fretting, when they think only of their country, and soon die; whereas the young [slaves] are light-hearted and frolicsome, and thus preserve their health better."[41]

The Dutch learned that children did tend to survive the passage better than adults. Many Malagasy children — even infants — were imported to the Lodge. The *Voorhout*'s second voyage brought back 33 children, the *Eemlandt,* 29 children; the *Jambij* even brought three babes-in-arms.[42] The Lodge's imported slave

---

[38] VOC 3991: "Monsterrollen van d' Officieren, Matroosen ende Soldaten" (31 May 1657), folios 387–390; excluding other slaves already at the Cape.

[39] Van Riebeeck, *Daghregister,* vol. 2, p. 277 (17 April 1658); I have added punctuation to the single sentence.

[40] AR VOC 4013: "Journaal. . . van 't jacht *Voorhout*," (1 July 1677), folio 979.

[41] Letters Despatched, Governor Bax to Heeren 17 (May 18 1678), in Donald Moodie (comp.), *The Record or a Series of Official Papers* . . . , (Cape Town: Balkema, 1960) p. 363.

[42] AR VOC 4029 (13 May 1687), no pagination; AR VOC 4013 (1 July 1677), folio 979; *Jambij:* CAD C.501: "Letters despatched [Cape to Patria]," p. 630 ff; and information from James Armstrong.

population was younger than the other imported slave groups at the Cape, at least for the first century. The fact that there were more women and hence more locally born children at the Lodge meant earlier creolization. As a result, in the first century of occupation one-third of the Lodge slave population was always children (see Chapter 6, Figure 6-5).[43]

After the voyages of the *Brak* in the early 1740s and throughout the remainder of the eighteenth century, according to cargo manifests and subsequent instructions to slaving captains the selection of slaves by age became less random. By 1781, the Cape Council of Policy, having learned from their contact with French slavers, indicated to the Cape Lodge slaving captain, F. R. Duminy, that the ideal age composition was: "two thirds adult and one third adolescent [*half-wassenes*]," termed by the French "*Capors*, [sic]" (capon, a castrated cock).[44] The ideal slave for the Cape trade was clearly indicated by this terrible triple pun: a prepubescent male who was destined never to have children. The actual meaning of capon is a male chicken that has been castrated for the purposes of improving the flesh for the table. While the Cape slave traders did not deal in eunuchs (who were the perfect slaves in Orlando Patterson's view), they had a close substitute in the "capon."

Burghers' and Patricians' Slaves

Selecting children was no less important to burghers and officials. The first imported slaves sold to burghers at the Cape were children, and so were the last (imported illegally in the 1820s).[45] Between these terminal dates there was little variation in the age composition. The burghers preferred youths for the same reasons they preferred male slaves. Enslaved boys made up a disproportionate segment of the imported cargoes. The rearing costs due to future offspring were still obviated by this selection, and the new owners obtained boys at an age at which they could still receive instruction and be better assimilated into the work force. The assimilation of capons into the adult slave work force was a rather rapid process when the cargo slave population is compared to the landed population of a few years later (see Figure 3-6).[46]

---

[43] AR VOC 4032: "Opnemingh van Compagnies groot en kleen vee, mitsgaders der materialen, bouw gereedschapppen en andere goederen in 1693 bevonden " (31 December 1693), folios 65–73 ; CAD: Attestaties C.336: ". . . verklaring na gedane monsteringe bevonden te hebben onder te naeme 's Comp: leijfeijgenen" (*Ultimo*, August 1714), folios 457–475.

[44] Franken, *Duminy Diaries*, 14.

[45] For example, the first commandant of the colony, Jan van Riebeeck, owned among other slaves, two "Arabian slave girls from Abyssinia" Cornelia (10) and Lijsbeth (12), see W. Blommaert, "Het invoeren van de slavernij aan de Kaap," *Archives Year Book* 1, 1 (1938): 6.

[46] Data for cargoes from DO: "Transporten," and CJ Obligatien, 1671–1724; census data from AR VOC 4097 opgaaf (1 and 2 May, 1725), sommaria.

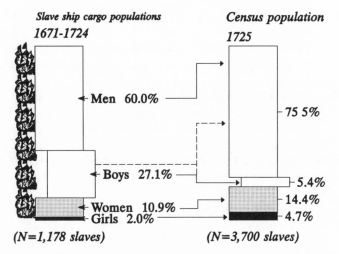

**Slave ship cargo populations
1671-1724**

**Census population
1725**

← Men 60.0% ——

━ 75 5%

←Boys 27.1% ——

━ 5.4%

━ 14.4%

←Women 10.9% ——
←Girls 2.0% ——

━ 4.7%

(N=1,178 slaves)

(N=3,700 slaves)

Figure 3–6. Slave ship cargoes (1675–1725) and the landed slave population, (1719).

Company officials' slaves were the oldest slaves imported into the colony. Most of these slaves were "second-hand"; they had been slaves for some time in the Indies, and some were sold to the Cape on the occasion of their masters' retirement. These *oorlam* slaves were not only seasoned and older therefore, but they also had experience of bondage overseas. Their enslavement had taken place many years before. Raw, or "saltwater" slaves, as they were termed in the New World, were called *baaren*, or *nuweling*, slaves at the Cape.[47] *Oorlam* and *baaren* were both corruptions of Malay words: (*oorlam* from *Orang-lami*, signifying old or "known" man, and *baaren* from *Orang-barn*, a new man).[48]

The Psychology of Orphanhood: A Case Study

Six-year-old Manomia of Bengal, baptized Clasina,[49] was put on board a Dutch ship in 1742 with her parents, bound for the Netherlands, when the governor of the Dutch station in Bengal, the Honorable Mr. Zigterman, retired with his immediate family and his servants. But when the ship called at the Cape, Manomia was inexplicably "left" with a patrician slave trading family, the Blankenbergs, with the express promise that she would be sent for later when the Zigtermans were settled in Holland.[50] She never was sent for. In an interview with the Cape court about her enslavement, she gave the most revealing firsthand

---

[47] VOC 4013: "Daghregister van Voorhout" (1 July 1677), 979.

[48] Otto Friederich Mentzel, *Life at the Cape . . .* , trans. Margaret Greenlees (Cape Town: Van Riebeeck Society, 1919), p. 79.

[49] Theal, RCC, "Cradock to Bathurst," 10: 4, 45-60.

[50] The Blankenbergs had been slaving at the Cape since the early eighteenth century.

account available of the psychology of the slave-orphan trade from the slave's perspective:

[Question] 1. Her name, age, and where born?

Clasina: Clasina, my age I do not know, but I believe full 70 years, I was born in Bengal, was six years old when I came to the Cape.

2. How she and her parents became the slaves of Mr. Zigterman?

C: My mother suckled Mr. Zigterman's child, and I was born in his house;[51] Mr. Zigterman brought me with my father and mother to the Cape.

3. Had she ever seen either her mother's or her own certificate of freedom?

C: No, at that period I was but a child, my mother did not show me them, and on her going to Holland she promised to return for me in two years, but in the interval she died.

4. If so, when, where, with whom, and by what means?

C: [No reply]

5. Does she not know that she was left [transferred] by Mr. Zigterman to Mr. Blankenberg?

C: Yes, because Mr. Blankenberg was agent to Mr. Zigterman.

6. Does she not know that she was presented [transferred] by Mr. Blankenberg to Johanna, the wife of Mr. P. J. Truter?

C: No, I was persuaded that my mother would in two years return to fetch me.

7. Was she not given [transferred] to the said daughter by Mr. Blankenberg before the marriage?

C: I was with her before this marriage.

[Questions 8 and 9 concern details of her own children.]

10. Does she know nothing further relative to her case?

C: Nothing but that I received two letters from my mother, since which she died.[52]

The letters referred to above had been, I presume, taken from Manomia's possessions just before the court proceedings. They had mentioned that her mother was "a free person," and that her father had died after arrival in Holland. The old Mrs. Blankenberg had read these letters to her repeatedly, since Manomia could not read. Her advocate J. T. Neethling, admitted that he had seen the letters, and "declared to have found nothing relating to her freedom, but that her mother would come for her."[53] What is significant is that there was no real moment of enslavement, no actual record of her slave status. The court's euphemisms,

[51] In the reformed faith, this had serious implications. The owner was obliged to baptize *and* educate Manomia. Thanks to Dominee Strijdom, her baptismal certificate was found, but we know that she was never taught to read.

[52] Theal, *RCC* 10: 55–56, "Interrogatories framed and delivered . . . 21st of June 1811, before Messrs. C. Matthiessen and P. Diemel, Commissioners from the said Court."

[53] Theal, *RCC*, 10: 56–57, no. 9., "Interrogatories framed and delivered."

"left," "given," and "presented" show how her slave status was only gradually affirmed through probate and marital contract of the owners. Her youth and her de facto servitude and her forced abandonment by her parents (both of whom died) resulted in the perpetual enslavement of this orphan and all her descendants. Since, according to Cape law, slavery followed the condition of the mother, her 3 children and 22 grandchildren were all also denied freedom. The two missing letters are important pieces of evidence, but what rounds out the story is that the "old Mrs Blankenberg" had read these letters to her, since she could not read. The orphan's new owners comforted her, even had her baptized, but at the same time never taught her to read. From the owners' viewpoint the psychology was perfect.

The Owners' Justification of the Slave Trade

At first the Cape system of importing slaves was random and piecemeal. As Company knowledge of the slave trade deepened (informed by British and French slavers), selection of slaves by age was refined to an exact formula. Yet there were so many exigencies on the trade that no cargoes were refused. The enslavement of children was justified as rescuing abandoned or orphaned children from a worse fate. This was well expressed in the laconic language of François Duminy, the Cape's most experienced slaving captain, who wrote in the *Meermin*'s log in Walvis Bay on 21 February 1793: "Sieur Pinard [a Cape Town patrician] has brought [on board] a little black boy and a little Damara negress, whom he says he received as a present from their mother and accepted them for the sake of humanity rather than let them die of starvation! It appears that his kind heart is fairly at one with his interest!"[54] On the homeward expedition of the same voyage, S. V. van Reenen, a Cape Town patrician merchant who had come along for the adventure and for ivory, explained: "They [the native people] also offered . . . to barter several of their people in exchange for tobacco and beads. After long persuasion he was induced to barter two little children, eight and nine years of age, whom they said were orphans, and were so thin that they could barely walk. They were put on the horses and brought on board."[55]

The new English slave-owning settlers used a similar form of justification, as when Samuel Eusebius Hudson wrote in his diary in 1799 that he had purchased his first slave child on the oceanic trade. The purchase had become for him, if not a philosophical necessity, for him, certainly a grandiloquent humanitarian gesture:

February 1st: Reconciled myself to the Idea of purchasing a slave, a traffic my whole soul condemned, but when we can rescue a poor wretch from a cruel servitude with a determination to render him those comforts to make slavery

---

[54] Franken, *Duminy Diaries*, 294; cf. the French, 262. New free trade statutes in 1792 allowed Cape slavers to trade on the West coast of Africa.

[55] J. L. M. Franken, *Duminy Diaries*, 294; cf. the French, 317.

bearable it becomes an act of charity and which humanity need not blush at. Such is my intention by this Boy who I hope will feel with gratitude and repay my care with fidelity. If so he is mine for Life and should providence call me hence I hope this will always make known my intention that to him and all the slaves I may at that time [be] possessed of, are free providing I find them worthy of that freedom, some there are to whom it would prove a curse. To such it will be madness to emancipate them.[56]

Children survived the slave trade better than adults, but slave holders had to balance this advantage against the increased cost of raising imported slave children to their maturity. Agricultural patriarchal slave owners, therefore, preferred to buy adult male slaves (in or close to their "prime"); urban patrician owners could better afford the rearing and nurturing costs of younger slaves and had more use for such partially assimilated imported slaves. The principal difference between burgher and patrician slave owners was the *range* of ages the respective buyers preferred. Children brought in via the slave trade were the most assimilable into the households, and, therefore were the perfect slaves from the viewpoint of the domestic concerns of most Cape slave owners. These, after seasoning, would be resold at a profit. However, all imported slaves, in one way or another, were scheduled for a perpetual childhood. Orphans, whether young or old, male or female, made the perfect psychological candidates for incorporation into their new Cape "families." The idea of rescuing orphans gave the more sentimental paternalist slave owners ample justification for their purchases, and at the same time these owners still felt they could roundly condemn the whole traffic that had made the system possible.

[56] Robert C.-H. Shell (ed.), *Hudson Journal*, (South African Library: Lloyd copy), (1 February 1799): 20–21.

FOUR

A Family Matter
The Sale and Transfer of Human Beings

IN ALL SOCIETIES based on slavery, the legal transfer of an enslaved person from one free person to another presents a host of vexed ethical, rhetorical, historiographical, and methodological problems.[1] It is not surprising that the actual sale of human beings is simultaneously the most sensitive and difficult topic in slavery. The personality and property aspects of the individual slave are relentlessly juxtaposed. This has led to quite different interpretations in different societies. Paul Bohannan, the eminent anthropologist, in an influential 1959 article claimed that in Africa (at least among the Tiv people in Nigeria) slave owners always exchanged slaves for other slaves and never for money.[2] Following Bohannan, there was a strong suggestion in the Africanist literature that owners did not buy enslaved persons in precolonial Africa for money, but incorporated them "into the family." Since African persons, in this view, were never commodities, Africanists have glossed over the transfer of slaves from one person to another under the rubric of "lineage" or "descent" transfer mechanisms.[3] Such family transfers were never part of any "market" and are thus seen as presenting the "benign" face of internal African slavery.

American scholars, on the other hand, have critiqued analogous incorpora-

[1] I would like to thank James C. Armstrong, Stanley Engerman, Harvey Feinberg, Leonard Guelke, Shamil Jeppie, Edmund S. Morgan, Christopher Saunders, Leonard M. Thompson and the members of his SARP seminar, Robert Tignor, and Anthony Whyte for commenting on previous drafts. I would especially like to thank James Armstrong and William Worger for providing me with copies of their Cape slave sales transfers.
[2] Paul Bohannan, "The Impact of Money on an African Subsistence Economy," *The Journal of Economic History* 19, 4 (December 1959): 491–503.

[3] Suzanne Miers and Igor Kopytoff (eds.), *Slavery in Africa, Historical and Anthropological Perspectives* (Madison: University of Wisconsin Press, 1977), pp. 14, 64, 72 and *passim;* John Grace, *Domestic Slavery in West Africa, with Particular Reference to the Sierra Leone Protectorate, 1896–1927* (New York: Harper & Row, 1975), pp. 1-20.

tion and intergenerational transference of slaves among the families of the antebellum South as evidence of paternalism. Africanists and Americanists have developed different rhetorics for describing the same phenomenon, and there are differences, too, in their argumentation. In the American literature, intergenerational family transfers are usually explicitly excluded from discussions of "market."[4] Part of this omission is evidentiary convenience, as centralized auction records are easier to collect than probate documents scattered in wills in various court houses. This has led to a misleading picture. At the Cape in the 1820s, the auction sales accounted for less than half of all transfers. While 2,842 slaves were auctioned in Cape Town between 1823 and 1830, "no less than 3,859 [slave] transfers were effected . . . under wills, donations, inter vivos, and like gifts and private agreements."[5] American scholars have invariably emphasized the auctions and the out-of-hand sales. In this they were following the well-trodden path of the abolitionists.

The stakes of the debate are high, for it relates directly to the long-term effects of the systematic breaking up of slave families and the geographical relocation of slaves through sale. In the 1960s, the sociologist (and later U.S. senator) Daniel Patrick Moynihan cited slavery as a cause of the destabilization of the contemporary African-American family. He saw the persistence of a mother-centered household in the African-American population as a result of the selling off of male slaves and the splitting up of slave families in the nineteenth century. His argument caused an uproar among scholars and policy makers in the African-American community. Other scholars have come down on both sides of the debate.[6]

We know surprisingly little about the domestic slave market and the slave family in slave societies other than in North America. With almost fifty years between monographs on the domestic trade in the well-studied antebellum South, it is hardly surprising that comparative treatments have yet to appear.[7] This applies most forcefully to Africa. The historian Herbert Gutman noted:

---

    [4] This partly reflects the better survivability and accessibility of antebellum bills of sales. William L. Calderhead, "How Extensive Was the Border State Slave Trade? A New Look," *Civil War History* 18 (March 1972): 48, 51–52.

    [5] This represents an upward estimate of my previously published findings; cf. Robert C.-H. Shell, "A Family Matter: The Sale and Transfer of Human Beings at the Cape, 1658 to 1830," *International Journal of African Historical Studies* 25, 2 (1992): 285–336; CAD SO 10/18 (17 February 1834): "Addenda," notes by G. I. Rogers, pp. 184–186. Since my initial findings were based on ratios, the only findings substantially different are the orphanage rates, which are now amended.

    [6] The literature is well reviewed by Richard Sennet, "The Family in Slavery, 1750–1925" *New York Times Book Review* (17 October 1976): 3–13.

    [7] Joseph Calder Miller, *Slavery: A Worldwide Bibliography, 1900–1982* (White Plains, N.Y.: Kraus International Publications, 1985), p. 447 and supplements in the journal *Slavery and Abolition;* see also the comprehensive bibliography on the antebellum market in John David Smith, *Black Slavery in the Americas* (Westport, Conn.: Greenwood Press, 1982), pp. 1122–1131.

Studies of the frequency and cause of slave sales in other regions are clearly needed. . . . A study . . . which explored the mechanisms by which the relocation of [slave] labor was accomplished would be most worthwhile. Finally, the simplifying assumption that the threat of sale touched all slaves equally, clearly needs improvement. An estimate of the age and sex distribution would add substantially to our understanding of this matter. In short, what is needed is not an abandonment of a statistical approach to the problem of slave sales, but rather a more careful one — an approach more sensitive to the assumptions — than has yet been offered.[8]

Robert Fogel and Stanley Engerman have argued that the antebellum domestic market had a small impact on the slave family, and Michael Tadman later argued that it had a high impact. These authors drew their estimates of the domestic sale of slaves from a wide range of sources. From the federal censuses they inferred the extent of both the breaking up of slaves' families and the interregional movement of slaves. There is no dispute that there was considerable migration of owners *with* their slaves in the antebellum South. Consequently, further assumptions had to be made about whether interregional movement was a result of owner migration or of the speculative sale and export of slaves. The fulcrum of the American debate still lies here.[9] The literature has generally rested on one or another of these assumptions, with the bulk of the literature siding with the high-impact argument, which I call the abolitionist view.

Where contemporary American scholars have relied on actual market or plantation records, critics have challenged the records' typicality. For instance, the New Orleans slave sales, used as a source since the 1930s, have long been questioned on grounds of typicality.[10] The principal methodological problem is that the typicality of a sale cannot be satisfactorily established without many interlocking and, therefore, vulnerable assumptions. One must note that no one has been able to trace individual slaves through various transfers, or to present a typical slave experience in the domestic slave market, although a variety of ingenious techniques have been used with the slave narratives.[11]

---

[8] Herbert Gutman and Richard Sutch, "The Slave Family," in Paul A. David et al. (eds.), *Reckoning with Slavery: A Critical Study in the Quantitative History of American Slavery* (New York: Oxford University Press, 1976), pp. 111–112.

[9] F. V. Carstensen and S. E. Goodman, "Trouble on the Auction Block: Interregional Slave Sales and the Reliability of a Linear Equation," *Journal of Interdisciplinary History* 8, 2 (Autumn 1977): 315–318; I have not dealt with the interregional movement of Cape slaves for reasons of space, but see Robert C.-H. Shell, "Slavery at the Cape of Good Hope, 1680-1731," 2 vols. (New Haven: Yale University Press, 1986), esp. "Regional Distribution Due to the Domestic Market," vol. 1, pp. 112-115.

[10] Michael Tadman, *Speculators and Slaves: Masters, Traders, and Slaves in the Old South* (Madison: University of Wisconsin Press, 1989), pp. 22-25; Robert Fogel and Stanley Engerman, *Time on the Cross* (Boston: Little, Brown and Company, 1975) vol. 1, pp. 49-50.

[11] Until the publication of Michael Tadman's *Speculators and Slaves*, the most quoted source on the domestic trade in the antebellum South had been William L. Calderhead's "How Extensive Was the Border State Slave Trade? A New Look." U. B. Phillips' works are among the

There is still no study that suggests that the market itself might have had changing effects.

In both the Americanist and Africanist literature, the same problem — the transfer of slaves — has branched into two debates: the Americanists have ignored family transfers and local sales, while the Africanists assumed family transfers. The twain have never met. For both shorthand and rhetorical purposes, I refer to the American view as "abolitionist," and to the Africanist school as "apologist." As I will attempt to show, only an intensive study of linkable individual records can yield answers to the penetrating questions Gutman asked and bring the apologists' and abolitionists' languages and arguments into a closer congruence.

Toward a Redefinition of the Domestic Market

The slave market was a type of market that economists term "exotic." The reasons for this classification are that not all slaves appeared on the market, and pure market forces did not operate with slaves. In this chapter, I consider all slave transactions to be part of the transfer mechanism, and I define the transfer process as that hypothetical area within which *any* change of ownership of slaves takes place.[12] A redefinition of the domestic slave market should include all types of legally sanctioned conveyancing of slaves within some clear geographical boundaries. My target of study is the effect that the transfer process within the colony had on the slaves' families and the owners' families, from 1658 to emancipation in 1838.

The Type and Changing Nature of the Documents

After all this methodological throat clearing, it is embarrassing to begin with an admission of the inadequacies of the Cape data. Cape transfers cannot reveal the long-term symbolic and psychological impact of sale — of course — no records can. In an important sense, slaves were only slaves because owners insisted that enslaved persons had the legal potential of being sold. Every time an owner transferred an enslaved person, slave status was legally affirmed. Every transfer reminded all slaves of their legal identity as potential chattel. Selling people thus had a hegemonic side effect: in any society, the sale of people undermined those

---

most thoroughgoing studies of their kind; see also Frederick Bancroft, *Slave Trading in the Old South* (New York: Frederick Ungar, 1959; original publication, 1931), especially chapter 3, pp. 45 ff.; Fogel and Engerman, *Time on the Cross*, vol. 1, p. 44 ff.; and also Laurence Kotlikoff, "Towards a Quantitative Description of the New Orleans Slave Market," paper presented to the University of Chicago Workshop in History, 1975. The abolitionist viewpoint is amply provided by Ethan Allen Andrews, *Slavery and the Domestic Slave Trade in the United States . . .* (New York: Books for Libraries Press, 1971; reprint).

12 Harold S. Sloan and Arnold J. Zurcher, *Dictionary of Economics*, 5th ed. (New York: Barnes and Noble, 1970), p. 276.

persons' identity and self-worth, and diminished their dignity. Even with the best sources, however, the historian can only obliquely capture such devastating effects.

Although the Cape slaves' psychological reactions to the market cannot be directly or systematically recovered, as they can in the slave narratives of the antebellum South, one can still gauge the immediate social effects of the market in greater detail. Changes can, most significantly, be traced through the abolition of the slave trade in 1808.[13] The Cape colony's small size, enclosed nature, annual household censuses, and excellent record keeping at the level of individual slave transfers are big advantages for an enquiry into the market. Some slaves can be traced by means of transfers throughout their lives.[14]

Because slavery was abolished in Holland in the Middle Ages, slave markets in the Dutch colonies in Asia began in 1609 with no contemporary precedents or extant systems. Roman Dutch law and Indonesian and Indian customs provided distant working models for the Cape slave market.[15] At first, Dutch East India

---

[13] There is scant mention of the effects of the domestic market in the 1,000 meters of criminal records, although I have not systematically ransacked these sources. The equally voluminous civil cases are untouched. They are possibly the most likely sources for determining such reactions. For slave reactions, I have relied on settlers and travelers' accounts and the few slave narratives I have unearthed. For a full discussion of these sources, see the sales appendix to chapter 1 in Shell, "Slavery at the Cape of Good Hope: 1680–1731," vol. 2, pp. 297-313.

[14] This enquiry is based on two discrete data bases (1658–1732, 1767–68, and 1788, N = 4,536, including ship-to-shore transactions; and 1823–1830, N = 4,027), small subsets of a minutely documented domestic slave market. The coded material is based on the Cape slave transfers, "Transporten en Scheepenkenissen," (1658–1713, hereafter "Transporten"); Court of Justice (CJ) records, sometimes called Notarial Protocols (1713–1732, 1767-68, 1788); inventories and *vendu* lists in the Master of the Orphan Chamber (MOOC) records 1658–1732, 1763; slave sales between 1823 and 1830, Slave Office (SO) 10/6 through 10/20, but especially 10/18. This last data set was initially created by sworn appraisers appointed by the British Crown, and constituted "all [auction] sales that could be ascertained to have taken place during the period defined in the Emancipation Act," which was "the eight years preceding the 31 of December 1830." Cf. George McCall Theal, *History of South Africa since 1795* (Cape Town: Struik, 1965 reprint), vol. 6, pp. 74–75. Each slave transfer in the early data set has been coded with 33 variables: date of sale, name, category of sale, sex, price, family relationship, and characteristics of both seller and buyer. The second data set, which is not quite symmetrical, has been coded with 20 variables, some the same — such as date of sale, sex, price, family relationship — and some "new" variables, including slave's occupation. No "origins" were given in the nineteenth-century originals, nor was there any information about the buyers and sellers. The combined data sets comprise just over 6,042 individual transfers. All tables and graphs are drawn from these data bases. Aggregated data from the censuses (*opgaafs*) are invoked in certain figures. I am grateful to William Worger for his generous gift of the nineteenth-century data while I was a graduate student at Yale. James C. Armstrong also provided some rare data for 1767–68 and 1788. Neil Lazarus, Anthony Whyte, Mary Caroline Cravens, and Susan Shell helped me with the arduous and exacting task of inputting of the data into the SPSSPC format.

[15] C. Graham Botha, *The Collected Works of C. Graham Botha, History of Law, Medicine and Place Names in the Cape of Good Hope* (Cape Town: Struik, 1962), vol. 2, p. 170.

Company clerks notarized all slave transfers at the Cape. From 1658 through 1713 all slave sales were interfiled with freehold property in the records of the Dutch East India Company. Today, these slave transfers are in the Municipal Deeds Office, not in the Cape archives. Clerks described each slave transfer with the same fidelity and detail as they used for the most valuable landed property. They recorded slaves' human aspirations, too, to some extent.[16]

After the 1713 smallpox epidemic, slave transfers were also filed with the Master of the Orphan Chamber, which had been established in the seventeenth century to be legal guardian to orphaned children. After 1714, the Council of Policy empowered the Orphan Chamber to protect the transference of property of all free individuals in the devastated colony.[17] It also, later, administered all intestate succession of slave owners — the bulk of slave transfers — until 1833, when the Orphan Chamber ceased to function, significantly, the same year as the emancipation decree. The Orphan Chamber disappeared along with slavery.[18] Also after 1713, the Court of Justice oversaw slaves sales that were unrelated to inheritance. In addition it supervised petty debts and sales of movable items, providing transfer documents akin to IOUs, which the Dutch called *schultbrieven* (literally, debt letters). Because of the smallpox epidemic, there was some confusion about registration of sales and transfers; the Cape Political Council brought order out of chaos by 1722.[19] Company clerks wrote out transfer deeds before filling in the details, and slave transactions increasingly became a formality, with a fixed fee assessed for the transfer. Transfers were recorded in a formulaic but no doubt speedier fashion, though without the details of slaves' lives that would have been useful to historians. By 1732 the authorities either saw no further need to maintain a central repository of slave deeds at all, or could not afford to do so. Clerks still notarized the sale, but they gave the individual buyer the only deed, and the Company did not retain a copy, or at least, none has survived. These notarial documents are found in the Deeds Office transfers, Master of Orphan Chamber and *vendu* (public auction) series.

After 1731, independent notaries at the Cape could draw up conveyancing documents for slaves; the buyer obtained the original and the notary kept a copy. When these notaries died, all their papers, by law, had to be deposited in the Cape

---

[16] For some examples see J. L. Hattingh, "Kaapse Notariële stukke waarin slawe van Vryburgers en Amptenare vermeld word (1658–1730) — 1," *Kronos* 14 (1988): 43-65; and Hattingh, "Kaapse Notariële stukke waarin slawe van Vryburgers en Amptenare vermeld word — II: Die Tweede Dekade 1671–1680" *Kronos* 15 (1989): 3-48.

[17] Kathleen M. Jeffreys and S. D. Naude (eds.), *Kaapse Plakkaatboek, 1652–1806,* (Cape Town: Kaapse Argiefstukke, 1944–1949) vol. 2, p. 26 (19 June 1714) "Versorging van weeskinders."

[18] The emancipation decree became effective in 1834. C. Graham Botha, "Intestate Succession," in *The Collected Works of C. Graham Botha,* vol. 2, p. 61.

[19] Jeffreys and Naude, *Kaapse Plakkaatboek,* vol. 2, p. 94 (29 September 1722).

archives.[20] The slave owner was also given a deed, but only a few such transfers have survived in miscellaneous or private collections in the Cape archives; these few are extremely useful, however, since they contain all prior deeds to a particular slave.[21] On 26 April 1816, local officials, prompted by the philanthropic lobby in England, began a registry of Cape slaves and all sales, drawn from deeds and the old censuses. The details of the slaves, apart from ages, were at first poorly recorded. Only gradually did the British system of slave record keeping come to rival in precision the older Dutch East India Company system.

The Actors in the Domestic Market

From 1658 to 1795, the Dutch East India Company had oversight of the domestic market. It sponsored special ships in the oceanic trade to replenish the supply of Lodge slaves. The Company rarely participated as a *seller* on the domestic market, ostensibly because of Dutch Reformed religious scruples (see Chapter 11). The strictly observed instruction of 1685 read: "Perfect order will prevail over the slaves of the Company: the lodge slaves may never be exchanged, sold, alienated or exported by anybody no matter what his station."[22] According to the Synod of Dordt, slaves in the household (and the Lodge was considered the Company's household) had to be baptized and educated and treated as other servants. They had to be paid a *peculium* (paid mostly in kind at the Cape) and could never be sold. The Company in general honored these principles. Up to 1685, the Company did sell imported slaves to early settlers on the basis "of need," and they sold slaves again in the early 1780s, as an investment. The Company sold these slaves directly from their slave ships in quayside auctions.[23] If they refrained from selling on religious grounds, the Company never participated as a buyer in the domestic market on economic grounds. Their self-sponsored slave trade, using Company

---

[20] These are called Notarial Protocols and are housed in special collections in the archives (CAD NP). See Margaret Cairns, "The Notarial Protocol as a Source for Genealogical History," *Familia* (1973). The Cape archives are busy computerizing this invaluable collection. I am grateful to David McCellan for his help in showing me these documents.

[21] CAD M49 (N): "Transfer Deeds of Sales."

[22] Anna Jacoba Böeseken (ed.), *Belangrike Kaapse Dokumente* (Cape Town: South African State Archives Publications Committee, 1966), vol. 1, p.217, "Memoriën en Instructiën, 1657–1699."

[23] According to the Synod of Dordt (1618–19), slaves within a Dutch Reformed household could never be sold. The Company's slaves housed in the Lodge were considered part of the Company's "household" and were routinely baptized. Consequently Lodge slaves hardly ever appeared on the domestic market. Perhaps this religious zeal wavered following the collapse of the Amsterdam stock exchange in 1773, after which there were several times when the Company sold imported slaves. So far as I know, no slave *born* in the Lodge was sold for any reason whatsoever.

ships, proved the least expensive way of acquiring slaves for the Lodge. Slave prices on the other end of the oceanic trade were always lower than on the domestic market. The Lodge was not part of the Cape's internal slave market system.[24]

The Company, and after 1795 the British state government, did, however, have an increasing oversight role in the administration of the trade, they notarized and regulated every single transfer, and they collected revenue from stamp duties and flat transfer fees from the independent notaries. In short, both were the regulators and indirect beneficiaries of all revenues of the domestic slave market.

The Cape domestic slave market directly excluded the Company Lodge, but it served three other slave-owning groups within the colony. The first group was the urban patrician officials of the Company, slave owners in their own right who also managed all aspects of the oceanic trade, but who lost their power after 1795 with the first British occupation. Second was the fastest growing group, the rural and increasingly patriarchal burghers. The largest of the three slave-owning groups, they ran all their plantations and even their urban concerns with slave labor. The third and smallest group was the predominantly urban free blacks, a subgroup of the burghers that included ex-slaves, Chinese ex-convicts, and Indian and Indonesian political exiles who mainly used the market to free their kin. All buyers and sellers on the domestic market came from one of these groups. And each group behaved in the market in different ways (see Figure 4-1).[25] The free blacks purchased fewer slaves off slave ships than expected, and they sold fewer than they bought in the internal market. They manumitted and purchased with the intent to manumit at an extraordinary rate. The Company officials were the "middlemen"; at any given time barely three dozen Company officials engaged in the slave trade, but they sold almost one-third (31.4 percent) of all slaves. They were the Cape's slave speculators. Offsetting their speculative character, they also manumitted more slaves than one would expect. The burghers, for their part, were the final buyers, the end users. They manumitted the fewest slaves of all.

The Changing Functions of the Domestic Market

The Cape domestic slave market came to have five discreet functions. First, the market ensured the investment in slaves by providing a fiscal and legal recording mechanism for sale and inheritance. Second, it was the only avenue for the

---

[24] Crew members of Company ships did sell slaves to burghers on the sly.

[25] Data for burghers from VOC 4118 (1731), n.p.; officials data from LJ, p. 323; free black data from R. Ross, *EEC*, p. 118; (N = 2,020). This was not a distribution that one could have expected to have occurred randomly. Chi square = 389.15035 with four degrees of freedom; significance .0000 (variables *are* dependent); minimum E. F. 5.419; number of missing observations = 226. In all cross tabulations, if one value is missing, pairwise deletion of data occurs. Totals (N) in subsequent figures will vary slightly, as each variable has a different proportion of missing values. I have heroically assumed such missing values were randomly distributed.

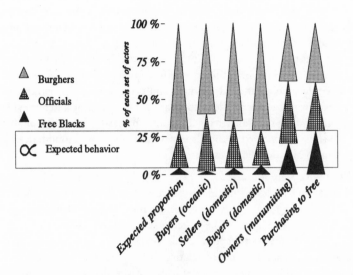

Figure 4–1. Behavior of groups in the domestic slave market.

acquisition of creole slaves.[26] Third, it played a minor disciplinary role for owners and, later, for the state. Fourth, it provided revenue to the state in fees and duties. And fifth and finally, the domestic market was an arena in which the state's power to confiscation property (sequestration) could be exercised. These functions changed dramatically as the colony evolved.

Slaves' Liquidity

The price of a skilled slave at the Cape was roughly equivalent to the cost of setting up a humble frontier loan farm (see Chapter 5). The purchase of a slave was thus a considerable capital investment. As early as 1671, one colonist exchanged an unskilled young slave, Isaaq, for a minimal frontier "kit," four draught oxen, and a broken-down wagon.[27] Slave owners — thanks to the domestic slave market —

---

[26] I use the word in its Spanish sense of locally born. I use the word mulatto for slaves born of a union across racial lines.

[27] I emphasize this point since the purchase of a slave was always a choice. Capital outlay to purchase a slave could also begin an alternative free frontier existence. According to Leonard Guelke, the authority on the subject, "setting up on the frontier" would have included a horse, some cattle, some sheep, a wagon, annual rent for a loan farm, miscellaneous equipment, coffee, and so on — all in all, about 200 Rixdollars; see Guelke, "The White Settlers, 1652–1780," in Richard Elphick and Herman Giliomee (eds.), *The Shaping of South African Society, 1652–1820* (Cape Town: Longmans, 1979), p. 64. At least one slave owner made this choice; for the swap of a slave for a wagon and oxen, see Leon Hattingh, "Die Notariële Stukke van de Tweede Dekade (1671–1680)," *Kronos* 15 (1989): 16 (13 September, 1671). The high price of a skilled slave at

were able to render their slaves into some form of negotiable asset. Edmund Morgan, a historian of colonial America, in bleakly highlighting the dual advantages of the marketability and transferability of slaves, pointed out how slavery lured seventeenth-century Virginians away from the use of indentured servitude: "Slaves offered the planter a way of disposing his profits that combined the advantages of cattle and servants. . . ."[28] Cattle could be sold or bequeathed, while servants could only be worked for the term of their indenture. Slaves and their offspring could be bought, sold, worked, and bequeathed. The domestic market offered slave owners a variety of legal mechanisms for investing and retrieving their capital, but mainly for transferring naturally increasing human capital: slaves. Until 1834, slaves appeared to the Cape slave investor to be a sound, flexible, and above all safely transferable investment.

The Creole Slave Market

The oceanic slave trade was the main source of new slaves for Cape slave owners until 1770, when, for the first time, locally born (creole) slaves outnumbered imported slaves (see Figure 4-2).[29] Creole slaves, all of whom once had intact families in the colony, do not appear on the market in their expected proportions; their market appearance decreased relative to their expected proportions. In the period 1658 to 1808, domestic market sales and transfers encompassed both the resale of foreign-born slaves and the sale of creole slaves, but up until 1770 slave owners bought most slaves directly off the slave ships. After the abolition of the oceanic slave trade in 1808, the domestic market was no longer the subsidiary market: it became the only source for all creole and previously imported slaves. However, there was a decreasing tendency to put creole slaves on the market. Slaves born in the colony increasingly enjoyed better familial expectations and were less likely to be sold (see Figure 4-2).[30]

The Domestic Market as Punishment for Slaves and Owners

The domestic market was said to serve a disciplinary function, but I believe this was minor at the Cape, although disciplinary sales do occupy a prominent place in

the Cape must also be emphasized: the highest price paid for a single slave in the Colony's first 75 years was 360 Rixdollars. He was a 30-year-old male slave owned and trained by a blacksmith. A nineteenth-century blacksmith slave could cost anything from £150 and up.

[28] Edmund S. Morgan, *American Slavery, American Freedom* (New York: Norton, 1975), p. 310.

[29] This figure is based on tallies of inventories and transfers that represent not only my own work (for the years 1658–1731, 1833), but also that of many other scholars, some of whom have sent me their tallies and other inventory data. These include: Nigel Worden (1722-1799, Stellenbosch), Margaret Cairns and Frank Bradlow (selected tables), James Armstrong, William Worger (1823–1830), and John Mason (1833). I have also drawn on the early work of Leon Hattingh and Anna J. Böeseken.

[30] Shell, "Popucape." Expected percentages derived from 760 individual slaves sold in estate sales; observed percentages from 2,240 sales. An assumption is made that estate slaves are a representative sample of all creole transfers.

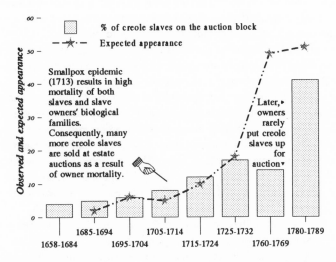

Figure 4–2. Creole slaves' observed and expected appearance on the domestic market, 1658 to 1789.

the settlers' and travelers' accounts and in the secondary literature, which report that the threat of sale offered owners an effective psychological spur to punish "recalcitrant" slaves.[31] A punitive sale would remind other slaves that it could happen to *them*. Such a practice had its counterpart in the American South. According to Michael Tadman, even presidents sold slaves in this way.[32] The American practice of "selling a slave down river" had an early South African equivalent in "selling a slave upcountry." Otto Mentzel, writing of the late 1730s, noted this: "In my time, a farmer named Michael Otto (commonly known as Michael Ox) owned the best farm in Hottentots Holland, noted for viticulture; but he was savage, tyrannical to his slaves . . . When any farmer had a disobedient slave, the mere threat to sell or give him to Michael Otto unless he improved, was often more effective than other punishments would have been since every slave was afraid of this man."[33] No slave owners gave Michael Otto any slaves. Of the 22 slaves he owned, he had acquired most through marriage to his second wife, Anna Siek. She had inherited the *Vergelegen* plantation with all its slaves. Otto bought

---

[31] Calderhead, "How Extensive Was the Border State Slave Trade? A New Look," 52–53.

[32] Tadman, *Speculators and Slaves,* 16.

[33] Otto Friederich Mentzel, *A Complete and Authentic Geographical and Topographical Description . . .* , trans. G. V. Marais and J. Hoge, rev. ed. (Cape Town: Van Riebeeck Society, 1944), vol. 3, p. 50.

only 5 slaves, 2 from a deceased owner's estate. Otto's plantation therefore was no large reservoir of "troublesome" slaves. His reputation for savagery among Cape slaves rested on his having killed his most valuable slave while in a drunken fit.[34]

Elsewhere Mentzel offers his view of selling a slave as punishment: "The most sensible course . . . is to send [the recalcitrant slave] to the auction and dispose of him at any price."[35] Carl Peter Thunberg, a Swedish botanist visiting the Cape in the 1770s, pointed out that masters chose to cede their slaves to local officials if they proved too "troublesome."[36] In 1797, Lady Anne Barnard, the wife of the second-in-command of the colony, provided a convincing anecdote of an owner selling a slave out-of-hand for discipline's sake.[37] Nevertheless, disciplinary sales seem to have been rare, or perhaps the clerks and auction masters were entirely in collusion with the sellers, for the texts of the transfers do not describe or hint at such a practice. In a small colony, of course, slave owners would be aware of the character of a particular slave, and certainly of the character of other slave owners.[38] Slaves sold out of their region would have been suspect, and slave purchasers were not fools.

A sorting of all slaves by name, ascending dates, and decreasing price (a crude test of this notion) reveals only one such slave sale for disciplinary reasons. This was the only transfer document to admit candidly that the market was being used to get rid of a slave.[39] Rosa of Bengal first appeared on the market in 1723, being sold from Daniel Jonas to an indentured servant, Harman Guttner. Johannes Zacharias Beck, a burgher tapster, bought Rosa with her child in 1725,[40] and five years later initiated her dramatic shore-to-ship swap for an imported slave, Maij of Madagascar. Rosa left the Cape without her child on the *Rudge*, a ship loaded with hundreds of slaves and bound for the River Plate. Her last Cape owner stipulated

---

[34] CJ 3029 (1718–1725, no pagination): Titus of Bengal (22 July 1722); Alexander of Madagascar (24 June 1724); Caesar of Madagascar (24 June 1724); Jason, unknown origin (13 October 1723); CJ 3030: Fortuijn van Madagascar (26 October 1729); J. Hoge, "Personalia of the Germans at the Cape, 1652–1806," *Archives Year Book* 9 (1946): 304; *opgaaf* of 1731 RA KA 4093 (old VOC document class), Stellenbosch district, entry no 9.

[35] Mentzel, *Description,* vol. 2, p. 130.

[36] Carl Peter Thunberg, *Travels at the Cape of Good Hope, 1772–1775* (Cape Town: Van Riebeeck Society Second Series, no. 17, 1986), pp. 206–207, 269; Nigel Worden, *Slavery in Dutch South Africa* (London: Cambridge University Press, 1985), pp. 110–111.

[37] Anne Barnard, *The Letters of Lady Anne Barnard Written to Henry Dundas from the Cape of Good Hope* (Cape Town: Balkema, 1973), p. 93.

[38] CAD C.339: "Attestatien" (11 November 1721), folio 729, October of Mallebar was sold to the Company.

[39] The data base was sorted interactively in a three-level sort: the criterion variables were toponym, name of slave, date of transfer (ascending order), and price (descending). I then visually inspected the data for matches of sellers and buyers.

[40] DO: "Transporten," (9 May 1710), (15 March 1723); CJ 3077 (2 May 1725): folios 113, 203.

to the English captain, Francis Williams, that she "must never be allowed freedom and was no Christian."[41]

As late as 1772, Cape owners remained convinced that the best way to rid themselves of a problem slave was to sell him or her not upcountry (where they would be suspect), but in another country.[42] Because the colony was small in the eighteenth century, and because of its position as a refreshment station for oceanic slave trading, unsatisfactory slaves were simply swapped or resold to oceanic slave traders en route to the Americas.

Resale of a slave with a bad reputation within the small colony was not easy. The seller had to go to extraordinary lengths, for example, to dispose of a slave felon. There was a law that a slave convicted of a crime had to be sold in chains. The only surviving eighteenth-century poster advertisement for any slave sale was for such a slave: "On Saturday morning the 1st August within this Castle at 10 o'clock it is intended to sell for cash by public auction on behalf of the Honorable Court of Justice a certain slave named Alexander of Bengal, aged 16 years. . . . The buyer must undertake to keep the slave in chains for six successive years in accordance with his punishment. Only on this express condition can he be alienated or transferred to another. Those interested should come on the day and hour specified and thereby make a profit."[43]

In the nineteenth century, the selling of "bad" slaves upcountry came to the notice of the British authorities. They wished to stop the introduction "of the worst [slave] characters into those parts of the colony in which there exists the least control over them. . . . We are certainly aware that a practice prevails at the Cape of purchasing slaves of bad, perhaps of infamous, character for a low price in Cape Town and removing them to the remote parts of the country."[44] Most surprisingly, there is no direct evidence for this in the transfers, but incidental evidence points away from the likelihood that the practice was prevalent. All low-priced slaves were very young, very old, or "sold in a state of infirmity."

According to William Wilberforce, the famous abolitionist, Cape slaves especially feared the fate of being sold upcountry. In a celebrated episode of 1814, Wilberforce told the British House of Commons that a female slave belonging to a Cape Town Dutch person had been treated harshly: "Her mistress threatened that

---

[41] CJ 3080 (5 May 1730): folios 76, 158.

[42] See the case of Judith van Eeden selling Manna of Boegies to Sri Lanka, in H. C. V. Leibbrandt, *Requesten* (Memorials), 1715–1806 (Cape Town: South African Library, 1989); vol. 1, pp. 425–427 (No 43 of 1772); the same sentiments applied in the American South: slave criminals were always sold "out of state"; cf. Calderhead, "How Extensive Was the Border State Slave Trade?" 52–53.

[43] As quoted in Victor de Kock, *Those in Bondage* (London: Allen and Unwin, 1950), p. 42.

[44] George McCall Theal, *Records of the Cape Colony* (Cape Town: Struik, 1967, reprint; hereafter *RCC*), 33: 109, "Report of the Commissioners of Enquiry to Earl Bathurst upon Criminal Law and Jurisprudence."

she would take her children from her, and sell them to the Boors [*sic*] of the interior. The dread of that worst of all evils so worked upon her mind, that to save them from this fate, she took them four in number, down to the sea where she succeeded in drowning three of them, and was in the act of destroying herself and the remaining child when she was discovered."[45] Cape officials went to elaborate lengths to refute his report.[46]

The transfers nearly always mention the residence or district of both buyer and seller. Cross-tabulating the residences of all buyers and all sellers shows that interregional movement of slaves due to sale from owner to purchaser was rare, and many of the instances can be linked to moves of younger members of the slave-owning family. These were, of course, not disciplinary upcountry sales. Slaves went from ship to farm, or from port speculator to rural owner; they were rarely resold out of their district.

Whether the incidence of such upcountry sales was low or not, slaves dreaded being sold there. "[Wilhelmina] complained that her master was going to sell her into the country to a man named Bickenaar, out of spite because he, having asked her to have connexion with him, she had refused. The master stated that she herself expressed a wish to be sold and therefore he was going to sell her. After some difficulty, however, the Guardian [of Slaves] prevailed upon him to give Wilhelmina 14 days time to look out for a master in town and she having found one within that time was transferred *much to her satisfaction*."[47] One may conclude that even if the actual number of upcountry sales was small, there was a profound fear of the possibility felt among slaves. The phrase "sold upcountry" certainly had entered the colonial idiom.

For the Cape authorities the domestic market also served an important symbolic function in exerting control over all slave owners. Through the market process, the state encouraged a particular way of managing slaves; from as early as 1686, Cape courts routinely punished owners convicted of mistreating or even killing their slaves by forcing the public auction of all their surviving slaves.[48] This was the first intrusion of the state into the domestic market. The state removed slaves from the danger of retribution and punished the owner in a material way. The courts also clearly stipulated that such slaves could not be sold to any family members of the offending owner. In one example, the four surviving slaves of Gottlieb Opperman, a German brewer who had tortured one of his slaves to death

[45] Theal, *RCC,* 14: 484, Hansard's Parliamentary Debates (22 July 1822), "William Wilberforce Speech."

[46] Theal, *RCC,* 11: 176–183, 188, 344–349; 16: 65, 379–381.

[47] PRO (Kew) Slave Protector's Reports, Cape Town, CO 53/50: p. 138, no. 128 [no date, pencilled no. 161–162], emphasis added; cf. CO 53/54 (9th January 1832), Case no. 258.

[48] G. C. de Wet, et al. (eds.), *Resolusies van die Politieke Raad* (Pretoria: Government Printer, 1958–1993, hereafter *Resolutions*), vol. 3, p. 146 (24 September 1686).

in 1731, all testified against him. So did his wife and daughter. The court ruled that Opperman's slaves had to be sold by public auction. The sale had the following state-imposed condition: "that they never came under the power of the family of the accused."[49] In this attenuated and indirect but effective way, the authorities both fostered and enforced a colonywide paternalism toward slaves. The lesson was clear for the slave owners: maintain efficient slave governance or lose the livelihood of your family.

The state's role in the market increased in the nineteenth century but became contradictory. On the one hand the imperial state, in occasional fits of philanthropy, passed legislation to protect the slave family in the domestic market. On the other hand, local authorities used the domestic market and the state's power of sequestration to confiscate slaves and maintain the credit equilibrium of the colony. The imperial and the local colonial state had opposite effects on the slave family. Together, they transformed the market.

The Domestic Market as a Source of State Revenue
The state derived considerable stamp revenue (2.5 percent) and the auctioneer's salary from Cape slave auctions, as well as revenue from all individual out-of-hand slave sales.[50] There were two types of auctions: the first was discretionary, the second mandatory, the result of the owner dying intestate. The state ran both, and it undertook to pay the seller immediately and allowed the buyer as much as six months to pay the purchase price with interest. By 1822, the state employed four full-time roving auction masters. These *Vendumeesters* were reputed to be the wealthiest men in the colony thanks to activities closely akin to today's "insider trading." The state worked against the domestic market by imposing taxes and interest payments on the auction of slaves. Taxes retarded the market, and the state credit scheme led to many more state sequestrations of owner's estates and confiscations of slaves.

Right behind the auctioneer waited the Insolvency Chamber, of which body Samuel Hudson, an English immigrant, noted in 1806: "The Insolvency Chamber undertakes to dispose of the Goods, Chattels, Houses and Slaves of all unfortunate persons who cannot pay their debts."[51] Between 1 January 1821 and 31 July 1826, the sequestrator's office confiscated no fewer than 873 slaves and

---

[49] AR VOC 4117: (12 July 1731), folios 810–811, *"Moogen werden verkogt by publicque vendutie, met conditie om nooijt weeder te koomen onder de magt van zijn gevangenis huijs vrouw ofte kinders."*

[50] For a fuller discussion of the Cape auction system, see Robert C.-H. Shell (ed.), Samuel Hudson, "Auctions — Their Good and Evil Tendency," parts one and two, *Quarterly Bulletin of the South African Library* 39, 4 (June 1985): 147–151; and *Quarterly Bulletin of the South African Library* 40, 1 (September 1985): 12–18. See also Shell, "S. E. Hudson on Funerals," *Quarterly Bulletin of the South African Library* 44 (December 1989): 56–63.

[51] Shell, "Auctions," part 2, 14.

sold them to pay debts.[52] Undersheriffs, sheriffs, and marshals of the sequestrator's office confiscated hundreds of slaves in these years. The *mesne* (the face-to-face phase of the sequestration proceeding) had roots in medieval law. All property had to be removed from, and be secured from the owner. Slaves, as property, had to be "protected" from being retaken by their masters. As one commentator explained: "Slaves [of sequestrated owners] are placed either in the custody of the messenger or when greater security is required, in the town prison."[53] By probating slaves early or transferring them to junior (even infant) members of the family, owners could avoid all such risks.

The Owners' Perception of the Market

In the Cape slave owners' view, the domestic slave market most closely resembled the market in cattle. For the patriarchal owners' expectations to be realized, all slave owners had to be empowered to transfer their slave labor to the next generation. This was to them the prime and enduring and most jealously protected function of the increasingly intricate domestic slave market. The local government, which assuredly served the interests of slave owners, as well as all commercial interests, too, had to maintain the credit equilibrium of the colony. The state and all commercial creditors looked first to slaves to ensure that balance. Thus, as I have noted, the owners' best strategy was to distribute their slaves early to their children; entire slave families were often transferred to a newly born child. Such transfers were termed *inter vivos* sales by the government Slave Protector.[54] By 1806, Hudson observed that some transfers of slaves coincided with an important rite of passage in the young owners' lives, their marriage: "When the [married] parties commence housekeeping, in case they have no Slaves of their own brought up with them, the parents generally present them with some of the younger part of their own establishment [of slaves] which can be most conveniently spared."[55]

In a discussion of the legal transfer of slaves, there is also the issue of Calvinist guilt. All Cape Dutch Reformed slave owners understood that it was their duty to educate all their household slaves in the teaching of Christianity. They also knew, from the Synod of Dordt and the subsequent *Statutes of India*, that baptized slaves should *not* be sold. The idealistic and egalitarian vision of John Calvin struck directly at the root of slavery: the institution's market. Dutch Reformed slave owners solved this problem in three ways. First, most stopped baptizing their slaves. Second, they manumitted baptized slaves on their deathbed. Third, they transferred their slaves by inheritance or *inter vivos*. In their minds, transfers by

---

52 Theal, *RCC,* (31 July 1826) 28: 241; Theal only summarizes the 45 pages of documents.

53 Theal, *RCC,* (6 September 1826): "Bigge to Bathurst," 28: 46–47.

54 CAD SO 10/18: "Addenda" (17 February 1834), pp. 184–186.

55 Robert C.-H. Shell, "S. E. Hudson on Marriages and Other Customs at the Cape," *Kronos* 15 (1989): 56.

inheritance were not equivalent to selling slaves. Therefore inheritance solved many of the ethical problems of slave ownership.

Significantly, the Dutch Reformed Church's restrictions on the domestic slave market were removed by the English governor in 1812 in response to other Christian slave-sellers' complaints.[56] From 1812 to 1823, there were no religious restrictions on the domestic market at all, but by then owners were worried about the increasing British abolitionist view that associated Christianity and freedom. For a few pious owners, the reluctance to sell creole and house-born slaves was partly grounded on religious scruples. Wilberforce, who believed that most Cape owners did not think in that way, addressed the House of Commons on 25 July 1822 on the subject of "Slavery at the Cape of Good Hope": "If I had not received the intelligence from a source of information, on the authenticity of which I can implicitly rely, I should scarcely have credited, what however is an undoubted fact, that it has of late become a practice to train up these poor creatures [Cape slaves] in the Mohammedan faith. . . . It is alleged that the Mohammedan religion is to be preferred for slaves . . . to Christianity because . . . it tends to prevent the female slave from being inseparably bound to her husband, as she would be by the Christian rule of wedlock."[57]

Taboos against selling creole slaves were grounded in the paternalism of the owners, religious observance, and, conceivably, some domestic affection between owner and slave. But the increasing reluctance of owners to sell their slaves derived most of all from the economic dependence of the owners' families on their slaves and the slaves' future offspring. This situation became most pronounced after 1808 and the cessation of legal slave imports. Bird, the Comptroller of Customs summed up these views well when he wrote in 1822: "The acquisition of a male slave is a life interest; that of a female is considered to be a perpetual heritage."[58]

The Slaves' Perception of the Market
In their most negative view of the market, slaves knew that owners regarded them primarily as a dynastic capital investment, and in consequence, ill-treated slaves sometimes took revenge by murdering not their masters, but their fellow slaves, for such an act would be a double loss to the owner. John Barrow, the British auditor-general at the Cape after 1795, recalled an eighteenth-century Cape slave who articulated these motives in court:

---

56 Robert C.-H. Shell, "The Establishment and Spread of Islam at the Cape from the beginning of Company Rule to 1838," honors thesis, University of Cape Town, 1975, p. 43; Richard Elphick and Robert C.-H. Shell, "Intergroup Relations: Khoikhoi, Settlers, Slaves and Free Blacks," in R. Elphick and Herman Giliomee (eds.), *The Shaping of South African Society, 1652–1820*, rev. ed. (Middletown, Conn.: Wesleyan University Press, 1989), pp. 185–193.

57 Theal, *RCC*, "Slavery at the Cape of Good Hope, 25 July 1822" 14: 477.

58 W. W. Bird, *State of the Cape of Good Hope in 1822* (Cape Town: Struik, 1966 reprint), p. 349. This Bird is sometimes confused with Col. C. Bird, his successor and no relation.

Conceiving that he not only had served his master sufficiently long, and with great fidelity, but a sufficient length of time, exclusive of the several sums of money he had given him, to entitle him to his freedom, he was one day tempted to remonstrate on the subject and to demand his liberty, which however, the master, with more harshness than was necessary, thought fit to refuse. The following morning the Malay murdered his fellow slave. On being taken, and brought up for examination before a commission of the Court of Justice, he acknowledged that the boy [i.e., slave] he had murdered was his friend, . . . he calmly observed that having considered the most effectual revenge he could practice on his master was, not by taking away his [i.e., his master's] life, but by robbing him of the value of a thousand Rixdollars in the loss of the boy and another thousand by bringing himself, in so doing, to the gallows, the recollection of the loss would prey upon his [the owner's] avaricious mind for the remainder of his life.[59]

In the middle of the continuum of slaves' perspectives, the artisan slaves regarded their own skills and value on the market as their prime bargaining point.[60] By the early nineteenth century, slaves were the only artisans of the colony, and the Dutch guild system, which had fostered apprenticeship and considerable craftsmanship in Holland, had atrophied among the colonists. One disappointed traveler noted that no settler would "put his hand to any kind of handicraft."[61] Skilled slaves at the Cape became "super" artisans, and many urban artisan slaves (many of whom were so valuable they were appraised for raising a mortgage for their owner) bargained for their de facto independence. Owners allowed artisan slaves to live separately and even to keep some of the money they had earned for their masters. Their continued presence and skills enhanced the value of a household, and in consequence, the domestic slave market held few threats for them, for owners rarely sold their artisan slaves. Speculation with such slaves was inconceivable.[62] One English official wrote in 1818 of the 2,000 Cape Town artisan slaves, their "value is now become enormous, out of reach of speculative enterprise."[63]

Finally, at the opposite end of the continuum, the slaves regarded the market as the primary means by which they could liberate themselves. Ironically, it was their very marketability that gave them the opportunity for freedom and self-fulfillment. Thousands of petitions dating before 1789 from slaves for their civic freedom remind us that the world did not have to wait for the French Revolution for the concept of civic freedom to be introduced. These Cape slaves saved the money from their *peculia* (the money to which a Cape slave was entitled) to purchase their own freedom through the domestic market. Eventually this

---

[59] John Barrow, *Travels into the Interior of South Africa*, 2nd ed. (London: Cadell and Davies, 1806), vol. 2, p. 93; a summary of this tradition is also in John Schofield Mayson, *The Malays of Cape Town* (Manchester: J. Galt & Co., 1861), p. 30.

[60] Mayson, *The Malays of Cape Town*, 12.

[61] A. Gordon-Brown (ed.), *James Ewart's Journal* (Cape Town: Struik, 1970), p. 27.

[62] Speculation is used in its technical economic sense of buying in anticipation of a price rise.

[63] Theal, *RCC*, "Nourse to Sidmouth," (12 January 1818), 11: 446.

tradition — in Cuba a right called *coarticion* — was formalized at the Cape in imperial legislation in 1830.[64] Although this aspect of the market proved to be a declining function, it was hardly insignificant.

A Taxonomy of Slaves

Legal transfers of slaves typically occurred at different stages in the slaves' life cycle and affected the slave family in different ways (see Figure 4-3).[65]

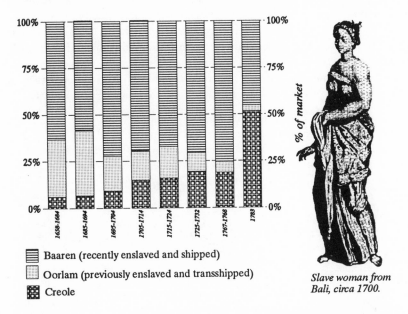

Baaren (recently enslaved and shipped)

Oorlam (previously enslaved and transshipped)

Creole

Slave woman from Bali, circa 1700.

Figure 4–3. Types of slaves on the domestic market, 1658 to 1783.

Recently enslaved persons, who were termed *nuweling* or *baaren* in the early period and in the British period called "green" slaves, comprised, on average, 16 percent of all slaves on the domestic market. Their passage through the oceanic trade and the domestic market undid all their family structures. *Oorlam* slaves, slaves in the eastern possessions of the Company before their importation, had a high (65 percent) chance of being resold in their first year in the colony. These transshipped slaves were unusual in the secondary literature but were common in reality (slaves transshipped from the Caribbean to North America would be a comparative analogue: Tituba, the slave in the Salem witch trial in 1693, for example, had been transshipped from Barbados). The passage to the Cape had already sundered the overwhelming majority of their family connections. They were then sold alone,

---

64 William Wright, *Slavery at the Cape* (London: Rodwell, 1831), p. 19.
65 Shell, "Saledeed." (N = 4,122).

because they had already lost their families. Creole slaves did not appear on the domestic market in their expected proportions.[66] Robert Wilson, a British lieutenant-colonel visiting the Cape in 1806, testified that a clear tradition of not selling creole slaves continued to the eve of the abolition of the oceanic slave trade. The creole mother-child relationship was especially protected: "The number of slaves in the service of each family is a cause of some surprise, and particularly as there are *so many women and children*. This is indeed a burthen imposed by an honorable aversion to sell those who have been born under their roof."[67]

There are two complicated but important actuarial conclusions to these findings. First, the oceanic trade drove the internal market and led the way in destroying slave families. Second, imbalanced sex ratios on the oceanic trade also structured the family formation of survivors. Creolization — considered solely in comparison with the oceanic trade — preserved to some degree slave family formation, and creole slaves increasingly stayed with their own families as well as within their owners' families.

A *Taxonomy of Transfers*

A slave sold in a deceased owner's estate probably remained in the same family and in the same region, but one sold in an auction for purely speculative purposes was sold to the highest bidder, regardless of who the buyer was or where he or she lived. There were, in effect, three major categories of domestic slave transactions: discretionary, mandatory, and donation sales. The worst type from the slave's perspective were those transactions in which the seller had no discernible reason for selling the slave except to raise money quickly. Such discretionary sales resulted in a single slave being sold individually to the highest bidder, and, therefore, had the most dramatic consequences for the slave, who changed owner and "home," *and* had to leave family and fellow slaves behind.

Mandatory sales, those sales in which the seller was personally obliged or financially or legally forced to sell all his or her slaves in a "lot," arose because of an owner's repatriation or retirement to Europe, or because of death or insolvency. Slaves in these sales generally stayed on the estate or were simply transferred to kin of the owner. They were sold as a group, and most stayed together.

The best outcome for slaves followed the rare donation transfers, sales in which the slave owner made a gift of freedom to a slave or transferred the slave to

---

[66] Perhaps this is obvious, but these results are based on total proportions; the market effects on the slave family are based on two "populations at risk": *all* imported slaves, and *only* the creole slave population.

[67] CAD: Lt.-Colonel Robert Wilson, "Description of the Cape Colony in 1806," unpublished manuscript, VC 58 no. 59, p. 14 (emphasis added).

another person, with manumission to follow. Money did not always change hands (see Figure 4-4).[68]

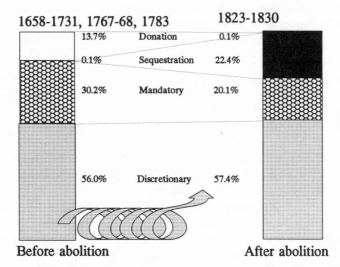

Figure 4–4. Changing functions of the domestic market, before and after abolition.

The discretionary sale category increased only marginally, but the mandatory sale category enlarged considerably over time. Specifically, the sequestrated sales increased from just over zero to nearly one quarter of all sales in the 1820s. This was a result of the colony wide depression after 1821. By the second decade of the nineteenth century, one of the biggest dangers to the slave family came not only from the whim of individual speculating owners, but also from the local state's efforts to guarantee the commercial credit equilibrium of the colony.

The donation transfers almost disappear. From independently collected manumission data for the years between 1808 and 1821, one can see this decline occurred after the oceanic slave trade was abolished.[69] Once the supply of oceanic

---

[68] Shell, "Saledeed"; Shell, "1823Sale." (Before abolition, N = 4,122; after abolition, N = 4,027.)

[69] I am aware that Andrew Bank has recently argued that manumission rates went up in the 1820s. This is true only for the urban population of Cape Town. First, the urban slave population was losing slaves to the rural areas at this time. Bank used a shrinking denominator. Second, urban manumissions in this period and place were drawn from more male and far older cohorts of slaves than in the ancien régime manumissions. The colonywide manumission rate was in fact going down in the 1820s. The main reason was that owners were manumitting far fewer women after the abolition of the slave trade in 1808. Andrew Bank, "Slavery in Cape Town, 1806 to 1834," M.A. thesis, University of Cape Town, 1991; see also Bank, "The Decline of Urban Slavery in Cape Town, 1806 to 1843" (University of Cape Town: Centre for African Studies, 1991), pp. 171 ff.

trade slaves stopped, all slaves — but especially female slaves, the source of all future slaves — had a much smaller chance for manumission. There was a dramatic reduction in the number of slaves transferred with the intention of manumission. Such donation transfers had nearly always meant not only freedom, but also reunification with other members of the slave family.

Discretionary Sales

Discretionary sales most often occurred shortly after the slaves arrived in the colony. Most common were cash sales. Hidden in this category were what one might term speculative sales. Individual slave transfers can be linked to show the rates of profit.[70] Such speculative sales were transacted by the port's slave dealers, who regularly bought slaves off the slave ships and resold them at their leisure for profit. Until the first British occupation in 1795, there were no "professional" slave traders in Cape Town, that is, persons who made their living solely from trading,[71] although, according to the abolitionist literature, such figures were common in the American antebellum South.[72] Many individuals at the Cape did, however, indulge in such sales for profit in a small way.[73] The most active of the slave speculators in the seventeenth century was the Cape Town burgher councilor Jan Dircks de Beer. He sold at least 98 slaves on the domestic market in 14 years. When he died in 1701, there were 25 unsold slaves in his estate.[74] Although not a large number, these 123 slaves equalled about one-eighth of all the colony's imported slave force in those early years. In the early eighteenth century, one physician, Johannes Theophilus Rochlits, dealt in slaves as a profitable sideline.[75] For Rochlits, slave dealing actually became more important than his medical career. After three years of slave trading in which he sold 25 or perhaps more slaves, he retired to the Netherlands with his young wife.[76]

---

[70] For a more detailed treatment of the seventeenth-century data and a full listing of all speculators and their rates of profit, see J. L. Hattingh, " 'n Ontleiding van Sekere Aspekte van Slawerny aan die Kaap in die sewentiende Eeu," *Kronos* 1 (1979): 34-87.

[71] Theal, *RCC*, "Report of the Commissioners of Enquiry upon the seizure of the *Stedcombe*, Schooner, by Captain Evatt, Commandant of Algoa Bay, for a Breach of the Laws for the Abolition of the Slave Trade, in the year 1822" (Mauritius, 10 July 1827), 32: 182.

[72] Tadman, *Speculators and Slaves,* 179-211.

[73] Hattingh, "Ontleiding van Sekere Aspekte van Slawerny," 48, Table 3. Nothing in the eighteenth-century (1700–1731) material contradicts Hattingh's extremely careful work.

[74] Jan Dircks de Beer started selling slaves on 8 September 1687, see DO: "Transporten," *passim,* and his estate, MOOC 10/1/18 (3–5 March 1701), MOOC 8/1/36 (29 February? 1701), MOOC 8/1/63 (1 March 1701).

[75] DO: "Transporten," (6 March 1687; stopped selling on 9 September 1726).

[76] Johannes Theophilus Hugo Rochlits was born in 1700 and arrived at the Cape in 1721 on the *Hoognes* as a Company soldier; see *Resolutions,* vol. 6 (11 May 1723), p. 320 note 235, and also *Resolutions,* vol. 7, p. 226 note 61. In 1723 he requested burgher rights, claiming that "he could earn his living by practicing as a surgeon"; CAD C.230: *Requesten* (no. 42 of 1723), 183–184. In the following year, he married the 15-year-old Maria Kleijnveld. From 17 April 1723 to

Although many travelers visited the Cape in the period from 1658 to 1808, none provided any written description of such imported slaves for sale in a Cape Town household's holdings. However, we do know about the high numbers of slaves in Cape Town homes.[77] According to a wide range of primary and secondary sources, there were as many as 20 slaves in many urban "establishments."[78] A pen-and-wash drawing of the home of a well-known trader in slaves, the slave trading captain, François Duminy, offers the only visual description. In the drawing a long, high wall and a barred seven-foot iron gate surround the house. The slave quarters have narrow slits for windows. The slave quarters are in the foreground of the compound for better observation from the large windows of the "big house." Both slave quarters and the doublestoried big house are flat-roofed to avoid arson — a cynical architecture perhaps, but one well-suited to the domestic slave trade centered in the port.[79]

In household "pens" like this, many slave arrivals spent their first months or years at the Cape. Almost half the imported slaves had their first experience of the Cape in the urban pens of part-time slave speculators. These slave dealers provided a service (if a ghoulish one) to the Cape slave-owning community. Speculators took on the risk that the slaves might die in the first vulnerable months, and they prepared the slaves for their life at the Cape, for which service they could charge as much as a 100 percent profit, though profits were usually much lower. These "prepared" slaves were sold alone; they had to leave any family behind. The remainder of imported slaves traveled directly from the slave ship to the plantation or to the urban holding and were not put up for sale unless their owner suffered a misfortune or died intestate.

Swapping of Slaves During the seventeenth century, Cape owners frequently swapped slaves. The "price" depended on the occupational or physical attributes of the slaves. On 24 October 1695 a skilled slave, Arent van Madagascar, was swapped for two unskilled slaves, Manuel and Dominingo, both from Malabar.[80]

---

18 October 1725, he sold at least 25 slaves on the internal market at regular intervals. We know that the transfers are incomplete in these years; CAD CJ 3076 to CJ 3078, *passim*.

[77] Antonia Malan, "The Archeology of Probate Inventories," *Social Dynamics* 16, 1 (1990): 6.

[78] Johan Georg Bövingh, *Kurze Nachricht von den Hottentotten oder denen Heyden . . .* , (Hamburg: Caspar Jahkel, 1710 [rare]; 2nd edition, 1714), p. 2; Captain James Cook, *A Voyage Toward the South Pole and Around the World* (London: W. Strachan and T. Cadell, 1777) vol. 1, pp. 77–78; Mirza Isfahani, Abū Ṭālib Ibn Muhammed Khān, *The Voyages of Mirza Abu Taleb Khan in Asia, Africa and Europe in the Years 1799, 1800, 1801, 1802 and 1803, written by himself in the Persian Language. Translated by Charles Stewart* (London: Longman, Hurst Rees and Orme, 1810) vol. 1, p. 68; Barrow, *Travels into the Interior of Southern Africa*, vol. 2, p. 92.

[79] J. L. M. Franken (ed.), *Duminy Diaries* (Cape Town: Van Riebeeck Society, no. 19, 1938), plate facing p. 73.

[80] DO: "Transporten" (24 October 1695), folios 1–2. Ironically, although the new owner had no money, one slave in the transaction did: the deed stipulated that Dominingo should "be allowed to keep the money in his possession."

On 25 November 1701, Governor Willem Adriaan van der Stel, the most frequent trader in the colony, swapped Anna and Marritje of the Cape, age 5 and 4, for a 15 year-old slave.[81] The last swap was recorded in 1767, when Reinhart Keith, a sailor, swapped Rosetta of Bengal to Dominicus Rosa, a well-known Cape Town slave trader, who gave Anthony van Bengal to Keith. The owners reversed the swap a few days later.[82] In Bohannan's formulation of the domestic market, swapping was the most common form of slave transfer among the Tiv. Swapping was common at the Cape in the seventeenth century, rare in the eighteenth century, and disappeared altogether in the nineteenth century.[83] Overall, swapping represented the smallest category of slave transfers.

Bartering of Slaves Lack of specie in the early Cape, as later in certain regions of the American South, encouraged bartering of slaves for material goods. Ethan Allen Andrews, the American abolitionist, recalled how "horses, mules, cattle and swine are driven into the Atlantic states, where they are often exchanged for young negroes."[84] Barter transactions afford a more vivid indication of the material value of a slave in contemporary terms than does the opaque currency of Cape Rixdollars. In the early period, almost anything of value was acceptable in exchange for slaves. For example, in 1689 Thomas Dirkcx van Schalkwijk, a wealthy patrician town councilor, sold Valentijn of Madagascar, a 25-year-old slave, to Joost Strijdom, a market gardener in Table Valley, for 80 wagon loads of firewood.[85] Livestock and agricultural products were more common bartering mediums in the rural areas than in the towns. In 1686 Gerrit Cloete, a patriarchal farmer in Stellenbosch, exchanged 38 breeding ewes for 19-year-old Adam van Madagascar; this amounted to 2 ewes for each year of the slave's age.[86] In 1710 the wealthy burgher Johannes Phijffer received four leggers (120 gallons) of "prepared" wine for his 24-year-old slave, Pedro van Cochin, from the wine farmer Class Westhuijsen.[87]

Barter sales, like swaps, declined rapidly and disappeared. After the smallpox epidemic of 1713, owners could buy slaves at an auction only for cash. In most of the transfers, the Dutch phrase "the last penny with the first" (*den lasten pennig met den eersten*) appeared on the document. In this respect, the Cape market was no different from the slave markets in the American South, where slave traders, intent on a quick sale, wanted to avoid expensive interest payments.[88] The reasons were quite different at the Cape, however. Cash prevented most, but not all, later

---

[81] DO: "Transporten," van permutatie of mangelinge (25 November 1701), p. 114.

[82] CAD CJ 3048 (28 May 1768) 122–3; (2 June 1768), 126.

[83] Bohannan, "The Impact of Money on an African Subsistence Economy," 501-503.

[84] Ethan Allen Andrews, *Slavery and the Domestic Slave Trade in the United States . . .* (New York: Books for Libraries Press, 1971), p. 49.

[85] DO: "Transporten" (5 December 1689), pp. 240–241.

[86] DO: "Transporten" (7 September 1686), n.p.

[87] DO: "Transporten," T296 (7 April 1710).

[88] Tadman, *Speculators and Slaves,* pp. 52–53.

disputes about slave runaways, or a slave's ill health.[89] Cape landed property, in contrast, was invariably purchased with a down payment and installments.[90] The informality of swap and barter may have been typical of small, informal communities, where everyone knew everyone else and where raising capital was difficult; however, policies of no credit, and no refunds without litigation, came to regulate the increasingly strict Cape domestic market. The few swaps and barters were for single slaves, whose family ties (if they had them) were destroyed. Swap transfers were too few to have a great impact on slave family structures, however, and no slave families were ever swapped or bartered. Although swapping slaves has a somewhat informal aspect since no money was exchanged, swapping people could destroy family ties every bit as efficiently as cash sales could. Indeed, a single swap transaction could destroy two sets of ties.

The Rise of Credit Sales and Slave Mortgages There were no public lending institutions at the Cape until the founding of the Lombard Bank in 1792. Some individuals used their slaves as peripatetic bank deposits, selling them when they needed cash. In August 1731, Anna Maria Brits, widow of Germanus Gerrits van Oldenburg, "cashed in" her slave, Carel van Batavia, when the wealthy free black, Robert Schot van Batavia, foreclosed on his 1725 loan to her deceased husband.[91] Such practices evolved into the mortgaging of slaves. Johannes Craa, hard-pressed by creditors, mortgaged his slave, Anthony van Mallebar, to the church council for 410 Cape guilders in December 1731. Anthony was the first Cape slave to be mortgaged,[92] but over the course of the eighteenth century the practice grew in the Cape slave society, especially among elderly slave owners, and by 1806, Samuel Hudson, an English slave owner, claimed that owning slaves "for the aged, 'tis their bank."[93]

A few hard-pressed owners sold mortgaged slaves at upcountry auctions. G. J. Rogers, the Protector of Slaves, noted in 1818: "the *vendu* [auction] masters not being bound by their instructions to inquire whether slaves intended to be sold by public auction are mortgaged or not, mortgaged slaves have been sold and transferred without mortgages being paid off."[94] Indeed, money raised on mortgaged slaves was considerable, as one official put it in 1831: "It [slavery] affords the

---

[89] See, for example, the canceled sale of Martha of Bengal, who was "found to be sick" (*siekelik was ingemeijnt*), MOOC 10/3/2: "Carel Strang" (29 April 1726), n.p. I am certain that the civil court cases would shed more light on this subject.

[90] The terms of higher purchase are interfiled with the property transactions from 1652 to 1795, see DO: "Transporten," *passim.*

[91] CAD CJ 3080 (11 August 1731), folio 92, no. 184.

[92] CAD CJ 3081 (4 December 1731), folio 852.

[93] Robert C.-H. Shell, "'Slaves,' an Essay by Samuel Eusebius Hudson," *Kronos* 9 (1984): 68.

[94] Theal, *RCC,* "Rogers to Colonial Secretary" (10 August 1818) 12: 26; and "Letter from C. C. Bird," 12: 28.

slave owners also greater facility than any other species of property for raising money upon mortgage, and the sum of money secured in this way amounted in the year of 1823 to twelve million three hundred and seventy five thousand Guilders, and the numbers of Slaves pledged to 4,089."[95] A petition from the major slave owners in 1827 revealed that "fifteen thousand [nearly 45 percent] of the most valuable slaves were mortgaged."[96] By the eve of emancipation, thanks to the increasingly intricate domestic market, slaves had become more than a negotiable commodity at the Cape; they were the *principal* mortgageable assets of the colony. This gives a new meaning to the word "bondsman."[97] Under the new mortgage regime, slave families were much less likely to be affected by transfer from an owner and were more likely to be disturbed by the local state's power to confiscate slaves to maintain equitable credit in the colony. This is a quite different picture from the abolitionist version of how the market worked. Where slave families were broken up at the Cape, it was in spite of their owner's interest, not because of the owner's speculation.

Mandatory Sales

In some transfers of slaves, the owner was compelled to sell *all* his or her slaves simultaneously. Such sales are sometimes called "distressed" sales in the American literature. Clerks at the Cape only sometimes noted such transfer of such slaves in the land transfers. In cases where they did not note the transfer of slaves in the landed property transaction, one must link slave transfers to property transfers to establish the impact of the transfer on the slave family itself.

Slaves usually had some warning of a pending mandatory sale. In cases in which the owner had died, a few weeks, sometimes months, would separate the death of the owner and the legal transfer of the slaves. While the executors resolved the estate, all the slaves stayed at "the house of mourning [*sterfhuysje*]." Mandatory sales included not only sales of intestate property, but also cadastral sales, that is, sales of slaves with property; repatriation sales, when owners emigrating to the Netherlands were selling their slaves; and, finally, insolvent and sequestrated estate sales.

A Note on Inheritance Patterns and Slave Transfers In the old South, at least in Virginia, where the rule of primogeniture was in effect until the Revolutionary War, this must have preserved the integrity of the Virginian slaveholdings far more efficiently than in the Cape inheritance system. This changed, however. As Ray Keim pointed out, primogeniture fell away at the time of the American Revolution.[98] The entailing of American slaves remains to be examined in detail, but as

---

95 Theal, *RCC*, "Report of the State of Slavery," 35: 375–376; 27: 445.

96 Theal, *RCC*, "Petition of Holders of Slaves," 34: 85, 234.

97 CAD SO 9/1–3, "Day Book of Mortgages"; SO 9/4-5, "Returns of Mortgages reported at the various Slave Registry offices"; and SO 9/9-37, "Register of [slave] Mortgages."

98 Ray C. Keim, "Primogeniture and Entail in Colonial Virginia," *William and Mary Quarterly* 25 (1968): 544–586.

Allan Kulikoff has shown, inheritance of slaves was crucial in the rise of at least the Maryland gentry.[99] One can therefore only guess how the nineteenth-century transformations in owners' inheritance patterns affected the slaves in later American holdings. Presumably the system worked *against* the integrity of the slave family, but this is only my speculation. In this respect, the American and South African systems developed along quite different lines. One may surmise that the American system, which was transformed into one of partible inheritance among the offspring, fragmented the slave family. The Cape system, favoring the surviving spouse with a half share, became more manorial and family centered and consequently favored the integrity of the slave family.

A strict and particular partible inheritance rule favoring the surviving spouse was in force at the Cape throughout the colonial period. At the death of a free adult, landed and movable property (including slaves) in the estate had to be appraised by the Orphan Chamber. The total value of a deceased owner's estate was divided in the following way: half the estate went to the surviving spouse (regardless of sex), and the other half was divided among the children of the deceased. This changed only in minor ways in the nineteenth century. At emancipation widowed spouses received one-third and a child's share.[100] This was what was supposed to happen, but since the Cape was never a fully monetized economy, other arrangements were often made. Most often the surviving spouse preferred to maintain sole ownership of the land. Only if hard-pressed would the spouse denude the estate of movables by auction, including his or her portion of the slaves; the spouse would then use the proceeds to pay out the offspring but would retain the integrity of the landed property at all costs. "Keep the farm" was the rule of the eighteenth century as well as the refrain of the nostalgic farm novels of the 1930s.[101] The death of an economically distressed slave owner could, therefore, result in a diaspora of most of the plantation's slaves. This was an exceptional disaster both for owners and for their slave families at least in the early period. By 1795 the disposal of estates was more common according to John Barrow, the

---

[99] Allan Kulikoff, *Tobacco and Slaves: The Development of Southern Cultures in the Chesapeake, 1680-1800* (Chapel Hill: University of North Carolina Press, 1986), pp. 263-313.

[100] Robert C.-H. Shell (ed.), "Hudson on Funerals," *Quarterly Bulletin of the South African Library* 44 (December 1989): 56–63. The situation was slightly more complicated than in the standard accounts cf. C. Graham Botha, "Early Cape Matrimonial Law" and "Intestate Succession," in Botha, *The Collected Works of C. Graham Botha: History of Law, Medicine and Place Names in the Cape of Good Hope* (Cape Town: Struik, 1962), vol. 2, pp. 50–59, 60–80.

[101] The popular Cape notion that constant subdivision of property led to population pressure and frontier movement is not borne out by either the wills or the land transfers of this period. They reveal consolidation of property, via the *erfpacht* (an extra grant of freehold property initiated in the 1720s), and concentration of land holdings in a few hands. People were "squeezed" on to the frontier by the gentry. Comparatively few farms, except the extremely large manorial estates of the Van der Stels, were ever broken up.

auditor-general, who commented that he had never seen such frequent buying and selling of estates.[102]

In modestly prosperous times, at least half the slaves would stay on the estate. Furthermore usually one heir, at least, would move onto the estate, sparing his share of the slaves any move. Female heirs stayed on the estate until they married. More important, if the young heirs had not reached their maturity, their slaves would be inviolate until such heirs reached their legal maturity at 25 years. One can say that, unless times were severely depressed times or an individual was financially distressed, most of the slaves on a plantation or in a holding would stay there. The exact proportion of slaves leaving the estate would be a function of the number of heirs who had reached their majority, or it could be a function of the number of heirs who had reached their majority and had decided to forsake the plantation way of life. Often, younger sons wanted to spend time on the frontier and left their slaves with their parents.

Deceased Estate Sales Widows but not widowers were overrepresented among the sellers, compared with their frequency among buyers on the domestic market.[103] Women who became heads of households through the death of their spouse may have sold more slaves because they felt unable or unwilling to "manage" slaves on their own. Eva, the Khoi widow of Pieter Meerhof, ceded her slave, Jan Vos, to the church in the 1660s, which in turn hired him out to another burgher.[104] Francina Bevernagie, widow of Jacob Mouton, asked the Company in 1743 to "take over" her slave, Hans of Bengal. She felt that although he "had been tried . . . the evidence was faulty." She added that she wanted only to "prevent further mischief."[105] Many older widows (not intending to remarry) sold both land and slaves and reinvested the capital in a small urban concern. For example, the widow of Wouter Mostert, Hester van Lier, sold all her market gardens and slaves and moved to Cape Town.[106] But not all widows sold their slaves. Widows formally manumitted more slaves than did other groups of owners.[107] And in addition, a few dynastically ambitious widows were quite aggressive slave buyers, themselves, for a good "stock" of slaves made a handsome dowry. The Cape partible inheritance system must have led to considerable familial tensions; all

---

[102] Barrow, *Travels into the Interior of Southern Africa,* vol. 2, p. 206.

[103] Robert C.-H. Shell, "Slavery at the Cape of Good Hope: 1680–1731," Ph.D. dissertation, Yale University, 1986, vol. 1, p. 103.

[104] J. L. Hattingh, "Kaapse Notariële stukke . . . ," *Kronos* 14 (1988): 63 (23 October 1669).

[105] Leibbrandt, *Requesten* (no. 89 of 1743), vol. 1, p. 75.

[106] DO: "Transporten," T174 (22 March 1681); T184 (15 January 1682); T196 (20 August 1683) and for the slaves, see T1103 (5 April 1682) and (4 March 1682).

[107] Richard Elphick and Robert C.-H. Shell, "Intergroup relations: Khoikhoi, Settlers, Slaves and Free Blacks," in Richard Elphick and Herman Giliomee (eds.), *The Shaping of South African Society, 1652–1820* (Cape Town: Longmans, 1979), pp. 140–141.

relationships, those among the family and step-family members, also between family members and slaves, were suddenly subject to self-interest as at no other time in the life cycle of a Cape slave-owning household. This must have strained family relations.

Cape women retained their maiden names after marriage, making kin relationships between buyer and seller not always apparent from the surname alone, and because the pool of original settlers was small, there was a high degree of familial interrelationship among families. Moreover many widows remarried at the Cape, creating a correspondingly large and bewildering set of step-relations. The historical record is not easy to follow, and the genealogy of all participants in a deceased estate auction have to be investigated individually.[108] Since the genealogical record is not complete, any statistical summary would be misleading. There are therefore numerous practical research difficulties; for example, there is no apparent familial relationship between the widow Johanna Starrenburg née Victor, and Johannes Pretorius and Josina Pretorius, to whom she sold three slaves. Yet the buyers were her own sons from a previous marriage to Johannes Pretorius.[109] In another example, Barbara de Savooije, the twice-widowed spouse of Elias Kina and Christiaan Ehlers, sold all her slaves to the offspring of her two previous marriages, Magdalena Kina, Susanna Kina, and Christina and Ernst Christiaan Ehlers.[110] With Pieter Joubert, who predeceased his father, all his slaves were bought by family members, including one slave, Dominingo from Mallebar, who was bought back by Pieter's father, a reversal of the usual direction of family transfer.[111] From the estate of Helena Siebers, Anthony Wagenaar, her widower, bought three slaves, an example of a lateral transfer.[112] Such individual slave transfers also have to be linked with the landed property registers to see if the slaves' families were broken up.[113] Even if slaves passed out of their former owners' hands, they might have stayed on the same property as part of a cadastral transfer when the farm was sold to a new owner.

A difference in names between seller and buyer does not mean that slaves were separated from their own families, nor does such a difference imply that slaves were even separated from their owner's family. A random sample of 30 estate sales suggests that in all estate sales at least some — in a few cases all — slaves were

---

[108] Shell, "S. E. Hudson on Marriages and Other Customs at the Cape," 49.

[109] CAD: MOOC 10/1/48 (18 May 1709) n.p.; MOOC 10/1/49 (21 May 1709); see C. Pama, and C. C. de Villiers, comps., *Geslagregisters van die ou Kaapse Families* (Cape Town: Balkema, 1981), vol. 2, p. 733.

[110] *Resolutions,* 8: 29, note 100; MOOC 10/3/81 (21 February 1729).

[111] MOOC 10/4/103 (8–9 November 1730).

[112] MOOC 10/3/72 (24 September 1727).

[113] Leonard Guelke and Robert Shell, comps., "The Deeds Book: The Cape Cadastral Calendar" (New Haven, Conn.: Opgaaf Project, 1990). Nineteenth-century data are not included in this publication.

transferred to an immediate family member.[114] Transferring slaves to other family members occurred mainly in long-established Cape families, for an obvious reason: newer immigrant slave owners had fewer family connections at the Cape. Family relationships, while not evident from the names of the buyers and sellers, are nearly universal in slave transfers from the early period. This is an example of one of those problems faced by historians in which the more research is done, the larger the proportion of owner family linkages becomes. However, a research strategy *not* based on genealogical lines would generate only out-of-hand sales. Moreover, linking slave sales to the discrete land transfers (an arduous task) has established that there were high persistence rates of slaves on properties. Transfers both in deceased estates and in cadastral sales were not as meticulously filled in as the discretionary sales records, primarily because slaves were transferred to family members and hence did not require the complicated identification of name, exact age, and origin, since the slave had earlier been fully registered to a family member. In both sets of circumstances, the slaves' families maintained their integrity.

Extremely rarely, family slaves were sold at auction at inflated prices. Later abolitionists depicted such rare cases in the familiar slave auction dramas, but they presented them as being typical.[115] By the early nineteenth century, passing on "family" slaves to close relatives or leaving them on the estate had become a fixed Cape tradition. Contemporaries elevated this practice to "a matter of honor," an important social code in slave societies, as Orlando Patterson has so clearly argued.[116] But I suggest that such familial traditions have far more important implications for the patriarchal and manorial order under which most Cape slaves had come to live by 1808. Holding the slave family together was important to the owner if for no other reason than as Barrow observed in 1798, "The Cape proprietor endeavors to enrich himself by . . . increasing his stock of slaves."[117]

The abolition of the oceanic slave trade was the crucial turning point for the Cape slave family. Even despite the new shortage of slaves, the owners' paternalistic traditions were not abandoned, although they came under increasing pressure as the demand for slaves grew as part of the supply was cut off. Most of the slaves in a deceased estate were still "reserved" for family members, although often a few had

---

[114] This is including step-family.

[115] Robert Semple, *Walks and Sketches at the Cape of Good Hope* (Cape Town: Balkema, 1968), pp. 44–47.

[116] Wilson, "Description of the Cape Colony in 1806," 19. Orlando Patterson has underscored how important honor was to the slaveholding ideology: "One part of the ideology referred to the master's own conception of himself, and it is generally agreed that its pivotal value is the notion of honor, with the attendant virtues of manliness and chivalry." Orlando Patterson, *Slavery and Social Death: A Comparative Survey* (Cambridge, Mass.: Harvard University Press, 1982), pp. 94 ff.

[117] Barrow, *Travels into the Interior of Southern Africa*, vol. 2, p. 88.

to be sold in a painful domestic "triage."[118] Of course, not all families followed the paternalistic tradition. Many colonists' offspring wanted to realize the considerable cash invested in the slaves of the deceased estate, and they disregarded the custom of passing slaves on to family members. These owners would sell to the highest bidder, perhaps even to a stranger. But such sales, which involved separating the slave from the owner's family, were exceptions. Bird, quite unsympathetic to slave owners, recorded in the early 1820s an observation consistent with the statistical breakdown of slave transfers of the time: "The public or private sale of slaves of good character rarely takes place, except by the distress or insolvency of the owner and by the Orphan chamber, or other executors, on a distribution of the property of a deceased person; and when it does in a family where kindness has prevailed, the scene of woe is dreadful."[119] The owners' financial well-being was, after 1808, entirely dependent on their increasingly expensive slave force, since with the end of the slave trade, future slaves of the colony could legally be obtained only through natural reproduction.

Repatriation Sales Slaves who journeyed to the Netherlands with their owners were considered free on arrival, but because the Company required owners to pay an expensive return-passenger fare for each such slave, most owners who returned to the "fatherland" sold or manumitted their slaves at the Cape before sailing. Dutch East India Company minister Petrus Kalden, so busy on his estate at Zandvliet (present-day Faure) that he persistently neglected to give his Sunday sermons in Stellenbosch, was permanently recalled by the Company to the Netherlands in disgrace.[120] The Company sold his estate in 1709, and the transfer clearly records that his farm included "nine slaves."[121] Such sales presented the least disturbance to the slave, as there was no move, no breaking of ties. No law enforced this pattern; it simply became a Cape tradition. Owners who left the country usually did so without disturbing the slave community on their estate, or in their urban concerns, because the efficiency and resale value of the plantation or holding depended on the stability and persistence of the slave labor force.

Cadastral Transfers Slaves who were transferred with landed property, like feudal serfs, stayed on the land after the sale. These "cadastral" transfers rarely

---

[118] Bird, *State of the Cape of Good Hope,* 348.

[119] Bird, *State of the Cape of Good Hope,* 78.

[120] Anna J. Böeseken, *Simon van der Stel en sy Kinders, 1658–1700* (Cape Town: Nasou, 1964), p. 203; Adam Tas, *The Diary of Adam Tas,* ed. Leo Fouché et al., trans. J. Smuts (Cape Town: Van Riebeeck Society, 1969–70), p.241.

[121] In this historic transaction, even the free European overseer was "sold" with the estate; see DO: "Transporten" (1 March 1708); the farm "Zandvliet" sold by Petrus Kalden to Michiel Romond with nine slaves, and one knecht.

receive any attention in either the Africanist or the Americanist literature.[122] In an early Cape example, in 1671: "Matthijs Cooijmans from Herental, a free burgher, sells to Jochum Marquart from Gorcum and Henry Barentz van Leeuwarden, his house, stables, cultivated lands, in size 27 morgen . . . and includes 22 draught oxen, one mare with a foal, *a slave named Anthonij van Angola,* unthreshed corn and other things at hand: two wagons, two plows and other equipment."[123] H. M. Robertson, an economic historian of the early Cape, has pointed out the medieval origins of some aspects of Cape law, and cadastral transfers of slaves do have a feudal aspect.[124] But it is more likely that they were related to the efficiency of the small Cape plantation. Cadastral slave transfers were sometimes recorded within the landed property transfer record itself, transferred as "part and parcel" of the estate. Many deceased estate auctions that reserved slaves for heirs and family members were really cadastral sales, with the clerks not identifying the slaves but simply recording them as "slaves and equipment." The anonymity suggests that officials increasingly approved such flimsy legal instruments.[125] Yet, cadastral transfers became a main form of transferring of slaves at the Cape. Under such a system, it would be difficult to determine exactly who was a slave. Significantly, in the Colony's first newspaper, the slaves in a sale were advertised *after* the property and its furniture: "On Wednesday the 15th October, 1800 and following days will be sold by Public Sale the place called the HOOGE KRAAL . . . at the same time, Furniture, Men and Women slaves, Farming Utensils, cattle, and sundry other articles."[126] The following advertisement dated 1970 suggests that this system endured well after slavery ended: "PAARL: 531 Morgen, grain wine and sheep farm, 200,000 wine grapes . . . Well built owner's house, foreman's house, usual outbuildings. . . . Price R255,000.00 includes winery sheds and 10 convicts."[127]

---

122 "Usually land and slaves were sold separately, but about 15 percent of the states land sales also involved the slaves who worked the land. Since traders had little interest in such a sale, this type of transaction has been left out of the accounts of this study"; Calderhead, "How Extensive Was the Border State Slave Trade?" 48, 51–52.

123 J. L. Hattingh, "Die Notariële Stukke van de Tweede Dekade (1671-1680)," *Kronos* 15 (1989): 15 (5 February 1671). In the IOU to the Church Council, who partly financed the sale, the slave was not mentioned; cf. "Editor's note."

124 H. M. Robertson, "Some Doubts Concerning Early Land Tenure at the Cape," *South African Journal of Economics* (1935): 158–172.

125 DO: "Transporten," no. 185: "Jacob van de Voorden to Guilliam Heems" (5 October 1682): T693, T696, T725 and throughout the series; some inventories were also in the following form: "Twelve slaves and one female, large and small, young and old," MOOC 8/1/50 (12 March 1700), n.p.

126 *The Cape Town Gazette and African Advertiser* (20 September 1800), and in *every* number.

127 *Cape Times* (20 October 1970); ibid., and ensuing correspondence (2 December 1970 [*sic*]). I am grateful to Keith Gottschalk for providing this reference.

Cadastral transfers did not occur only with large rural estates. In August 1729, for example, Jacobus Maarshoorn sold his Table Valley shoemaker's shop and tannery with tools, shoes, and a resident slave cobbler, Cupido from Batavia, for 3,000 Cape guilders.[128]

Cadastral sales did not force slaves to uproot themselves from kin, home, friends, or even from their products. The increasing frequency of cadastral sales in the transfers is compelling evidence for a gradual de facto enserfment of rural and urban Cape slaves and their offspring. No abolitionists mentioned cadastral sales, and some local officials denied them, as when G. J. Rogers, the Protector of Slaves, wrote in 1834: "There are no instances at the Cape where slaves have been sold with land in the same lot for one sum."[129] Three years away from the general emancipation decree, another official, the incorruptible utilitarian John Thomas Bigge, one of the royal commissioners, more accurately summed up the situation: "Slave owners in the colony have imbibed very strict notions of their right in property in slaves. It is incorporated more or less with every inheritance, marriage portion, or territorial acquisition, *and may be said to constitute the chief value of each.*"[130]

It was a subtle transformation of the slave transfer mechanism from individual to individual to a new type of transfer in which slaves were increasingly associated with the landed property they worked. Slave families were protected under this regime compared with out-of-hand transfers, and their intergenerational dependence on the owner's family must have deepened. That dependency was mirrored by the increasing dependency of all owners on their slave force. Paternalism operated like a vise.

Liquidation Sales In the early colonial years, liquidation sales, the most distressed of mandatory sales, were most frequent between 1713 and 1720, a period that saw severe economic depression, a smallpox epidemic, and many livestock diseases; during that time many persons were forced into insolvency.[131] In 1718, one of those, Maria van Brakel, the widow of Jacob Jansz Louw, could not maintain the butcher's shop her husband had bequeathed to her a few years before, and as a result, the Table Valley concern was liquidated and sold along with three male slaves.[132] Such liquidation sales, which also meant the owner's ruin, occurred

---

[128] CAD CJ 3079: "Marshoorn to Labuscagne" (30 August 1729), p. 122, folio 57; This recalls Varro's definition of a slave as an "articulate tool" as quoted in William D. Phillips, Jr., *Slavery from Roman Times to the Early Transatlantic Trade* (Minneapolis: University of Minnesota Press, 1985), page 21.

[129] CAD SO 10/18: "Addenda" (17 February 1834), p. 184.

[130] Theal, *RCC,* "Report of the State of Slavery," 35: 375–376

[131] Richard Elphick, *Kraal and Castle: Khoikhoi and the Founding of South Africa* (New Haven: Yale University Press, 1977), p. 233.

[132] "Liquidation of butcher's shop and three male slaves"; CAD CJ 3074 (31 December 1718), folio 216, p. 424; see also *Resolutions* (14 June 1718), 5: 287.

in periods of depression, when the domestic market was inactive. While slaves in such sales always changed their owner, they did not change households.

In the nineteenth century, severe economic depression gripped the Cape after 1821, when Napoleon Bonaparte died on his exile island of St. Helena. Supplying the huge garrisons there from 1815 onward had started the Cape's modest export economy, and his death threw the Cape economy into a deep depression.[133] The results were insolvencies and the dislocation of some slaves' lives and families at the Cape. Slaves in such liquidated estates were almost always sold as a group and invariably stayed on in the "establishment," however.[134] The insolvency category of sales included sequestrated estates and sales resulting from slave owners' being convicted of violent crimes or being expelled from the colony. Such sales must have come as a relief to some of the slaves; they removed slaves from the thrall of an owner's poverty, or removed all the slaves in the holding from the clutches of a what may have been a savage master or mistress. Although the proportion of mandatory sales increased in periods of depression, the rate of *all* domestic sales dropped.

Donation Sales

Manumission Transfers Donation transfers of slaves included manumission sales and outright gifts of slaves from one individual to another. In a manumission sale, a regular sale with the expressed intention of manumission, usually some free member of the slave's family bought and freed the slave.[135] Sometimes the manumission bond, required by the Church's poor fund, was not paid, and the official manumission request and *vrijbrief* (letter of freedom) were not filed. In such cases the slave was, in Cape law, still a slave and the transfer was only an expression of intent. But if the emancipating family member did not enforce the slave status of the transferred slave — and none did — the slave was, for all practical purposes, "free."[136] The context of the document, or more often its linkage with others, reveals the true relationship between buyer and slave. One such example was the sale of Claas van Mallebar, "in all respects free [*vrij van de been*]" bought by his free mother, Cecilia van Macassar, from the estate of the Cape

---

[133] Marcus Arkin, "Supplies for Napoleon's Gaolers: John Company and the Cape–St. Helena Trade during the Captivity, 1815–1821," *Archives Year Book* 1 (1964): 165–230; and Arkin, "Agency and Island: John Company and the Twilight Years of the Cape–St. Helena trade, 1822–1836," *Archives Year Book* 1 (1965): 265–330.

[134] At the Cape, the word *establishment*, literally a building, came to refer to slaves *and* the building; cf. Shell, "'Slaves,' an Essay by Samuel Eusebius Hudson," 67.

[135] I would like to stress that these transfers do not account for all manumissions. The legal instruments of formal manumission were a memorial and a *vrijbrief*. These were achieved without a transfer. The few manumission transfers discussed here are a small subset of all manumissions.

[136] The only way to enforce slave status would be to sell the slave; Leibbrandt, *Requesten* (no. 90 of 1737) vol. 2, p. 605.

farmer Hans Casper Gerringer.[137] By avoiding the ever-increasing manumission bonds, on which the Church poor fund insisted, many free blacks saved considerable money in their quest to free their kin.[138] Such "sales" had the most satisfying outcome for the slaves — freedom and being reunited with their family, lovers, or friends.

Once a free black made a purchase, the slave was, with some few exceptions, absorbed into the small and highly urbanized free black community. Church records of baptismal witnesses, signatories to manumission bonds, and executors of wills all reveal that this small community was bound both by extensive and persistent family and friendship circles.[139] Slave transfers also confirm this pattern. Slaves entering the free black community via the domestic market were incorporated into their families and later manumitted de facto, if not always de jure.

The quality of the freedom within those families is another question. Some male Chinese "free blacks," Mentzel recalled, "practice polygamy and obtain their wives by the purchase of female slaves,"[140] but one must also record that the Chinese were scrupulous in obtaining a formal manumission after such slave purchases. The following astonishingly candid manumission request submitted in 1768 illustrates this perfectly: "Liminionko, Chinaman, banished on Robben Island, and Lemuko, a countryman, holding his power-of-attorney, prays that his [Liminionko's] slave, Dina, and the two children whom he has procreated by her, might be manumitted [the previous sale transfer from a patrician slave trader attached to the request]."[141]

Nearly all of the free black transactions involved people in the urban area of Table Valley. In the port, free black fishing syndicates, chandlery concerns (which the Chinese monopolized), haberdashery shops, and restaurants were profitable enough to generate capital to pay for, and informally free, many slaves.[142] Even if one counts only formal manumission requests, one has to conclude that, considered proportionally, free blacks bought and freed many more slaves through the domestic market than any other group of slave owners from 1658 through emancipation.

Lack of money was not always an obstacle to free blacks in their quest to free their kin. Cecilia of Macassar, for example, not only freed her son, Jan Holdsmidt

---

[137] MOOC 10/2/10 (3–7 April 1719).

[138] Elphick and Shell, "Intergroup Relations," pp. 135–136.

[139] DRCA baptismal records (*Doopboeke*); Leibbrandt, *Requesten, passim;* and MOOC, *passim.* There are hundreds of such cases in these classes of documents.

[140] Otto Frederich Mentzel, *A Complete and Authentic Geographical and Topographical Description . . . ,* trans. G. V. Marais and J. Hoge, rev. ed. (Cape Town: Van Riebeeck Society, 1944), vol. 2, p. 150.

[141] Leibbrandt, *Requesten,* vol. 2 (no. 124 of 1768), 687

[142] Mentzel, *Description,* vol. 2, p. 92, 150.

of the Cape, but also friends. Lena of Bengal and Cecilia had been fellow slaves in the governor's "establishment" many years before. On her son's manumission deed, it stipulates that she bought Jan from the agent of Willem Adriaan van der Stel in 1714, and therefore Jan Holdsmidt of the Cape was technically a slave of his own mother for 14 years.[143] Tijntij from Bali, a Cape Dickensian character, must have found it hard to obtain money, yet he bought Bastiaan van Timor from the Chinese free black, Quodjonko — Tintij's sacrifice must have been rewarded in private, since he remained a convict isolated in the Lodge. He could have had no other purpose than to free Bastiaan unconditionally, since convicts housed in the Lodge could not keep slaves there.[144]

Sometimes the parent-emancipator died after the sale, before any formal manumission request went through. The following request reveals that legal limbo of semi-freedom:

Mangis and Elizabeth, both of the Cape, ex-slaves of the deceased Anna Schalkwijk, state that they had been bought free by their mother, Magdalena of Batavia, for a certain sum, they were therefore emancipated on the 21 October 1740, as shown by the annexed document, but in consequence of her severe illness and subsequent death there had been no time to obtain the necessary authority from the Government, they therefore pray that the emancipation may be confirmed and liberty letters given to them. The annexure says that the undersigned, Magdalena of Batavia, in presence of the seven witnesses, manumits her two slaves, Mangis and Elisabeth. Signed by herself with a cross.[145]

Fathers, too, bought their children to free them, although these cases were few.[146]

Apart from the few chandlery, fishing, and restaurant enterprises owned by free blacks and ex-convicts, it is difficult to say how free blacks generated the capital for so many slave transfers and manumissions. Their sacrifice in using their savings to free others can only be regarded as dazzling. This sacrifice nudged many into an honorable, but binding, poverty.

---

[143] CAD CJ 3078 (23 September 1728), p. 322, folio 191. Cecilia of Macassar was a slave of van der Stel's on 29 May 1695, when she had her daughter, Flora of the Cape, baptized. Similarly Lena, her friend ("Magda*lena* of the Cape") and her mother, Cecilia of Bengal, appear in the baptismal registers 13 June 1706 as slaves of W. A. van der Stel, DRCA G1 1/8, pp. 82 ff. Cecilia bought and manumitted them all; DO: "Transporten," (28 December 1713), no. 168, n.p.

[144] Bandiet thans in 's Companje's slawelogie alhier bescheijden. CAD: CJ 3078 (24 March 1728), folio 165, page 277; note: transfer signed in Chinese characters.

[145] Leibbrandt, *Requesten* (no. 82 of 1748), vol. 2, p. 753; and ibid. (no. 42 of 1744), vol. 2, p. 529, the case of Helena van de Caab who wished to manumit "her two children, still her slaves. . . ."

[146] Leibbrandt, *Requesten* (no. 31 of 1782) vol. 2, p. 699, s.v. "Louw."

There is little evidence that free blacks engaged in slave speculation. Although they did sell slaves, they bought slightly more than they sold.[147] The individual sale transfers confirm that free blacks played a crucial role in freeing slaves throughout the eighteenth century and into the early nineteenth century. Abolitionists traditionally have associated the domestic slave market with the breaking up of slave families, but one must point out that free blacks also used the domestic market to form, often to reunite, families. This avenue, for all intents and purposes, did narrow after 1808, at which point the colonywide manumission rate dropped precipitously, when slaveholders could no longer buy slaves from the trade and became increasingly unwilling to part with slaves. Transfers expressing an intention to manumit all but disappeared.

Gift Transfers Slave gifts often marked celebrated events within the family of the patriarchal owner. Slave owners in Brazil, for example, sometimes freed a favored household slave when they had one of their own children baptized.[148] At the Cape, similar ritual gestures of generosity took place. The following deed of sale drawn up on the fourteenth of May 1686 reveals this clearly: "The free settler, Jan Broertjie, declares in front of the undersigned witnesses, to give in full ownership to Willem Jansz, fellow free settler and the donor's son-in-law a small slave girl of seven years of age, named Marie van de Caap, *born in his own house,* which slave he gives as a dowry for his legal daughter, Anna Pieters Broert[jie], on the condition that she ultimately frees the slave."[149] Not all such gifts resulted in immediate freedom for the slave. The recipient of the slave could choose the moment of emancipation.[150]

Giving a slave to another person was not only a patriarchal gesture or one limited to the rich patrician owners in the port. The free black Jubij Poelij gave his wife, Sobagaan from Bali, an entire family of four slaves.[151] (This was one of four complete slave families documented in the early transfers.) As the price of all slaves rose in the early nineteenth century, such gestures ritualizing and affirming family events of the owner still appear in the records.[152] Whatever their numerical weight in the transfers, even a few such gift transfers reflect an evolving dynastic paternalism.

---

[147] See the cross tabulation in Figure 4-1.

[148] Stuart B. Schwartz, "The Manumission of Slaves in Colonial Brazil: Bahia, 1684–1745," *Hispanic American Historical Review* 54 (November 1974): 621.

[149] DO: "Transporten" (14 May 1686), n.p. (emphasis added).

[150] Ibid. (14 May 1686), n.p.

[151] Ibid. (23 June 1705), p. 100.

[152] Shell, "S. E. Hudson on Marriages and Other Customs at the Cape," 56.

Chronological Patterns of the Domestic Trade

The domestic traffic in slaves was in lockstep with the agricultural and commercial maritime rhythms of the colony. Consequently the percentage of slaves on the domestic market varied substantially from one period to another. These differences ranged from more than 12 percent of the unsold slaves in 1699 (massive speculation in the oceanic trade by the governor) to fewer than 1 percent in 1713 (small pox). To the slaves, this would mean that at some times the probability of being sold was considerable, while at other times, it was negligible. The peak years of the domestic trade correspond to economic boom years and periods of assisted settler immigration. Heavy trading in the oceanic slave trade resulted in heavy trading in the domestic market. In speculative oceanic trade sales, slaves were bought from skippers by local officials, then resold to Cape burgher slave owners.[153] In its boom years and trading surges, the early Cape domestic market resembled its counterpart in the later American South.[154]

Troughs in the domestic trade activity, on the other hand, correspond to periods of low immigration, demographic setbacks (for example, smallpox epidemics), and economic depression.[155] Sales of slaves in the 1720s were active, sales in the late thirties, forties, and early fifties were slow; there was a long depression in the 1740s, started by a measles epidemic in which one-fifth of the slave force died. During this period, Mentzel recorded, "most" slave transfers came through inheritance.[156]

Large new French garrisons at the Cape in the 1770s brought new money and a surge in oceanic slave trading, and the domestic market picked up again. The Dutch authorities briefly kept centralized records of domestic slave trading.[157] After 1795, with an even larger British garrison at the Cape again, both the oceanic and the domestic markets in slaves were stimulated.[158] Oceanic traders landed approximately 700 to 1,000 slaves annually in the last years of the Cape oceanic trade, but after the abolition of the slave trade in 1808, not surprisingly, slave

---

[153] See Hattingh, "Ontleiding van Sekere Aspekte van Slawerny," 34–78. These speculative sales are extremely difficult to count, as the slave has to be traced through several transfers. *Any* variation in the spelling of the slave's name, eg. "Anthonica" for "Antonica," makes for bad matches in a computer sort. Name changes due to baptism can conceivably be linked, but this has not been attempted here.

[154] Tadman, *Speculators and Slaves*, 115.

[155] Elphick, *Kraal and Castle: Khoikhoi and the Founding of South Africa*, 233; Mary Isabel Rayner, "Wine and Slaves: The Failure of an Export Economy and the Ending of Slavery in the Cape Colony, South Africa, 1806-1834," Ph.D. dissertation, Duke University, 1986.

[156] Mentzel, *Description*, vol. 2, p. 125, 126.

[157] CAD M49 (N): "Transfer Deeds of Sales"; CJ 3047 (1767); CJ 3048 (1768); CJ 3118 (1783); CJ 3063 (1783).

[158] Barrow, *Travels into the Interior of Southern Africa*, vol. 2, 92–93.

prices went up sharply.[159] Slave purchasers then depended wholly on a slow domestic market. Cornelis de Kiewiet said that "hard times came in 1820 and stubbornly stayed."[160]

When times were economically adverse, the slave was far less likely to be separated from family, locale, and friends. In only one period of depression (1704 to 1709) did many slaves come on the market. When the settlers, after a particularly severe harvest, complained about the corruption of the officials, the officials were recalled and, incidentally, forced to sell their slaves. In that tumultuous period, almost a quarter of the colony's slaves came onto the domestic market, mostly in the form of cadastral transfers, with the sale of their plantations. This was the exception to the general rule: boom conditions resulted in a volatile market; depression entailed a stagnant market.

Seasonal Patterns of the Domestic Trade

Shipping movements around the Cape, which underlay the relationship between the economy and the slave trade, led the inhabitants of the Cape to divide the year into "good months" and "bad months." For example, in levying fines the Cape court often postponed collecting fines "until the next fleet."[161] Good and bad months also led to a reciprocal seasonal relationship between the oceanic slave trade and the domestic slave market. More than 95 percent of slaves arrived in the Cape in the "good months" between December and June, when the Southeaster brought the returning, fully laden Company and international slavers scudding toward the Cape. Fully 24 percent of the annual quota of imported slaves arrived in March. Indeed, some slaves were named after their month of arrival.[162] Prospective slave purchasers — especially those from the interior — who missed these good months would have to pay higher domestic market prices in the winter months, when few if any ships called. Slave shortages in winter were acute, since many slaves died then. In the winter months, urban

---

[159] Theal, *RCC,* (27 November 1826), 29: 427. Annexure 8 "Average Prices" were in 1795: £60; 1806: £75; 1826: £150.

[160] Cornelis de Kiewet, *A History of South Africa Social and Economic* (London: Oxford University Press, 1941; reprint 1966), p. 38.

[161] Otto Friederich Mentzel, *Life at the Cape . . .* , trans. Margaret Greenlees (Cape Town: Van Riebeeck Society, 1919), p. 75; the most frequent use of these terms is in the AR "Civiele Proccess Stukken," *passim,* where fines and repayments were commonly held over to the "good months"; cf. Donald Moodie, comp., *The Record, or a Series of Official Papers Relative to the Condition and Treatment of the Native Tribes of South Africa* (Cape Town: Balkema, 1960), pp. 363, 385: "Judgement postponed until the fleet arrival [*fiat uijtstel tot de vloot*]"; Barrow, *Travels into the Interior of Southern Africa,* vol. 2, 11.

[162] This might be the origin of the Cape *moppie,* or song: "January, February, March. . . ."

peculators sold "fleet" slaves they had held onto deliberately.[163] Prices
d a peak in early spring, when there were few available slaves (see
e 4-5).[164]

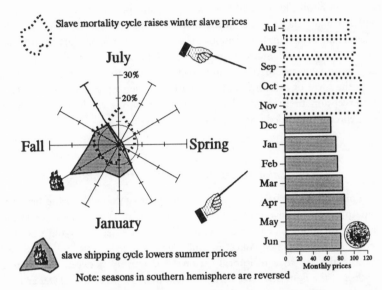

Figure 4–5. Seasonal fluctuations in the domestic and oceanic markets.

After the end of oceanic slave trade in 1808, seasonal mortality and agricultural timetables were more closely related, with the peak of slave sales occurring
in spring (October) and autumn (May). Without the summer supply surges of the
oceanic trade, the seasonal price structure flattened. There was less seasonal
speculation after 1808.[165]

---

163 Peter Kolbe, *The Present State of the Cape of Good Hope: Containing, the Natural History
of the Cape* . . . (London: Johnson Reprint Company, 1968), vol. 2, p. 69. The diary of Adam Tas
also shows the frenetic agricultural activity during the summer months; Tas, *The Diary of Adam
Tas*, passim. See also *Almanach der Africaansche Landbouwers en Hoveniers* (Cape Town: South
African Library, 1984), pp. 1–14; for slave mortality I have relied on Hans Friedreich Heese,
"Mortaliteit onder VOC Slawe, 1720-1782," *Kronos* 11 (1986): 7-14. Unfortunately the records
of the Office of the Fiscal, which detailed privately owned slave deaths, were lost in the nineteenth
century. See "Introduction" to AG Inventory, CAD.
164 Data for mortality from H. Heese, "Mortaliteit onder VOC Slawe, 1720–1782,"
Kronos 11 (1986): 12; Shell, "Saledeed." (For sales figures, N = 1,870; for mortality, N = 2,253;
for prices, N = 4,122.)
165 Shell, "Saledeed"; Shell, "Popucape." Although Rixdollars were used in the eighteenth
century and pounds sterling in the nineteenth, the means are still comparable. (For data from
1656–1731, 1767–68, and 1783, N = 1,870; for 1823–1830, N = 4,027.)

The Overall Effect of the Domestic Market on Slave Family Life

The oceanic slave trade to the Cape, with its unusual highly skewed sex composition, doomed most male slaves to lives without female companionship. This was the primary limitation on, and explanation for, limited family formation among slaves at the Cape. If the slave had been in a family before enslavement, that family was immediately sundered. Fewer than 1 percent of slaves arrived in families, and there were no husband-and-wife couples. Most slaves were bachelors and were fated to stay that way. The oceanic slave trade destroyed families at the point of enslavement, and also limited all subsequent family formation.

If — and there is no way to know this — every slave woman more than 15 years old had formed a relationship with a male slave, then 92 percent of all slave women who appeared on the early domestic market (1656 to 1732) would have been separated from their male partners. Of all the women on the market between 1823 and 1830, 98.7 percent had their conjugal relationships sundered.

After 1823, slaves married in a Christian church were not permitted to be separated. Article seven of this legislation stipulated: "After the celebration of [slave] marriages, it is forbidden for the Parties to be sold separately."[166] But it was only in the preceding year, 1822, that slaves had first been allowed to marry. Also, the new legislation protected only "Christian" slave marriages, not Muslim marriages, as Wilberforce had pointed out. And despite the new protective legislation, in fewer than 6.2 percent of all individual sales of women older than 15 was a "husband" in fact also sold to the new owner. About 86 percent of slaves' spousal relationships did not survive in the early period, and 94 percent failed in the nineteenth century. In 1,506 sales, only 20 "husbands" were mentioned. While the conjugal link was all but eliminated, many more slaves were sold in mother/child families *after* the abolition of the slave trade. This — to my mind — is surprising (see Figure 4-6).[167]

The Proportion of Female Slaves in the Domestic Market

With one exceptional decade (1670 to 1679), slave women appeared on the early market slightly more often than expected. The situation in the 1670s was a consequence of the arrival of one large cargo of male slaves from Madagascar; because the early slave population was small, a single shipment of male slaves could dramatically alter the sex composition of the slave population of the entire colony. In the nineteenth century, although there was some slight fluctuation, on average the sex ratios among the slaves up for sale and in the slave population were similar.

---

[166] Cape Proclamation (18 March 1823), by His Excellency General the Right Hon. Lord Charles Henry Somerset. Original in South African Library.

[167] Shell, "1823Sale"; Shell, "Saledeed."

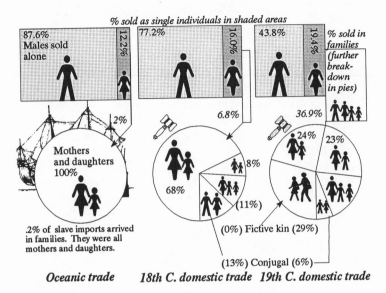

Figure 4–6. Effects of phases of the market on slave families.

When slaves appeared on the market in the nineteenth century due to events like the death of an owner or sequestration, and not speculation, such a pattern would apply (see Figure 4-7).[168]

Separation from Children

In the seventeenth and early eighteenth centuries, slave children (up to 15 years old) appeared on the market more frequently than one would expect from their proportion in the general slave population (see Figure 4-8). The reason was that proportionally more children were imported than were in the landed population (see Chapter 3). Imported slave children in the early period, already orphaned by the slave trade, were quickly resold for speculation.

In a few cases in the early period of slavery, a mother separated from her child was reunited later when the new owner could afford to buy the second slave. In October 1725, Cornelis Victor sold an adult female creole slave, Flora van de Kaap, and her daughter, Maria, to Sophia van der Merwe on condition that neither could be resold.[169] Flora's 11-year-old son, David van de Kaap (whose existence and relationship with his mother is known only from the baptismal records of many years before) was able to join her only after the estate of Cornelis Victor was wound up a year later. The transfer stipulated that the sale to

---

168 Shell, "Popucape" and "1823Sale."
169 CAD CJ 3077 (18 October 1725), p. 296, folio 167.

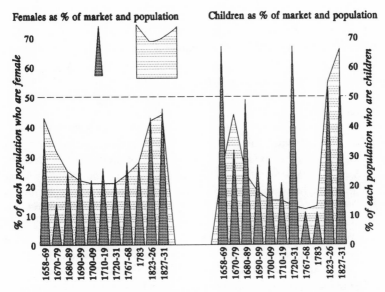

Figure 4–7. Sex and age composition of slaves on the market and in the general population, over time.

Sophia van der Merwe was at the behest of the owner: "on instruction of Jacoba Junius in fulfillment of the wishes of her husband."[170] The linkage of these records, showing an effort to keep the slave's family together, was a fluke, but there may have been more such cases. Creole slave families were more often protected than other slave families; creole slave children were the least likely of all to be sold. In general, only slave children directly off the slave ships were sold without their parents.

Between 1823 and 1830 children appeared on the domestic market in almost the same proportions as in the slave population. The same legislation that sought to protect married persons from separate sales much more effectively forbade sale of "the Children of such marriages, without the Parents, (or the Survivor of them) until such Children shall have attained the age of 10 years, except under a decree of the Court of Justice."[171] A significant fluctuation in 1828 was caused by the extremely small number of slaves on the market in that tumultuous year of the Hottentot emancipation, when slave owners, anticipating labor shortages, were reluctant to sell any slaves; this was also the year in which a new transfer system was inaugurated (see Figure 4-7).[172] The probable explanation is that there was little

170 CAD CJ 3078 (16 October 1726), p. 117, folio 64; David's baptism: DRCA G1 8/2 (10 November 1715), p. 177.

171 Cape Proclamation (18 March 1823), by His Excellency General the Right Hon. Lord Charles Henry Somerset.

172 CAD SO 10/18: "Addenda, G. J. Rogers" (17 February 1834), pp. 184–190.

speculation of slave children after the new ordinances. The matching age composition of the nineteenth-century domestic slave sales and the population at risk for sale is also consistent with the random events of death and sequestration of owners. The sale of slave children was still part of the domestic market process, but after 1823 far fewer children were sold apart from their mothers, although most were sold apart from their fathers. There were now more father-child separations than in the early period.

Over time, there were two significant changes in slave parent-child relationships. First, the proportion of all transferred slaves in families changed dramatically, from 6.5 percent in the early period, to 34 percent in the nineteenth century, and second, the type of family structure that survived the market also changed. The mother-daughter relationship was the most likely to survive in the early period (67.3 percent). Indeed, mother and daughter transfers overshadow transfers of all other types of relationships combined. Spousal relationships evident in transfers dwindled in the nineteenth century from 13.1 percent in the seventeenth and eighteenth centuries to 6.2 percent in the 1820s. One type of slave whose family ties were consistently broken was the unskilled adult male slave. For them, there were longterm effects on self-esteem and identity and, no doubt, a progressive — and perhaps irreversible — sense of familial alienation.[173] At emancipation, most adult male slaves were still bachelors (see Figure 2-7).

Orphans

The number of slave orphans on the domestic market is not known. Children appearing alone on a transfer might already have been separated from their parents through death or, up until 1808, the oceanic slave trade. Orphans were transferred on their own, and clerks never mentioned foster parentage; the orphan status of slaves was not mentioned in any Cape slave transfer document, nor did the Reformed Church, which placed both settler orphans and free black orphans in foster homes, keep records of orphaned slaves.[174] The Cape Orphan Chamber was founded in the seventeenth century but never concerned itself with slave orphans. (There was no orphanage of any kind at the Cape until 1815.[175]) Slave orphanhood simply was not recognized.

---

[173] Alexander Mitscherlich, *Society without the Father: A Contribution to Social Psychology* (New York: Schocken, 1970), pp. 268–304.

[174] The only slaves to receive material help from the Church were the elderly and sick slaves of a later governor, Ryk Tulbagh, who left 5,000 guilders to the church for this specific purpose; see Maria M. Marais, "Armesorg aan die Kaap onder die Kompanjie, 1652–1795, " *Archives Year Book* 1 (1943): 62.

[175] Johannes Petrus Serrurier, *Eene Leereerde, uijtgesproken op Dinsdag, den 26 September 1815 by gelegentheid der inwijding van 't gestigte weeshuis van de Kaap de Goede Hoop* (Cape Town: Gouvernments Drukkery, 1815).

Consequently, I have used orphan estimates for the American slave population to establish some bounds. This is an unsatisfactory "fix," however, as these figures are disputed.[176] Assuming that antebellum orphan rates were roughly analogous to those of the Cape, one would expect that between 1 and 2 percent of all Cape slave children under 13 were orphans. In 1823, this would be approximately 225 orphan slaves in the population of 5,821 young male slaves and 5,418 young female slaves, with about 13 up for sale that year, assuming random sales.[177] Yet 41 slaves under 13 years of age were sold in this year without their parents, thus orphaning, one assumes, 28 more slave children than expected. This would mean that, over a decade, a slave child would have an equal chance of being orphaned by the deaths of his or her parents *or* by sale. Most children transferred without their families were between 11 and 13 years old. Katie Jacobs, a 100-year-old slave, remembered her own mother's transfer when she was a young girl: "When my *baas* [boss], through old age, was unable to continue farming, he distributed most of his chattels among his sons, whom he had set as farmers in the neighborhood. I and some cattle and horses were given to *baas* Kootje; my mother and some more cattle were presented to another son in Frenchhoek. From that day I never saw my mother, nor do I know what became of her."[178]

Some mothers were sold apart from some of their children with special permission of the government. Perhaps Rebecca of the Cape was specifically coached by her owner when, in 1826, she "represented to the Guardian that she had been living for some time in the family of the Rev. Mr. Fallows and that she was anxious to purchase herself and her youngest child; and as she was pleased with her situation, and had hopes that if Mr. and Mrs. Fallows returned to England they might take her with them she preferred leaving her other children with Mr. Brink by whom she was certain they would be well treated and with whom their father resided."[179]

The largest group of slaves sold away from their parents were males aged 11 to 40. Whether they were sold on the oceanic or the domestic trade, they were usually sold alone. All their family relationships were broken. The process worsened in the nineteenth century despite some protective legislation. Adult and younger male slaves undoubtedly bore the brunt of the slave market, not only

---

176 Paul A. David, et al., *Reckoning with Slavery: A Critical Study in the Quantitative History of American Negro Slavery* (New York: Oxford University Press, 1976), pp. 130-131; Fogel and Engerman, *Time on the Cross*, vol. 1, pp. 50–51.

177 Theal, *RCC*, 16: 489; 28: 464.

178 Robert C.-H. Shell (ed.), "Katie Jacobs: An Early Oral History," *Quarterly Bulletin of the South African Library* 46, 3 (1992): 95.

179 Theal *RCC*, (27 December 1826) 29: 86, "Return of a Case in which the Guardian of Slaves has made application to the Court of Justice to be allowed to transfer a Female slave, without three of her children, who are under the age prescribed by law."

through the rupture of spousal relationships, but also through the orphaning of children. Women and children were increasingly, but never wholly, protected from separation (see Figure 4-8).[180]

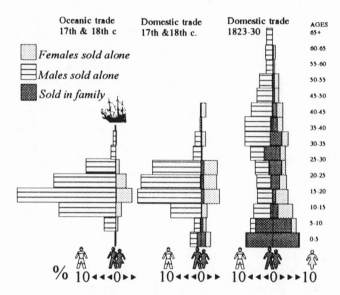

Figure 4–8. Changing population pyramids of the oceanic and domestic slave trades.

The Abolitionist View Reconsidered

A Cape abolitionist pamphlet tells a heartrending but revealing story that shows how Cape owners tried to keep slaves within their family — that is, to keep *female* slaves:

A variety of articles were exposed for sale, over which Humanitas cast a careless eye; for, as they were composed chiefly of household requisites and implements of husbandry, there was not any thing in them calculated to engage his attention. Scarcely, however, had he finished his vacant survey of the above varieties, before his eye was arrested by another portion of property, ranged in a line with the horned cattle which flanked the enclosure, the whole of which was to be disposed of by the fall of the hammer. This was a group of unfortunate beings whose forefathers had been stolen from the land of their birth, and these their hapless progeny were, therefore, adjudged worthy to be branded by the opprobrious name, and treated with the barbarity, of slaves and beasts of burden. . . From this abstraction he was roused by the plaintive and heartrending moans of a female; he turned, almost

---

180 Shell, "Saledeed"; "1823Sale."

mechanically, and beheld an interesting young woman of colour, standing apart from her companions in captivity, the intensity of whose grief might be better conceived of by the agony which shook her frame, than expressed by the cold language of narration. Close by her side stood another female, whose dress bespoke her of respectable connexions, but her countenance wore not the reprobatory hue (as some men seem to think a tawny skin is) possessed by the others, and yet her sorrow was not less intense than her's whose complexion had made her a slave. In her arms she held a sweet infant, which at intervals she pressed to her bosom in convulsive agony, as she gazed with phrenzied emotion on the black for whom her tears flowed so profusely. The scene was, in all its parts, a painfully interesting and novel one. Humanitas felt it so; and, prompted by a strong desire to ascertain, if possible, the cause of so powerful a sympathy on the part of a white person, so unusual, even in the female breast, in the brutalizing regions of slavery, towards a slave, he enquired of some who were connected with the sale for a solution of the mystery. A few words informed the inquirer that the white person was the daughter of the late farmer, whose effects were not to be disposed of, and that the slave over whom she so affectionately wept was her foster-sister. From infancy they had been associates — in childhood they were undivided. The distinction which colour made in the eyes of some, to them was not known. The marriage of the farmer's daughter was the first cause of separation they had ever known, and even then a pain such as sisters only feel at parting was felt by each of them as they said — Farewell! She had retired with her husband to a distant part of the colony, and there received the mournful intelligence of her father's death, and the account of the public sale of his property; included in this, she was certain, would be found the slave in question: *her father's insolvent circumstances rendered this unavoidable.* With an affection which distance, fatigue, and danger could not affect, she had travelled four hundred miles, cheered by the hope of being able to purchase her freedom. The pleasing delusion which strengthened and encouraged her, during the fatigue and her toilsome journey, fled as she reached the spot where already her beloved foster-sister stood exposed for sale. . . . 'Once, twice,' responded he who held the hammer — 'is there no advance?' He cast his eyes round the assembly with the inquisitiveness of his calling — neither wink, nod, or voice, gave answer to his question. A dead pause ensued — it was fearful, but short. The hand of the auctioneer was again raised — when the poor slave, in a tone of sublimated agony, shrieked out, 'Jesus, help me!' and, clasping her hands wildly, fell senseless on the ground. . . . The stranger bended over the prostrate female, and, having raised her from the earth, took her hand and led her to her foster-sister, whose agony was still intense, to whom he presented her, saying, 'Receive your friend, no longer as a slave, but as your companion.'[181]

The anonymous abolitionist was using the high drama of the woman and child being sold as a vehicle for his message, a mise à scène which also inspired a

---

181 Emphasis added, Anonymous, "The Tourist" (Cape Town: South African Library, South African Bound Pamphlets, n.d. [1831?]), pp. 1-10.

contemporary artist (see Figure 4-9).[182] The reality of the "rescue" by the mistress—although poignant—reveals clearly how the highly gendered maternalism worked even under the auctioneer's hammer.

Conclusions — the Reality of the Domestic Market

Ever since the first attempts at intensive agriculture at the Cape, officials and settlers had insisted that the colony suffered from an inadequate labor supply. The solution was slavery. The oceanic traffic in slaves and the domestic slave market that allowed slave owners to invest in slave labor inevitably led to dislocation of slave family ties, although not on as massive a scale as has sometimes been supposed. The sundering of families was highly gendered. The domestic transfer of slaves passed on slave wealth from generation to generation within owners' families. This dynastic system allowed for the growth of alliances between slaveholding families who perpetuated the slave-owning way of life. At the same time, the system of cadastral transfers forged a society with increasing aspects of serfdom. Slaves de facto, if not de jure, were transferred with the plantation or the urban "establishment," and in consequence, slave families often were able to stay together. The single most surprising fact about the domestic market is the continuity of most of the Cape slave force on the holding. Whole generations of slaves born on large estates, plantations, and in urban households must have watched several free but poor overseers (knechts) and owners come and go.[183] Ramsay MacMullen, a social historian of Rome, has argued that the free poor in Rome were far more insecure than the slaves, and that they, and not the slaves, occupied the lowest rungs on the social ladder. This could have been only partly true in the early Cape and the antebellum South, since a developing ideology of racism reserved a privileged place for all the poor whites.[184]

Slave women and children were increasingly protected from familial dislocation; males older than 11 years of age were not — unless they were skilled artisans. Daughters were always relatively protected from separation from their mothers. Creole slaves throughout the colony enjoyed relative stability; so, too, the lives of male artisan slaves in Cape Town were undisturbed by transfers. It was the imported and unskilled male slave who was the most likely to remain without a spouse or to be sold away from his family. The persistence of slaves on the landed property or remaining attached to their owners' families was common. Still, slave family dislocation, no matter how statistically "small," was for those it touched a

---

[182] This picture accompanies an abolitionist pamphlet on the domestic slave trade. A slave woman being sold was the favorite target of abolitionists. Anon., "The Sale of Slaves at the Cape," *The Tourist* (1831) South African Bound Pamphlets, Courtesy of South African Library.

[183] Shell, "Slavery at the Cape of Good Hope," vol. 1, 281–287.

[184] Ramsay MacMullen, *Roman Social Relations, 50 B.C. to A.D. 284* (New Haven: Yale University Press, 1974), pp. 92–93.

human tragedy. In the South African colonial society, settlers' families, until the introduction of concentration camps in the Anglo-Boer War (1899 to 1902), were always secure from imposed dislocation; their slaves were not.

The effects of the market on slaves were important on personal, psychological, and practical planes. The Cape records do not, and cannot, reflect all of the psychological effects of the market. The fear of sale, without doubt emphasized by some discipline-minded owners and in confiscations practiced by the courts, must

Figure 4–9. "Sale of slaves at the Cape of Good Hope, [1831]".

have undermined every slave's sense of security and identity. On the practical plane, although the breaking up of mother-child relationships through the domestic market became less prevalent. In strong contrast to the deleterious effects of the market on slave families, the transfer records reveal that slaves and free blacks often used that same market to liberate themselves and other slaves and to reunite them with their families in freedom. However, this process dropped off markedly in the nineteenth century, when the end of oceanic trade reduced the supply of slaves and raised prices.

Despite the conditions that tended toward some slave family stability, the rising proportion of inheritance and cadastral transfers of slaves along with land, and even of sequestrated slaves, had a malevolent character — the sale of people as a part of landed property. The resulting system increasingly looked like serfdom and slavery combined. Also, the intergenerational continuity of slaves on an estate fostered a binding paternalism. The domestic market thus had even more pernicious effects on the whole society than the abolitionists suggested.

Above all, each sale was seen to compromise the identity of all enslaved persons; to sell a human being was to confirm the system of slavery. But the roles of the local and imperial states were at cross purposes here. On the one hand, the rise of sequestration transfers presaged the intrusion of the local authorities in slave family lives. On the other hand, the imperial authorities were seeking to protect the integrity of the slave family; the cessation of the oceanic slave trade eliminated a whole class of speculation transfers, and the legislation of the 1820s aimed at protecting the slave family.

The most effective measures abolitionists used to undermine slavery were appeals to universal sentiments concerning the integrity of the family. Using images of broken slave families was their means to a good end. Wilberforce in his most impassioned speeches used two such examples from the Cape domestic trade. Whether they were true is trivial, whether they were typical is a more profound question. It is true that many males were sold alone; the domestic market did break up families and did orphan children. The equally important and more invidious significance of the domestic slave market lay in two emerging effects. That slave transfers at the Cape ensured the integrity of the slave owners' family inheritance, sponsoring a dynastic, paternalistic mode of family management of slaves, had a limited effect on abolitionist audiences, since both inheritance and paternalism were linchpins of nineteenth-century European middle-class society. That the rise of slave sales through sales of land and transfer by inheritance ensured the perpetuation and prosperity of the slave owners' families and allowed for gentrified dynastic expectations is of significance for the history of slavery in the Cape and cast a shadow beyond emancipation day. The emergent Cape slave society, therefore, came to resemble other, very different, slave societies on the African continent. The transfer of slaves at the Cape increasingly became a household issue and very much a family matter.

F I V E

Knowing One's Place
The Apportionment and Geographical
Dispersion of Slaves

AMONG THE MOST pivotal questions that have to be answered to understand any slave society are those of the statistical apportionment of slaves and the geographical dispersion of the slave holdings. From the early work of Kenneth Stampp to the recent work of Robert Fogel, there is considerable agreement among scholars of slavery that the culture of slaves on large plantations differed significantly from that which prevailed on small holdings.[1] Historians' judgments of slave societies are based on their knowledge or assumptions about these distributions. For example, many people still have an image of the American South as a "plantation society." They are invariably surprised to learn that the typical American slave in 1860 did not live on a plantation, but in a small holding of seven or eight families.[2] What type of slave society was the early Cape? Did most slaves live in the country or the towns? How many Cape slaves faced their owners on the various holdings? Were they constantly under the broad thumb of their owners, or did they have some autonomy in their own quarters? Knowing the answers to these questions allows one to establish the form of slave management that was most likely, and thereby to make inferences about what the day-to-day life was like for enslaved persons.

Anthropologists and historians have identified two kinds of slave societies. The first is the plantation slave society, such as that in Zanzibar, Jamaica, Cuba, Barbados, the Dutch Antilles, and Haiti. Plantation societies were mostly island economies where there were few remaining native people, where low rates of free immigration prevailed during the slave regime, and where agricultural labor was performed by imported, enslaved people. Plantation slave societies are further characterized by a low (10 percent) level of urbanization and a high (80 percent) proportion of slave women in the agricultural work force. The second type of slave

---

[1] Robert Fogel, *Without Consent or Contract: The Rise and Fall of American Slavery* (New York: Norton, 1989), pp. 51, 169, 178.

[2] Fogel, *Without Consent or Contract*, 31.

society, household slavery, occurred mostly in mainland areas where there were alternative forms of labor — either native or immigrant — such as in seventeenth-century Virginia, in Peru, Mexico, some parts of Brazil, and in early South Africa. Household slavery was further characterized by a high proportion of urbanized slaves (50 percent) and an equally high proportion of female slaves in domestic service. Most slave societies fall somewhere along the spectrum between these two categories. Moreover, slave societies can move from one end of the spectrum to the other, as the American slave society did between the Revolution and the ante-bellum period. Since all slave societies change, it is the purpose of this chapter to trace three key characterization variables for the Cape: the size of holdings, the extent of the urbanization of the slave force, and the extent of enslaved persons in domestic service.

The Geographical Distribution of Cape Slaves

Most geographical explanations of slave distributions are economic, based on person to land ratios, and are strongly biased toward rural depictions of slavery. Johann Heinrich von Thünen, a German economist of the nineteenth century, postulated a model economy he called "the isolated state," which resembles the Cape slave society up to the 1770s in important respects.[3] His model consists of a single city in the center of a large plain, whose inhabitants exchange manufactured goods for the agricultural products of the hinterland, with wagons as the sole means of transportation. Various agricultural products are grown in concentric circles around the city. The location at which each crop is grown is determined by the cost and the possibility of transportation of the goods to the city. Conse-quently, land use ranges from the growing of perishable vegetables nearest the city — where the division of labor is most marked — to grazing livestock in the most distant circle. This is a pattern similar to that of the early Cape, with its market gardens in Table Valley surrounding the port of Cape Town, wine and wheat farms in the immediate hinterland, and cattle and sheep ranches in the remoter frontier regions (see Figure 5-1).[4]

---

[3] Johann Heinrich von Thünen, *Der isolierte Staat in Beziehung auf Landwirtschaft und Nationalokonomie*, 3 vols. (Jena, Germany: Fischer, 1930).

[4] Adapted from Leonard Guelke, "A Computer Approach to Mapping the *Opgaaf*: the Population of the Cape in 1731." *South African Journal of Photogrammetry, Remote Sensing and Cartography* 13 4 (1983): 228-229. See also Richard Elphick and Robert C.-H. Shell, "Intergroup relations: Khoikhoi, Settlers, Slaves, and Free Blacks," in R. Elphick and Hermann Giliomee (eds.), *The Shaping of South African Society, 1652–1820*, rev. ed. (Middletown, Conn: Wesleyan University Press, 1989), p. 117.

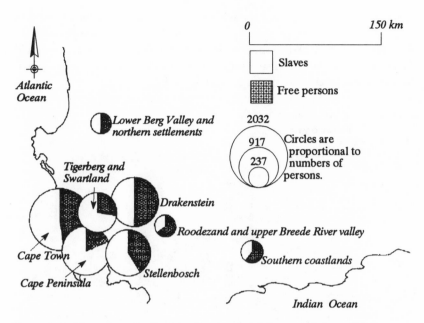

Figure 5–1. The urban distribution of enslaved and free populations, 1731.

This model of the "isolated state" helps in understanding most features of the distribution of Cape slaves and the division of labor that emerged at the Cape. All that has to be added to the model is the specific distribution of rainfall, which determined the choice of crop and the farm type. Nearly all slaves lived within the 20-inch rainfall line, a strip running along the coast from just north of the Cape Peninsula and steadily broadening along the southern littoral.[5] Before the invention of windmills, settlement followed easy access to surface water. Since there are no navigable rivers in South Africa, ox-drawn wagons dominated all transportation until the discovery of diamonds in the interior in the 1860s ushered in the railroad era.

The location of mountain ranges and escarpments in the colony determined what could be grown and transported and also had important consequences for the quality of all rural slaves' lives. Since the Cape is extremely mountainous, most rural slaves (especially those in the Western Cape) lived out their lives on farms in deep valleys, separated from each other and far away from the few towns and villages of the interior. Katie Jacobs, a slave born in the Malmesbury district in the nineteenth century, was separated from her Malagasy-speaking mother by sale to

[5] Leonard Guelke, "A Computer Approach to Mapping the *Opgaaf:* The Population of the Cape in 1731," *South African Journal of Photogrammetry, Remote Sensing and Cartography* 13, 4 (1983): 227–237.

an owner in the next valley and not only never saw her again but also never heard from her.[6] While Cape historian Wayne Dooling has convincingly argued for a "moral community of slave owners" in the rural area of Stellenbosch, one should also bear in mind that individual members of that moral community were isolated. The mountainous terrain of the Cape, albeit beautiful, combined with the extravagant land tenure system (see Chapter 1) to impose a tyrannical isolation on most rural households (see Figure 5-2).[7]

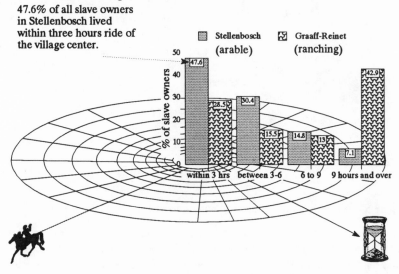

Figure 5–2. Distance on horseback from the markets of Stellenbosch and Graaf-Reinet, 1831.

The Urban Character of Cape Slavery, 1652–1795

The Cape was never an isolated state, of course. The port was a hypermarket for fresh produce, serving hundreds of ships' crews annually. This circumstance alone resulted in Cape slavery having a decidedly urban character. The medieval German saying, "*Stadluft macht frei*" — roughly, "city air makes for freedom" — never applied in colonial Cape Town. In addition to the port market, there were several other reasons for the unusual urban concentration of slaves. Most poor free settlers preferred working on their own in agricultural pursuits in the interior and

---

[6] Robert C.-H. Shell, "Katie Jacobs: An Early Oral History," *Quarterly Bulletin of the South African Library* 3, 46 (March 1992): 95.

[7] Neville Christopher Fleurs, "A Comparative Study of the Treatment of Slaves at the Cape of Good Hope and in the West Indies, 1806-1834" (Pretoria: University of South Africa, 1984), p. 38.

therefore quit the port when they could. Although there were urban poor whites and a few urban freed slaves from the beginning of the settlement, there were never sufficient numbers of them to do all the menial jobs, such as fortification building and stevedoring. As late as 1767, over 40 percent of all the colony's slaves were housed in the busy port (see Figure 5-3).[8]

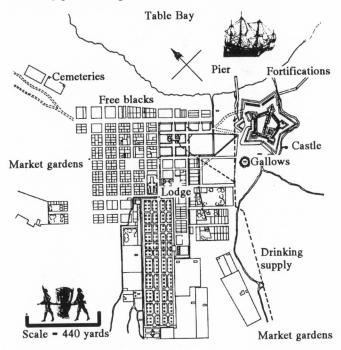

Figure 5–3. Cape Town in 1767.

Further, for a full century after 1717 there was no assisted European immigration to South Africa. Cape Town therefore never became a Boston, a bustling city of European immigrants, but instead became a colonial residency city with an administrative and mercantile core served by slaves working market gardens and doing domestic labor. Moreover, during the slave trade, all imported slaves started the South African phases of their lives in the urban pens of the patrician slave traders. The port was therefore both a depot for the oceanic slave trade and the main distribution center for all the Cape's imported slaves. Cape Town was also a strategic port, the coveted Gibraltar of the Indian Ocean. Consequently there were nearly always large garrisons that had to be fed, housed, and warmed (collecting firewood was a common household occupation for male

---

[8] Based on a map of Cape Town in 1767, CAD Map room.

urban slaves). The Dutch East India Company itself kept hundreds of slaves housed in the Lodge in the port for various tasks, such as running the Company's market garden plantation, building the port's considerable fortifications and performing the town's unattractive chores, such as removing slurry to the beach (see Figure 5-3).

Throughout the period from 1652 to 1770, slaves were concentrated in and around Cape Town and the market centers of the interior. While the absolute number of slaves in the port was high, the percentage of Cape slaves living in the port slowly dropped as the Cape slave society changed from the household type of slave society to a more rurally based plantation system. The completion of the metamorphosis was interrupted by the externally imposed political event of emancipation (see Figure 5-4).[9]

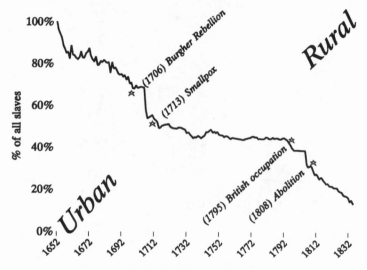

Figure 5–4. The extent of urbanization of slaves at the Cape, 1652 to 1832.

The "Problem" with Urban Slavery

A sizable fraction of the Cape slave labor force (1,000 slaves in Cape Town alone in the period from 1652 to 1706) was in the urban service sector, a type of slave holding that has received too little attention in the comparative literature.[10] Urban slaves belonged to bakers, butchers, boardinghouse keepers, tapsters, and firewood

[9] Shell, "Popucape"; this is based on a reiterative calculation of the sum of 90 percent of all Lodge slaves, plus the number of slaves belonging to urban officials and burghers.

[10] Richard C. Wade, *Slavery in the Cities: The South 1820–1860* (New York: Oxford University Press, 1972), pp. 30–33.

collectors, the leading service occupations of the early Cape. Throughout the Dutch period and well into the British period, the employment of male slaves to perform urban services was, nevertheless a matter of controversy. Even simple, biblical tasks like drawing water and hewing wood were subject to multiple regulations. Illicit woodcutting by slaves for seventeenth-century masters led to the first attempt by authorities to curtail the mobility of urban slaves through the introduction of a pass system (*licentiebrief*), which required that all unaccompanied urban slaves carry a signed letter describing that slave and his or her task, to be produced on demand.[11] The individual householder was responsible for his or her slave's pass. Similar pass systems were introduced in the states of the American South, but not until the nineteenth century.[12] The earlier introduction of a pass system for slaves in South Africa suggests that Cape slave owners considered their urban slaves more refractory, or more prone to rebellion, than their American counterparts did, or possibly the greater proportion of urban slaves in the Cape population led to these earlier measures of social control.

Economic competition between urban slave owners and poor free Europeans without slaves in the same occupation soon led to fierce rivalries. In Cape Town, settler bakers without slaves competed directly with slave-owning bakers, and the have-nots filed an earnest petition on 11 May 1706: "Some licensed free bakers complain that some others keep three or four slaves running about the Cape and near their houses to sell bread, in that way injuring them in their earnings. As they have no slaves of their own to send about in a similar manner, they wish to be protected by the Political Council."[13] In response, the Council decided that each baker could keep only one slave and that all bakers "should mark their bread," presumably so miscreants could be identified.[14] This is the first indication that urban slave labor was resented. Two years later, after the successful settler revolt, the same burgher bakers made pointed remarks about the use of slaves by Company officials interloping in the private baking business, directly requesting "that servants of the Company might not receive a [baking] license" and that "all [bakers] might be forbidden to send their slaves along the

---

[11] Otto Friederich Mentzel, *A Complete and Authentic Geographical and Topographical Description . . .* , trans. G. V. Marais and J. Hoge, rev. ed. (Cape Town: Van Riebeeck Society, 1944), vol. 2, p. 91; Kathleen M. Jeffreys and S. D. Naude (eds.), *Kaapse Plakkaatboek, 1652–1806* (Cape Town: Kaapse Argriefstukke, 1944–1949), vol. 2, pp. 130–131 (10 July 1676); vol. 1, 162–163 (8 April/11 June 1680); see also vol. 2, 68 (16 November 1717); vol. 2, 105–106 (14 November 1724); vol. 2, 115 (1727).

[12] Robert S. Starobin, *Industrial Slavery in the Old South* (New York: Oxford University Press, 1975), p. 91; Wade, *Slavery in the Cities*, 81, 148.

[13] Hendrick Carel Vos Leibbrandt, *Journal, 1699–1732* (Cape Town: W. A. Richards & Sons, Government Printers, 1896), p. 91.

[14] Jeffreys and Naude, *Kaapse Plakkaatboek*, vol. 1, 348–349 (11 May 1706).

streets."[15] In 1727 the licensed burghers bakers of Cape Town, having eliminated the illegal Company competition, complained once more, this time about
Chinese "free black" slave-owning bakers: "certain [unnamed] settlers and Chinese bakers were sending their boys about the streets to sell different sorts of
cakes, and [we] pray that this should be forbidden as it causes the memorialists
great injury."[16] The complainants had shifted their ground somewhat. By this
time they were complaining that certain urban groups should not own slaves, not
that urban slaves were a problem in themselves. Such petitions were entirely
successful; by the nineteenth century free burgher bakers, untrammeled by
competition, employed close to 30 "baker" slaves.[17]

Similar complaints about other urban service slaves continued throughout
the eighteenth century until the authorities were persuaded to ban owners from
using slaves in certain service occupations altogether. In 1794, the penultimate
year of the Dutch occupation, urban slave hawkers were only allowed to sell
"eatables," nothing else,[18] and by January of 1808, all hawking by slaves was
forbidden.[19] After 1809, slaves could no longer act as "coolies" or porters unless
registered by the Fiscal (the official charged with the slaves' welfare), who issued
to the slave a numbered ticket to be worn on the head, "so that everyone may see
the same."[20] Before 1795, the Lodge slaves had done all the portering and
stevedoring; after that year, these occupations were open to the private, albeit
licensed, enterprise of slave owners, free blacks, and poor whites. Penalties for
failing to comply were severe for slaves: a public flogging and three months of
hard labor.[21]

In the American South, according to Richard Wade, an American urban
historian, the fear of the loss of control of urban service slaves was uppermost, but
in seventeenth-, eighteenth-, and early nineteenth-century Cape Town, mercantilist attempts to limit competition, status considerations, *and* fear of the loss of
control swirled around the employment of service slaves. But although a wide
variety of persons complained volubly about urban slaves, urban slavery continued
to flourish at the Cape until the end of slavery, and the town was transformed both
architecturally and culturally by their presence (see Chapters 9 and 12). Cape
Town was always full of slaves. Historical archeologist Antonia Malan, tallying

---

[15] Leibbrandt, *Journal* (17 January 1708), 91.

[16] Hendrick Carel Vos Leibbrandt, *Requesten (Memorials) 1715–1806* (Cape Town: South
African Library, 1989) vol. 1, pp. 60–61 (no. 4 of 1727/28).

[17] CAD SO 10/18.

[18] George McCall Theal, *Records of the Cape Colony* (London: Government Printer, 1905;
hereafter *RCC*): D. Denyssen, "Statement of the Laws of the Colony of the Cape of Good Hope
regarding Slavery" (16 March 1813) Article 54, 9: 146–161.

[19] Theal, *RCC*, "Statement of the Laws," Article 56, 9: 155.

[20] Theal, *RCC*, "Statement of the Laws," Article 57, 9: 155.

[21] Theal, *RCC*, "Statement of the Laws," Article 57, 9: 155.

household inventories, was shocked that the average number of slaves in eighteenth-century Cape Town households was so high.[22] By 1821, most people in Cape Town had direct experience of slavery and urban servitude; the average number of people per house was 11, of whom nearly half were enslaved or had been slaves. While there were complaints, there was never a problem with urban slavery (see Figure 5-5).[23]

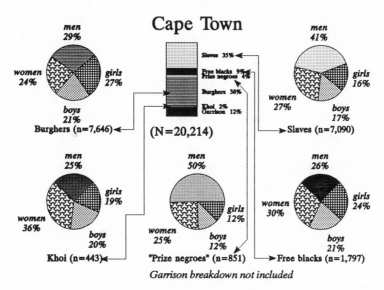

Figure 5–5. Population and status groups in Cape Town in 1821.

The Exodus of Slaves from Urban Areas after 1795

While economic factors explain much about how slaves were initially distributed, the picture became more complicated once the institution of slavery was attacked politically, as it was in Europe from the 1770s onward. After 1795, many

---

[22] Antonia Malan, "The Archaeology of Probate Inventories," *Social Dynamics* 16, 1 (June 1990): 6.

[23] CAD CO 6135 (1820); CAD CO 5968, p. 151a; W. W. Bird, *State of the Cape of Good Hope in 1822*, pp. 109, 357. The number of households in Cape Town was 1,553; the average number of persons per house was 11. The 2,000 men of the garrison were housed seperately. Many officers boarded in private houses. They would have increased the average number per house.

urban slaves were relocated to rural areas as the demand for agricultural labor was intensified by the general prosperity ushered in by the British occupation, and the abolition of the oceanic slave trade further intensified this redistribution. Cape slave owners, cut off from their supply of imported enforced labor after 1808 but encouraged by a booming economy, started moving into the interior with their slaves, partly in search of new lands and also, after 1828, to escape the growing abolitionist chorus and other strands of Enlightenment thought that threatened to abolish not only slavery but their way of life.

Urban slaves were also displaced by an influx of skilled European immigrants who chose the urban life. The first and second British occupations (1795 to 1803 and 1806 to 1815) led to a growing garrison strength and naval presence that allowed for a temporary boost in urban slaveholdings, an extension of the labor-intensive market gardens throughout the peninsula, and, more important, an extension of slavery into the arable farms further inland. Consequently, the first British occupation witnessed the most intense oceanic slave trading of all periods at the Cape (see Figure 2-1). There was a profound shift of slaves (some with their owners) away from the town. This does not mean that there was a decline in urban slavery because slavery was incompatible with urban life, as Andrew Bank, a Cape historian has argued, but more simply it was a redistribution of slave labor.[24]

Immigration after 1795 and the Redistribution of Slave Labor

After 1808 there was no more importation of slaves and no replacement of agricultural slave labor, except through natural increase. Also, immigration from Europe accelerated after 1816, when it became subsidized by the British government. However, most of the new immigrants, who were scheduled to be buffer populations on the eastern frontier, failed in their agricultural enterprises and fled to the towns. Established employers of urban labor therefore had a ready alternative to slave labor and so could sell, move, or rent a portion of their slaves to the rural areas. Arriving English and Irish apprentices were engaged and trained not by the slave owners or other settlers, but by the urban slaves themselves. This circumstance was so unusual to visiting British royal commissioners that they interviewed several Cape slave artisans in 1825. The following extract of an interview with the urban saddler slave Carel illuminates all these points:

---

[24] Andrew Bank, "The Decline of Urban Slavery in Cape Town, 1806 to 1843" (University of Cape Town: Centre for African Studies, 1991).

Q: What trade do you follow?

A: I am a Saddler and Upholsterer.

Q: Have you an apprentice?

A: I have.

Q: What is his name?

A: Paddy Farel, he came to the Colony with Mr. Ingram.

Q: Is Farel indentured to you?

A: No, he is indentured to Mr. Heyward, Mr. Durham's clerk, but I paid the sum of 150 Rixdollars to Mr. Ingram six months after the boy landed in the Colony, and in consideration of this I am to have Farel's services for seven years and to feed and clothe him during that time, and I am to teach him my trade.[25]

By 1833, one-sixth of all Cape slaves were in the newly settled Cape districts, and Cape Town was rapidly losing slave laborers. The greatest demand in the new districts, according to the auction records, was for young men in manual labor and for young women in domestic service. Women who were sold in the new districts did the same type of work that they did in the old, although there was also a slight increase in the demand for female manual labor as well. Katie Jacobs, who was a creole household nanny slave, also had to do manual labor and don men's clothing. Whether her owner forced her to do this, or whether it was her own ruse is exquisitely ambiguous:

The work was more arduous than on the old farm, for the land had never been cultivated, and was overgrown with innumerable big bushes. For the first year, I had to take my pick and shovel and fall in regularly with the men at sun rise to clear the land. In the evening I assisted in the kitchen. At other times of the year I herded cattle. This job I hated most of all, not only because it was monotonous and I dreaded somewhat to be alone so far from home, but because I had to don men's clothes. I always tried to avoid meeting strangers for fear of being discovered as a girl in men's clothing. By lighting a stumpy clay pipe, which I purposely kept when accosted by strangers, and by pulling my slough hat well over my eyes, I managed for a number of years to pass as a boy. One day I was identified. A Mr. Van Niekerk, a frequent visitor to the farm, happened to pass the grazing grounds on his way to Cape Town. He approached me and warned me not to let the cattle stray into his fields, unless I wanted a good *sjambokking*. As usual I had taken the precaution to light my pipe and to draw my hat somewhat carelessly over my eyes. Mr. Van Niekerk had acquired a reputation far and wide among the slaves for the ease and naturalness with which he cursed and swore at anything or anybody on the slightest provocation. That morning, he was apparently in a bad temper, for he

---

[25] Theal, *RCC*, "Evidence of Carel, a slave of Mr. de Klerk to the Commissioners of Enquiry," 21: 448–449; cf. ibid., 21: 450–451, the case of Jacob van Hedenrick, the shoemaker slave who sacked his free Irish apprentice, Mahoney, for "drunkenness."

swore at me as I had never heard him swear before. While at the height of his paroxysm he suddenly stopped, stared hard at me for a few seconds, burst in a loud laugh and exclaimed, 'My G — [od], its Grietje of Mr. M[ostert].' I felt ashamed to think that I had been discovered, and from that day I hated herding cattle more and more.[26]

The British occupation, in stimulating the Cape economy, brought about an expansion of slavery throughout the colony. The increased demand for slaves at the Cape after 1795 (expressed in their steeply rising prices, see Figure 1-6) was accelerated by the abolition of the slave trade in 1808 and further boosted by European immigration after 1816. Free immigration to the towns led to a substantial geographical restructuring of the slave force.[27] In 1795 more than 80 percent of the slave force was still concentrated within 150 miles of the port city of Cape Town, but by 1806, slaves were distributed in a wider pattern that generally followed the contours of the high rainfall areas along the coast. A larger proportion of the slaves was also found in the inland areas of Graaff Reinet, and in the "new districts" established after 1795 (see Figure 5-6).[28]

Prize Negroes

After the abolition of the oceanic slave trade, the redistribution of slaves was almost entirely a consequence of the migration of farmers or the operations of the

---

[26] Shell, "Katie Jacobs," 95–96. Katie, as a slave woman, was unusual in being asked to perform manual labor; according to numerous sources, slave women at the Cape unlike their counterparts in the American South, were excused from all field work. The most probable explanation for her wearing men's clothes was that the farmer was ashamed of using a slave woman for shepherding and wished to disguise her, but it is possible that Katie herself chose them. Of the several Van Niekerks who were in the area, the one mentioned here was most likely A. B. W. van Niekerk, owner of Mossel Bank, the farm slightly to the south of Kalabas Kraal; he would have had to cross "Wolve Dans" to get to the road leading to Cape Town. He calls her Grietje, which was possibly Katie's household name; her baptized name was Katie. It was typical for slaves to take on an entirely new name when they were baptized.

[27] This may be clearly seen in Figure 5-4. The census years highlighted by the graph were chosen for several reasons. First, 1793 was the last year during which the Company imported slaves. Second, 1806 was the penultimate year during which the British were allowed to import slaves. Third, 1826 was the year of a slave owners' revolt. A detailed and useful discussion on the changing boundaries of the various districts may be found in Theal, *RCC,* "Report of the Commissioners of Inquiry to Earl Bathurst upon the Administration of the Government" (6 September 1826), 27: 342–397. One year before emancipation the British authorities took a detailed census of all slaves by region. PRO CO 53/57 (31 August 1833) folios 149–150.

[28] CAD A45 (1795); Theal, *RCC* 6: 7 (1806); Theal, *RCC* 28: 464 (1826); PRO CO 53/57 (31 August 1833).

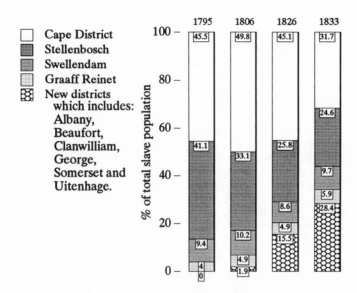

Figure 5–6. Percentage of slaves in each district, 1795, 1806, 1826, 1833.

domestic slave market. A semi clandestine and unsuspected slave trade after 1808, hidden in the contemporary euphemism of "prize negroes," provided substitute labor for Cape Town's market gardeners and mercantile classes and also boosted the Lodge's waning population.[29] "Prize negroes" were illegal slaves captured at sea by the royal navy after the abolition of the slave trade in 1808 and landed at Cape Town where they were supposed to be liberated. However, they were housed in the Lodge along with the other slaves.[30] One valuable prize negro, Vicenti King, a doctor, liberated himself much to the chagrin of the Lodge director (see Figure 5-7).[31]

But it was not business as usual, prize negroes were then "apprenticed" to established slave owners for 14 years. W. W. Bird, a philanthropic author, writing in 1821, voiced some genteel doubts about whether loaned out prize negroes were entering the ranks of formal slavery.[32] We still do not know how many there were, but Christopher Saunders, the Cape historian, has estimated that

---

[29] CAD CO 6135, "Summary of the Population at the Cape of Good Hope" p. 23; although prize negroes arrived in Cape Town in 1808, they were not registered until 1816.

[30] Sierra Leone was the other depot for prize negroes.

[31] *Cape of Good Hope Gazette* (1 June 1827).

[32] W. W. Bird, *State of the Cape of Good Hope in 1822* (Cape Town: Struik, 1966 reprint), pp. 356–357.

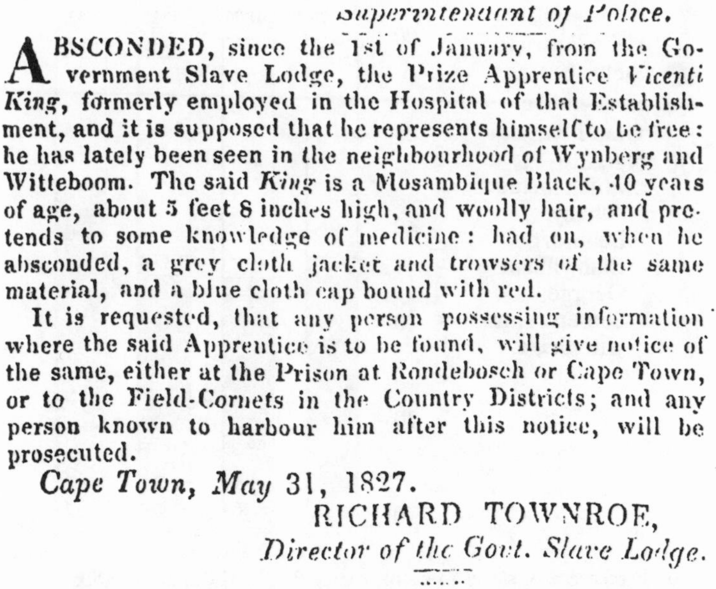

Superintendant of Police.

ABSCONDED, since the 1st of January, from the Government Slave Lodge, the Prize Apprentice *Vicenti
King*, formerly employed in the Hospital of that Establishment, and it is supposed that he represents himself to be free:
he has lately been seen in the neighbourhood of Wynberg and
Witteboom. The said *King* is a Mosambique Black, 40 years
of age, about 5 feet 8 inches high, and woolly hair, and pre-
tends to some knowledge of medicine : had on, when he
absconded, a grey cloth jacket and trowsers of the same
material, and a blue cloth cap bound with red.

It is requested, that any person possessing information
where the said Apprentice is to be found, will give notice of
the same, either at the Prison at Rondebosch or Cape Town,
or to the Field-Cornets in the Country Districts; and any
person known to harbour him after this notice, will be
prosecuted.

Cape Town, May 31, 1827.

RICHARD TOWNROE,

Director of the Govt. Slave Lodge.

Figure 5–7. Escape of a "prize negro" doctor in 1827.

at least 5,000 were imported to the Cape between 1808 and 1856. Many of
the prize negro women bore children, so the net increase to the total slave
population must have been considerable. The prize negroes rapidly creolized (see
Figure 5-8).[33]

The fastest growing areas in terms of slave population were in the Eastern
Cape, the area where the 5,000 British settlers established themselves. In 1826
John Thomas Bigge, a royal commissioner, suggested that a slave registry office be
established at either Grahamstown or Uitenhage, both because of the substantial
relocation of slaves into the area and because of suspicions about slave raiding in
the area.[34] "Apprentices" was a term also applied to "starving" native people,
whom farmers attached to their farms, sometimes for life. The auctioning of slaves
was most common in the old districts, which fed the new districts in an eastward
direction, a pattern analogous to that in the American South, where the older, soil-
exhausted states exported slaves to the new regions (see Figure 5-9).[35]

---

[33] CAD CO 6138 (1811–1826); Bird, *State of the Cape,* 109.

[34] Theal, *RCC,* "Report of the Commissioners of Inquiry to Earl Bathurst upon the
Finances" (6 September 1826), 27: 496–497.

[35] PRO CO 53/57 (31 August 1833) 149–150; CAD SO 10/18 (N = 4,027).

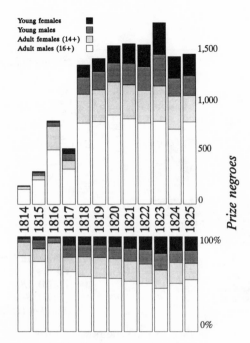

Figure 5–8. "Prize Negroes" at the Cape, 1814–25.

The Three Slave Populations

There were three distinct slave populations at the Cape in ascending numerical importance, each in specific, but overlapping areas. First were the Company Lodge slaves, 90 percent of whom worked in the urban Lodge in 1693. These Lodge slaves, who worked a 40-acre urban plantation, remained the largest single distribution of slaves until 1828 (see Chapter 6). Second were the slaves belonging to the patrician officials, who had large rural plantations until 1706, and who were thereafter mainly urban. Third were the slaves who belonged to the urban burghers and the urban free blacks (subsumed under burghers). The urban and rural burghers, however, came to own the majority of slaves by about 1740. These groups' relative proportions and absolute numbers changed over time (see Figure 5-10).[36]

The Distribution of the Patrician Slaves
The local officials introduced slavery to the colony; the rural slave plantations they founded are among the most prized properties today (most are museums), and for the first 54 years of the colony's existence, they collectively owned the most slaves.

---

[36] Shell, "Popucape."

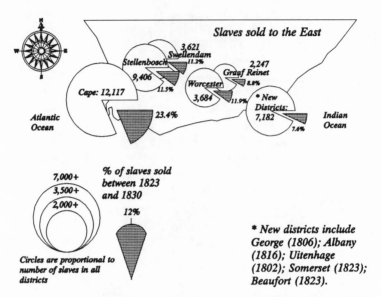

Figure 5–9. Distribution of slaves in 1833 and percent of slaves sold in each district, 1823 to 1830.

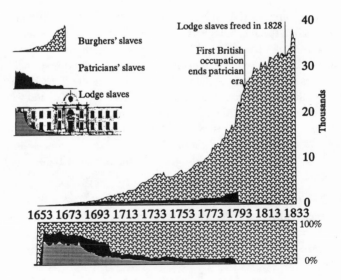

Figure 5–10. The three Cape slave populations, 1653 to 1833.

Since the directors of the Company forbade their colonial officials to farm (and owning slaves in large groups was a dead giveaway of such activity) officials, who were in charge of the record keeping, suppressed records of their large slave holdings. Since officials were permitted to own a few domestic slaves, they did report some slaves, and historians understandably, albeit erroneously, accepted their understated holdings as such and dismissed them as insignificant. Their huge slave holdings have to be reconstituted on a slave-by-slave basis from the few records that were not sent to Holland (see Figure 5-11).[37] The pattern of local officials clandestinely owning many slaves became an established feature of slavery at the Cape and continued into the British period, when local British officials also avoided enumerating their holdings. Sir George Yonge, a British Governor, like Willem Adriaan Van der Stel a century before him, was an enthusiastic patron of the slave trade. Since most officials (Dutch and British) lived in the port, our ignorance of officials' slaves has also led to a underestimation of the number of urban slaves.

The Burghers' Household Slave Distributions

Between 1652 and 1795, even the largest individual settler slave holdings were still considerably smaller than the Company's single urban slave force in the Lodge. The Cape distributions resemble those of early colonial America more closely than they do any other society. By 1650 only 3 percent of the population was "negro," which included freed slaves in the Southern states of colonial America; midway through the colonial era, it was 15 percent. Even by 1770 slaves were only 40 percent of the entire population in the South. The percentage of slaves in the Cape population was therefore high by colonial American standards, but it was low in comparison with the Caribbean.[38] Most slaves in the Old South were owned in small household distributions.[39] The majority of slaves at the Cape were owned in small distributions too (see Figure 5-12).[40]

---

[37] The slave holdings of officials have to be reconstituted from transfers in the archives of the Deeds Office, the Notarial Protocols in the Cape archives, and from baptismal records in the Dutch Reformed Church archives (the senior officials, who were also the colony's main slave traders, invariably baptized their house-born slaves — and from these records one can garner the imported mothers' names). These slaves then have to be linked to the paymaster schedules [*monsterollen*] of the Company, kept in the Hague.

[38] Robert Fogel and Stanley Engerman, *Time on the Cross* (Boston: Little, Brown, 1975), vol. 1, p. 22.

[39] Most of my comparisons are first drawn from the American South, then from Brazil, and lastly from the Caribbean.

[40] AR VOC 4018 (collated 14 February 1683), folios 115–116; VOC 4052: "Generale opneem der vrijeluijden, derselver bezitting enz. aen de Caeb (1705)," folios 454 ff.; VOC 4083 (3 May 1720); VOC 4113: "Sommarium," (1–2 May 1730).

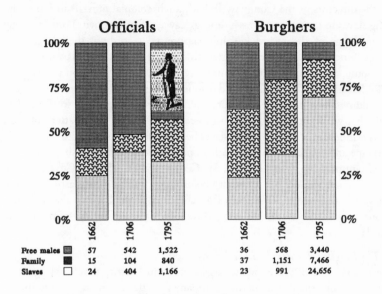

Figure 5–11. Company officials and burghers, families and slaves, 1662, 1706, 1795.

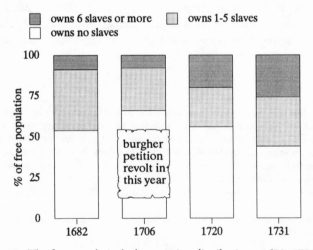

Figure 5–12. The free population's slave owning distributions, 1682, 1706, 1720, 1731.

Members of the Slave-owning Class

More and more Cape households owned slaves; owning slaves became an increasingly prevalent way of life. A wide variety of owners of dwellings, shops, boarding-houses, alehouses, warehouses, market gardens, plantations, wine and wheat farms, frontier and fishing posts, and "loan farms" reported having slaves.[41] In 1706, only 34 percent of the free population owned slaves; by 1731, a generation later, at least 56 percent did.[42] Slave owning became more concentrated. "Gentry" owners, those who owned more than 16 slaves apiece, had only 19 percent of the slave force in 1682, but more than 50 percent of the 4,333 slaves in 1731.[43] The concentration of slave ownership was slightly more pronounced than the concentration of more general wealth based on holdings of land, livestock, equipment, and crops.[44] Within three generations, a small minority, less than 7 percent of the free population, had come to hold title to most of the slaves in the colony.

There is thus no evidence whatsoever for the popular notion of an early colonial "*herrenvolk* democracy" among a "master race" of European settlers. This golden age mythology found in the *plaasroman* (farm novel) of the 1930s could only have been latter-day compensation for the glaring inequality among early European settlers.[45] Cape society perfectly illustrated Vilfredo Pareto's iron law: no matter how evenly goods are distributed initially, after a single generation ownership will be concentrated. In 1658 land (and slaves) were doled out equitably (if one can use the two terms without being guilty of an oxymoron); after three generations, most slaves and private wealth were in a few hands. Slaves in the seventeenth century were distributed among a quite economically diverse group of people, but by 1731 nearly half of all slaves at the Cape were already owned by relatively few wealthy people.

These broad tallies are based on the census enumerations of slave ownership as reported by heads of household. However, when one collates the enumerated slaves with the property holdings (which were never enumerated on the census) the

---

[41] G. C. de Wet, *Die Vryliede en Vryswartes in die Kaapse Nedersetting, 1657–1707* (Cape Town: Historiese Publikasie-Vereniging, 1981), pp. 62–105.

[42] AR VOC 4052: folios 454 ff: "Generale opneem der vrijeluijden, derselver bezitting enz. aen de Caeb (1705)," AR VOC 4115: "Generale opneem der vrijeluijden, derselver bezitting enz. aen de Caeb," (1 and 2 May 1732), folios 995 ff.

[43] AR VOC 4017: "Lijst der vrije luijden en haeren ommeslag," (14 February 1682), 114; AR VOC 4115: "Generale opneem . . . enz." (1731), folios 995 ff.

[44] Leonard Guelke and Robert Shell, "An Early Colonial Landed Gentry: Land and Wealth in the Cape Colony, 1682–1731," *Journal of Historical Geography* 9, 3 (1983): appendixes, 284–286.

[45] George M. Fredrickson, *White Supremacy: A Comparative Study in American and South African History* (New York: Oxford University Press, 1981), pp. xi–xii, 154–155, 166–167, 178–179, 198, 270.

face-to-face situation on the farm and in the urban holding appears quite differently.[46] Unfortunately, the census entry alone cannot tell us about the distribution of slaves on the properties, which is the key question for understanding a slave society. Historians of Cape slavery, working solely with the censuses, have assumed that the individual Cape slave holding was much larger than it was. This has affected the way they assumed Cape slaves were "treated" and how they assumed all slave-based enterprises (urban, rural, and mixed) were managed. The point is an arithmetic one: in cases where the slave owner owned more than one property, the number of slaves on each property was always much smaller than the census entry. The ostensibly large Cape slave distributions, when disaggregated from the census, universally reveal themselves to be small slave holdings spread over several properties.

The census entry of Hendrik Schneuwindt illustrates this statistical artifact. In January of 1701 the census was taken and he reported 14 adult male slaves and 3 adult females.[47] Schneuwindt died in November of the same year and left a detailed inventory, revealing three farms, a market garden along the Liesbeeck River (this was the main farm, identified in the inventory as the *hofstede*), a subsidiary freehold farm in the Tigerberg region, and also a loan farm in the frontier reaches of Tigerberg. Each of these farms required slave labor. One of his daughters, who had married his neighbor Abraham Diemer in 1697, was already running the Tigerberg farm, and those slaves, included in the January census, were not included in the November inventory of the *hofstede*. His widow, Abigail Vroom, inherited the main farm, for which she reported only 6 slaves.[48] If one relied solely on the rough census entry that reported that Schneuwindt owned 17 slaves, inferences about owner-slave relations would be entirely different from the reality of only 6 slaves at the *hofstede*.

This difference becomes more important as the census holdings became larger in the eighteenth century. Another wealthy owner, Hendrik Ostwald Eksteen reported 102 slaves in 1731. But one cannot make the assumption that there were 102 slaves on Eksteen's plantation. His reported census slaves have to be separated and placed on the various properties he owned. With 18 properties, 18 children (by three marriages), and 102 slaves, Eksteen can be said to have realized the patriarchal ideal.[49] He left 1 property and at least 5 slaves to each of his children, thereby founding an enduring dynasty. Eksteen is typical of Cape slave

---

[46] These are listed in another archive, the Deeds Office; Leonard Guelke and I have published a summary of these, available in most Cape libraries and universities, see Leonard Guelke and Robert C.-H. Shell (comps.), "The Deeds Book: The Cape Cadastral Calendar" (New Haven, Conn: Opgaaf Project, 1990).

[47] AR KA 4022 (January 1710), folio 13.

[48] CAD MOOC 10/1, no. 21 (8 November 1701).

[49] AR VOC 4115: "Generale opneem der vrijeluijden, derselver bezitting enz. aen de Caeb," (31 May 1731), folios 995 ff.

owners who reported large slave distributions. They held title to these slaves, but the slaves were under the direct control of the offspring, not the patriarch.

The owner of the largest number of slaves in the eighteenth century was Martin Melck, who reported 204 slaves on his census return in 1770, but Melck had 11 properties scattered all over the colony. This was neither absentee ownership nor plantation slavery, but rather a special type of household slavery, with secondary estates and slaves already in the hands of the next generation — in other words, an *inter vivos* transfer of ownership (see Chapter 4). By retaining title to all the estates and all the slaves until the last possible moment, the patriarch maximized his power over his own children. That the census picture was so different from the situation on the land, where only a handful of slaves faced each youthful, future owner or overseer, is the central fact of Cape slavery and is the basis for all subsequent sociological and psychological assumptions I have made about the family and the incorporation of slaves into the settler household.

The ratio of slaves to free heads of household increased only slightly up to 1795, even when one includes as heads of household the sizable "poor white" and "free black" groups in the free population, many of whom owned no slaves at all. After abolition of the slave trade, the ratio decreased. Over the period 1658 to 1828, the average ratio of all slaves (including those belonging to the Lodge and officials) to all free heads of household was .96 to 1.[50] The percentage of the Cape population that was enslaved (excluding the Khoisan) changed according to the patterns of immigration to the colony. In periods of assisted European immigration (1658 to 1717, 1816 to 1826), the percentage of enslaved persons was always below 50 percent. Once the oceanic slave trade was the main form of immigration (1717 to 1808), the percentage of enslaved persons hovered just over 50 percent, although it was affected by periodic epidemics (measles in 1739, small pox in 1755, 1763, and 1812). After 1808, when the importation of slaves stopped, European immigration overtook the slave population quickly — by 1826 settlers outnumbered both slaves and prize negroes.[51] Forced and assisted immigration changed and shaped the Cape slave society (see Figure 5-13).[52]

Distribution of Slaves by Sex

Looking at the slaves rather than the owners in the early period, several surprising distributions emerge. The first is what may be called a "von Thünen" pattern of slave distribution by sex. In the early period, slave women, always at the center of

[50] Nigel Anthony Worden, *Slavery in Dutch South Africa* (Cambridge: Cambridge University Press, 1985), pp. 11–12.

[51] Shell, "Popucape."

[52] Shell, "Popucape" (excluding the "free" Khoikhoi).

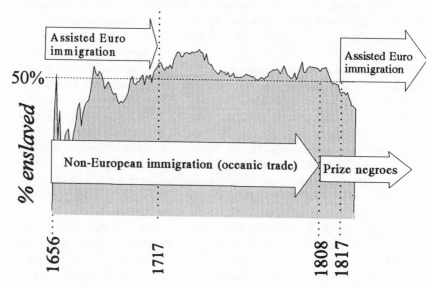

Figure 5–13. Percentage of total population enslaved, 1656–1825.

the early Cape economy, were found in decreasing proportions the further one moves from the port. The most labor-intensive forms of activity at the Cape were around the town, where most of the slaves resided, while the land extensive activities such as ranching went on in the frontier regions, where only a few male and even fewer female slaves were employed.

By 1795, women were found in increasing proportions in the rural areas as the slave population creolized and the higher fertility of the rural slaves resulted in an evening out of the sex composition.[53] Until 1808 the Cape district, which included the port, still contained the imported (predominantly male) slaves, boosting the percentage of males in the slave population in that area. After the abolition of the oceanic trade, slave women were found in increasing proportions in the rural areas as all slaves became more and more difficult to obtain (see Figure 5-14).[54]

Distribution of Slaves by Age

Dynastic ownership and management of slaves bridged simple urban and rural dichotomies and also followed clear Von Thünen regional wealth and age patterns. The wealthier, older owners lived in the port while their progeny, the young,

---

[53] I suspect that wet nursing was predominantly an urban phenomenon.
[54] CAD A45 (1795), p. 2; PRO CO 56/56 (31 August 1833).

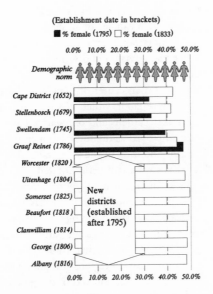

(Establishment date in brackets)
■ % female (1795) □ % female (1833)

Figure 5–14. Percentage of slaves who were female, by district, 1795 and 1833.

inexperienced owners, lived in the interior. Mentzel called such wealthy urban owners *nachtwerkers* (night-workers) — people who lived in town but owned estates in the country, that were managed by their children and worked by their slaves.[55] In the early period, 1652 to 1808, there were also Von Thünen regional age patterns among the slaves, with the younger "prime" slaves at the urban center of the economy, while the older slaves (*uijtgeleefdes,* literally "lived-out slaves") ended their lives in the less arduous jobs of shepherding and cattle herding on the frontier. Thus, in the period 1652 to 1795, the older established and experienced owners had young slaves, while the young slave owners started their slave holdings in the interior with older, more dependent slaves. This was a pattern that made a lot of sense from the patriarchal slave owner's viewpoint, since both the slave and free youth were serving apprenticeships, although of a very different kind.

Old slaves, when they are mentioned at all in the early travel literature, are almost without exception found on remote ranches tending sheep or cattle. One eighteenth-century shepherd, who claimed to have arrived with Jan van Riebeeck, lived to be 100 years old. In his case the sinews of dependence were so thickened that although his urban daughter purchased him and brought him to the town, he soon returned to his former owner, who paid him a small wage until he died.[56]

[55] Mentzel, *Description,* vol. 2, 85.
[56] Mentzel, *Description,* vol. 2, 131.

The travelers were accurate in this regard: in the 1820s the mean age of all slave herdsmen was 50 years, and the mean age of all slave shepherds was 51.7 years.[57] Older slaves were more dependent on their owners, and, consequently, such slaves did not require experienced supervision and were nearly always spun out to the frontier farms for a semiretirement.

In the early period, the urban center of the Cape, Table Valley, absorbed a large proportion of young slave labor, which was used for highly intensive agricultural production on market gardens and on nearby, larger arable farms, while young slave women were employed as domestic labor in the boardinghouses and taverns of the port. After the abolition of the slave trade in 1808, this regional age pattern changed. Older slaves were still being rotated out to the frontier for the traditional shepherding tasks, but many more younger slaves were being sold in the frontier areas as well. There were enough younger slaves sold on the frontier in the 1820s to depress substantially the mean age of all slaves sold in those new regions. By the 1820s the traditional regional age pattern of the colony's slave force had inverted (see Figure 5-15).[58] The original (non-British) settlers in search of new land were moving into the Eastern regions and taking their slaves with them. By 1838, one-sixth of the slave population was in the new Eastern districts. This population movement of slaves was almost equivalent in numbers of persons to the Great Trek, but it has been obscured by three major changes in administration along with changes in their individual record-keeping practices, and changes in district boundaries.

Distribution of Slaves by Somatic Factors

An important aspect of the distribution of slaves at the Cape was that from the beginning to the end of slavery, the division of labor was based not only on age and sex but also on perceived criteria of racial descent (mulatto status), creole status (whether born at the Cape or imported), and geographical origin. When owners filled out their transfer deeds of sale they never forgot to transcribe the slave's creole status and geographical origin. Phenotype, origin, and racial descent early on became preoccupations of Cape slave owners. This found expression in a "naive anthropology" in which behavior was attributed to racial descent or geographical origin. Both positive and negative stereotypes of slaves emerged early at the Cape.[59] This preoccupation also became a cornerstone in the geographical struc-

---

[57] CAD SO 10/18: "Return of slaves sold at public auction between . . . 1823 and . . . 1830."

[58] Shell, "Saledeed" (N = 4,316); "1823sale," (N = 4,027). The mean age in each period was different. I have put them on the same plane (a singulate mean) for comparative purposes.

[59] Robert C.-H. Shell (ed.), " 'Slaves,' an Essay by Samuel Eusebius Hudson," *Kronos* 9 (1984): 51–52 and notes.

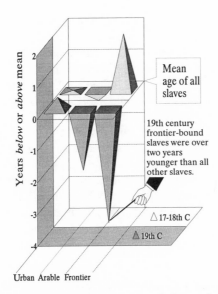

Figure 5–15. Regional differentiation of slave ages, before and after abolition.

turing of the early Cape slave labor force. Because of the wide range of origins of Cape slaves, a regional division of slave labor based on origin and descent is more readily apparent in South Africa than it is among the African slaves of the American South (nearly all creole by 1808), the Caribbean, or Brazil.

Travelers support this observation, but were inclined to exaggerate: Admiral Stavorinus, for one, described one large plantation in the late eighteenth century: "Between these [houses] he had a blacksmith's and carpenter's workshop, and a cartwright's manufactory, together with other work-people, necessary for so large and troublesome concern. But few of them were Europeans, the largest number were oriental slaves, who had cost him a great deal of money. Among others he showed me a slave who understood smith's work, and making of tires or wheel bands, whom he had purchased for fifteen hundred Rixdollars, or three thousand six hundred Gulden."[60] Two Cape historians, Margaret Cairns and Frank Bradlow, carefully went through the estate inventory of Martin Melck and found that of his 204 slaves, 51 percent were creole (perhaps of "oriental descent"), 28 percent were Africans, and only 21 percent were Indian or Indonesian and could satisfy Stavorinus' observations about the "largest number."[61] Nonetheless, the

---

[60] J. S. Stavorinus, *Voyages to the East Indies by the Late John Splinter Stavorinus, Esq., Rear-Admiral in the service of the States General . . .* (London: G. G. & J. Robinson, 1798), vol. 1, p. 62.

[61] Frank R. Bradlow and Margaret Cairns, *The Early Cape Muslims: A Study of Their Mosques, Genealogy and Origins* (Cape Town: Balkema, 1978), p. 96.

slave transfers remain unambiguous: in cases where the slave owner had only one occupation and only one property, a well-defined division of labor based on racial descent and origin is apparent. For example, Indonesian slaves were highly represented in the manufacturing sector of the economy, providing nearly 40 percent of all the manufacturing labor, a disproportionate distribution that suggests that the division of slave labor was based on perceived attributes of origin.

As among the Lodge slaves, creole status always overrode status based on origin. Slaves born at the Cape were more highly represented in manufacturing than in any other sector of the economy. Within the creole group, which was always increasing (see Figure 4-2), the slave artisans of partial European ancestry were especially favored in the hierarchy of privately owned slaves. This is a point confirmed by Mentzel, who noted "that some of the [mulatto slaves] are taught certain trades and become skilled artisans."[62] This naive anthropology found expression at Cape slave auctions and in the proportions of slaves sold to urban and rural regions. There was a slight but significant tendency, in the first 75 years at least, to sell both male and female slaves from Africa or Madagascar "upcountry" (see Figure 5-16).[63]

From a Typology of Holdings to a Division of Labor

In the early period there was only a slight division of labor among the slaves. On the typical smallholding, a single slave had to do a wide variety of jobs; Cape slaves were expected to be Jacks (and Jills) of all trades. Up to 1795 the occupation of the slave is rarely mentioned on transfer deeds and one has to rely on the occupation of the owner as a rough guide for the occupation of the slave. By the 1820s, the majority of slaves were creole and their origins and descent went unrecorded on the transfers, but their occupations were routinely recorded and one can speak of a clear division of labor.

---

[62] Mentzel, *Description*, vol. 2, 130. Mulatto slaves were called *halfslag*, literally half-breed, in the original church documents, rarely *mesties*. The term did not apply to the offspring of "races" other than European; a slave born of an Indian mother and a Malagasy father, for example, would not be a *halfslag*, but a *casties*. Only a slave with a European father would be called *halfslag*, or mulatto. In the late eighteenth century, such slaves were sometimes called "bastards," but bastard increasingly came to refer to the offspring of Khoi mothers and slave fathers. Cf. DRCA 1, 1/1 through 1/8.

[63] Shell, "Saledeed," (N = 4,316).

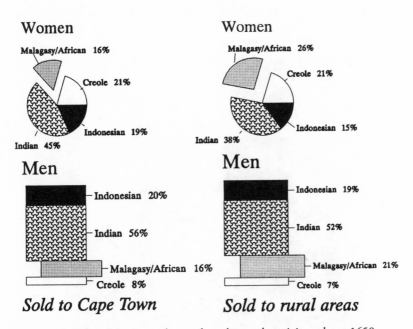

Figure 5–16. Sales of slaves to urban and rural areas, by origin and sex, 1658–
1731.

Domestic Service

The service category of slave labor includes female slaves used in a domestic
capacity in the settler's household. The early inventories of estates and early slave
transfers disclose that the greatest concentration of female slaves was in the urban
and periurban areas, but by the nineteenth century slave women were distributed
throughout the colony.[64] Their role as nanny, servant, and mother was not only
economic but also social and biological (see Chapter 10). Male slaves, in contrast,
were nearly always kept outside of the home in the early eighteenth century. To
obtain a numerical estimate of domestic slaves is, unfortunately, almost impossible, because they cannot be systematically disentangled from the rest of the
holdings. Domestic labor was highly gendered in the early period, less so by the
nineteenth century. For the early patriarchal Cape slave owner, at least, all females
(both free and slave) were to be found in the home.

This pattern changed in the second half of the eighteenth century. A revealing pencil sketch from the 1770s reveals that a wealthy patrician slave owner,

___

64 For specific examples, see CAD MOOC 8/1/49: urban (*"huijs en erf"*) estate of Barrilje
and Dina van Soetermeer (5 February 1700); 10/3/59: urban estate of Elizabeth Beijer.

Hendrik Cloete, employed a young liveried male household slave in a most trivial task, holding the stem of the pipe while the owner puffed away. The picture was not satirical and it even had a self-congratulatory note by the subject scribbled across the bottom (see Figure 5-17).[65]

Figure 5–17. Household slave at Groot Constantia, 1772.

The practice of using male slaves in this particular domestic capacity, seems to have caught the imagination of travelers; Robert Percival, an English officer visiting the Cape in 1804 noted: "They prefer a pipe to either the dessert or a cheerful glass; and the pleasures of conversation, from the time a Dutchman's pipe is put into his mouth, are with him altogether at an end. He never speaks a word afterwards, except to call [to his male slaves] . . . for another pipe of tobacco."[66]

The introduction of the sedan chair also meant more male domestic servants (see Figure 5-18).[67] This Sombartian extravagance was too much for some

---

[65] Notice the slave's uniform and the Sombartian extravagance of the scene. The circumscription by the subject, Hendrik Cloete, reads: "It is your tobacco I am smoking with such enjoyment at the card table." G. J. Schutte (ed.), *Briefwisseling . . . , 1778–1792* (Cape Town: Van Riebeeck Society, 1982), frontispiece. Courtesy of the Van Riebeeck Society.

[66] I know they were male slaves, since Percival uses their names; Capt. Robert Percival, *An Account of the Cape of Good Hope* (New York: Negro Universities Press, 1969 reprint), p. 265.

[67] Scanned and enhanced detail from E. C. Godée-Molsbergen, *South African History told in Pictures* (Amsterdam: S. L. van Looy, 1913), page 52, for attribution see p. 48: "Gezigte van het Stadthuijs aan Cabo de Goede Hoop . . . , 1764" Johannes Rach painting of Cape Town in 1764 in the private collection of Mr. Van Stolk of Rotterdam.

Figure 5–18. Cape sedan chair, 1761.

observers. Samuel Hudson, an English immigrant writing in 1806, scoffed at how the household slave force was being regendered by joking about the ideal urban holding of a young married pair:

My Lady must have at least if she is of any consequence Two Boys for her [sedan] Chair. They must attend her in their gala Dresses with their Strips of Red Bazil[68] Skin stitched with White with Leather rozes and all the exterior finery of a London Market team (except the Bells) her chair gaudily painted with devices and lined with cut Velvet or Damask. These have lately been much disused by the Introduction of a large assortment of European Chairs of London construction whose neatness and elegance have cut up the splendid antiquity of these other cumbrous conveniences. In addition to these [two boys] she must have a boy as an errand boy. But sometimes a girl is thought more suitable for this purpose as she can be easily initiated into the grand secret of confidential service by acting upon all occasions with more [t]act and from her sex having the power to introduce herself into the families of her mistresses' friends and learning the whole domestic concern of the establishment. This is a consideration not to be overlooked by a young woman beginning life. Dear curiosity being the most prevailing principle among the females of southern africa, this forms the first part of the establishment. My Gentleman must have his Boy to attend him to the Billiard Table, light his pipe, hold his Horse, carry his Umbrella and learn the secrets of others. A Stable Boy or two to keep his Animals in nice Order, clean his Horses and to do the greater part of the domestic affairs of the House such as brush the furniture, rub the floors,

---

68 Alternative spelling of "basil" from the French *basane*. According to a contemporary quotation in England: "An inferior leather . . . tears almost like paper." *Oxford English Dictionary*, p. 690, s.v. basil.

deck the table and wait at different meals. A cook compleats the family party. . . . Many here at the commencement [of their marriage] had Ten twelve and some Twenty Slaves. The very value of which would form a solid basis to the making a fortune when properly employed.[69]

Although the travelers and people like Hudson wished to make fun of the domestic extravagance of the original Dutch settlers, in the nineteenth century the employment of male slaves as domestics did increase substantially in the older areas, thus domestic slave gender roles did change. But in the newly settled districts the proportion of all male slaves employed as domestics remained as low as they were in the early eighteenth century (see Figure 5-19).

The geographic origins of the service slaves in the colony were significantly different from the origins of slaves in the other sectors of the economy and this pattern changed according to the changing slave trade. For example in the early period, slaves from the Indian subcontinent comprised nearly 40 percent of the service group, while providing only 27 percent of the agricultural work force. Malagasy slaves, on the other hand, were sold more frequently to the agricultural sector than the service sector (see Figure 5-12). These statistically significant differences hint that the assignment of slave labor was not due to a random process but was the result of a deliberate choice by the owner based on perceived stereotypes. After 1770, when more slaves from the east coast of Africa were imported, occupation by origin changed again, according to travelers' reports, but the nineteenth-century transfers, while recording occupations, do not list the origins of individual slaves, since most slaves — but by no means all — were by that time creole (see Figure 2-3.).

The Artisanal Sector

Slave owners in the manufacturing sector were primarily masons, blacksmiths, and carpenters, the three leading trades. Most of them lived in Table Valley and owned small businesses there. However, there were a few such owners in the rural areas; two blacksmiths in the village of Stellenbosch owned skilled slaves, and even in the more remote Drakenstein district a blacksmith established himself with slaves. One rural owner had a peripatetic entourage of 16 slave masons, with whom he covered the colony.[70]

Slaves involved in manufacturing also collected shells for lime and made all the bricks for the ever-expanding colony. Just as among the Lodge slaves assigned to the "general works," there was no gender deference in the building trade, and there was a 15-year-old age restriction, according to Mentzel: "When the clay is reduced to a pulp, it is kneaded by hand into rough bricks which are then placed into molds to receive the proper shape. All the work is done by slaves; slave

[69] Robert C.-H. Shell, "S. E. Hudson on Marriages and Other Customs at the Cape," *Kronos* 15 (1989): 56–57.

[70] C. Spoelstra, *Bouwstoffen voor de Geschiedenis der Nederduitsch-Gereformeerde Kerken in Zuid-Afrika* (Amsterdam: Hollandsch-Afrikaansche Uitgewers-Maatscappij, 1906–1907), vol. 2, p. 453 (31 October 1717).

children of both sexes, when fifteen or sixteen years of age, assist in the work of carrying the molded bricks and arranging them in regular layers. With their assistance a slave [mason] can make a couple of thousand bricks a day."[71]

Manufacturing was not confined to the urban areas. The early transfers of slaves to the large plantations do not disclose which slaves did what, but the estate inventories of farm equipment, down to the butter churns in the pantry, suggest that successful plantation owners also employed slaves in manufacturing, building, transport, and handicrafts. For example, there was a wagon maker's shop and smithy on Blauweblomkloof, the farm of Frans Hendrik Batenhorst[72]; there was a carpenter's shop and smithy (with blast furnace) on the farm of Jacob Malan and Catherina Morkel[73]; the farm of Maria Vosloo and Jan Andries Dissel boasted a smithy, and so on.[74] Only for the nineteenth century, however, is there a clear picture of the artisanal structure of the colony (see Figure 5-19).[75]

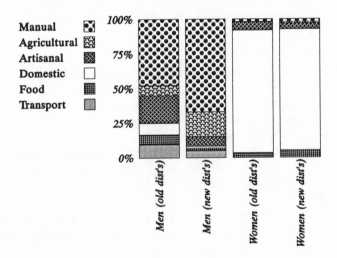

Figure 5–19. Occupations of Cape slaves by region and sex, 1823–1830.

[71] Mentzel, *Description*, vol. 2, 90–91; the argument about gender deference — namely that Europeans arrived in the colonies with some racial baggage, since they made distinctions between white men and women in regard to the type of labor each could do but put black women into the most strenuous gang labor — is made in chapter 6; see also Stanley L. Engerman and Eugene Genovese, *Race and Slavery in the Western Hemisphere: Quantitative Studies* (Princeton, N.J.: Princeton University Press, 1975), pp. 514–515.

[72] CAD MOOC ST 18/30 (5 March 1762).

[73] MOOC ST 18/31 (3 February 1780).

[74] MOOC ST 18/32 (23 June 1731); see Mentzel, *Description*, vol. 2, 91.

[75] Shell, "1823Sale." I have attempted to inject a picture of change over time by comparing the older and new districts.

The Professional Sector

To characterize fully the division of labor among the slaves belonging to persons in the professional sector is not feasible in either period. The various governors, those in the upper echelons of the administration, doctors, lawyers, and even the ministers of the Dutch Reformed Church were so bound up in the speculative side of the slave trade that to disentangle the slaves they used for themselves from the slaves they bought quickly to resell is virtually impossible. To cite one difficult case among many: a private surgeon, Johannes Theopholis Rochlits, who was at the Cape for only a short time in the 1720s, sold more than 25 slaves in the space of two years,[76] but only one or two of these slaves, according to C. Graham Botha, an early social historian of the early Cape, could have been connected to the practice of medicine.[77] The professional sector may have specialized in the hiring out of slaves prior to reselling them, which could explain what these urban, professional owners might have done with so many slaves. According to Hudson, there were so many underemployed slaves in Cape Town (the way station for imported slaves, see Chapter 4) that some householders, during the southeaster wind, sent their slaves to water the gravel streets three times a day.[78]

The Agricultural Sector

Slave holdings at the Cape gradually became more agriculturally based and more rural. There were three types of farms: market gardens, plantations and frontier ranches. Each type of farm was characterized by its distance from the market, and since the market gardens surrounded and even penetrated the port, the agricultural sector cannot simply be equated with "rural."

The Market Garden Holding All the market gardens (which ranged from 0.1 to 5.0 morgen, or 11.25 acres), were near the port or inland villages, where the crops in greatest demand were green beans, peas, lemons, limes, and other varieties of fresh produce to feed the scurvy-ridden crews of the ships passing the Cape twice each year. Since these farms' crops were never reported on the census, the identification of market gardens has gone virtually unnoticed by Cape histo-

---

[76] For Rochlits' purchases, see CAD CJ 3076: "Obligatien, Transporten van Slaven, ens.," (March 1723 to August 1724); CAD CJ 3077: "Obligatien, Transporten van Slaven, ens.," (October 1724 to December 1725).

[77] Col. G. Botha mentions in his article on the medical profession at the early Cape that house calls by physicians were rare; most of the entries in the bookkeeping of Cape doctors refer to medicine being sent out "*par son ordre*" by "*envoyé,*" with the name of a slave messenger being entered into the record; see C. Graham Botha, *The Collected Works of C. Graham Botha, Volume Two: History of Law, Medicine and Place Names in the Cape of Good Hope* (Cape Town: Struik, 1962), p. 181.

[78] Robert C.-H. Shell (ed.), "S.E. Hudson on Buildings," *Quarterly Bulletin of the South African Library* 47, 4 (June 1993): 139.

rians.[79] Many of the prize market gardens were on the slopes of Table Mountain (on the outskirts of Cape Town), and a few well-known market gardens, like Schotschekloof (the present day "Malay quarter") and Tamboerskloof, were in Cape Town itself. The Lodge slaves were originally meant to tend the Company's own urban market garden, but during the regime of Willem Adrian van der Stel (1699 to 1706) this walled area in the center of the city became an experimental farm and, finally, a botanical garden, which it remains today.[80]

There were only eight market gardens during the first 75 years of this period, ranging in size from one-half acre to 12 acres; thereafter they proliferated.[81] Although market gardens were small and few, farm for farm and acre for acre (representing only 2 percent of the original 440 freehold farms) market gardens employed many more slaves than other agricultural enterprises at the Cape. Slaves stationed on these market gardens had to do double duty as planters and sellers,[82] and such farms generated a fortune. W. W. Bird described one in 1821:

Leeuwenhof — the Lion's den — is what in England would be called a good estate, yielding to its owner ample means of living like a gentleman. The rents arise from the daily sale of every description of fruit and vegetables to the population of Cape Town; this is done to a great extent by slave boys, who go with two large baskets twice a day, backwards and forwards, filled with whatever is seasonable, from the garden, and with eggs and milk from the farms. From some gardens five or six slaves are constantly so engaged, and at particular seasons, each will bring home twenty or thirty rixdollars a day.[83]

More isolated rural farmers could supplement their labor force with occasional Khoi labor.[84] Not so with the urban market gardeners who required steady year-round labor. Even "rural" Stellenbosch by 1820 was considered a center of market garden activity. Only in the areas immediately surrounding the towns did slave holding become virtually universal. The proliferation of market gardens was partly responsible for this particular distribution of slaves (see Figure 5-20).[85]

---

[79] The only method of identifying them is to look at the descriptions of the individual properties in the Deeds Office where the clerks identified every *tuijn* (garden); Guelke and Shell, "The Deeds Book."

[80] The "Buiten-" prefixes in the names of four streets in contemporary Cape Town indicate the borders of the old town. The present boundaries of the "Gardens" suburb are another rough guide to the erstwhile market gardens. A contemporary map illustrates the location of the market gardens, cf. George McCall Theal, *Chronicles of the Cape Commanders . . .* (Cape Town: W. A. Richards, 1882), facing p. 298.

[81] See Cape Town Deeds Office, property transfers labeled as a "*tuijn*."

[82] Mentzel, *Description*, vol. 2, 88.

[83] Bird, *State of the Cape*, 157–158.

[84] Bird, *State of the Cape*, 174.

[85] Adapted from N. A. Worden, *Slavery in Dutch South Africa* (Cambridge: Cambridge University Press, 1985), p. 13, Table 2.2.

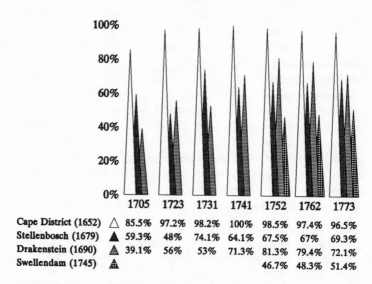

		1705	1723	1731	1741	1752	1762	1773
Cape District (1652)	△	85.5%	97.2%	98.2%	100%	98.5%	97.4%	96.5%
Stellenbosch (1679)	▲	59.3%	48%	74.1%	64.1%	67.5%	67%	69.3%
Drakenstein (1690)	▲	39.1%	56%	53%	71.3%	81.3%	79.4%	72.1%
Swellendam (1745)	▲					46.7%	48.3%	51.4%

Figure 5–20. Percentage of farms with at least one slave, 1705–1773.

Market gardeners had both steady and seasonal consumer support, thanks to the thousands of scorbutic sailors and soldiers who passed through the port each summer, some on the way to the East, others returning from there. Market garden owners were jointly responsible for the purchase of 5 percent of the total domestic market of slaves, mostly men in their prime. The number of market farms increased dramatically during the latter half of eighteenth century in response to a boost of maritime traffic after 1770 (see Figure 2-2). While the male slaves around the port labored outside to produce and deliver vitamin C for the sick seafarers, the female slaves in the ubiquitous Cape Town boardinghouses ministered to the needs of the revitalized sailors and officers. Again, the result was to concentrate young slaves in and around the port.

The Freehold Plantations The second type of farm was the intensively culti-vated, freehold, arable farm (5 to 200 morgen), with wine, wheat, rye, and barley the predominant crops. This farm type has been extensively analyzed by the Cape historians Nigel Worden, Mary Rayner, Pamela Scully, Robert Ross, and Peter van Duin.[86] Wine production, which only slowly developed an export base, enjoyed a spectacular boom in the 1820s that, according to Mary Rayner, brought about a hyperexploitation of the slave workers in the rural vineyards, and from Andrew

---

[86] See Worden, *Slavery in Dutch South Africa*, for slavery in the Stellenbosch district; Robert Ross and Peter van Duin, *The Economy of the Cape Colony in the Eighteenth Century* (Leiden: Intercontinenta, no. 7 (1987), pp. 1–166.

Bank we can infer a relocation of many urban slaves to the wine-growing regions.[87] According to complaints from wine producers in this period, they were in a mood close to desperation, as no additional labor could be found for these labor-consuming farms. Ordinance 50 (1828), which liberated the Khoi from serfdom, also posed an additional labor crisis for the rural Cape farmer, who had barely recovered from the abolition of the oceanic slave trade.

The Loan Farm There was, finally, extensive ranching of sheep and cattle on the arid frontier escarpments, a type of farm (with a minimum size of 6,000 morgen) that the Cape historian Leonard Guelke has described in great detail.[88] These farms employed few free people and even fewer slaves. Typically on such a farm an overseer or a son of the owner supervised a few Khoi serf herdsmen, or, a few older slaves who had been "farmed out" would be there on their own. Such farms provided the prototype for agricultural activity after abolition as farmers turned to an alternative way of life — ranching without purchasable slaves.

The Chances of Regional Dislocation Through Sale

The first "move" of an imported slave was from the slave ship to the new owner. These new owners were chiefly in the market garden areas of Table Valley (39 percent) and the Liesbeeck Valley (5 percent), while farmers of arable land in the Tigerberg region received 3 percent of the slaves, and the remainder of the Cape district (all rural areas) received 37 percent of the "green" slaves. The intensively cultivated Hottentots Holland region received 6.7 percent of imported slaves, the area around the town of Stellenbosch 5 percent and the frontier area of Drakenstein (opened in 1690) 4.3 percent. Over half of the imported slaves were whisked out of the port within days of their arrival, the other half remained, some to be resold at a later date (see Chapter 4).

A slave had a greater chance of being sold if he or she lived in Table Valley or in the Cape district, but such a sale rarely entailed a move outside that district. The proximity of the slave to the market center of Cape Town thus entailed a greater risk of sale, but a smaller chance of regional and familial dislocation. Most slave sales occurred within districts; both seller and buyer were generally in the same district, and more particularly within the Cape district, which included the urban and periurban areas of Table Valley. Over two-fifths of all slaves sold came from the Cape district; of these, 41.6 percent remained in that area and 14.5 percent went

[87] Mary Isabel Rayner, "Wine and Slaves: The Failure of an Export Economy and the Ending of Slavery in the Cape Colony, South Africa, 1806–1834," Ph.D. dissertation, Duke University, 1986.

[88] Leonard Guelke, "Frontier Settlement in Early Dutch South Africa," *Annals of the Association of American Geographers* 66, 1 (March 1976): 25–42.

to Cape Town. More than half of the Cape district slaves sold on the early domestic market stayed in the same district. Slaves sold in other districts tended to stay in those districts.

In the early period, sales increasingly involved a direct transfer from slave ship to farm, but in some cases newly imported slaves stayed in the town for an interim speculation period before being sold "up country." Up to 1808 and the end of the oceanic trade, nearly all creole slaves stayed where they were born. Throughout both periods, sales were most likely in the urban and periurban areas, and the probability of slave's being sold was always highest in Cape Town where slaves were sold almost every week in the popular auctions in Church Square. These were held under a large tree, next to the Lodge and facing the rear edifice of the Dutch Reformed Church.

Individual Slave Distributions by Holding

Although the Lodge had an average size of 400 slaves, all other slave distributions at the Cape remained small. Owners who owned many slaves nearly always also owned several properties, and slaves were distributed in modest household distributions among these properties. Generally, older slaves were found in the remote interior. In the early period, age was directly related to distance from the market centers, but after 1808 many younger slaves also found themselves in the new more remote districts. In the beginning, slave women were kept at the urban center of the economy, and only a handful were moved into agricultural activities in the nineteenth century. Gender-based domestic labor remained stable until the nineteenth century, when more male slaves came to be used in the household.

An important analytical point for understanding Cape slavery in this period is that the primary distinctions between slave holdings were not only between urban and rural, but also among types of slave holdings. The differing proportions of slaves from different origins within these types of holdings shows that the division of labor was based on gender, racial descent, creole status, and geographical origin. All Cape slaves were kept in small distributions, and slave women were in the domestic environment while slave men were outside. Patterns of domestic dependency, although they changed somewhat, remained highly gender-based. Establishing distributions is the key to unlocking the secrets of any slave society. If the "availability" of land led to the introduction of slavery and serfdom into South Africa, the type of land, the availability of rainfall and surface water, and the distance from the market centers are good guides in explaining how slaves and serfs were distributed in the Cape colony.

As the institution of slavery became threatened politically, the earlier, largely urban distribution, which had had clear economic causes, gave way to one that was increasingly oriented to the interior and was politically motivated (in the sense that it was a reaction to emancipation). After 1795, more and more owners moved to the edges of the colony's interior. As emancipation loomed, some slave owners readied themselves for what would be called the Great Trek, when one-fifth of all settlers moved out into the frontier. While the prevailing interpretation (with due respect to Theal) of that movement is that it was an attempt to acquire more land, Esther, a slave mother in 1833, had quite another interpretation: she complained that Louis Trichardt, one of the famous leaders of the Trek, was planning to take her daughter, Laurissa, into the interior, "beyond the land boundaries of the colony" to avoid "the Act of Parliament for the Abolition of Slavery."[89] Another leader, Piet Retief, wished to travel overland to South Africa's oldest continuous slaving area, Mozambique, and before setting out he interrogated his own imported Mozambican slaves about conditions in their homeland. For the Cape patriarch in the 1830s, slavery had to be mobilized. Geography was to be the epic, heroic, but not final solution for the preservation of their way of life.

[89] PRO CO 53/58 (4 January 1834), Albany District B2. I am grateful to Rachel Vandervoort for this reference.

SIX

The Company Slave Lodge
An Urban Plantation

COMPANY SLAVES, whether immigrant or creole — that is, imported or locally born — always began their Cape careers in the Lodge. The Lodge, therefore, defined the life and character of the Company slave. The Lodge was the largest slave holding at the Cape. In the big, windowless[1] building, a symbol of isolation, lived more slaves than in all other slave households *combined* from the establishment of the colony in 1652 until 1695. The Lodge, as a single large holding, thus represents a perfect contrast to the typical small holding of slaves at the Cape (see Figure 6-1) and allows us to see how slaves were treated outside an individual owner's household.

The Company slaves, an unusual group at the Cape, have no clear counterpart in the comparative literature of slave societies. The nearly autonomous slave community that evolved in the Lodge was perhaps unique in the history of slavery. The Lodge slaves resembled, in some respects, the Roman *familiae Caesaris*, the emperor's slaves who did all sorts of administrative and manual work in ancient Rome.[2] Like the *familiae Caesaris*, the Lodge slaves were urban, but unlike their Roman counterparts, their work was both agricultural, tending the Company's vegetable plantation of nine acres in the center of the town, and municipal, fixing the roads and seeing to the removal of the town's slurry every night.

The Lodge slaves were different from any of the Cape settlers' holdings in a number of respects. Most of the Company slaves were housed together in the slave Lodge. There were as many female slaves as male slaves — in the seventeenth century, there were more. Although the Company slaves performed a variety of domestic, clerical, and hospital chores, heavy manual labor was the lot for most of them — women included; in strong contrast to the burgher's slave holdings, there

---

[1] Windows were added in the nineteenth century, see chapter nine.

[2] P. R. C. Weaver, *Familiae Caesaris: A Social Study of the Emperor's Freedmen and Slaves* (London: Cambridge University Press, 1972), 224–226.

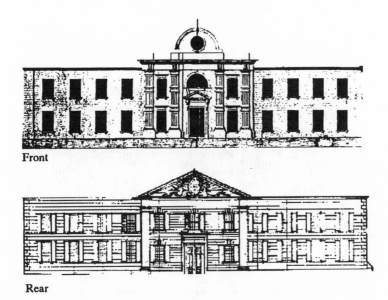

Front

Rear

Figure 6–1. The Lodge façade and rear view, 1804.

was little gender deference in the Lodge. Mortality for slaves in these occupations — "general works," as they were euphemistically called — was high; men died faster than women. Also, runaway slaves were mostly men. Throughout the period of slavery there was a clear excess of deaths and runaways over births among the Lodge slaves. Replenishment was through the slave trade. The Lodge, in effect, was a demographic sinkhole (see Figure 6-2).[3]

Both conception and death had clearly defined seasonal profiles. Death visited the Lodge in the coldest, rainiest months and dropped to a very low rate in summer. Conceptions occurred in the spring. Mention is usually made of visiting seamen using the Lodge as a brothel, but the mulatto conception cycle does not tally with the fleet arrivals. In fact, conceptions were the lowest in the months of heaviest fleet movement at the Cape. The mulatto conception rates in the Lodge were based on the equinoxes, as in most other populations, and the Lodge women chose local European partners (see Figure 6-3).[4]

---

[3] Mortality: Hans F. Heese, "Mortaliteit onder VOC slaven, 1722–1782," *Kronos* 11 (1980): 13; Pretoria, UB CA 88 C.291 (microfilm), pp. 96–251; Theal, *History*, 4: 103; (N = 501; 830; 1,535). Fertility: DRCA G1 8/2 Doopboeke; G1 4/34: tabulation of all baptisms; (N = 1,050). The Dutch Reformed Church has deposited copies of these documents in CAD. See Robert C.-H. Shell, "Slavery at the Cape of Good Hope, 1680–1731," Ph.D. dissertation, Yale University, 1986, pp. 431–436.

[4] Fertility: DRCA Kaapstad Doopboeke GR1 1/1, 8/1–2; shipping: DO: "Scheepenkennissen en Transporten" (1658–1731).

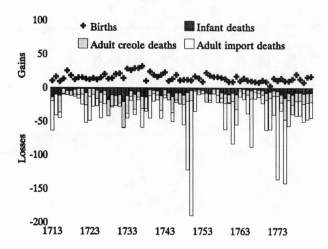

Figure 6–2. Fertility and mortality in the Lodge, 1713 to 1782.

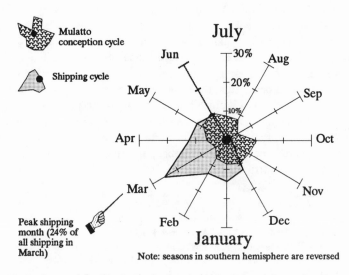

Figure 6–3. Seasonal fertility in the Lodge and shipping activity at the Cape, 1680 to 1731.

The Company slave Lodge, sometimes called the "Loots" or "Logie,"[5] was a large two-story building centrally located at the head of the town's main thoroughfare, backing onto the Company's 9 acre vegetable plantation and across the street from the large Company hospital that served the crews of passing ships. The new Castle, the primary defense and administrative center of the colony with a floorplan to rival an Egyptian pyramid, was a monument to Lodge labor (see Figure 6-4).[6] Numerous Company operations depended on Lodge slave labor.[7] How this unique community operated, how it was managed, and what its mores, standards of conduct, and relationships were like are all important questions for the study of Cape slavery. Over the whole period the Lodge population averaged 476 slaves (see Figure 6-5).[8]

---

[5] The standard translation for the Dutch term is a lightly constructed building, usually made of wood; Van Dale, *Groot Woordenboek der Nederlandse Taal*, ed. C. Kruyskamp ('s-Gravenhage: Martinus Nijhoff, 1982, 10th edition, Van Dale Lexicografie), s.v. "*Loods*." This referred to the original building, destroyed by fire in 1679. The building that replaced this was more heavily constructed, having walls four feet thick. The building was renovated many times and sometimes substantially rebuilt (see Chapter 9).

[6] The old fort was considered too small and a new Castle was constructed with stone walls which was completed in 1674. Scanned and enhanced from E. C. Godée-Molsbergen, *South African History told in Pictures* (Amsterdam: S. L. van Looy, 1913), page 33. Original in Rijkarchief.

[7] Much of the history of the building may be garnered from "The Memorandum of the Historical and Aesthetic Aspects of the Old Supreme Court Building," Appendix C in *The Report of the Committee of Enquiry Concerning the Old Supreme Court Building, Cape Town, and the Widening of Bureau Street* (Pretoria: Government Printer, 1953–54) G. P. S. 11369–1953–4 — 48. I am grateful to Paul Mills for his generous personal gift of this source. See also O. Geyser, *Die Ou Hooggeregshofgebou* (Cape Town: Tafelberg, 1958), pp. 1-40, and C. A. Lückhoff, *Die Ou Hooggeregshofgebou: die ingeligte openbare mening en die toekoms van die gebou* (Cape Town: Balkema, 1954).

[8] A wealth of sources invites inquiry into the inner workings of the Lodge and allows the historian almost physically to enter the Lodge. A detailed analysis of the social workings of the Lodge is possible because notes, resolutions, and sometimes even essays often accompanied periodic full censuses of the Lodge population. In the Company slave censuses, the Company clerks often provided each slave with a toponymic identification and occupation. Moreover, each occupational group of slaves was headed by the legend "half-" or "full-breed," that is *halfslag* or *heelslag*. Each category of slave was also broken down by sex. See, for example, AR VOC 4030: "Generale Opneming en monster rolle van's Comp: Soo slaven als bandieten" (1 January 1693), folios 359–367. The church scribes used a similar classification scheme throughout the period, that affords comprehensive identification of the racial descent and genealogies of most of the Company slaves, who were obliged to attend services, see DRCA, Kaap Notule, 1665–1695, Doop Register, GR1 vol. 1/1. When the settlers did have their slaves baptized, their race was not mentioned; see for example, DRCA: GR1 1/8, p. 86: the slaves of Theunisz Dirksz van Schalkwijk and Gerrit Jansz van Aart.

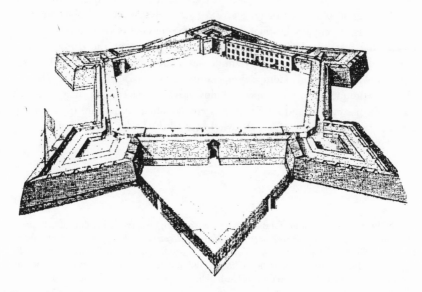

Figure 6–4. The new Castle.

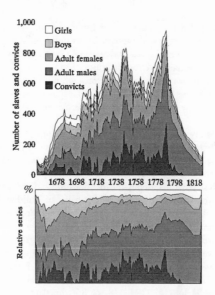

Figure 6–5. Demographic profile of the Lodge, 1658 to 1828.

The Intramural Lodge Hierarchy

At the top of the Lodge's hierarchy were the Europeans, though the European personnel kept themselves segregated from the day-to-day operations of the Lodge as much as possible. No European Company personnel lived in the Lodge, for example. The only Europeans there — a reflection on the status of the slaves — were lunatics and criminals. The Lodge doubled as an adjunct asylum and prison for almost its entire history. It first housed "lunatic" Europeans in 1710; by 1804 there were three rooms set aside for such persons who had proved an "embarrassment" to both the authorities and the other settlers. The lunatics' rooms were next to the Lodge's own prison room (a prison within a prison),[9] and this set of miserable rooms flanked eight lavatories. The insane added an Hieronymus Bosch-like touch to the already macabre Lodge community. If Michel Foucault, the French historian, is correct in saying that European contemporaries considered the mad to be socially dead, and bearing in mind Orlando Patterson's similar definition of slaves, then the Lodge, in housing both, was the colony's central symbol and repository for the socially dead.[10] Architecturally the Lodge was a rectangular panopticon. With none of its inhabitants able to see out and with no one outside able to see in, it could, in a sense, be ignored, even though it was located on Cape Town's busiest thoroughfare, in the center of the town, a shameless fortress, in effect, of human misery.

Europeans were in overall command of the Lodge and were responsible for security. The four Company employees in charge of the slave Lodge were the Fiscal,[11] the commissioner of the Company slaves, and the two upper foremen[12] who acted as quartermasters and the gatekeepers,[13] their only on-site chore being

---

[9] Lunatics were first housed in the Lodge in 1710; Hendrik Carel Vos Leibbrandt, *Journal 1699–1732* (Cape Town: W. A. Richards & Sons, Government Printers, 1896) p. 216; the rooms reserved for "lunatics" can be seen in Figure 9-1, a diagram of the 1804 Lodge, next to the prison within a prison.

[10] Michel Foucault, *Madness and Civilization: A History of Insanity in the Age of Reason* (New York: Vintage, 1973), passim. Orlando Patterson, *Slavery and Social Death: A Comparative Study* (Cambridge, Mass.: Harvard University Press, 1982), pp. 38 ff.

[11] There is no satisfactory translation of the word *fiscal.* The Fiscal was third-in-command of the colony and had authority over all the slaves. According to W. W. Bird, who gives the best account of the Fiscal's duties: "The fiscal is an advocate of the court of justice, holding a situation, with respect to government something similar to that of the attorney-general in England . . . the slave population is under his immediate charge. . . . Such is the awe of a fiscal in the breast of a slave, that were the governor to pass by during a street quarrel (of slaves), the disputants would persevere; but on a mere report of the fiscal's being near at hand, all is instantly hushed to peace and order." W. W. Bird, *The State of the Cape of Good Hope in 1822* (Cape Town: Struik, 1966), pp. 16–17.

[12] In Dutch, *opper-mandoors.*

[13] CAD C.335: "wegens d' huijshouding van de E. Comp. Slawe Logie" (13 February

the removal of the Lodge key every night, an effective safeguard against arson, which was a common form of revenge for Cape slaves against their owners.[14] According to earlier sources, the slave underboss (*onderbaas*) went to fetch the key in the morning from the Fiscal's house,[15] which would suggest that at least one Lodge slave stayed outside the Lodge at night. Few Europeans entered the Lodge by choice, except during the one hour each night when the Lodge became an active brothel for the local garrison — again an overt symbol of the complete ostracism of Company slaves from human society. None stayed the night.[16] About 85 percent of Company slaves lived in the Lodge; the others were temporarily stationed at various smaller "outposts" — Rondebosch, Paradijs (Bishopscourt), Klapmuts, Hottentots Holland, and Kuilsrivier — and a favored handful went to the top local officials. Company slaves preferred the nonsegregated outpost appointments, yet the operation of these stations was similar to that of the Lodge, except for the presence of European soldiers.

Hierarchies based on descent and origin dominated the social interactions in the Lodge. Despite their rapid turnover — occasioned by runaways and high mortality — the Lodge slaves maintained a strictly military order, which John Blassingame, an American historian, has pointed out was also the main mode of slave management on large plantations in the American South.[17] The armylike chain of command was superimposed on both sexes; descent, creole status, and geographic origin were interpolated into the hierarchy to form this quite new society.

The Culture Brokers
At the top of the Company slave pyramid were the *tolks* (slave interpreters), who were accorded the most extensive privileges in the Lodge hierarchy. They were of necessity "full-breed," for linguistic reasons. Mockadan Sijmon, for example, an Arabian interpreter of the Malagasy language, was after years of work given a house in Cape Town, and he lived there with a slave concubine who was excused from all

---

1710), p. 11; C.338, Attestatiën: "Winter Kleeding" (1 August 1719), folio 376; C.339, Attestatiën: "Zoomer Kleeding" (6 or 16 October 1720), folio 253; C.339, Attestatiën: "Winter Kleeding" (21 May 1721), folio 503.

[14] Otto Friederich Mentzel, *A Complete and Authentic Geographical and Topographical Description . . .* , trans. G. V. Marais and J. Hoge, rev. ed. (Cape Town: Van Riebeeck Society, 1944), vol. 2, p. 116.

[15] CAD C.335: "wegens d' huijshouding . . . ," 11; see also Anna J. Böeseken et al. (eds.), *Suid-Afrikaanse Argriefstukke: Resolusies van die Politieke Raad* (Cape Town: Cape Times, 1957–1975; hereafter *Resolutions*), vol. 5, 115 (17 November 1716).

[16] Mentzel, *Description*, vol. 2, 116.

[17] John W. Blassingame, *The Slave Community: Plantation Life in the Antebellum South* (New York: Oxford University Press, 1979), pp. 289–290, 323–327. Even after the Civil War, plantation gangs were headed by "captains" as they were before; see Merle Prunty, "The Renaissance of the Southern Plantation," *Geographical Review* 45, 4 (October 1955): 470.

other work.[18] He received extra rations and trading items to use on slaving expeditions to Madagascar, and was even permitted to travel to Europe.[19] At the Cape, he sported a top hat and shoes — ordinarily slaves at the Cape went barefoot. He retired to Batavia in 1681 after an enraged escaped Lodge slave torched his house.[20] The only infringement on his liberty was that the Dutch retained his passport.[21]

Although the Dutch once termed Sijmon "a *black*," they also called him a "free-born Arab."[22] Officials finally resolved (after a closed session) to treat him as "a prisoner of war."[23] They did not list him on the Company payroll, nor on the freeman census, nor on the slave census (although he was supposed to be a Lodge supervisor when not on a slave voyage).[24] Sijmon therefore was an anomaly. Stolen at sea from the British for his linguistic skills, he became a friend of the Cape governor and an indispensable guide on Company slaving expeditions in Madagascar.[25] He was so valuable in these early years of slave trading that the Company officials dared not fit him into the slave hierarchy for fear of embarrassing him; therefore, he had no particular place at all in the Cape community. Mockadan Sijmon was therefore a double outsider: he was "outside" both slave and free populations, a classic culture broker.

As the Cape slave trade to Madagascar increased, more multilingual slaves and convicts emerged, eager to fill the coveted post of interpreter. Among them were Aje of Clumpong, who spoke 11 languages; Moegadua of Macassar, who spoke 8; and Jongman of Bali, who spoke 5[26]; but none ever achieved Sijmon's special status, and all stayed inside the Lodge. Some interpreters were *mestiço*. The French Jesuit astronomer Father Guy Tachard, who visited the Cape in 1686 on his way to Siam, explained that the slave interpreters the Company provided for the French visitors were "*metis* [*sic*] that is to say, were born of a Portuguese man

[18] For Mockadan Sijmon's career, I have relied heavily on James Armstrong's fascinating "A Note on Interpreters" in Armstrong, "Madagascar and the Slave Trade in the Seventeenth Century" (Université de Madagascar: Colloque d' Histoire Malgache, 13–18 Avril 1981 à Mahajanga), pp. 20–21; but also see "Isbrand Goske vir sy Opvolger" in Anna J. Böeseken (ed.), *Belangrike Kaapse Dokumente*. "Memoriën en Instructiën, 1657–1699" (Cape Town: South African State Archives, 1967), vol. 1, pp. 135–136.

[19] AR VOC 4013: "Dag register van de Voorhout" (25 May 1677); "Isbrand Goske vir sy Opvolger," in Böeseken, *Memoriën en Instructiën*, vol. 1, p. 35.

[20] "Isbrand Goske vir sy Opvolger," 1: 35.

[21] "Isbrand Goske vir sy Opvolger," 1: 35.

[22] In Dutch, "*swart*" (emphasis in original).

[23] "*Oorlogsgevangene*," see "Isbrand Goske vir sy Opvolger," in Böeseken, *Memoriën en Instructiën*, vol. 1, 35.

[24] Armstrong, "A Note on Interpreters," 20; "Isbrand Goske vir sy Opvolger," in Böeseken, *Memoriën en Instructiën*, vol. 1, 35.

[25] Armstrong, "A Note on Interpreters," p. 20; "Isbrand Goske vir sy Opvolger," in Böeseken, *Memoriën en Instructiën*, vol. 1, 35.

[26] Hendrick Carel Vos Leibbrandt, *Letters Despatched*, (Cape Town: W. A. Richards & Sons, Government Printers, 1986), pp. 29–30 (no. 48 of October 1696).

and a Siamese woman."[27] Later documents confirmed the privileges accorded to interpreters. Jan Bosman, the interpreter on the Company ship, the *Barneveld* in 1720, was allowed to buy and sell a slave on his own account. Notably, this was not an under-the-counter transaction: the commissioner of slaves himself signed the document.[28] Interpreters were key personnel and the Company had to look after them first.

Internal Authority

The closer a slave was to being European, the higher up in the hierarchy he or she was. The somatic norm worked in administrative as well as domestic hierarchies. Below the interpreters in status were the mulatto "boss-boys" — part European, the products of out-of-wedlock slave liaisons — who had local jurisdiction over the Company slave force.[29] In 1693, an overseer was referred to in the records, as "Jacob Cornelisz(oon), mulatto," in charge of four male and six female "full-breeds" and six female "full-breeds" at the Company post at Rondebosch.[30] The 1710 report on the housekeeping at the Lodge mentions but does not name mulatto overseers at both Rondebosch and Cape Town.[31] The practice of using mulatto overseers was widespread in other Dutch possessions as well. In 1709 a visiting commissioner, Heer Simons, explained to the new Cape governor, Louis Assenburg, that the full-breed eastern slaves in Columbo were always supervised by a European *and* a mulatto overseer.[32]

Below the overseers were the *mandoors*, most of them mulatto or creole, born and raised in the Lodge.[33] In the 1714 slave census, seven mandoors were named: only one, Francis van de Kust, had a toponymic suffix suggesting full-breed status (van Coromandel).[34] One mandoor had a "modern" name, Arie Boer de Groot, suggesting European descent; another was listed as Abraham van de Caap — the

---

[27] Father Guy Tachard, as quoted in E. Strangeman, *Early French Callers at the Cape* (Cape Town: 1936), p. 200.

[28] CAD C.338: "De onder volgende Slaven en Slavinne op den 21 Feb. 1720 uijt het Scheep Barneveld Ontvangen," folios 753 and 761.

[29] They were *onderbaasen*, literally under bosses; see CAD C.335: "wegens d' huijshouding van de E. Comp. Slawe Logie," 11. Hereafter I will not put the offensive terms "full-breed" and "half-breed" in quotes.

[30] AR VOC 4030: "Generale Opneming . . . ," folios 359–367, recto.

[31] CAD C.335: "wegens d' huijshouding . . . ," p. 11.

[32] C. J. Simons, "Opstel van eenige Poincten . . ." (19 April 1708), in C. Graham Botha (ed.), *Collecteana* (Cape Town: Van Riebeeck Society, 1924), p. 28.

[33] *Mandoor* is a corrupted form of the Portuguese *mandador*, which means foreman, overseer, or driver; see Raven-Hart's note 301 in François Valentyn, *Description of the Cape of Good Hope . . .*, ed. E. Raidt, trans. Maj. R. Raven-Hart (Cape Town: Van Riebeeck Society, 1973), vol. 2, p. 243.

[34] CAD C.336 Attestatiën: "Verklaring na gedane monsteringe bevonden te hebben onder te naeme 's Comp: leijfeijgenen" (*Ultimo*, August 1714), folios 457–475.

Cape toponym disclosing his Cape-born creole status. Other mandoor names, like Sambo, directly indicated mulatto status.[35] The remaining names provided no clue about descent, creole status, or origin, except for the negative evidence that they had no toponymic nomenclature that designated full-breed status.[36] A 1717 report on the new slave Lodge provides conclusive evidence: Abraham Cranendonk, the commissioner of slaves, separated the rooms of the resident "creole mandoors" from the offices of the free "Dutch mandoors" (porters and quartermasters).[37]

Movement up the Lodge slave hierarchy could be rapid; there were many openings in the Lodge due to deaths and escapes. In one example among many, Johannes Kemp, who had been seized in Ceylon in 1688 and condemned to slavery at the Cape,[38] was listed as a convict among Company slaves working on the "general works."[39] After a five-year stint (dated from his arrival in 1688), just after the census of 1693 the governor himself appointed him a mandoor of the Lodge.[40] According to the crime records in 1705, Kemp was mandoor of the Company slave masons, which was an elite corps of Lodge slaves.[41] Responding to his 1710 request for the right to work his passage back to Batavia, the Dutch official mentioned — in Johannes's favor — that he was mulatto (*"mestiço"*).[42] Some mulatto slaves had free European relatives outside the Lodge, which further added to their favored racial status, especially in the few cases when such free persons had died and left their estate to their close relatives still languishing in the Lodge.[43] There was definitely a lottery aspect to Lodge manumissions (see Chapter 12).

The Lodge mandoors, like the even more fortunate interpreters, enjoyed several privileges. They had separate lodging on the ground floor of the Lodge, and they all had extra clothing rations. The admiral of the 1709 return fleet, Johan van Hoorn, asked the Cape governor, Louis van Assenburg, about the slave rations

---

[35] According to the Oxford English Dictionary, sambo is used in Asia and America to refer to persons of mixed race. The editors opine that the word *Sambo* with a capital *S*, used as a nickname for American slaves, comes from the Foulah word for uncle. William Foltz claims this is a common name in West Africa (private communication).

[36] CAD C.336, Attestatiën: "Verklaring na gedane monsteringe . . . ," folios 457–475.

[37] "*Inlantse*" means creole; Company creole slaves — with one exception — were half-breeds; see also *Resolutions* (30 March 1717), 5: 162.

[38] *Resolutions*, (8 April 1710), 4: 164.

[39] AR VOC 4030: "Generale Opneming . . . ," folios 359–367, recto.

[40] *Resolutions*, (8 April 1710) 4: 164.

[41] AR VOC 4053: "Criminele rechtsrollen" (Thursday, 19 February 1705), folio 658, verso, (8–16 February 1705), folios 504–505, and verso, folio 509.

[42] *Resolutions*, (8 April 1710), 4: 164.

[43] See, for example, the case of Frans van Leeuwen, born at the Cape and a soldier in the Company's employ who left part of his estate to Pieter Cornelisz[oon] and Johan Smiesing, "slaves of the Company." LM 17: 1124a (no. 45 of 1726).

the governor told the admiral: "The mandoors and other head-men [*hoofden*] always received double issue of clothing."[44] In the detailed report about the housekeeping of the slave Lodge, drawn up in the following year, the nine mandoors listed received more than clothing alone; small personal supplies were also among a mandoor's perquisites.[45]

The account books meticulously written up biannually by the European *opper-mandoors* also suggest that the mandoors handled the clothing rations for *all* the Lodge slaves, distributing these items to the rank and file,[46] and withholding supplies as a means of discipline. Mentzel noted, for example, that the Company slaves' "weekly dole of tobacco is often kept back."[47] The mandoors supervised the daily rounds of the Lodge. Illustrating the barracks-like nature of the Lodge hierarchy, the anonymous author of the 1710 report on "the housekeeping of the Lodge" used military terms throughout to describe the quotidian routine of the slaves. For instance, the report stipulated that at six o' clock every morning "the mandoors, each with their own number [of slaves] which they commanded should assemble on the usual square."[48] Drummers and trumpeters kept the time of the Lodge.[49] According to the census of 1714, each of the seven mandoors had an average of 66 slaves under his jurisdiction, which was called a "company" of slaves. Some mandoors commanded more slaves than others; the exact distribution of slaves probably related to the type of work at hand, which varied considerably from day to day.[50] At day's end, the mandoors conducted roll-calls for their respective companies. After that, a prayer was said by the mandoors. Finally, the Lodge's big, heavy outer doors were closed and locked, and the key was taken away.[51] By the 1740s there had been a slight adjustment to the daily schedule: "At nine P.M. the gates are [briefly] reopened to permit the soldier and sailor visitors to the woman slaves to depart, for no stranger is permitted to spend the night with the slaves."[52] One may assume that before 1740, some patrons stayed over. Pieter Kolbe, the wayward astronomer who had traveled to the Cape to chart the southern heavens

---

[44] Johan van Hoorn, "Vraagen door den Heer Johan van Hoorn," in Valentijn, *Description*, vol. 2, 242–244.

[45] CAD C.335: "Wegens d' huijshouding . . . ," 11.

[46] CAD C.338, Attestatiën: "Winter Kleeding" (1 August 1719), folio 376; C.339, Attestatiën: "Zoomer Kleeding" (6 or 16 October 1720), folio 253; C.339, Attestatiën: "Winter Kleeding" (21 May 1721), folio 503.

[47] Mentzel, *Description*, vol. 2, 129.

[48] CAD C.335: "Wegens d' huijshouding . . . ," 11.

[49] AR VOC 4030: "Generale Opneming en monster rolle van 's Comp: Soo slaven als bandieten" (1 January 1693), folios 359–367. The positions were full-time; there was even a retired trumpeter.

[50] CAD C.502: Letters Despatched, "Companje Slaven" (16 April 1688), folio 72.

[51] Cad C.335: "Wegens d' huijshouding . . . ," 11.

[52] Mentzel, *Description*, vol. 2, 116.

but stayed to write two volumes on the native Khoi, confirms similarities to the army model of the Lodge by pointing out that at the end of the daily round a barrack bed awaited the slaves: "The Bed-Steads for the slaves, in this Lodge, are fix'd up against the Walls, and have much of the form of Barracks." These beds could not have been comfortable, since, as Kolbe added, the slaves "chuse to lye upon the bare ground rather than upon a bed."[53]

Some multilingual mandoors occasionally did double duty and acted as spies in the Company fort's top-security jail, nicknamed the *donkergat* (dark hole).[54] In 1705, when a gang of Chinese convict slaves from the Lodge were awaiting trial, a "*mestiço* mandoor" who understood Chinese was locked into the cell with the prisoners to eavesdrop on their pretrial conversation. In the following weeks the court used his testimony to condemn his fellow slaves: they were sentenced to death.[55] Every slave in the Lodge had to know where the principal loyalties of the mulatto slave mandoors lay. Their attitudes may have been, as Stanley Elkins noted, similar to the complex attitudes of "prominents" — inmates who identified with their captors — in the concentration camps of the Second World War.[56]

The mandoors' function was also akin to the role of the noncommissioned officers in modern armies, a parallel that John Blassingame, an historian of the American South, has suggested in another context.[57] To the mulatto mandoors fell the task of face-to-face discipline. Keeping the Lodge running smoothly was an easier task for such slaves. As early as 1693 one-quarter of the Lodge children were mulatto. In contrast to the imported Lodge slaves, the creole mulattos had been born and educated in the building, their mothers lived there, and they were acculturated to the ways of the Lodge. Also, being creole, they had a significantly enhanced chance of outliving their imported fellow slaves and becoming, in another of Blassingame's terms, "veterans"; their greater longevity alone made them the rational choice for their position.[58]

Slave "officer-boys" (*officier jongens*) were below the mulatto mandoors in the hierarchy. In August 1719, the officer-boys numbered 56. They were in charge of the male slaves (of which there were 280 in 1719).[59] From 1718 to 1721 — the

---

[53] CAD C.335: "Wegens d' huijshouding . . . ," 11; Peter Kolbe, *The Present State of the Cape* (London: Johnson Reprint Co., 1968), vol. 2, p. 345.

[54] So named because no light whatsoever penetrated this underground dungeon. One can still visit this sad spot in the Castle and experience the pitch dark when the guide switches off the modern lights: the authentic smell also remains.

[55] AR VOC 4053: "Criminele rechtsrollen" (Thursday, 19 February 1705), folio 658, verso.

[56] Stanley Elkins has fruitfully explored the comparison of the antebellum plantations and the Nazi concentration camps; see Elkins, *Slavery: A Problem in American Institutional and Intellectual Life* (Chicago: University of Chicago Press, 1963), pp. 115–127.

[57] Blassingame, *The Slave Community*, 323, 326.

[58] Blassingame, *The Slave Community*, 324.

[59] CAD C.338, Attestatiën: "Winter Kleeding," folio 376.

period for which the relevant documents have survived in a consecutive series — the ratio of officer-boys to men was one officer for every five to eight male slaves, a convenient platoon size.[60] The names of these officer-boys were not recorded, so no inferences about their origin or descent can be made. That the officer-boys were not identified by name on the slave lists (unless the name of the subsection of the list was that of an officer-boy, which is a possibility) would suggest that their appointment was in the hands of the mandoors themselves.[61] Weakly supporting this line of thought, the European Company personnel did not seem aware of the existence of officer-boys. When distinguishing the mandoors from the other head slaves, they simply referred in the broadest terms to "the other headmen."[62] Allowing the mandoors to appoint their own underlings would have made sense as a way of reinforcing the mandoors' power and influence. Whether the group of officer-boys came into being during this period, or whether they had been a permanent part of the Lodge hierarchy is hard to answer. Company clerks refer to officer-boys as a group in only one type of document, the Lodge quartermaster's account books. According to these books, officer-boys received a larger allotment of clothing than the slaves below them in the pyramid.[63]

The mulatto mandoors and the officer-boys were responsible for the control of the Lodge on a microeconomics level. Over and above all outright perquisites, the officer-boys had the responsibility of distributing all essential items (other than clothing, which the mandoors parcelled out) for *all* the slaves. For example, the summer supply of copper slave buttons (12 gross, or 1,728 buttons) was given only to the officers to distribute as rewards to obedient and otherwise deserving slaves.[64] The system of a racial-descent hierarchy, indirect rule, and army-style internal discipline cost the Company nothing except the overhead associated with a few bits of clothing, buttons, and the like.

A "button currency" may have existed among the slaves, since among the most frequently promulgated Cape regulations were rules forbidding the

---

[60] CAD C.338, Attestatiën: "Winter Kleeding," folio 376; C.339, Attestatiën: "Zoomer Kleeding" (6 or 16 October 1720), folio 253; C.339, Attestatiën: "Winter Kleeding" (21 May 1721), folio 503.

[61] This would make sense, since there *were* a few half-breeds in 1693 who were not mandoors, yet who headed the various "gangs," see AR VOC 4030: "Generale Opneming . . . ," folios 359–367, recto (but this is conjecture on my part).

[62] "*De ander hoofden*"; see van Hoorn in Valentijn, *Description*, vol. 2, 242; see also Kathleen M. Jeffreys and S. D. Naude (eds.), *Kaapse Plakkaatboek, 1652–1806* (Cape Town: Kaapse Argriefstukke, 1944–1949), vol. 2, p. 91: "the *mandoors*, or those who have jurisdiction over the slaves" (1722).

[63] According to a personal communication from Professor Leon Hattingh, these documents did exist before this period; an examination of any of the account books for clothing illustrates some of the officer-boys' privileges.

[64] Mentzel, *Description*, vol. 2, 129.

settlers — but especially the Company soldiers and sailors — from buying "clothing and accoutrements" from Company slaves.[65] Sailors, settlers, and soldiers were fined 50 Rixdollars (half the price of an ox wagon) for the first such offense; second offenders, 100 Rixdollars; third offenders were tried as "receivers of stolen property" and, if convicted, could be banished from the colony. Kolbe mentioned that the Lodge slaves would sell anything for the sake of drink: "They make away both with their bedding and the cloaths allow'd 'em for daily Wear, in Extravagances for the Swallow."[66] The constant publication of statutes against selling Company issue and the heavy penalties to be levied suggest that this trade continued. By the 1790s, convalescing patients in the Company hospital (the same institution, incidentally, where the real Robinson Crusoe recovered) were found "completely naked," Company slave nurses having removed and sold their clothing and even their bedding. By 1794, Company slaves were selling every rationed item, including mattresses, clothing, and floor mats.[67] Thus, although the slave officers might have attempted to control the microeconomics of the Lodge, it is quite apparent that the lower-ranking Lodge slaves had developed a thriving, if dangerous, black market.

Murders and theft committed outside the walls of the Lodge by Company slaves were dealt with by the Court of Justice. It is suggestive, if not ominous, that no murders, rapes, or other violent crimes in the Lodge itself were reported in the crime records, though not every record has been consulted.[68] The implication is that the Lodge inmates dealt with such matters themselves. The omnipresent mandoors had to keep an all-night vigil in the kitchen and report any irregularities — even a slave lighting a lamp — to the authorities in the morning.[69] Perhaps these reports were oral; there are no records of this procedure. In short, although arguing from silence is always problematic, in terms of violent and minor intramural crimes, it seems that the Lodge inmates had developed their own rough system of justice.

The Work Hierarchy
Much more is known about the origins and descent of the next rank of the hierarchy in the Lodge: the artisan slaves. In March 1681, Rijklof van Goens wrote

---

[65] "*Klere en deksel*"; see Jeffreys and Naude, *Kaapse Plakkaatboek*, vol. 1, 148–149. Copper slave buttons were first issued at the Cape between the 16 and 30 December 1677.

[66] Kolbe, *State of the Cape*, vol. 2, 345.

[67] Jeffreys and Naude, *Kaapse Plakkaatboek*: (5–6 July 1700) vol. 1, 320; (1704) vol. 1, 340; (1715) vol. 2, 62; (30 May 1716) vol. 2, 64; "Verbod op die ruil of koop van siekes se klere of ander besittings" (8/19 November 1791) vol. 4, 60-61, see also 238.

[68] James Armstrong has supported this point (private communication, January 1983). The crime records of the period 1652–1795 occupy close to 1,000 running meters of shelf space in the Rijksarchief and obviously have not been thoroughly ransacked.

[69] Jeffreys and Naude, *Kaapse Plakkaatboek*, vol. 2, 65.

a memorial for the governor, Simon van der Stel, suggesting that the highly paid garrison artisans be replaced by Company slaves to be specially trained for the task. This would be "cheaper for the Company," he explained.[70] But cost was not the only or even the most important issue: racial arrogance was also involved. H. A. van Reede in 1685 prepared a lengthy set of instructions for van der Stel in which he devoted several pages to the problem of the 58 slave children under 12 years of age who after genealogical investigation, had been found to have a Dutch or German father.[71] These slaves, van Reede said, should be considered apart from the other slaves: "While these mulatto children cannot bear the guilt of the evil-doings of their parents, together with the fact that the indisputable children of our own nation cannot be made into slaves, we must take measures to find a solution."[72] These "measures" included training the mulatto slaves as artisans, with freedom to be bestowed on them at the age of 25. As free persons, the mulattos would then work for the Company as much-needed artisans and as other skilled workers, for example, "wagon drivers, tailors, cobblers, smiths, wood-cutters, wheel-wrights, herders, supervisors, foresters, and gardeners."[73] But these eugenic notions of visiting Company officials were not respected by the local officials who oversaw the Lodge.

In August 1710 Andries Barendse, a mulatto, filed a request that, since he had been born at the Cape in the slave Lodge and had "worked for the Company for over 20 years of good service as a mason," he was entitled to freedom. The Council of Policy agreed and stipulated: "according to the instructions left behind by the late Commissioner General, the Lord Hendrik Adriaan van Reede, that if such a slave had accumulated 40 years of service as a Company slave, he was entitled to his freedom."[74] Since Andries happily met this condition as well,[75] he was given a three-year contract to work as a mason for the Company at 10 guilders a month —

---

[70] Rijklof van Goens, "Memorie van R. v. Goens jr. vir Simon van der Stel" (20 March 1681) in Böeseken, *Memoriën en Instructiën*, vol. 1, 147–156.

[71] "Van Duij[t]sche vaders geteelt"; see H. A. van Reede tot Drakenstein, "Instruksie vir Simon van der Stel . . ." (16 July 1685) in Böeseken, *Memoriën en Instructiën*, vol. 1, 189.

[72] H.A. van Reede, "Instruksie vir Simon van der Stel," vol. 1, 189.

[73] H. A. van Reede, "Instruksie vir Simon van der Stel," vol. 1, 189. Despite the many references to van Reede's instructions in the period 1680–1730, few half-breed slaves were freed at age 25; however, this does not imply that van Reede's suggestions were a dead letter, as James Armstrong has argued (private communication, 1985); rather, it implies that local officials worked around the considerable inconveniences of van Reede's provisions. The favorable attitude toward Company (and free) half-breeds did not depend on van Reede alone, but was an attitude shared throughout the Dutch East Indies. See Heather Sutherland, "Mestizos as Middlemen? Ethnicity and Access in colonial Macassar," unpublished paper, 1980.

[74] *Resolutions* (19 August 1710), vol. 4, 170.

[75] Leibbrandt, *Journal*, 241.

1 guilder above the starting salary of a teenage Company soldier or sailor.[76] Despite the parsimonious attitude of the local officials toward freedom for Lodge mulattos, the artisans were always at the head of the line when it came to the allocation of "easy" work. In 1693, Jan van der [*sic*] Caap, listed as a mulatto, was stationed at the dispensary, helping to distribute medicine. Andries, another mulatto, worked at the Company butchery.[77] In the 170 years of the Company's existence, only 108 of its slaves obtained their freedom; not all were mulatto.

Some overlapping hierarchies spoiled the symmetry of the Eurocentric descent system. In the middle ranks of the Lodge slaves' occupations were persons of either mulatto or full-breed status. Isaa, a full-breed (origin unknown), worked in the Company pharmacy; Jan Maleijer, a full-breed, was posted to the blacksmith shop.[78] The "Malays" had a reputation for artisanal skills.[79] The Company kitchens were exceptions in the general practice of using mulattoes in favored skilled or domestic positions. Perhaps these kitchens were less than salubrious places to work in and therefore should not be included in the same privileged "domestic" category as, say, positions in the domestic service of the governor and other top officials. The Company hospital kitchen, which fed 250 or more,[80] was staffed entirely by full-breeds — for example, "Asiam Chinees," "Pedro Mauoa [from Portuguese Goa]," "Niman van Bali," and "Meheitzou van Madagascar."[81] Bolstering this theory, Sevelen, a full-breed from Madagascar, presided over the kitchens of the slave quarters, where the single largest group of slaves was Malagasy.[82] Or perhaps the company purposely selected an ethnic potpourri of cooks to serve the culinary habits of the cosmopolitan patient and slave populations. In the middle ranges of jobs, the descent hierarchy, based on notions of European racial superiority, came up against the hierarchy of geographic origins, based on a separate notion that slaves from specific areas had special skills. A few anecdotes cannot prove the simultaneous existence of two discrete hierarchies based on descent and origin, but a cross tabulation can (see Figure 6-6).[83]

---

[76] C. R. Boxer, *The Dutch Seaborne Empire* (New York: Knopf, 1965); see "Some Salary Scales of Seafaring Personnel 1645–1700," p. 301.

[77] AR VOC 4030: "Generale Opneming . . . ," folios 359–367, recto, Jan is no. 204; Andries, no. 203.

[78] AR VOC 4030, "Generale Opneming . . . ," folio 363 verso, nos. 202 and 199.

[79] Richard Elphick and Robert C.-H. Shell, "Intergroup relations: Khoikhoi, Settlers, Slaves and Free Blacks," in R. Elphick and Herman Giliomee (eds.), *The Shaping of South African Society, 1652–1820* rev. ed. (Middletown, Conn.: Wesleyan University Press, 1989), pp. 152–153.

[80] Mentzel, *Description*, vol. 1, 112–113.

[81] AR VOC 4030: "Generale Opneming . . . ," folio 363, verso, nos. 193–195.

[82] AR VOC 4030, "Generale Opneming . . . ," folio 363 verso, no. 196.

[83] Compiled from AR VOC 4030: "Generale Opneming . . . ," folios 359–367, recto; and AR VOC 4032: "Opnemingh van Compagnies Groot en kleen vee, mitsgaders der materialen, bouw gereedschapppen en andere goederen in 1693 bevonden" (31 December 1693), folios 65–

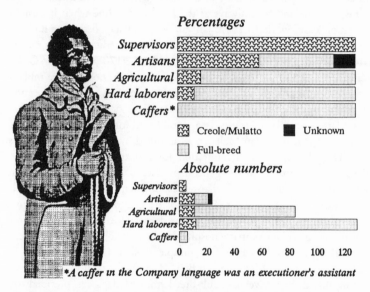

A caffer in the Company language was an executioner's assistant

Figure 6–6. Occupations of male adults in the Lodge by descent, 1693.

The racial hierarchy is most noticeable at the extreme ends of the assigned, ranked tasks: no full-breeds were supervisors; no mulattos were Caffers (executioner's assistants, an extremely lowly position). Only one probable exception to this rule has emerged: Francis van de Kust, a mandoor in 1714. Only in the middle ranks is there some competition between the origin and descent hierarchies, perhaps as a sign of confusing, hard-to-prove bloodlines. For instance, in the clerical category full-breeds outnumbered mulattos by two to one, but in all the other "soft" occupation categories the mulattos are present in a greater proportion than one would expect from a random distribution of descent and occupation. Although individual full-breed slaves might rise higher in the Lodge system, and individual mulatto slaves might sink lower, there were statistically significant boundaries. No individuals of either group appeared in the extreme top and bottom levels.

The most unpleasant tasks of all — collecting salt, mining, grave digging,

---

73; DRCA baptismal and other records allowed identification of the racial descent of most of the 371 slaves. To Dutch officials, "full-breed" indicated no European descent. A "Caffer" in the Company language, was an executioner's assistant. The Cape hangman, pictured here, head of the "Caffers" complained to Lady Anne Barnard that the English had done him out of a job, since they abolished torture in 1798. Lady Anne Barnard, *The Letters of Lady Anne Barnard* (Cape Town: Balkema, 1973), page 68. Courtesy of South African Library.

and removing the town's excrement — were invariably reserved for those full-breed male slaves from the most unpopular areas. Van Reede (who disliked people from Indonesia) instructed Simon van der Stel in 1685 that the "Javanese, Macassarese and other stubborn nations" (*hardnekkige natien*, literally stiff-necked nations) should be kept apart from the other slaves and assigned to hard-labor farms.[84] Such scorned people were also housed in windowless basement quarters, those closest to the depths of the earth. When the Dutch began a slave station at Rio de la Goa (present day Maputo) in the 1720s, they separated the full-breed African slaves from the "land of Terlate" from all the other Lodge slaves. Mentzel, who once delivered salt to the Lodge, and thus became one of the few Europeans to enter the place and write about it, confirms the status of "these Terlatens, as the Europeans called them"[85] and also illustrates that the customary Cape practice was to combine territorial and racial attributions: "[Terlatens] are a foul, evil-smelling race, with villainous slits in their faces which they have cut into all sorts of patterns. Their quarters are in the basement of the Lodge, apart from the other slaves. To them are allotted the dirtiest and most unpleasant tasks."[86] By the 1740s, the Dutch were associating certain types of labor with certain "races." Experience in the Lodge could also influence a slave's place in the Lodge hierarchy. The lowest slaves were full-breed from an unpopular area, but whether the slave was a "new-boy" or a "new-girl" made a certain difference.[87]

The Caffers: The Company's Vigilantes and Executioners

The jobs of executioner's assistants and a type of police force — technically acting as the executive arm of the Fiscal — were filled by the Caffers. The Caffers were low in the Lodge hierarchy, just above the convicts, but they held a quite anomalous position in the colony, somewhat removed from the intramural hierarchy of the Lodge. The South African word Caffer has a curious and pertinent etymology. Originally the word was an Arabic noun meaning "ungrateful"; by association, those who did not believe in Allah were ungrateful. All non-Jews, non-Christians, and non-Muslims — people "not of the book" — were thus considered "Caffers." Because the Arab Muslims came into contact with many African pagans, there arose an association in the Muslim mind between caffers and pagan Africans. This association was exported to the Indonesian Archipelago by Arab and Gujerati traders. The Portuguese, and later the Dutch, picked up the term. Since the first

---

[84] Van Reede, in Böeseken, *Memoriën en Instructiën*, vol. 1, 217.

[85] Otto Friederich Mentzel, *Life at the Cape* . . . , trans. Margaret Greenlees (Cape Town: Van Riebeeck Society, 1919), p. 59.

[86] Mentzel, *Description*, 125.

[87] CAD C.337 (17 February 1717): 45–46; CAD C.336 (5 December 1716): 955.

slaves of Europeans in the Indonesian Archipelago were African, such slaves were termed "Caffers" and were used for police duties. It was from the Dutch possessions in the Indonesian Archipelago that the word was re-exported to Africa, to Cape Town. In the nineteenth century, the British — probably picking up the word (and original derivation) from the Arabs on the east coast of Africa, reintroduced the term, this time applying it to all Africans on the Eastern frontier. In present-day South Africa the word remains the gravest slur: in a bar its use will provoke a fight.

In 1682 the Caffers were full-breed slaves from Angola, although this identification is tenuous.[88] In 1693 the Caffers were also all full-breed slaves, but by that time, we know only their "full-breed" descent, not their place of origin.[89] According to their toponyms, however, Caffers were mostly from the Eastern regions. In 1714 there appeared in the Company slave census one "Biscob van Macassar, Caffer."[90] In most documents of 1682 through 1786, "Caffers of the Justice Department," as they were actually called, were Asian full-breeds. In 1786 an "Asian Caffer" out on patrol, who had run "amok," killing several people — including two provosts — had a price of 100 Rixdollars "dead or alive" put on his head by the Fiscal Gabriel Exter.[91] This incident nicely illustrated the Cape's system of categorizing people by descent and origin. Exter advised the Council of Policy a few days later that the "asiatics were the least trustworthy," and that "*other blacks* inclined for that kind of work should be appointed (my emphasis)."[92] In the interim, four European constables were taken on.[93]

Although the Caffers occupied a despised echelon of the slave hierarchy, the Company issued them superior clothing — special police uniforms with waistcoats. They were also the only slaves allowed to bear arms.[94] According to Mentzel, they "are armed with a sword with iron hilt, carry . . . a *palang* or heavy club, wear a gray uniform consisting of a short coat with blue lapels, a waistcoat and trousers,

---

88 David Tappen as quoted in R. Raven-Hart (Comp. and ed.), *Cape Good Hope, 1652–1702* (Cape Town: Balkema, 1971) vol. 2, 242.

89 AR VOC 4030: "Generale Opneming . . . ," folios 359–367 recto, esp. folio 364: "Caffers van de Justitie, Jongens: Heelslag."

90 CAD C.336, Attestaties: "Verklaring na gedane monsteringe bevonden te hebben onder te naeme 's Comp: leijfeijgenen" (*Ultimo*, August 1714), folio 460 recto (no. 78).

91 Hendrick Carel Vos Leibbrandt, *Requesten (Memorials) 1715–1806* (Cape Town: South African Library, 1989), vol. 1, pp. 20–21 (26 September 1786). According to James Armstrong, a 1727 Company census also lists the Caffers separately — in fact, first (private communication).

92 Jeffreys and Naude, *Kaapse Plakkaatboek*, (26 September 1786) vol. 3, 190–191; Leibbrandt, *Requesten* (26 September 1786) vol. 1, 20–21 (my emphasis).

93 Leibbrandt, *Requesten* (1 November 1786), vol. 1, 22.

94 Jeffreys and Naude, *Kaapse Plakkaatboek* (17–19 August 1686), vol. 1, 219–220; (2 January 1687), vol. 1, 230; (14–15 January 1688), vol. 1, 246–247; (21–22 January 1692), vol. 1, 268; extract from daily journal (22 April 1692), vol. 1, 273.

and receive some petty perquisites as well."[95] And unlike the other slaves — Company and privately owned, who were subject to various curfews, the Caffers were permitted — actually required — to roam around the Cape day and night, enforcing the curfews.[96] This they did, executing rough justice on all — even Europeans who were guilty of the smallest infringement of Cape law. For instance, on one night in February 1705, the Caffers apprehended Jan van der Brugge, a prominent settler, while he was rolling a barrel of wine on the beach to sell to an English ship riding in the roadstead, a "crime" that breached the Company monopoly. Everyone at the Cape expected the Caffers would rough up such mercantilist miscreants.[97] Of course, the "privileges" accorded the Caffers were a compensation related to the public perception of *Company* Caffers, who were hated and feared (not respected) throughout the colony.

It fell to the Caffers to carry out the ghoulish sentences the Court of Justice concocted. The punishments handed down by these courts followed Old Testament principles: an eye for an eye; sometimes, when slaves were concerned, an eye for a tooth. In February 1724, the court sentenced a slave for murder *and* arson, and ordered the Caffers to "cut off his right hand" (the murder weapon), after which he was to be "half-strangled and killed on a slow fire" (the punishment for starting a fire).[98] For even minor crimes — such as smoking a pipe in the street — the Caffers were instructed to inflict severe floggings. Because of the fire hazard in Cape Town, any person, "without distinction" (*zonder onderscheid*), found smoking a pipe in the street was to be "soundly" beaten by the "Caffers."[99] A high proportion of the sentences handed down by the Court of Justice ended with the words "to be handed over to the executioner and to be beaten by the Caffers."[100]

An interesting illustration is the murder trial of Christiaan Godlieb Opperman, a German brewer at Rondebosch who, in early February 1731, tortured one of his slaves, Dam, so severely that he died.[101] Opperman submitted a letter to the court from his knecht (manservant, see 11) informing the governor that Dam,

---

95 Mentzel, *Description*, vol. 2, 124.

96 For the Company slaves, see CAD C.335: "wegens d' huijshouding . . . ," 11. The slaves belonging to the burghers, free blacks, and officials were subject to colonywide curfews; see Jeffreys and Naude, *Kaapse Plakkaatboek* (21–22 February 1660), vol. 1, 57–58; a 9 o'clock curfew (3 July 1686), vol. 1, 215; (15 October 1715) vol. 2, 62. A ten o'clock curfew was introduced in 1727 in the general *placcaaten*, vol. 2, 126.

97 AR VOC 4053: "Processtukken" (19 February 1705), folio 658 verso.

98 Leibbrandt, *Journal* (12 February 1724), 296.

99 Jeffreys and Naude, *Kaapse Plakkaatboek* (1708) vol. 2, 7; in 1794 this was specifically addressed to slaves only, see vol. 4, 249 (article 27).

100 See various "sententies" in the "Processtukken" 1652–1795.

101 AR VOC 4117: "Processtukken, Interogatie van Opperman" (15 May 1731), folio 838 verso. See "Surgeon's report," folio 829 recto. Opperman had used medieval German torture methods, which had ensured that the ordeal went on for several days; see folio 830 verso.

after having run away twice, had been beaten by the Caffers and had died.[102] Opperman's implication was that Dam had died at the hands of the Caffers. The letter piously asked for permission to bury the slave's corpse.[103] Members of the Court of Justice, accompanied by the Fiscal — the official charged with the well-being of slaves — went out to the brewery in a surprise visit and asked to inspect the corpse. Opperman demurred, whereupon a council member, Johannes Rhenius, turned to the Fiscal and said in a stage whisper: "Mister, be so good as to fetch the executioner and the Caffers."[104] Rather than face the Caffers, or "scum," as Opperman called them later from a cell in the Company prison, he barricaded his house and holed himself up in the attic with an array of loaded weapons.[105] In the style of Gene Hackman, he also refused to doff his hat when the officials arrived. He consented to come down and be taken into custody only when assured that the men surrounding his house were from a European garrison and were not the dreaded Caffers.[106]

The Caffers' reputation grew. C. H. Buytendag, a Stellenbosch patriarch charged by the regional magistrate, Van der Merwe, with "atrociously abusing" his household servants, was sentenced to be deported in the 1780s. Buytendag appealed to the governor, claiming he "would turn over a new leaf." Governor Plettenberg, fearing reprisals, relented, but insisted that Buytendag move to the port, whereupon Buytendag's wife, Maria Theron, and eldest daughter approached the Fiscal to bring charges and to complain of further drunkenness and beatings. One evening while the family was sitting down to supper, Boers, the Fiscal, entered, accompanied by Caffers ("the hangman's black assistants," as the townspeople called them) who knocked Buytendag off his chair, bound him, and took him, with cries of his wife and children in his ears, to a waiting ship preparing to sail to Batavia (exile was the worst punishment in the *ancien regime*).[107] Buytendag appealed to the Batavian authorities so skillfully that he was sent back to the Cape in the same year of his banishment. He died en route, however, and became one of the Cape patriots' most noted martyrs.[108] The Caffers' humiliating intru-

---

[102] "Processtukken, Interogatie van Opperman" (15 May 1731), folios 846 ff.

[103] "Processtukken, Interogatie van Opperman" (15 May 1731), (dated February 1731, exhibited May), folio 846 recto. The text of the letter is written half in German and half in Dutch and addressed to his knecht (manservant) Andreas: "*ihr Könnet ihm* [the Fiscal] *wohl sagen daf er* [Dam] *der Drosser ist, die Zweimahl kurtze auf ein ander van die Caffers gegeselt ist, leket wohl, Ich bin euer freund,* [signed] *G.C. Opperman.*"

[104] "*Mijn Heer, weest so goed van de geweldiger en kaffirs hier te laaten koomen,*" "Processstukken, Interogatie van Opperman" (15 May 1731), folio 838 verso and folio 837 recto.

[105] "*Canaille,*" "Processstukken, Interogatie van *Opperman*" (15 May 1731), see also Opperman's "Duplique" (13 October 1731), 882 verso.

[106] "Interogatie van Opperman" (15 May 1731), folio 837 verso and folio 841.

[107] *DSAB*, vol. 5, 109.

[108] I am grateful to Robert Ross for pointing out this reference.

sion into the domestic arena of a patriarchal burgher's family life was the principal reason for the colonywide public agitation over this incident.

The Caffers sometimes used their position of power for their own purposes. Victor de Kock, an early Cape historian, tells an amusing story of how a Caffer in Stellenbosch unlocked the jail to free a friend who had stolen a sheep from Adam Tas, a wealthy settler.[109] On another occasion, a Caffer constable was arrested for allowing two slaves to escape from that same Stellenbosch jail. He defended himself by claiming that the "prison had no locks and was otherwise defective."[110] These anecdotes prompt one to ask why Caffers were used in such a sensitive security post? Moses Finley has argued that slaves predominated in the police forces of classical Athens, because none of the citizens wanted the unpopular job with its unsocial hours and ever-present dangers.[111] Similar sentiments probably prevailed at the Cape, where the grisly sentences of the Court of Justice must have added a further negative inducement, to create a wholly unattractive occupation. The Greek slave police, the *toxotai*, were perfect for their job. Because they were always imported from Scythia, they had no blood ties with the citizenry, which was presumably a safeguard against corruption. At the Cape, as in other such slave societies where there was a constant shortage of nonslave manpower, compelling slaves to defend their masters' way of life and property was not unusual.[112]

During the period 1680 to 1795 almost one slave per month was publicly executed in Cape Town. The decaying corpse would be rehanged by the Caffers in numerous places to afford a peripatetic exposure to the general population. In one 1721 example, drawn from a rather full Cape chamber of horrors, the court sentenced Franciscus Xaverus van Tranquebar to be crucified upside down and for the coup de grace to be withheld; at death, the Caffers were to drag the cadaver "backwards and forwards" through the main byways and streets of Cape Town, taking it to the outskirts of the town (at the present-day traffic department headquarters, Gallows Hill, Greenpoint), there to be hanged, first on a wheel (*Rad*) and then on the gallows, "and there to be left until the birds of the heavens and the air itself consume the body."[113]

The Caffers' area of jurisdiction never clashed with the mandoors' or with the slave officer-boys'. In the 1714 slave census, Caffers are scattered throughout the

---

[109] Victor de Kock, *Those in Bondage: An Account of the Life of the Slave at the Cape in the Days of the Dutch East India Company* (London: Allen & Unwin, 1950), p. 168.

[110] Leibbrandt, *Letters Despatched* (15 March 1704), p. 234.

[111] Moses I. Finley, *Economy and Society in Ancient Greece* (New York: Penguin, 1983), pp. 103, 122.

[112] Bernard H. Nelson, "Confederate Slave Impressment Legislation, 1861–1865," *Journal of Negro History* 31 (October 1946): 392–410.

[113] VOC 4091 (1721): "Sententie," folio 1242. According to artists of the period, the gallows were visible from the sea, although this might be artistic license; see the line drawings of E. V. Stade.

various work gangs — under a mandoor.[114] In a face-off with a mulatto mandoor, a full-breed Caffer had to give way. In the 1693 and 1727 censuses, the Caffers were regarded as a separate group, not attached to any work gang.[115] Even the Lodge slaves — no matter how lowly — regarded them as being beyond the pale, but were undoubtedly under their rule (see Figure 6-7).[116]

Figure 6–7. A Caffer and a Lodge slave, 1764.

Their high profile in the daily activities of the colony resulted in their job, personality, status, and race becoming blurred, contributing to a well-defined, negative stereotype for the Caffer.[117] The position of the Caffers was full of ambiguity. On the one hand they were despised, on the bottom of the Lodge's hierarchy, on the other, they were allowed to behave much like free men: they were free of curfews, were able to carry arms, and were mandated to inflict punishment. Any other slave who lifted a hand against a settler, according to laws passed in 1754 and republished in 1794, would have forfeited his life.[118]

---

[114] CAD C.336: "Verklaring na gedane monsteringe . . . ," folios 457–475.

[115] AR VOC 4030: "Generale Opneming . . . ," folio 364. See note 88.

[116] Scanned and enhanced detail from E. C. Godée-Molsbergen, *South African History told in Pictures* (Amsterdam: S. L. van Looy, 1913), page 52; for attribution see p. 48: "Gezigte van het Stadthuijs aan Cabo de Goede Hoop . . . , 1764" Johannes Rach painting of Cape Town in 1764 in the private collection of Mr. Van Stolk of Rotterdam. I believe that the left hand figure is a caffer with a waistcoat and carrying a *Palang* for prodding the other lodge slave. The disposition of the two figures is most unusual, but appropriate for the upside-down world of the Lodge.

[117] For example, in 1795 the Dutch inhabitants complained to the new British administration that the gruesome activities of the Caffers were causing their women to miscarry.

[118] Leibbrandt, *Journal* (12 February 1724), p. 296; Jeffreys and Naude, *Kaapse Plakkaatboek*, vol. 4, 244 (20/22 August 1794) article 2.

Convict Labor: Punishing Europeans by Identification with Slaves

Two other categories of persons associated with the Lodge, political prisoners and petty criminals sentenced to slavery, were in a social no-man's-land where European male convicts mixed with political prisoners, mainly from the Indonesian Archipelago, and petty criminals, mainly Chinese. All were sentenced to a period of hard labor and slavery in the Cape's penal colony, Robben Island, but they would sometimes be transferred to the Lodge.[119] Besides being a refreshment station for passing ships, from 1658 to 1795 the colony doubled as a secure dumping ground for political and civil troublemakers from the Dutch East Indies.[120] Convicts[121] from the Dutch East India Company's possessions in the East were dispatched to the Cape to work out their sentences "without remuneration."[122] There were a few Singhalese and Javanese convicts,[123] but most were Batavian Chinese. (The Chinese at the Cape were numerous enough by 1706 to have become an identifiable subset of the population.[124]) Initially, most Chinese immigrants to the Cape started their new lives at the Lodge.

The growing settler population was not allowed to use the Company's convicts for their own labor needs, but the precedent of coerced labor, sanctioned by the Company and local officials, served as a model for their own relationships with workers. The convicts the Company put to quarrying, building fortifications, and collecting lime and salt, were rapidly supplemented, after 1685, by a growing slave force in the slave Lodge. At first slaves and convicts were housed together in the Lodge, and their status became blurred in the annual Lodge censuses, although separate lists were occasionally drawn up.

After 1699, the "most dangerous convicts" were stationed offshore for security on Robben Island, South Africa's hard-labor quarrying colony, which was also

---

119 "*Bannelinge* and *bandieten*"; see Robert C.-H. Shell, "The Establishment and Spread of Islam at the Cape from the Beginning of Company Rule to 1838," honors thesis, University of Cape Town, 1975, Chap. on convicts.

120 CAD CJ 3318: "Bandiete Rolle," passim; see also the petitions for freedom in Leibbrandt, *Requesten*, 2 vols. "A-E," and "F-O," 3 vols. "R-Z," are unpublished manuscripts. in the Cape Archives, s.v. Leibbrandt's Manuscripts; one is obliged to use these sometimes carelessly transcribed works, since the originals have been withdrawn for binding.

121 "*Bandieten.*"

122 "Zonder loon," in CAD C.501: "Letters Despatched, Lijste de geregelde Maccasarschen Princen en Groten en dieselven dienaren" (5 September 1686), folios 508 ff.

123 Especially in the seventeenth century; see CAD C.501: "Letters Despatched, Lijste de geregelde Maccasarschen Princen en Groten en dieselven dienaren" (5 September 1686), folios 508 ff.

124 AR VOC 4053: "Criminele rechtsrollen" (Thursday, 19 February 1705), folio 658 verso; the only known article on this topic is James Armstrong, "The Chinese at the Cape in the Dutch East India Period, 1652–1795" mimeo (12 June 1979).

reserved for European convicts, slave criminals, and political exiles.[125] Only in times of dire labor shortages were these hard cases shipped across the bay to work in Cape Town households. One can gauge how acute the labor shortage was at times like these by the fact that the governor himself was once obliged "to set a personal example" by digging a trench.[126] Toward the end of the seventeenth century, the growing colony was less dependent on convict labor and heavily dependent on slave labor. Indeed, once the slave trade was firmly established, the Cape authorities asked their superiors in Batavia to avoid sending convicts to the Cape, as they were an "expensive nuisance."[127] Notwithstanding such pleas, convicts continued to arrive at the Cape until the end of the Dutch East India Company's rule in 1795.[128] All Cape households had from the beginning of the colony the example of Company-sanctioned convict labor before them, used for tasks from the provision of salt to the removal of domestic excrement. In fact convict labor never ceased to be used in South Africa.

The racial mixing among convicts and political prisoners does not suggest a departure from the usual racial attitudes of the Dutch — far from it. Forcing European prisoners to live with low-status and enslaved groups was part of their punishment. For Europeans, only the most severe crimes — or insanity — warranted such a sentence. David Tappen, a scholar who was captured and forced to serve on a Dutch ship, described the South African Alcatraz on a return voyage from Batavia in 1682: "On the said Robben Island are set the rebellious rulers brought from the East Indies, where they must end their lives in very bad conditions, since very many of them who are now at the . . . [Cape] must now work like the . . . slaves for their living, and often get more kicks than ha'pence for their hard tasks such as carrying wood and stones, burning lime, etc. . . . To this Robben Island come not only the rebellious East India rulers and other black [*sic*] folk but also the rebellious Dutch are kept in slavery there for some years."[129]

A prisoner list, dispatched to Holland 5 September 1686, shows that although the prisoners had been given sentences of a given number of years, the records of their sentences were conveniently mislaid. In a note appended to Jacob van Macassar's name appeared these words: "the length of his banishment and his crime are not to be found."[130] Next to Arie van Bengal's name was the legend: "not

---

125 Simon A. de Villiers, *Robben Island: Out of Reach, Out of Mind* (Cape Town: Struik, 1971).

126 Leibbrandt, *Journal* (7 October 1705), p. 80; (12 October 1705), p. 81.

127 Leibbrandt, *Letters Despatched* (No. 56, 1 July 1699), p. 125.

128 CAD CJ 3318: "Bandiet Rollen," passim. The greatest number of convicts (Chinese) arrived in the 1740s to build the breakwater; ibid., pp. 400-457. On 7 October 1795 the Company had a list drawn up of the Asian convicts in the Lodge, ibid., n.p.

129 David Tappen, *Cape Good Hope, 1652–1702*, vol. 2, 242.

130 CAD C.501: "Letters Despatched, Lijste de geregelde Maccasarschen Princen en Groten en dieselven dienaren" (5 September 1686), folio 511.

found in the Company books."[131] These records disclose that sentences of convicts were quite commonly "mislaid." To be blended in with the slaves and then forgotten was clearly part of the punishment for convicts sent to the Cape. Jannas of Tagal wrote indignantly to the Council of Policy that he had been "now nineteen years in banishment here, while his sentence was 10 years."[132] Ripa Nagara wrote that he had arrived in the Company ship the *Herstelling* in 1723, "having been sent away by his brother from India to remain away as long as the latter lived, his brother is already dead sixteen years, but as yet he has not received back his liberty."[133] Slavery was also part of the punishment for these prisoners; many, whose records were "lost," became slaves for life.

The geographically isolated Cape was a perfect exile for overthrown political leaders from the Eastern possessions. At the top of the prisoner-slave hierarchy, for example, were a few important ex-sultans. Some were given the right to live quietly at the Cape with large retinues of slaves to attend to their creature comforts,[134] and they were never sent to Robben Island or to the Lodge. The lives of the other prisoner-slaves were grim. An important status distinction was whether the slave was wearing chains or not.[135] While some prisoner-slaves were put on Robben Island or sent to work on the Castle's moat or fortifications, and a few were exiled to remote Company outposts, most went to the Lodge.[136] Racial stereotypes operated even within this hierarchy, as well. For instance, Chinese prisoner-slaves in the Lodge had an especially dangerous job, building the breakwater; many died doing that work.[137]

---

[131] "Lijste . . . ," (5 September 1686), folio 509.

[132] Leibbrandt, *Requesten,* vol. 2, 605, (no. 33 of 1743).

[133] Leibbrandt, *Requesten,* vol. 1, 19, no. 77 of 1785; vol. 1, 374, no. 26 of 1743.

[134] Some of these political prisoner-slaves were only hostages of the Dutch and had been forgotten at the Cape; see "Daim Manjampa." If a prisoner-slave master died, his servant would remain at the Cape as a slave of the Dutch; for an example of such a "slave of a slave," see CAD C.501: "Rervat, servant of the deceased Carra Roepa . . ." in "Letters Despatched, Lijste . . ." (5 September 1686), folios 508 ff.; see also Robert C.-H. Shell, "The Establishment and Spread of Islam at the Cape from the Beginning of Company Rule to 1838," honors thesis, University of Cape Town, 1974, pp. 15–28.

[135] For example, see the phrase "*In de ketting gebannen*" (banned in chains) appended to Anthoin Nillam van 't Nalle and Franciscus van Mallebar. The type of crime that resulted in chaining was not one that our own notions of justice would recognize. Franciscus was in chains because of adultery, for example, see CAD C.501: "Letters Despatched, Lijste . . ." (5 September 1686), folio 509.

[136] Tappen as quoted in Raven-Hart, *Cape Good Hope,* vol. 2, 245; AR VOC 4030: "Generale Opneming . . . ," folios 359–367, recto and esp. folio 360 verso.

[137] CAD CJ 3318 and 3321: Roster of "Bannelinge and Banditti," passim, n.p.

Lodge Women and the Hierarchy of Work

Unlike the situation for slave women who were privately owned, there was no special place reserved for women in the Lodge. One could argue on grounds of sexual degradation that they were at the bottom of the Lodge hierarchy (see Chapter 10). The Lodge slave censuses disclose that the slave women were under the overall supervision of a male mandoor at their work places outside the Lodge.[138] In the Lodge itself, the women were under an equivalent authority figure, the *matres* — literally, a schoolmistress — who lived in a separate room strategically located next to the chamber set aside for the Lodge's schoolgirls. Her duties exceeded those of the traditional "schoolmarm," and matron seems a more appropriate term.[139] In the two references in which matrons are mentioned by name, it is clear that they enjoyed the same, or greater, privileges of manumission as the male mulatto mandoors. As mothers themselves, they also had children to free. Both matrons mentioned were also mulattos, and both were allowed to purchase and free their children. Armozijn van de Caab, the matron before 1711, was manumitted by Governor Willem Adriaan van der Stel because of good service; she asked the Company to free her daughter, Marie van de Caap, who was still in the Lodge.[140] The Company granted her request, but required that the slave girl work for the Company for three years before being sold to her mother at the price Lord van Reede had laid down in 1685 for all such mulatto slave children.[141] In August 1728 another matron, Christijn van de Caab, freed her 13-year-old child, Johanna Barbara van de Caab, before she raised the matter of her own freedom.[142]

Below the Lodge matron in the female hierarchy was the *ondermeesteress* (undermistress); these were also women of mulatto status.[143] Women in these supervisory positions somehow managed to obtain cash as well as their other customary perquisites. For example, the Company instantly freed Anna van Dapoer van de Caap, who had worked for "ten unbroken years" as an under-mistress in the Lodge, when on 23 September 1727 she presented as an item of exchange for her own freedom a male slave, Julij van de Kust, whom she had bought out of her own pocket for this purpose. The Company surgeon, Jan van Schoor, examined the slave and pronounced him "upstanding and healthy."[144]

---

138 AR VOC 4030: "Generale Opneming . . . ," folios 359–367, recto; CAD C.336, Attestaties: "Verklaring na gedane monsteringe . . . ," folios 457–475.
139 *Resolutions* (27 March 1717) vol. 5, 162.
140 *Resolutions* (3 April 1711), vol. 4, 203.
141 *Resolusies* (3 April 1711), vol. 4, 203.
142 *Resolutions* (31 August 1728), vol. 7, 440.
143 *Resolutions* (23 September 1727), vol. 7, 362.
144 CAD C.344, Attestatiën: (1727), folio 579.

Anna van Dapoer had to work another twelve years as a free woman, until 1739, before she had enough cash to free her children, Jan and Frans.[145]

This exchange system, the Cape equivalent of the Cuban *coartición*, entitled any slave to purchase freedom at a stated price.[146] But unlike the Cuban custom, the Cape Lodge practice usually involved an exchange of persons, rather than money (the Tiv in Nigeria always exchanged persons for persons; see Chapter 4). A Cape slave's chances for freedom were statutably greater if the slave were mulatto, of European descent.[147] The purchase price of an exchanged slave was high; such a slave might be worth four draft oxen and a wagon, or several horses.[148] Perhaps Lodge officials created an artificially high premium for exchange slaves, or the price included a bribe.

Each of two female slave officers, the last and lowest group in the Lodge's female administrative hierarchy, had an average of 79 "work-maidens" under her supervision, many more underlings than her counterpart officer-boy. Perhaps this suggests greater compliance among the Lodge women. Like her male counterpart, the female officer received more clothing than the other slave women. In addition, the women received bolts of linen, plus each officer, male and female, received a length of cotton cloth, which was presumably part of the general paternalist scheme of the Lodge.[149]

While male slaves lived according to strict army-style regulations, Lodge slave women lived in a family-control mode of slave management, but there was much overlapping. The family metaphor was amplified through the offices of external (European) "mothers" and internal (slave) "mothers."[150] External mothers were surrogate mothers outside the Lodge, usually European officials' wives, who perhaps served as ombudspersons, and sometimes advocates. In 1687, the Council of Policy appointed and charged four external mothers with seeing that the "maidens" (under 14) and "younger girls" (under 8) of the Lodge were well-mannered and skilled in the handicrafts of the "fatherland," specifically the sewing of linen and the making of woolen clothes.[151] Internal mothers looked after not

---

[145] Leibbrandt, *Requesten* (no. 3 of 1739/1740), 4.

[146] David W. Cohen and Jack P. Greene (eds.), *Neither Slave nor Free: The Freedman of African Descent in the Slave Societies of the New World* (Baltimore: Johns Hopkins University Press, 1972), pp. 25, 285.

[147] Van Reede in Böeseken, *Memoriën en Instructiën*, vol. 2, 205; see also A. Hulshof (ed.), "H. A. van Reede tot Drakenstein, Journaal van zijn verblijf aan de Kaap," *Bijdragen en Medelingen van het Historisch Genootschap* 62 (1941): 202 ff.

[148] For the equivalent prices, see the testament of Anna van Banchem, CAD MOOC (14 June 1726), 10/3/no. 57.

[149] CAD C.338, Attestatiën: "Winter Kleeding" (1 August 1719), folio 376.

[150] "*Binne*" and "*buijten*" mothers; *Resolutions* (23 June 1716), 5: 89. I am grateful to Anna J. Böeseken, whose help here has led to a fundamental revision of this section.

[151] *Resolutions* (15 September 1687) 3: 171. A month later the number of external mothers was increased to six, see *Resolutions* (23 October 1687) 3: 173–174.

only their own children but also other mothers' children housed in the Lodge crèche, and slave children who were patients in the Lodge hospital. When a slave child became sick, the biological mother, if at an outpost, would be called back and placed in the Company hospital with her child, but only if the child were seriously sick. According to the complete hospital records of 1710, 19 Lodge slave children were bed patients, yet only one mother was recalled from her work to look after her child.[152] The Company also consulted internal mothers about conditions in the Lodge, which suggests that they may have had some control over the other female slaves.[153] They did not, however, receive any extra rations.[154] It is doubtful that the position continued through the remainder of the eighteenth century; all we know is that the internal mothers disappear from the historical records.

The Company made few distinctions between the types of labor men and women could do. The Company had no hesitation in assigning Lodge slave women to the most grueling tasks. For example, at the Company mine at Silvermine (on the road to present-day Kommetjie), a mine that was worked around the clock,[155] a small undivided hut was set aside for the men and women slaves.[156] Women in contemporary England had proved efficient miners, because they could crawl through the narrow coal tunnels dragging carts by ropes between their legs without discomfort. The legend accompanying an illustration of Silvermine reveals that the Dutch made a distinction between the maximum number of Europeans (50) and slaves (150) who could safely be in the mine at one time, but no mention is made of women, a further indication that no gender deference was shown to Company slave women with regard to manual labor.[157]

The only evidence of gender differentiation for Lodge slave women was the Company's decision not to let them work in the Company hospital as nurses because of the "rough soldiers and sailors" there who were often afflicted with "Venus sickness (venereal disease)." Such nursing work was "wholly incompatible for a woman," the internal mothers had complained in a written request 10 February 1710.[158] The Council of Policy agreed, in response, to use fewer women in the hospital, but it did so on epidemiological grounds rather than from contemporary Dutch notions of gender deference.[159]

---

[152] AR VOC 4063: "Rolle van 's Compagnie Slaven die siek in't hospital leggen" (*sedert ultimo* August 1709 *tot* 9 May 1710), folio 837.

[153] *Resolutions* (23 June 1716), 5: 89.

[154] CAD C.338 (1 August 1719), folio 376; C.339 (6 or 16 October 1720), folio 253; C.339, (21 May 1721), folio 503.

[155] "*Bij daege en bij nagt.*"

[156] Hulshof, "Journaal . . . ," 148.

[157] AR: Kaartenafdeeling no. 813 "Model van een Bergwerck off Mijn" (1686); see also VOC 4022, folios 667–668.

[158] "*Geheel incompatibel voor een vrouws persoon*"; *Resolutions* (10 February 1710), 4: 131.

[159] *Resolutions* (23 June 1716), 5: 89.

Pairing of Men and Women in the Lodge

In the beginning of the colony, the Company's slave women were in a vastly different situation from slave women owned by private citizens. First, they were not under the direct domestic supervision of any settler or European official. Second, there were almost as many slave women as men in the Lodge, sometimes more. Indeed, until the French Huguenot families arrived in 1688 Lodge slave women outnumbered *all* the settler women. As a result of the high number of women in the Lodge, slave men always had a chance of finding a spouse among the inmates. As early as 1671, slave women in the Lodge, in contrast to their counterparts owned by settlers, who were not permitted to marry until 1823, could "be effectively married" to Lodge slave men. But there were no Dutch Reformed church weddings in the Lodge. One had to be baptized and freed before one could legally be married.[160] According to Commissioner Adriaan van Reede's carefully worded instructions issued in 1685, "[slave] man and wife were to be left together" and to be "married in their manner."[161] A slave couple who wished to be wed in this manner had to seek permission to be placed on the "marriage list." The official church of the colony never sanctioned or even recorded such slave marriages, and the mandated "lists" of such Company slave couples do not appear in the voluminous Company books or censuses of company slaves.[162] Scholars of the period have suggested that local officials regarded van Reede as an aristocratic busybody and all but ignored his heavily touted reforms.[163] Only one year after van Reede had left the colony, the local authorities were using the Dutch word *wijven* (female of the species) to describe these Company slave spouses and not the expected term *vrouwen*, the contemporary word for the settlers' wives. This is suggestive linguistic evidence that the unions were not considered to be in the same category.[164]

---

160 Isbrand Goske, "Memorie voor den E. Hr. Pieter Hackius" (1671), in Böeseken, *Memoriën en Instructiën*, pp. 101, 108, 208 for compulsory recording of slave marriages; *Resolutions*, 5: 162. These marriages were not official; they were not recorded in the marriage register, and who conducted the ceremony is a mystery. Only one other document refers to the married company slaves — significantly, only a few years after van Reede's visit; see CAD C.502: "Letters Despatched, Companje Slaven" (16 April 1688), folio 72.

161 Van Reede did mention in 1685 that Company slaves should unofficially marry other company slaves "after their own fashion" (op haar wijse), but that such couples should be warned that they could not marry another partner, "without danger of severe punishment"; Van Reede, in Böeseken, *Memoriën en Instructiën*, vol. 1, 205.

162 The Dutch Reformed Church archives recorded all company slave baptisms but no such slave "marriages"; DRCA, passim, 1652–1795.

163 Personal communication with Richard Elphick and James Armstrong.

164 Jeffreys and Naude, *Kaapse Plakkaatboek* (17 December 1686), vol. 1, 224; It is true that *wijf* could mean wife, but the word was not a true cognate; it was more properly a term for gender differentiation in the animal and plant kingdoms. In Afrikaans, the word came to have the latter as its leading sense; see J. Verdam, *Middel Nederlandsch Handwoordenboek*, s.v. *wijven*.

Getting on to one of these marriage lists also meant the slaves moved to new quarters, since the Lodge architecture was based on both gender and age (see Chapter 9). The "pairing" of slaves spilled over into the work place, too. Even the heaviest labor contingent on the general works in 1693, where one would expect to find a higher proportion of males (who were physically more capable of the heavy labor), suggests pairing: six mulatto men were listed next to seven mulatto women, while 60 full-breed men were listed next to 61 full-breed women. Thus, for each half-breed male slave there was one half-breed female slave; for each full-breed female slave there was one full-breed male. Only two extra "overlapping" women spoiled the otherwise perfect symmetry of pairing based on descent criteria. Whether further racial pairing was organized by the Company or the slaves themselves is unclear.

By 1792 the Lodge population had not had an infusion from the slave trade for almost a generation. The lack of replenishment and also the continuing high mortality in the Lodge had turned it into a virtual old-age home, with older inmates taking a familial interest in the few surviving young. In short, the Lodge had become an aging, communal, extended family. That, at any rate, was the opinion of the director of the Lodge, Christiaan Godlieb Höhne, who submitted a detailed report to the Council of Policy in that year:

Thirty six of the lodge slaves were incapable of doing any hard work owing to old age or physical disability; they were responsible for cleaning the lodge and nursing the small children. Some were in sick beds, others were about to become mothers. . . . Some of the aged and infirm Company's slaves . . . are totally blind and have to be led by the arm, and others are lame and must be carried. . . . Many are so weak or deformed that no outsider would care to be burdened with them; in the lodge . . . they received compassionate treatment. He himself had often beheld with great emotion how the younger slaves, never forgetting the days when they had been nurtured by these now aged folk, regarded them with deep affection and esteem, it was always a comfort to the young to know that they too, would be able to spend the evening of their lives in the sanctuary of the slave lodge.[165]

In 1795 there were no births at all in the Lodge.[166] This was the first year of the first British occupation. Perhaps because of the changing colony personnel, or perhaps because there were so few children, one Cape Lodge custom was dropped: no more Lodge slaves were baptized in the Dutch Reformed Church, since the Church of England did not require education of all baptized slaves. The school for Lodge slaves was not abandoned, however, as W. W. Bird recorded a Lodge schoolmaster being paid by the British Army.[167]

---

[165] The full text is in Cruse, *Opheffing van die Kleurlingbevolking*, pp. 214–221; also quoted in de Kock, *Those in Bondage*, pp. 37–38.

[166] DRCA G 1 4/34, "Bijlae."

[167] W. W. Bird, *State of the Cape*, Appendix P, 335.

The Lodge: An Old-Age Home, 1795–1828

When the creole slaves Eva (74) and Maria (73), both in the Lodge, rose on a December morning in 1824 to have their names registered in a census in the Lodge courtyard, they might have had cause to reflect that they were the oldest surviving women in the Lodge. They were older certainly than any man there, or *any* imported female slave. Only one 67-year-old male, who had possibly been one of their younger schoolmates, survived as long as these two women. Both women were invalids. What makes their biographies compelling is that their entire lives had been spent in that single building, a very bleak fate for any human being. They must have known each other as well as it possible to know another human being, and both would certainly have known every nook and cranny of the Lodge.

They were listed far apart on the census, but this need not indicate anything special. Eva had been born and baptized in 1750 and Maria in 1751. The Lodge population had been almost four times larger then and very much younger in its age profile than it was in 1824. In each of their respective birth years, many hundreds of Chinese convicts (*bandietten*) had been housed in the Lodge, people they would have grown up with and whose language they must have listened to with astonishment. The 1755 smallpox epidemic nearly emptied the Lodge of inmates and almost certainly carried away the parents of Eva and Maria. The pox did not harm the pair when it revisited the Lodge in 1767 and again in 1811, since they had both been immunized by the first epidemic. Approximately 60 children of mixed descent, including mulatto children, were in school at the Lodge in those years. The schoolmaster, Christoffel Stents, was the only manumitted slave to request to stay on at the Lodge after he won his freedom. Under his tutelage the students had learned the Dutch Reformed catechism and how to read and write.

From 1760 to 1764, Malagasy slaves had come into the Lodge. In 1771, nearly 100 slaves arrived from Bengal with a new language, and their new looks must have startled the 20-year-old women. Maria certainly remembered the year 1781, when Appolina, her only recorded child, was born. Two years after the 1824 census, another, more energetic, census taker recorded more details. Both women had aged faster than the calendar allowed: they were by appearance at least 83. Both were recorded, in the column registering "State of health," as "worn out." Their occupations were recorded as "invalid," and in the "Remarks" column, each was described as "not able to support herself."[168]

The Lodge was, in 1824, run entirely by the British military establishment for whom the Lodge had been a "prize" of their 1806 occupation. Richard Bourke, a British official responsible for the census and governor-to-be, wrote a letter to

---

[168] George McCall Theal, *Records of the Cape Colony* (London: Government Printers, 1905), "List of Government Slaves" (June 22, 1826), 26: 504–508.

Earl Bathurst to request that people like Eva and Maria be treated well: "I submit to your Lordship the propriety of . . .continuing the use of the Lodge as a Hospital of charity to those sickly and worn out Individuals, who are not capable of labour. . . . It is proposed that the expense of supporting the old and infirm slaves should continue to be borne, as at present, by the Military Chest."[169] The Lodge, although still run on army lines, had ceased to function as a labor source in all senses.

A *Military Model of Control for Men, a Family Model for Women*

The Lodge chain of command running from the *onderbaasen* through the man-doors and down to the officer-boys, comes close to Blassingame's "army" model for a plantation slave society, but it must be remembered this was an urban group. What makes the Lodge distinctive is how finely drawn the hierarchy was, and how descent and origin were so smoothly and systematically interwoven as boundaries demarcating the upper and lower echelons.

To the Company mulattos went most of the benefits of the system: extra clothing, less unpleasant work — skilled, or semi-skilled jobs, or supervisory roles — and, most important to a slave, greatly enhanced chances of winning legal freedom.[170] The Company slaves were ranked first by gender, racial descent, creole status, and then by place of origin. Mulatto slaves were always above the other slaves in the Cape hierarchy and enjoyed privileges analogous to those of an army officer class. Attributions based on the origins of the slaves gradually transmuted into simpler group attributions, and by the 1740s both territorial and descent classifications were absorbed into overarching ranked racial and descent stereo-types, but this was not unique to the Cape. Much of the same racial stereotyping occurred throughout all of the possessions of the Dutch East India Company,

---

[169] *RCC,* "Bourke to Earl Bathurst," (June 22 1826), 26: 494–495.

[170] Scholars of comparative slavery have often pointed out the inadequacy of using manumission as an index of mildness of treatment, noting, for example, that often slave owners manumitted their slaves not for humanitarian motives — as Frank Tannenbaum, the father of comparative slavery, implied — but to get rid of them once they were too old to work. Without abandoning manumission as a key area of inquiry, a further qualification of the Tannenbaum interpretation of manumission emerges at the Cape: the company manumitted half-breed Company slaves simply because of racial arrogance. Some high-ranking Dutch officials consid-ered it unpalatable that miscegenated descendants of Europeans were enslaved. For an illuminat-ing discussion of the overall topic, see Eugene D. Genovese, "The Treatment of Slaves in Different Countries: Problems in the Applications of the Comparative Method," in Eugene D. Genovese and Laura Foner (eds.), *Slavery in the New World: A Reader in Comparative History* (Englewood Cliffs, N.J.: Prentice Hall, 1969), pp. 202–210.

where certain groups of slaves were traditionally thought to be especially suited for specific occupations. Under the British, the origins of the Lodge slaves continued to be recorded. The primacy of European descent in the social hierarchy was not unique to either Dutch or British South Africa, but European descent privileges did become more deeply entrenched in South Africa than elsewhere. Other Dutch colonial settlements never developed significantly large European settler populations with the numerical muscle and economic and political-military power to establish a similar social order. At the Lodge, there were Europeans in charge, but they did not live in the Lodge. Women and children within the Lodge struggled to live with as much dignity as possible. A few established relationships with local settlers and soldiers and thereby obtained their freedom. Even without such a liaison, the principal responsibility of all Lodge women was to their children, whom they always tried to free. For the Lodge women the family was beset with a bewildering variety of constraints, but even in the twilight of the Lodge, women organized themselves around a nucleus of family governance and caring for the young. This attitude, as noted by officials, pervaded the entire Lodge compound and, to a certain extent, must have softened the nasty, brutish, and hierarchical reality of Lodge life. The Lodge slaves were freed in 1828 along with the Khoi serfs. Even at the end, the Lodge was to serve as an example to the settlers, who were facing the first rumblings of the general emancipation.

SEVEN

The Metaphor of Family
The Management of Involuntary Labor

ALL INVOLUNTARY LABOR is based ultimately on violence. This is an obvious but inadequate explanation for how slave societies worked. All slave owners everywhere needed special strategies to manage and control their involuntary workers, and there were as many methods of management and control as there were slave societies. Most slave societies actually used several types of management simultaneously. At the Cape, patrician local officials managed male Lodge slaves by using a military system. The same officials managed their own slaves at home by using paternalism. The farmers and frontier-bound *trekboers* came closest to using patriarchal control, with violence more in the foreground. But all systems (including the Lodge) had aspects of familial control.[1]

For Cape settlers on their isolated farmsteads and in their urban holdings, the security provided by the Dutch East India Company's military personnel was not always enough. Nor could the typical Cape settlers use a draconian "army" model of slave control like the one so effectively employed in the Company's Lodge or, indeed, on the large plantations of Zanzibar, the Caribbean, Brazil, or the American South. The naïve neoabolitionist view, which some still hold, that Cape slavery depended principally on whips and chains, is an insufficient answer to the question of control.[2] Power did not come only from the barrel of a gun or the tip of a whip. Physical coercion alone, so universally associated with involuntary labor, can never explain why slavery worked in South Africa.

---

[1] Since women often managed slaves and serfs, paternalism seems too gendered a term.

[2] Cf. Nigel Anthony Worden, *Slavery in Dutch South Africa* (Cambridge: Cambridge University Press, 1985), p. 106, where he writes, "The corporal punishment of slaves was the most common form of control. By inducing fear of pain, masters obtained co-operation, albeit grudgingly"; see also Robert Ross, who writes, "The social system of slavery was kept in being by the continual threat of rigorous punishment. It is as if the machine of production required to be oiled by the blood flogged out of the slaves' backs," in Ross, *Cape of Torments: Slavery and Resistance in South Africa* (London: Routledge and Kegan Paul, 1983), pp. 32–33.

Violence at the Cape: The Universal Backstop

Chains, whips, fetters, and rhinoceros-hide whips called *sjamboks*[3] were used not only on slaves, but also on the Europeans and the Khoi. This was so from the beginning of the colony. In 1705, Jan Pietersz Roltz van Amsterdam, a Dutch East India Company sailor who was an overseer on the farm of Jan de Long in the Drakenstein district, was found guilty of desertion, was sentenced to be "beaten by the Caffers [slave policemen from the Lodge], to be locked in chains, and to work for six months without pay."[4] Also in that year Jochem Hartman Frank van Holstein, a European, was found guilty of stealing carrots from the Cape Town garden of Lambert Adriaanus and was sentenced to run the gauntlet, composed of the entire garrison, three times. In addition, he was sentenced to spend five years in chains on Robben Island (the penal colony at the Cape).[5] European Company personnel who ran afoul of the law were thrashed and chained as well. According to Samuel Hudson, under the British administration at the Cape after 1795 similarly severe corporal punishment was meted out to British soldiers.[6] In fact, the whole society was based on violence, and slaves were part of that society.

Khoi men and women accused of a crime were, initially, tried and sentenced by their own leaders, even when the crime had been committed against the settlers. But this practice of self-government and indirect rule changed in 1671, when Sara, a Khoi girl, committed suicide, an act the Dutch authorities deemed an offense against the European laws of the colony. Her memory was therefore suitably dishonored: her corpse was dragged through the streets and exposed on a forked post as "food for the birds." After that precedent, the Cape court passed its own sentences on Khoi criminals, including "thrashing, branding, and periods of forced labor up to fifteen years."[7] Corporal punishment was never exclusive to slavery at the Cape.

Ironically, from the earliest introduction of slaves into the colony in the 1650s, slaves were the only group specifically protected by statute from being whipped and chained. In 1658, the cat-o'nine-tails was forbidden on land, only to

---

[3] *Sjambok*, a Malay word, originally Urdu, was what the slaves called the infamous Cape instrument of corporal punishment. A *sjambok* is a strong and heavy whip, about four feet in length, made of solid rhinoceros or hippopotamus hide; it was also used for driving cattle. As of 1985, the *sjambok* was still in wide use in South Africa.

[4] AR VOC 4053: "Processtukken" (13 January 1705), folios 657 and verso.

[5] "*Om door het guarnisoens volk driemal door de spitsgarde te loopen*"; AR VOC 4053: "Processtukken" (begun 27 December 1704), folios 487 ff. and verso.

[6] SAL manuscript: Samuel E. Hudson, "Memorandums and Occurrences," p. 10.

[7] Richard Elphick, *Kraal and Castle: Khoikhoi and the Founding of South Africa* (New Haven: Yale University Press, 1977), p. 184.

be used on slave ships.[8] In the beginning, severe punishment was reserved for *equals*, and for *men*. Dutch authorities limited punishment of privately owned slaves to "domestic correction," the same type of punishment a husband and father could apply to his wife and children, individuals not equal to him in status. No punishment could legally be used against slaves that was not one that would be meted out to the women and children of the immediate family. Chains and whips were forbidden. The wording of the relevant statute is clear: "The owner is allowed, in the case of a slave making a mistake, to correct such a slave with domestic punishment, it is not permitted to set a slave in irons, or worse, to torture or otherwise maltreat the slave."[9] The slave was not seen as an adult, and male slaves were never seen as men. Slaves, like everybody else at the Cape, were whipped when it was deemed necessary, but the Company reserved this executive right for itself alone; others were under pain of heavy penalties. Slave owners who whipped slaves were interrogated and punished by the Company officials as the following dialogue drawn from a three-day interrogation of slave owner, Christiaan Gottlieb Opperman, in 1731 illustrates:

> Question: "Have you not lived long enough in this place to know that no master is permitted to inflict on a slave anything other than a mild punishment [*matige kastyding*] and that blood must never be drawn?"
> Answer: "Yes, that I know very well, but the slave boy was only mildly punished."[10]

Accused of a sadistic intent towards his slave, this slave owner acknowledged that he had forced his slave to tread acorns in a bucket for three hours. He defended his actions on two grounds: the punishment was "mild," and it was, he explained, a typical punishment of children in Germany: "Treading acorns is merely a child's chastisement, for in Germany even the smallest children are made to kneel upon stones as punishment in school."[11] Three months after the Opperman case, all the laws against "barbaric treatment and striking of slaves" were repeated in a comprehensive statute.[12]

Such laws were by no means dead letters. At the same time that Samuel Johnson, in London, was musing about how in America the "loudest whelps for liberty" were coming from "the drivers of negroes," this legal restraint was a prominent and heartfelt grievance for Cape settlers in the "patriot uprising" of 1779. In that year, the local "patriots" directly petitioned the executives of the

---

[8] Kathleen M. Jeffreys and S. D. Naude (eds.), *Kaapse Plakkaatboek, 1652–1806* (Cape Town: Kaapse Argiefstukke, 1944–1949), vol. 1, p. 37 (28 August 1658).

[9] "*Domestijke straffe*"; J.A. van der Chijs (comp.), *Nederlandsch-Indisch Plakkaatboek, 1602–1811* ('s-Gravenhage: M. Nijhoff, 1885), vol. 1, p. 573.

[10] AR VOC 4117: (15 May 1731), folio 834 verso.

[11] AR VOC 4117 (16 August 1731), folio 859.

[12] Jeffreys and Naude, *Kaapse Plakkaatboek*, s.v. "Mishandeling van Slawe" (10 July 1731), vol. 2, 149–150.

Dutch East India Company in Holland for the right "to allow the settlers to punish their slaves themselves."[13]

Some evidence suggests that owners who took the law into their own hands and used harsh methods excessively were not only punished by the Company but were also frowned upon and shunned by the Cape society as a whole. Examples of such notoriously cruel owners were Michael Otto and Gottlieb Opperman, both well established as disliked persons in the colony. As Cape historian Wayne Dooling has pointed out, there was a well-developed moral community of slave owners at the Cape.[14] When Opperman, a German brewer, was found guilty of murdering his slave in 1731, the court granted his wife a divorce. This was a rare domestic excommunication. He was barred from the conjugal company of his wife with the phrase "a separation of board and bed." He was barred from seeing his children. Finally, the court stipulated that slaves who had borne witness against their master were never to come "under the thrall of any member of the former family."[15] Such actions by the Company officials, especially after a slave fatality at the hands of a careless, sadistic master, were stern reminders to owners not to mistreat their slaves. If the owner did so, all the slaves in his or her holding could be forfeited — as they indeed sometimes were.[16]

Maltreated slaves could also bring complaints before the Fiscal, the third-in-command in the colony and the official protector of slaves during the Dutch period.[17] In 1731, a wealthy free black man, Robert Scott of Bengal, who used chains on his female slaves "on private authority," was brought to book on a

---

[13] André du Toit and Herman Giliomee, *Afrikaner Political Thought: Analysis and Documents, 1780–1850* (Cape Town: David Philip, 1983), p. 255, article 6.

[14] Wayne Dooling, "Law and Community in a Slave Society: Stellenbosch District, c. 1760–1820," M.A. thesis, University of Cape Town, 1991; Otto Friederich Mentzel, *A Complete and Authentic Geographical and Topographical Description . . .* , trans. G. V. Marais and J. Hoge, rev. ed. (Cape Town: Van Riebeeck Society, 1944), vol. 3, p. 110.

[15] "*Skeiding van tafel en bed*"; see J. Hoge, "Personalia of the Germans at the Cape, 1652–1806" *Archives Year Book* 9 (1946): 303. Hoge claims that the wife petitioned for divorce because Opperman was mistreating her and her children; Opperman died in the year following the divorce.

[16] AR VOC 4117: "Dictum ter Rolle" (27 October 1731), folios 911–912 verso. It should be noted that no slave owner at the Cape in the Dutch period was ever put to death for the murder of a slave, no matter how compelling the evidence. This changed in 1824 when Lord Charles Somerset, the governor, confirmed the death sentence of Willem Gebhardt, who had killed a slave. Gebhardt, like Opperman, based his defense on manslaughter. What especially galled the colonists was that the prosecutor's case was based on slave testimony. Richard L. Watson, *The Slave Question: Liberty and Property in South Africa* (Hanover: Wesleyan University Press, 1990), p. 25.

[17] Bird, *State of the Cape of Good Hope in 1822* (Cape Town: Struik, 1966 reprint), pp. 16–17, et seq.

complaint brought to the Fiscal's attention by Scott's own slave women.[18] Ninety-nine years later, chains were still illegal: in 1830 Spatie, a 38-year-old slave born at the Cape, complained to the Protector of Slaves that her master, J. D. Cilliers, had fastened her with a chain placed around her neck, in which state she remained from 11 o'clock in the morning until the evening. The owner was fined 5 pounds, a small fee, but embarrassing.[19]

There were also material interests for the slave owner to consider in resorting to physical punishment as a means of control. A serious beating could incapacitate a slave. The death of a slave resulted in the loss of valuable property. Even losing a single slave might entail an owner's financial ruin. Mentzel recalled just such a case: "The last slave that Michael Otto lost because of brutal punishment had been a wagon-maker's apprentice, for whom he had paid a thousand florins. It was the loss of this man that put the idea in his mind of getting rid of his farm and of drinking away his money."[20]

Incapacitated free labor, on the other hand, could always be replaced cheaply. In this cynical but no doubt correct view, the expensive slave was the least likely of all servants to be whipped or maltreated. These sentiments remained in force until the nineteenth century,[21] when Samuel Hudson, an immigrant English slave owner noted: "Many instances of cruelty [to slaves] have been brought to light, even murder, but in a colony like the Cape of Good Hope they are not very common. A man's interest is too much concerned, and the loss of a slave is of very serious consequence to him. Therefore their treatment is made subservient to their dear interest from no motive of humanity or honoribility."[22]

Instead of being driven by whips, many slaves at the Cape, especially shep-herds and cattle herders, worked without direct supervision at all. Travelers in the interior invariably expressed astonishment at finding solitary slaves in charge of distant holdings. They pointed out slaves who displayed great ingenuity in farm management, and recorded stories of slaves who had jurisdiction over other free servants. Anders Sparrman, a Swede who had few good words for Dutch slave owners, wrote in the 1770s that "It was curious to see how the only slave that was then at Zaffraan-craal, and *who had the absolute management of the farm*, how

---

18 Van der Chijs, *Nederlandsch-Indisch Plakkaatboek*, vol. 1, 573; "*op prive authoriteijt*," AR VOC 4117: "Dictum ter Rolle" (27 October 1731), folio 911; see also Jeffreys and Naude, *Kaapse Plakkaatboek* (6 August 1658), vol. 1, 36–37.

19 PRO CO 53/50: "Slave Protectors' Reports" (3 May 1830), No 25.

20 Mentzel, *Description*, vol. 3, 49. Christiaan Gottlieb Opperman had all his slaves confiscated because he had maltreated one, see AR VOC 4117: "Eijsch en Conclusie" (12 July 1731), folios 810 verso and 811.

21 Henry Lichtenstein, *Travels in Southern Africa* (Cape Town: Van Riebeeck Society, 1930), vol. 1, 74–75.

22 Robert C.-H. Shell (ed.), "'Slaves,' an Essay by Samuel Eusebius Hudson," *Kronos* 9 (1984): 53.

skillfully, I say, with the assistance of two hottentots who dwelt not far from the place, he had brought the water in rills or channels down to the fields of wheat as well as to the garden and had made dams at these places, so that they may be overflowed and water, whenever it was requisite, by which means they appeared clad with a delightful verdure."[23] As Otto Mentzel pointed out, any harsh punishment could induce such slaves to run away.[24]

Comparative evidence suggests that Cape slaves were not unique in this regard. In early South Carolina, for example, slaves looked after extensive cattle ranches without supervision. Peter Wood, a historian of South Carolina, believes that the American institution of the independent "cowboy" may owe its etymology to the Carolinian practice of employing unsupervised West African slaves as cowhands. These slaves knew how to ride horses from their cattle-ranching experience on the West African savannas.[25] Farming techniques such as intercropping might similarly have been introduced into the American South from Africa by enslaved Africans. If violence had been the principal or universal method of ensuring slave obedience, such initiative on the part of slaves would have seemed strange, and innovations would have been unthinkable. Whips and chains did not force the Carolinian slaves to stay on their ranches, nor did physical sanctions force the Cape slave to devise irrigation schemes. In short, hegemonic power on the slave holding was expressed in a variety of other ways. In the small slave distributions of the Cape, violence was the last resort and indicated a temporary and dramatic failure of paternalism.

Some Cape masters did, nevertheless, whip their slaves. There is no systematic evidence as to whether bondsmen were whipped more often than the autochthonous Khoi workers or the European indentured servants. In general, whips and chains were used as a final resort. Violent death was the ultimate punishment for slaves, but also for free persons. In this light, scholarly debates about "whipping indices" and such seem beside the point in analyzing Cape slavery.[26] Neither corporal punishment nor the threat of death was reserved for slaves alone.

---

[23] Anders Sparrman, *A Voyage to the Cape of Good Hope . . .*, ed. Vernon Forbes (Cape Town: Van Riebeeck Society Second Series, No. 7, 1977), vol. 1, p. 274 (emphasis added); see also vol. 1, 73 (1986 edition).

[24] Mentzel, *Description*, vol. 3, 110.

[25] This would explain why the word *cowboy* has a *boy* (that is, *slave*) suffix rather than the expected *-man*. Cf. Peter H. Wood, *Black Majority: Negroes in South Carolina, from 1670 through the Stono Rebellion* (New York: Norton, 1975), pp. 30–32; see note 58.

[26] For a provocative discussion of this topic, see Robert Fogel and Stanley Engerman, *Time on the Cross*, 2 vols. (Boston: Little, Brown, 1975), pp. 144–147; and for dissenting views see also Paul A. David, et al. *Reckoning with Slavery: A Critical Study in the Quantitative History of American Negro Slavery* (New York: Oxford University Press, 1976), pp. 57–69, 91–93; Herbert G. Gutman, *Slavery and the Numbers Game: A Critique of Time on the Cross* (Urbana: University of Illinois Press, 1975), pp. 18–41.

The chains of slavery were, in the main, psychological — a more subtle but no less certain, form of cruelty. Slavery was not one whit more "benign" because of this, only more complicated and cynical. As Emmanuel Kant said, "Paternalism is the cruelest tyranny." The toleration that most slaves showed for the paternalism of their masters was not an indication that they accepted their subservient status as just, nor does it support a "moonlight and magnolias" interpretation of slavery. Eugene Genovese has specifically denied this: "[The slaves'] acceptance of paternalism allowed them, even in so unjust a relationship, to perceive that they had rights, which the whites could trample on only by committing a specific act of injustice. The practical question facing the slaves was not whether slavery itself was a proper relation but how to survive with the greatest degree of self determination."[27]

South African slaves had been coerced into slavery, but there were alternatives, albeit hard to achieve. For example, they could run away to one of the maroon societies at Faure, Hanglip, and on Table Mountain itself. Several small, stable maroon societies in the colony offered succor to runaway slaves, and these havens survived throughout the period. The 60-slave Hanglip community who lived in a cave, which Robert Ross, the Cape historian, delineated so well, lasted for a century, virtually undisturbed until slavery ended in 1834 (see Figure 7-1).[28] Runaways could also choose to quit the colony entirely, or they could join the Griquas, a frontier group of natives, runaway slaves, and renegade settlers. Slaves also from time to time engaged in small revolts.[29]

Alternative societies and the option of rebellion did thus exist for the minority who could not, or would not, accept their position in the paternalistic slaveholding society, but most male slaves and nearly all female slaves did accede to the paternalism imposed by their masters. There were, after all, risks to running away. Commandos searched them out, rewards were offered, and punishments inflicted. Probably the biggest risk was death itself. The arid and inhospitable terrain offered few secure hiding places. The South African system of slavery evolved without serious challenge, as did most slave societies, with the solitary exception of Haiti.

Slave owners, some of them immigrants with no colonial experience of slavery, devised a system in which the culturally diverse Cape slave population

---

[27] Eugene D. Genovese, *Roll, Jordan, Roll: The World the Slaves Made* (New York: Vintage Books, 1976), p. 125, the "moonlight-and-magnolia" reference is on page 123. See also T. E. J. Wiedemann, "Slavery," no. 19 in *Greece and Rome, New Surveys in the Classics* (Oxford: The Clarendon Press, 1987), p. 48, where he writes of ancient slavery: "This emphasis on violent resistance [in slave studies] runs the risk of masking the fact that most slaves, most of the time, accepted their situation."

[28] Shell, "'Slaves,' an Essay by Samuel Eusebius Hudson," 62–63; and Ross, *Cape of Torments*, 54–72; author's own photograph.

[29] Several revolts were betrayed at the last minute by fellow slaves; Ross, *Cape of Torments*, 4 and passim.

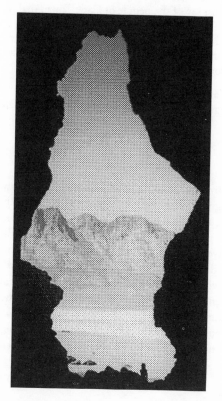

Figure 7–1. The runaways' cave, Hanglip.

could work efficiently, without excessive reliance on physical punishment. With relatively few slaves to manage in the typical holdings, the type of discipline had to be more subtle and flexible than the blunt military system used by the officials in the Company Lodge, who *did* control slaves through physical coercion, deprivation, and degradation. The Cape experience of slavery suggests that the size of the holding greatly influenced the mode of management. Larger holdings relied on more physical sanctions; the smaller holdings on fewer. Since most slave holdings at the Cape were small, family management was a much more subtle and more appropriate means of control than physical punishment would have been. There were also pronounced regional and racial components to the type of control exerted. This was apparent to travelers, as Robert Percival wrote in 1804:

The treatment of the different classes of slaves at the Cape is by no means the same. The domestic slaves at Cape Town live equally happy as our own [British] servants, and only retain the name of slaves. . . . Far different is the case of the poor

Negro, Cafre, and African slaves, who are employed at hard labour, and out of their houses; but I must say of the people of Cape Town, that they treat them well in comparison to the farmers and planters of the country parts. . . . With respect to the punishing and chastising of slaves, those unfortunate creatures belonging to the Country Dutch are at the mercy of their lords and masters and are often beaten most unmercifully for the slightest fault.[30]

A chorus of 1,000 slave women reported that by far the most violence (at least in the years before emancipation) was on agricultural holdings (see Figure 7-2).[31]

The Family as Metaphor

Cape slave owners, by incorporating slaves into their family government were not inventing something new. They were invoking an ancient institution, the Roman family; the Cape equivalent came to have much in common with the Roman *familia*. Friedrich Engels pointed out that this social unit of the family originally included all the slaves belonging to the head of the household: "The original meaning of the word "family" (*familia*) is not that compound of sentimentality and domestic strife which forms the ideal of today's philistine; among the Romans it did not at first even refer to the married pair and their children, but only to the slaves. *Famulus* means domestic slave, and *familia* is the total number of slaves belonging to one man. . . . The term family was invented by the Romans to denote a new social organism whose head ruled over wife and children and a number of slaves."[32]

As late as 1688, this sense of the word *family* was used by Gregory King, the

---

[30] Captain Robert Percival, *An Account of the Cape of Good Hope* (New York: Negro Universities Press, 1969 reprint), pp. 292–293.

[31] Rachel van der Voort, "Daughters of Bondage," senior thesis, History Department, Princeton University, 1993, Appendix 1. Based on PRO CO "Slave Protector's Reports" (1831–1834), all recorded occupations (N = 401). The line drawing is from John Barrow, *Travels into the Interior of Southern Africa, in Which Are Described the Character and the Condition of the Dutch Colonists . . .* 1st ed. 2 vols. (London: J. Lee, Cadell, 1802). All subsequent editions appeared without this picture. All first editions I have ever seen have this picture, the frontispiece, torn out. The only extant copy is in the Library of Parliament, Cape Town. I am grateful to the librarian for permission to reproduce here. The caption to the original is critical to my interpretation. "The Dutch mode of punishing the Hottentot Slaves by flogging them till he has smoaked as many pipes of tobacoo as he might judge the magnitude of the crime to deserve." The person being flogged is *not* a formal slave, but a native serf. The use of pipes of tobacco as timing devices dates back to the time before pocket watches. Fiscals in the Dutch Indonesian possessions used pipes for public floggings as early as 1619. The owner, in the shade, considered this beating a four pipe problem.

[32] Friedreich Engels, *Der Ursprung der Familie des Privat-eigenthoms und des Statts* (Zurich: Hottingen, 1884), p. 33 (my translation).

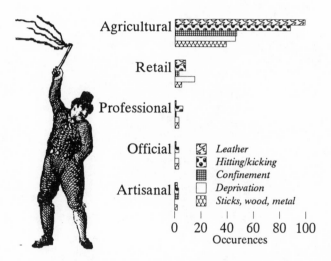

Figure 7–2. Occupational and regional aspects of slave owner violence, 1830 to 1834.

English statistician, in his compilation of the British population, to denote servants and retainers as well as kin.[33] The Dutch shared this sense in their own cognate word, *familie*. In the first quarter of the eighteenth century, Pierre Rousseau, a wealthy magistrate of the Drakenstein district, signed a contract with a school teacher, Gerrit Daveman, stipulating that "Daveman was obliged to teach his entire family up to and including his slaves."[34] This sense of "family," as an institution that included slaves and servants in the immediate household, provided the Cape slave owner with the most effective means of managing his slaves (see Figure 7-3).[35]

In the colonies, where ecclesiastical and secular institutions were yet undeveloped and weak, the family took on added importance. It filled the voids created by the transplanting of a society. The household provided, for slaves who had been uprooted from their own culture and kin, the only "home" there was. The slave

---

[33] Gregory King, *Natural and Political Observations upon the State and Condition of England,* as quoted in Dorothy George, *England in Transition* (London: Pelican, 1969), p. 10.

[34] "*Mits dat hij gehouden zal zijn . . . zijn geheele Familie tot Slaaven daaronder begreepen als Schoolmeester te moeten onderwijzen*" quoted in J. Hoge, "Privaatskoolmeesters . . . ," *Annals of the University of Stellenbosch* 19: 26.

[35] This patrician family portrait, painted on the top of a Cape Town flat-roofed house, shows the slaves and the children in the same plane — the background of the family. Courtesy Stellenbosch Museum.

Figure 7–3. The Graaf Family, 1762.

remained, in all civic and legal matters, an outsider, but the slave owner always insisted that the slave was part of the family, which was presented to the slave as a poor but tangible consolation.[36]

The State and the Family

Colonial authorities went to sometimes eccentric lengths to foster the institution of the family. In colonial Massachusetts, for example, bachelors were rounded up to form wholly artificial "families" — families without women![37] Later in New

[36] For the Cape there is no treatment of the legal status of slaves like A. Leon Higginbotham's *In the Matter of Color: Race and the American Legal Process* (New York: Oxford University Press, 1978). However, we can rely on the summary of the old Cape laws drawn up in the nineteenth century by the Fiscal D. Denijssen, see George McCall Theal, *Records of the Cape Colony* (London: Government Printers, 1905; hereafter *RCC*): "Statement of the Laws of the Colony of the Cape of Good Hope regarding slavery" (16 March 1813), 9: 146–161; and the general *placcaaten*, which regulated the everyday activities of all in the colony, see Jeffreys and Naude, *Kaapse Plakkaatboek*.

[37] Edmund S. Morgan, *The Puritan Family: Religion and Domestic Relations in Seventeenth Century New England* (New York: Harper & Row, 1966), p. 144.

England an attempt was made to place all single people in family homes.[38] In colonial South Africa, the Company maintained detailed lists of free, single European men,[39] and Company clerks (called "soldiers-at-the-pen") closely monitored their lives until they were safely married. These lists, of persons assumed to be potentially unstable characters — "singletons," as they were dubbed — were kept as a security measure.[40]

Since colonial authorities at the Cape viewed the family as the bedrock of the society and the economy, persons outside the orbit of the family were subjected to official scrutiny and nudged into some kind of family setting. There were no orphanages in the colony until 1815, and free orphans were carefully placed with families. A colonial institution, the Orphan Chamber, came into being in the seventeenth century to protect the interests of all free orphans. The upkeep of such orphans was paid by the Church council (the *Diaconij*).[41] For a time, the Dutch East India Company also imported young women from orphanages in Rotterdam to form families at the Cape,[42] just as the Virginia Company, in a similar impulse, had considered importing women to Virginia.[43] The authorities in both colonial America and colonial South Africa independently considered the family to be an essential ingredient for a well-ordered society. Orphanhood for slaves was not recognized, because orphaned slaves belonged to the paterfamilias.

Elements of family government were subconsciously fused into the everyday language of the time. One cannot accurately interpret the society without recognizing that the dominant metaphor of Cape colonial life was the family. This is also what Emmanuel Le Roy Ladurie, the French social historian, has termed the

---

[38] Morgan, *The Puritan Family*, 145.

[39] AR VOC 4032: "Rolle der vrijluiden die bij anderen in dienst, als mede die voor de kost en ook buijten dienst gehuijsvest zijn te weeten" (31 December 1693), folios 233–236.

[40] "*Eenlopendes*"; AR: Radermacher Collection, no. 507, "Letters of Jan de la Fontaine" (30 January 1732) and Appendices. In a sample — using a random number generator — of 202 free men in 1731, it was found that 23 percent of the singletons (*eenlopendes*) never married nor acquired property in freehold or loan; see Leonard Guelke and Robert C.-H. Shell, "An Early Colonial Landed Gentry: Land and Wealth in the Cape Colony, 1682–1731" *Journal of Historical Geography* 9, 3 (1983): 283, note 37.

[41] Incidentally, such payments were prorated by the "race" of the child: thus free black orphans received half the support that free European orphans did. This racial dispensation was decided on in 1705; see Maria M. Marais, "Armesorg aan die Kaap onder die Kompanjie, 1652–1795," *Archives Year Book* 1 (1943): 61–62; see the clear example in C. Spoelstra, *Bouwstoffen . . .* (Amsterdam: Hollandsch-Afrikaansche Uitgewers-Maatscappij, 1906–1907), vol. 2, 275. Marais' conclusions (p. 64) attempt to gloss over this point.

[42] George McCall Theal, *History of South Africa*, (Cape Town: Struik, 1964) vol. 3, pp. 315–316.

[43] Sigmund Diamond, "From Organization to Society: Virginia in the Seventeenth Century" in Stanley N. Katz ed., *Colonial America: Essays in Politics and Social Development* (Boston: Little, Brown, 1971), p. 22.

"*Domus*" — the home.[44] The family was used as a trope in all aspects of colonial life. Thus, Holland was termed the "fatherland"[45]; even male nurses were "sickness-fathers" (*siekevaders*)[46]; female slave nurses were "sickness-mothers" (*siekemoeders*)[47]; surrogate slave mothers in the Lodge were termed "inside mothers" (*binne-moeders*), surrogate mothers (free women) outside the Lodge were termed "outside mothers" (*buiten-moeders*), and so on.[48] The language of the period was shot through with such references.

The passage written in 1687 makes no sense to someone not aware of how important family and domesticity were to the seventeenth- and eighteenth-century Cape mentality: "Further to the service of the Company, it is understood that the outside and inside mothers [of the Lodge] should be apprised that the slave girls and daughters of this place are to become fully familiar with all the fatherland's handicrafts . . . and should be placed in the home of a council member there to learn such trades.[49]

In the seventeenth century, the Cape family was only beginning to evolve; nevertheless, there is compelling evidence that the Cape *familia* was, even as early as the 1690s, a well-established institution. Slave women themselves were the first to acknowledge — at least on the surface — this mode of management, while male slaves sometimes rejected it outright (despite what it cost them). On a Friday evening in March 1692, a slave girl, Marie of the Coast of Coromandel, was working in the kitchen with her mistress, Catherina Everts van der Zee, on a market-garden farm at Wittebome (near present-day Wynberg), when a household slave, Claas van Mallebar, passed through the kitchen on his way to chop wood in the yard. Mistress Catherina scolded Claas for not fetching the cows in time for her baking and refused to believe his excuse that he had been on the mountain looking for them. Whereupon Claas turned and spat out: "You old dog, go and fetch them yourself!"[50] Catherina attempted to strike Claas, but he lifted his axe and buried the weapon in her neck. The fatal blow, according to the surgeon's report, almost

[44] Emmanuel Le Roy Ladurie, *Montaillou: Cathars and Catholics in a French Village, 1294–1324* (Paris: Penguin, 1980), p. 24.

[45] CAD C.502: "Letters despatched, Cape to Patria," (18 April 1687), pp. 336–337; Anna J. Böeseken et al. (eds.), *Suid-Afrikaanse Argiefstukke: Resolusies van die Politieke Raad* (Cape Town: Cape Times, 1957–1975; hereafter *Resolutions*), vol. 3, p. 171 (15 September 1687); ibid., vol. 3, 256 (Monday, 16 June 1692).

[46] *Resolutions* (23 June 1716), vol. 5, 88; CAD C.337, "Attestaties:" (20 February 1717): 49–50.

[47] *Resolutions* (30 March 1717), vol. 5, 162.

[48] *Resolutions* (Saturday, 28 June 1687), vol. 3, 167; *Resolutions* (15 September 1687), vol. 3, 171. CAD C.502: "Letters despatched, Cape to Patria" (16 April 1688), pp. 72–73.

[49] *Resolutions* (15 September 1687), vol. 3, 171.

[50] "*Jou oud hond, Jij moogste den selvs gaan haalen!*"; AR VOC 4030: "Confessie: Claas van de Kust Mallebar" (14 March 1692), folio 328.

severed her head.[51] This nightmare unfolded in front of Marie, and she ran through the house, shouting, "Boss, Boss! Mother is dead! Mother is dead!"[52]

What Marie was shouting, in the unquestionable authority of her distress, was already a fact of life at the Cape: some of the slaves simultaneously considered their owners as mistresses and mothers, masters as fathers. So, also, the prosecutor of the case, in attempting to come to a suitable sentence and searching the European precedents for similar crimes, settled on "patricide" (even though the victim was a woman). In this case of a slave killing his mistress, the prosecutor had to make a suitable distinction, but one that decidedly followed the precedent for patricide. His summation concluded:

So the prosecutor holds as self evident that a slave owes more submission and obedience to his patron or patroness than a child towards his parents. Therefore all instances of disobedience, rebellion and other graver crimes among slaves towards their owners must be punished much more severely than similar crimes by children towards their parents. Consequently, the murder by the accused of his mistress must be regarded as more severe than patricide (*Vadermoord*) [*sic*]. In different areas of the world, different punishments are imposed for matricide: in Germany, to be broken on the rack, or to have their flesh pinched off their bodies by red hot tongs . . .[53]

The prosecutor, after listing all the regional variants of punishments for matricide, citing chapter and verse of many contemporary legal authorities, finally settled on having Claas broken alive on the rack. The dismembered parts were to be put on public display in a barrel "to be consumed by the birds of prey and the elements."[54]

What is significant here, and new for the Cape, is not the grisly punishment itself, but the choice of matricide/patricide as the closest analogue for a slave's killing of his mistress. The punishment was in keeping with punishments in other old-regime European societies. It had a somewhat liturgical quality.[55] In dealing with the murder of an owner by a slave, the court had invoked what was to it the nearest legal parallel — murder within the family. That two culturally and socially dissimilar persons, Marie from India, a household slave, and the Dutch-trained public prosecutor, expressed converging opinions of the same crime is compelling evidence in support of the Cape notion of the "father in the master," or here, the "mother in the mistress."

51 AR VOC 4030: "Relaas: Willem ten Damme" (14 March 1692), folio 307.

52 "*Baas, Baas! Moeder is dood! Moeder is dood!*"; AR VOC 4030: "Relaas: Marij van de Kust Coromandel" (14 March 1692), folio 306 verso.

53 AR VOC 4030: "Eijsch en Conclusie" (18 March 1692), folio 310 verso and 310.

54 AR VOC 4030 (18 March 1692), folio 310 verso and 310.

55 Charles Taylor, "Foucault on Freedom and Truth," in David Couzens Hoy (ed.), *Foucault: A Critical Reader* (London: Blackwell, 1986), pp. 71–72.

The governing authorities continued to encourage the family mode of management well into the late eighteenth century. When Major General J. H. Craig of the new British occupation wrote to the Dutch Court of Justice in 1796 on the thorny issue of treatment of slaves, seven members replied: "It may also be observed, that in every Family (with very few exceptions) the number of Slaves is so great that the safety of the family depends on them. . . . The measures we recommend are the following, viz. that masters should zealously endeavor to conduct themselves as Fathers rather than as Judges in their Families."[56]

Travelers to the Cape in the eighteenth and nineteenth centuries increasingly referred to the phenomenon of the Cape family. They remarked on the strangeness, the novelty of the new domestic arrangements, which were without a parallel in contemporary European society. Lady Anne Barnard, a newly arrived British socialite in 1795, wondered about the appropriate protocol in the Cape slave-society family. She was unsure whether she should give a necklace to a slave woman who belonged to her hosts *before* handing out gifts to the natural members of their family. She therefore asked the owners' guidance on this minor point of colonial etiquette. Their reply was apropos: "They both laughed and cried aloud: "Not to think anything of that — that she [the slave woman] had been born in the house, and was a sort of child of the family — and that if I had the beads, to give her them."[57] Augusta de Mist, the European-born 18-year-old daughter of the revolutionary Commissary General J. A. De Mist, wrote in her diary in 1803 of the strange spectacle of frontier families traveling to Cape Town to get married or baptized: "Many take the whole household, wives, children, slaves and animals all go along. Their journey takes as long as a month, and is quite patriarchal."[58] This same organization of the family was labeled by the German zoologist, Henry Lichtenstein, in 1803 as "the patriarchal mode of life" at the Cape.[59] As Cape historian John Mason correctly points out, it was "the standard form of social organization" at the Cape.[60]

Perhaps our clearest glimpse of the fully fledged Cape *familia* is from 1806, when Samuel Eusebius Hudson, an English slave owner who had left his own family (wife and daughter) in England, wrote from Cape Town:

---

[56] Cf. *RCC*, "Letter from Court of Justice to Major General Craig" (14 January 1796), 1: 307; for Craig's letter see *RCC* (7 January 1796), 1: 298.

[57] A. M. Lewin Robinson (ed.), *The Letters of Lady Anne Barnard to Henry Dundas from the Cape and Elsewhere* . . . (Cape Town: Balkema, 1973), p. 137.

[58] Augusta Uitenhage de Mist, *Diary of a Journey to the Cape* . . . (Cape Town: Balkema, no date), p. 23.

[59] Lichtenstein, *Travels in Southern Africa*, vol. 2, 22–23.

[60] John Mason, Jr., "The Slaves, the Hotnots [*sic*], and What Not: The World the Tourists Saw," paper presented South African Research Project seminar, Yale University (17 April 1985), pp. 20–23. Mason is working on a comparative study of Cape Town and Charleston in the period 1795 to 1834. I am indebted to him for this reference.

My family consist principally of Mosambiques and that not a few — seldom having less than twenty — and I can with truth assert my slaves have the character of being superior to most in the colony. I have seldom occasion for punishment and they are well aware of its being regularly inflicted when they deserve it. I treat them as my Children and they return it with gratitude and affection. I have had repeated proofs of this when I have been confined to a sick bed [and] unable to assist myself my slaves have been indefatigable in their Attendance and when I have suffered a momentary pang from the acuteness of my disorder, the big drops have chased each other down their sooty cheeks and their very looks expressed the thousand terrors that assailed them for fear of losing the Father in their Master.[61]

There were apparently no upper limits to the number of bondsmen in this family management scheme. Hudson, for instance, reveals that he had 22 slaves in his "family." Nor did the slave and serf family members have to be under one roof. Lichtenstein wrote of Jacob Laubscher's farm: "Indeed, [Laubscher] maintained a sort of patriarchal household, of which some idea may be gained by stating . . . The family itself, including masters, servants, hottentots, and slaves, consisted of a hundred and five persons, for whose subsistence the patriarch had to provide daily." Such huge patriarchal estates resembled, as Lichtenstein, a German, observed, barely concealing his admiration, "a state in miniature."[62]

The incorporation of the free Khoikhoi natives into the family management scheme was a natural extension of the slave family model. Early in the eighteenth century, Khoisan people had worked for the settlers in peripatetic gangs, moving from farm to farm, doing piecework and being paid off.[63] By the nineteenth century, freedom of movement for Cape Khoi workers was a thing of the past.

While we know that outright coercion was used to keep Khoi laborers on the farms, the family system also worked with them. Lichtenstein described Rhenosterfontein, a prosperous Cape farm in the Sneeuwbergen, as a place where "family harmony reigned among master, mistress, slave and Khoi,"[64] and when Hudson went to the Eastern frontier in 1818, he wrote in his daily journal: "Have hired a hottentot and his wife with four children, so I should be provided with a family."[65] To modern readers this Cape settler family system seems a grotesque mixture of Old Testament sentimentality and cynicism. To the Cape slave owner, however, such family government was not only practical, it was also an ideal way of life. The family metaphor provided a natural justification for the incorporation of

[61] Shell, " 'Slaves,' an Essay by Samuel Eusebius Hudson," 47.

[62] Lichtenstein, *Travels in Southern Africa*, vol. 1, 57.

[63] Adam Tas, *The Diary of Adams Tas*, ed. Leo Fouché et al., trans. J. Smuts (Cape Town: Van Riebeeck Society, 1969–70), pp. 117, 123, 125, 127.

[64] Lichtenstein, *Travels in Southern Africa*, vol. 2, 23.

[65] CAD A 10: Hudson, "Journal" (Tuesday, 3 February 1818), n.p.

servile groups (first slave and then free) into the domestic hegemony of family, household, and estate. Into this family system the Cape slave and serf were physically and involuntarily incorporated.

The Slave as Perpetual Child

An English visitor to the Cape in 1808, Lieutenant Colonel Robert Wilson of the Twentieth Light Dragoons, noted with some surprise that Cape slave owners considered it "a matter of honor" not to sell a house-born slave.[66] Perhaps this goes some way toward explaining why house-born slaves were seen as having a special place within the family. To sell such slaves to outsiders would have perverted the paternalism (see Chapter 4). The phrase "born in the same house" invariably referred to a slave's special status in the slave-owning family and was also a distant reference to the biblical patriarch Abraham, who was obliged by God to circumcise the slaves born in his household (see Chapter 11). The best way to obtain such a slave was through the estate of a deceased slave owner, but even then these highly prized slaves tended to go to relatives, not strangers.[67]

The family metaphor occasionally became reality, though this was rare. Cape slave owners stopped just short of what anthropologists call lineage slavery (where slaves became recognized members of the family and lineage). Still, Cape slave owners considered slaves, especially female slaves, "part of the family" and went to considerable lengths to keep them within the bounds of that institution. A Dutch visitor to the Cape in 1806, H. G. Nahuys van Burgst recorded that "An English officer had become acquainted with a beautiful white slave girl and had made a bid for her to the owner at more than her price, but the latter, having often importuned his beautiful slave in vain with his unchaste demands, now in a spirit of vengeance refused to allow her freedom . . . I met this slave girl myself and the account here given I heard from her own lips, as well as from people who were in the know about all this."[68]

A bachelor, Jan Vosloo, "one-time master woodcutter in the honorable Company's forests," petitioned the Political Council in November of 1707 that he "had eleven years previously had born in his house a slave girl Lena van de Caap, the mother of whom was a Company slave woman assigned to look after him in the forest."[69] From that time, Vosloo said, presumably long after the mother had returned to the slave Lodge in Cape Town or died, he had looked after the slave girl

---

[66] Robert Wilson, "Description of the Cape Colony in 1806," unpublished manuscript (Cape Archives: Verbatim Copies 58, no. 59, p. 19.

[67] See Chapter 4 on the domestic market.

[68] H. G. Nahuys van Burgst, *Adventures at the Cape of Good Hope in 1806* (Cape Town: Friends of the South African Library, 1993), 83.

[69] DO: "Transporten en Schepenkennis" (1 November 1707), T 1707/8 no. 163.

(repeating the phrase "in his house"), providing for her every need, providing a teacher for reading and writing — Vosloo himself was illiterate and signed his name with a cross — feeding and clothing her, and so on. He had heard a rumor that the Company now claimed Lena and planned to take her back into Company service and put her under the care of Kaij Jesse Slotsboo, an ensign at the fort, who had a well-established family.[70] Vosloo objected to this plan, claiming that the 11-year-old was still an "infant" (*infantie*), and offered whatever money the Company required for the slave. The Company, not without some compassion, evidently perceived the real relationship between Lena and Vosloo and stipulated that once the price was paid her manumission would be effective, but that Vosloo would be responsible for her care and feeding "until her marriage day." By including the latter paternal provision, the Company implicitly suggested that Vosloo had the same responsibility to Lena as toward his own daughter (which is what Lena was).[71]

When Matthijs Perara wished to return to Ceylon in March 1718, he asked to be allowed to take with him Lodewijk, the young son of the deceased slave Catharina of Columbo (Columbo was in Ceylon), whom Perara had looked after for five years and four months "as if he were his own son."[72] He begged with "folded hands" to be permitted to take the boy to Ceylon without paying the cost of the passage.[73] After two months the Company, probably after some investigation, acceded to the request, but altered the record forwarded to Holland — the settlers' petitions were not as a rule copied and sent to the various chambers — and formally resolved that Matthijs Perara be allowed to take his "son" (*Zoon*) on condition that they both did "ship's work."[74]

Examples of genuine emotional ties between owner and slave exist in the historical record as well. What, for example, is one otherwise to make of Hendriksz van Rheenen, a Stellenbosch farmer, who in 1726 left his entire estate to his imported slave, Carel van Bengal?[75] Or of the following "family" that Lady Anne Barnard came across in 1797 near present day Paarl:

. . . the room filled with slaves — a dozen at least — here they were particularly clean and neat, *Myfrow* [my woman, the mistress] sat like Charity tormented by a Legion of devils, with a black babie in her arms, one on each knee and three or four larger ones around her, smiling benign on the little mortals who seemed very sweet

---

[70] DO: "Transporten en Schepenkennis" (1 November 1707), T 1707/8 no. 163.

[71] DO: "Transporten en Schepenkennis" (manumission effective 10 April 1708), T 1707/8 no. 163.

[72] "*Gelijk als sijn eijgen naturlik kint.*"

[73] The following records, Union Buildings (hereafter UB): "Requesten en Nominatien," were in the process of being rebound in Pretoria when I consulted them there. They therefore have two references: since they have been in Pretoria for at least seven years, it is best to give both the "new" and the "old" acquisition numbers: UB C.225 (10 March 1718), folios 251–252; and UB C.1079, 92–93.

[74] *Resolutions* (10 May 1718), 5: 281–282.

[75] *Resolutions* (29 January 1726), 7: 224, note 57.

creatures and develish [*sic*] only in their hue — she and her husband having (for a wonder) no children of their own, they mean to leave their slaves free and to give amongst them all their fortune, of course, these people are likely to be well served for life.[76]

Long after slavery had ended, such familial attachments continued. Lady Duff-Gordon, an English visitor to the Cape, wrote in 1862, 28 years after the abolition proclamation, of an ex-slave who had become richer than his former master, Willem Klein, and who regularly sent presents to Klein. When the former master traveled to Cape Town, he visited the slave, who had been born in the owner's father's house and who had been "*his boy* and playfellow." The former slave "seats him in a grand chair and sits on a little wooden stool at his feet." Klein begged him as *huisheer* (master of the house) to "sit properly" to no avail, the ex-slave saying: "No, I shall not. I cannot forget."[77] Ironically, the former owner tried to impose an air of equality on the situation by invoking the former privilege of slave-holding authority.

Such cases are no doubt exceptions, inversions within a subtle system of family management so charged with all the human emotions of dependence and domination that occasionally the institution of slavery faltered and the slave became master. At no other point within a slave system do the distinctions of personality and property unravel so revealingly as in these few examples of intense domestic affection between master and slave.

But even when slaves were incorporated along physical, sexual, and emotional byways into the settler family, this never entailed equality with other members of the household. Even the young daughters of settlers, Mentzel notes, were allowed to punish adult household slaves.[78] The natural children of the slave owner therefore enjoyed the same rights of domestic chastisement of slaves as the *paterfamilias*. And even though slaves enjoyed much intimacy — sharing confidences with their young mistresses and masters, accompanying them to school, fighting with them, perhaps having sex with them — these encounters were all cul-de-sacs. They were epiphenomena of that spectacular but false intimacy peculiar to a master-and-slave relationship. At some point in every slave's life, usually at the young master's or mistress's maturity, there arose a simultaneous realization that while the master or mistress was bound for adulthood, the slave — in the settlers' eyes — was scheduled for perpetual childhood and dependence, and the demeaning obscurity that went with that fate.

---

[76] Robinson, *The Letters of Lady Anne Barnard to Henry Dundas*, 86. The slaves did not after all inherit the fortune, but they did receive "financial help"; see Margaret Cairns, "The Weigt Slaves of Wagenmakers Vallei and Their Emancipation," *Quarterly Bulletin of the South African Library* 42 (June/July 1988): 146.

[77] Lady Duff-Gordon, *Letters from the Cape* (Oxford: Oxford University Press, 1927), p. 92.

[78] Mentzel, *Description*, vol. 2, 110.

Clothing the Slave as a Child

The clothing slaves wore was also a sign of the imposed distinction between adult-master and child-slave.[79] In ancient Rome the school cap was the badge of adult slavery.[80] At the Cape — even in winter — slaves, including liveried footmen, were forced to go barefoot.[81] By the early nineteenth century, slave women, at least, were wearing "pointed shoes" in Cape Town, but men continued without "shoes or stockings," part of the pervasive pattern of demeaning male slaves.[82] Roman children wore school caps, Cape children went barefoot — slaves in both societies were forced to adopt aspects of dress symbolic of children. Incidentally, from both an economic and a symbolic perspective, the Cape system was more practical: shoes were hard to come by and expensive; caps cost money and could be "lost."

Slave headgear was an early target of legislation. In 1642 Van Dieman, a high-ranking Dutch official, proclaimed that throughout the Dutch possessions, slaves could wear hats only if they had proved to the commissioner of marriages in a written test that they could "clearly understand Dutch." The commissioner of marriages was the logical choice to invigilate such examinations since this officer routinely administered them to female slaves bound for marriage through manu-mission (see Chapter 12). Slaves who wore hats without the requisite examination would have the offending hats confiscated and would also be beaten.[83] Carl Peter Thunberg, a Swedish traveler in the Cape in 1770s, observed that this practice still continued at the Cape.[84] To get around these prohibitions, Cape slaves, by the

---

[79] For a fuller discussion, see Robert C.-H. Shell, "De Meillon's People of Color: Some Notes on Their Dress and Occupations with Special Reference to *Cape Views and Costumes: Water-colors by H. C. de Meillon in the Brenthurst Collection* . . . (Johannesburg: The Brenthurst Press, 1978).

[80] Mentzel quoting the *Berliner Monatschrift* of 1784, in *Description*, vol. 2, 112.

[81] "Without shoe or stocking — the badge of slavery" in Shell, " 'Slaves, an Essay by Samuel Eusebius Hudson," 52; see also Shell, "De Meillon's People of Color," 1; George Barrington, *A Voyage to Botany Bay, with a Description of the Country, Manners &c.* (London: H. D. Symonds, 1794), p. 34.

[82] Anon., *Gleanings in Africa* . . . (New York: Negro Universities Press, 1969 reprint), p. 270; Robert Semple, *Walks and Sketches at the Cape of Good Hope* (Cape Town: Balkema, 1968), p. 38.

[83] Van Dieman's *Placcaat* (1642) in van der Chijs, *Netherlandsche-Indisch Plakkaatboek*, vol. 1, p. 575.

[84] See the account of Mockadan Sijmon, the slave interpreter who wore a hat, in Chapter 6 on the Lodge slaves. See also Karl Peter Thunberg, *Travels at the Cape of Good Hope, 1772–1775* (Cape Town: Van Riebeeck Society Second Series, No. 17, 1986), p. 26 and note 21; Victor de Kock, *Those in Bondage: An Account of the Life of the Slave at the Cape* . . . (London: Allen & Unwin, 1950), p. 49. Jacob van Reenen, one of the four "Cape Patriots" chosen to go to Holland, made a request to import "hats and shoes" for his slaves in 1782. There is no evidence that permission was granted. See Vernon Forbes's comment in Thunberg, note 21. Van Reenen, one of the richest men in the colony, was also one of the most "progressive" farmers and probably an exception; see Coenraad Beyers, *Die Kaapse Patriotte 1779–1791* (Cape Town: Juta, 1929), p. 86.

nineteenth century, started to wear handkerchiefs and turbans, symbols of the alternative culture they were creating.[85]

The slave was also regarded as a child in legal matters. In the published statutes of the Cape of this period, crimes perpetrated by slaves were considered in the same way as crimes perpetrated by the children of the family. To quote a statute first issued on the eleventh of February 1687: "Should the delinquent be a child of the household, *or a slave,* the parent or master will be responsible for the fine."[86] Mentzel noted in support of this that "a master is responsible for any damage committed by the slave."[87] In Cape law, as in ancient Roman law, the slave, whatever his age, was legally regarded as a junior member of the family.

From the moment the slave was brought into the home of the master, he or she was faced with a well-organized domestic power structure, in which each slave had a well-defined place, with function stereotyped by origin and price pegged. In the theater of the slave-holding household, the everyday language, the naming patterns, and even the wardrobe of the slave had hegemonic elements. The Cape colonial society was governed by the family: not all power came from the barrel of a gun.

The slave at the Cape lived in a deracinated world in which every last detail of life, from day-to-day tasks to personal names and apparel, was determined by others. Still, the slave's personality was not wholly crushed, as Orlando Patterson has so cogently argued, it was only limited. The slave did have some room for expression. There was room enough to believe in himself or herself as a junior member of the household, and sometimes more. In the more paternalistic "families," formal freedom was held out as a tempting incentive to adopt the mores of the family: in the patriarchal family, this never happened. Both types of families clearly associated adulthood and freedom. If you were a slave, you would never become free. If you were a slave, you could not become an adult. If you were free, you could be an adult. The permutations of the formulas for family control were endless and universal. In the domestic arena, a careless shrug, failure to raise a cap, or to lower the voice, resulted in domestic retribution. This was the mundane yet critical threshold of accommodation, which probably changed from day to day, from task to task, and even from mood to mood.

Managing a slave-holding household was a juggling act; out of synchronization it could result in the slave's assuming an adult anger. This explains why escape, arson, rape, and murder were commonplace fears at the Cape. Because many Cape slave owners were immigrants and new to slave owning as a way of life, there were

---

[85] Shell, " 'Slaves,' an Essay by Samuel Eusebius Hudson," 60; Semple, *Walks and Sketches,* 38.

[86] Jeffreys and Naude, *Kaapse Plakkaatboek* vol. 1, 231 (11 February 1687); and CAD C.687: "Orig. Plakkaatboek" (30 April 1688), 32 (emphasis added).

[87] Mentzel, *Description,* vol. 2, 130.

probably many "bad" slave owners in addition to the usual complement of psychopaths, the lot of all societies. The resulting frequent ruptures in the Cape's social fabric gives Cape slavery a pernicious character. What held the entire slave society together — so far as the typical settler was concerned — was the Cape family.

Not all slaves accepted the masters' hegemonic vision willingly or totally — there were far too many slave arsonists, runaways, and suicides to allow for argument on that unnecessary point. Slaves consented when it was practical and rebelled when their situation became intolerable. Slavery was an unjust as well as a secularly unstable human transaction, but at least it remained just that — an arrangement that could be broken if rights were trampled upon. A slave's seemingly sycophantic acceptance of the master's mores on one level often disguised a wholesale rejection of all the master's values on another level. Cape slavery worked altogether too well for thousands of slave-owning families, for 176 long years. Considering the influence of the family in ordering most human lives, there is little wonder that deference, dependence, and compliance became cultivated mannerisms for many slaves.

In the process of slavery at the Cape, both master and slave changed. In the emotional inferno of the new family order, each was forced to accommodate to the other's behavior. A unique cuisine and a new language — Afrikaans — were among the only positive byproducts of this interaction. Each successive generation refined the family mode of management, and also honed the slaves' responses to it, and the creolization of the slave force accelerated this process. Within the slave society, the psychological ramifications of family management could only have been Byzantine. The social costs and hidden injuries for future generations are plainly incalculable.

*E*IGHT

T*he Script of Subordination*
The Everyday Language of the Household

*"Sticks and stones may break my bones,
but words will never hurt me" — child's refrain.*

As THE FRENCH HISTORIAN Roland Mousnier has suggested, economic distinctions were only one subset — although an important one — of early modern European society.[1] This applies especially to the colonial world. The Cape may be most appropriately perceived — through Mousnier's comprehensive vision — as a society of orders. That society of orders was shaped anew in the theater of the colonial household. Only at the elemental domestic level could the emerging society digest the new colonial hierarchical criteria of slavery, racial descent, and group stereotyping of a variety of ethnic origins and combine them with the established criteria of wealth, age, and gender. In this interpretation of Cape slavery, slaves were by no means outsiders, or marginalized, or even in a separate category. They became an integral part of a fully articulated but constantly changing hierarchical society.

Slavery presented the early officials and settlers with a new challenge: to incorporate new population elements into the traditional hierarchical ordering of European society. The most pernicious aspect of the evolution and transmission of the domestic "script" was that it was unchallenged and universal, and it therefore became unconscious. Codes of behavior and the baton of culture itself, the household language, were passed from mother to daughter, from owner to slave, from *baas* to serf, and from father to son. Robert Percival, writing in 1804 understood this clearly: "For want of a liberal education, their course from infancy to manhood seems an uninterrupted course of degeneracy. One of their first lessons, as I have elsewhere observed, is to domineer over, and insult the unfortunate slaves, who are subject to all their whims and caprices. Observe the Dutch children, and those [children] of the slaves playing and mixing together, you will see the former at one moment beating and tyrannizing over the latter, and at the next caressing and encouraging them; so that from an early period they acquire an

---

[1] Roland Mousnier, *Social Hierarchies: 1450 to the Present* (London: Croom Helm, 1973).

arbitrary and capricious habit of mind."[2] By the nineteenth century, the new language of the household had developed into colonywide ways of thinking.

The many diverse strands of the Cape's mixture of Eurasian and autochthonous cultures had enabled first the officials and then the settlers to enforce the new hierarchy on not one but many enslaved peoples. This infusion of different people strained the settlers' and officials' means of incorporating them into traditional metropolitan-ranked social hierarchies. The result, as has been noted, was a new and distinct division of household and farm labor based on origin and descent. This chapter does not attempt to uncover the entire archeology of attitudes based on gender, descent, and origin. Such attitudes developed before the Dutch occupation of the Cape in 1652. They were present early in the history of the Eastern possessions of the Company, and perhaps even earlier — in Europe itself.[3] Some attitudes, such as those toward gender, were shared among the various cultures at the Cape, but the overall colonial combination was new.

The Cryptography of Household Names

At the Cape each slave was given a first name and a toponymic identification (a name denoting origin, for example, Rangton *van* [from] Bali).[4] Whether this system originated in the Eastern possessions of the Company — or in Europe itself — is not clear. When the Dutch first occupied the Cape in 1652, the system was immediately apparent.[5] For centuries, individuals within the metropolitan Dutch society identified themselves by using a regionally specific toponym. Subsequent Dutch surnames were a composite of a patronym and town toponym preceded by the preposition *van*. A contemporary example might be Leonard Blussé van Oudekaas. The Dutch went to this trouble partly because a town name plus a surname would be a unique identifier, but also because they believed in the syllogism that because people came from a different region, they *were* different. Most people, even in the twentieth century, want to know a stranger's place of origin, a curiosity stemming from humans' near universal

---

[2] Captain Robert Percival, *An Account of the Cape of Good Hope* (New York: Negro Universities Press, 1969 reprint), p. 280.

[3] Winthrop D. Jordan, *White over Black: American Attitudes towards the Negro, 1550–1880* (New York: Penguin, 1969), p. 257.

[4] DO: "Transporten en Schepenkennis" (vols. 1–25); see the individual slave transactions for confirmation of these naming patterns; see also J. L. Hattingh, "Naamgewing aan Slawe, Vryswarte en ander Gekleurdes," *Kronos* 6 (1983): 5–20.

[5] Jan Antonisz van Riebeeck, *Daghregister gehouden by den oppercoopman, Jan Anthonisz van Riebeeck*, ed. D. B. Bosman and H. B. Thom (Cape Town: Balkema, 1952–1957): "*blanke mestice*" (white mestiço), vol. 3, p. 284; "*als swarten ende mesticen,*" vol. 2, 13; and also Maria van Bengal's marriage, vol. 2, 330, 344.

propensity for classifying. If we have knowledge of a person's origin we can anticipate — or think we can — his or her behavior. At the Cape, a different skin color would only have strengthened a purely regional association and, finally, become a racial stereotype.

The method of identification used in the colonies was probably based on popular notions of character attribution by origin — at the town, provincial, or national level — notions popular in Europe at that time. Vestiges of this even transplanted themselves to colonial New England, where the word Yankee, for example, was derived from the Dutch name Jan Kees, a stereotypical Dutch freebooter from New York. (It became a negative regional nickname first for people in New England, later for those in all the Northern States, and finally for all people from the United States.) Toponyms in Holland were sometimes coupled with given names or a patronym, although occasionally there were "modern" surnames, with no regional or patronymic connotations.[6] This naming process continued until the Napoleonic period, when the Dutch government first registered all the people in a national census. Thereafter, nicknames, patronyms, and toponyms congealed into the forms they have today.[7]

The Dutch East India Company named their colonial employees, subjects, and slaves systematically in their documents. Perhaps the Company found such toponymic nomenclature bureaucratically useful for governing polyglot subjects and administering of its widespread colonies. The Company payrolls exemplify the system: officials and personnel in 91 percent of the cases have both a patronymic and a toponymic suffix. The names of four hunters listed on a 1685 Company payroll illustrate the system: Laurens Pieters*zoon van Coedingen*, Dirk Roeloffs*zoon van Stockholm*, Jan Roeloffs*zoon van Copenhage[n]*, Marten Matthijs*zoon van Stockholm*. Toponyms allowed the authorities to identify their thousands of peripatetic employees. The Company paymasters would never confuse the two Roelofszoons when these two Scandinavian hunters came in from the veld to sort out their different pay packets. When an employee died, the hometown of surviving relatives was also included in the name. Even the heads of Cape government had such identification: "Simon van der Stel van Mauritius . . .

---

6 To illustrate this toponymic naming system with the archeology of the Afrikaans language, the current Afrikaans translation of the English word *surname* is *van*, which also has another meaning, "from." Thus, the Afrikaans and Dutch words share the same root, and the Afrikaans is probably an etymological vestige of the widespread use of toponyms to identify and ultimately name people after their hometown or region.

7 See Dutch examples in B. N. Leverland, *Zo Schreven onze Voorouders: Nederlands Schrift tussen 1450 en 1700* ('s-Gravenhage: Centraal Bureau voor Genealogie, 1980), pp. 8–51; also Eugene D. Genovese, *Roll, Jordan, Roll: The World the Slaves Made* (New York: Vintage Books, 1976), pp. 444–445. I am extremely grateful to Robert Ross for his help in this section.

Commandeur," or "Andries d'Man van Amsterdam . . . Administrateur en Coopman." The naming system was used throughout the society, from top to bottom.[8]

Names of European Company personnel and Company slaves appear together on a document drawn up in December 1693 that clearly illustrates how the slaves were incorporated into the Company's naming system. In the section of the census listing a slave gang at the Klapmuts slave post, a European Company overseer with a toponymic suffix appears above several slave laborers who are *only* given toponymic surnames:

Andries Rodever van Oostenburg . . .

Valentijn *van* Madagascar . . .

Kintza *van* Madagascar . . .

Ziena *van* Ceijlon &c . . .[9]

According to cargo manifests, captured slaves never identified themselves to their Dutch captors by region or origin. Without exception the detailed slave lists drawn up on board the Company slave ships that plied the East coast of Africa and Madagascar included no slave toponyms, only the two-level given name of the slave, such as "Andia Nomba" and "Kindu Rinevau."[10] Both these slaves — according to the daily journal kept on one slave ship, the *Soldaat* — were bought at the town of Maringado in Madagascar in 1697, but were listed without any toponymic nomenclature at that place.[11] "Kintza van Madagascar," on the Klapmuts list, was bought as "a young boy" in Maningaer during the 1676 voyage of the *Voorhout*, and was listed at the point of embarkation without a toponymic suffix, simply as "Kintza." The only logical conclusion is that sometime *after* disembarking at the Cape, the slaves were given new names by the local Dutch officials, who removed any second element of a slave's native name and added a suitable toponymic suffix to the slave's given first name.

Slaves with special physical characteristics might not have had a toponym at all, but instead a physical description — usually of a defect — was included in their name, for example: "Minte de Stomme" (Minte the Mute), "Kleijne Klaas," (Small Klaas); and "Hannibal, Siek en Melaats" (Hannibal, Sick and Leprous).[12] The crude physical description rendered any further toponymic additions super-

[8] A. Hulshof (comp.), "Compagnie's dienaren aan de Kaap in 1685," *Bijdragen en Mededelingen van het Historisch Genootschap* 63 (1942): 356.

[9] AR VOC 4032: "Opnemingh van Compagnies Groot en kleen vee . . ." (31 December 1693), folios 65–73. For a regional classification of slaves and free men in the same document, see François Valentijn, *Description of the Cape of Good Hope* . . . , ed. E. Raidt, trans. Maj. R. Raven-Hart (Cape Town: Van Riebeeck Society, 1973), vol. 1, p. 171.

[10] James C. Armstrong, "Malagasy Slave Names in the Seventeenth Century," Université de Madagascar, Colloque d' Histoire Malgache, 13–18 April 1981, p. 7.

[11] Armstrong, "Malagasy slave names," 7.

[12] AR VOC 4030: "Generale Opneming en monster Rolle van 's Comp: Soo slaven als bandieten . . ." (1 January 1693), folios 359–367 recto.

fluous. According to James Armstrong, who has made a study of the Malagasy language, some slaves (perhaps those who refused to give their names) were named at the point of embarkation by the Company interpreter, for a physical or personal attribute such as "short" or "cheeky" — Kintza, for example, means stubborn.[13] Identification was also an attempt to distinguish similarly named slaves from each other. For example, in the slave gang at the Klapmuts station there was a "Lamara," who had the usual toponymic suffix "van Madagascar." In the same gang appeared "Lamara Swartkop" (Lamara Black Head). At the nearby slave station at de Kuijlen, there was yet another "Lamara"; this time, there was only one resort: a three-level name, "Lamara Taboijne van Madagascar."[14] In her case the naming system used was the same as the one for Europeans. Many examples indicate both the consistent internal logic and the universality of the three-level naming system.[15]

The Relevance of the Toponym

Probably reasons of domestic security first prompted Roman jurists to insist, in Roman law, which the Cape followed, that the geographic origin of each slave be stated on the document of legal transfer.[16] Either because the Cape slave owners were following the Roman codes by custom, or because they had found this information on the origin of the slave to be essential, in all the Cape transfer documents the slave's origin was meticulously recorded, *not* the slave's occupation, though one might reasonably expect that in a purchase of a worker, that even a perfunctory description of occupational skills would have priority in the legal transfer document. In the early years at the Cape, however, only a handful of Company slave-trading documents recorded the occupations of individual slaves (for example, one enthusiastic Dutch slaving captain recorded purchasing a "potter" in Madagascar).[17] In general, no such information was used in the slave transfers until the 1820s.

---

[13] Armstrong, "Malagasy slave names," 4; personal communication, May 1984.

[14] AR VOC 4030: "Generale Opneming," folios 359–367 recto.

[15] AR VOC 4032: "Opnemingh van Compagnies Groot en kleen vee, mitsgaders der materialen, bouw gereedschapppen en andere goederen in 1693 bevonden" (31 December 1693), folios 65–73; CAD C.336, Attestaties: "Verklaring na gedane monsteringe bevonden te hebben onder te naeme 's Comp: leijfeijgenen" (Ultimo, August 1714), folios 457–475.

[16] J. A. van der Chijs (comp.), *Nederlandsch-Indisch Plakkaatboek, 1602–1811* ('s-Gravenhage: M. Nijhoff, 1885), vol. 3, 132, "Nopens het verkoopen van Lijfeigenen" (15–17 April 1684). Slaves from certain regions could not be sold at all; see "Verbod tegen het verkoopen van Balische lijfeigene . . ." (25 September/24 November 1665), vol. 2, 405; and "Verbod tegen den invoer te Batavia en elders van slaven, afkomstig van het eiland Celebes . . ." (27 April/1 May 1685), vol. 3, 147–148.

[17] Armstrong, "Malagasy slave names," n.p.; but in the subsequent schedules of landed slaves, these occupational categories disappear; see for example, AR VOC 4030: "Generale Opneming" (1 January 1693), folios 359–367.

Typically, the more distant and unfamiliar the area of origin was, the more sweeping (and derogatory) the qualities attributed to its people. This was a system present in Europe, but it was probably universal. For example, the Dutch East India Company officials in 1700 considered men from the Hague ("Hagenaars") and from the province of Zealand ("Zealanders") to be "industrious," and Huguenots from France — of the same religious faith — "ill-behaved," "poor farmers," and "lazy." The governor himself believed that the French of "all the nations at the Cape were the least to be trusted."[18]

The geographical xenophobia and solipsistic patriotism of the Dutch was also drawn upon to ascribe dispositions and capabilities to slaves from specific areas. Such character attribution by origin appears frequently in the Cape crime records. On 20 January 1713, for example, the prosecutor summarized why an entire gang of runaway slaves from one set of regions should be put to death. Religious, regional, and national character attributions were seen to coalesce: "the Muslims from the regions of Macassar, [Sam]Bouwa, Bali and East of Java, who descend on Batavia, or are sent into slavery there, which nations are afflicted by an innate treacherous disposition, deserve for their treachery and [these] attacks to be cleared from this earth by a painful death."[19] The prosecutor clinched his case by appealing to a "higher," racial level of explanation, that this was the sort of crime "one expected from the vengeful and cursed scum of Asiatics."[20] Edward Said has persuasively pointed out the fundamental racial thinking behind such examples of "orientalism."[21] It is easy to appreciate that the mild regional attributions used among Europeans could be easily transmogrified into fully fledged racial stereotyping in the colonial setting, but one must also appreciate that Europeans were not alone in such ways of thinking, only more capable of enforcing their visions.

Such group attribution did not have to apply to a large geographical area. One of the smallest geographical units used as a toponym for slaves was Bougies, a small coastal area in the Celebes island group in the Indonesian Archipelago. Cape colonial householders ascribed regional capabilities even to slaves from this small area. Bouginese slaves became renowned throughout the Dutch East Indies for both artisanal skills and treachery.[22] Generally, toponyms and regional

---

[18] C. Graham Botha, *The French Refugees at the Cape* (Cape Town: Struik, 1970), pp. 55–56, 160; see also Simon van der Stel, "Instructie . . . des Casteels de Goede Hoop . . ." (30 March 1699), in C. Graham Botha (ed.), *Collecteana* (Cape Town: Van Riebeeck Society, First Series, 1924), pp. 16–17.

[19] *"Natie"*; *"aangebooren, veradelijk inborst"*; AR VOC 4071: "Processtukken, Eijsch en Conclusie" (20 January 1713), folio 541 verso.

[20] *"Uijt dit wraaklustige, en vervloekte schuijm van Oosterlinge"*; AR VOC 4071: "Processtukken, Eijsch en Conclusie" (20 January 1713), folio 541 verso.

[21] Edward W. Said, *Orientalism* (New York: Pantheon, 1978).

[22] Samuel Abraham Rochlin, "A Forgotten Name for the Cape Malays," *Bantu Studies* 8 (1934): 95–97.

dispositions for slaves referred to the widest possible geographical area, while toponyms given to Northern Europeans referred to the smallest possible area. Probably nothing more complex than parochial pride, solipsistic reasoning, and limited geographical knowledge by the Europeans was responsible for this difference.

Group Attribution, Descent and Origin in Naming Patterns

Naming slaves by origin may have been an everyday convenience for dealing with individual slaves, but officials and labor settlers also ascribed attributes to whole groups — even nations — by origin. For example, in a memorial written in March 1676 for Simon van der Stel, the incoming governor, Isbrand Goske, described the Malagasy slaves as "a brave and industrious people"[23] H. A. van Reede tot Drakenstein, a visiting commissioner to the Cape, wrote in his report to the Dutch East India Company executives in 1685 that "because . . . the [slaves, exiles and convicts] especially those from Java, Macassar . . . [are] extremely dangerous . . . they must be watched carefully."[24] The aristocratic Van Reede, who had a dim opinion of the lower ranks of his own people, added a generous note on the slaves from Madagascar, whom he had found to be "physically strong, industrious, quick in intelligence, and not truculent . . . and who through leadership and education by our own people could be expected to deliver good service. Yes, better than our own *nation*. . . ."[25]

Specific skills became associated with certain regions. Van Reede also mentioned in 1685 that "slaves from Madagascar were especially suited for farming and agricultural pursuits,"[26] and local officials evidently complied or agreed with him because a few years later, in 1693, Malagasy slaves were more highly represented in the agricultural slave force stationed on Company farms and in the Company's extensive gardens in Cape Town than in stevedoring, fortification building, or domestic or clerical work.[27]

These attitudes toward descent and origin were often imported into the colony. In a revealing memorial written on 19 April 1708, C. J. Simonsz, a visiting Dutch East India Company commissioner from Ceylon, pointed out to Louis van

[23] "*Volck*" Isbrand Goske, "Memorie van Isbrand Goske vir sy opvolger," in Anna J. Böeseken (ed.), *Belangrike Kaapse Dokumente: Memoriën en Instructiën, 1675–1699* (Cape Town: South African State Archives, 1967), vol. 1, p. 135.

[24] A. Hulshof (ed.), "H. A. van Reede tot Drakenstein, Journaal van zijn verblijf aan de Kaap," *Bijdragen en Mededelingen van het Historisch Genootschap* 62 (1941): 236.

[25] Hulshof, "Journaal," 238 (emphasis added).

[26] Hulshof, "Journaal," 238.

[27] AR VOC 4030: "Generale Opneming" (1 January 1693), folios 359–367 recto.

Assenburg, the new Cape governor fresh from Amsterdam, how a division of labor based on origin and race might work as well at the Cape as it had in Ceylon. Especially significant are his concluding comments urging that *halfslag* (half-breed, or mulatto) slaves be used for the skilled occupations:

Also the convicts, especially the Easterners, could be used to great advantage as Woodcutters in the Company's forests, as in Columbo [Ceylon] this is done by some 20 of this caste . . . and although the Company's Eastern slaves [there] are not by far so strong as the Madagascar [slave] here, the heavy masonry work . . . is however also done by them . . . moreover they are for the most part used on the ship's wharf, carpenters shop, and with the copper-smiths and coopers and in the armory. . . . You would not have to worry that all such skilled work could be better performed here, especially if you made use of the half-breeds for these types of work.[28]

A significant difference between the naming patterns for slaves and for free persons is that slaves invariably had a toponym only, while Europeans typically had a patronym and a toponym. The system for slaves of mixed race, who were listed in a separate subgroup *above* "full-breed" slaves, fell somewhere between the other two. Since the racial descent of "half-breeds" overrode the regional ranking system, their names often had no toponymic suffix, and they are sometimes indistinguishable from European names of the same period.

There was a marked tendency for the Company clerks to use matronyms when recording slave names in the Lodge records, perhaps arising out of the Roman-Dutch legal notion that slave status at the Cape descended matrilineally. Thus one finds names such as Frans van Marretje van Calmeronde; the matronymic identification could also extend into two generations: David van Christijn van Magdalena Smith, or Christoffel van Christijn van Helena Abramsz[oon]. The combination of patronymic and matronymic elements was possibly an echo of the Dutch Reformed religious tenet that both parents had to be known for baptism, but this was rare. A few slaves had their father's name in both the first and last parts of their name: Jan Frans (patronym) van Anna (matronym) Hendriks (patronym).[29] These naming systems were unique to the Lodge.

If Company clerks used matronyms, then the Lodge slave mothers used Christian patronyms at the one place they could — the baptismal font. The baptismal records also reveal that slave mothers invariably chose the first names of their offspring from the European pool of New Testament, or Protestant, names.[30] This practice ensured that, on reaching adulthood, all creole Lodge slaves would

---

28 Cornelis Joan Simonsz, "Opstel van Eenige Poincten" (19 April 1708), in Botha, *Collecteana*.

29 Examples drawn from CAD C.344 (1727), p. 128. I am grateful to James Armstrong for this important point and the reference.

30 DRCA: Kaap Notule, 1665–1695, Doop Register GR1 vol. 1/1, pp. 27–28.

have Christian first names drawn from the same name pool of the owners. Creole Lodge slave names were thus in sharp contrast to those slaves imported to the Lodge who either retained their native names, or had classical or Old Testament slave names bestowed on them, for example, "Titus," "Augustus," "Solomon," "Moses," and so on.[31]

European fathers of Lodge slaves rarely turned up for the baptism ceremony.[32] The slave names in the Church's baptismal register suggest that the absence of the European father allowed the slave mother considerable leeway in naming her offspring. Often the slave mother named her son after the father, sometimes after a putative father. For instance, on 12 April 1682 Catharina van Bengal had her son baptized with no fewer than three patronyms: "Mauritsz[oon] Herman Jacobson." In the blank space reserved for the father's name, the deacon — attempting to clarify the identity of the father for the curious — added the marginal annotation: "Bartholomeus Herman — *so they say.*"[33] So while the father often was absent while the mulatto child grew up (which in itself must have compounded the other deleterious psychological effects of slavery, see 128), at least the child entered adolescence with a name which was indistinguishable from the settlers.

A partial list from the 1693 census of Company slaves reveals a variety of mulatto slaves' names among the men assigned to "general works":

Johannes Barentzoon
Anthoni Verlagen
Hendrik de Kleijne
Pieter Rosendaal
Frans van de Caap[34]

Barentzoon, Verlagen, and Rosendaal were names of early Cape settlers or Company personnel. Such slave patronyms illustrate how a few slave mothers successfully drove a genealogical stake into the baptismal records.[35] A few of these slaves, once free, became settlers and kept their Lodge names.

Such were the attitudes of the Dutch in this period that all mulatto slave half-breeds were considered, ipso facto, superior to the more numerous full-breeds and hence were listed above other groups of slaves. The term half-breed was not used for slaves whose parents both came from continents, regions, or countries outside Europe. For instance, the local officials did not consider a slave child born of a Bengali mother and an African father to be a half-breed, although the formal logic

---

31 DO: "Transporten en Schepenkennis" (vols. 1–25), transactions regarding slaves.

32 DRCA GR1 vols. 1–1/1–5 passim.

33 "*Soo men segt*" DRCA, GR1 vol. 1/1 (11 January 1680), pp. 27–28 emphasis added).

34 AR VOC 4030: "Generale Opneming" (1 January 1693), folios 359–367 recto.

35 C. Pama (comp.) and C. C. de Villiers, *Geslagregisters van die ou Kaapse Families* (Cape Town: Balkema, 1981), vol. 2, p. 797; Hulshof, "Compagnie's dienaren," 347–369, passim.

of the term half-breed implies this. Such locally born slaves of mixed descent had no special nomenclature and were lumped together with full-breeds. Mulatto slaves, therefore, are treated throughout this book as a subset of the creole slaves. The distinctions of half- and full-breed are evident not only in Company records but in Church records as well.[36]

Some creole slaves were half-breeds, although this is not always discernible from the name of the slave alone, since two full-breed slaves could parent a creole ("van der Kaap") child. The 1693 Company slave census, which lists 371 slaves by first name, descent, and origin, makes it possible to distinguish between adult creole slaves of partial European descent (half-breeds) and all other creole slaves whose parents originated somewhere else. Surprisingly, there was only one adult full-breed creole slave, Claes van de Caap, listed with other full-breed slaves on the Hottentots' Holland company slave post. The existence of only one creole full-breed among so many slaves suggests that most creole slaves — at least in the Lodge — were of European descent, a fact that shocked a visiting commissioner in 1685, but no one else.

In 1714 "Claes van de Caap" was one of 55 slaves (out of 371) to survive the 21 years between censuses.[37] His survival might not have been a coincidence, since creole slaves acquired immunity in childhood to the local diseases. Nor, of course, had creole slaves suffered the trauma of the journey of the middle passage. Many slaves who died, died within weeks of their arrival at the Lodge. Creole slaves should have been highly valued independently of their racial genealogy, based on their life expectancy alone. However, since coincidentally nearly all creole slaves in the Lodge were half-breeds of European descent, Company officials, possibly ignorant of the epidemiological explanation for the longevity of creole slaves, may possibly have ascribed their biological advantage to the European bloodline. We do not know.

The Dutch adopted much of the terminology of the Portuguese slave societies in the East, such as *casties* (pure-breed), *mestiço* (half-breed), *mandoor* (actually the Portuguese *mandadoor*), *kaffer* (actually Arabic for ungrateful), and *Mardijcker* (slave freed for defensive purposes). The Luso-Hispanic racial classification system, in which each genealogical fraction, and shades of color within each fraction, of the slaves' "white" ancestry is recorded — with such terms as *quadroon, octoroon, caboclas, cabrochas* — had no place at the Cape.[38] Only the words *mesties*, and

---

[36] The Church was more diligent in this respect than the company; Cf. DRCA, GR1 vol. 1/1; AR VOC 4030: "Generale Opneming" (1 January 1693), folios 359–367 recto; and CAD C.336, Attestaties: "Verklaring" (30 August 1714), folios 457–475.

[37] AR VOC 4030: "Generale Opneming" (1 January 1693), folios 359–367 recto; CAD C.336, Attestaties: "Verklaring" (30 August 1714), folios 457–475.

[38] For a full list of these Brazilian terms, see Gilberto Freyre, *The Masters and the Slaves: A Study in the Development of Brazilian Civilization* (New York: Knopf, 1971), pp. 477–500. For a

casties were used in this way. *Mardijcker*, although frequently used in the secondary literature of the Cape, is only rarely found in primary documents.[39]

In strong contrast to Brazil, where descent terms were applied to all people, at the Cape they almost always referred only to slaves, never to settlers and only rarely to free blacks.[40] Claims about the significance of the differences in descent rules among various slave societies (whereby status in the community is determined by racial genealogy) have been debunked by such anthropologists as Marvin Harris, but perhaps prematurely.[41] The Cape presents a new variant. If you were free, you were either "black" or "white" — even light-skinned people, such as Chinese or Arabs, were considered black at the Cape.[42] "Blackness" was not a matter of skin color as such, but of non-European descent. If you were a slave, you were either a half-breed or a full-breed from a specific region. These attitudes continued to develop through the eighteenth century and into the early nineteenth century. Robert Ross has suggested that there is no evidence in the later eighteenth century to support the classification of half-breed.[43] However, in one example in 1794, the Cape authorities issued a statute protecting "half-breeds" and others of European descent from being "jostled on public byways." A few years later Lady Anne Barnard mentioned that the taint of half-breed was still a serious social impediment.[44] The Cape descent rules are paramount in the

---

comprehensive body of indexed printed documents for this period — with a glossary of some similar terms in each volume — see Anna J. Böeseken et al. (eds.), *Suid-Afrikaanse Argiefstukke: Resolusies van die Politieke Raad*, 8 vols., 1652–1732 (Cape Town: Cape Times, 1957–1975).

[39] See for example I. D. du Plessis, *The Cape Malays: History, Religion, Traditions, Folk Tales* (Cape Town: Balkema, 1972), p. 31.

[40] "*Vrijzwarten*"; see the 150-odd annual lists of settler families and their effects, termed the *opgaafs*.

[41] Marvin Harris "The Origin of the Descent Rule," in Eugene D. Genovese and Laura Foner (eds.), *Slavery in the New World: A Reader in Comparative History* (Englewood Cliffs, N.J.: Prentice Hall, 1969), pp. 48–59.

[42] For example, "Mockadan Sijmon . . . vrijgebooren Arabier" is termed "Seeker *swart*" ("a certain *black*," *black*, according to the editor, was added later) as quoted by Goske, "Memorie van Isbrand Goske vir sy opvolger" (Maart 1676), in Böeseken, *Memoriën en Instructiën*, vol. 1, 135 and footnote 19. For the Chinese as black, see Abraham de Vijf, who was baptized as a free Chinese in 1703 (C. Spoelstra, *Bouwstoffen* . . . [Amsterdam: Hollandsch-Afrikaansche Uitgewers-Maatscappij, 1906–1907], vol. 1, p. 34) but was listed as a "free black" in 1706, cf. G. C. de Wet, *Die Vryliede en Vryswartes* (Cape Town: Historiese Publikasie-Vereniging, 1981), pp. 208, 213.

[43] Robert Ross, D. van Arkel, and G. C. Quispel do not mention the point that Europeans at the Cape classified the slaves according to breed: see Robert Ross, D. van Arkel and G. C. Quispel, "De Wijngaard des Heeren? Een onderzoek naar de wortels van die blanke baasskap," in Zuid Afrika (Leiden: Martinus Nijhoff, 1983), pp. 32-37.

[44] George McCall Theal, *Records of the Cape Colony* (London: Government Printer, 1905; hereafter *RCC*), 9: 153 (20 August 1794); Lady Anne Barnard, *The Letters of Lady Anne Barnard* . . . , ed. A. M. L. Robinson (Cape Town: Balkema, 1973), p. 174.

history of domestic slavery at the Cape.[45] No doubt over time they were contested and changed.

If you were a half-breed slave at the Cape, you stood a reasonable chance of passing for "white" if manumitted. The Cape rules fell somewhere between the Manichean North American hyperdescent rule, by which any "black" — that is, non-European — blood whatsoever resulted in "black" status, and the Luso-Hispanic descent rule in which there is a careful, fractional gradation of race and color, leading to what Gilberto Freyre, the Brazilian social historian, believed was a more "open" society for his country.[46]

Slaves as Children

An examination of the ordinary language of the slave household shows how the slave was seen as a child. No matter what their age — or status — all Cape slaves were "boys" or "girls."[47] But unlike free boys and free girls, the Cape slave-holding household offered no hope to slaves of ever being seen as an adult. This crude paternalistic device seems near universal in slave societies, at least from ancient Greek and Roman times (note the Greek vocative *pai;* the Latin, *puer*).[48] This practice was so accepted at the Cape that slaves, when referring to one another in the crime depositions, used the same demeaning language — or else the court clerks simply transcribed their testimony in that way.[49]

All burghers or officials were addressed extremely formally, even in the privacy of a personal diary as, for example, "Mister van der Heijden" or "Monsieur van der Stel."[50] But all Cape slaves were known in the community by their first name. In the status-conscious early Cape, only children, slaves, serfs, cattle, and pets were addressed by their first names. Slaves' names were provided by the slave trader or the new owner, and the legal transfer was the place to rename (*hernaam*) a slave. The daily, communitywide, repetitious use of the first name and no other was an important part of the process of socializing slaves into their status of unending childhood. The process is still in wide use with the one million domestic servants in South Africa today, as it was until recently in much of the American South.

[45] For example, see the critique of George Fredrickson's highly touted work, Richard Elphick, "A Comparative History of White Supremacy," *Journal of Interdisciplinary History* 13:3 (Winter 1983): 503–513.

[46] Freyre, *The Masters and the Slaves* xviii, xxx, 3–11.

[47] That is, "*jongen, meijden.*"

[48] T. E. J. Wiedemann, *Slavery* (Oxford: Clarendon Press, 1987, pamphlet), p. 25.

[49] AR VOC 4030: "Confessie: Claas van de Kust Mallebar" (14 March 1692), folio 328.

[50] Adam Tas, *The Diary of Adam Tas*, ed. Leo Fouché et al. trans. J. Smuts (Cape Town: Van Riebeeck Society, 1969–70), pp. 38–42; 96–97.

Cape Slave Naming Patterns

When Robert Semple visited Cape Town in 1804 he correctly noted the significance of the naming pattern for Cape slave owners:

It may be here observed that the whole heathen mythology is ransacked to find them names, which are in general bestowed in a manner not the most honourable to those deities at whose altars one half of the human race formerly bowed down. Thus Jupiter cleans the shoes, Hercules rubs down the horses, and Juno lights the fire. Yet [this] is not done through any disrespect towards these once remarkable names, as those in Scripture are applied with as little ceremony, and in as unappropriate a manner, Sampson being daily sent for water, and Solomon up to the Table Mountain to cut firewood.[51]

One might think that naming slaves might have reflected conscious — if jocular and harmless — references to patriarchal or imperial patrician life-styles, which the slaves made possible, but there was actually a more sinister logic to the choice of Cape slave names. Naming slaves was a domestic ruse to diminish the dignity of slaves in daily life and to establish differences among slave groups. There were six distinctive types of first names for slaves. These types represented a spectrum (see Figure 8-1). Facetious names were at the exclusionary end (the bottom), while owners' names, represented the other, more inclusive end (the top).[52]

Facetious Names

The settlers' facetious spirit found its fullest expression in ridiculous or pejorative nicknames given to slaves, faithfully copied in the transfers. The most common name was Fortune (*Fortuijn*), presumably an ironical reminder of where the household wealth lay. Pickle Herring[53] was the nickname of one slave; Winter Butter was another, a racial joke referring to the slave's pale skin color.[54] The list is as endless as it is demeaning: Thickleg (*Dikbeen*), Long-time-coming (*Lang onderweg*), Watch-out (*Pasop*), Sweet Potato (*Pattat*), Teawater (*Theewater*), Blixem (*Blucksam* — an expletive), Welcome (*Wellekom*), Sabbath Ape-child, (*Domingo Aapkind*), or simply Ape (*Aap*), Evil (*Slegt*), Clever (*Slim*), and *Servidor* and

---

51 Robert Semple, *Walks and Sketches at the Cape of Good Hope* (Cape Town: Balkema, 1968 reprint of second edition), p. 34.

52 Shell, "Saledeed"; (N = 4,122). "Foreign" indicates foreign Christian names, such as "Francisco"; "toponym" indicates toponyms used as first names, such as "Africa van Guinea."

53 "*Peekel Haaring*"; DO: "Transporten en Schepenkennis" (12 February 1687); In eighteenth-century Suriname, "Peekel Haaring" was also used as a slave name. I am grateful to Natalie Davis for pointing this out to me.

54 "*Winter Botter*"; DO: "Transporten en Schepenkennis" (10 April 1688). Butter made in winter used to be pale in color due to the absence of vitamin A in the winter diet of cows. I am extremely grateful to Helen Armstrong for this explanation.

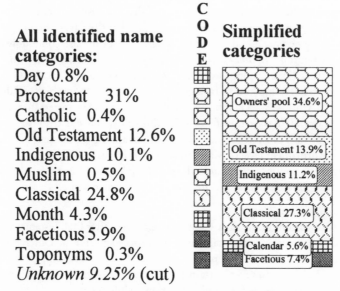

All identified name categories:	CODE	Simplified categories
Day 0.8%		
Protestant 31%		Owners' pool 34.6%
Catholic 0.4%		
Old Testament 12.6%		Old Testament 13.9%
Indigenous 10.1%		Indigenous 11.2%
Muslim 0.5%		
Classical 24.8%		Classical 27.3%
Month 4.3%		
Facetious 5.9%		Calendar 5.6%
Toponyms 0.3%		Facetious 7.4%
Unknown 9.25% (cut)		

Figure 8–1. The spectrum of slave names at the Cape, 1656 to 1762.

Shitato, which require as little translation as they require imagination. Presumably this thigh-slapping humor was explained, or perhaps the joke grew old, but the names stuck. When the slave was sold again, the name reappeared in the records.

Calendar Names

In between the facetious and classical or biblical names were calendar names, which, unlike West African day names, were at least partly facetious. Friday was the most common day name, perhaps because the person on whom Daniel Defoe had based his famous character — the real Robinson Crusoe — had convalesced at the Cape. But month names were the most popular calendar names, especially for enslaved persons from the Indian subcontinent (see Figure 8-3). One oceanic slave trader, after selling a particularly large lot of slaves from the quayside in Cape Town, and having exhausted his imagination and classical learning, reeled off, as their own, the names of the months, in order of the slaves' appearance on the auction block.[55] This month-naming practice, repeated quite often in the eighteenth and nineteenth centuries, may explain the haunting yet quite maddening

---

[55] DO: "Transporten en Schepenkennis" (13 May 1699).

lyrics of an old Cape dirge, or *Moppie* — "January, February, March, April, . . ." — which the slaves sang to help themselves get through the quotidian ordeals of Cape slavery. Possibly, the moppie had an educational purpose, too.

Classical Names

One scholar of the American South has argued that the slave owners' use of classical and historical names for their slaves was evidence that the slaves stood in the same relation to their owner as did the owner's dogs, at that time also commonly named for classical figures.[56] In this way, too, the slave owner invited the slave-owning class into a cultural "joke," (supposedly) hidden from the slave. That the Cape slave owners considered this joke to be a good one is attested to by the 81 Tituses, 53 Cupidos, 50 Coridons, 35 Hannibals, and 39 Scipios in sale transfers from the early period. In the 4,076 slave transfers used in this study, only one Cromwell and one Diogenes testified to a different level of education among the masters. Most names were at the firmament level of Mars and Venus.[57] To name a slave after a god or an emperor was a common household device; the joke would be revealed when the slave came upon livestock or pets that had his or her own name.

Old Testament Names

It was also a custom in the early Cape to name slaves after Old Testament figures. The Old Testament provided many important precedents for the Dutch Reformed tradition, so it is difficult to separate sacred from profane naming practices (see Chapter 11, 337). However, certain names such as Solomon and Moses, were never used by the settlers for naming their own children.[58]

Indigenous Names

Some slaves were allowed to keep their given, indigenous names. This was true for all imported Lodge slaves, but a few private owners also allowed their slaves to keep their given names. Since the Lodge was internally run (except for baptisms) one assumes that allowing the slaves to keep their names was a form of Lodge autonomy. Among private owners this practice was rare and did not extend to the second, creole generation. Such names as Affans, Assar, Caftiaan, Chachista, Cosambij, Doole, Galba, Jo-ombie, Jofta, Moensat, Nalk, Origo, Orsous, Pagolet, Pantsiko, Pasi, Soutanij, Thijmon, Towaijo, and Trimmatas all fell out of use.

Inclusion and the Owners' Pool of Names

Only a tiny minority of urban patrician owners baptized their slaves and used the same name pool as they did for their own natural children. But some owners used

---

[56] Cecil D. Eby, "Classical Names among Southern Negro Slaves," *American Speech* 36 (May 1961): 140–141.

[57] DO: "Transporten en Schepenkennis" (22 February 1729).

[58] See the genealogical record: Pama, *Geslagregisters*, passim; J. Hoge, "Personalia of the Germans at the Cape, 1652–1806," *Archives Year Book* 9 (1946): passim.

names from their own pool and did not baptize their slaves. Aside from baptizing slaves, using family names for slaves represents the highest level of inclusion into the owners' domestic circle. These naming patterns, when cross-tabulated with the sex and age of the slave, provide several statistically significant and revealing patterns (see Figure 8-2).[59]

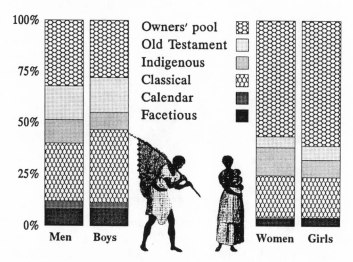

Figure 8–2. Cape naming patterns, 1656–1784.

What is most surprising is that the big variation is by sex, when one might reasonably have expected to find creole status and age the determinants. Female slaves, whether young or old, had the highest percentage of owners' names. Young boys were named, like men, with names drawn from outside the owners' pool. But here one is also seeing up the "*capon*" effect, because young male slaves were more often targeted in the oceanic slave trade. The socialization of male slaves as outsiders, at least so far as the names reveal, started early.

Slave women born in the colony were much more likely to have names from the owners' pool. Imported African slaves, male and female, were the next most likely to have owners' names, but it must be remembered that the African slaves arrived early in the colony's history — in the first two decades — when there was still a strong idealistic and inclusive Reformed tradition. African slaves also had the biggest proportion of facetious names (see Figure 8-3).[60]

Creole slaves, some of whom were born in the owner's house, are a special subset, as they were rarely sold (see Chapter 4). Their naming patterns are also

---

[59] Shell, "Saledeed."
[60] Shell, "Saledeed."

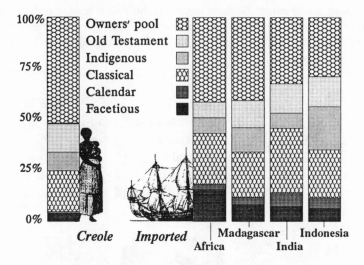

Figure 8–3. Names of slaves by creole status and origin, 1656 to 1784.

revealing. Girls were named most closely in accordance with their owners' own naming patterns, then women. Creole boy slaves had fewer owners' names than the men, but all male slaves were obviously scheduled for the periphery of the household. The socialization of creole slaves was fierce, the patterns stark. Young creole boys had the highest percentage of facetious names of all groups apart from imported African slaves (see Figure 8-4).[61]

Some slaves did see through the naming schemes and rejected the facetious names — usually reserved for imported slaves — in favor of names of their own choosing. For example, in the more detailed crime records a slave might be identified by a formal and a self-chosen name, as "Scipio of Bengal, known round about as Kees."[62] Such a name was called a *skuilnaam* (literally, "a hiding name"). Over time, more and more slaves rejected their slavish names, and by the nine-teenth century, slave aliases and Muslim names were common, for example, Dort van de Kaap, Achmat van Bengal, Abdul Malik van Batavia, and so on. These illustrate the growth of an alternative culture, but the three-level naming pattern nevertheless remained constant.[63]

Slaves were named, for ease of identification, by origin, and if this conflicted with a similar name, as noted earlier, a physical identification was added and

---

[61] Shell, "Saledeed."

[62] "*Scipio van Bengal, in de wandeling genoemt, Kees.*"

[63] AR: "Processtukken," 1680–1795, passim. For the nineteenth century, see the Cape Town street directories.

finally, if there was still some repetition of names, yet another name. The three-level naming system for full-breed slaves at the Cape, similar to the European system, differed in the frequency and geographical range of the use of toponyms: slaves invariably had a broad toponym; Europeans usually had a narrow toponym. Creole slaves' naming pattern followed the system of the contemporary dominant European order, but still disclosed the slave's descent status. Mulatto slaves' names were almost indistinguishable from owners' names. Once manumitted, there was no change in their names and they smoothly entered the ranks of the free — and sometimes became slave owners themselves.

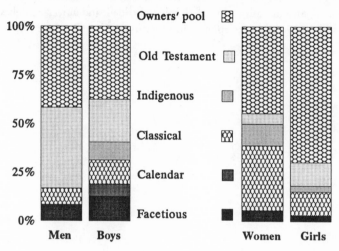

Figure 8–4. Creole naming patterns, 1656 to 1784.

These points go some way toward explaining the plethora of racial and ethnic slave stereotyping found scattered throughout the later eighteenth- and nineteenth-century sources on the Cape.[64] The early practice of systematically recording the region of origin suggests that this was considered the single most useful bit of information about a slave, even when the age was sometimes left out on the transfer. As the slave population became increasingly creolized, the system was modified, but by then some identities had become established. For instance, some favored, locally born slaves were still considered "Malay" in the nineteenth century. Like the European Christian master class, they too, forged an identity based on descent.

---

[64] Some examples are Percival, *An Account of the Cape*, pp. 286–291, and James Ewart, *James Ewart's Journal* (Cape Town: Struik, 1970), pp. 27–30; and Semple, *Walks and Sketches*, 43–54; and see a discussion of this point in Robert C.-H. Shell (ed.), " 'Slaves,' an Essay by Samuel Eusebius Hudson," *Kronos* 9 (1984): 46, note 3.

The slave names at the Cape were descriptive tags that constantly reminded householders of their slaves' racial descent, origin, language, sometimes even parenthood, but always their slave status. The more facetious names were most often reserved for male imported slaves, young and old, but even creole male children were often named in this way. Based on the evidence of naming patterns, slave women were on the inside track in Cape household slavery. Their total incorporation into the household as nannies, concubines, or wives prompts a comparison with other lineage slavery systems on the African continent (see Chapter 4). The slave naming system was certainly only a minor part of the total hegemonic apparatus the owners had constructed, but it was an aspect carefully adumbrated, meticulously recorded, deeply imbedded, and universal. Relics of the system still survive, as any telephone directory in the Cape Province will bear out.

Nine

Arson and Architecture
The Vernacular World the Slaves Made

THE EFFECTS OF SLAVERY on Cape society were not only political and economic on the one hand, psychological and subtle on the other, they were also visible in the structure of houses and the architectural designs that have existed in the Cape to the present. The size of a house, the number of rooms, the shape of a roof, even the width of alleys between houses expressed some response to slavery. Out of the unlikely ingredients of slavery, Dutch Reformed definitions of the household, and the ensuing domestic arrangements, the people of the Cape slave society developed a unique, creole vernacular architecture.[1]

The Creole Origins of Cape Architecture

The flat-roofed houses of Cape Town have been termed Moorish; the imposing gables and steeply pitched thatched roofs of the slave-owning Cape estates and farmsteads have characteristically been called Cape Dutch; slave houses, or *pondoks*, have been termed *kapstijlhuizen* — their origins imputed to the Mediterranean *barracas* — or the *jongenhuis*, which has been onomatopoeically bowdlerized into *jonkerhuis* (the house belonging to the eldest son); even the corbelled stone

---

[1] Cape architecture has attracted interest resulting in several monographic and pictorial descriptive treatments. The ambition of many middle-class people in the Cape today is still to own or build such a home, albeit cramped on some tiny suburban plot. Rare is the South African home without its coffee table book on "Cape Dutch" architecture, but few books mention the slaves who built and ran these households. The undeniable beauty of Cape architecture captured the attention of the outside world some time ago, but Europe was always credited as being the source of that beauty. In the nineteenth century, for example, John Ruskin was allegedly moved to comment on the special beauty of the domestic architecture of the old Cape and to claim its special contribution to the vernacular architecture of the whole world. W. A. de Klerk, *The Puritans in Africa: A Story of Afrikanderdom* (New York: Penguin, 1975), p. 13.

houses of the frontier *trekboer* have been termed Mediterranean. Whatever their origins, they were said to be remote from South Africa.[2] The trope of "European origins" — and the over-priced genre of Cape architectural books that it gave rise to — served a dual purpose of legitimizing and, indeed, glorifying the European presence while simultaneously denying the existence of domestic slavery and serfdom. But the Cape's new colonial architecture was in fact based on defensive, managerial, even hegemonic considerations; the colonial architecture only superficially followed transplanted European patterns.[3]

A fresh interpretation of the origins of Cape architecture is sorely needed. I believe the design of Cape buildings was principally a response to the local environment, the strong wind known as the Southeaster, the related danger of fire and arson, the local materials, and above all, to the social tensions within the slave society with its high proportion of imported male slaves. In a slave society that had such small distributions of slaves, and hence a statistically circumscribed domestic character, the local vernacular architecture was a vital element in the growth, maintenance, defense, management, and, not least important, celebration of the institution of slavery.

The Example of the Lodge

The slave Lodge, which housed the majority of the colony's slaves until 1706 and was the largest single slave holding from 1658 to 1828, served as an architectural prototype for the housing of all slaves in the colony. The slave Lodge predates the Company's stronghold, the Castle, and therefore is probably the oldest surviving building in South Africa. The Lodge was always expanding — housing 1,000 slaves, convicts, and lunatics at its peak — and scholars have identified no fewer than seven phases of construction.[4] It is the first example of a building in South

---

[2] The Dutch and Moors have not had everything their own way. In 1962, Jan van der Meulen, the German-born former director of the South African Cultural Museum, produced a three-volume work on Cape architecture, "Die Europäische Grundlage der kolonial Archtektur am Kap der Guten Hoffnung," Ph.D. thesis, University of Marburg, 1962; he emphasized Germanic origins for all Cape architecture. His work deeply influenced Hans Fransen, whose joint work with Mary Cook is currently the standard reference on Cape architecture; Hans Fransen and Mary Alexander Cook, *The Old Buildings of the Cape* (Cape Town: Balkema, 1980).

[3] By superficial, I mean fitments, doors and styles of gables. The significant changes to my mind were roofs and the layout of the rooms, placement of the kitchen and the development of the werf.

[4] The following is based on "Memorandum on the Historical and Aesthetic Aspects of the Old Supreme Court Building: Annexure C," in *The Report of Committee of Enquiry Concerning the Old Supreme Court Building, Cape Town and the Widening of Bureau Street* (Pretoria: Government Printer, G.P-S11869-1953-4-48), pp. 1–8.

Africa devoted to high-density housing. No Cape building underwent as many architectural modifications. The first Lodge — made of wood and thatch in the 1650s to house several hundred Angolan slaves — was rebuilt in 1669 both because it had fallen into disrepair and because it had become too small, a favorite refrain of the patrician officials in charge of the Lodge. The second Lodge was built of plastered baked bricks and was a single story with a pitched, tiled roof and ceilinged rooms. In August of 1679, this Lodge was destroyed by a fire presumed to have been started by slaves. The Company regarded the fire as doubly terrible, as a Lodge slave who could both read and write was burned alive in the blaze.[5]

By the time of Simon van der Stel's governorship in that year, the old and new buildings had been combined to form a quadrangular building enclosing a covered courtyard, which is thought to have been the dining area of the slaves. In February of 1705, a "gang" of several Chinese Lodge slaves were apprehended for stealing from the town's burghers over a period of many months. Records of their interrogations reveal their ingenious escape route from the Lodge and also something of its the architecture. By standing in a human pyramid in the courtyard, they reached the *pannedak* (tile roof) after which they clambered down the small *rietdak* (thatched awnings) and over the "small" Lodge wall into the street.[6]

By the time of François Valentijn's visit to the Lodge a few years later, the building had a flat roof, that he reported, was then fully 30 feet high.[7] The building was enlarged in 1716 after a successful slave voyage to Madagascar and in anticipation of the establishment of a permanent slave station in Mozambique. A curved portico and classical pediments were added, perhaps as a jocular reminder of the Roman life-styles which the institution made possible. The walls, two feet three inches thick, were thought strong enough to support a second floor. After the abandonment of the Mozambique slave station in 1732, the Council of Policy decided that the Lodge should be expanded again, and the flat roof design was continued. In 1753 the councilors resolved both to lengthen and broaden the slave Lodge to the canal of the hospital and to the edge of the Church cemetery. This was the final enlargement of the Lodge, which could now easily house a thousand slaves. Narrow five-inch slits with iron crossbars (the Lodge housed several hundred small children) served as "windows," but most external walls had no slits at all. It was so dark inside the Lodge during the day that when L. M. Thibault, the French-trained architect, went inside on one summer day in 1803, he was obliged to carry a lantern.[8] The appointment of a European in-house surgeon and a Lodge director with offices on the northeast quadrant was the occasion for the first full windows of the Lodge and also for further doors.

---

[5] O. Geyser, *Die Ou Hooggershofgebou* (Cape Town: Tafelberg, 1958), p. 7.

[6] AR VOC 4053 (16 February 1705), p. 510 verso.

[7] François Valentijn, *Description of the Cape of Good Hope* . . . ed. E. H. Raidt, trans. Maj. R. Raven-Hart (Cape Town: Van Riebeeck Society, 1973), vol. 1, p. 101.

[8] Geyser, *Die Ou Hooggershofgebou*, p. 15.

The internal architecture of the Lodge was based on the age, racial descent, sex, origin, respectability, and health (both physical and mental) of its inmates. School-children were segregated by sex and age, and slept next to the schoolroom, overseen by a mulatto matron. Mulatto mandoors (overseers, see 180–185) were stationed at the only exit to the street; young bachelor slaves were in the east wing; spinsters were in the west wing; "married" slave couples in their own quarters.[9] In 1710 special rooms were set aside for "lunatics" (not only Lodge slaves, but also free Euro-peans).[10] By 1800 there were still two lunatic rooms. Next to the lunatics' rooms were rows and rows of outside latrines, the stench of which compelled Mentzel, who was delivering salt to the Lodge, "to beat a hasty retreat."[11] The planned second story of the Lodge, according to the Fiscal in 1717, was to be given over "to the best and most respectable paired slaves."[12] Mentzel was probably unaware of this plan when he noticed that "the male and female slaves were supposed to occupy different apartments, but generally they live promiscuously as man and wife. A number of hammocks, given by the sailors to the female slaves, are hung around a small court and are occupied by various couples."[13] The basic separation of the sexes in the Lodge continued through to the nineteenth century, as Hudson observed in 1806: "The Government slave Lodge . . . is capable of holding six hundred slaves, very commodious, divided into two wards, one for the males, the other for the females with an overlooker and attendants."[14] The most despised slaves (imported Africans from East Africa) were housed in the damp cellars, which were prone to flooding because of the same underground spring which normally provided the drinking water for the Lodge in a well in the courtyard.[15]

The Lodge slaves were dissuaded from nocturnal arson by the simple and effective, if cruelly irresponsible, device of removing the only key at closing time. It was deposited at the Fiscal's house, nearly a mile away. Mandoors kept all-night

---

[9] The marriage was not solemnized in church; Anna J. Böeseken (ed.), *Belangrike Kaapse Dokumente: Memoriën en Instructiën, 1675–1699* (Cape Town: South African State Archives, 1967), vol. 3, p. 205 (16 July 1685): A. Hulshof (ed.), "H. A. van Reede tot Drakenstein, Journaal van zijn verblijf aan die Kaap," *Bijdragen en Mededelingen van het Historisch Genootschap* 62 (1941): 206; Victor de Kock, *Those in Bondage: An Account of the Life of the Slave at the Cape . . .* (London: Allen & Unwin, 1950), p. 114.

[10] Leibbrandt, *Journal, 1699–1731*, p. 216.

[11] Otto Mentzel, *A Complete and Authentic Geographical and Topographical Description . . .*, trans. G. V. Marais and J. Hoge (Cape Town: Van Riebeeck Society, 1944), vol. 1, pp. 116–117.

[12] "*De beste ordentlijkse gepaarde slaven*"; Anna J. Böeseken et al. (eds.), *Suid-Afrikaanse Argiefstukke: Resolusies van die Politieke Raad* (Cape Town: Cape Times, 1957–1975; hereafter *Resolutions*), vol. 5, p. 162. In 1685, van Reede also suggested separate quarters for the "married" slaves, cf. H. A. van Reede tot Drakenstein, "Instruksie . . ." (15 July 1685) in Böeseken, *Memoriën en Instructiën*, vol. 1, p. 205.

[13] Mentzel, *Description*, vol. 1, 116.

[14] R. Shell, ed., "Hudson's Cape Town" *QBSAL* 47, 4 (June 1993): 144.

[15] This has been filled in with concrete.

vigils in the Lodge kitchens to guard against internal fire. With no exit, if a fire ever had broken out, the building would have become a hecatomb. Fortunately, after 1679, there were no further fires in the Lodge.[16] The Lodge became the primary site of architectural innovation for the difficult problem of housing and managing slaves within an urban setting. It is not surprising that the patterns established there, like segregating the slaves by age, sex, and descent group, and locking up the slaves at night,[17] became commonplace throughout the colony (see Figure 9-1).[18]

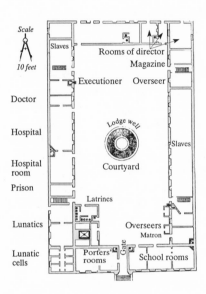

Figure 9–1. Plan of the ground floor of the Lodge, 1804.

The Early Development of Cape Vernacular Architecture, 1652–1736

Settlers who owned only a few slaves — nearly everybody started off small — could not afford to house their slaves separately as the Company did. At the outset of the colony, the domestic inclusion of all slaves within private houses was a

---

[16] Mentzel, *Description,* vol. 1, 116.

[17] Captain Robert Percival, *An Account of the Cape of Good Hope* (New York: Negro Universities Press, 1969 reprint), p. 117.

[18] Based on a plan in the William Fehr Collection, the Castle, Cape Town.

matter of economy, not preference. According to both James Walton and Hans Fransen, two architectural historians, the early Cape house was a simple rectangular room with the entrance at one end, windows along the sides and the chimney on the side opposite the entrance. Its only external (and occasional) adornment was a cross on the roof over the door, which signified a Christian inhabitant (see Figure 9-14). This architectural signature disappeared completely by the beginning of the eighteenth century.[19] This was the prototype of the Cape vernacular "longhouse," in the argot of the Cape's architecture and is symbolized by the letter I (for its shape). For structural and spatial reasons, the longhouse flourished in the rural areas. When the basic house was enlarged, two or more rooms would be joined together, resulting in L- and U-shaped houses in the urban areas, which allowed for a courtyard, and T- and H-shaped houses in the rural areas (see Figure 9-3).

In this early period, everyone on the holding, male and female slaves and the owner's family, lived together in a single room, perhaps with a rudimentary partition (*porte de divisie*); families shared beds and all slaves shared the house. Only much later do lockable bedrooms appear in the sources, as when Sparrman shared a bed with a burly Hanoverian knecht near Paarl in the 1770s: "Being but two Christians among twelve or fourteen male slaves, we bolted the door fast, and had five loaded pieces hung over our bed."[20] Rangton of Bali, a freed slave, refused to pay his landlord rent because his room had no lock.[21]

Living space was scarce and cramped in the private dwellings of the early Cape, whatever their architectural form. In 1681 the free black Louis van Bengal, housed his slaves "with other people" in the attic room (*zolder*) of his house.[22] Because of the shortage of living space, levels of intimacy were high. Claas van de Kust Mallebar, returning from putting clay on his owner's new house on a cold day in 1692, stopped in at the house of his master's relative, a settler named Pieter Jansz van Marseveeren, and asked his wife whether he and his fellow slaves could spend the night, since it was late. Her reply suggests that such an arrangement was not unusual: "Why not! You can sleep in the straw over there." The wife was already in one bed, with her sister, and since the two other male slaves made a beeline for the one available bunk in front of the fire, Claas was obliged to sit on the chest next to

---

[19] Fransen and Cook, *The Old Buildings of the Cape*, 2–4; James Walton, *Old Cape Farmsteads* (Cape Town: Human and Rousseau, 1989), pp. 11–15.

[20] Anders Sparrman, *A Voyage to the Cape of Good Hope . . .* , ed. Vernon S. Forbes (Cape Town: Van Riebeeck Society Second Series No. 7, 1977), vol. 1, pp. 101–102.

[21] Robert C.-H. Shell, "Rangton van Bali (1673–1720): Roots and Resurrection," *Kronos* 19 (1992): 192.

[22] One settler, suspecting that his runaway slave was hiding in such a room, and surprising the other inmates at 5 a.m., was greeted with some carefully aimed human excrement; see CAD C.330, *Attestatien* (3 January 1681), p. 353.

the women, with whom he proceeded to have an intimate conversation, which soon got out of hand. Claas did not relish the straw.[23]

The seventeenth-century curfew laws of the colony stipulated that owners should see that their slaves were kept "within *the* house" after the nightly curfew.[24] Slaves found on the streets after curfew would be jailed if they could not produce their letter of permission, a prototype of the notorious pass system.[25] The authorities, anxious at least to reduce expensive policing costs in the town, preferred urban owners to keep their slaves living within the main house. This was in clear contrast to policies toward the Khoi, who from 1658 were not allowed in the homes of settlers by Company edict.[26] From the beginning, the native people were the outsiders in an architectural sense, while the slaves were the insiders.

We know that even some male slaves shared the living quarters of well-to-do masters in the seventeenth century. Cornelis Brust van Alkman, a down-at-heel Dutch East India Company soldier, attempted to break into Henning Hussing's sumptuous Cape Town home at midnight on the sixth of June 1692. He forced the window of the main room with a marlin spike and was in the process of climbing through when he found himself — in his own words — in the arms of a "black boy," who with evident satisfaction handed him over to the Company authorities and the Caffers for punishment.[27]

An even more rudimentary house, the *pondok* (or *kapstijlhuijs,* from the German *kapsteilhaus,* a roof(cap)-style house), served as a temporary home that could be abandoned by the owner's family and subsequently used for slave quarters. Such houses were tiny with small low walls and steeply thatched roofs, the eaves of which were only a few feet above ground but the low walls could always later be elevated. The average floor space of the *kapstijlhuijs* was 15 feet by 21 feet and walls were so low, that one could stand upright only in the center.[28] This style of house fell out of use at least in Cape Town, in 1715 when the

---

[23] "*Waarum niet? Jij kund daar in 't Stroo well slaapen*"; AR VOC 4030: "Confessie: Claas van de Kust Mallebar" (14 March 1692), folio 328 verso.

[24] "*Binne 't huijs*"; emphasis added.

[25] "*Licentiebrief*"; Kathleen M. Jeffreys and S. D. Naude (eds.), *Kaapse Plakkaatboek, 1652–1806* (Cape Town: Kaapse Argiefstukke, 1944–1949): (13 January 1661), vol. 1. p. 64; (3 July 1686), vol. 1, 215; (13 April 1697), vol. 1, 299.

[26] Jeffreys and Naude, *Kaapse Plakkaatboek,* "Verbod teen die Veehandel van Vrijburgers met die Hottentotten" (24 October 1658), vol. 1, 44–45.

[27] "*Swarte jongen*"; AR VOC 4030: "Confessie: Cornelis Brust v. Alkman" (8 July 1692), folio 338.

[28] James Walton, "The South African *Kapstijlhuis* and some European Counterparts," *Restorica* 10 (December 1981): pp. 2–8. James Walton suggests that the house was similar to the Mediterranean *barracas,* but it seems that this was a type of human dwelling that was universal where labor and material were in short supply. The significant salience between these and other universal dwellings lies in the spatial arrangement of the Cape rooms, especially the placement of the kitchen.

authorities issued a *placcaat* (a statute on a poster) forbidding further building of new houses with walls lower than 15 feet.[29] But the style continued in the frontier areas and was used throughout the colony for housing slaves on the farmsteads. The slave lodge at the van der Stel farmstead Vergelegen, built between 1699 and 1706 to house 100 slaves (and probably knechts — European contracted labor — as well), was based on a longhouse version of the basic model. Anne Markel and Martin Hall, historical archaeologists currently excavating the farmstead, have claimed that this lodge was based on the *hallehuijs*, a model used in the medieval Netherlands to house farm workers, but considering the van der Stel's family history, Indonesian or Mauritian housing prototypes are equally likely. Several floor fireplaces with wooden hooded vents provided the heating for this large building.[30] The tentlike character of these Cape slave dwellings is directly confirmed by Peter Kolbe and E. V. Stade for the rural areas, and obliquely confirmed for the urban areas by oft-repeated statutes of the period that accused pipe smokers of carelessly igniting the "low eaves" of the houses in the town with their discarded lunts. Some *kapstijlhuizen* still exist in outlying areas in the Overberg and Clanwilliam districts.[31] The entrance was at one end and two small unglazed windows on the other end faced into the prevailing wind, the Southeaster. The *kapstijlhuijs* was subdivided by a partition, and cooking was done outside behind a screen, or sometimes in another *kapstijlhuijs* set at a right angle to the first, an arrangement that reduced drafts and provided a modicum of safety against the ever-present danger of the cooking fire, which when fanned by a 100 mile-an-hour "Cape Doctor" could quickly become uncontrollable.[32]

As soon as a slave owner could afford to, he would move his male slaves into an adjacent dwelling, while enslaved women usually stayed under the owner's roof. The women slept where they worked — in the kitchen. As Otto Mentzel, a German immigrant of some years' standing, noted: "It is usual at the Cape for a couple of slave girls to bring their beds into the kitchen at night time, sleep there, and clear out again in the morning."[33] Mentzel's observation is supported by an examination of both the written and the pictorial record and from the picture of slave holdings emerging from detailed research of inventories of urban and rural

---

[29] Jeffreys and Naude, *Kaapse Plakkaatboek*, vol. 2, 45 (1715) Item 35.

[30] This is based on some preliminary archeological work on the site. Personal communication, March 1993, with Carmel Schrire.

[31] Walton, "The South African *Kapstijlhuis*," pp. 2–8.

[32] Peter Kolbe, *The Present State of the Cape* . . . (London: Johnson Reprint Co., 1968), vol. 2, p. 52; Jeffreys and Naude, *Kaapse Plakkaatboek*, (2 December 1697/10 January 1698) "Nopens de bou van huise," vol. 1, 303–304.

[33] Otto Friederich Mentzel, *Life at the Cape* . . . , trans. Margaret Greenlees (Cape Town: Van Riebeeck Society, 1919), p. 40.

households.[34] The greater proportion of male slaves on rural estates throughout the eighteenth century would have strained the sleeping capacity of even the largest rural main house, when one calculates the number of slaves per room. Owners in rural areas were obliged to house their slaves separately because there simply was no commensurate increase in the number of rooms in the main houses of the rural farmsteads (see Figure 9-2).[35]

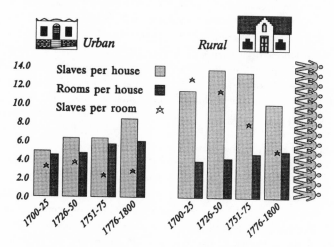

Figure 9–2. The number of slaves and rooms in urban and rural households, 1700 to 1800.

The Hearth as Focus: The Kitchen Hypothesis

If one visualizes the kitchen as the focal point of the early Cape home — the space where slave women slept and mistress and slave met most often — the development of all Cape architecture appears more straightforward. The importance of the kitchen arose from the importance of the fire and the simultaneous desire to separate the inside servants from the family. Sometimes, as Walton notes, an external kitchen was used as a separate slave quarters.[36] (In colonial America, the

---

[34] Historical archaeologists such as James Deetz, Margot Winer, Antonia Malan, and L. Y. Brink have begun intensive and systematic work on the estate inventories, cf. Antonia Malan, "The Archaeology of Probate Inventories," *Social Dynamics* 16, 1 (June 1990): 1-10; Margot Winer and James Deetz, "The Transformation of British Culture in the Eastern Cape," *Social Dynamics* 16, 1 (June 1990): 55–75.

[35] Antonio Malan, "The Archeology of Probate Inventories," *Social Dynamics* 16, 1 (June 1990): 7; (N = 570 inventories); free blacks excluded in original research. Slaves per room is a projection based on three rooms, including the *voorhuijs*, being reserved for the owner's immediate family.

[36] Private correspondence with James Walton (28 June 1993).

kitchen was often separated from the main house, and separate slave quarters emerged there, too.) Even when separate Cape slave quarters were built, they would face the same yard as the house of the owner, like the *jongenhuijs* on the Groot Constantia farmstead which in 1799 housed at least 25 slaves.[37] The town house of the Fiscal Joan Blesius, who owned 39 slaves, had separate slave quarters with slits for windows, facing the courtyard and the back of the house.[38]

The slave women did the cooking and were bent over, hard at that task for most of the day. Wrought iron cranes and "idle backs" which adorned West European open hearths, were never fashionable in South Africa because, as Walton notes with candor, "the ever-present slave rendered such labor saving devices unnecessary."[39] Whether the women were forced to sleep in the kitchen, or chose to is not clear — the kitchen was the warmest place in the chilly Cape homes, and its dominance by the women slaves influenced the management of the household and the holding profoundly. (In colonial America there was often a summer (external) and a winter (internal) kitchen. On the restored Belle Grove plantation in Virginia, for example, the winter kitchen had a large bed for the cook.) The women slaves thereby avoided the crowded male slave quarters, but were more closely under the impress of the owner's family, especially the mistress. Like the mandoor supervisors in the Lodge, the slave women became the informal sentries (and beneficiaries) of the big house's fire. By the nineteenth century the women slaves nearly always slept there (wet nurses however, slept outside the door of the mistress's room), and a taboo had been established forbidding the male owner from entering the kitchen at night. Samuel Eusebius Hudson, a newly arrived English resident, entered into his diary on 3 April 1799: "The inhabitants labor under a great inconvenience, few having a fireplace in any room except their kitchen, which is occupied by their slaves, and of course is not approachable by the master of the family."[40] Even in 1822 women slaves, either creole or "Malay," were the preferred live-in house servants, but by that time there were also male domestics, who were needed to carry the cumbrous sedan chairs.[41]

---

37 Also termed *slavenhuijsjes*, for some examples, see CAD C.331: "Attestatien" (2 April 1681), p. 41. Thÿs van der Merwe has shown that the term *jonkerhuijs* is probably incorrect; see van der Merwe, "Hendrik Cloete en die Argitektuur van Groot Constantia," *The Annals of the South African Cultural History Museum* 3, 1 (September 1990): 12. *Jongenhuijs* (slave house) was probably bowdlerized into the more respectable *jonkerhuijs*, house of the eldest son.

38 The slave quarters of the Blesius house (off Hof Street) have recently been excavated and restored.

39 James Walton, *Homesteads and Villages of South Africa*, (Pretoria: Van Schalk, 1952), pp. 28–29.

40 SAL Manuscripts: Samuel Eusebius Hudson, "Memorandum of Occurrences . . . ," p. 68; I have deposited an edited typescript of this manuscript in the South African Library, page references are to the edited manuscript.

41 W. W. Bird, *State of the Cape of Good Hope in 1822* (Cape Town: Struik, 1966 reprint), pp. 73–74.

In the rural T-shaped house, the kitchen and the owner's bedroom were separated by the *voorhuijs*, an enlarged entrance parlor, at the junction of the T. Alternatively, the house could grow longitudinally into the Cape longhouse pattern, in which the kitchen fire was as far away from the front door as possible (see Figure 9-3). If the kitchen became a separate dwelling or the longhouse were abandoned by the owner, the male slaves would be housed there, and the fireplace in the separate building would probably be used as a combination domestic hearth, stove, and smithy. This would explain why separate slave quarters nearly always have a chimney.[42] In J. V. Thiel's 1707 sketch of slave quarters at Vergelegen, two chimney stacks are represented on the slave quarters; in Johan Christiaan Frederiqui's 1798 aquarelle of the Meerlust farmstead and *werf* (the area around the main house sometimes enclosed by outbuildings or a perimeter wall, or both) no fewer than three chimney stacks are represented on the flat roof of the slave quarters, one belching smoke during the day.[43] In the early slave houses, windows are represented by artists, but increasingly, ventilation slits came to serve for windows in separate slave quarters, similar to slave houses in Curaçao and to the Lodge in Cape Town.[44] The emerging Cape pattern (and it was by no means universal) was that female slaves were housed in the kitchen attached to the main house, while the male slaves were housed in separate and inferior quarters, guardians of pigsties, dovecotes, and fowl runs and placed as far from the wine cellar as possible, although there may have been many permutations on individual farms (see Figure 9-3).[45] External quarters deteriorated in quality in some areas. Catherina Nel complained scornfully to the authorities in 1795 that her wealthy neighbor, Hendrik Ostwald Eksteen, had only built a *pondok* for his slaves, and much too near her property.[46] In one frontier holding in the 1830s a male and a female slave, Mina and Adonis, shared "a straw hut."[47]

No sources indicate where the slave children slept, but one may surmise that at least very small children slept with their mother and then left the house during

---

[42] Walton, *Old Cape Farmsteads*, 94.

[43] Walton, *Old Cape Farmsteads*, 92, 94.

[44] These ventilation slits were invariably enlarged. Examples can be seen in the Lodge on the north wall and on some farms, for example, Harmonie en Onrus; Walton, *Old Cape Farmsteads*, pp. 94–109.

[45] The original farm was granted in 1692; Adam Tas, the burgher revolutionary, came into possession by marrying the widow of the late owner, Hans Jurgen Grimpe. Based on H. Fransen and M. A. Cook, *Old Buildings of the Cape* (Cape Town: Balkema, 1980), p. 184; Phillida Brook Simons, *Cape Dutch Houses: A Concise Guide* (Cape Town: Struik, 1987), pp. 108–109; J. Walton, *Old Cape Farmsteads* (Cape Town: Human and Rousseau, 1989), pp. 12, 19, 92–94, 98–99.

[46] Hendrik Carel Vos Leibbrandt, *Requesten (Memorials) 1715–1806* (Cape Town: Cape Times, 1905), vol. 4, p. 1537 (30 January 1795).

[47] PRO CO 53/55 (16 August 1832) Somerset District, B16, n.p. I am grateful to Rachel van der Voort for this reference.

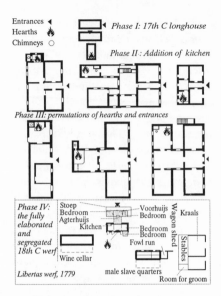

Figure 9–3. Diagram of Libertas plantation, showing segregation of slaves by 1779.

the day. Such creole slaves were closer to the owner's family and would later have first pick of the kitchen's hearth. The phrase "*in zijn huijs geboren*" (born in his house), found in a wide range of Cape documents, always heralded various patriarchal dispensations for such a slave and suggest that at least when the slave woman came to term she always slept inside.

As the rate of creolization increased there were many more slaves, both male and female, who became domestic slaves in the town and the country. Mentzel, writing of the 1740s, noted that "in the town there are some household slaves of a far superior type. They are well-behaved, diligent and devoted to their masters, who return this fidelity with kind treatment and many presents."[48] In 1783 Commissioner Hendrik Breton wrote that "on various farms, that I expressly visited, I found a far from simple life, and nothing except signs of prosperity, to the extent that, in addition to splendor and magnificence in clothes and carriages, the houses are filled with elegant furniture and the tables decked with silverware and served by tidily clothed slaves."[49] An American-born visitor, Robert Semple, noted in 1804: "It may be seen that the slave lodges in general under the same roof as *his* master. He [the slave] is fed with what comes from his [the master's] table,

48 Mentzel, *Description*, vol. 2, 130; Robert Wilson, "Description of the Cape Colony in 1806," unpublished manuscript, CAD VC 58 no. 59, p. 14.

49 As quoted in Robert Ross, "The Rise of the Cape Gentry," *Journal of South African Studies* 9 (1983): 206.

mingling with it a greater portion of rice."[50] But a few pages before he had written: "With respect to the slaves, they are lodged sometimes in the house, but more generally in small apartments connected with, or but slightly separated from the main building."[51] I believe one way to reconcile Semple's observations is that by 1800 a clear distinction had arisen between household slaves and others. Separate slave quarters emerged for imported male slaves, while the female slaves and perhaps a trusted creole male slave were kept within the house. The Koopmans' de Wet house in central Cape Town is a classic example of such an arrangement, with an internal room for the female slaves and a staircase leading to the courtyard that faced the separate male slave quarters. Off the kitchen was a "servant's hall" where the sedan chair was kept (see Figure 9-4).[52] Robert Percival, a British officer visiting Cape Town in the first British occupation, noted the clear distinction made in the urban architecture between the creole domestic slaves and others: "There are separate ranges and yards set apart for the slaves, strongly palisadoed [*sic*] and barricaded to prevent any communication with the former. Here, those slaves who are not highly in their confidence, or not bred up to household offices, are locked up every night."[53]

The fear of what imported slaves could do within the confines of the home is brought home by an anecdote of Samuel Hudson's, recorded in 1806:

Another instance which occurred very soon after I arrived at the Cape: a man of respectability and one who in every respect was considered a very humane good master to his slaves. He had invariably treated them with kindness. He purchased a man from the captain of a Danish ship lately arrived from Tranquebar. At the time

---

[50] Robert Semple, *Walks and Sketches at the Cape of Good Hope* (Cape Town: Balkema, 1968 reprint), p. 38.

[51] Semple, *Walks and Sketches,* 34.

[52] This architecture still serves a purpose: the museum authorities at the De Wet house today have seen fit to set aside the male slave quarters for the male black janitorial staff while the white female custodial staff has the internal room for office space. None of the slave quarters is open to the public. The casual visitor might well leave without knowing that the house, in its heyday, was full of slaves. Although the curators have faithfully followed G. E. Pearse's *Eighteenth Century Architecture in South Africa* drawings, there is much circumstantial evidence that what was labeled "a store room," at the rear of the second story house, was really a slave room. In the English script, the words *store* and *slave* are almost indistinguishable. The cross on the first *t* in "store" could have been the top most element of an *a* in any italic script, while the *v* and *r* are always difficult to decipher in the original script, which is not cited by Pearse. There is no reason whatsoever for a storeroom to have two entry ways *and* an expensive staircase into the courtyard. It is far more likely that this room was a slave room, most probably for the women slaves of "the establishment." Unfortunately, both the acknowledged slave quarters and the "store room" have been closed to the public for many years, although according to Lalou Meltzer, a museum worker, there are plans to restore them. G. E. Pearse, *Eighteenth Century Architecture in South Africa* (Cape Town: Balkema, 1968), page 10, Figure 6.

[53] Percival, *An Account of the Cape of Good Hope,* p. 117.

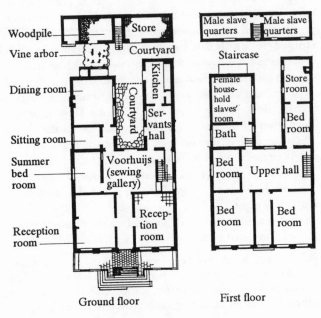

Figure 9–4. The layout of a typical big house, Cape Town.

he bought him, the boy told him he was no slave, but, considering this as a fabrication to prevent his sale, he concluded the bargain with the unprincipled Dane. The good and tender treatment of the master had in some measure reconciled the man to his new situation but he always insisted that he was not a slave. Things remained in this state for some time. It was a usual custom of Sundays for the slaves to take it in their turns to have holiday and one Sunday this boy having some particular engagement applyed to his master for permission to spend the day from home. He was refer'd to the head man who was [a slave] over looker[54] of the slaves and manager of the business, who on being apply'd to, told him it was not his turn to go out. This caused a second application to the master who said if Herries[55] had refused him he must have cause for so doing and he could not interfere. The boy said: "I am no slave and yet you treat me as one" and in language not very decent insisted on going out which the master as strongly insisted he should not, at the same time ordering the boy to quit the room immediately — he did so but it was with the most diabolical intention — he went to the shop secured a slaughtering knife (his master was a butcher) ran up stairs

---

[54] That is, an overseer.
[55] The name of the overseer.

followed by one of his fellow servants, but before he could prevent him, he had stab'd his master in several places and then turned on the slave who had endeavoured to prevent him in his horrid attempt and stab'd him, but not mortally.[56] The mistress, hearing the cry of her husband, snatched up a young child and rushed into another chamber and fastened the door. The sanguinary wretch followed and was in the act of forcing the door when Herries ran up stairs and with one blow of the cleaver — with which he had armed himself — nearly severed the boy's arm from his shoulder. He was then secured and carried bleeding to the trunk [*tronk*, jail]. The master died immediately and on the Monday the boy was brought to trial, condemned to be hanged, to have his head struck from his body, to be hung by the heels and his head placed between his legs. This sentence was immediately executed and after being exposed there for the day his body was carried to the Salt River and there placed on a gibbet as food for the crows and other birds of prey.[57]

Domestic architecture at the Cape was increasingly based on gender, but as the slave population was creolized, another form of household segregation crept in to separate creole slaves (and their owners) from imported slaves. Even well after the slave trade was abolished, W. W. Bird, the Comptroller of Customs, noted such domestic distinctions remained in force.[58]

If it is true that a broad range of Cape slave owners kept their female slaves within, and their male slaves outside but close to the "big house," this finding has implications for the domestic acculturation of all slaves at the Cape. Unlike the fieldhands of the American South who, according to American historian Albert Raboteau, at least enjoyed some cultural autonomy in their separate quarters, female slaves at the Cape were forced by reason of space to be under the broad thumb of their owner and family and to share their domestic culture.[59] The process was reciprocal, however. Cape slave women helped create a creole culture, cuisine, and language — kitchen Dutch — through the centuries-long architectural arrangements around the Cape kitchen. By 1833, the kitchen architecture was complete. Lady Herschel, a newcomer to the Cape, remarked on the novelty of the new arrangements:

So off we set & arrived at a Farm house where the Lady good-naturedly took us in, but never rose from her seat beside her tea wasser [see cover], which they sip from morning to night. She beckoned to the rooms we might occupy & issued orders for

---

56 Robert Percival, who repeats this story, albeit in a shorter form, adds that the slave who assisted was rewarded with his liberty; see his slightly different, and inferior account in Percival, *An Account of the Cape of Good Hope*, 290–291.

57 Robert C.-H. Shell (ed.), " 'Slaves,' an Essay by Samuel Eusebius Hudson" *Kronos* 9 (1984): 69–70.

58 W. W. Bird, *State of the Cape*, 73–74

59 Albert J. Raboteau writes: "It is clear that the slave community had an extensive religious life of its own, hidden from the eyes of the master. In the secrecy of the quarters . . . the slaves made Christianity truly their own." Raboteau, *Slave Religion: The Invisible Institution* . . . (New York: Oxford University Press, 1980), p. 212.

roasting fowls for our dinner, but took no further notice of us that night. The next morning we found her at her tea table as if she had never moved, & if you like to imagine a mass of human flesh supported in an arm chair, with perhaps a string around the waist to fasten petticoats & a huge shawl thrown over the shoulders & a common calico cap, you have a tolerable notion of the most respectable farmers *fraus* [i.e. *vrouwen,* wives] . . . The three front rooms of these Houses are generally spare rooms. The Back Hall is the family parlour, out of which there is always a dismal looking den of a passage leading to the kitchen where you dimly see black forms of all sizes & all degrees of dirt trotting about on their mistress's errands, & on this night especially dozens of faces peeped over each other's shoulders to see how the strangers ate & drank.[60]

At the Cape, imported male slaves and the native people were always the outsiders, all creole and women slaves, the insiders.

The Development of Urban Architecture, 1736–1808

Scant attention has been directed to Cape urban architecture — indeed, not a single volume is devoted to this topic — and, in contrast to the assiduous preservation of the rural patrician estates and some careful and imaginative work in the town of Stellenbosch, the smaller and humbler seventeenth- and eighteenth-century urban dwellings of the Cape are not only being allowed to crumble away, but they have also been ruthlessly bulldozed.[61] Many of the examples of early urban Cape Dutch architecture were owned by people who were born not in Europe, but on the rim of the Indian Ocean Basin. Koornhoop on the Liesbeeck River was owned by the wealthy Robert Schott van Bengal, who also owned a market garden in Cape Town, Schottsche Kloof.[62] And the "pearl" of all Cape architecture, Stellenberg, was owned by Christina of the Canarie Islands, once a slave, whom Simon Van der Stel, a governor of the colony, had freed shortly before

[60] Brian Warner (ed.), *Lady Herschel: Letters from the Cape, 1834–1838* (Cape Town: Friends of the South African Library, 1991), pp. 128–130.

[61] Under the implementation of the Group Areas Act, the most historic quarter of Cape Town, Castle Ward (or District Six), was bulldozed before the eyes of an astonished Cape Town shortly after I. D. du Plessis, the Afrikaans poet and a powerful patron of the area, had died. Although bulldozed, crumbled, and neglected, these urban dwellings have been described in an ethnographic vein, to which has been added a dash of righteous nostalgia. The urban, flat-topped buildings have been dubbed "Arabian" or "Moorish." Many of the surviving examples are in the Bo-Kaap, what used to be called the Malay Quarter. A fanatical central government intent on schemes of self-styled Aryan purity simply destroyed more than half of Cape Town's most historic creole buildings. The purpose was to allow poor whites who worked for the government to buy prized urban real estate cheaply.

[62] DO: TN 1705 (1725).

his own death.[63] Most freed slaves owned houses in Stellenbosch and Cape Town, but a handful owned farms in the interior. Kronendal, now a fashionable restaurant in Hout Bay, was owned by Ansiela van Bengal, originally one of Jan van Riebeeck's household slaves; Lanzerac, the famous Stellenbosch hotel, was owned by Louis van Bengal; the farms of Honswijk, Kijkuijt, and Sonquasdrift are among other celebrated rural homes owned by freed slaves. A sustained examination of the property deeds has revealed almost one hundred free black homes.[64] Such details of free black ownership are rarely mentioned in the literature. The same scholars who fastidiously ignore widespread freed slave ownership of early Cape houses and farms proudly point out that there were no architects at the Cape until the late eighteenth century and that, in the view of one famous author, the settler owners were their own architects.[65] One Wellington tradition from the farm Welbedacht has it that one slave's building skills became so famous that his owner hired him out as an architect and builder. No fewer than three farms have been attributed to this anonymous enslaved architect.

The Disappearance of European House Patterns

One might reasonably expect to find at least some carryover from the urban architecture of Holland in the busy port of colonial Cape Town. Since canal frontage was scarce in Holland, Dutch canal houses became elongated vertically with the front door and gable on the side facing the canal and the main bulk of the house extending away from the canal. In Cape Town, sea frontage was as scarce as canal frontage was in Holland. The Company warehouses perched on the breakwater, clearly depicted in E. V. Stade's 1710 drawings, do resemble their Dutch metropolitan counterparts and also resemble contemporary waterfront architecture of the port of Willemstad in Curaçao. A lively real estate market of sea frontage properties can also be reconstructed from the records of the Cape Deeds Office, and indirectly from statutes as early as 1714 (the year after a smallpox epidemic) forbidding any speculation on Cape Town property.[66] In short, waterfront property, both in Holland and at the Cape was a scarce resource that fundamentally affected the shape of the earliest buildings.

---

[63] Presumably she named the house after her patron. DO: TN 1192 (1717).

[64] DO: "Transporten," passim. Leonard Guelke and Robert Shell (comps.), "The Deeds Book: The Cape Cadastral Calendar" (New Haven, Conn.: Opgaaf Project, 1990), passim.

[65] C. de Bosdari, *Cape Dutch Houses and Farms* (Cape Town: Balkema, 1971), pp. 15, 77; James Deetz has defined vernacular architecture in this way: "buildings built without architect's plans." I prefer the etymological meaning of *vernacular*, from the Latin *verna* (slave), cf. James Deetz and Patricia E. Scott, "Building, Furnishings and Social Change in Early Victorian Grahamstown," *Social Dynamics* 16, 1 (1990): 80.

[66] Jeffreys and Naude, *Kaapse Plakkaatboek* (19 June 1714) vol. 2, 25–32, esp. (10 June 1714), vol. 2, 32.

All the material conditions necessary for a continuation and elaboration of Dutch urban architecture were in place in Cape Town and yet this did not happen. Instead, arson and the high winds of the Cape transformed and dominated the colonial urban architecture. If the most important element in canal front architecture in Holland was water, the principal elements in Cape urban architecture were fire and wind. Fire threatened everybody and everything, Company and private buildings. Some fires were accidental, but from the beginning many were deliberately set. In the same year that the class of free burghers was established by the Company, Khoisan people set fires in the settlers' houses and hay ricks. As a result, the Company actually forbade colonists from having any Khoi inside the houses of free burghers.[67] By the 1680s slaves were indirectly being accused of arson, and burghers were encouraged to build high walls and to plant thorn bushes around their homes.[68] Even slaves themselves were sometimes targets of other slaves — Mockadan Simon, the favored Company slave interpreter and foreman of the slave Lodge, had his own house torched by an irate Lodge slave in the 1680s. The fire was set because of Simon's close association with the governor and because of all the favors he enjoyed (not only the house, but also a concubine, and the right to be excused from work from time to time).

Individuals were not the only target of slave arsonists — Cape Town itself was at risk. The first serious slave revolt in Cape Town (in 1688), led by a free black, Sante van Sante Jago (Cape Verde), and a slave, Michiel, had as its ambitious aim to "burn one house after the other, to ashes." The Company issued a *placcaat* and set a reward of 20 Rixdollars to help find the arsonists, dead or alive.[69] Stellenbosch burned down in 1710, shortly after E. V. Stade painted his famous pen-and-wash picture of the village.[70] If it was arson, nobody was ever caught.

Because of the fear of fire, there were even plans to build extensive canals in Cape Town. The first canal was dug in 1687 in front of the town homes, not for transportation but for "household use and to extinguish fires."[71] Others followed: present-day Adderly Street used to be called Heerengracht (Lords Canal), Kaisergracht (Emperor's Canal) was another. The boundary streets of Cape Town still bear the old canal suffixes, such as Buitengracht (outside canal). These were not canals in the European sense; they were a sluice system for diverting water from the streams running off Table Mountain to provide water for drinking, irrigation, and fire control.

---

[67] Jeffreys and Naude, *Kaapse Plakkaatboek,* "Verbod teen die Veehandel van Vrijburgers met die Hottentotten" (24 October 1658), vol. 1, 44–45.

[68] Jeffreys and Naude, *Kaapse Plakkaatboek,* "Reëlings Nopens die beskerming van huise teen brand" (2 July 1686), vol. 1, 214.

[69] Jeffreys and Naude, *Kaapse Plakkaatboek* (10 March 1688), vol. 1, 249.

[70] DNTD, Van der Graaf Collection, "Stellenbos" [1710].

[71] Botha, *Social Life and Customs in the Eighteenth Century,* 22–23.

Fire and Punishment

So often had private buildings in Cape Town been set alight that the Company issued an edict on 2 July 1686 forbidding the construction of urban houses with low eaves, which — so the authorities claimed — were easily ignited by "malicious slaves and Hottentots." Harsh punishments for smoking in public places followed.[72] Convicted arsonists were put to a slow death over a fire and had a chamber pot jammed on their heads as a humiliating symbol of the dousing of the firebrand. Kolbe provides a horribly vivid example of what happened to a recidivist slave arsonist in 1714:

A slave at the Cape, in my time, there, attempted more than once to burn down his master's house. For this, being seized, he was sentenced to be roasted alive: and the execution was performed in the following manner. A stout post being fix'd upright in the ground, he was fastened to it by a chain, which at one end was fastn'd about his waist; at the other, to the post with such a length between the post and his body, that he might make one round about the post. Then was kindled a large fire round about him, just beyond the stretch of the chain. The flames rose high: the heat was vehement. He ran for some time to and again about the post; but gave not one cry. Being half roasted, he sunk down.[73]

Mentzel recorded what happened to a gang of 16 slave arsonists in 1736:

The whole gang of incendiaries was captured little by little. The prisoners were placed in the Donker gat [the "Dark Hole" in the Castle, see p. 183], where three of them cut their throats, having been enabled to do so by one of the gang, who with insolent boldness, went into the Castle in broad daylight and threw a sharp knife into the dungeon. He threw it in by the only opening the dungeon possesses — a tiny air-hole half a yard long and a quarter of a yard high, that is above the door. Even this hole is guarded by iron cross bars. Of the remaining incendiaries, five were impaled; four were broken on the wheel; that is to say each arm and each leg was twice beaten in two with an iron club, and then they were bound living on the wheel; four were hanged, and two women were slowly strangled while the hangman's assistants waved a burning bundle of reeds about their faces and before their eyes.[74]

Mentzel, who had suffered personally through the fire added with obvious relish: "In warm weather it is usual for slaves impaled and broken on the wheel to live between two or three days and nights, but on this occasion it was cold and they were all dead by midnight."[75] Sparrman, writing in the 1770s, confirmed that live impaling was reserved for incendiaries: "The spike in this case is thrust up along

---

[72] Jeffreys and Naude, *Kaapse Plakkaatboek* (10 January 1698), vol. 1, 302–303 refers to the earlier statutes.

[73] Kolbe, *The Present State of the Cape,* vol. 1, 363.

[74] Mentzel, *Life at the Cape,* 102.

[75] Mentzel, *Life at the Cape,* 102.

the backbone and the vertebrae of the neck, between the skin and the cuticle, in such a manner, that the delinquent is brought into a sitting posture. In this horrid situation, however, they are said to be capable of supporting life for several days, as long as there comes no rain, as in that case, the humidity will occasion their wounds to mortify, and consequently put an end to their sufferings in a few hours."[76] Such executions took place by torchlight, and all the town's slaves would be compelled to watch.

All the arsonists who were caught were imported slaves. This partly explains why the major architectural innovations at the Cape took place during the duration of the slave trade. The great fires at the Cape — in Stellenbosch (1710), Cape Town, (1736, 1790 and 1798) — took place during periods of the greatest numbers of imports. These periods of heavy importation, in turn, were caused by boom conditions in the local economy. But not all such periods were followed by fires. There were, for example, no major fires between 1736 and 1790. Perhaps the other conjunctures of fires and high import rates were a coincidence and the problem was more simply, that every generation had to be reminded anew of the dangers of fire. Nevertheless, temporary bans on importing male slaves from the East were imposed in 1767 and 1784 (see Figure 9-5).[77]

The Urban Owners' Response to Fires
Since there were no fire insurance companies at the Cape until the nineteenth century, all fire damage was made good by the Company, as Kolbe noted in 1710: "If any of the settlers suffer by fire in their houses or barns, and such settlers are not rich, the Company always largely and readily contributes to the repair of the Damage. The Company, in such cases, furnishes the best part of the materials for rebuilding, and orders its own artificers and servants upon the work; and the sufferers see themselves quickly [back] in [the] status quo."[78] Because of the cost of such rebuilding, the Company assumed a proactive role. From the earliest years of the colony, in a dubiously conceived co-option measure, the Company had insisted that the work of putting out fires was performed by the urban slaves themselves. As Mentzel noted: "All slaves whether belonging to the Company or to private owners, must assist in putting out the fire. The slaves carry the hoses, work the pressure engine, and fetch water. . . . Soldiers do not take part in putting out a fire; on the contrary, the gates of the castle are then closed and all the military are held in readiness to put down any possible rioting by the slaves."[79]

---

[76] Sparrman, *A Voyage to the Cape,* vol. 2, 257.

[77] Jeffreys and Naude, *Kaapse Plakkaatboek* (28 September 1767), (2 September 1784), vol. 3, 164. Fires (1658, 1770, 1794) PB 1: 43, 373; 3: 78; 4: 233; (1679) Geyser, p. 7; (1710, 1714) Dominicus, p. 68; (1740, 1787, 1790) Leibbrandt, *Requesten,* vol. 5, s.v. "fires."

[78] Kolbe, *The Present State of the Cape,* vol. 1, 360.

[79] Mentzel, *Description,* vol. 1, 133–134.

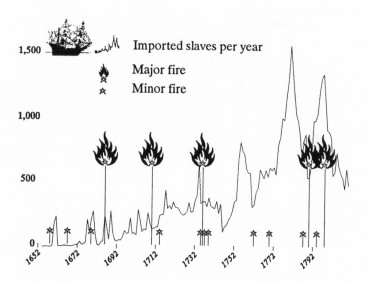

Figure 9–5. Imported slaves and the occurrence of major and minor fires, 1652 to 1808.

After 1722 the Company enrolled the free blacks and free Chinese in an unpaid and compulsory fire brigade. This new administrative ruse pitted ex-slaves against slaves. Its ostensible purpose was to make the free blacks responsible for putting out the fires that the slaves may have started, perhaps in the hope that the free blacks would police the slaves, or at least inform against them if there were a hint of an arson plot. Individual free blacks — in a disciplinary measure — were compelled to have a "pass" whenever they wished to leave town for more than a few days. Arson resulted in more measures of social control being imposed over both the free blacks and the slaves. Not until 1828 did Ordinance 50 finally liberate the 546 free black males from the burden of the *pompklompie* (the pump group), as the brigade is still remembered among the Cape Town community.[80]

---

[80] I am grateful to the fire department of Cape Town, which provided me with an anonymous typed manuscript of the history of the fire brigade. I have deposited it in the South African Library. Anthony Whyte provided the number of free blacks in 1828 (private communication, June 1991).

The Introduction of the Flat Roof

In 1717, the same year that the directors of the Company decreed that the colony would no longer have assisted immigration of people from Europe (and that labor, by default, would be based on slavery, see pp. 4–7), the local authorities recommended that urban householders abandon thatched roofs; directions were issued also for making a watertight, fireproof flat roof. The Company's urban patrician officials took the lead in developing the new arson-proof urban architecture. The various statutes were based on experiments carried out by the Fiscal (the official in charge of all the slaves, see 177). Leeuwenhof, the home of the first Fiscal, and currently the home of the administrator of Cape Province, "the most important house to have been built in Table Valley at that time," was among the first flat-roofed houses at the Cape.[81] Flat roofs, as any builder knows, mean leaks, and the Cape citizens took pride in concocting special plaster mixtures to make their fireproof flat roofs impervious to rain.[82] The first burgher house built with a flat roof went up in 1717, but the owner, in a desperate attempt to make his roof watertight, had soaked the roof in whale oil, which of course defeated the primary purpose.[83] Once the Fiscal's domestic experiments were completed, the Council of Policy in 1717 called for roof of hard burned bricks laid over laths, on top of which applied three arson-proof agents — sea shells, lime, and brick dust — and two waterproofing agents — cocoanut oil and *Bengal Gor*, a sediment of sugar.[84]

Following the example of the Lodge, all other Company buildings in Cape Town were gradually rebuilt in the flat-roofed style, but it was not until 1732 that a wealthy burgher, Hendrik Müller, a slave-owning tailor and a former fire master of the town, built the first successful flat-roofed house in the private sector.[85] Mentzel, the German tutor who lived in Cape Town for some time, wrote that "Müller, who had amassed a small fortune by trade, pulled down his corner house in the Market Square and put up a new three-storied building with a flat roof."[86]

Müller's example was slow to catch on, for the walls of a flat-roofed house have to support more dead weight than walls supporting a pitched roof. Financial considerations also retarded the switch to the new architectural style. Then, in 1736, Cape Town had its first "great fire." Many gabled and thatched Company buildings and private homes were razed. Mentzel's boss, Herr Alleman, had his

---

[81] Philida Brooke Simons, *Cape Dutch Houses* (Cape Town: Struik, 1987), pp. 25–26.

[82] Samuel Hudson had such recipes in his personal notebooks; cf. CAD A10, Hudson, "Notebook, recipes &c."

[83] Fransen and Cook, *The Old Buildings of the Cape*, 1.

[84] *Resolutions* (12 April 1718), vol. 5, 275–276; C. Graham Botha, *Social Life in the Cape Colony*, including *Social Customs in South Africa in the 18th Century* (Cape Town: Struik, 1973 reprint), p. 26.

[85] *Resolutions* (12 April 1718). vol. 5, 275–276.

[86] Mentzel, *Description*, vol. 1, 133–134.

own house burned down, so Mentzel was an eyewitness and recorded what might be considered the pivotal period for vernacular urban architecture:

In 1736 there was a plot formed by some fugitive slaves to set the town on fire with the object of robbing, pilfering and murdering to their heart's content during the confusion. They began in the South Eastern corner so as to take advantage of the prevailing South Eastern Wind, which was likely to fan the flames, and set fire to a shoemaker's workshop that contained rawhides undergoing the tanning process. The fire spread rapidly to several burgher dwellings, three of which were burned down to the ground, including that of Lieutenant Allemann. Thereafter Herr Alleman rebuilt in the style of the tailor Müller; many others followed suit to minimize the risk of fire, and houses in the new style were put up by the warehouse master, Swellengrebel, the dispenser Henning, the assistant Fiscal Reder, and various rich burghers. The number of new houses is constantly on the increase and it is quite probable that in the course of time the thatched roofs will disappear altogether.[87]

The household slaves of Herr Alleman were not part of the plot but partook of some of the spoils, Mentzel wrote: "When we went over the same ground the next day we found the Terlaten slaves [from Mozambique] making merry with a feast of roasted fowls. They ate the birds — which must have tasted very juicy, being cooked in that way — right up to the bones."[88]

After the disaster of the 1736 fire, the Company decreed that all Company buildings should have flat roofs. Of these, the Greenmarket Square Stadhuijs (Town House) depicted by the French artist, H. C. De Meillon is the most noteworthy, because it is the only building embellished with motifs designed by slaves.[89] Robert Semple, who knew nothing of its history, observed that by 1804 it had become the favorite place for Cape Town slaves: "it is ornamented with pilasters and a portico, which may be called the slaves' portico; for here when unemployed, especially in rainy weather, or towards the close of summer evening, they assemble together in groups, and talk over the hardships of a life of slavery."[90] This building was the symbolic seat of government, the burgher senate and also, by coincidence, where the fire engines were kept (see Figure 9-6).[91]

Detailed work on inventories by Cape historical archaeologists confirms that the floor plans of all urban houses became more complicated with more internal supporting walls and more rooms after 1736, a process which steadily increased in the eighteenth century, if the household inventories are a good guide. There were

[87] Mentzel, *Description,* vol. 1, 134–135; cf. the same incident described in Mentzel, *Life at the Cape,* 100–101.

[88] Mentzel, *Life at the Cape,* 101.

[89] Anna H. Smith, *Cape Views and Costumes* (Johannesburg: Brenthurst Press, 1978), Plate 1, p. 23; Plate 5, p. 30.

[90] Semple, *Walks and Sketches,* 17–18.

[91] Bird, *State of the Cape,* 159.

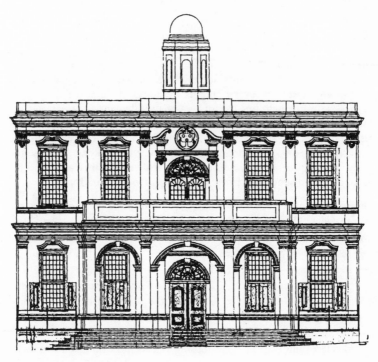

Figure 9–6. The Stadthuijs, 1822.

more rooms in the Cape Town home than in the rural farmsteads (see Figure 9-2).[92] The *voorhuijs*, which separated the kitchen from the other rooms, became fashionable at this time. There, the female slaves would sit on long benches doing their embroidery and knitting after they had cleaned the house. According to L. Y. Brink, the architectural historian, these new Cape floor plans were "found only very rarely in the Netherlands."[93]

More Cape Town houses were being used every year as boardinghouses and unofficial canteens for the increasing numbers of sailors and officials visiting the Cape. Using the conservative length of a fortnight for the average ship's call and accepting F. C. Dominicus's estimate of 147 for the average ship's crew, one can readily appreciate that the Capetonians had a seasonal opportunity to make much money from housing the "Lords of six weeks," as Charles R. Boxer called these

---

[92] L. Y. Brink, "The Voorhuijs as a Central Element in Early Cape Houses," *Social Dynamics* 16, 1 (1990): 52.

[93] Brink, "The Voorhuijs as a Central Element," 51.

sojourners. By 1731, there were also many boarding houses that catered exclusively to the nonseasonal frontier trade (*buijtenlui*).[94] In addition, many wealthy Capetonians were using rooms in their homes as storehouses for petty goods and private offices.[95]

Another reason for the changing architecture in Cape Town houses was the slave trade. The urban patriciate would buy slaves and keep them in their urban "pens" until there was an acute shortage of slaves on the market in the winter months. According to a wide range of primary and secondary sources, there were as many as 20 slaves in such wealthy urban "establishments."[96] An anonymous pen-and-wash drawing of the home of François Duminy, a well-known trader in slaves and a slave-trading captain employed by the Company, is the only visual description we have. According to the drawing, a long, high wall with a barred seven-foot iron gate surrounded the house. The slave quarters, like the Company Lodge, had narrow slits for windows. The slave quarters were in the foreground of the compound for better observation from the large windows of the "big house." Both slave quarters and the double-storied "big house" were flat-roofed to avoid arson and surrounded by a protective *ringmuur*. This was a cynical architecture perhaps, modeled on the Lodge, but one well-suited to the domestic slave trade centered in the port (see Figure 9-7).[97]

Figure 9–7. Duminy's house.

[94] Leonard Guelke, Robert Shell, and Anthony Whyte (comps.), "The de la Fontaine Report" (New Haven, Conn.: Opgaaf Project, 1990), introduction.

[95] Some officials preferred to have their pay banked in the Netherlands. Their agents would send out goods on the ballast-light outward-bound fleets; Percival, *An Account of the Cape of Good Hope*, 117.

[96] Johan Georg Bövingh, *Kurze Nachricht von den Hottentotten oder denen Heyden . . .* (Hamburg: Caspar Jahkel, 1710, rare; another edition 1714), p. 2; Captain James Cook, *A Voyage around the World* (London: Strachan & T. Cadell, 1777), vol. 1, 77–78; Mirza Isfahani Abū Tālib Ibn Muhammed Khān, *The Voyages of Mirza Abu Taleb Khan in Asia, Africa and Europe in the Years 1799, 1800, 1801, 1802 and 1803, written by himself in the Persian Language*, trans. Charles Stewart (London: Longman, Hurst Rees and Orme, 1810), vol. 1, p. 68; John Barrow, *Travels into the Interior of Southern Africa* (London: Cadell, 1806), vol. 2, 92; Antonia Malan, "The Archeology of Probate Inventories," *Social Dynamics* 16, 1 (1990): 6.

[97] J. L. M. Franken (ed.), *Duminy Diaries* (Cape Town: Van Riebeeck Society, No. 19, 1938), plate facing p. 73.

Whether accidental or arson, fire remained a problem with many implications. A fierce dispute between the burgher councilors and the owners of the pubs
and canteens erupted in 1752. Irate burgher councilors claimed that "slaves and
low class Europeans" were in the habit of getting drunk in the new canteens in the
center of town: "With burning lunts they walk about the streets and beat them
against the door posts; they carry coals of fire from one tap to another, and
constantly wander about inside those houses and outside with lit pipes . . .most of
the Cape houses are thatched with reeds, and if they were to catch fire the whole
turn would be burnt down to the ruin of inhabitants." The burgher councilors
wanted to segregate the town's canteens by establishing all canteens along the
seafront, away from the slave Lodge. "Heavy punishments," they added, "would
not only intimidate that class of people, but also prevent any accidents."[98] The
canteen owners objected that the danger from fire came from all houses at the
Cape, "especially those inhabited by the Chinese and other light folk," and that if
the burgher councilors succeeded in segregating the canteens along the waterfront,
the Company would "lose much revenue."[99]

The numerous alleys of Cape Town are also a legacy of fire control in the
eighteenth century, as Mentzel noted:

It is customary in the town of the Cape to leave a passage of four feet between each
house. The main object of this arrangement is to permit the rainwater from the
roofs to find its way to the road, but it has a most beneficial effect in the case of fire.
It enables the firemen to get between the houses and play the fire hose upon every
part of the burning building. The four foot passage is an absolute protection of the
new type of house with solid flat roofs especially if it is higher than the burning
house; in fact these flat-roofed dwellings form an excellent vantage point . . . hence
fires can be more easily got under [control]. Upon the outbreak of fire many of the
neighboring houses spread old sails over the side of the roofs adjacent to the fire,
and if these sails are well soaked with water the extension of fire is checked.[100]

Fully one hundred years before a municipality was thought of, the organization, administration, and layout of the town was increasingly predicated on fire
control. *Brandmeesters* (fire masters) were chosen from among the most respectable
people in the town, and each was entrusted with a "ward," a district over which the
brandmeester had considerable authority to enter and inspect houses on a weekly
basis. There was also someone assigned to the all-night fire watch *(de ratelwag)*
who, in case of fire, rang the bells of church and Castle.[101] By 1762 there were no
fewer than 24 published statutes concerning fire regulations, which every urban

---

[98] Leibbrandt, *Requesten* (no. 68 of 1752), vol. 1, 85–86.

[99] Leibbrandt, *Requesten* (no. 73, 18 July 1752), vol. 2, 680.

[100] Mentzel, *Description*, vol. 1, 134.

[101] H. C. Dominicus, *Het Huiselik en Maatschappelik Leven* . . . ('s-Gravenhage: Martinus
Nijhoff, 1919), p. 68.

householder was expected to memorize.[102] Despite such measures, however, fire and arson continued in the town. An impoverished Cape Town businessman, Andries Nolte, complained in 1760 that "his dwelling house has lately been most maliciously set on fire by his late slave, January van Boegies, so that, as well as all the goods it contained, the tannery and horse stable, which he had used for his saddler's business, were all laid in ashes, and he had been plunged into the extremist poverty."[103]

1798 was the year of Cape Town's second great fire, which was more devastating to property and the most far-reaching in terms of architectural changes. Again it was assumed that slave "incendiaries" were responsible. A curfew was ordered — 8 o'clock for slaves, 9 o'clock for soldiers, 10 o'clock for "inhabitants." It was declared that any slave or soldier informing on the arsonist would be set free or be discharged. Samuel Hudson, one of the earliest English colonists, provided a vivid description of that fire:

About half past ten o clock this evening I was roused from my bed with an alarm of Fire. The Drums beat to Arms, the Bells were rung and the whole Town thrown into the greatest consternation. Parties of Light Dragoons rode through the streets to rouse the Inhabitants. I threw some few clothes on and sallied forth but gracious God what a sight presented itself. . . . Some houses were much injured, one reduced to a heap of ruins. The wind was blowing a tremendous hurricane from the South East which carried the flames to a considerable distance and caused the fire to spread so rapidly, at times apprehensions were entertained for the fate of the whole town. . . . Some of the soldiers had the temerity to continue in the stores drinking the brandy from the ground whilst the roofs and floors were in a falling state and every aperture red with conflagration, the very spirits blazing as it flowed, and these wretches blowing the flame away whilst they quaffed the almost boiling beverage. One man was carried out by force and was with difficulty prevented from making another attempt . . . death would have been the consequence and [he] was so miserably scorched that he expired soon after he was carried to the Hospital and this I believe was the only accident of the kind that happened.

A few days later Hudson wrote:

21st: A Proclamation was issued this morning ordering all slaves under severe punishment to be in their houses by Eight o' Clock of an evening and the Inhabitants not to be found in the streets after ten o'clock at which times a Bell is rung at the Church. Soldiers to be in their Barracks at nine o'clock and any person having occasion to be out later then the time specified must get a permission from the General or chief Magistrate as no excuse will be accepted for not complying with the above order. Three thousand Rixdollars reward is offered to any person

---

[102] Jeffreys and Naude, *Kaapse Plakkaatboek* (16/20 November 1762) "Instruksies i.v.m. die bestrijding van brand," vol. 3, 42–50.

[103] Leibbrandt, *Requesten* (no. 127 of 1760), vol. 2, 834.

who will confess of his or her accomplices, their names kept secret, and if a slave, to receive besides the above reward his liberty, and, if a soldier, his discharge. These advantages I hope will bring the Incendiaries to condign punishment for I am afraid there is a numerous set who have determined these damned measures.[104]

After much deliberation the town authorities decreed in 1804 that no private houses whatsoever were to be built with thatched roofs. The steeply pitched, black thatched Cape roof now disappeared, and in its place went up the flat roof. The glamorous front gable fell away, too. A wavy parapet along the top of the facade became the urban counterpart of the glamorous rural Cape gable.[105] According to the artistic record, by 1831 there was only one thatched-roof building with a bacchanalian, central gable left in central Cape Town, a historic tavern in Greenmarket Square; it too would burn down. Its gable was purely decorative: there was no door under the gable (see Figure 9-8).[106]

Figure 9–8. Gabled canteen in central Cape Town, built 1714, burnt down 1860.

After the second great fire, the Cape authorities studied reports of the great fire of London of 1666 for clues to retarding the spread of fire. They learned that

---

[104] SAL Manuscripts, Samuel Eusebius Hudson, "A Memorandum of Occurrences . . . ," p. 68.

[105] Only two examples survive in Cape Town, one is the Bo-Kaap Museum in Wale Street, the other, around the corner in Buitenkant Street, was an upholstery shop in 1985. The owner has added some external shutters of his own making.

[106] Scanned and enhanced image from George Duff, "Willem Berg's Canteen, Dorp Street, 1717" in Hymen W. J. Picard, *Gentleman's Walk* (Cape Town: C. Struik, 1968), second plate following page 61.

the London fire had spread from one outside shutter to the next, and so decreed that all new houses in Cape Town would have inside shutters instead of outside ones. The new urban architecture of Cape Town was now almost complete. The houses had plain square facades, unadorned by external shutters or central gables (see Figure 9-9).[107] The only feature of the urban Cape house that extended beyond the plain unshuttered facade was an external light, the *bolig* (upper light), that every inhabitant was to light at dusk. The authorities believed darkness allowed slaves and free blacks to gather together and plot. Private homes thus provided all the street lighting in Cape Town throughout the eighteenth and early nineteenth centuries.

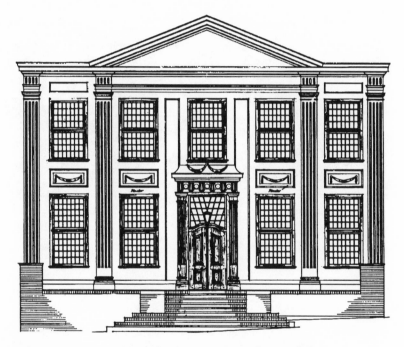

Figure 9–9. Koopmans de Wet façade, Cape Town, showing *bolig*.

Local conditions (such as the Southeaster, which magnified the potential of even the smallest fire) and the tensions of the Cape slave society, rather than imported European influences in house design, transformed urban Cape architecture into what it was: a defensive architecture. With no gables, no thatch, and

---

[107] Scanned and computer enhanced image, based on G. E. Pearse, *Eighteenth Century Architecture in South Africa* (Cape Town: A. A. Balkema, 1968), Plate 29.

indeed no roof — in the customary sense of the word — the ordinary Cape Town house was, by statute, destined to be plain. It resembled the architecture of the Mediterranean by coincidence. No clearer evidence for this may be found than in the comparison of three townscapes, the first done by E. V. Stade in 1710, which clearly does show European influences; the second, a flat roofed townscape by Samuel Hudson in 1806, on the eve of the abolition of the oceanic slave trade; and finally, the waterfront drawn by Sir Charles D'Oyly on the eve of emancipation in 1831 (see Figure 9-10).

Figure 9–10. Waterfront scene, 1831.

The Development of Rural Architecture, 1706–1808

Arson was more easily controlled in the rural areas, since both slaves and the Khoi were more intimately dependent on the farm family and under their focused supervision. Unlike the town, the country offered the runaway arsonist no assured anonymity. The rural slave population was also increasingly isolated by distance, mountains, and language. Conspiracy and escape were more difficult to organize. Runaway slaves, *drosters*, were ruthlessly and successfully hunted down by commandos (burgher militias); and only the most isolated native people would harbor

runaway slaves. Because of the small numbers in the typical Cape slave holding, incorporation of the slaves into the family structure on isolated farms was more complete. If a rural slave attempted arson, he or she had to run away.

The large mansions on rural Cape slave farmsteads were a feature of the early period and were owned and built by patrician Company officials. For example, the largest houses in the first century of occupation, Groot Constantia and Vergelegen, were both owned by governors of the colony, and were part of a father-and-son architectural contest that long dominated the metropolitan-creole rivalry in the design of houses at the Cape. The creole design of the son's single-story farmstead house eventually prevailed throughout the Cape; even Constantia (the father's three-story farmstead) was rebuilt in the new single-story form. In 1706 the disgruntled and patently envious burghers called the patrician houses, with their characteristic exaggeration, "palaces." Despite their complaints about the officials' palaces, all wealthy rural burghers spent their life aspiring to own such stately houses.

Some slaves must have stayed in these rural mansions, although a museum guide vociferously denied this to me in 1981.[108] At Groot Constantia most of the male slaves were probably housed in the basement. This would provide a tentative explanation for the "secret tunnel" leading from under the front of the house to the *werf.* The owner's family could hide in the tunnel if the slaves became rebellious. But this tunnel was unusual; the general Cape solution to domestic slave rebellion was separate quarters. The earliest mention of rural "slave houses" occurs in 1679.[109]

It is important to realize that slaves on big rural estates were kept both within the house and without. According to François Valentijn, a visiting *predikant,* Willem Adriaan van der Stel had slaves who were exiled Indonesian royalty serving as his live-in housekeepers at Vergelegen in 1706.[110] Vergelegen was therefore among the earliest farmsteads to have large external slave houses, termed a slave Lodge, as well as internal domestic servant quarters.[111]

Khoi workers who settled on European estates built their own houses in the neighborhood of the main house. Adam Tas, a Stellenbosch burgher, remarked on the separate quarters for his Khoi workers in 1706, but nowhere mentioned in his detailed diary where his own slaves — whom he referred to as "our people" (*onze*

---

[108] Delft: *Nederlandsche Topografische Dienst,* Van der Graaf Collection: E. V. Stade, "*Constantia, de hofstede van den Heer Simon v.d Stel*" M/1/984, (1710).

[109] "*Particuliere slaven huijsen*"; Jeffreys and Naude, *Kaapse Plakkaatboek* (30 November 1678), vol. 1, 152.

[110] Valentijn, *Description of the Cape of Good Hope . . .* , vol. 1, 151–152.

[111] Hendrik Carel Vos Leibbrandt, *Precis of the Archives of the Cape of Good Hope: The Defense of Willem Adriaan van der Stel* (Cape Town: W. A. Richards & Sons, 1897), p. 111.

volk) — slept. Extant plans of his farmstead, Libertas, show no separate slave quarters until 1779.[112] Perhaps at least some of them slept inside the house (see Figure 9-3). Only much later, in the 1770s, do reports of separate houses for slaves on the big burgher estates start appearing regularly. Admiral Stavorinus, a well-informed visitor to the Cape at this time, was so impressed by Martin Melck's farmstead and its housing arrangements for the slaves that he wrote: "A little higher up stood a range of buildings, calculated for the slaves, of whom he had full two hundred; for he declared to me he did not know the exact number. Everyone [slave] had a separate brick dwelling to sleep in." Perhaps Melck had modeled his farmstead on the Lodge, or believed in the integrity of the slave family, or had pronatalist convictions. Whatever the reason, Stavorinus added: "Those that were married were kept apart from the others."[113]

Melck's farm, exceptional in its size, heralded an expansion of separate quarters throughout the colony through a hand-me-down system. As Robert Ross, a Cape historian, has clearly shown, more new farmsteads were built in this period than in any comparable period, and in such cases the old main house, I surmise, would be used for slave quarters.[114] This building boom had several underlying and connected causes, but it was principally based on the prosperity occasioned by the French garrison presence, a diplomatic arrangement that also ushered in many East African slaves, a trade the French controlled. In addition, the Statutes of India which were reissued in 1770, greatly expanded Christian responsibilities to servants and slaves within the household. These could be partly obviated if owners regarded only the household slaves as technically part of the household. Although deliberately not out of sight, the field slaves, by now mostly from Africa, were definitely out of their owners' mind in their separate quarters. These factors resulted in a desire to organize the Cape farmstead along the lines of the early patrician farmsteads such as Vergelegen. Imported slaves were given separate quarters as soon as the owner could afford them. Either a new main house (*hofstede*) was built, in which case the old house was given to the slaves, or new slave quarters were built. Over a period of one hundred years, some estates went through multiple transformations. Most of the gables, indicating a new "big house," date to the period after 1770 (see Figure 9-11).[115]

---

[112] Adam Tas, *The Diary of Adam Tas*, ed. Leo Fouché et al. (Cape Town: Van Riebeeck Society, 1969–70), p. 139.

[113] J. S. Stavorinus, *Voyages to the East Indies by the Late John Splinter Stavorinus, Esq., Rear-Admiral in the Service of the States General . . .* (London: G. G. & J. Robinson, 1798), vol. 2, 62.

[114] Ross, "The Rise of the Cape Gentry," 206.

[115] Ross, "The Rise of the Cape Gentry," 206.

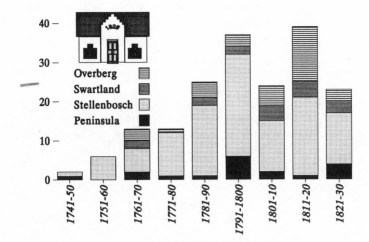

Figure 9–11. The building of rural gabled farmsteads, 1741 to 1830.

Rural Arson

Admiral Stavorinus stated that fire was a problem on Martin Melck's farmstead, without being specific about any alterations having been made.[116] Reactions to arson were informal rather than statutory, as they were in the town. The rural thatched roofs and gables were not at risk as they were in the hurly-burly of Cape Town, where arsonists sometimes got away scot-free. The main architectural precautions taken against fire in the rural area were that, after 1706, the over-whelming majority of all rural mansions, even the largest, were built with a single story and without a basement. Although there were a few multi-story houses — Groot Constantia and Koelenhof are seventeenth century examples — almost without exception Cape rural houses had a single story (see Figure 9-12).[117]

The *brandzolder* (fire ceiling) was developed in the rural Cape to contain the damage of a roof fire.[118] The coals and embers would fall on the *sparretjezolder*, a thick mat of dried clay pressed into an armature of dried reeds and strung across heavy beams. If the fire was small, only the thatch roof would be lost.[119] The

---

[116] Stavorinus, *Voyages to the East Indies . . .* , vol. 2, 62.

[117] G. E. Pearse, *Eighteenth Century Architecture in South Africa* (Cape Town: Balkema, 1968), plate 58.

[118] Groot Constantia burned to the ground in 1925 because it had no *brandzolder;* cf. de Bosdari, *Cape Dutch Houses and Farms*, 21.

[119] The *brandzolder* became a storage loft and even a granary with an external lockable staircase. According to Walton, "lack of trust in the servants was apparently the reason for the unusual arrangement of the stairs"; Walton, *Homesteads and Villages of South Africa*, 8; see Plate 9 of his book.

brandzolder was possibly the clearest innovation of rural Cape vernacular architecture and the most significant departure from contemporary European architectural norms. Double-story houses and basements required expensive, flammable wooden staircases, and these became a rarity in the spacious households of the rural Cape.

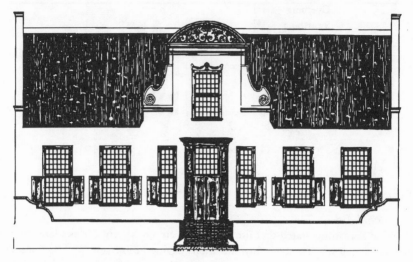

Figure 9–12. Stellenberg, Claremont.

Among all the structures on the *werf,* the Cape bell tower most clearly symbolized the rural slave society. Even the largest *haciendas* in the Yucatán or the most luxurious *landhuizen* in Curaçao could not boast of slave bell towers such as are found on Cape farmsteads. The large Cape bell tower was also associated with fire and danger.[120] F. C. Dominicus claimed that the early Cape slave bells were salvaged ship's bells that were used to warn neighbors of impending attack by the Khoisan.[121] When fire broke out, too, the slave bell was rung to call all the farmstead slaves to put out the blaze. The Cape slave bell and its impressive tower are exact replicas of the Cape church bell. This appropriation of ecclesiastical architecture may be seen in several lights: the bell symbolized the owners' Christian connections; the bell served to set the quotidian routines of the farmstead, from sunrise to sunset. While the church bell called the faithful to church, the farm bell tower called slaves to work and, on the wine-producing farms, announced the times for their *dops* (measures of wine). The architectural device was not only unmistakably hegemonic and symbolic of both work and religion, but it was also

---

[120] There is not a single article on this architectural topic; Margaret Cairns has been collecting the inscriptions on the bells.

[121] F. C. Dominicus, *Het Huiselik en Maatschappelik Leven . . .* , 40, note 1.

Pavlovian in its division of the day into *dop,* work, *dop,* work, and *dop.* Just as Charles Randolph Boxer wrote of Brazil, that "the place of the cathedral, more powerful than the king, was taken by the farmstead big house,"[122] so too the Cape farmstead, with its oversize bell, not only presided over the *werf* aesthetically, but also came to dominate an increasing arena of human experience psychologically, a communion of labor (see Figure 9-13).[123]

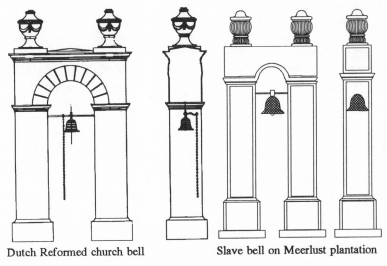

Dutch Reformed church bell   Slave bell on Meerlust plantation

Figure 9–13. Slave bell tower on Meerlust plantation and local Church bell.

The central gable came to be the dominant feature of all rural architecture in South Africa. De Bosdari claims that the purpose of the Cape front gable was new: it served to keep the front door free from the drip of the eaves, to allow light into the attic, and mainly to protect the ornate, expensive front door from burning thatch in the event of fire.[124] By 1700 Christian crosses on roofs had disappeared, along with the other genuine European derivation — the end gable.[125] The front gable flourished in the rural areas of the Cape in the late eighteenth century. The cross was to be replaced by a decorative motif, most

---

[122] Charles Randolph Boxer, *The Golden Age of Brazil, 1695–1750: Growing Pains of a Colonial Society* (Berkeley: University of California Press, 1962), p. 192.

[123] Scanned and copied images from G. E. Pearse, *Eighteenth-Century Architecture in South Africa* (Cape Town: Balkema, 1968), Plates 71, 99, cf. plates 80, 86.

[124] de Bosdari, *Cape Dutch Houses and Farms,* 24; interview with James Walton, August 1990.

[125] Walton, *Old Cape Farmsteads,* 12–13.

commonly the date of construction. The front gable grew larger and more elaborate, and finally matching gables reappeared on the ends of the houses in addition to the front. Barns and other outbuildings, down to humble dovecotes, chicken coops, and pigsties, also sported matching, but always inferior, gables. Slave quarters however, rarely had front gables. The main front gable and its efflorescence of ornamentation came to have the same social cachet and significance for a Cape settler as a coat-of-arms had for a medieval European nobleman. The main gable became a secular, domestic steeple, sometimes emblazoned with a fleur-de-lis or an ethnic signifier of the resident owner.

The modern viewer is perhaps charmed by the elegance of these buildings, but it is their size that awes. The Cape estate houses were larger by far than the grandest *landhuizen* of the Dutch Antilles. One is apt to forget that they grew from a meager, mixed economy that could scarcely afford them. Perhaps this extravagance partly explains why the farmers of the Cape were typically deeply in debt in the seventeenth and eighteenth centuries.[126]

The rural farmstead owner always had overriding defensive and hegemonic considerations when choosing the design and layout of his property. The more prosperous farms had a low stone wall (*ringmuur*), a neatly whitewashed perimeter of nearly half a mile in total length, enclosing all the outbuildings and a copse of imported trees, following a pattern that dates to the seventeenth century.[127] The wall decisively separated the owner's oasis of "civilization" from the ever encroaching wilderness, or the "*bos*" (the bush). This wall enclosed the *werf*, the basic defensive unit of Cape rural architecture. One seventeenth-century Stellenbosch farm even had an entirely appropriate name, Harmonie en Onrus (Harmony and Chaos). The estate, apparently renamed in happier times as Beverly Hills, now serves as an integrated nightclub.

Many farms were not only cultural oases in the settlers' eyes, but real oases as well. The house and its associated outbuildings always dominated the only available water source in the immediate area. Outside of the high rainfall areas of the Western Cape, farms often were, and still are, named after their most important asset, their water: thus, Brakkefonteijn (Brack Fountain), Droogevallei (Dry Valley), Elandsfontein (Buck Fountain), Geelblommetjefontein (Yellow Flower Fountain), Klaarstroom (Clear Stream), Riviersonderend (River-without-end), Soebatsfontein (Beg-for-Fountain), and even simply Watergang (Watercourse). Possession and defense of the water sources proved to be the most efficient way to displace the Khoisan populations. Displaced Khoi men were thereby forced deeper into the interior to search for alternative sources of water, while their womenfolk stayed behind or were cajoled into a penurious and vicelike domestic clientage.

---

[126] Guelke, Shell, and Whyte, "The de la Fontaine Report," passim.

[127] Walton, *Old Cape Farmsteads*, 12–13.

Early Khoi women camped next to the settler's "big house," are clearly depicted on a seventeenth-century sketch.

The frontier's corbelled house design, shaped like an igloo, also had local origins. The *trekboers* modeled their dwellings on the Khoi buildings they saw around them. The only difference was in the materials they used — stone, mud, and clay. From a distance the corbelled house was indistinguishable from a Khoi house. The floor was packed earth, sometimes sealed with cow dung or ox blood. Here slave, serf, and *trekboer* shared the same house design, and sometimes the same living space.[128]

By 1808 the main features of the new creole architecture were in place, its development having been based on local conditions and material, the geographical distribution of imported slaves, and the native people, rather than on transplanted European patterns (see Figure 9-14).[129]

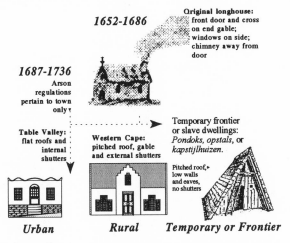

Figure 9–14. The development of vernacular architecture at the Cape, 1652 to 1808.

Without exception, all gabled houses were slaveowners' houses. The elaborate 80- and sometimes 90-foot gable visible to a horseman on the horizon signaled to a largely illiterate colonial population that here was a house of substance. This was the Cape version of the "big house" of the Americas, rivaling in majesty and elegance, if not economic viability or even plain creditworthiness, the *casa grande* of Brazil, the *hacienda* of the Yucatán, the *landhuis* of the Dutch Antilles, and the

---

128 Sparrman, *A Voyage to the Cape of Good Hope,* vol. 1, 265.

129 The tiny image of the seventeenth-century house with the cross has been scanned and edited to enhance the picture (Spier, 1686). My ideas for this diagram have been derived from the work of James Walton, *Old Cape Farmsteads,* pp. 12, 31, 126.

fantastic classical plantation house of the American South. Set before the backdrop of the spacious veld, functionally unrelated to its remote European, urban, canal-front origins, the whitewashed creole gable became the perfect colonial facade. The Cape gable symbolized the remorseless privatization of the water resources, and it presided visually and aesthetically over a landscape of conquest and coerced labor.

T E N

Tender Ties
Women and the Slave Household

T HE "IMPORTANT" AREAS in which men were so prominent in colonial history — commerce, legislation, wars — only superficially seem to outweigh the "ordinary" activities that women performed, such as fashioning garments, cooking, and, more important, running families and households.[1] But the latter work rather than the former constituted the daily round and, one might add, provided the psychological touchstone of all colonial life. There was more truth and pre-Freudian wisdom than sentimentality in the Spanish proverb, "The hand that rocks the cradle, rules the world."[2] In short, the choices slave and free women made and the constraints they lived under shaped the families, the households, and the psychology of the slave society of the colonized Cape.

The Lodge Women and their Freedom

Most reports of slave women at the Cape concern a small, atypical group, the Company's Lodge slave women. For settler historians the Lodge was a primary site for reconstructing sexual and racial differences. How the Lodge slave women perceived potential sexual partners is a difficult but important question. The detailed crime records rarely provide a glimpse inside since the Lodge ran itself (see Chapter 6). Attitudes have, perforce, to be inferred from behavior, which has to be reconstructed from the baptismal records,[3] and also deduced from Europeans'

---

[1] William Cronon et al., "Women and the West: Rethinking the Western History Survey Course," *Western Historical Quarterly* 17, 3 (July 1986): 275; I am grateful to Stanley Engerman and Shula Marks for reading a previous draft of this chapter.

[2] Joseph Vogt, *Ancient Slavery and the Ideal of Man* (Cambridge: Harvard University Press, 1975, translated by Thomas Wiedemann), p. 109.

[3] At first the Company slaves were listed together with the settlers, but after 1693, they were listed separately, see DRCA: Kaap Notule, 1665–1695, Doop Register, GR1 vol.1/1–5.

commentary originating outside the walls of the Lodge.[4] Some contemporary settler sources argued that while the women slaves of the settlers may have been coerced by their mistresses to make love with European visitors, the Lodge slave women's own slave spouses forced them to sleep with visitors, both settlers and the famous "lords of six weeks," the soldiers and sailors with money and a brief time to spend it in Cape Town, the "tavern of the seas." In 1686 Ambrose Cowley, an English visitor to the Cape, said Lodge "husbands" were easily persuaded to offer their wives: "If a slave of the Company's should have a mind to have carnal knowledge of one of their women, let him but give her husband a bit of Tobacco-Roll of about three inches long, he will fetch her forthwith to the slave and cause her to lie with him."[5] Otto Mentzel, who delivered salt to the Lodge regularly thus was one of the few settlers to pass through the Lodge's portals, claimed that male slaves actually forced their partners to take a European lover;[6] elsewhere he suggests that not all Lodge women were "loose," but that those who were scrupulously insisted on advance payment from their patrons.[7] He would not have been in the Lodge at night, and it is not known whether his views were based on rumor.

There is another interpretation of these accounts of the Lodge women: possibly the initiative lay with the women. In 1686 a freed female slave informed the governor that under the promise of marriage she had borne one of the soldiers of the Company four children, and that she had frequently asked permission from the Council to marry the soldier. From the Lodge slave woman's perspective, a liaison with a free European man could mean freedom. Freedom, to the desperate Lodge slaves, was more important than endogamy. The court resolved that the reputed father was to support the children, and while it did not order him to marry the slave, he was never to be permitted to marry anyone else.[8] Several travelers and other sources insist that Lodge slave women willingly courted European sexual attention. Pained Political Council members in 1681 protested that the slave women in the Lodge flaunted their European lovers in public,

---

[4] On the merits of these sources, see Richard Elphick and Robert C.-H. Shell, "Intergroup relations: Khoikhoi, Settlers, Slaves and Free Blacks," in R. Elphick and Herman Giliomee (eds), *The Shaping of South African Society, 1652–1820*, rev. ed. (Middletown Conn.: Wesleyan University Press, 1989), pp. 129ff.

[5] Ambrose Cowley, as quoted in R. Raven-Hart (comp. and ed.), *Cape Good Hope 1652–1702* (Cape Town: Balkema, 1971), vol. 2, 310.

[6] Otto Friederich Mentzel, *A Complete and Authentic Topographical Description . . .* , trans. G. V. Marais and J. Hoge, rev. ed. (Cape Town: Van Riebeeck Society, 1944), vol. 2, 124; see also Elphick and Shell, "Intergroup Relations," 127.

[7] *"Kammene Kas, Kammene Kunte"* (If you have no money, I have no —); Mentzel, *Description*, 3: 99.

[8] C. Graham Botha, "Early Cape Matrimonial Law," in *The Collected Works of C. Graham Botha* (Cape Town: Struik, 1962), vol. 2, p. 57.

"dancing, stark naked even on Sundays, in full aspect."[9] Charles Lockyer, who visited the Cape in 1711, claimed that "There is little notice taken of the sailors who lodge in their rooms, and as for the women themselves, they are so fond of white children, that they would willingly have no other, whence the breed is highly improved, many of them being as white as Europeans."[10] Johan Daniël Buttner, a doctor who stayed at the Cape in the 1720s, also commented on the mixed-race children in the Lodge; they were, so he said, the result of willing sexual mixing from "men of many nations."[11] However, there is little statistical evidence for the sailor and prostitute model of behavior. Conceptions (based on the date of baptism minus nine months) show that both mulatto conceptions and "full-breed" conceptions were not correlated with the visits of the "Lords of Six Weeks" (sailors and marine personnel who arrived in Cape Town in March with the outward and homeward bound fleets) but rather with other seasonal patterns. In those critical six weeks, Lodge mulatto conceptions were well below average. Lodge women who had mulatto children mainly conceived them after the ships had left (see Figure 6-2). The implication is that they chose local, European partners.

More compelling evidence for the idea that slave women intent on freedom approached men settled or permanently stationed at the Cape comes from the Church records. Records kept by the independent church scribes show that Company slave women took great pains to drive a genealogical stake into the baptismal records of the colony. They always named their invariably absent European lover as the father of the child for which they were seeking baptism, and they did this by providing their child with an embarrassingly exact patronym.[12] Whether the naming was a boast or an act of retaliation, whether the slave women had been coerced into the relationship by their slave spouse or had been willing partners, the result was the same: what Mentzel later termed a "*mestiço* class" in the Lodge.[13] If their bid for freedom failed, the next generation might fare better. It was a desperate wager.

Were the slave women of the Lodge defying the growing racial order by flaunting their European partners? Or were they simply establishing for their offspring the best possible future in a colony where the advantages increasingly depended on light skin color? With society becoming increasingly racially based in

---

9 "*Moeder naact*"; Kathleen M. Jeffreys and S. D. Naude (eds.) *Kaapse Plakkaatboek, 1652–1806* (Cape Town: Kaapse Argiefstukke, 1944–1949), vol. 1, pp. 179–180 (26 November 1681).

10 Charles Lockyer, *An Account of the Trade in India* (London: Samuel Crouch, 1711), p. 297 (emphasis added).

11 Johan Daniel Buttner, *Accounts of the Cape . . .* , ed. G. S. Nienaber and R. Raven-Hart (Cape Town: Balkema, 1970), p. 66.

12 Robert C.-H. Shell, "Slavery at the Cape of Good Hope: 1680–1731," Ph.D. dissertation, Yale University, 1986, p. 134.

13 Mentzel, *Description*, vol. 2, p. 125.

the colony, perhaps the genius of the Lodge women lay in their success in making that distinction as difficult and troublesome as possible for the ruling order. Although there is little evidence for this theory of biological altruism (and there is not likely to be any), it makes more sense than the traditional notions of general Lodge promiscuity. But above all, by securing a European sexual partner the slave women sometimes could provide their offspring with immediate and incomparable civic advantages. No better example of this can be found than in the story of Manda Gratia (origin unknown), a matron in the Lodge in 1714, who married a burgher, Guilliam Frisnet. Through the marriage, she managed to free nearly all of her previous offspring. One freed mulatto son promptly joined the Dutch East India Company and set sail for the East Indies, the first slave emigrant from the colony.[14]

The Legal Position of Lodge Slave "Marriages"
After 1685 all mulatto females in the Company's Lodge were, in fact, encouraged to marry "a man from the Netherlands." Van Reede, a visiting commissioner, was simply embarrassed by the many mulatto children of European descent who were born into slavery. The men they married would first be expected to pay back the cost of their paid upkeep and education, then to free the women, and, finally, to marry them in the Christian church. In this way enslaved women of European descent came to be rescued from slavery.[15] The process of settlers formally marrying Company mulatto slave women became common enough for the Company to resolve to exact compensation from the bridegroom. The men were, after all, acquiring property from the Company. Not all bachelor settlers could afford this expense, and consequently antenuptial contracts were sometimes written, whereby the settler or soldier promised that, should his slave bride die before him and leave no heirs, half of the estate of the marriage would go to the Company as compensation for her education and upbringing. As can be seen from the following 1689 extract from just such a contract, the woman's metamorphosis from slavery to freedom and incorporation into the settler family was as carefully monitored as any other humdrum accounting transaction: "Andries Oelszen, free settler at Stellenbosch presently intending to marry Sara van de Caap, the Company's mulatto [*halfslag*] slave, declares that in the event of his bride's pre-deceasing him and in the event of her leaving no legal heirs, that a half of the estate, including land and movables, should be given over to the company, at the death-house [*sterfhuijsje*],

---

[14] CAD C.336 (31 August 1714), p. 471, no. 388; her son was a schoolmaster, ibid., no. 245; another was a pupil, ibid., no. 267; her manumission request has not been found, but she is listed as the wife of Frisnet in RA KA 4060 (19 April 1720) Opgaaf, Entry 219 Cape District; see also Hendrik Carel Vos Leibbrandt, *Requesten (Memorials) 1715–1806,* (Cape Town: South African Library, 1989), vol. 4, p. 1262 (no. 45 of 1727) for the fate of her children.

[15] A. Hulshof (ed.), "H. A. van Reede tot Drakenstein, Journaal van zijn verblijf aan de Kaap," *Bijdragen en Mededelingen van het Historisch Genootschap* 62 (1941): 206–207.

before the debts of the estate are settled, to acknowledge and pay off the Company's role in bringing up and feeding the above-mentioned bride."[16]

According to van Reede's racial and actuarial calculations in 1685, a mulatto slave woman 22 years of age cost 150 guilders.[17] Many European men were willing to pay.[18] Full-breed women slaves had to wait much longer (sometimes forever) for their manumission.[19] Officials must have presumed that no European would want to marry a "full-breed" [*heelslag*], because no provisions were made for such a nuptial event. One source suggested such unions were, in fact, "illegal."[20] Because of the long-term shortage of women at the Cape, mulatto Company slave women always had some chance of being manumitted and then married to a European. This was encouraged officially at the same time that regulations forbade any concubinage of settlers' or visitors' full-breed slaves.[21]

The Settler Women and their Slave Women

To understand the multiple, pivotal roles of the free women and their slaves in early South Africa, one must first have some idea of their distribution, their numbers. Only a handful of Company personnel were allowed to bring their wives and families to the Cape, and no free women worked for the Company in a full-time capacity.[22] European women never appear on the Company payrolls, except as midwives or "external mothers" (the specially appointed guardians of the Lodge women).[23] When adventurous individual women were caught after having disguised themselves as men and joined the Dutch East India Company to come to

---

16 DO: "Transporten en Schepenkennis" (31 December, 1689) 18/90, pp. 292–293.

17 Hulshof, "Journaal," 207.

18 Hans Friedreich Heese has painstakingly documented all such cases; see H. F. Heese, *Groep sonder Grense* (Bellville: Wes Kaaplandse Institute vir Historiese Navorsing, 1984), passim, especially Appendix A, pp. 41–75.

19 Hulshof, "Journaal," 7.

20 Hulshof, "Journaal," 189–223; F. C. Dominicus, in his classic work on domestic life of South Africa in the eighteenth century, claims that it was forbidden for a European to marry "a pure breed," see Dominicus, *Het Huiselik en Maatschappelik Leven van de Zuid Afrikaner in der Eerste Helft der 18de Eeuw* ('s-Gravenhage: Martinus Nijhoff, 1919), p. 79, but I have been unable to find the original source.

21 Hulshof, "Journaal," 1–245; cf. Jeffreys and Naude, *Kaapse Plakkaatboek* (30 November 1678), vol. 1, pp. 151–152. Since all Company "half-breed" slaves were baptized, an assumption has been made that references to "heathen" slave women are equivalent to references to "full-breed" slave women.

22 Leonard Blussé, *Strange Company: Chinese Settlers, Mestizo Women and the Dutch in VOC Batavia* (Providence: Foris, 1988), pp. 172–173.

23 See, for example, A. Hulshof (comp.), "Compagnie's dienaren aan de Kaap in 1685," *Bijdragen en Mededelingen van het Historisch Genootschap* 63 (1942): 347–369.

the Cape, they were tried and sent home — even though several male settlers "instantly asked for their hand in marriage."[24] A mere rumor of female passengers on the outward bound fleets from Europe would be enough to bring a throng of hopeful settler bachelors to the quayside to view the "roast pears," as European women immigrants were called by the Dutch.[25]

Once the Dutch East India Company decided not to support family immigration to the colony after 1717, the importance of the existing pool of free settler women began to increase, a dynamic process that continued through the eighteenth and into the nineteenth century. Continued male immigration increased the unbalanced sex ratio. Women in the Cape were scarce and much sought after. The original pool of settler women comprised only a few hundred wives and daughters of French Huguenots, women imported by the Dutch East India Company from orphanages in Rotterdam, and wives and daughters of the original Dutch settlers and top officials. These few hundred free women imported prior to 1717 constituted the main demographic pool of settler women. This was small when compared to several thousand male employees of the Company and the even more numerous free male settlers. From 1652 to 1808, more than 15,000 slave women were imported to the Cape (see Figure 10-1).[26]

Most slave women in the American South worked in the fields. Emily Burke, a visitor to nineteenth-century Georgia, noted that slave women and men alike "run their ploughs side by side, and day after day . . . and as far as I was able to learn, the part women sustained in this masculine employment, was quite as efficient as that of the more athletic sex."[27] In precolonial West African patriarchies, women had routinely worked the ground, and whether the differently gendered work patterns in the antebellum South and the Cape were legacies of slaves' geographic background is not known.[28] In contrast, most slave women at the Cape (except for a few Company Lodge slaves) worked in their owners' homes.[29] Cape slave women were imported from the east coast of Africa, Madagascar, the Indonesian Archipelago, and India right up until 1808. The Cape adult slave sex ratios were among the highest ever recorded for a slave society, averaging between 720 to 150 men per 100 women, depending on the year. Few worked in the fields in the seventeenth and eighteenth centuries. Only 5 percent of

---

[24] Donald Moodie, *The Record* (Cape Town: Balkema, 1960 reprint), 18 June 1687, p. 421; François Valentijn, *Description of the Cape . . .* ed. E. H. Raidt, trans. R. Raven-Hart (Cape Town: Van Riebeeck Society, 1971), vol. 1, p. 208; Kathleen M. Jeffreys (ed.), *Kaapse Archief Stukken Lopende over het Jaar 1779* (2 February 1779), p. 288.

[25] Blussé, *Strange Company*, 160–161.

[26] Shell, "Popucape." This excludes the Khoisan but includes the Company garrison.

[27] Jacqueline Jones, " 'My Mother was Much of a Woman': Black Women, Work, and the Family under Slavery," *Feminist Studies* 2, 8 (Summer 1982): 241, 255, 261.

[28] Jones, " 'My Mother was Much of a Woman,' " 241, 255, 261.

[29] E. S. Morgan, *American Slavery, American Freedom* (New York: Norton, 1975), p. 235.

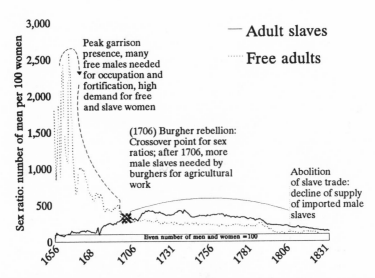

Figure 10–1. Sex ratios of slave and free populations, 1656 to 1831.

all slave women were kept as domestic servants in the American rural South; in South Africa, the percentages were almost exactly reversed.[30] I believe that this difference in gender roles and work, whatever it origins, led to substantially different slave cultures and slave societies. In addition, at the Cape the further inland one went, the fewer free and slave women there were. Free women preferred the environs of the market and the port, and the slave women were obliged to live with their mistresses (see Figure 10-2).[31]

The scarcity of members of her own sex had several important consequences for the typical Cape settler woman. The demographic realities empowered them and, to a lesser extent, their slave women. All free women benefited from the Cape inheritance system, by which widows received half of their spouse's estate, with the other half divided among the children. In colonial New England, by contrast, the entire estate went to the children. There, the widow, who rarely remarried, was lucky if she retained a room in her former house, and she was sometimes ignored by her own children.[32] In practice the Cape widowed spouse, husband or wife,

---

[30] Jones, " 'My Mother was Much of a Woman,' " 241.

[31] 1690, 1711, 1730, 1750, 1770: Richard Elphick and Herman Giliomee (eds.), *The Shaping of South African Society, 1652–1820* (Middletown, Conn.: Wesleyan University Press, 1989), pp. 196, 200; C. Beyers, *Kaapse Patriotte*, pp. 240–249; 1808, 1825: CAD CO 6135.

[32] Alexander Keyssar, "Widowhood in Eighteenth Century Massachusetts: A Problem in the History of the Family," *Perspectives in American History* 8 (1974): 89, 91, 93–94, 111–112, 117.

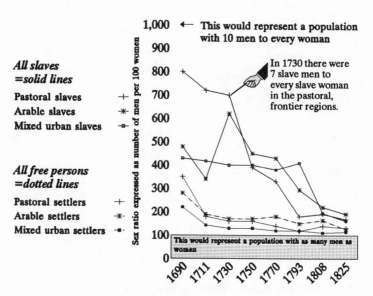

Figure 10–2. Sex ratios for all adult slaves and all free adults, by region.

struggled to keep the landed estate and the household slaves. He or she generally preferred selling off the movables to pay out the heirs' share. Perhaps it was a coincidence, but as settler women became less scarce in the nineteenth century, the Cape widow's share of an estate fell to one-third of the entire estate plus a child's share. With a large family, this meant a substantial financial loss for a widow. Nevertheless, in the early years at the Cape, widows became for a particular phase of their life some of the principal landholders of the colony. In that usually short phase they made their next marital choice skillfully.[33] Conforming with the practice in colonial Virginia, but in strong contrast to New England's patterns, nearly all Cape settler widows quickly remarried. Because of the particular Cape inheritance system, they became a principal channel for accumulating capital in the colony.[34] The Cape settler woman's de jure legal position as a minor under metropolitan Roman Dutch law was at odds with her de facto demographic scarcity. As a consequence of this scarcity and the particular system of inheritance,

---

[33] Leonard Guelke, Robert Shell, and Anthony Whyte (comps.), "The de la Fontaine Report" (New Haven, Conn.: Opgaaf Project, 1990); Leonard Guelke and Robert Shell (comps.), "The Deeds Book: The Cape Cadastral Calendar" (New Haven, Conn.: Opgaaf Project, 1990); DO: "Transporten en Scheepenkennis" (1658-1795).

[34] Leonard Guelke and Robert C.-H. Shell, "An Early Colonial Landed Gentry: Land and Wealth in the Cape Colony 1682–1731," *Journal of Historical Geography* 9, 3 (1983): 207 ff.; Morgan, *American Slavery, American Freedom*, 119–120, 164–170, 304.

the economic and social position of settler women became much stronger than it was in Europe and in other colonies such as early New England and even, one hazards, Virginia.[35]

Widows were the most empowered of the free Cape women, but widowhood was not a recorded phase of a slave woman's life. Free widows could make independent and judicious marriage decisions and other life choices. For example, widows sold or manumitted more female slaves than other settlers did. The available sources do not tell us why — whether, accustomed to having a dominant patriarchal spouse "run" the slaves, they felt or were unable to manage their slaves on their own; whether slavery was distasteful to them, as it was to some settler women of the Antebellum South[36]; whether manumission of slave women by free women was a genuine expression of domestic affection; or whether widows' sale of slaves was simply a way to avoid some of the probate problems in the Cape succession system.[37] Reformed Christianity, too, could have played a part in their choices; Cape women were more likely to be church members and communicants than Cape men, a similar gendered orientation to Church as that in colonial New England.[38] Conceivably Cape widows felt a need to express their piety through the profound act of freeing another woman. Whatever the reasons, Cape settler women in their widowhood rid themselves of their slaves through manumission or outright sale when they could afford the gesture (see Figure 10-3).[39]

Slave Status Inherited through the Mother
One of the most sweeping changes to affect life in all the European colonies was that children came to follow the legal status of the mother, not the father. For instance, in all the North American colonies (except, briefly, Maryland) the legal condition of the mother dictated the status of the child[40] — a colonial *reversal* of the rule of English common law that the status of the father determined the status of offspring. The Virginia House of Burgesses passed a law in 1662 stipulating that "Whereas some doubts have arisen whether children got by any Englishman upon a negro woman should be slave or Free, Be it therefore enacted and declared by this present grand assembly, that all children borne in this country shall be held bond

---

35 Herbert Moller, "Sex Composition and Correlated Culture Patterns of Colonial America," *William and Mary Quarterly* Second Series, 2 (1945): 113–153.

36 See Anne Firor Scott, *Southern Lady: From Pedestal to Politics* (Chicago: University of Chicago Press, 1970), pp. 46 ff.

37 Shell, "Slavery at the Cape of Good Hope," 102–104.

38 DRCA: Kaapstad Notule GR1 1/1 and 2, "Ledematen"; Stephen R. Grossbart, "Seeking the Divine Favor: Conversion and Church Admission in Eastern Connecticut, 1711–1832," *William and Mary Quarterly* Third Series, 46 (1989): 696–740.

39 Anna H. Smith, *Cape Views and Costumes: Water-Colours by H. C. De Meillon* (Johannesburg: The Brenthurst Press, 1978) 37, 8. Courtesy of the Brenthurst Library.

40 Stanley M. Elkins, *Slavery: A Problem in American Institutional and Intellectual Life* (Chicago: University of Chicago Press, 1963), p. 55.

Figure 10–3. Woman and slave going to church, c. 1820.

or free only according to the condition of the mother."[41] This was in keeping with the logic of the colonial saying, "Motherhood is a matter of fact, but fatherhood is a matter of opinion."[42] The principal purpose of such legislation was to thwart

[41] Warren M. Billings (comp.), *The Old Dominion in the Seventeenth Century: A Documentary History of Virginia, 1606–1689* (Chapel Hill: University of North Carolina Press, 1975), p. 172.
[42] Edgar T. Thompson, "Virginia," in E. T. Thompson (ed.), *Race: Individual and Collective Behavior* (New York: Collier Macmillan, 1958), p. 262.

claims of freedom being made on behalf of mixed-race slave children by free fathers. The change was the most important legal device in maintaining hereditary slavery. Whether the father was free or slave, the offspring remained a slave.

The Cape system was always based on uterine descent — the mother's status taking precedence — because Roman law, not English common law, was practiced there. A set of laws passed on 10 April 1770 in Batavia, part of the comprehensive Statutes of India, did attempt to address the more flagrant cases of the reproductive exploitation of women slaves in all Dutch colonies of the Dutch East India Company; one article directed that a woman slave who had lived in concubinage with her European owner and all children of that union should be freed at the death of the father/owner.[43] But this law, close to English common law in principle, was not observed. (I have made a distinction between reproductive, sexual, and gender exploitation, where reproductive exploitation means that the child-bearing or nurturing services — such as wet-nursing — are the target of exploitation; sexual exploitation means the exploitation of the body, and gender exploitation is the exploitation of the status of women. All could exist together in a single act of exploitation, or separately.)

Slavery at the Cape worked in the same way as that in the American colonies, the principal difference being that in America, the legislation had to be introduced. Uterine-descent slavery at the Cape, as in Virginia, was the final solution to the problem of mixed unions with the slave population. Free fathers of slave children had to buy their wife's and children's freedom.

Sources before 1770 indicate that some Cape settler women allowed their female slaves to be maintained, housed, and sometimes even paid a wage by European males, usually military bachelor personnel. Such slave women were known at the Cape as "courtesan slaves"; they did not live in the household of their owners, but with the free men, who paid for their children's upbringing.[44] The absentee owner was "paid" by owning the children.[45] This custom of courtesan slaves continued after 1770, despite the provision made for their eventual freedom in the 1770 Statutes of India. By the early nineteenth century, slave women in the household were even foisted on casual visitors to Cape Town. Robert Percival, an English officer at the Cape in 1804, wrote of one Cape settler woman who coerced a slave woman to have sexual intercourse with a male houseguest by pushing the reluctant

---

[43] This law is not found in the incomplete *Kaapse Plakkaatboeken*, but nevertheless it did have a profound influence at the Cape; see H. C. Vos's correspondence and "Extracts from the Statutes of India," especially article 8 in George McCall Theal, *Records of the Cape Colony* (Cape Town: Struik, 1967; hereafter *RCC*), vol. 9, pp. 130–134; and see also CAD SO (20 January 1766) 17/1, n. p.

[44] Robert C.-H. Shell (ed.), " 'Slaves,' an Essay by Samuel Eusebius Hudson," *Kronos* 9 (1984): 52; Anon., *Gleanings in Africa . . .* (New York: Negro Universities Press, 1969 reprint), p. 64.

[45] Mentzel, *Description*, vol. 2, 30.

slave into the bedroom and locking the door: "The Dutch ladies have no reluctance to their slave girls having connections with their guests, in hopes of profiting
by it, by their being got with child."[46]

In 1806, Samuel Hudson, an English slave owner, observed that sometimes it
was the resident male owners who directly took advantage of their domestic female
slaves[47]:

I know one Gentleman — if he can by such conduct deserve the name — that at
the time I left the Colony was considered among the richest of the Inhabitants,
held one of the first situations in the English Government was generally respected.
Yet this very Man at his first outset was in possession of a white (or nearly so) Slave.
He had children by this Woman several [of] which as they grew up from their color
were considered very valuable. The connection continued with her own children
and even with his Grandchildren. My very nature shudders whilst I relate this
horrid trait of beastiality in a Man in other respects highly respectable. This is a
well established fact and it was always remarked Mister W . . .'s [ellipsis in
original] Slaves were considered the finest in the Colony and were they brought to
the Hammer would fetch extravagant prices. Many of them had all the features of
Europeans not with [out a] tinge of their Ancestors' complexion. Several of these
Girls were let out by the Month to Europeans who made them Servants of all work.
But from the cunning and artfulness of their behavior too generally became
Mistresses and expensive ones in the end. *Under these circumstances all children
from such connections are born Slaves.* Many of whom remain so when every Man
certainly has it in his Power to prevent This Shamefull badge by giving a hundred
Dollars to the proprietor at the birth of the Child. But they calculate on the
chances there are of Its dying and some bold blooded Mortals look with indifference on the fruits of this shameful prostitution.[48]

Few Cape women slaves availed themselves of the escape hatch provided by
the emancipation clause in the 1770s Statutes of India, for good reason. Local slave
owners and the local court system would not allow them such simple access to
freedom. Steyntje of the Cape, a creole slave, was the solitary woman to bring a
civil suit under this clause. And she was, in the end, successful. Her long ordeal
illustrates just how difficult it was to prove parenthood in those prescientific times.
She suffered through more than ten years of humiliating court appearances before
she obtained freedom for herself and her various children, each of whom had been
fathered by a different settler owner. Steyntje was an extraordinary person of great
personal charm, courage, and beauty. We know this both from the number of her
female friends who testified on her behalf, the number of settler wives she

---

[46] Robert Percival, *An Account of the Cape of Good Hope* (New York: Negro Universities
Press, 1969 reprint), p. 291; Shell, "Slaves," 51 (emphasis added).

[47] Elkins, *Slavery*, 55.

[48] Shell, ed., Hudson, "Slaves," 68–69.

displaced, and the number of European men who vied to buy her or to possess her in other ways. One Danish captain was so smitten that he offered to buy her on the spot and take her home. The case became a cause célèbre and ultimately went to the Privy Council in England. All the court papers, revealing among other things a passionate ménage à trois, were published in 1827 for Cape Town readers (who were expected to wade through the 179 pages of court proceedings).[49] One must conclude that Cape slave owners, up to the 1820s and the final resolution of Steyntje's case, felt free to exploit their slaves reproductively. It is quite apparent that a few owners preferred their slaves to be of European descent and arranged, apparently, to father such children themselves; eugenic notions were so strong that the European owners themselves took on the task of improving the slave stock. This sexual and reproductive exploitation of slave women resulted in a preferred group of mulatto slaves.

Hudson wrote on the eve of the Steyntje episode that the effort "to improve their breed of livestock" had "produced a race perfectly white": "The mixture of Europeans with the Slave Girls of the Colony has produced a race perfectly white which are in high esteem — each Family priding themselves in the fair complexions of their Maids and Youngers. 'Tis too frequently the case that their Masters & Mistresses encourage these connections to improve their breed of Live Stock & many an English Countenance you may perceive running through the Streets of Cape Town without shoe or stocking — the badge of slavery and a reproach to some of our Countrymen in not having released them from the bonds of slavery.[50] In the seventeenth and eighteenth centuries, some fathers did free their slave offspring, but by the nineteenth century, with a decline in the number of slaves available on the market, manumission declined. This change marks a striking degradation of parental values and attitudes. Whether or not it reflects the steep rise of slave prices after the abolition of the slave trade, for slave owners, property rights to a person had won out over any parenting impulses.[51]

Even after the revolutionary Batavian administration (1803 to 1806), which had brought some aspects of the Enlightenment to the Cape, and after the subsequent second British occupation, the Cape persevered with the uterine-descent law for slave status. Article 83 of the general codification of Cape slave law in 1813 was based squarely on Roman precedents: "The children of a female slave born previous to the time prescribed for [manumission], or pending the fulfillment of the condition, are slaves."[52] The imposition of English colonial rule, one

---

[49] *Papers Relating to the Manumission of Steyntje and Her Children, with an Appendix*, South African Bound Pamphlets (Cape Town: George Greig, 1827).

[50] Shell, ed., Hudson, "Slaves," 51–52.

[51] Percival, *An Account of the Cape*, 285, 291.

[52] Daniël Dennijson, "Statement of the laws of the Cape of Good Hope regarding slavery" (16 March 1813), in Theal, *RCC*, 9: 146–161.

would assume, would logically have introduced English common law, with its emphasis on patrilineal descent. However, this would have been quite revolutionary for the Cape slave society. The British instead acquiesced to local custom and let the Roman Dutch legal practice stand.

By 1822, the new Cape custom of *not* freeing mulatto slaves had resulted in a new category of slaves or, as one contemporary official, W. W. Bird ambiguously put it, a "class" or a "race" of slaves called "the Africander." Bird elaborated: "The Afrikander women are the favorite slaves of the mistress, arranging and keeping everything in order, and are entrusted with all that is valuable — more like companions than slaves; but the mistress rarely and the slave never, forget their relative situations, and however familiar in private, in the presence of another, due form prevails." These Afrikander slaves considered themselves superior to slaves with no European descent. Bird concludes: "The Africander slave girl would consider herself disgraced by a connection with a negro, or the production of a black infant."[53]

Since the condition of slavery remained based on uterine descent at the Cape through the Dutch, British, and Batavian occupations, the manumission of a slave woman was a profound act. Manumission freed not only the slave women, but also, by default, her future children and their offspring.[54] The sex ratio of the manumitted slave population at the Cape increased in the nineteenth century. Fewer women were freed after 1808, and free fathers increasingly were content to leave their mulatto offspring in bondage.

Family size and age at marriage
As a departure point for examining the demographic changes that the transplanted female settlers underwent, it is useful to establish the respective sizes of families in their European and colonial contexts. This provides unambiguous "before" and "after" pictures. Because most Cape settler families had migrated so far, sometimes even leaving family members behind, the early Cape family size was, according to the local censuses of the 1680s, slightly smaller than the average family size in Europe during the same period.[55] But after the first generation, the size of settler women's families changed dramatically. The first change for women transplanted from Europe to the Cape was that they tended to marry younger and consequently bore more children than their European counterparts. This colonial transforma-

---

[53] W. W. Bird, *State of the Cape in 1822* (Cape Town: Struik, 1966 reprint), pp. 73–74; see also Percival, *An Account of the Cape,* 285–286.

[54] Elphick and Shell, "Intergroup Relations," 140–141.

[55] A. M. van der Woude in Peter Laslett (ed.), *Household and Family in Past Time* (Cambridge: Cambridge University Press, 1972), pp. 309, 311. For the Cape, see AR VOC 4017: "Lijst der vrije luijden en haeren ommeslag . . ." (14 February 1682), 114; AR VOC 4018: "Generale rolle der vrije luijden en haeren verdere ommeslag" (31 January 1683), 210.

tion may be exactly measured with one immigrant group, the Huguenots (see Figure 10-4).[56]

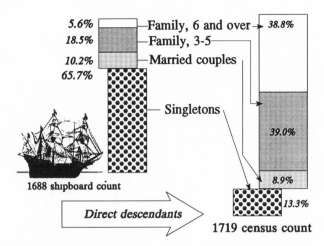

Figure 10–4. Family size for Huguenots at embarkation and a generation later.

The French Huguenot women were typical of all free settler women; there was a dramatic increase in the numbers of sons and daughters in every free group of European descent. No similar pattern emerged in the slave population until after the abolition of the slave trade (see Figure 10-5).[57]

There was a significant change in behavior after 1700. A new family reconstitution study of approximately 1,300 families in the first hundred years of the early Cape shows that the number of children born to the average settler woman increased from 5.3 children in the generation of 1705, to 6.2 for the generation of women in 1731. This amounts to an average of one extra child in one generation.[58] Such a rapid change in demographic behavior did not go unnoticed by contemporary European visitors. In 1710 Peter Kolbe, the German naturalist and astronomer, was moved to comment, in the vivid chauvinist language of his time, on the reproductive efforts of the transplanted European settler women: "The

[56] Their clearly distinguishable French names on the ships' passenger lists and later on the census of 1719 have been linked, individual by individual, to form clear "before" and "after" family distributions. 1688: C. Graham Botha, *The French Refugees at the Cape* (Cape Town: Struik, 1970), appendixes.

[57] Shell, "Popucape." The tiny free blacks are included in these aggregate totals but their inclusion does not affect this statement; their numbers were all relatively small, as was their increase.

[58] See appendix in Shell, "Slavery at the Cape of Good Hope," vol. 2, 313ff.; Leonard Guelke, "The Anatomy of a Colonial Settler Population: Cape Colony, 1657-1750" *The International Journal of African Historical Studies* 18, 4 (December 1992): Table 10.

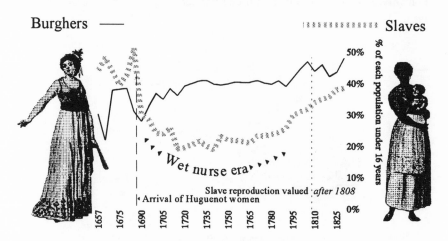

Figure 10–5. Age composition of slave and free populations, 1657 to 1825.

European women in the *Cape-Colonies* are generally modest, but no Flinchers from Conjugal Delights. They are excellent breeders. In most houses in the Colonies are seen from six to a dozen Children and upwards; brave Lads and Lasses with Limbs and Countenances strongly declarative of the ardor with which they were begotten."[59] Colonial life then, entailed several consequences for the settler woman. The most important demographic consequence is that the Cape settler women, like their counterparts in colonial America, began to marry much earlier than women in Europe. The age at first marriage for Cape women dropped well below European norms. This had the immediate result of a longer period during which it was socially acceptable to bear children. Contemporary travelers were shocked at the early Cape marriage pattern among European settlers. For instance, Kolbe hinted that a 14-year-old European mother was nothing unusual at the Cape.[60] This practice continued at the Cape at least until the early nineteenth century. Robert Semple, writing in 1804, confirmed that the age of marriage remained low: "The [settler] women are sometimes married here very early, sixteen years may be fixed upon as the most general age at which they become wives, and often mothers; and ten, twelve, and even eighteen children are not uncommonly the produce of one marriage."[61] Samuel Hudson remarked in 1806: "Marriages take place when the parties are very young. Warmth of Climate gives warmth of Constitution and

---

[59] Peter Kolbe, *The Present State of the Cape of Good Hope* (London: Johnson Reprint Company, 1968 reprint), vol. 2, 340 (emphasis in original).

[60] Kolbe, *State of the Cape*, vol. 2, 338–339.

[61] Robert Semple, *Walks and Sketches at the Cape of Good Hope* (Cape Town: Balkema, 1968), pp. 29–30.

Prudence on the part of the Parent seldom throws any Obstacles in the Way of the young people."[62] The Cape settler women married at a much younger age than the colonial New England women, who, since Thomas Malthus's time, have been regarded as providing benchmarks for early marriage and high fertility.[63]

Traditionally, demographers have seen the age at first marriage as a key index of the economic opportunity within a society.[64] Simply put, when times are hard, people wait longer to get married. Because of the favorable economic conditions, based on land availability and the Mediterranean climate, settler women were marrying earlier than was the case in any comparable European society. And not only were women marrying earlier, but also more were entering into marriage. Or, as demographers put it, the nuptiality rate (the proportion of the population who enter into marriage) of Cape women had risen from contemporary European norms of 90 percent to almost 100 percent. Few, if any, Cape European women remained spinsters in this period.[65] In short, there were few economic constraints to keep settler women at the Cape from marrying and having lots of children.

The Cape settler women, then, departed from what John Hajnal, the influential demographer, has termed the "western European marriage pattern," that is, late marriage and a low nuptiality rate.[66] The Cape settler women conformed to the typical "Eastern European or Asian" marriage pattern, in which early and universal marriage was the rule for women. The difference between the two patterns had arisen because of different economic constraints. In Western Europe the demographic regime of late marriages and a part of the population never marrying was a consequence of economic constraints on fertility and nuptiality. Marriage was delayed until the individuals concerned attained sufficient capital to buy their own land, farm, or house. In Eastern Europe, by way of contrast, land was collectively owned or worked. The actual possession of land was never a constraint on individual behavior. On the other hand, the availability of labor was a constraint on working the land. So, Hajnal argues, Eastern European societies tended to maximize output by maximizing the number of children they had. At

---

[62] Robert C.-H. Shell (ed.), "Samuel Hudson on Marriages and Other Customs at the Cape" *Kronos* 15 (1989): 49–50; John Hajnal, "European Marriage Patterns in Perspective," in David V. Glass and David E. C. Eversly (eds.), *Population and History: Essays in Historical Demography* (London: Arnold, 1965), p. 102.

[63] In America the ages at first marriage were 22.3 years in the second generation and 24.5 years in the third generation; see Philip Greven, *Four Generations . . . in Colonial Andover, Massachusetts* (Ithaca, N.Y.: Cornell University Press, 1970), pp. 200–201, 271. Anthony Flew (ed.), Thomas Malthus, *An Essay on the Principle of Population* (New York: Pelican Classics, 1970), pp. 106 ff.

[64] T. H. Hollingsworth, *Historical Demography* (Ithaca, N.Y.: Cornell University Press, 1969), pp. 102 ff. and footnote 3.

[65] C. Pama (comp.) and C. C. de Villiers, *Geslagsregisters van die ou Kaapse Families* (Cape Town: Balkema, 1981), passim.

[66] John Hajnal, "European Marriage Patterns in Perspective," 101–143.

the Cape, land was readily available and the unbalanced sex ratios ensured that nearly all women would get married. This combination led the Cape settler women to conform to the Eastern European marriage pattern, although the underlying causes were quite different. The net result — a higher proportion of colonial settler women marrying, *and* marrying earlier — was a rapidly increasing settler fertility. This was a pattern distinctly different from contemporary Europe and more pronounced even than North American colonial trends.[67]

Because of the small pool of original (pre-1717) female settlers, there arose an astonishingly high degree of family intramarriage, when the settler family is considered in its matrilineal aspect. By this I mean looking at Cape families in terms of lines of descent through the mother. The Cape genealogists do not arrange families in this way: they arrange all their data in patrilineal form, which they term the *Stamvader* (tribal father) approach.[68] The degree of matrilineal intrafamily marriages among Cape settler families increased over time and a wide and complex network of interlocking credit and mortgage obligations further tightened settler family bonds.[69] The high rate of personal debt in the capital-starved early Cape, partly a result of over investment in slavery and the flight of local money into the oceanic slave trade, ensured that the sinews of family interdependence became stronger.[70] The Cape settler society rapidly became a "tangled cousinry," to borrow a neologism from the distinguished American historian, Bernard Bailyn in his apt description of seventeenth-century Virginia. As one can learn from Cape genealogists, almost every settler family was related to every other at the Cape.[71] Samuel Hudson, who prided himself on being an after-dinner raconteur, illustrates through one of his feeble jokes just how widespread intramarriage had become by the first decade of the nineteenth century:

[67] Laslett, *Household and Family in Past Time*, pp. 125–128, 170–171, 191–203 (England); 264, 331–333 (France); 551–560 (Colonial America).

[68] M. P. de Chavonnes and G. W. van Imhoff, *The Reports of Chavonnes and His Council* (Cape Town: Van Riebeeck Society, 1918), pp. 121, 125; see also the "Opinions on Immigration" (1750) ibid., pp. 149 ff.

[69] Pama and de Villiers, *Geslagsregisters*, passim; for the hierarchical organization of the colony, see Mentzel, *Description*, vol. 2, pp. 75–92, 115–123; an annotated hierarchy of the entire colony is found in Guelke, Shell and Whyte, "The de La Fontaine Report"; the original document is in Holland, AR: "Rademacher Collection, Letters of Jan de la Fontaine" (30 January 1732) and Appendices.

[70] Because slaves were a risky investment, slave sellers — with some few exceptions — insisted on cash. Since there was little available currency at the Cape and there were no banks, a complex family-based credit system materialized in the colony. This system can be reconstructed from the "Sureties" and "IOUs" (Obligatien), interleaved with the property transfers in Cape Town; DO: "Transporten en Schepenkennis," vols. 1–25.

[71] Pama and de Villiers, *Geslagsregisters*, esp. s.v. "Retief," "De Villiers," "Bosman," "Mostert."

In this Colony intermarriages are so frequent that the whole of the Inhabitants are related. I recollect when General Janssens first took upon him the Government of the Cape of Good Hope [1803] he was consulting with a very worthy Friend of mine, a Mister Rhenius, concerning the necessity of newmodeling the constitution and if possible indicating the vices and corruptions of the generality of the People. An Herculean labour it would have proved. "How," cries His Excellency "is this to be done?" My friend whose penetration was equal to the goodness of his heart said: "General, this may be done by banishing root and branch four of the principal Families of the Cape: The Van Reinens, the Cloetez, the Bredaus and the Exteens." Now these Families were so interwoven with each other and with nearly the whole of the Colony that there must have been a general clearance. This the Governor was convinced of and gave up the Attempt.[72]

The Cape settler families became larger, more interconnected, and more clannish than their counterparts in Europe or even colonial America. Cape settler women gave rise to a new social order in the colony. Within two generations they had dramatically changed the demographic patterns from the respective home countries they had left behind. A new organization of the basic building block of society, the family, had been instituted. A few hundred European women comprised the genetic pool from which European settler society emerged in Southern Africa until 1820, and the extended, matrilineally interrelated Cape family had emerged and would continue to evolve. The patriarchal ideal provided the inspirational bedrock of future settlers' expectations of domestic life.

Household Size

If completed *family* size changed dramatically, a change in *household* size was also evident from early on. The census household included all people (slave and free) on the immediate property of the head of household, and also included people on a second and sometimes a third piece of property (see Chapter 5). From the second generation in the Cape, the census "household size" of the settler family in 1680 was more than one and a half times the size of households in contemporary Europe.[73]

After some fluctuation in settler family size occasioned by the arrival of the French Huguenots (1688 to 1701) and by the smallpox epidemic of 1713, the mean household size (family plus servants and slaves) was almost twice as large as the mean family size. Household size reached a peak in the late 1730s and then dropped after a measles epidemic, which affected mainly the slave population. The subsequent period was compounded by a severe depression (1742 to 1754), which

---

72 Shell, "Samuel Hudson on Marriages," 49–50.
73 Van der Woude in Laslett, *Household and Family in Past Time*, 309, 311. For the Cape see AR VOC 4017: "Lijst der vrije luijden en haeren ommeslag . . ." (14 February 1682), 114; AR VOC 4018: "Generale rolle der vrije luijden en haeren verdere ommeslag" (31 January 1683), 210.

retarded slave buying. After another smallpox epidemic in 1755, the settler family size remained relatively constant until 1808 (see Figures 1-3, 10-5).

The Slave Wet Nurse and the Slave Nanny

The Cape household size (in the main house) was large partly because of the number of indentured servants families had, but primarily because of the slaves, especially female slaves, living in the house.[74] The first clear indication that female slaves were being used *inside* Cape homes for the care and welfare of the settler families comes from 1713, with the first smallpox epidemic at the Cape, when George McCall Theal, an early historian of South Africa, noted: "In May and June there was hardly a family in the town that had not one sick or dead. Traffic in the streets was suspended, and even the children ceased to play their usual games in the squares and open places. At last it was impossible to obtain nurses, though slave women were being paid at the rate of four to five shillings a day."[75]

That the Cape household size was boosted by the presence of female slaves is not only an arithmetical point but also a biological one. The introduction of slave women into the homes of the settlers allowed for the rise of the slave wet nurse and nanny at the Cape. In this way slave women were not only brought into the bosom of the family, so to speak, but also actually became in a literal sense the bosom of the settler family. Many of the requests for manumission of slave women mention that they were or had been nurses or even "foster mothers." Such slave women were considered, according to their owners, "part of the family."[76] Seventeenth-century settler requests for the right to return to Holland often included the price of the passage for a wet nurse. For example, Joan Steen, Fiscal of the return fleet of 1692, paid passage for a wet nurse, or *minnemoer*, for his suckling child.[77]

It would seem that the early settler women had learned about lactation amenorrhea sometime around 1713. Perhaps they learned this from their slave women from the eastern possessions or from the local Khoisan mothers, who practiced extended lactation themselves.[78] Simon Schama has shown that wet-nursing was frowned on in metropolitan Holland at this time,[79] but settler women

---

[74] See Shell, "Slavery at the Cape of Good Hope," 276–287.

[75] George McCall Theal, *History of South Africa* (Cape Town: Struik, 1964), vol. 3, pp. 477.

[76] Mentzel, *Description*, vol. 2, 108; C. Graham Botha, *Social Life in the Cape Colony* (Cape Town: Struik, 1973), pp. 40, 83.

[77] Anna J. Böeseken et al. (eds.), *Suid-Afrikaanse Argiefstukke: Resolusies van die Politieke Raad* (Cape Town: Cape Times, 1957–1975; hereafter *Resolutions*), vol. 3, p. 256 (16 June 1692).

[78] Richard B. Lee, "Lactation, Ovulation, Infanticide and Women's work: A study of hunter-gatherer population regulation" in Mark Nathan Cohen *et al* (eds.), *Biosocial Mechanisms of Population Control* (New Haven: Yale University Press), 1980, pp. 321-348.

[79] Simon Schama, *The Embarrassment of Riches: An Interpretation of Dutch Culture in the Golden Age* (Berkeley and Los Angeles: University of California Press, 1988), pp. 539–540; Blussé, *Strange Company*, 187 (birth intervals), 191 (wet nurse). Only Thunberg, among all the sources, disputed the Cape practice of slave wet-nursing, but Sparrman, traveling at the same

had slaves to employ who could feed their infants. Cape settler women clearly perceived that there was some sort of link between lactation and ovulation. They believed that they had to physically inhibit their lactation. Kolbe provided direct evidence for the inhibition of lactation when he claimed that the majority of Cape settler women had devised various ways to stop lactation (and consequently they were always complaining bitterly about soreness of their breasts). So prevalent was this phenomenon that Kolbe devoted several pages to the horrible effects of the various local procedures.[80]

The difference in fertility between lactating and nonlactating mothers is due to the mother's production of the hormone prolactin during each episode of suckling. Prolactin effectively inhibits ovulation: mothers who do not lactate ovulate more frequently than women who are lactating and are therefore more likely to produce more children. During lactation there is thus a period of natural infertility, the length of which varies depending on local customs for nursing. The condition can continue for 18 months, or even as long as four years with one child.[81] A wet nurse who suckled her own child for, say, 18 months and then her mistress's child for a similar length of time might experience a protracted period of infertility. The generally accepted maximum period for lactation amenorrhea is four years. Not surprisingly, Cape settler women (whose lactation was stopped) and wet nurses (who hardly ever stopped lactating) had quite different fertility rates. Infertility due to lactation is not constant, or reliable, but it does appear to be statistically significant with aggregated statistics over the long term. The wet-nursing custom, admittedly an implausible explanation at first, probably accounts, at least in part, for the high fertility of the Cape settler women (circa 1700 to 1807) and the hitherto unexplained low fertility of the slave women at the Cape. One must remember that they inhabited the same epidemiological and domestic environments and shared the same or similar diets.

The starkly different fertility rates of settlers and slave nurses were thus linked by the suckling process. The Cape wet nurse, by lactating for the biological mother, ensured that the biological mother would be ovulating again sooner than if she were breast-feeding. Therefore the birth intervals between her children would be shorter, and the net result would be that she would tend to have many more children than her female slave. This practice is not unique to the Cape.

---

period, noted in clear contrast that the colonists preferred "Malays as [wet]nurses"; see Carl Peter Thunberg, *Travels at the Cape of Good Hope, 1772–1775* (Cape Town: Van Riebeeck Society Second Series, No. 17, 1986), p. 33, but see editor's note 52; Anders Sparrman, *A Voyage to the Cape of Good Hope . . .* , ed. Vernon S. Forbes (Cape Town: Van Riebeeck Society Second Series, No. 7, 1977), vol. 1, p. 218.

[80] Kolbe, *Present State of the Cape*, vol. 2, pp. 340–341.

[81] For a discussion of this point, see Alan F. Guttmacher, *Pregnancy and Birth* (New York: Signet Books, 1962); I am grateful to Helen Armstrong for many further details on this subject.

Demographers have suggested, for instance, that the use of community wet nurses similarly explains why the Hutterite women in North America have the highest recorded fertility rate.[82] From 1713 through 1808, the slave wet nurse was an integral part of the settler family — a surrogate mother.

Slave transfers, data from the household censuses, and the purchase order of Cape slaves provide some circumstantial evidence about which slaves were used as wet nurses. Settlers *never* purchased a female slave as their first slave; slave women typically were the third or fourth slave, in order of purchase, in a listing of over 4,000 slaves. Nearly all slave women purchased by wealthier colonists were bought by those who were just married or about to have a child, oblique support for this explanation of Cape settler and slave demography.[83] In 1719 the number of heads of household who owned adult female slaves, among whom were some wet nurses, was 179; the number with no female slaves was 601, but those households that reported female slaves had, on average, more than twice as many settler children (see Figure 10-6). A century later, colonists openly advertized for wet nurses.[84] Wealth, of course, or some other factor might explain the coincidence of the greater number of settler children in households and the presence of slave women. Or there might have been some wet nurses and nannies among the native people brought into the poorer households, but no sources mention this until 1811. Cape census takers failed to record any native people at all until 1798.[85]

The evidence from the settler birth intervals, or child spacing, is perhaps more convincing. Despite the slightly later age at first marriage for the 1731 group of settler women, their completed family size was larger, not smaller, as one might otherwise have supposed. In 1705 the average age at first marriage for settler women at the Cape was 17.2 years; in 1731, a generation later, it was 18.5 years, yet the 1731 settler women had a larger completed family size.[86] The presence of slave wet nurses in the household best explains the shorter birth intervals for these 1731 settler women.

Mentzel, writing of the 1740s, says that the use of a slave nurse or a slave nanny was common. The roles of midwife, wet nurse, and nanny would all be

---

[82] Christopher Tietze, "Reproduction Span and Rate of Reproduction Among Hutterite Women," *Fertility and Sterility* 8 (January-February 1957): 89–97.

[83] Slave transfers sorted by individual owner's surname, first name, sex of slave, and date of purchase: a four-level sort. The multiple-level sort was done with the aid of a spreadsheet and then linked slaves were counted; Elphick and Shell, "Intergroup Relations," p. 32, Table 4.4.

[84] AR VOC 4081 (2–4 May 1719), folios 813 ff. The slave nurse was drawn by Lady Anne Barnard in 1797. The advertisements are all from a century after the census: *Cape of Good Hope Gazette* (13 January 1826), (26 April 1826), (27 April 1827), (29 June 1827), (14 September 1827), (28 September 1827).

[85] James Ewart, *James Ewart's Journal* ed. A. Gordon Brown (Cape Town: Struik, 1970), p. 26.

[86] Guelke, "Anatomy," Table 5.

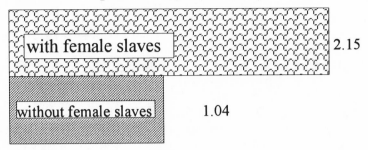

Free children per head of household (1719)

with female slaves — 2.15

without female slaves — 1.04

Ads for wet nurses (1820s)

TO LET, a healthy Wet Nurse.—Apply to H. GNADE Zirkedwars-street.

TO LET, a young and healthy Wet Nurse, with a Child. Inquire at Dr. VAN OOSTERZEE, Church square.

WANTED, a Wet Nurse; one without a Child will be preferred.—Apply to Dr. LIESCHING. Jun. No. 60, Loop-street.

Healthy Wet Nurse to Let; also, a clever Sempstress and Ironer.—Apply to J. G. ROUX, No, 4, Keerom-street.

Figure 10–6. Number of free children per household related to presence of female slaves, 1719 and newspaper ads a century later.

performed by a single slave woman. The slave nurse-nanny was there to assist at the birth; she suckled the child; she carried the settler's infant to be baptized; she was the child's companion when it was time to go to school. During this period, "Such a slave is very well treated," Mentzel noted. Elsewhere he added: "In addition to good food, she gets many presents with the prospect of manumission for good service in the bringing up of several children."[87] Mentzel here provides the second and perhaps the most important part of the explanation for the low fertility of the slave women: a statistical artifact. Slaves who were manumitted tended to be women and children, mainly women in their own childbearing years (16 to 40 years old). When they left the census "slave" population, they were, henceforth, recorded as "free." Since wet nurse slaves were the most likely of all slaves to be manumitted and were also of childbearing age, their enfranchisement as free persons and their reappearance in a different column on the census with their freed children makes it appear that all slave women had fewer children.[88]

---

[87] Mentzel, *Description*, vol. 2, 108–109.
[88] Elphick and Shell, "Intergroup Relations," 205, Figure 4.1.

The most frequent mention of the wet nurse occurs in the *requesten* for manumission from the seventeenth and eighteenth centuries. Wet nurses had to be mentioned for their fares and their compulsory manumissions to be arranged, since all slaves automatically became free when they reached the Netherlands. For example, one Fiscal, Diderik Johan Schook, asked permission in 1755 to take Mina of Batavia to Holland as "a nurse for his infant." Frederick Wilhelm Storch, a burgher, asked for passage in 1778 for a female slave, Melatie van Maccasser, for his "infant, Otto."[89] Taking a wet nurse to Holland was a considerable financial sacrifice[90]; a repatriating family that could afford only one slave passage might well select the family wet nurse.[91] In 1789, a lengthy paternalist request from a Cape slave owner discusses the manumission arrangements for two generations of wet nurses in one settler family:

Hendrik van der Graaf, Captain-Lieutenant of Artillery has notwithstanding every effort, not been able to find any other wet nurse for his infant boy than the female slave of the Company named Catryn, the daughter of Hanna, the daughter of Catryn, who has been given by you [the Company] in service to the Reverend Christianus Fleck, minister of the Cape Congregation. She has been born and educated in the house of memorialist's late father-in-law, the Rev. John Frederikus Bode, to whom as well as her mother, Hanna, gave so much satisfaction with their services and conduct, that the collective children and heirs of memorialist's father-in-law, from an upright sense of obligation, addressed themselves to your honours, in order to exchange Hanna, for a strong male slave, manumit her [Hanna] and give her liberty. This was graciously conceded by you, and given effect to by the heirs, memorialist proposes with your permission to repatriate with his wife and child in the expected return fleet, but he will be prevented from doing so if he cannot take a nurse with him, on whom he can implicitly depend. For that purpose he would by preference, chose the aforesaid Catryn, because his wife is very much attached to her and also because of the great care which she has hitherto shown to her nurseling and which (the infant child) *now always claims marks of grateful acknowledgement.* Memorialist therefore prays to be permitted to exchange Catryn for a healthy male slave, and to pay for her child the usual amount in order to manumit both.[92]

The author of this request and his father were members of the patrician class of Cape Town. Other families who manumitted slave women may well have been unable to write or unwilling to express themselves so explicitly. An ambiguous

[89] CAD C.502: "Letters despatched, Cape to Patria" (18 April 1687), pp. 336–337; Leibbrandt, *Requesten,* 3 (20 March, 1756): 1080; Ibid., (20 January 1778), page 1112.

[90] Victor de Kock, *Those in Bondage: An account of the life of the slave at the Cape in the days of the Dutch East India Company* (London: George Allen & Unwin, 1950), page 61; Leibbrandt, *Requesten* (no. 35 of 1771), vol. 1, 265.

[91] For numerous examples, see Leibbrandt, *Requesten,* 1713–1806.

[92] CAD LM 16: 1054 (no. 187 of 1789), (emphasis added).

Figure 10–7. A slave woman and her children, 1798.

sketch by Lady Anne Barnard in 1798 suggests that the dedicated wet nurse was still part of the household in 1798 (see Figure 10-7).[93]

The last clear evidence of the dedicated Cape wet nurse comes from a Boston-born visitor to the Cape, Robert Semple, who wrote in 1804: "The [settler]

---

[93] This appears to be a wet nurse rather than "a slave woman and her children." Notice "the sleeping dog lying" under the slave woman. There is considerable artistic approval of the entire scene. Source: Lady Anne Barnard, *The Letters of Lady Anne Barnard* (Cape Town: Balkema, 1973), p. 173.

women seldom suckle their children; the most prevailing practise is to consign them over in manner to a faithful female slave, who suckles, overlooks them, brings them up; in a word becomes a second mother to them." Semple suggests, though, that by the time wet-nursing was no longer universal; "Happy are they, and reason have they to be grateful, who have not suckled the milk of slavery, nor found it necessary to divide their attentions between the mother who gave them birth and the one who preserved their existence"[94] The *requesten,* a set of sources rich in descriptions of wet nurses, stop in 1806, the occasion of the second British occupation, but so too do the travelers' mentions of the Cape wet nurse. Hudson, who would never have failed to mention such a topic as wet nurses, only affirms the importance of the Cape slave dry-nurse (nanny) in the settler family for the first decade of the nineteenth century, bemoaning the duplication of habits picked up by "these discarded children":

The young children are generally placed with the female slaves, few [settler women] taking upon themselves the office of mother. This in my opinion lays the first foundation for all the vicious habits they contract of them: caresses and instances I could bring forward when the licentious curses of these domestic slaves are considered more by these discarded children than [those of] their real mothers are . . .the first thing they learn then, is to deceive the parent and keep their intercourse with their *enameraldos*[95] a secret so that by the time they are able to discriminate they are initiated into all the mysteries of duplicity and not frequently of dishonor."[96]

It may well be that with the abolition of the slave trade in 1808, the wet nurse function was abruptly abandoned because fertile slave women were needed to produce slave offspring and, therefore, could not afford to nurse settlers' infants, as well. The only legal supply for slaves after 1808 was by birth, through slave women already in the colony. Slave wet nurses do not completely disappear after 1808, but rather than remaining a part of the typical Cape household, they were specially hired. *The Cape of Good Hope Gazette,* the official newspaper, ran the following advertisement in 1829: "TO LET: a healthy Wet Nurse, without a child, about 8 months from her child bed, being also a clever seamstress, and irons well."[97] John Thomas Bigge, one of the royal commissioners at the Cape in the 1820s, believed that the hiring of slave wet nurses had became popular as a result of the hardships of the colony.[98] The most compelling evidence that slave wet nurses continued to

---

[94] Semple, *Walks and Sketches,* 30.

[95] *Enameraldos* (Spanish), a young lover.

[96] Shell, "Samuel Hudson on Marriages," 52 and note 19.

[97] As quoted in Howard Philip, "Cape Town in 1829," *Studies in the History of Cape Town* 3 (1984): 7.

[98] Theal, *RCC,* "Report of the Commissioners of Inquiry to Earl Bathurst upon the Finances" (Cape of Good Hope, 6 September 1826), 27: 444; and for the wet nurses, cf. ibid., 27: 422.

Figure 10–8. Katie Jacobs, 1910.

be a factor in the nineteenth century comes from the testimony of an ex-slave, Katie Jacobs (see Figure 10-8), who, in her ninety-sixth year, recalled the circumstances surrounding her manumission in 1834:

My first child died in infancy. I was a healthy woman, and as my missus was in rather delicate health, I became foster mother to her first-born son and heir. During this time I was well looked after, and became one of the family; that is, I was made to sleep on the floor of the dining-room near the bedroom door to be at hand when the baas wanted a drink [of milk]. My missus wept at the idea of my leaving her. "No; you must stay!" she cried. "Think of my son, whom you have suckled and nursed, and who has now grown so fond of you."[99]

Nonetheless, in the records of slave sales of the 1820s, which were compiled with actuarial accuracy, only a tiny percentage of women slaves were registered as "nursemaids."[100] A variety of sources, both literary and quantitative, demonstrate that Cape settlers' slave women busied themselves with not only nursing and child care, but also with crocheting, embroidering, sewing, knitting, laundering, and cooking.[101] Jacqueline Jones, writing of the American South, points out that tasks like these could also occupy slave women during their confinements.[102] The seventeenth-century Batavian slur that such household slave women were "*naai mandjes*" (*naai* means to sew *or* to have intercourse; *mandje* is a basket or basin) also recalls that such activities could serve a dual purpose.[103] Of all the occupations of female slaves derived from sale transfers, only a small number can be classified as nurturing occupations. Not a single "wet nurse" is mentioned, but since wet-nursing (after 1808) was only part of the female slave's life, perhaps this is not conclusive (see Figure 10-6).

After the end of oceanic slave trade in 1808, slave women in the colony were no longer adjunct mothers to the settler families, but were mothers in their own right. One may conclude that the female slave between 1713 and 1808 played an important role in the reproduction and also the socialization of the settler family. This simultaneously resulted, I have noted, in restricted slave fertility.[104] So important was the wet nurse to the slave society that two terms entered the colonial creole language: *minnemoer* or *mina* (love-mother) and *aiya* (old nursemaid). These words have survived, as has the nanny herself.[105] In 1980, there were just under a million nannies in South Africa.[106]

Diet, Venereal Disease, Abortion, and Infanticide Other factors that limited slave fertility — poor diet, venereal disease, abortion, and infanticide — are men-

---

99 "The Life of Katie Jacobs, an Ex-Slave," *African People's Organization Newsletter, (Xmas Number 1910).* Christmas Number (1910): 8–9. The picture shows Katie Jacobs in a family portrait with her grandchildren. Katie was orphaned by the domestic slave trade. It is one of four known photographs of Cape slaves. Source: Courtesy of South African Library.

100 CAD SO: "Slave Transfers," 18/6 (N = 3,484 slaves).

101 Mentzel, *Description,* 2: 125.

102 Jones, " 'My Mother was Much of a Woman,' " 243.

103 Personal communication with Leonard Blussé, 9 January 1992.

104 Only a minute analysis of the wills of the Cape colonists will yield additional data that might more fully support the existence of wet nurses and nanny in the Cape slave family.

105 *Minnemoeder* shortened to *Minnemoer* and sometimes to *mina* has an entirely Dutch etymology; cf. J. Verdam, *Middelnederlandsch Handwoordenboek* ('s-Gravenhage: Martinus Nijhoff, 1979), s.v. "minne" as "Zoogmoeder," p. 360, while *aia,* sometimes *aiya,* according to C. Graham Botha, was Malay.

106 Jacklyn Cock, *Maids and Madams: A Study in the Politics of Exploitation* (Johannesburg: Ravan Press, 1980), pp. 26–27 and passim.

tioned rarely in the sources, and consequently it is difficult to estimate their effects. Diet does not seem to have been a factor for the early period (1657 to 1808), when slave women were an integral part of the domestic household and prepared and often shared the meals, although not at the same table as the owner's family. Even in the nineteenth century many slave women were cooks, and most female slaves had household occupations (see Figures 2-6 and 10-9).[107] Since contracting

Figure 10–9. An old ex-slave woman, 1932.

---

[107] This picture of "an old slave of the household of Mr. [Melt J.] Brink's parents" appeared in the *Cape Times Supplement* on 2 August 1932. Notice her burgher dress. Courtesy of the South African Library.

venereal disease resulted in corporal punishment, few afflicted with such an illness would come forward voluntarily.[108] The same was obviously true for infanticide. Victor de Kock, an early historian of Cape slavery, who reports that if a person guilty of infanticide was brought to justice through a slave's information, the informant was freed as a reward and received the considerable sum of 200 Rixdollars. Punishment for offenders was severe. One female slave who strangled her half-caste child was tied up in a bag and drowned in the waters of Table Bay.[109] But despite the treasured rewards for betraying a slave mother guilty of infanticide, not one slave came forward, at least so far as the detailed manumission records show.

The vehemence with which one particular infanticide was mentioned in legislation suggests that the crime was rare in the eighteenth century, but it was perhaps more common in the nineteenth century, when reporting of the act increased.[110] In 1806, Hudson wrote: "I am credibly informed by people of respectability that prior to the English first taking the Cape of Good Hope many a poor Unfortunate babe found a Grave in the Sea from inhuman depraved Mothers."[111] In the second British occupation, one desperate slave woman took her children "four in number, down to the sea, where she succeeded in drowning three of them, and was in the act of destroying herself and the remaining child when she was discovered."[112] An officer in the ninety-third regiment said he had seen the bodies of no fewer than 13 infants washed up by the tides on the Cape Town beach. Seventy-four Cape Town ward masters thereupon swore that "only" 8 dead infants had been found in the urban area since 1795. Others signed separate depositions for the investigation stating that only 2 rural infanticides had been uncovered in the same period.[113] Infanticide occurred in other slave societies as well and also in societies that had no slaves. Eugene Genovese, an American social historian, suggests that infanticide, at least in the American South, seems not to have been "a major problem."[114] At the Cape, too, there is little evidence that it played any significant role in reducing the count of newborn slaves, though the practice assuredly existed.

---

[108] "An emancipated female slave infected with the venereal disease to be cared for in the slave lodge and corporally punished when released, but a second time taken in[to the] hospital, be confined or punished more severely"; CAD SO 17/1 (23 December 1803), n.p.

[109] De Kock, *Those in Bondage*, 184, 185.

[110] Jeffreys and Naude, *Kaapse Plakkaatboek* (15 March 1740), vol. 2, p. 171; (24 April 1753), vol. 2, p. 246.

[111] Shell, "Samuel Hudson on Marriages," 53 and note 23.

[112] Theal, *RCC.*, 14: 484.

[113] Theal, *RCC.*, "Letter of R. B. Fisher to William Wilberforce" (13 September 1813), 11: 176–183; "Letter from Bathurst to Lord Charles Somerset" (24 September 1816) 11: 188, 344–349; and on the trial of a female slave, Hester for the murder of her three children in 1819, see "Somerset to R. Wilmot" (20 October 1823), 16: 379–381.

[114] Eugene D. Genovese, *Roll, Jordan, Roll* (New York: Vintage Books, 1976), p. 497.

Sexual Exploitation

The psychosexual implications of the slave nanny and, especially, of the slave wet nurse are a matter of high controversy in the literature on slave societies. Gilberto Freyre, the original, if currently unfashionable, social historian of Brazil, has argued that the sexual preference for black women among sons in slave-holding families in Brazil was a direct development of the intimate relationship the white child had with the black wet nurse.[115] The evidence for his theory rests on anecdotes; Freyre never establishes the statistical presence of wet nurses. Freyre maintains that, in Brazil, some European men not only preferred blacks but also were "incapable of enjoying themselves" with white women. Freyre tells the story of a wealthy and important rural family of Pernambuco, that was unable to arrange a marriage for their son, for the well-known reason that he "wanted" only blacks.[116] C. R. Boxer quoted an eyewitness account of the Dutch invasion of the same region of Pernambuco in 1637, when "many of the pot-bellied sugar planters fled southward with their pretty mulata mistresses riding pillion behind them, while their neglected white wives struggled, disheveled and barefoot, through swamp and scrub."[117] Jonathan Gathorne-Hardy, a social historian in England, pursued a similar line of argument in his account of the importance of the nanny in Victorian Britain, hinting that the attraction of the younger gentry for women of "lower class" origin is based on a relationship between the infant squire and his "lower class" nanny.[118]

We know nothing at all of the sexual preferences of the slave women; still, there is considerable evidence that well-to-do Cape slave-owning families, like some of their counterparts in Brazil, perceived similar "problems" with their sons' adolescent sexual orientation and behavior. Mentzel noted: "Wealthy . . .[boys] who, through force of circumstance, have to remain at home during these impressionable years between 16 and 21 *more often than not* get entangled with a handsome slave girl belonging to the household. These affairs are not regarded as very serious. The girl is sternly rebuked for her wantonness, and threatened with dire punishments if she dares to disclose who was responsible for her condition; nay, she is bribed to put the blame on some other man."[119]

---

[115] Gilberto Freyre, *The Masters and the Slaves: A Study in the Development of Brazilian Civilization* (New York: Knopf, 1971), pp. 278–279.

[116] Freyre, *Masters and the Slaves,* 279.

[117] C. R. Boxer, *The Golden Age of Brazil, 1695–1750,* (Berkeley and Los Angeles: University of California Press, 1962), p. 16.

[118] Jonathan Gathorne-Hardy, *The Unnatural History of the Nanny* (New York: Dial Press, 1973), p. 56 (published in England under *The Rise and Fall of the English Nanny*).

[119] Mentzel, *Description,* vol. 2, 109–110, (emphasis added).

A few married owners lived polygamously, with a free wife and slave concubines in the same house. This resulted in some predictable domestic dramas. Hudson related one in 1806:

A farmer in the district of Stellenbosch of some repute had frequently had some serious quarrels with his wife respecting a slave maid who unfortunately happened to be more desirable than her mistress which had caused heart-burnings and jealousy and many severe chastisements whenever opportunities offered by the absence of the husband. At last matters arrived to such a pitch that this furious woman was determined at all events to rid herself of this encroacher upon her rights by the most cruel and unheard of piece of barbarity. Her husband was in the field being with his slaves in cultivating his ground at a considerable distance from the house. This poor wretch had been baking and had just taken the hot bread from the oven when her merciless mistress came into the kitchen and accused the girl of being with child by her master. She denied it & assured her tyrant that he had never taken any such liberty with her. Frustrated by her denyal, she vented her fury on the poor wretch who patiently bore the cruel treatment of the devil in human shape, not content with beating her maid unmercifully, she called in a strong boy [i.e., slave] who was employed about the house and made him hold the maid whilst she crammed hot bread down the throat of the unfortunate slave 'till she had choaked her. The poor boy begged of his mistress to forbear, that the maid was dying. "So much the better!" said the hardened wretch, "I have now my wish." The slave actually died under the fangs of this harpy. Not content with having taken her life, she cut her open to be convinced whether her suspicions were well founded or not — where slept the thunder at this awful moment?[120]

In another case a slave woman took exquisite revenge on a master who had shown little sexual restraint in his youth. Her erstwhile owner complained to an English visitor, Lady Duff-Gordon, in 1862 of the misery he had undergone as the result of the "ingratitude" of his "slave-girl," Rosina. He had had two children with her. After the emancipation of slaves in 1834, Rosina stood outside his house and "read the [emancipation] statute in a loud voice on every anniversary of the day." Every time she met him on the street, she kissed him "by main force," exclaiming: "Aha! when I [was] young and pretty slave girl you make kiss me then; now I ugly, drunk, dirty old devil and free woman, I kiss you!"[121]

Domestic propinquity within the household sometimes led to sexual encounters also between young adolescent settler daughters and their male slaves. In 1695 a slave, Jan van Batavia, made love to a 14-year-old settler girl, Adriana van Jaarsveld, who was staying in the Drakenstein home of his owner. The slave was

---

[120] Shell, "Slaves," 54–55.

[121] Lady Duff-Gordon, *Letters from the Cape* (Oxford: Oxford University Press, 1927), p. 112.

severely scourged and banished from the colony.[122] Early on a spring morning in 1712, after the field slaves had left for work, Robert van Batavia, the household slave of Gijsbert Verweij, attempted to seduce the owner's 17-year-old grand-daughter, Neeltje Olivier. According to the accused, the victim was provocatively squatting on her heels mashing rice to feed the chickens.[123] The voluminous documents of this case disclose that he had been watching her on several similar prior occasions. The ensuing verbal exchange, centering around the word "*melktert*" (custard pie), was sufficiently ambiguous (in Robert's view) to suggest that he was given at least some "encouragement." While the full extent of these domestic interracial liaisons may never be known, references to such incidents appear from time to time in the crime records, the daily fort journal, and even the austere Church records.[124]

The most spectacular case of an interracial liaison was one in 1714 between the 24-year-old Maria Mouton from Middelburg in Zealand, who had a love affair with her slave, Titus of Bengal. She, with Titus and several slave accomplices, murdered her husband of eight years, Franz Joost of Lippstadt.[125] The Cape court sentenced Titus to be publicly impaled through the anus until death. While impaled he was given a flask of rice brandy (*arrack*) by several onlookers, one of whom duly chided him lest he become too drunk. The diarist recorded Titus's sardonic answer: "It did not matter as he sat fast enough and there was no fear of falling." The diarist of this event concluded: "It is true that whilst sitting in that deplorable state, he often joked, and scoffingly said that he would never again believe a woman."[126]

Very rarely was a liaison between an adult settler woman and a slave man referred to in the Church records. However, in September 1716 the distant Drakenstein Church council decided that "from widely circulating rumors, and despite repeated admonishments, it was clear that Van Bruel's wife was living a very evil [*seer boos*] life with her slave and that she was consequently called before the church, and told that unless she desisted and sold the slave, she would be excluded from the communion."[127] In her defense, reminiscent of St. Augustine's human plea "Give me chastity and continence, but not just now," she said she

---

122 Elphick and Shell, "Intergroup Relations," p. 131.

123 AR VOC 4069: Processtukken, "Recollement van Matschinge" (2 September 1712), folio 538 and verso.

124 Hendrik Carel Vos Leibbrandt, *Journal, 1699–1732* (Cape Town: W. A. Richards & Sons, 1896), pp. 260–261.

125 Pama and de Villiers, *Geslagsregisters*, vol. 1, 367.

126 Hendrik Carel Vos Leibbrandt, *Letters Despatched* (Cape Town: W. A. Richards & Sons, 1896), pp. 260–261 (3 September 1714).

127 C. Spoelstra, *Bouwstoffen voor de Geschiedenis der Nederduitsch-Geref. Kerken in Zuid-Afrika* (Amsterdam: Hollandsche-Afrikaansche Uitgewers-Maatscappij, 1906–1907), vol. 2, p. 431.

would comply, but as her husband was having difficulty selling her slave paramour, would the Church be patient?[128] Mentzel recorded a case later in the eighteenth century, at Salt River near Cape Town, in which the settler proprietress of a wine shop had given birth to a black child. She declared to her quite well-educated husband, and everybody else, that she had been frightened during pregnancy by unexpectedly meeting a black slave.[129] The overall impression is that such liaisons between adult settler women and male slaves were rare.

Travelers' anecdotes may not be reliable, since it must have been tempting for writers to titillate metropolitan readers with prurient tidbits, as when Mentzel claimed such unions were more common in the town, where "they were not so strict," than in the country.[130] There is no way to verify such statements. Carl Peter Thunberg, a Swedish botanist visiting the Cape in the 1770s, mentioned that "the daughters of the colonists are sometimes with child by their father's black slaves. In this case, in consideration of a round sum of money, a husband is generally provided for the girl, but the slave is sent away from that part of the country."[131] Anders Sparrman, Thunberg's fellow countryman and a usually trustworthy source, provides another anecdote of this sort of sexual liaison. The overall impression from all the sources, however, excluding the crime records, is that these travelers were trying to amuse and excite their readers and that there were actually few such liaisons.[132]

Recent research on interracial marriages in the antebellum South has eschewed any reliance on anecdotal sources.[133] The welcome practice of quantifying primary records has now caught hold in South Africa, and thanks to the careful genealogical work of the Historical Institute at the University of the Western Cape, we know that only two liaisons between a "full-breed" (*heelslag*) or mulatto [*halfslag*] male slave (or ex-slave) and a settler woman ever resulted in marriage.[134]

---

[128] Spoelstra, *Bouwstoffen*, (6 December 1716), vol. 2, p. 431.

[129] Mentzel, *Description*, vol. 3, 104.

[130] Mentzel, *Description*, vol. 3, 104.

[131] Thunberg, *Travels at the Cape*, 50–51 and note 33; but one wonders what would have happened to the infant — would the mother have had it baptized or have had it aborted? See also Nigel Anthony Worden, *Slavery in Dutch South Africa* (Cambridge: Cambridge University Press, 1985), pp. 148–149.

[132] Sparrman, *A Voyage to the Cape*, vol. 1, 94.

[133] Gary B. Mills, "Miscegenation and the Free Negro in Antebellum 'Anglo' Alabama: A Reexamination of Southern Race Relations," *Journal of American History* 68, 1 (June 1981): 16–34.

[134] Marguerite de Savoye married Christoffel Snyman, and Maria Roos married David Hoon in 1794. Hoon's father was a slave from Madagascar, and his mother, Rachel of the Cape, was the daughter of Indian parents. The only Conservative party member on the "all white" President's Council in 1988 was a fifth-generation descendant of this couple. Private communication with Hans Heese, (5 December 1988).

The runaway interracial couple celebrated in André Brink's famous South African novel, *An Instant in the Wind*, was, disappointingly, based on an Australian story; there was no such Cape incident, despite the novel's deliberately misleading introduction.[135] One must remember that there was no law against a settler woman's freeing a mulatto slave and marrying him. There was only an increasingly powerful custom against doing so. As was true in other European colonial slave societies, Cape women were protected from any "aberrant" wishes by new colonial customs.[136] A number of Cape settler men and free black men, on the other hand, did free and marry slave women, but men historically have been freer than women to act on their sexual preferences. Where women were free to act was in their marriage choice. One must conclude that Cape free women never "married down" in the increasingly race- and status-conscious Cape. The one choice white women traditionally had — the marriage choice — although truncated by descent, was resolutely exercised at the Cape.

The early and very rare domestic liaisons between settler women and male slaves should not be regarded as evidence of racial fluidity in the colony, as some scholars suggest. All such encounters were forbidden by statute, and the male perpetrator was harshly punished *if and only if* he was a black slave. For example, the courts did not sentence any European settlers to death for concubinage with, or rape of, a female slave. The same courts did, however, sentence many male slaves to banishment or death between 1658 and 1795 for the merest suggestion of a sexual advance against a settler woman.[137] Jan van Batavia, for example, who had made love to a settler girl, was sentenced to be scourged and banished to Mauritius, there to be chained for 20 years, while Mrs. van Bruel, the amorous European settler woman who had lived a "very evil" life with her slave, was simply barred from Church communion for her transgressions.[138] The language of a 1705 death sentence for a Stellenbosch house slave who had an encounter with a European farmer's daughter discloses that the disparate status and race of the partners bore heavily against the accused slave in such liaisons, "and that [this crime was committed] by a black slave on a free girl of European breed &c."[139] The

---

[135] Information from Ralph Austen's taped interview with André Brink, August 1991.

[136] Herbert Moller, "Sex Compositions and Correlated Culture Patterns of Colonial America," *William and Mary Quarterly* Second Series, 2 (1945): 135.

[137] The Cape crime records of this period cover over 1,000 meters of shelf space in the Rijksarchief; obviously not all could be consulted. See some published examples in Moodie, *The Record*, pp. 380–385, especially Cupido of Bengal (p. 384) who had a "criminal conversation" with his master's daughter (3 February 1681); also Anna Böeseken, *Uit die Raad van Justisie* (Pretoria: Staatsdrukker, 1986), passim.

[138] Elphick and Shell, "Intergroup Relations," 131.

[139] *"En dat door een swarte lijfeigenen aan een vrije dogter van Europeansche geslag"*; AR VOC 4053: "Eijsch en Conclusie" (4 June 1705), folio 580. It must be noted that these were the words of the sentence of the court. The prosecutor used a very different construction in his phrasing:

predominance of male slaves in the colony, many of whom had little opportunity for heterosexual gratification and only some of whom had had daily domestic contact with settler women from childhood, no doubt increased the likelihood of such encounters.[140] That male slaves were housed separately from their owners was probably the main reason, but not the only one for the rarity of liaisons between white women and black men.

Marriages of Privately Owned Slaves

Slaves were allowed to marry each other only after baptism and freedom. A slave woman who, by habits of devotion and fidelity, had attached herself to a slave man was called by local officials his *wijfie*, a word meaning the female of any animal species, not wife.[141] Even under the Batavian administration between 1803 and 1806, which was ostensibly inspired by the ideals of the French revolution and which introduced civil marriages, the Cape marriage board, after obtaining the names and addresses of the couple, asked each of them: "Are you a Christian, and not a heathen or a slave?"[142] Robert Semple said that by the first decade of the nineteenth century slaves were using their own marriage ceremonies, completely outside the colonial order;[143] by the 1820s, Muslim *imams* were routinely performing ceremonies for all slaves who wanted to be joined in matrimony.[144] By 1822 those slaves not choosing the Muslim marriage rite simply dubbed themselves man and *vrouw* (wife) and observed fidelity.[145]

Legally sanctioned slave marriages did not exist until passage of the Nineteenth Ordinance of 1823. Even then, slave couples had to be Christian to be married. Few slaves rushed to the Christian altar, from which they had been barred for so long, and early Dutch prohibitions and Batavian ordinances continued to operate long after the Nineteenth Ordinance had been passed. Also slaves (as "children" of their master) had to have their owner's permission to marry. Isaac, 25 years of age, a slave carpenter who had been born at the Cape, complained in December 1829 that his master Hendrik Frans Hiltzeroth had refused to consent to his marriage with a free black woman, Louisa Bril. On enquiry the master failed to give such "good and sufficient proof that the proposed marriage would be

---

"that this [crime] was perpetrated (by a slave and heathen) on a girl of European, and Christian descent . . ." "(*Het welke (als bij een slaaf en onchristen) aan een dogter van Europeesche en Christene geslagte [sic] gepleegd . . .*"). Race and religion were clearly close analogues in the minds of the court officials.

[140] Elphick and Shell, "Intergroup Relations," p. 132, Table 4.4.

[141] Leibbrandt, *Requesten,* vol. 2, 872 (no. 62 of 1789 and no. 55 of 1789).

[142] Jeffreys and Naude (eds.), *Kaapse Plakkaatboek,* vol. 6, 218 (Publicatie: Article 8 B, 1804); cf. ibid., 223 (Article 23).

[143] Semple, *Walks and Sketches,* 39.

[144] Robert C.-H. Shell, "Rites and Rebellion: Islamic Conversion at the Cape, 1808 to 1915," *Studies in the History of Cape Town* 5 (1984): 28.

[145] Bird, *State of the Cape,* 74.

injurious to the well-being of the slave," whereupon the assistant guardian told him that unless he gave written consent, a marriage license would be issued without the master's permission. The owner duly gave his consent in writing, and it was handed over to the clergyman of Uitenhage District, but that clergyman refused to solemnize the marriage of the slave on the grounds that the matrimonial court did not permit a slave to pass through the court with a free person (pursuant to the twenty-second section of the proclamation of 20 September 1804).[146] Isaac promptly applied to missionaries at Bethelsdorp, and they acceded to his request. However, an official noted that a marriage solemnized by a missionary was not considered in this colony "a legal marriage." It is not surprising that by 1831 only three legal — that is, Christian — marriages had been solemnized among 35,000 slaves.[147]

In the early years of the colony (1652 to 1717), the slave most often wholly incorporated into a settler family was a mulatto female slave who had married a bachelor settler or a Company employee. Typically such a slave was first baptized, then manumitted, and only then married to the settler, who was sometimes also her former owner. The ex-slave then became the mother of his children and thus acquired full burgher status. The ubiquitous members of the Basson family, of modern South Africa, for instance, all descend from Ansiela of Bengal, a household slave of the colony's first governor, Jan van Riebeeck.[148] Ansiela married Arnoldus Willemsz Basson, a visitor to the van Riebeeck household, in 1669, and bore him seven children, in addition to some she had borne before.[149] Recently, more than 1,000 self-styled Afrikaner families were surprised to find, in Hans Heese's 1984 book, *Groep sonder Grense (Community without Boundaries)*, that they are descended from women who were slaves in the first generations of conquest.[150] The humiliation of these descendants was so intense that they promptly took the genealogist to court in a million-Rand law suit. I have tabulated Heese's identifications and compared them with the number of adult slave women who were manumitted. The quite independently collected data match. Many slave women who were manumitted were marriage-bound. That there were more marriages of

[146] PRO (Kew) CO 53/50 no. 60, pp. 24–25 and memorandum page 31 (14 December 1829).

[147] William Wright, *Slavery at the Cape of Good Hope* (New York: Negro Universities Press, 1969 reprint), pp. 14, 106.

[148] W. Blommaert, "Het invoeren van de slavernij aan de Kaap," *Archives Year Book* 1, 1 (1938): 7.

[149] Ansiela's record illustrates on an anecdotal basis that slave women, freed of wet-nursing duties, could have as many children as settler women; cf. Pama and de Villiers, *Geslagsregisters*, vol. 1, p. 24.

[150] Hans Friedreich Heese, *Groep sonder Grense: Die rol en status van de gemengde bevolking aan die Kaap, 1652–1795* (Bellville: Wes Kaaplandse Instituut vir Historiese Navorsing, 1984).

slaves to settlers than manumissions may be explained by Heese's inclusion of Khoi women who married settlers (see Figure 10-10).[151]

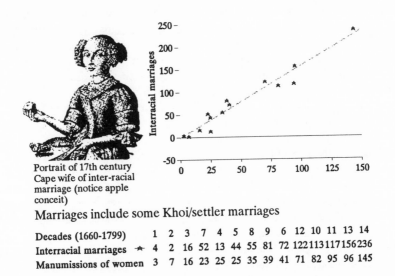

Portrait of 17th century Cape wife of inter-racial marriage (notice apple conceit)

Marriages include some Khoi/settler marriages

Decades (1660-1799)	1	2	3	7	4	5	8	9	6	12	10	11	13	14
Interracial marriages	4	2	16	52	13	44	55	81	72	122	113	117	156	236
Manumissions of women	3	7	16	23	25	25	35	39	41	71	82	95	96	145

Figure 10–10. Correlation of marriages and manumissions, 1658 to 1800.

The choice of such slave marriage partners was not random. Preferences based on race and origins were involved. Of the 191 slave women who married or lived with men of German descent in the seventeenth and early eighteenth century, the majority (59.7 percent) were creole (Cape-born), many possibly mulatto. The next largest group of slave spouses was from the Indonesian Archipelago (22.5 percent), and 15.2 percent of the slave wives were from India, all from Bengal. Perhaps the most stunning difference lies in the fact that "full-breed" Malagasy women and the tiny contingent of African slave women, who together constituted a large portion (18.6 percent) of all imported Cape slave women, represented fewer than 3 percent of these wives. German settler men preferred mulattos over *heelslags* and slaves from certain regions over others.[152] These findings are fully in accord with what Hermanus Hoetink, a historian of the Dutch Caribbean, has called the preference for the "somatic norm." According to Hoetink, spouses preferred their partners to resemble themselves in body type and skin

151 Shell, "Manucomb"; manumissions: N = 603; r² = .94715 with marriages independent; Marriages: N = 1,083; H. F. Heese, *Groep sonder Grense* (Bellville: Weskaapslandse Instituut Vir Historiese Navorsing, 1984), appendixes.
152 Data for marriages from Elphick and Shell, "Intergroup Relations," 129–130; data for the slave population from the transfers.

color.[153] Cultural affinities and linguistic factors must have played a part as well. For example, the preferred creole slaves, having been born in the colony, would also have spoken Dutch as their first language, whereas imported Malagasy women would not.

On the other hand, George Bataille, a French anthropologist, has maintained that opposing somatic features fire the erotic imagination.[154] Anders Sparrman said that in the Cape hinterland of the 1770s at least one Hanoverian immigrant had a hierarchy of sexual preference by race in which "the blackest" were the best and "white Dutch women" the worst of all:

I arrived in the evening at a farmhouse, the bailiff [*knecht*] of which welcomed me in the most friendly manner, with a hearty slap of the hand, in the African style. He entertained me with milk, and an account of his love affairs and intrigues. . . . He also gave me a scale or list (which by his desire, I took down in my pocket book, as the result of his own experience) of the constant order of precedence in love which ought to be observed among the fairest sex in Africa: this was as follows. First the Madagascar women, who are the blackest and handsomest; next to them the Malabars, then the Bouganese or Malays, after these the Hottentots and last and worst of all, the white Dutch Women.[155]

Interracial sexual liaisons, and later marriages, too, became increasingly embarrassing to Cape settler society, especially to the free settler women, many of whom had slave ancestry. Attitudes toward free black women became increasingly antagonistic. Even on such matters like dress, the settlers sought to control their behavior. In 1765 the local authorities took scornful notice of the colony's 118 free black women who, by their dress, placed "themselves not only on a par with other respectable burghers' wives, but often pushed themselves above them."[156] The all-male Political Council, possibly prompted by settler women, deemed such behavior "unseemly and vexing to the public." Henceforth no free black women were to appear in public in colored silk clothing, hoop skirts, fine laces, adorned bonnets, curled hair, or even earrings.[157] Emancipated female slaves were ordered to wear no material other than chintz and striped cotton and to be "well-behaved, if christened, [or] married and at other occasions in church, [to wear] a habit [*kledje*] of black silk."[158] Even in freedom, ex-slaves were managed in such domestic matters as dress.

---

[153] Hermanus Hoetink, *Slavery and Race Relations in the Americas: Comparative Notes on Their Nature and Nexus* (New York: Harper & Row, 1973), pp. 205–210.

[154] Georges Bataille, *Eroticism*, (San Francisco: City Lights, 1986 reprint).

[155] Sparrman, *A Voyage to the Cape*, vol. 1, p. 72.

[156] Elphick and Shell, "Intergroup Relations," 218; there were 118 free black women in 1760.

[157] Elphick and Shell, "Intergroup Relations," 215.

[158] CAD SO 17/1 (12 November 1765), n.p.

A few decades later, in 1798, Lady Anne Barnard, the wife of the colony's second in command, wrote at the apogee of interracial marriages, of one pretty quadroon bride-to-be who was ostracized by the Dutch settler women so pointedly that she left the colony: "The Dutch ladies will not visit her, I dare say, she has a dash of the *Blew*, her mother's mother having been a slave, & as we are as proud as *Lucifer* on point of birth there is no quality or virtue not even the *virtue of being rich* which is not spunged [*sic*] out by the word slave born or half cast."[159] There was a head-on clash between evolving racial attitudes of the time and the continuing shortage of European women at the Cape. The marital trajectories of the Colony's few slave women cannot be regarded as real evidence of racial fluidity, for in those regions of the colony where European women were more numerous, the incidence of mixed unions and interstatus marriages was proportionally low. According to Heese's tabulations, just over 1,000 ex-slave and native women married free burghers of European descent in the years 1652 to 1795 (and only two male ex-slaves married free women of European descent).[160] When one considers that 65,000 slaves were imported into the Cape and almost an equal number were born into slavery, it is clear that the chances of a slave's entering the ranks of colonial society were small and highly gendered, and, moreover, that they declined with time.[161]

Attitudes of Women toward their Slaves

The attitudes that settler women held toward the slaves in their household varied over time. In general, their attitudes deteriorated, I believe, when the function of the wet nurse declined, but the development of these attitudes was by no means straightforward. It is at first astonishing to find that, despite the importance of the female slave to the settler population, female slaves on the auction block did not on average obtain high prices, contrary to the claims of several European observers.[162] The quantitative data and the travelers' accounts are in conflict on this matter. An analysis of the distribution of slave prices by age and sex shows that female slaves were more expensive than their male counterparts only until they reached the age of menarche. After menarche they reached a price plateau that was clearly lower

---

159 A. M. Lewin Robinson (ed.), *The Letters of Lady Anne Barnard to Henry Dundas* (Cape Town: Balkema, 1973), p. 174 (emphasis in original).

160 Heese, *Groep sonder Grense*, 41–75.

161 I have calculated the number of slaves imported into the colony by applying a reiterative formula to the annual *opgaafs* from 1658 to 1808, making algebraic assumptions about fertility, mortality, and runaways. I hope to publish this rather technical work somewhere, but at this time can find no home for it. I would be glad to provide the details to anyone interested.

162 Sparrman, *A Voyage to the Cape*, 74; Bird, *State of the Cape*, 348.

than the corresponding male price curve. Research on slavery in America confirms that prepubescent female slaves, who were more skilled at agricultural pursuits than similarly aged male slaves, were also sold at higher prices on the auction block only up until menarche (see Figure 10-11).[163] Menarche, the sign of the incipient risks and costs of pregnancy, made slave women on average less valuable than men of a similar age. Despite the key domestic position slave women held in Cape slave society, the early slave age-price distribution does suggest that owners did not value adult female slaves highly.[164] Perhaps the male Cape slave owners, who were the principal buyers at slave auctions, simply regarded domestic services and child-rearing as less important than field labor.

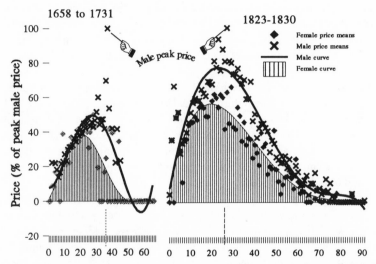

Figure 10–11. The age-price curves for male and female slaves, before and after abolition.

Sale transfer documents reveal that the high proportion of male slaves bought from the oceanic slave trade led to a male-to-female slave sex ratio that was among the highest in the colonial world.[165] Settler families, for sentimental reasons, rarely

---

163 Shell, "Saledeed"; "1823sale." Since mothers were sold with their children for a single price, all mothers unfortunately had to be excluded from both graphs. This graphic is therefore only suggestive. In the lefthand graph the slightly higher price for prepubescent girls is attributed to their earlier physical maturity; see Robert Fogel and Stanley Engerman, *Time on the Cross* (Boston: Little, Brown, 1974), vol. 1, 77.

164 Unfortunately it is not possible to derive the same graph from the nineteenth-century data, because then women were nearly always sold with their offspring in a joint sale and for a single price.

165 Shell, "Slavery at the Cape of Good Hope," 79–81.

allowed their wet nurses or nannies to reach the auction block. Nannies were, indeed, the most valued slaves, and they were rarely if ever sold. When they were sold in the sale of a distressed estate, they fetched high prices often, in an auction drama that caught the attention of travelers. Most of the slave women who were, in fact, up for auction were possibly "reject" slave women. They may have been infertile and so not able to produce more slaves, or perhaps they were "too truculent" for their owners. Such conjecture could explain their anomalous prices, but any such theory faces a heavy sea of conflicting evidence from the travelers.

We know from a variety of sources that settler children were brought up deeply imbued with the slave-holding ethos. Mentzel noted that settler parents encouraged even their youngest daughters to inflict domestic punishment on the slaves.[166] In contrast, Sparrman noted that some slaves refused to "be disciplined by the weaker sex. Many a master and mistress of a family who have happened to forget themselves with respect to this point, have . . .been made to pay for this mistake with their lives."[167] Some adult mistresses would nevertheless physically assault their female slaves. In 1833, on the eve of emancipation, Colonie, a 30-year-old housemaid on the farm Boschijemans Vallei near Waaihoek, complained to the Protector of Slaves that "on a certain morning in the course of last week she was unwell and could not attend to her usual work, that about 8 o'clock her mistress ordered her to clean her shoes, which Colonie did and brought them to her bedroom, which she then began to clean, while she was busy therewith, the mistress was angry that the hall was not clean and on entering the bedroom began to beat Colonie with the fist upon her head and mouth and knocked out one of her teeth."[168]

The expectations and limits on behavior which the slave owning society inculcated in young women, both slave and free, cannot be ignored. An anonymous British officer indicated that inculcation of slave-holding values had deepened by the early nineteenth century, so that "accustomed to be surrounded with female slaves from their infancy, they [young settler women] no sooner begin to move, than they find they are not allowed to assist themselves, but have attendants at their call, over whom they are soon taught, by the powerful examples they see around them, of exercising the imperious tones of command; this, by degrees, is confirmed by habit, and carried with them into active life, when they become mothers in their turn."[169] Samuel Hudson, writing of the same period, observed that young settler women had high expectations of a gift of slaves at their maturity and marriage. Ambitious society brides of Cape Town in the 1800s, for example, insisted on an "establishment" of slaves as part of their marriage settlements.[170]

---

166 Mentzel, *Description*, vol. 2, 110.
167 Sparrman, *A Voyage to the Cape*, vol. 2, 343–344.
168 PRO (Kew) CO 53/57 (14 October 1833), n.p.
169 Anon., *Gleanings in Africa*, 257–258; see also Semple, *Walks and Sketches*, 37–38.
170 Shell, "Samuel Hudson on Marriages," 56.

Robert Wilson, an English officer visiting the Cape in 1806, saw the settler women as benevolent in their attitude toward their slaves: "Although the European mother prefers her own race, she would think herself unworthy to be a parent if she could neglect an infant or not treat it with kindness because it was the offspring of a slave."[171] Analysis of slave sales and manumissions also sheds a kinder light on the attitudes of settler women. Adult settler women, at least the widows, manumitted (and sold) their slaves much more frequently than did men. Moreover, settler women freed adult slave women more often than they freed young men. There is sometimes even evidence of genuine affection (expressed best in the manumission records). But the overall impression from the existing sources is that the settler woman's attitude was unleavened with compassion or sympathy for her housemaid — either as a slave, personal servant, and nurse for her children, or as a woman.

The settler women came to occupy a commanding social position both because of their scarcity and because of the particular system of partible inheritance at the Cape, and their scarcity in the short run empowered them to maintain their dominant position over the long term. For instance, there was, at the Cape what E. S. Morgan, writing of Virginia, has termed "widowarchy." Some Cape widows remarried as many as three times, and in remarrying they acted as the conduit of large fortunes. Because of their small numbers and enhanced social position, Cape settler women nearly always married up the social scale; anthropologists would say they practiced an almost perfect hypergamy. There is also some evidence that free white women increasingly ostracized free black women on grounds of racial or slave descent, even though some of the "white" women were not of European descent themselves. In short, settler women took advantage of their own scarcity to empower themselves, and, in doing so, helped forge and maintain the colonywide hierarchy based on racial descent. Although there were individual sympathetic gestures of settler women to slave women, on the whole these gestures were matriarchal, statistically insignificant, and did not challenge the regime of Cape slavery (see Figure 10-12).[172]

Many slave women in the orbit of settler women were treated well on a day-to-day basis, because they were members of the household. If any slaves were present in the main household at night, those slaves would in all likelihood have been the slave women. Such women slaves therefore enjoyed the largest fireplace in

---

[171] Lt.-Col. Robert Wilson, "Description of the Cape Colony in 1806," unpublished manuscript, CAD: VC 17, p. 15.

[172] This is Bell's cartoon masterpiece of Cape slavery and family life. The settler wife is in the center of the picture. In her left hand she holds keys the symbol of property. The right hand gestures imperiously. Her generous figure envelops the home. The cowering, cap-in-hand slave ironically holds the whip, the symbol of slavery. The owner, a diminutive figure, has his back to the viewer. Artist: Charles Bell, Courtesy of Brenthurst Library.

Figure 10–12. Untitled, [1831].

the house, in the kitchen. This does not mean that domestic work was not arduous and exploitative, however. Further, slave women were apparently sexually exploited by male owners as concubines, and also often reproductively exploited in their respective capacities as wet nurses and, after 1808, as breeders of slaves and, hence, of property.

Slave women had tasks not in the fields but within the house. In this respect Cape slave women were treated differently not only from Cape slave men but also from their female counterparts in the American South, many of whom were required to do heavy agricultural work. Throughout the period the Cape slave women were manumitted proportionally more often than their male counterparts. The favorable ratio dropped after 1808, but it never inverted. Slave women, once baptized, stood an incomparably better chance than slave men of being incorporated into the ruling class through a formal Christian marriage. Many freed slave women entered colonial society and enjoyed all the perquisites of settler status. Slave women thus had a clearly perceived stake in the system, and they made use of all their advantages. But after 1808, when slave women's function as a wet nurse declined, and when the scarcity of all women at the Cape became much less of a problem, their opportunities to become free and to have free children declined.

Notions of gender *and* sex undercut the potential for slave solidarity at the household level. From the outset of colonial occupation, slave women were more closely woven into the settler family household than were slave men. Their own domestic responsibilities to their own children probably resulted in low runaway rates, a pattern also observable in the American South.[173] In the period up to 1838, the cultural and emotional influence of the slave women on settler families far outweighed that of the male slaves. It was the slave women of the settlers who were the most likely of all slaves to betray slave rebellions. It was the slave women who went running to the owner when there was "trouble." There seems to have been little change in the individual slave woman's identification with the owner's household. That was where the power lay. That was where a slave woman would look for security for her children and for her own old age. Even after the general emancipation in 1838, Katie Jacobs stayed with her owner's family, despite her husband's entreaties and their dreams of an independent existence. As she put it: "Finally, my husband gave way, and we remained at the farm for three or four years."[174] The slave women tended to identify with the settler household more than with the other slaves in the holding. In the early period, they were often the surrogate mothers of the slave-owning class, and when they married a settler bachelor, they were the real mothers of future creole settlers. More than 1,000 women of slave and native descent married free persons of European descent and thereby passed into the "master" class.

The relatively few slave women at the Cape held a privileged but hitherto unrecognized position in the colony. Their influence over small and large matters in the daily life of the settler family was significant. Because their role in the owner's household was domestic, the legacy of slave women was vast, one of an unfathomable psychological magnitude. But they were intimately suborned into the domestic hegemony of the settler family and household, their very womanhood sacrificed to the domestic interests, predilections, and impulses of the settler men and their families. As a result of their respective roles in society, Cape women, slave and free, tended to consolidate the slave society rather than to challenge its injustices. Women, whether slave or free, proved indispensable in the complex web of production and reproduction that constituted the changing Cape slave-owning household.

---

173 Jones, " 'My Mother was Much of a Woman,' " 244.
174 "The Life of Katie Jacobs," 8–9.

ELEVEN

Religion, Civic Status, and Slavery
From Dordt to the Trek

A PAINTING ENTITLED *The Baptism of the Monomotapa* hangs in the Dominican House in Rome; it depicts the baptism of an African king in Portuguese Mozambique in August 1652. In celebration the Dominican convent in Lisbon had hosted a thanksgiving feast that King John IV and his court had attended. The assembly regarded the African king's baptism as a significant triumph for Christianity (see Figure 11-1).[1] There is another, late seventeenth-century image of Jesuit priests baptizing Angolan slaves as they boarded the slave ships from Luanda, on their way to Brazil — "gangplank baptisms," as they were called. As evidence of their baptism, the slaves wore about their neck a mark of the royal crown.[2] Taken together, these images suggest that the Catholic church in Africa baptized everyone, that baptism was offered both to royalty and to the humblest slaves. Monarchs, owners, and slaves were all brothers and sisters in Christ, if not in any other sense.

Another compelling but entirely different event occurred three thousand miles away in Dutch South Africa, in the Great Hall of the old fort at Cape Town on a Sunday morning in March 1666. Fourteen years after the foundation of the colony (and the baptism of the Monomotapa) a sad event unfolded. Following the usual sermon a European child was presented for baptism, and then a slave woman went up to the baptismal font to present her own infant. But before the presiding minister, the Reverend Johannes De Voocht, could dip his fingers in the baptismal water, up rose the Reverend Phillipus Baldeus, a visiting Reformed[3] minister and a

---

[1] George McCall Theal, *History of South Africa* (Cape Town: Struik, 1964), 2: facing p. 426.

[2] Such "gangplank baptisms" resulted in a "fee" for the priests; private communication with Joseph Miller. See Frank Tannenbaum, *Slave and Citizen: The Negro in the Americas* (New York: Knopf 1947), p. 64 and note 149.

[3] The term *Reformed* was chosen in the sixteenth century to distinguish those churches that had broken away from the Catholics and even the Lutherans, and were thus "reformed."

330

Figure 11–1. Baptism of the Monomotapa, 1652.

well-known intellectual on the Dutch East Indies run. He stopped the rite in front of the astonished Cape commander, his officers, and the small congregation. Baldeus explained that he was "better informed about such matters than anyone there" and that the practice of baptizing the children of slaves, then "in vogue at the Cape was decidedly wrong." De Voocht closed the baptism ceremony forthwith.[4]

[4] Anna J. Böeseken et al. (eds.), *Suid-Afrikaanse Argiefstukke: Resolusies van die Politieke Raad* (Cape Town: Cape Times, 1957–1975; hereafter *Resolutions*), vol. 3, pp. 340–341 (Monday, 22 March 1666); C. Spoelstra, *Bouwstoffen voor de Geschiedenis der Nederduitch-Geref. Kerken in Zuid Afrika* (Amsterdam: Hollandsch-Afrikaansche Uitgewers-Maatscappij, 1906–1907), vol. 1,

Why are these seventeenth-century images of baptism at odds? Part of what turns out to be an important but complex answer lies in colonial perceptions of what, for want of better words, I term the civic and communal consequences of baptism. This argument is by no means novel. It derives its inspiration directly from the seminal work of Frank Tannenbaum and Eugene Genovese.[5] In this chapter I wish to focus primarily on the colonial reconstruction of the civic, that is, the nontheological, entailments of baptism within the colonial community.

The Dispute Over Baptism

Reformed baptism, in Christian Europe before the Enlightenment and the French Revolution, was perceived as analogous to legal enfranchisement. Baptism was necessary for the right to inherit, the right to marry, the right to be buried in a Christian graveyard, and the right to bear witness. The Reformed rite of baptism, quite discretely from its ostensible purpose as a signifier of incorporation into the Church, also imbued the baptismal candidate with secular civil and legal advantages within the Christian society. By being denied the right to baptism in South Africa, most slaves were systematically excluded from the Christian community. Most slave owners distanced themselves from evangelical duties and Reformed piety; many slaves turned to Islam. As a result, there arose a distinct, colonywide polarity between the Christian settlers and the "heathen" slaves and autochthonous people. The issue of Reformed baptism thus became the linchpin in the complex identities of owners, slaves, and native people.

At the outset, it is crucial to appreciate that Reformed societies were defining themselves simultaneously with their escape from Catholic-Iberian hegemony after a long and bitter nationalistic war (1580 to 1609) and with their commercial expansion into the New World (1602). The process was also occurring at the same time that slavery was introduced into their new colonial possessions (circa 1609). These years defined the religious and legal identity of the Netherlands, and during this historical maelstrom Reformed Protestants forged new and more radically constructed conceptions of baptism that spilled over religious boundaries into the

---

pp. 29–31; George McCall Theal, *History of South Africa* (Cape Town: Struik, 1964), vol. 3, p. 153; De Voocht's own slave trading may be found in DO "Transporten en Schepenkennis," now in the Cape Archives: 30 September 1666, Willem van Bengal; 17 April 1669, Abraham of Angola; 30 September 1671, Thomas of Bengal; 29 March 1672, Jacob van Coromandel and Cupido of Bengal; 4 April 1672, Claas of Ceylon. The unlucky slave infant was baptized the following Sunday on orders of the Cape Council of Policy.

[5] Most commentators on the debate believe that Tannenbaum was referring to the material "treatment" of slaves. However, he was not: he only spoke of access to citizenship, the sense of belonging to, and incorporation into, a community. There is no necessary connection between "treatment" and Tannenbaum's ideas of community and citizenship.

civic arena. If one were baptized into the Dutch Reformed Church, important civic consequences immediately ensued.

A 1609 letter written by Dominee Adriaan J. Hulsebos, the presiding minister at Jakarta, to the Amsterdam Classis, the presbytery most closely associated with the colonial church, started the Reformed colonial baptismal dispute. The issue Hulsebos raised would dog all colonial Reformed churches for almost two centuries. The letter asked: "What was to be done with household slaves within Christian households?"[6] The Classis passed the Hulsebos letter to the Provincial Synod of North Holland, of which it was a part. The Provincial Synod decided to present it to the Synod of Dordt delegates. When the Reformed delegates in the last months of 1618 assembled for the Synod of Dordt, where they would crush the Arminian Remonstrants — delegates who argued that grace was resistible and that Christ had died for all mankind — groups of Calvinist theologians from all over Europe, from England to Switzerland, gathered in the town of Dordrecht (Dordt for short) in the Netherlands. The Synod of Dordrecht was the last international meeting of the Reformed churches, and the meeting was especially important for that reason. Thereafter, Reformed synods would convene only at their separate national or colonial levels. Later national gatherings have always referred back to the Canons of the Synod of Dordt. Today the Canons of the Synod of Dordt still form the last and main part of the Reformed Standards of Unity.[7]

On a Friday afternoon in November 1618, two questions arose about pagan baptisms. The first question was whether senior merchants in the Dutch East India Company could perform baptisms. This would obviate the expense of an ordained minister. This "frivolous" question was not tabled. The second question read: "Whether children, born of heathen parents, who had become members of Christian households, ought to be baptized, when the householder promised to bring the child up in the Christian faith?"[8] Each group of delegates was to present its own independent written answer.

The most erudite group of Reformed scholars ever assembled was asked to provide a statement of their views on infant baptism and the spiritual incorporation of pagan slaves and free heathen persons into Christian households. The scholars were actually asked to "hurry up," since the Dutch East India Company outward-bound fleets were ready to sail, waiting for their answer.[9] The delegates failed to reach any real agreement. Each church delegation submitted separate findings, so there were opinions from the "Theologians of Great Britain," the

---

[6] W. van 't Spijker and C. C. de Bruin, et al. *De Synode van Dordrecht in 1618 en 1619* (Houten: Den Hertog, 1987), p. 165.

[7] Leroy Nixon, *Reformed Standards of Unity* (Grand Rapids, Mich.: Society for Reformed Publications, 1952), pp. 97–118.

[8] Hendrik Kaajan, *De Pro-Acta der Dordtsche Synode* (Rotterdam: T. de Vries, 1914), p. 224.

[9] Kaajan, *Pro Acta*, 248.

Children of Bondage

"Helveti" (Calvin's Swiss republics and Churches), "The Theologians of Bremen," and also documents from individual scholars, such as Giovanni Deodatus; in all, there were 18 separate opinions.

Perhaps because of the diversity of responses, their opinions never became part of the Standards of Unity, or part of the Reformed tradition. They are still not considered an integral part of the Canons of the Synod of Dordt. Consequently these diverse opinions, *De Ethnicorum Pueris Baptizandis*,[10] remained obscure to the mainstream Reformed tradition, yet they were vitally important in the development of Reformed colonial policy, which affected millions of slaves.[11]

All the opinions followed the precedent of the Old Testament patriarch Abraham. The Reformed head of household, not the Church and not the parents of the child, had the primary responsibility for baptizing slaves and heathens. This was the key difference. Baptism, a public imperative for the Catholic church, became a *household* choice for the Reformed Christian.[12] The opinions held that all heathen children in the household, whether slave or free, should enjoy the right of Christian instruction. (Delegates were divided over whether this instruction should take place before or after baptism.) Slaves or heathens who had one Christian parent could be baptized as infants — yet the Reformed clergy had a right to refuse baptism. Baptized slaves "should enjoy equal rights with other Christians." There was no stated objection to clergy owning slaves. Rights were not specified but implied: the right to testify in court (heathens, too, could initiate litigation, however); the right to enter into Christian matrimony; the right to

---

[10] The opinions constitute about 45 pages of Latin and have been separately edited and deposited in the South African Library.

[11] *De Ethnicorum* is not well known to contemporary scholars of slavery, and as it was written in Latin, the opinions on slave baptism have remained obscure until recently. I came across a three-line fragment in Latin in a rare copy of H. Cruse, *Die Opheffing van die Kleurling Bevolking: Aanvangsjare, 1652–1795* (Stellenbosch: Christian Student Union, 1947), p. 224. Cruse was citing from *Acta Synodi Nationalis Dordrechtanae,* Sessione Decimanona, edito Canani, but I subsequently found the entire Latin opinions in C. Spoelstra. *Bouwstoffen voor de Geschiedenis der Nederduitsch-Geref. Kerken in Zuid Afrika* (Amsterdam: Hollandsch-Afrikaansche Uitgewers-Maatscappij, 1906–1907), vol. 2, pp. 621–641; the originals reside in the Old Synodal Archives at Gravenhage, section 17 A: "Proceedings of the Synod of Dordt, 1618–19." The translated fragment from Cruse was enough to begin a new direction in the study of South African slavery, see Richard Elphick and Robert C.-H. Shell, "Intergroup Relations: Khoikhoi, Settlers, Slaves and Free Blacks," in R. Elphick and Herman Giliomee (eds.), *The Shaping of South African Society, 1652–1820*, rev. ed. (Middletown, Conn.: Wesleyan University Press, 1989), p. 188; Cruse's transcription was quite correct; cf. Kaajan, *Pro-Acta,* 249. The same fragment found its way into George Fredrickson, *White Supremacy: A Comparative Study in American and South African History* (New York: Oxford University Press, 1981), pp. 73, 81, 83 (although Fredrickson cites Cruse, he uses the translation from Elphick and Shell); and also into Orlando Patterson's global analysis of the institution of slavery, *Slavery and Social Death: A Comparative Study* (Cambridge, Mass.: Harvard University Press, 1982), p. 276.

[12] As I will show, the imperative evolved into a choice.

inherit; the right to burial in a Christian graveyard. Baptized slaves could not be sold to heathens, but could be passed to other Christians by inheritance or gift.

The most revealing sentence in the whole proceeding was written by Giovanni Deodatus, a Swiss professor of theology who was the "great defender of orthodoxy" at Dordt (see Figure 11-2). It was his declaration that struck at the root of slavery: "That those baptized should enjoy equal right of liberty with all other Christians and that, concerning the danger of apostasy, they be safeguarded, as far as it can be done, by the prohibiting for the future of all selling and transferring of them to another. . . ." The ellipsis in the last sentence was crucial. Should the last word be *heathen* or *person*? Precisely who constituted *another*? If the meaning were interpreted as *heathen*, owners could still sell their baptized slaves to other Christians; a baptized slave would remain partially marketable. If it were *person*, a baptized slave could not be considered a slave in the sense of being transferable property. When the document summarizing this proceeding first appeared in print in 1621, the editors chose the "heathen" interpretation: "Baptized slaves should enjoy equal right of liberty with other Christians and ought never to be handed over again to the powers of the heathens [*potestati ethnicorum*] by their Christian masters either by sale or by any other transfer of possession."[13]

Deodatus' next sentence was quite unambiguous, but it did not find its way into the 1621 published canon: "And let their masters use them [baptized slaves] as hired servants clearly according to the customs of other Christians."[14] An association between Reformed baptism and limitations on selling baptized slaves was clearly established at Dordt.

No delegates argued that slaves should be freed *immediately* after baptism or specified exactly when they should be freed. There was no clear agreement on the proper age at which slave should be baptized[15] and no mention of how these precepts were to be enforced. All these matters were left to the head of the household. Reformed evangelical duties had become domestic, quite imprecise, and therefore open to interpretation.

---

[13] This appeared in Isaaq Janz. Canin, *Acta ofte Handelinghedes Nationalen Synodi . . . tot Dordrecht, Anno 1618. ende 1619, met privilegie der H.M. Heeren Staten Generael* (Dordrecht: Canin, 1621); Kaajan, *Pro-Acta*, page 249 and note 2; Cruse, *Die Opheffing*, page 224, relying on, *Acta Synodi Nationalis Dordrechtanae*, 49; Elphick and Shell, "Intergroup Relations," 188, relying on Cruse. David Brion Davis in an early work had written: "Nor was there any ground for the belief that baptism entailed liberation." D. B. Davis, *Problem*, p. 205.

[14] Robert C.-H. Shell (ed.), *De Ethnicorum Pueris Baptizandis* (Cape Town: South African Library), pp. 19–20.

[15] As an example of the variety of responses, some held that heathens who were in the household of any owner ought to be baptized as infants (the English Puritan and Frisian views); others argued that heathens should be baptized as adults, *after* instruction (the majority view). Some delegates argued that the heathen should be given the choice of baptism after instruction, others argued against a choice. All were agreed that baptized heathens should not fall back into heathen hands, as this would damn the sacrament itself.

Figure 11–2. Giovanni Deodatus, 1576–1649.

Baptism at the Cape Becomes a Right of Racial Descent

The association between baptism and freedom and the lack of unity on the civic entailments of baptism, together with the Protestant tradition of clerical independence, presbyterian church governance, and a colonial rural diaspora, ensured varied interpretations of the Reformed baptism in the colonial world. The baptismal font was to become a hotly disputed place at the Cape. Baptism was seen not only as a signifier of spiritual salvation but also as a primary symbol of the civic incorporation or exclusion of slaves and people of non-Christian descent. This was a universal development in the Reformed colonial world, from Sri Lanka to New England, the Dutch Antilles, Suriname, Brazil (briefly), South Africa, and to the outer reaches of the Indonesian Archipelago.[16]

Reconstruction of Dordt at the Cape

The first recognizable mention of the Dordt opinions is found in a joint dispatch from the governor-general and the Council of Batavia,[17] dated 25 January 1664:

It had been a matter of many disputes among the church congregations here whether the children, born of unbelieving parents should be admitted to baptism, and that, after reference to the *Classis* in Holland, the question was decided in the affirmative, and in the following way: all slaves of the person with whom they live, whether the owner or not, are to be baptized, and must be obliged to educate them in the Christian religion; this being chiefly founded upon the example of the Patriarch Abraham, in whose faith all who were in his house were circumcised; and the observance has accordingly been long followed here. . . . You may therefore take this regulation for your guidance, and if you proceed in that holy work, there, as is done here, you will do well and act the part of a Christian.[18]

After the first font incident in 1666, Cape officials baptized all Lodge slaves, but each local administration asked and had to be told again, as if Cape officials hoped to be given a different answer on the baptism of slaves. The Cape Church renewed the 1664 edicts on the issue.[19] What is most striking is that there never was any discussion of how the obligation to baptize slaves should be enforced.

On 23 November 1674 the question arose, in a stormy session of the Cape Political Council, of what to do with slave children who had already been baptized as Catholics.[20] No resolution was reached, but the officials had never assumed any obligations toward such adult (more than 12 years old) imported slaves. An increasing number of Cape slaves from ships originating in Portuguese possessions spoke Portuguese and more important for the slave society, had been baptized in the Catholic faith and were, therefore, something of a cultural anomaly among the Cape slave population. Since Catholicism was not tolerated at the Cape until 1804, all these slaves learned to keep their Catholicism secret in the Dutch Reformed colony, disclosing their faith only to surprised Catholic visitors. Père Guy Tachard, a French Jesuit on his way to Siam, wrote enthusiastically of these

---

[16] Kaajan, *Pro-Acta*, 252 and note 1.

[17] Batavia directly governed the Cape Colony until 1732, after which the Company assumed direct control of the Cape.

[18] Donald Moodie (comp.), *The Record . . .* (Cape Town: Balkema, 1960), p. 273, note 1.

[19] Spoelstra, *Bouwstoffen*, vol. 2, 265.

[20] *Resolutions* (23 November 1674) 2: 119–120.

Cape Catholic slaves: "They who could not otherwise express themselves, because we understood not their language [the slaves spoke Portuguese] fell up on their knees and kissed our hands. They pulled chaplets and medals out of their bosoms to show they were Catholics, they wept and smote their breasts."[21]

Two years later, sometime between 28 December 1676 and 1 January 1677, the Political Council again debated the issue, and this time the local Cape officials added a new and significant element, that children who had European fathers, or a "black" father and half-European mother should, ipso facto, be permitted baptism. The councilors referred to an "Act" of 1666, but could only have meant the Batavian Act of 1664, received in 1664 and repeated in the 1666 session, following the font incident. There was no Act of 1666.[22]

In this surreptitious way local political officials (not ecclesiastical officers) introduced significant ethnic and racial descent rules into the sacrament of baptism. A convenient, but faulty, syllogistic interpretation of Dordt lay behind this shift. The Dordt delegates had emphasized the importance of the religious status of either parent of the heathen child. If one parent was Christian, the child would have to be baptized. But now arose a new association: the Cape Council of Policy was now equating European with Christian. Commissioner Van Reede, who is usually credited with the later introduction of privileges based on racial descent, was in fact following Cape practice of some ten years' standing.[23]

An undated letter, written sometime after October 1678 by Johannes Overneij, a Cape minister, and his deacon Elbert Di[e]mer to the Amsterdam Classis, sincerely asked for guidance on the issue of baptism of slaves. The letter suggests a total amnesia within the Cape Church. They admitted, "We have found nothing in our Church books here on this issue, but know nevertheless that particular resolutions on this issue have been passed by your honorable Synods."[24] As a result of the seemingly endless shuttle of correspondence on this issue, the Cape authorities and the churches of the Dutch East Indies now shifted the responsibility for baptizing heathen infants from the head of household, whom the Dordt participants had held responsible, to the father of the child, a subtle, widespread, and significant change in colonial clerical thinking.[25]

The *Heeren XVII* (the directors of the Company) had to tell Simon van der Stel, the first governor of the colony, in 1680, in the first year of his administration

---

[21] Father Guy Tachard, "Voyage de Siam," in E. Strangman (ed.), *Early French Callers at the Cape* (Cape Town: Juta, 1936) p. 82.

[22] *Resolutions* (28 December 1677), 2: 159–160.

[23] Spoelstra, *Bouwstoffen*, vol. 2, 70, footnote.

[24] Spoelstra, *Bouwstoffen* (Ongedateerde Brief), vol. 1, 27.

[25] See the meeting of ministers in New England and the Cambridge (Massachusetts) Synod in 1662 in E. S. Morgan, *Visible Saints: The History of a Puritan Idea* (Ithaca, N.Y.: Cornell University Press, 1963), pp. 130–131.

that "as to the baptizing of Slave Children, you will be guided by the practice at Batavia."[26] Nobody in Holland seemed willing to take responsibility, and the issue became one mediated by the Council of Policy, Batavia, and, lastly, the local clergy. Carl Peter Thunberg, writing in the 1770s, confirms that the responsibility of the head of the household, so emphasized by the Dordt Synod, had shifted to the father of the child, who, in an increasingly descent conscious society, might well consider it shameful to admit to his fatherhood of a slave, or, indeed, of any mulatto child: "In the baptism of children, the Cape clergy consider it as a circumstance of the first importance, that the fathers should be known and be present. If the child is a bastard, and its father does not discover himself, the infant remains unbaptized. If the mother is a black or a Hottentot, but the father a Christian, who requires it to be baptized, it is baptized."[27] As E. S. Morgan concludes his book on the Puritan family, "When theology became the handmaid of genealogy, Puritanism no longer deserved its name."[28] In South Africa in the seventeenth century, theology had become the handmaid of racial descent *and* genealogy.

In the aftermath of the settler revolt in 1706, the baptism of slaves took on an added urgency if for no other reason than the fact that slaves now outnumbered settlers. Engelbertus Fransiscus Le Boucq, the designated minister of the frontier colony of Drakenstein, wrote an outraged letter to the Amsterdam Classis in 1706 about the baptism procedures at the Cape:

1. Baptism is scandalously misused at the Cape, so much so that it is an abomination. . . . The ministers do not determine whether the fathers or mothers are Christian; nor pass the appropriate act of adoption, and simply baptize as the Pope does. Yes, a person could believe that if the Governor presented a sheep in the clothing of a person, then the ministers would baptize that sheep.[29]

2. That some adult slaves are too easily baptized, who do come from the best backgrounds but then [are] admitted to communion, which is contrary to Church Law.

3. The third misuse is that baptized slaves and their baptized children, who are fine members of the congregation, *are often sold and used in slavery* which is against Christian liberty . . . and this last practice is common throughout India as well.[30]

---

[26] Moodie, *The Record,* 376.

[27] Carl Peter Thunberg, *Travels at the Cape of Good Hope* (Cape Town: Van Riebeeck Society Second Series, No. 17, 1986), p. 142 and note 162.

[28] E. S. Morgan, *The Puritan Family,* p. 186.

[29] He was complaining of the practices of Willem Adriaan van der Stel, later recalled to the Netherlands, who was a baptizer of his slaves. See DRCA: Doopsregister, 1699–1706, passim.

[30] Spoelstra, *Bouwstoffen,* vol. 1, 63–65 (emphasis added).

Le Boucq's aggravation cannot be understood without knowing his part in the settler revolt of that year. The individual he was attacking in his letter and whom he wished to embarrass was the governor, who *was* a regular baptizer of his household slaves. Baptized slaves of the officials, emboldened by their baptism, had taken advantage of the other, more intimate rite of communion, and this infuriated the settlers. Le Boucq intended to highlight the hypocrisy of the governor, who did not automatically free his slaves after they were baptized. Local clergy who were deeply involved in improving their own plantations took advantage of the Le Boucq contretemps by advocating their version of who should be baptized: only children of Christian European parentage.

By about 1725, some Cape Christian slave owners came close to an Anabaptist position — in behavior, if not intellectual inclination — by denying their infant slaves the right to baptism, a heretical possibility that one theologian had foreseen at Dordt.[31] Otto Mentzel, writing of the 1740s, noted that "It is a matter for regret that the children born in slavery are neither baptized nor given any religious instruction. There is a common and well-grounded belief that Christians must not be held in bondage; hence only such children as are intended for emancipation are baptized."[32] Mentzel was correct. Moreover, the Church records show a clear trend toward fewer baptisms over the century (see Figure 11-3).[33]

Most slave owners abandoned evangelical efforts in their household. All settlers were orthodox enough when it came to the baptism of their own infant children; some were Anabaptists when it came to their slaves' baptism, but most did not bother with their slaves' baptism at all. According to the detailed baptismal registers of the Cape Church, few privately owned adult slaves were baptized in the period; almost no baptized slaves took communion (see Figure 11-3). By the late eighteenth century, pews specially built for slaves in the "Mother Church" (*Moeder Kerk*) of Cape Town were empty Sunday after Sunday.[34] By 1795 there were only

---

[31] The Anabaptists were members of various radical religious sects of the sixteenth century who rejected infant baptism. The term, which means rebaptism, was first used derogatorily by Huldrych Zwingli, from whose reformed Protestant community in Zurich the first "true" Anabaptists separated themselves in 1523. Anabaptist settlements survived in Moravia, mainly because they were well organized by Jacob Hutter. They were sufficiently strong to contribute to the migrations to North America, where their descendants came to be known as Hutterites.

[32] Otto Friederich Mentzel, *A Complete and Authentic Geographical and Topographical Description . . .* , trans. G. V. Marais and J. Hoge, rev. ed. (Cape Town: Van Riebeeck Society, 1944), vol. 2, 130. The issue must have been painful for Mentzel, since in an earlier volume he had noted: "I shall also pass over in silence the baptism of slave children and their instruction in the Christian religion. . . . It is a lamentable paradox to baptize schoolchildren, initiate them into the truths of the teachings of Christ . . . in ibid., vol. 1, 117.

[33] DRCA G1 4/34 Bijlae; 1690–1713: Doop Boeke G1 1/1, 8/1–7.

[34] Johannes Stephanus Marais, *The Cape Coloured People, 1652–1937* (Johannesburg: Witwatersrand University Press, 1968), p. 168.

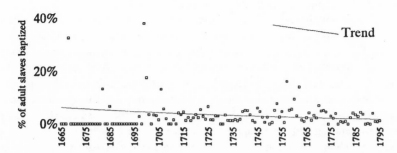

Figure 11–3. Baptism rates among privately owned adult slaves, 1659 to 1795.

six churches ministering to a potential congregation of 17,000 settlers, 20,000 slaves, and approximately 100,000 native people. Large and commodious though these churches were, nobody boasted that they could seat more than 200 people at a time; they certainly could not accommodate the 6,000-odd potential parishioners of the colony.

If a slave were admitted to the Church via baptism, such a slave had certain qualified rights to freedom, or at least the right not to be sold. If one accepts the Sumerian, Greek, and Roman definitions of a slave as property, then decreeing that a slave could not be sold, or limiting the conditions of sale in any way, would indeed be striking at the basis of slavery itself. Periodic reminders to the settlers from Batavia and, after 1731, from the fatherland to baptize their slaves were ignored. Batavian legislation in 1714 and 1715 resolved that slaves of Christians could be sold only to other Christians; legislation in March 1715 stipulated that the sale of all Christian slave children be forbidden — if such children came up for sale for probate reasons and no member of the family wanted them, the deacons of the Church were to take them on as wards. Slave children whose owner was their father could not be sold at all.[35] This legislation clearly prefigures the better known 1770 Statutes of India and harks back to Dordt.

While no slave owner, no matter how cynical, would dare claim that slaves had *no* right to baptism, the owner could justify a delay in baptism by arguing that slaves should be instructed before they were baptized. Then the slave owner could postpone, through endless domestic ruses, bringing the slaves into the Christian community and thereby avoid any risk of reducing the marketability of his slaves. This is not to say that all slaves were excluded from all household devotions, but they were excluded from the ones that mattered. Once the slaves reached adulthood, there was always the strong possibility that they would use their own

---

[35] Carel Wessel Theodurus, Baron van Boetzelaer van Asperen en Dubbeldam, *De Protestantsche Kerk in de Nederlandsch-Indië* (The Hague: Nijhoff, 1947), pp. 225–226.

judgment to steer clear of membership in a church in which slaves were not welcomed as baptismal candidates or as parishioners.

Almost without exception, commentators on the Cape mentioned that slave owners believed that if they baptized their slaves they would not be able to sell them. The first traveler to notice this was a visiting missionary, Johann Georg Bövingh. Shortly before 1714 he wrote: "Only a very few slaves are baptized. Although a separate [*seine*] congregation could easily be made from these people, since many have a substantial experience of Christianity from many years' contact and ask to be become Christians themselves, their masters — as I hear from many people — are not willing to agree, as slaves who are baptized cannot be sold again."[36] Thunberg, a Lutheran botanist, also made this association when he related the following anecdote: "A certain hatter in the town, who was a bachelor, had got two of his slaves with child. For the children he had by one of them, he in quality of their father, demanded baptism, and accordingly these were baptized and consequently freed; while the other girl's children remained unbaptized and slaves."[37] According to the 1770s Statutes of India, widely distributed throughout the Dutch commercial empire, both slave women and their children in this situation should have enjoyed eventual manumission, but they would have done so on the grounds of European parentage *or* baptism.[38]

Although baptism did not entail immediate freedom according to any reading of Dordt, this is what Cape slave owners came to believe. The slaves brought themselves, in their owners' eyes, a few steps closer to freedom through the embrace of Christianity. Thus, one can postulate a slave owner's vantage point: one might as well *not* evangelize among one's own slaves, because if emancipatory legislation were to come, it would probably benefit Christian slaves first (an entirely correct view as it turned out in the nineteenth century). Because of slave owners' correct understanding of *De Ethnicorum,* they always saw Christianity as narrowing the gap between master and slave. But even if a strict reading of Dordt were followed, it was always better from the owner's perspective if the slaves were not baptized, since then they would at least remain marketable. In South Africa, slaves were safer investments if they were *not* Christian, a conviction that continued until emancipation. In contrast, because American colonial legislatures had specifically nullified all civic entailments of baptism in the seventeenth and early

---

[36] Johann Georg Bövingh, *Kurze Nachricht von den Hottentotten* (Hamburg: Bey Casper Jahkel, 1714), p. 3: *Nur etlige wenige [Sclaven] sind getaufft da doch mit leichter Muhe aus diesen Leuten eine seine Gemeine konte gesammlet werden angesehen viel aus dem vieljarigen Umgange Schon eine zimliche Erfartnis haben und selbst Christen zu werden verlangen: so aber Ihre Herren wie ich van vielen gehoret nicht zugeben wollen die weil Sie wenn sie getaufft nicht wieder verkauft werden konnen.* I am grateful to Harold James for the prompt translation of this passage.

[37] Thunberg, *Travels at the Cape,* 268.

[38] George McCall Theal, *Records of the Cape Colony* (Cape Town: Struik, 1967; hereafter *RCC*), vol. 9, 131 ff.

eighteenth centuries, American slave owners could safely foster Christianity among their slaves. By the 1820s, the whole of the American South held the opposite conviction to that of South African slave owners: Christian slaves were better slaves for being Christians.[39]

Slave Baptism at the Cape in Practice

What is immediately apparent from the baptismal registers at the Cape is that individual Cape slave owners and the Dutch East India Company baptized their slaves in quite different ways. Of the 2,543 slave baptisms from 1652 to 1795, 1,715 baptisms were of slave children who belonged to the Dutch East India Company — an average of one per month. These Lodge slaves were considered part of the "household" of the Company, and all slaves born into the household of the Lodge were baptized. Visiting commissioners were always careful to make sure that the Lodge slaves were both baptized and instructed. As a result, the Lodge, considered solely as a Christian household, had the highest per capita proportion of baptized children in the colony. After the demise of the Company in 1795, Lodge children were no longer baptized, and the total number of baptisms in the colony dropped precipitously, dramatically revealing the small number of private individuals in the Cape congregation who did baptize their slaves (see Figure 11-4).[40]

A symbolic head of household, the most senior Company official, was present at all such baptisms in loco parentis. All slaves born into the household of the lodge were baptized within seven days of birth. For instance, a detailed 1693 census of the Lodge ends with the following single entry "slave number 369, a daughter of Sumassa, unbaptized." This infant slave had been born a few days before the census, between baptism Sundays.[41] Slaves with parents who were not Christian were also baptized — for example, the children of the (presumably) Muslim slave woman, "Fatima," one of many adult "heathen" Lodge parents whose children were baptized.[42] By not making enquiries about parentage after 1666, the Lodge officials were baptizing slaves in the way the Frisian and English Puritan delegation had suggested at Dordt, that is, baptizing *all* infants. I believe they were echoing those opinions rather than following them. Although Christian parentage was an important factor in advancing a candidate for baptism according to Dordt, in the Lodge environment, it was considered too troublesome to enquire into and, moreover, to establish.

Racial descent entered into all decisions on baptism in the Lodge after 1685,

---

[39] I am grateful to David Brion Davis for this point.
[40] DRCA: G1 4/34, G1 1/1–8, and Doopboeke (Cape district congregation only).
[41] AR VOC 4030 (1 January 1693), 367.
[42] AR VOC 4030 (1 January 1693), 367.

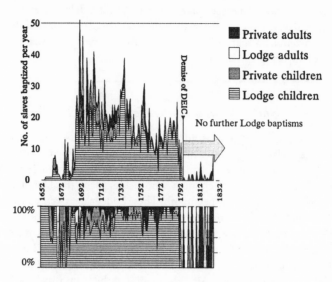

Figure 11–4. All baptisms in the Cape congregation, 1652 to 1832.

when a visiting commissioner, Adriaan Van Reede, was shocked to discover that several Lodge slaves were of obvious Christian and European parentage. Van Reede initiated a detailed genealogical enquiry into the 335 Lodge slaves, of whom 137 were men, 106 women, and 92 children (under 12 years of age), and he found that of the children, 25 boys and 19 girls, almost half, were descended from "*Neder Duijtse vaders.*"[43] Van Reede was convinced that the regulations should be changed. It was his racial arrogance, not his Christian belief, that had been outraged. His recommendations, which were followed until 1795, provided that no Lodge slaves were ever to be sold, exchanged, exported, or given to anybody, no matter how important.[44] All infants in the Lodge were to be baptized, but a note was to be made of their ancestry. They were then to be instructed in the Christian faith by specially appointed schoolteachers. Furthermore, all baptized slaves born at the Cape were to be free at age 40 years, so that "they would not sigh in perpetual servitude and slavery." Imported slaves were to be free after 30 years of service to the Company. Those of part-European stock were to be freed after 25 years (if male) and after 22 years (if female). All had to speak Dutch, to be confirmed in the Reformed faith, and to pay 100 florins to the Company (in installments, if need be).[45] Because the Company did not pay their Lodge slaves a

---

[43] A. Hulshof (ed.), "H. A. Van Reede tot Drakesteijn, Journaal van zijn verblijf aan de Kaap," *Bijdragen en Mededelingen can het Historisch Genootschap* 62 (1914): 213–214.

[44] Hulshof, "H. A. Van Reede tot Drakesteijn," 213–214.

[45] Hulshof, "H. A. Van Reede tot Drakesteijn," 210–211.

meaningful wage, this meant that an outside person would always be obliged to help out. Confirmation was referred to here, and again in 1770s, but in the manumission requests, only baptism was mentioned as the religious requirement for freedom.

All baptized slaves were entered in Church records in strict order of baptism. Between 1655 and 1691 slave and free baptisms were listed together; but after 1692 each slave was classified by age and racial descent, "full-breed" (*heelslag*) or mulatto (*halfslag*). In 1695 a new baptismal register was opened, with three categories of baptisms: "Names of Christian Children," "Slave Children of the Honorable Company," and "Slave Children of Free burghers or Company servants."[46] The clerks continued to follow this scheme through 1731.[47] Christian "free blacks" were not listed separately; they appeared next to people of European descent. Among free people there was a genuine Christian universalism. The separation of the lists reflects the slave status over race, although within the slave category, racial descent, not Christian parentage, was registered. If the Christian fathers of mulatto children owned up to their parenthood, the children might have been freed upon petition. The evolving hierarchy was strengthened according to a bewildering set of criteria. For slaves, descent, parentage, and owner's status all fed into the new baptismal regime. Baptized Lodge slaves certainly did not enjoy liberty immediately. Indeed, baptized Company slaves were not all freed. All one can say is that baptized Lodge slaves were never sold or alienated. While the Company did sell unbaptized slaves to the burghers on two occasions, in the 1660s and 1780s, they sold only newly arrived slaves. There is no record, no anecdote, no suggestion of the Company selling a baptized slave. But there is also no record of a baptized Lodge slave with both parents baptized enjoying equal status with other Christians as they were entitled to do. We know from Van Reede's observations that many blue- and green-eyed Christians remained in the Lodge as slaves.

Among the privately owned slaves, who were many times more numerous — slaves belonging to Company officials or free burghers — baptisms were predominantly performed for slave children. Of the few slave owners who did baptize their infant slaves, most were wealthy individuals. The highest numbers of these slaves were baptized in the seventeenth century. After 1800, as a proportion of the total slave population, these baptisms become statistically insignificant. In the late eighteenth century, many owners baptized their slaves not for religious reasons, but because they wanted them to inherit, or they wanted to legitimize them. The main purpose of these "secular baptisms" as I call them, was to legitimize and eventually free a slave who was also the offspring of a free man.

In Cape society there were few slaves who were baptized as adults and who

---

[46] DRCA G1, 8/1 Kaapstad Doop, 1695–1712, "Doop, Trouw en Ledematen."
[47] DRCA: G1 8/2.

took up positions in Cape Christian society (see Figure 11-4). Many patrician owners (wealthy urban owners) who baptized their slaves for purely religious purposes were selective. Not all of their household slaves were baptized. Whatever the reasons for baptism, the percentage of their slaves who were baptized declined dramatically, a graphic illustration of the declension of this particular form of evangelical piety among Cape slave owners (see Figure 11-5).[48]

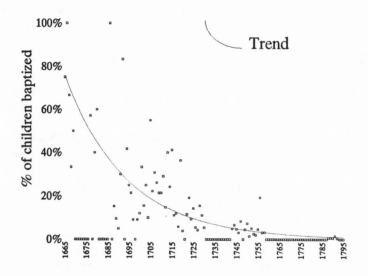

Figure 11–5. Baptism rates among privately owned slave children, 1665–1795.

Christian Instruction of Lodge Slaves
In the Reformed tradition, Christian instruction followed closely after baptism. As soon as they were able, baptized infants went to school. The 800 Lodge slaves were the most favored persons at the Cape in terms of both baptism and Christian education. Between 1665 and 1795, 1,715 Lodge slave children were baptized, and all went to school.[49] Even Thunberg, a Scandinavian traveler who rarely had a good word to say about the Dutch, claimed "though slaves are not usually instructed in the doctrines of Christianity, nor their children baptized, the Dutch East India Company takes care that the children born in the lodges of their own female slaves are baptized, and in some measure instructed in the Christian religion."[50] It is curious that only in this windowless, fetid building — the inevitable object of travelers' libidinous commentaries, an omnibus prison housing slaves

---

[48] DRCA: G1 4/34 Bijlae; G1 1/1–8 (Cape district only).
[49] CAD (formerly DRCA): G1 4/34 KA Bylae, 1832–1891.
[50] Thunberg, *Travels at the Cape*, 169 and notes.

as well as lunatics, a building that only a Hieronymus Bosch could have depicted — did Christianity obtain some real institutional purchase.

However one interpreted *De Ethnicorum* — with the responsible party being the head of household (the "strict" interpretation) or the parent (the convenient, settler interpretation) — the Company alone among the three groups of Cape slave owners felt obliged to baptize and instruct all its (Lodge-born) slaves. As evidence of this belief, the Company established a large Christian school for its slave children in the seventeenth century.[51] In the first decade of the colony, Jan van Riebeeck's brother-in-law, Pieter van der Stael, had founded a short-lived school for slaves. The primary objectives of this institution were the teaching of Dutch and Christianity. Other attempts had followed until, in the wake of Commissioner van Reede's visit to the Cape in 1685, the Company founded its school for all the Lodge slaves, which lasted until 1795.[52] In this institution the teachers were slaves, convicts, or free blacks. This caused some evident concern among the Cape clergy. For instance, the Reverend Le Boucq complained in 1706 that the "black [school] master, Daniel van Batavia, a branded . . . black . . . convict" should not be allowed to teach school in the Lodge."[53]

Being a schoolteacher in the Lodge was evidently a rewarding position for a slave. The only manumission records that include a request to stay in the Lodge were from schoolteachers. The 49-year-old Christoffel van Simosia submitted to the Political Council in 1751 that he had taught in the Lodge for 19 years and wished to be emancipated but to stay on as a schoolteacher. Similarly, in 1769, Christoffel Stents van Simosia, a slave in the Lodge, submitted that he had "acted as schoolmaster in the lodge for several years" and given satisfaction "as far as he knew." He wished to be manumitted and "at the same time he is prepared to continue as schoolmaster."[54] Here, then, was the beginning of a dedicated Christian slave intelligentsia — as a direct consequence of the opinions about Christian instruction expressed in *De Ethnicorum*.

The Lodge school was not a token gesture. Timeless techniques of instruction were used. For example, on Christmas day *all* slave children were given a cake (*Soete koek*), each of a different size. Special pens were handed out to the most deserving slaves. From the beginning, settler slaves were specifically excluded from

---

[51] See the list of schoolchildren in AR VOC 4030: "Generale Opneming en monster rolle van 's Comp: Soo slaven als bandieten . . . " (1 January 1693), folios 359 to 367 recto; and for the establishment of the school, see H. A. van Reede tot Drakenstein, "Instruksie vir Skoolmeester en kinders" (15 July 1685) in Anna J. Böeseken (ed.), *Belangrike Kaapse Dokumente: Memoriën en Instructiën, 1657–1699* (Cape Town: South African State Archives, 1967), vol. 1, 189.

[52] Cruse, *Die Opheffing* (Stellenbosch 1947), vol. 1, pp. 83, 101, 106.

[53] Spoelstra, *Bouwstoffen* (8 June 1707), vol. 1, 69.

[54] CAD LM 16, p. 984 (no.16 of 1751), p. 1010 (no. 15 of 1769/70).

this school.[55] A few Lodge slaves used their Christian education for their own ends. From as early as 1705, enterprising baptized company slaves escaped on ships to Europe and then promptly *wrote* to their friends in the Lodge to tell them of the "great difference between liberty and slavery." In one instance, the clerk went on to record that "many [slaves] are in that way tempted to escape, and in this first fleet of this year two slaves of the Company have again managed to run away."[56] Christian instruction and literacy had unforeseen but definite consequences for a few Lodge slaves.

Christian Marriage of Slaves

Marriage among different status groups is the perfect index of the openness of a society. After 1685 a baptized Lodge slave could marry another slave within the Lodge "in their manner," or even marry someone outside the Lodge, in which case they would have to be freed by the Political Council, not sold. The Company made the bridegroom "pay compensation" for bringing up the slave. It is important to stress that only women left the Lodge, and they left only through both baptism, manumission, and then Christian matrimony. Some male baptized Lodge slaves did enjoy emancipation, but only at their maturity (40 years of age), and each such slave had to provide a healthy slave in exchange. Comparatively few Lodge slaves were baptized as adults, and those few were women, who were baptized purely as a prelude to manumission and matrimony. Baptism was the sine qua non for Christian marriage.

Baptism also had other civic benefits. The question of whether baptized slaves in the Lodge could inherit was answered in the affirmative after Frans van Leeuwen, "a native of the Cape and soldier died on the *Koning Karel de Derde*" in 1721 and left a will specifying that his estate of 1,070 Guilders was to go to four beneficiaries. The Orphan Masters, who managed all probate cases, wrote to the Council of Policy in 1726 to "mention that the two first heirs were Cape born slaves of the Company and ask the Council's advice on how to act."[57] The Council replied that no obstacle ("*geen swarigheijd*") should be placed in the way of the slaves' receiving their portion.[58]

---

[55] Böeseken, *Memoriën en Instructiën,* vol. 1, 189, especially article 4: "*Alle andere slaven of Duijtsen in de Schole niet toelaten*"; the editor opines that the instructions were for the slaves of the Company, see note 1. See also *Resolutions* (22 December 1687), vol. 3: 179. Later in the eighteenth century, burghers were allowed to send their children to the Company school; see Kathleen M. Jeffreys, *Kaapse Archief Stukken Lopende over het jaar 1779,* pp. 93–94. I am grateful to James Armstrong for the last reference.

[56] Hendrik Carel Vos Leibbrandt, *Letters Despatched* (Cape Town: W. A. Richards & Sons, 1896), pp. 267–268 (27 May 1705). Robert Ross has indicated that there was a further case late in the eighteenth century.

[57] CAD LM 17 (no. 45 of 1726), p. 1124; the five-year delay between the death and the request is unexplained.

[58] *Resolutions* (26 March 1726), 7: 249-250.

One does not have to be an actuary or analyze life tables to realize that the chances that a locally born baptized Lodge slave would live to the age of 40, or that an imported slave would endure 30 years of service, were small. Mortality in the Lodge was so excessive that surviving to freedom was only a remote possibility. The horrendous demographic reality of the Lodge, so clearly captured by Hans Heese, rendered Christian baptism into its theological essence.[59] At the Cape slave baptism — even in the Lodge — was actually only a signifier of possible salvation.

Christian Instruction of Privately Owned Slaves

While the participants at Dordt had differed on the question of baptism, they had all agreed on the duty of all Reformed householders to instruct their slaves in Christianity. Clearly this duty was increasingly neglected by Cape slave owners. The only spontaneous and therefore sincere expressions of Christianity found in the sources are records of slaves singing Christian hymns or psalms. In the 1770s Anders Sparrman, the Swedish botanist, noted this when he entered a remote Cape settler farmstead:

About ten o'clock I took shelter from the rain in a farmhouse where I found the female slaves singing psalms, while they were at their needlework. Their master being possessed with a zeal for religion quite unusual in this country, had prevailed with them to adopt this godly custom, but with that spirit of economy which universally prevails among these people, he had not permitted them to be initiated into the community of Christians by baptism; since by that means according to the law of the land, they would have obtained their freedom and he would have lost them from his service.[60]

The majority of burghers did not care, or could not afford, to instruct their slaves in Christian doctrine. In the rural areas only two instances of a settler hiring a knecht-teacher to instruct his natural children *and* his slaves have been unearthed in the astonishingly large number of contracts drawn up between 1652 and 1795,[61] although many settlers educated their own children in this way.[62] By 1779

---

[59] Hans Friedreich Heese, "Mortaliteit onder VOC Slawe, 1720-1782," *Kronos* 11 (1986): 7–14.

[60] Sparrman, *A Voyage to the Cape*, vol. 1, 90.

[61] Hoge, whose authority on such matters is unquestioned, is quite definite about this: "*Die kontrak wat Pierre Rousseau, oud-heemraad van Drakenstein, met Gerrit Daveman gemaak het . . . is die enigste kontrak [only contract] waarin bepaal word dat die gehuurde skoolmeester ook die slawe van sy baas moet leer*" (emphasis added). J. Hoge, "Privaatskoolmeesters aan de Kaap in de 18de eeu," *Annals of the University of Stellenbosch* 12, B 1, (July 1934), continued in ibid., B 2 (June 1937), p. 26 and footnote 15. Hoge infers the second instance of slaves being instructed by schoolmasters from the estate inventory of Martin Melck in 1781, which mentions "a schoolroom," school benches, and other school equipment. However, Martin Melck was a Lutheran, not subject to the Reformed traditions. We also know from an independent source that Martin Melck was running a plantation with more than two hundred slaves; the plantation school probably served a similar function to that of the Lodge school, see J. S. Stavorinus, *Voyages to the East Indies . . .* (London:

a total of eight schools in the colony (mostly urban) reported 696 pupils, of whom only 82 were slave children.[63] Using the 1778 census as a rough guide, one may estimate that in that year 11.1 percent of all free children went to school, but only 5.3 percent of all the privately owned slave children attended school, including the slaves of officials and the handful of slaves belonging to Christian free blacks.[64] Samuel Eusebius Hudson, an English slave owner at the Cape in the early nineteenth century, recorded perhaps the typical Dutch attitude toward slave education: "Ask a Dutchman if he ever thinks of giving a slave any education to make them more useful in his concerns. "Education! Do you suppose me mad? Learn a slave to read and write? Put it in his power to do me every injury, make known all my secrets and give him a power to cheat me with greater security? No. No. The s[h]ambuck[65] is better than a Book for a slave."[66]

In their neglect, Cape slave owners did not go so far as their counterparts in the American South, where every southern state, except Maryland and Kentucky had stringent laws forbidding anyone to teach slaves reading and writing, and in some states the penalties applied to teaching free blacks as well.[67] Although Christian instruction was Company policy for the Lodge slaves until 1795, the burgher slave owners, who owned the bulk of the slave force at the Cape, became increasingly negligent in instructing their slaves in Christianity. Nevertheless, they did not pass any antiliteracy legislation.

The Frontier Diaspora

The Cape Company administrators, having once unsuccessfully clashed with the settlers in 1706 over their charges of personal corruption, shied away from any other potential confrontation. Baptism certainly remained such an issue, and therefore officials allowed the religion of the settlers' slaves to become an increas-

---

G. G. & J. Robinson, 1798), vol. 1, pp. 60–71; but see also Robert C.-H. Shell, "Slavery at the Cape of Good Hope, 1680-1731," Ph.D. dissertation, Yale University, 1986, pp. 267–268 for the case of the slave girl, Lena van de Caap, for whom the illiterate Company woodcutter, Jan Vosloo, must have hired a schoolteacher.

[62] Hoge, "Privaatskoolmeesters," 1–30.

[63] *Resolutions* (2 September 1779). I am indebted to James Armstrong for this reference.

[64] Coenraad Beyers, *Die Kaapse Patriotte 1779–1791* (Cape Town: Juta, 1929), p. 248.

[65] Originally an Urdu word, probably imported by Bengal slaves. At the Cape, the *sjambok* was a heavy rhinoceros-hide whip about four feet long, one inch thick, and tapering to a thick, half-inch tip. It invariably splits human skin and is the instrument of choice for corporal punishment used by the contemporary South African police force and also by many farmers.

[66] Robert C.-H. Shell (ed.), " 'Slaves,' an Essay by Samuel Eusebius Hudson," *Kronos* 9 (1984): 52.

[67] Elkins, *Slavery*, page 60.

ingly remote problem. The baptism of settlers' slaves was not their responsibility. Their perception of their role, difficult to document, seems to have been to "let sleeping dogs lie." They baptized the Company slaves according to the orders from Holland, and some of the lesser officials, perhaps setting a reluctant example, duly baptized their own slaves as well. It is mostly their Cape Town slaves who appear in the Cape baptismal registers. Perhaps to avoid embarrassing the settler congregation in Cape Town unnecessarily, the Company baptized their own Lodge slaves en bloc on "special" Sundays of the year. By 1725 baptism of slaves was almost entirely an urban phenomenon.

As the colony grew and the several congregations became increasingly scattered, settlers grew more lax about baptism, sometimes baptizing en bloc several of their own grown children at once on the rare occasions when they came to town. On these occasions, their slave children did not accompany the family to the church. The far-flung and always expanding settlement pattern, coupled with the thorny complexities surrounding the incorporation of the slave into the home and Church led the typical settler further and further away from the precepts of his cherished Protestant beliefs. These precepts, according to Calvinist teaching, stressed close ties between civic and ecclesiastical government. For example, as early as 1708 one Dutch minister, Johannes D'Ailly, complained to the Amsterdam Classis that he was no longer able to accomplish his parochial house calls because of the wide settlement patterns of the then still small district.[68] Some idea of the effects of geographical dispersion and isolation on the religious behavior of Cape settlers may be gleaned from the extraordinary petition of a 17-year-old woman, Johanna Magdalena Victor. She wrote to the Company authorities in 1742 invoking their protection from her patriarchal frontier father:

Johanna Magdalena Victor, daughter of Gerrit Victor, shows that her father has gone far inland, and wished to compel her to join him there, where she will see nothing but slaves and hottentots and be cut off from all Christians and the blessings of the Gospel; she had seen the improper conduct of her father when he was here [Cape Town], and this makes her dread going so far in to the veld; she therefore prays that as she is able to support herself, that she may be permitted to remain here in order to be taught the Christian tenets so that she may, with God and with honour, pass through this world; for similar reasons, Anna E. Bockelenberg [her aunt] begs that Johanna's little sister, named Maria, only seven years old, may also be left here, as she [the aunt] will undertake her maintenance and education; as to her sorrow she has found that her father is permitting not only these two girls, but their three brothers also, the eldest of whom is eighteen, to grow up as blind heathens.[69]

---

[68] Spoelstra, *Bouwstoffen* (9 April 1708), vol. 1, 121.

[69] Hendrik Carel Vos Leibbrandt, *Requesten (Memorials) 1715–1806* (Cape Town: South African Library, 1989), vol. 4, pp. 1279 (no. 50 of 1742); CAD LM 17, p. 1130; genealogical

Geographical remoteness from the metropolitan Church, together with the relative isolation of the individual homestead, drove the typically independent settler to an increasingly autodidactic relationship with his Bible. That environment was one unrelieved by regular pastoral visits.[70] The effect of rural isolation on the settlers is exemplified in the following extract from the diary of Willem B. E. Paravicini di Capelli, the aide-de-camp of the revolution-minded General Janssens. He toured the country in the early 1800s and visited the distant farm of Ignatius Ferreira:

Before leaving Ferreira, I should like to refer to this man more closely. Filled with pride at the degree of perfection he believes he has attained, he makes use in conversation of set phrases and Biblical quotations. Whenever his interests demand it, he quotes Bible texts sanctimoniously. Of this he gave a proof when the Governor asked his opinion of treating Hottentots and slaves inhumanly. Our hypocrite, who clearly felt that this question was aimed at him personally, tried to prove that the Hottentots were the race of Ham, accursed of God and doomed to slavery, and that it was the duty of a Christian to obey the word of God. However neat this subterfuge, he noticed that this application was not well received by the Governor. He blushed, slammed shut the Bible, laid it in its accustomed place on the mantle plank of the chimney and gave a new turn to his scriptural knowledge.[71]

If Reformed Christianity increasingly became a home brew for the Cape settler, the early seventeenth-century Cape slaves were fashioning their own version as well. François Leguat, en route with some French Huguenots to colonize the Indian Ocean island of Mauritius, provides the first, albeit Eurocentric, description of what some of the Cape slaves believed as early as 1698. Significantly, there were elements of Khoikhoi religious veneration in the Cape slaves' religion:

They say the [slaves] worship only one God, creator of all things, and that they likewise have a great Veneration for the Sun and Moon, as his Chief Ministers

---

details and ages added from C. Pama (comp.) and C. C. de Villiers, *Geslagsregisters van die ou Kaapse Families* (Cape Town: Balkema, 1981), vol. 2, pp. 1022–1023.

[70] The early Cape settlers had a reputation for being "religious," but this is extremely difficult to confirm. Much hard evidence points the other way. Recusancy rates were astronomical, and an analysis of the inventories reveals not only widespread illiteracy but also few household Bibles. In an attempt to create a reliable price series for the early Cape, I chose as an index "a shopping basket of common goods," viz. a feather mattress (*bulsak*), a horse, a sheep, a slave, and, finally, a Bible; the Bible had to be discarded from the list, as there were simply too few in the inventories. See also André du Toit, "No Chosen People: The Myth of the Calvinist Origins of Afrikaner Nationalism and Racial Ideology," *The American Historical Review* 88 no 4 (October 1983): 920–952; Du Toit, "Puritans in Africa?" mimeo, 1981; Du Toit, "Captive to the Nationalist Paradigm," mimeo (no date).

[71] W. B. E. Paravicini di Capelli, *Reize in de Binnen-Landen van Zuid Africa, Gedaan in den Jaar 1803* (Cape Town: Van Riebeeck Society, 1965), p. 231. This was his private journal; Paravicini was also entrusted with the official journal of the tour.

whose principal commission is to vivify the Earth and all the inhabitants . . .but this adoration is secret and interior. They have neither images, Ceremonies nor any other manner of sensible worship, and admit no other Law than that of nature. If they feast and Dance at the Renewing of the moon, it is not to show any respect for her, but like the Hottentots, to rejoice at the return of the Light. In a word they are perfect deists, whereupon I cannot forbear taking notice, by the by, though against all common Opinion that there is no real difference to be made between these People, and those we call Atheists.[72]

Bartholomaus Ziegenbalgh, a Danish missionary visiting the Cape in 1706, actually met with some Christian Cape slaves. He described their religion in his diary: "We were overjoyed to hear the Children of the Blacks answer so prettily to all the questions of the Christian Religion, but were much amazed to see that the [European] Christians use their slaves so hard, and (as it was said) deny 'em the very benefit of *Baptism* whereby they might be initiated into the Christian Faith."[73] When Ziegenbalgh later asked the settlers why they were straying from the path of righteousness, they replied that not everyone could "serve God so well in these parts of the world, as in his own country; and so they think they had rather put it quite off till they come home again."[74]

Slaves reacted against the imperceptibly closing doors of the colonial Reformed Church. According to a 1706 complaint by a rural official, Landdrost Starrenburg, on several occasions the slaves openly "molested and frightened" the Stellenbosch minister and made him "anxious" while he was coming out of his church on Sundays.[75] Nevertheless, they did inculcate some notions of Christianity: for instance, there were rare, dramatic religious oaths taken by slaves while on the gallows or being executed. One Portuguese slave at the Cape dramatically expressed his dual Portuguese and Catholic cultural heritage while being roasted alive by the Cape executioners. His words assuredly deserve a mention since they are the first recorded words of a Cape slave in an archaic Portuguese lingua franca: "*Dios, mio Pay!* [God, my father!]"[76]

George Schmidt, the first missionary (although not Reformed) to work in South Africa, wrote in December 1737 that the slaves were treated badly by nominal Christians; that "Godlessness was great in the land."[77] In the nineteenth

---

72 François Leguat, in R. Raven-Hart (comp. and ed.), *Cape Good Hope 1652–1896* (Cape Town: Balkema, 1971), vol. 2, p. 438.

73 B. Ziegenbalgh, *Propagation of the Gospel* (London: Joseph Downing, 1718), p. 11 (emphasis in original).

74 Ziegenbalgh, *Propagation*, 11.

75 Hendrik Carel Vos Leibbrandt, *Journal, 1699–1732* (Cape Town: W. A. Richards & Sons, 1896) (August 4 1706), p. 97; Leibbrandt, *Letters Despatched* (15 April 1707), 316–317.

76 This seems to be a dialect of Portuguese; Peter Kolbe, *The Present State of the Cape . . .* (London: Johnson Reprint Company, 1968), vol. 2, 363.

77 Schmidt, *Das Tagebuch*, p. 43.

century Johannes Theodorus Van der Kemp, an energetic missionary, came to be loathed by the settlers for his inclusive evangelism. He placed the "pernicious laws" of baptism at the Cape, as he called them, at the root of the colony's problems: "There is an ardent desire among them [slaves] to know the word of God, which shows to a remarkable degree its power to salvation in the hearts of many heathens, who are evidently baptized with the Holy Ghost, and with fire, tho' the customs and rules of this country do not allow them to be baptized with water."[78] Van der Kemp was an ardent abolitionist, if for no other reason than that he perceived that slavery was a barrier to Christianity. He was also an activist. His biographer cited the example of a deacon of the Dutch Reformed Church who refused baptism to his domestic slave, Suzanna, even when the aristocratic Van der Kemp directly petitioned him. The deacon refused on the grounds that Suzanna's "pride would grow insupportable when admitted to the community of Christians" and that moreover he would lose the right to sell her. Van der Kemp was outraged and administered communion to her without the rite of baptism. Local settlers thought his actions threatened not only the local Church but also the entire social structure. Their agitation drove them to an assassination attempt. They actually fired upon this missionary with their guns, but luckily he was not hurt.[79]

As a proportion of their population, fewer and fewer settler slaves were baptized.[80] In the seventeenth century, when there were many devout and Church-fearing immigrant slave owners (the French Huguenots started arriving in 1688), slave baptism rates were relatively high.[81] François Leguat, himself a Huguenot refugee, noted in 1698, perhaps not too impartially: "those that have authority over them, take care to instruct them in religion, and teach them to read and write, which the French refugees above all employ themselves about with a great deal of earnestness."[82] But this zeal, according to a swelling chorus of travelers, colonists, and officials, proved short-lived. In the long eighteenth century and the 38 years of the nineteenth century during which South Africa remained a slave society, no one endorsed Leguat's opinion or expressed sentiments similar to his. Only the Company, the governor himself, and a handful of devout Christian slave owners, mainly Company personnel and members of Cape Town's patrician

---

[78] As quoted in D. K. Clinton, *The South African Melting Pot: A Vindication of Missionary Policy, 1799–1836* (London, 1937), pp. 31–32.

[79] I am extremely grateful to Mary Caroline Cravens for this reference, as quoted in Cravens, "The New Culture Brokers: Women in the Nineteenth-Century Protestant Missions to South Africa, 1799–1914," senior thesis, History Department, Princeton University, 1993, p. 53. I. H. Enklaar, *Life and Work of Dr. J. Th. Van der Kemp, 1747–1811* (Cape Town: Balkema, 1988), pp. 116–117.

[80] CAD G1 4/34 KA Bylae 1832-1891, n.p. I am grateful to James Armstrong for a typed version of this document.

[81] CAD G1 4/34 KA Bylae 1832-1891.

[82] Leguat in Raven-Hart, *Cape Good Hope*, vol. 2, 438.

class, took the precepts of *De Ethnicorum* seriously, evangelized among their household slaves, and systematically baptized their own infant slaves throughout the period.

The settlement came to be divided between a religious patrician minority in the towns and a recusant patriarchal rump in the rural areas — usually Company personnel or wealthy patrician townspeople on the one hand, and the increasingly independent slave owners and *trekboers* on the other. By the end of the period hardly any rural settlers slaves, adults or children, were being baptized. More important, the number of slaves and free blacks taking communion remained negligible. By the 1770s Cape slave owners believed in the convenient moral solipsism that the baptism of slaves was "wrong." Sir John Cradock, a British governor, writing of that period claimed in a letter to Lord Bathurst:

My Lord, I have to submit to your Lordship that I felt it my duty to repeal a Resolution of the Council of Batavia, passed the 10th April, 1770, which by prohibiting the transfer or disposal of slaves who had been converted to Christianity, *completely stopped the progress of the Christian religion* among that class of persons, for it was not to be supposed that the Dutch inhabitants or others would encourage any exertion on this subject, whereby they were to suffer in their property. Until this repeal took place, every opposition would certainly be given to the conversion of any slave, *or even his appearance at any church*.[83]

One of the ironies of the colonial Reformed tradition was that the state, not the Church, came to protect the slaves' right to convert to Christianity. What is striking is that the discussion over baptism was carried on in the corridors of colonial administration, not in the local synods. The Fiscal Daniël Dennijson, who was third in command of the colony and who also had jurisdiction over the welfare of slaves, wrote to a counterpart in the second decade of the nineteenth century:

In compliance with the desire of his Excellency the Governor and Commander-in-chief contained in your letter of the 16th Instant respecting the alteration of a part of the existing laws, by which the owners of all slaves who have embraced the Christian Religion are forbid[den] to sell them; I have the honor to say...the reasons which have induced his excellency to fix his attention on their object, appear to be well grounded and too well confirmed by experience, for although a number of slaves are to be found in whom the principles of the Christian faith are imprinted from their childhood still however there is scarcely one who has got so far, as to be confirmed. It is true the sale of Christian Slaves, the trading with one's fellow believers can be considered as disallowable by Christian Morality, but the same Moral Lesson extended to the whole system of Slavery, and therefore so long as the Government here is under the necessity to [support] the greater evil of

---

[83] Theal, *RCC*, "Letter from Sir John Cradock to Lord Bathurst" (25 January 1813), 9: 130 (emphasis added).

slavery, it is not unjust if the lesser evils which can not be separated from the evil itself without increasing it should remain attached thereto.

Dennijson then offered the solution that had worked in the Americas:

The liberty of selling slaves who have embraced the Christian religion being allowed to all proprietors of slaves here, it will probably be seen, that many will be baptized and confirmed in the Christian faith, and his Excellency will thereby be enabled at the same time to grant to the increasing numbers of Christian slaves certain privileges tending to the promotion of good morals which it would have been useless hitherto to have done to the slaves not Christians, as for example legal marriage, the same as was allowed among the Romans however under the name of *Contubernium servorum;* the legality of children born in lawful Matrimony between slaves, liberty to attend public worship in the churches at certain times and others of that nature.[84]

The tensions caused by the incorporation of slaves into the Christian household, and controversy over the civic equality that *all* fellow Christians supposedly enjoyed, were greatly magnified after 1807. After that year the supply of new slaves to the Cape dwindled as the oceanic slave trade was suppressed and settlers were forced to turn to the domestic slave market and the natural increase of the slave force to buy slaves in a legal manner. It was during this period, with slave prices steeply rising, that the colonial reconstruction of *De Ethnicorum* was finally nullified at the Cape, only five years after the abolition of the slave trade. But by then many slaves, particularly in the urban areas, had turned irrevocably to Islam.[85] Urban Christian missions in South Africa, both English and Dutch, were almost total failures until well into the nineteenth century.[86]

The Growth of Islam

By the early nineteenth century convicted slaves at their execution were turning, in extremis, not to Christ but to Allah.[87] Before 1825, there are no records of the number of Muslims at the Cape; in that year, according to figures submitted by Cape Town *imams*, there were 846 male Muslim slaves and 422 female Muslim slaves. As John Thomas Bigge, the British royal commissioner, noted that this figure illustrated the "spread of Muhammedanism," one can be certain that there

---

[84] CAD AG 31 18/2: "Outgoing Letters of Fiscal, Dennyson to Governor" (30 September 1812), pp. 43–45.

[85] Robert C.-H. Shell, "The Establishment and Spread of Islam at the Cape from the Beginning of Company Rule to 1838," honors thesis, University of Cape Town, 1975.

[86] Robert C.-H. Shell, "Rites and Rebellion: Islamic Conversion at the Cape, 1808 to 1915," *Studies in the History of Cape Town* 5 (1984): 1–46.

[87] Robert C.-H. Shell (ed.), Hudson, *Memorandums and Occurrences*, no pagination.

were considerably fewer Muslim slaves before this date.[88] In addition to the number of Muslim slaves there were free Muslims in Cape Town in the same period, a total of 2,167 in 1825. However, by 1842, according to a Municipal census of that year, there were 6,435 Muslims in Cape Town, over one-third of the town's population.[89] Thereafter there was a slight decrease in the total number of Muslims — in 1875, for instance, there were only 5,335 Muslims in Cape Town. Although there are reasons to believe that this figure is artificially low, it can safely be said that the spread of Islam occurred mainly between 1770 and 1842 (see Figure 11-6).[90]

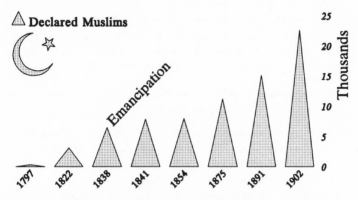

Figure 11–6. The growth of Islam at the Cape, 1797–1902.

Various unsatisfactory explanations have been advanced for this spread. John Centilivres Chase, a Cape colonial publicist, suggested that the most important cause was emancipation in 1838.[91] Samuel Abraham Rochlin, an antiquarian, claimed the spread could be explained by manumission: "the growing number of freed coloured folk."[92] Both explanations are advanced without evidence and, moreover, do not explain why slaves, once free, should profess themselves to be

---

[88] Theal, *RCC*, 35: 367.

[89] *Cape of Good Hope Almanac 1844*, front piece.

[90] Richard Elphick and Robert C.-H. Shell, "Intergroup Relations" in R. Elphick and Herman Giliomee (eds.), *The Shaping of South African Society, 1652–1820* (Cape Town: Longmans, 1979), pp. 148–150. John Schofield Mayson, *The Malays of Cape Town* (Manchester: J. S. Galt, 1861), p. 24; [G. 42-'76]: *Colony of the Cape of Good Hope. Census of 1875* (Cape Town: Saul Solomon & Co., 1876), p. 15; cf. [G. 6 — '92] *Results of a Census of the Colony of the Cape of Good Hope as on the Night of Sunday, the 5th of April, 1891* (Cape Town: Government Printers, 1892), p. xxvii.

[91] John Centilivres Chase, *The Cape of Good Hope and the Eastern Province of Algoa Bay* (London: Pelham Richardson, 1843), p. 141.

[92] S. A. Rochlin, "Aspects of Islam in Nineteenth Century Africa," p. 219.

Muslim when Islam was a heavily handicapped religion at the Cape. (Muslim marriages, for instance, were never recognized.) J. S. Marais's statement that "Islam did more than Christianity to bridge the gulf between slave and free-born,"[93] while not explaining the spread, does suggest that this spread might be related to slaves' exclusion from Christianity.

Ironically, the spread of Islam at the Cape during this period had its origin in a measure to promote Christianity, that derived very clearly from the Synod of Dordt. In the chapter on Slaves in the Statutes of India, dated 10 April 1770, article nine reads:

The Christians are held bound to instruct their Slaves, should they be so inclined or be capable of being persuaded without absolute compulsion in the Christian Religion, and have them baptized, on pain of arbitrary correction, and such as may have been confirmed in the Christian Religion, *shall never be sold*, but their Masters be under the obligation of emancipating them in the event of their departure from this country, or at their death, or to give them away, or bequeath them to others under the same obligation, or, on the other hand, to allow all such slaves to purchase their freedom themselves at prime cost or by taxation if born in the family, or [received as] presents from others . . .[94]

As I have noted, most slave owners at the Cape interpreted this clear legislation as a threat to their property. They believed that their slaves would become free if they became Christians, although all the legislation only stipulated that Christian slaves could not be sold. Cape slave owners, never energetic in attending "to a circumstance of so little consequence in their eyes as the religion of their slaves, thereafter neglected *all* form of Christian instruction for their slaves."[95] In 1804 Robert Percival, a British visitor, was told that the Dutch slave owners' "chief motive" for neglecting the religious instruction of their slave children, many of whom were their own children, was "for fear of them being lost to them on their becoming Christians."[96]

This attitude became known to the South African Missionary Society, whose single purpose was the Christian education of the slaves in the Colony. The society was founded in 1799 and led by the Reverend Vos of Tulbagh, himself a slave owner.[97] Vos, despairing of this attitude and its cause, the Statute of 1770, wrote the following letter to the authorities 9 March 1812: "Sir! exclusive of the false prejudice of the so-called Christians . . . there is another great obstacle in this country to the progress of Christianity, and Oh! how happy I be could I but see

---

[93] Marais, *The Cape Coloured People*, 172–173.

[94] Theal, *RCC*, 9: 131–132 (emphasis added).

[95] George Forster, *A Voyage round the World* (London: B. White, 1777), vol. 1, p. 60.

[96] Robert Percival, *An Account of the Cape of Good Hope* (New York: Negro Universities Press, 1969 reprint), pp. 274–275.

[97] Marais, *Cape Coloured People*, 168.

this obstacle removed by our highly respected government before my death. It is, namely, that a slave who is baptized may not be sold. This circumstance is the occasion that the proprietors of slaves, who may possess truly Christian hearts and entertain a desire of [them] becoming incorporated in the Church of our Lord Jesus Christ, object to their being baptized."[98]

Cradock, the governor, responded promptly to this appeal and repealed the clause in the same year. He clearly noted the irony "that a law intended for the promotion of Christianity and true religion had not been attended with the desired, but rather the contrary effect."[99] The repeal, however, had little effect, as other legislation reinforced the slave owners' belief that converting their slaves to Christianity was analogous to emancipating them. For instance, despite the repeal in 1812, legislation was proposed in 1817 by the colonial secretary, recommending that the children of Christian slaves who were married in the Church, after being educated in Christian principles, should no longer be considered transferable property.[100] However, on complaints from the owners this recommendation was not adopted, as "it was not at that period considered expedient by the local government to connect the religious and moral instruction of slave children or even of adults with any scheme for the ultimate attainment of their freedom."[101] The legislation that year was modified and limited to providing elementary education for Christian slave children, an obligation which remained burdensome to the owners. Christianity still held the promise and threat of equality and freedom. By 1823 it was decreed that Christian slave children should be sent to government free schools, but this "was not observed by the owners." Further legislation linking freedom and Christianity was passed in the same year, declaring that children born of an unmarried Christian slave woman were not to be separated from their mother until the child was nine years old.[102] Christianity thus continued to limit the marketability of slaves. Christianity for slaves involved several sacrifices from owners.

The growing scarcity of slaves at this point must be borne in mind. After 1808 the colony itself became the only source for slaves. Consequently, from 1808 to 1826 the price of slaves had risen 400 percent.[103] This high valuation ensured that any legislation that curtailed the domestic buying and selling of Christian slaves must have had a retarding influence on householders' decisions to baptize their slaves. The buying and selling of slaves increased substantially in the small

---

[98] Theal, *RCC,* 9: 133.
[99] Eybers, *Documents,* p. 18.
[100] Theal, *RCC,* 35: 365.
[101] Theal, *RCC,* 35: 365.
[102] Theal, *RCC,* 35: 364.
[103] Theal, *RCC,* 29: 427.

period for which figures are available: in 1816 there were 183 transfers in Cape Town, while in 1824 there were 679 (see Chapter 4).[104]

The growing pro-emancipation mood in Britain and the legislation curtailing the sale of Christian slaves, had, by 1830, resulted in the Cape slave owners' being "impressed with a belief in the claim to freedom which slaves acquired by becoming Christian," while other owners viewed "with apprehension any measure which might have a tendency to abridge the relative distance between master and slave."[105] Consequently, slaves received no Christian instruction. Bird claimed that in the few cases in which slaves did get a Christian education, it was confined to two commandments: thou shalt not steal and thou shalt not kill. This was taught, Bird added, "only because they [the commandments] guard and protect the property of the owner."[106] One result of this attitude was that, in an era of intense local and overseas missionary activity, of the 35,698 slaves in the colony, only 86 were baptized between the years 1810 and 1824, approximately 6 per year.[107] This percentage is so negligible it cannot be graphed.

At the time, the slave owners offered many lame excuses for why slaves were not receiving Christian education. Chief among these was that there "was a want of buildings adapted to this purpose."[108] While there was some truth in this, especially in the country,[109] it was overestimated, as Bigge pointed out in 1830: "This neglect of Christian instruction in the farmers might be attributable to the difficulties in which they themselves were placed, but it also prevailed among the inhabitants of the towns and villages where opportunities of instruction occasionally presented themselves."[110] Generally, however, little was done to convert and educate slaves in the country or the town.

At the same time, the number of Muslim slaves was increasing rapidly. Even in the country districts, away from the influence of the Cape Town *imams*, their numbers were considerable,[111] While in Cape Town, as was noted, there were over a thousand. Eric Aspeling, a later colonist, stated that the spread of Islam was directly attributable to the slave owners who, "studying their own interests, preferred their slaves embracing the Mahometan faith, in which case they would

[104] Theal, *RCC*, 35: 374.

[105] Theal, *RCC*, 35: 366.

[106] Bird, *State of the Cape*, 74.

[107] Marais, *Cape Coloured People*, 31, note 1; Theal, *RCC*, 35: 364; two districts, which included "free people of colour," were excluded from this figure.

[108] Theal, *RCC*, 35: 366.

[109] However, Christian slave education was "met with more encouragement in Stellenbosch" than in Cape Town; Theal, *RCC*, 35: 367.

[110] Imperial Blue Book No. 584 (1 July 1830): "Copies of reports relating to the condition of the Hottentots, Bushmen, Caffres and other Native Tribes of South Africa; the progress among them of Christian Missions," 9.

[111] Theal, *RCC*, 35: 367.

remain in bondage."[112] This judgment, although advanced without evidence, would seem to be accurate. Bird, writing in 1822, came to the same conclusion and added that whenever one asked a slave why he had become Muslim, the reply was: "some religion he must have and he is not allowed to turn Christian." Bigge drew similar attention to the owner's influence when he claimed: "It is strongly believed that the manifest preference shown by the slaves for Islam is regarded with indifference by the Masters."[113] Apart from remaining in bondage, Muslim slaves had other advantages for the owners. For instance, owners of wine-producing farms preferred their slaves to be Muslim, as they did not drink. Bird sums up this attitude: "It is made a question, still with worldly considerations only, whether the Muhammedan slave makes a better servant than the Christian. His sobriety, as it is affirmed, makes amends for some ill-habits attendant on Muhammedanism."[114] With the Cape undergoing an unprecedented wine boom in the 1820s, it is therefore not surprising that this should also emerge as a significant period for the spread of Islam, both rural and urban.

The colonial authorities, worried about the spread of Islam among the slaves, instigated an enquiry.[115] Although the quietist *imams* who were interviewed were more concerned about the persecution of Muslims in Cape Town[116] than about telling the commissioners about their spread of the religion, some further light was shed on why slaves adopted Islam. First, as Christian slaves were not officially allowed to marry until 1823,[117] *imams* would often conduct ceremonies for the slaves according to Islamic law. Moreover, they did not object to remarrying a male slave to another women if he and his first wife were separated by their master and sold (although the *imams* did not observe the same practice when it came to remarrying women).[118] Second, the quietist *imams* endeavored to make the slaves believe that although their bodies were held in slavery "yet that their souls are free and that they must trust in God to make them free when they die."[119] On their own, these attractions cannot be said to be responsible for the spread of Islam during this period, for they had been present long before 1770. However, added to

---

[112] Eric A. Aspeling, *The Cape Malays* (Cape Town: W. A. Richards & Sons, 1883), p. 3.

[113] Theal, *RCC*, 35: 366; Bird, *State of the Cape*, p. 349; James Backhouse, *Narrative of a Visit to the Mauritius and South Africa* (London: Hamilton, Adams, 1844), p. 82.

[114] Bird, *State of the Cape*, 349; Theal, *RCC*, 35: 366.

[115] "Evidence of Two Mahometan Priests," in "Papers Relative to the Condition and Treatment of the Native Inhabitants of Southern Africa within the Colony of the Cape of Good Hope, or Beyond the Frontier of that Colony," part 1 (18 March 1835); Theal, *RCC*, 35: 366.

[116] Theal, *RCC*, 28: 36–38; 35: 138ff.

[117] Between 1826 and 1834, the number of Christian slave marriages scarcely reached double figures; Marais, *Cape Coloured People*, 171; Bird, *State of the Cape*, 349.

[118] "Evidence of Two Priests," 210; Theal, *RCC*, 35: 367ff.

[119] "Evidence of Two Priests," 210; Theal, *RCC*, 35: 369.

the wine boom and the owners' indifference to Christian evangelism, the total influence might have been considerable.

The spread of Islam at the Cape, then, accelerated in 1770 with the enactment of specific legislation that prohibited the buying and selling of Christian slaves. As the domestic market became the only source of slaves after 1808, legislation curtailing the transfer of Christian slaves had sharper effects. Slave owners, never very energetic in the Christian education of their slaves, consequently neglected the practice completely. Despite a considerable global missionary effort, only a handful of Cape slaves were baptized each year. On the other hand, the number of male Muslim slaves increased rapidly. Although there were other, personal reasons for slaves' embracing of Islam, it is suggested that the rapid spread was caused by the slave owners, who believed that the adoption of Islam by their slaves would further distance them from Christianity and freedom. Muslim slaves would probably remain sober, and would certainly remain marketable. In an economy based on wine and slaves, such considerations were important.

Baptism and the Autochthonous People

Once one appreciates the full ramifications of Cape slave owners' fears of baptism for slaves, it is a short step to ask how these attitudes affected the autochthonous people. Attitudes of slave owners toward slaves can partly be explained and understood (if not excused) in that slaves were simultaneously property and persons, and that all slave owners stood to lose their property if their slaves were baptized and developed a Christian identity (with the accruing civic benefits). But this attitude toward baptism of slaves spilled over the threshold of chattel slavery and became a general attitude, as well, toward household and farm servants drawn from the autochthonous people. It is thus equally important when considering the influence of Reformed Christianity to realize that settlers came to perceive that baptism of natives narrowed the gap between Christian settlers and pagan indigenous domestic servants. The Dordt opinions on baptism had specifically addressed what the attitude of Christians toward all "heathens and pagans" in the household should be. The Dordt delegates nudged all Christians to instruct and convert such people. However, although there were some schemes to evangelize among the Khoi in the seventeenth century, these plans never came to fruition.[120]

The Cape minister Overneij candidly admitted shortly after 1678 that it had not been the practice to baptize autochthonous people at the Cape (except for one woman [Eva] and her children), that "these people were tangential to our reli-

---

[120] See Richard Elphick and Herman Giliomee (eds.), *The Shaping of South African Society, 1652–1820*, rev. ed. (Middletown, Conn.: Wesleyan University Press, 1989), p. 232, footnotes 7 and 10.

gion."[121] There were no full-time Reformed missionaries at the Cape before the 1790s. The only missionary was the Moravian, Georg Schmidt, who won a few converts at Genadendal between 1737 and 1744 before being expelled from the colony for baptizing the autochthonous folk.[122] When the pioneering Schmidt arrived in Cape Town in 1737 he went to a tavern where he overheard the patrons discussing his imminent arrival and what they saw as his incomprehensible mission. Before Schmidt revealed who he was, he overheard the patrons heatedly claim that the Khoikhoi could not possibly profit from any Christian education as they were "a stupid people"[123] and "anyway had no money."[124] The Company also evidently felt such Khoikhoi Christian education was unnecessary. The Company did not employ the autochthonous people in a Company capacity after the seventeenth century.[125] As Sparrman noted in the 1770s, "There is no doubt, but that the Hottentots might be easily converted to the Christian faith: but it is much to be doubted, whether anybody will ever trouble themselves with the conversion of these plain honest people, unless it should appear to have more connection than it seems to have at present with political advantages."[126] Elsewhere he noted the legal implications of baptizing autochthonous folk: "None of these ["Bastaard" people], nor any other illegitimate children are ever baptized, or indeed enquired after by the Christian ministers at the Cape, except in case that any one should present himself as the father, and make a point of the child's being baptized, and *thus give the infant the right of inheritance.*"[127] Settlers too, rarely instituted formal Christian education of the Khoikhoi on their farms, and certainly never did in their homes. The main reason was that the Reformed sacrament of baptism also conferred rights of a civic nature, marriage and inheritance.

Unbaptized offspring of autochthonous folk or of slave and native parents were by colonial definition illegitimate and were formally called "bastards." By 1800 a special column in the local census had been added to make room for this new distinction — that is, a special column for people who were born outside of a

---

[121] "*Doch dese natie is teenemal afkeerigh van onse Godsdienst*"; Spoelstra, *Bouwstoffen*, vol. 1, 28.

[122] See the recently transcribed, translated, and edited diaries of Georg Schmidt: Henry C. Bredakamp and J. L. Hatting (eds.), *Dagboek en Briewe van George Schmidt: Eerste Sendeling in Suid Afrika (1737–1744)* (Bellville: Die Wes-Kaaplandse Instituut vir Historiese Navorsing, 1981), see especially "Kort Berig . . ." pp. 479ff. The Cape ministers were obviously surprised that Schmidt was going to baptize the Khoi, and the governor himself raked Schmidt over the coals for doing the one thing he had forbidden the Moravian from doing; p. 485.

[123] [*dom volk*].

[124] [*en geld het hulle nie*].

[125] Bredakamp and Hatting, *Dagboek en Briewe*, 479; see also the conversation between the governor and George Schmidt, ibid., 485.

[126] Sparrman, *A Voyage to the Cape*, vol. 1, 208.

[127] Sparrman, *A Voyage to the Cape*, vol. 1, 263–264 (emphasis added).

Christian family. Thus, after the householder's name would appear his status: such as "unbaptized bastard [*ongedoopte bastaard*]" or "creole burgher."[128] Not immediately perceiving, or caring about, the derogatory connotations of the European word, some of the frontier unbaptized people took on the name "Bastards" until missionaries persuaded them to call themselves "Griqua" in the nineteenth century. In the plane of religious identity, the Cape society came to have four tiers: Christians, Muslims, pagan slaves, and unbaptized bastards. This hierarchy became so marked that the Fiscal Daniël Dennijson, who received complaints about the abuse of unbaptized free people from as far away as the frontier town of Uitenhage, wrote a letter to the governor on the 16 August 1813 pointing out that unbaptized autochthonous people and unbaptized "apprentices" and free blacks were still in a seriously disadvantaged legal position and urged him to legislate:

Sir! There are in this colony a sort of servants not unlike the Hottentots who hire themselves into the service of the inhabitants, but to whom the regulations proscribed respecting said Hottentots by the Proclamation of the 1st November 1809 does not extend, I mean the emancipated slaves and other free blacks *who have not been baptized or been confirmed in the Christian religion,* and among those are also Prize slaves or Apprentices. The decision of Disputes which may arise between such servants and their masters has appeared to me to be subject to uncertainty because that it is not the custom to place the latter on the same footing as European and Christian servants and still however the differences of their situation is not sufficiently proscribed by the local laws . . . the inconvenience of the uncertainty respecting the law to be observed is not felt by me alone . . .[129]

In short, baptism and civic rights were thus clearly associated in the settler mind for autochthonous folk as well as slaves. Excluding autochthonous persons and offspring of creole mulatto slaves and autochthonous persons from this primary sacrament was the simplest and most expedient way of maintaining the Christian settler / Muslim slave and Christian settler / heathen indigene hierarchies. This exclusion was greatly facilitated in that it conveniently began in the domestic arena of the settler households.

One question remains: why was there not a wholesale conversion to Christianity by slaves and autochthonous people in an effort to further their own interests? It should immediately be noted that slave mothers did occasionally present their children for baptism. But there were too few such cases, and some failed, as was seen in the 1666 incident described at the beginning of this chapter.

---

[128] CAD 1/5/226: "Opgaaf Rolle van Drakensteijn" (1800), n.p.: "*ongedoopte bastaard,*" "*gebore burger*"; even a brief history of the householder, e.g. "Christiaanz, Frans Abraham, sailor, became a burger in 1780."

[129] I am extremely grateful to Michael Ryan for pointing out this reference and photocopying it almost ten years ago. CAD: "Outgoing letters of Fiscal, Daniël Dennijson," AG 32 (16 August 1813), pp. 241–244 (emphasis added).

Clasina of Bengal was the solitary slave who brought suit under the Synod of Dordt's recommendation that baptized slaves ought to enjoy freedom with other Christians.[130] Brought to the Cape as a three-year-old, she was baptized in February of 1745, but she claimed her children's freedom and her own only when she was about to die in 1811, when she was fully three score years and ten.[131] She presented her baptismal certificate to the court, one of whose members, P. J. Truter, was her owner and was asked to recuse himself as an interested party.[132] J. T. Neetling was appointed as her advocate. Neethling instructed the court to search the Church books for Clasina's name and the word *person* which would signify her free legal standing. The document was found, but the Church pointed out: "in the register of baptisms that the word Person [*Persoon*] is more used in the same [*sic*] for the distinction of age [as different from children] than as the word Person is used as a law term."[133] Clasina was a child when she was baptized and was nevertheless referred to as a "Person," but nobody in the court thought to make this point. Further, the court claimed that Clasina was baptized *before* the Statutes of India had come into effect in the 1770s and that those laws had "no retrospective effect." This was flying in the face of legal history, since the 1770 statutes were reformulations of similar legislation repeated throughout the seventeenth and eighteenth centuries. One can only conclude from Clasina's case that the owners' fears of baptizing their slaves were exaggerated, for baptized slaves did not have any rights in civil court.

The precedent of Clasina's case made no difference to the colonists, but it might have prompted the repeal of the clause of the Statutes of India in the following year. Christian slaves could always be bequeathed, which is exactly how Clasina and her children had been passed from owner to owner and became separated from one another. Inheritance and probate law were used to circumvent liberty-affirming Reformed church policy. There are two wills from the patrician Eksteen and Kirsten families that stipulate a particularly finely attenuated form of liberty: although the slave in question and her children could never be alienated or sold, they would pass by inheritance from one relative to another, whom each slave was "at liberty to choose."[134] In this way the idealism expressed at Dordt was nullified in the colony.

---

[130] Some documents of this extraordinary case may be found in Theal, *RCC*, 10: 45–60.

[131] Theal, *RCC*, 10: 55.

[132] Theal, *RCC*, "Extract of a Resolution . . ." (14 February 1811), 10: 46.

[133] Theal, *RCC*, "To W. S. Ryneveld, Esquire, President and the members of the Worshipful . . . Court" (undated) 10: 48.

[134] Leibbrandt, *Requesten*, vol. 2 (no. 64 of 1790), 507; (no. 139 of 1783), 647.

The Cape Clergy and Baptism

The head of the household had the primary responsibility for baptism, but the clergy still had a role to play in instructing parishioners. The settlers must first have successfully excluded the slaves from Christian fellowship in the home environment — perhaps from Bible readings after supper, certainly from family prayers. This domestic exclusion must have been tacitly approved of or followed or accompanied by institutional exclusion, which raises the vexed question of the role of the Cape clergy, who have received little scholarly attention apart from occasional and unedifying hagiographies. Sparrman, a Lutheran, clearly blamed the Reformed Cape clergy for the generally low baptism rate among slaves and indigenes, but he was also decidedly puzzled, and contrasted the Cape baptismal practices with those of the Catholic church, the ultimate specter for Protestants:

I cannot comprehend the reason why the divines of the Reformed Church at the Cape are so sparing of a sacrament, which others, particularly the Papists, have endeavored to force, as it were, upon the heathens with fire and sword, and all manner of cruelties. The cloth does not, as far as I know, receive any benefit from the christening of children at the Cape, at least no particular benefit from the baptizing of illegitimate children, such conduct, therefore cannot fairly be ascribed to any self interest, nor indeed to mere neglect; a disposition which would but ill suit with that spirit of charity and universal benevolence, so peculiarly enforced by the doctrines of Christianity.[135]

Cape Church ministers never had the social standing or intellectual prowess and clerical independence of their New England counterparts. Cape clerics, in contrast to those in New England seemed to bow to their settler congregations. Were the Cape clergy examples of intellectuals grafting themselves onto powerful interest groups, of whom Antonio Gramsci complained?[136] Whatever the answer, the Church in early South Africa did not produce a body of independent charismatic intellectuals such as those who distinguished American colonial life. Edmund Morgan, who might have been writing of South Africa, has provided an explanation of sorts: "Historically the magnification of the minister's office has often gone hand-in-hand with a comprehensive policy of church membership, while a limited membership, emphasizing purity, has been associated with a restriction of clerical authority."[137] Before the appearance of Michiel Christiaan

---

[135] Interestingly, this extract was omitted from both the German and Dutch editions; Sparrman, *A Voyage to the Cape*, vol. 1, 264, and see editor's note p. 263, note 59.

[136] Antonio Gramsci, *Selections from the Prison Notebooks* (New York: International Publishers, 1975), pp. 5–9. Gramsci considered the clergy as the "most typical" of the intellectual class. Only a thorough modern prosopographical treatment of the Cape clergy could satisfactorily answer this query.

[137] Morgan, *Visible Saints*, 143.

Vos, a Cape Town-born patrician slave holder, on the Cape ecclesiastical scene late in the eighteenth century, it is difficult to talk extensively of piety among the early clergy in South Africa.[138] Theal's bibliographic comment on Vos's autobiography, *Merkwardige Verhaal,* is apropos: ". . . contains the first evidence that colonists believed that slaves had souls."[139]

The Church in colonial South Africa became institutionally weak, prone to corruption by the congregations, and was often staffed by eccentrics and bigots.[140] The Reverend Henricus Beck, for example, was accused of appropriating documents and Church lottery money, and even of taking the silver collection plate from the church when he retired.[141] The Reverend Petrus Kalden was accused of running a plantation rather than a parish; one burgher, Adam Tas, called him "the so-called preacher."[142] Nearly all had intermarried with powerful Cape patrician families of which they formed an important part. The following 1744 request, long after the gentry revolt of 1706 indicates both the clergy's dynastic connections and its lack of commitment to the church: the Reverend Franciscus Le Sueur had "bought at a public auction, in the estate of his late father in law, Johannes Swellengrebel [the first creole governor], an estate at Rondebosch named Eckelenburg [one of the finest Cape farmsteads]; as this incapacitates him from remaining in service any longer, he asks for his discharge."[143] George Schmidt, the Moravian missionary, met all the Cape ministers and sent the following judgment to Count Zinzendorf on 23 December 1737: "They are blind, and blind leaders whose stomach is their God. They believe in the conversion of the Hottentots less than they believe in the [conversion of the] devil."[144] Were the tensions between slavery, colonial life, and the Reform tradition too great for the individual ministers to bear? The doyen of archival South African historians, Anna Böeseken, points out that in the frontier

---

138 Jonathan Neil Gerstner, *The Thousand Generation Covenant: Dutch Reformed Covenant Theology and Group Identity in Colonial South Africa, 1652–1814* (Leiden: E. J. Brill, 1991), pp. 90 ff.

139 See Michiel Christiaan Vos, *Merkwardige Verhaal* (Amsterdam: H. Höveker, 1867), pp. 137–138; 215.

140 For example Petrus Kalden, the Stellenbosch *predikant,* was recalled to Holland along with the other officials convicted of corruption in the settler revolt of 1706. Besides drawing a salary, he owned a large plantation, Zandvliet, with many slaves and indentured servants, and had a house in Cape Town. See *Resolutions* (23 April 1707), vol. 3: 463; ministers who appealed to the Khoi were termed contemptuously "Hottentot converters" and were sternly reprimanded by the whole Church council, see Leibbrandt, *Requesten* (no. 105 of 8 October 1743), vol. 2, 527–528.

141 He was also unpopular because he had married Samuel Elsevier's daughter. There is some evidence that he attempted to convert some Khoi, *Dictionary of South African Biography,* vol. 1, pp. 60–61.

142 *DSAB,* vol. 2, 355.

143 Leibbrandt, *Requesten,* (no. 32 of 1744), vol. 2, 676.

144 Schmidt, *Das Tagebuch,* 43. I am grateful to Richard Elphick for pointing out this reference.

church of Land van Waveren, the offspring of slaves and the autochthonous people began to be presented for baptism only in 1770s, when the minister became "mentally ill." In one case the mother, Anna van de Caap, was a Company slave, whose right to baptism was protected by the Company.[145]

How little the individual ministers cared about their own duties to their own slaves is illustrated by an anecdote from James Walton's work on Cape homesteads. In 1806 J. J. Kicherer assumed the role of minister in Graaf Reinet. He found the church in a deplorable condition, and in accordance with a resolution of the church council, two slave carpenters were purchased to effect the necessary repairs. The slaves, according to Walton, were housed in cellars under the rear part of the *pastorie* and therefore should have been, by even the narrowest architectural definition, considered as part of the household.[146] In 1812 the *pastorie* was repaired, and three years later the slave Outong was sold by the church for his purchase price of 1800 Rixdollars. So church ministers and authorities apparently did little themselves to evangelize among the church's own slaves and certainly did not hesitate to resell them, disrespecting the Synod of Dordt. It is little wonder, then, that the eminently well-balanced historian J. S. Marais would baldly state: "During the eighteenth century nothing that is worthy of mention was done by the church or any missionary society towards the Christianization of slaves."[147]

No local ecclesiastical body emerged (missionary or parochial) that was strong enough to overcome the increasing reluctance of Cape slave owners to baptize their slaves. The slaves were particularly disadvantaged in South Africa, because a cost-conscious commercial enterprise, not a sovereign nation, administered the colony for most of the period of slavery. The humblest sovereign country had at least some evangelical ambitions, even if they were often prompted by geopolitical rivalries and broader hegemonic concerns of statehood. But such arguments had little purchase at the commercial way station of the early Cape. As a result, the modest Cape clergy proved inadequate for Christianity's highest calling, bringing the gospel to everyone.

Declension and Recursive Identities

The Cape Reformed Church as an institution became almost quiescent toward slaves and servants at the Cape, because of the society's overriding attitudes based on perceived rights of property as vested in the slaves of the settler congregations.

---

145 Anna J. Böeseken and Margaret Cairns, *The Secluded Valley: Tulbagh: 't Land van Waveren, 1700-1804* (Cape Town: Perskor, 1989), pp. 77–78.

146 James Walton, *Homesteads and Villages of South Africa* (Pretoria: Van Schalk, 1952), p. 54.

147 Marais, *Cape Coloured People*, 168.

This led to an increasingly subservient local clergy and, moreover to an under-staffed clergy. The individual freedom on which Reformed Christianity was predicated and the presbyterian form of church organization resulted, in colonial practice, in the freedom of parishioners to exclude slaves, the largest sector of the population, from Christian baptism, fellowship, communion, and, above all, Christian civic status.

The dark chasm that would open between all blacks and the emergent constitutions of the Boer republics in the later nineteenth century ("No equality in church and state") was already an ominous and established fissure in the seven-teenth, eighteenth, and early nineteenth centuries. This fissure first appeared at the household level between Christian master and pagan slave; then, significantly, it was transposed between the Christian settlers and the autochthonous people, and between the settlers and all those of mixed descent — in short, between Christian settlers and all who were being gradually incorporated into the domestic settler economy. Thus, the incorporation of domestic labor, which had its own hege-monic functions and inclusive framework, stopped short of spiritual incorporation in the Reformed colonial household. The real gateway to civic status and the solitary evangelical precept of *De Ethnicorum* was for all intents and purposes ignored. When Anna Steenkamp, a *Voortrekker* woman and niece of the Afrikaner martyr Piet Retief, wrote from Natal in 1844 of why the settlers had quit the colony in the emancipation era, she was pointing to a long tradition: "placing slaves on equal footing with Christians was contrary to the laws of God and the natural distinction of race and religion."[148] The problem was not so much that the slaves had been freed but that they and others had been made equal to "Chris-tians." However, the last word should belong to a slave. Katie Jacobs, an ex-Cape slave who was interviewed in 1910, claimed that her master had not allowed her to be baptized and she had never understood why. Even after emancipation, she and her husband had to go out of their district, to an eccentric pastor in Durbanville, to be baptized.[149]

If, Calvin argued, men and women had only behaved themselves in the beginning, they would never have needed such complicated institutions as church and government, but since they had fallen, they needed both. With respect to the problematic inclusion of slaves within the household, the Cape settlers — in their behavior if not their words (of which there are too few) — repudiated Calvin. Slaves became more important for the settlers' way of life than the Calvinist Christ. If the precepts of neo-Calvinist thinking had not been abandoned at the Cape, the result might have been a moral, free community that transcended slavery and race. That slaves were property as well as persons was tragic for South African

---

[148] As quoted in Elphick and Giliomee, *The Shaping of South African Society*, 507.

[149] Robert Shell, ed., "An Oral History of a Cape Wet-Nurse: Katie Jacobs" *Quarterly Bulletin of the South African Library* 46, 3 (March 1992): 97 and endnote 15.

Reformed Christianity, for in the dramatic tug-of-war between chattel and spirit, that proceeded in every slave-owning household from the inception of the colony, chattel nearly always won, and Christianity, which had enjoyed perhaps its most vital constituency among slaves of the Roman Empire, lost that essential constituency in the Dutch colonial world. This resulted in a religiously and racially bifurcated society.

Moreover, the settlers' attitude toward slaves was easily transmogrified into similar attitudes toward people of mixed race and autochthonous descent, in parallel attempts to deny them any civic status. Whatever the popular conception of the links between Calvinism and racial attitudes in South Africa (and they seem invariably to be erroneously or shallowly associated by certain scholars who dislike the settlers *and* Calvin and wish to taint both with a recursive smear), the physical and spiritual inclination of a substantial section of Cape settlers during this period was away from Calvinism, away from his recommended ecclesiastical government, away from the city, and certainly away from modern European influences, ecclesiastical or otherwise. Christian slave-owning settlers deliberately loosened their theological moorings and drifted into a fog of spiritual declension and rustic isolation on their slave estates, large and small. The rough beast (apologies to Yeats) that emerged in the seventeenth- and eighteenth-century towns and farms of colonial South Africa was not slouching toward Bethlehem (also a village in the Orange Free State), but toward quite another place.

TWELVE

Free at Last
Manumission and the Cape Household

MANUMISSION WAS a most dramatic and profound act. The owner was supposed to strike the slave on the back in a last symbolic gesture of humiliation as the slave was literally propelled into freedom — the last slap that wholly changed the life of the slave.[1] It was also a juridical act in which the property rights in the

---

[1] The individual manumission data were gleaned from the "*Transporten en Scheepenkennis*" (1652 to 1732) and probate documents, MOOC (1658 to 1732); the published Resolutions (1652 to 1744); the Requesten (1713 to 1806); George McCall Theal, *Records of the Cape Colony* (Cape Town: Struik, 1967; hereafter *RCC*), vol. 32: 136–147 (25 June 1827), "Return of Slaves Manumitted before the Registrar and Guardian at Cape Town from the 26 December 1826 to the 24 June 1827"; ibid., 32: 148–151 "Return of Slaves Manumitted before the Assistant Registrars and Guardians in several Country Districts. . . ." (25 June 1827); ibid., 29: 88–93 "Return of Slaves manumitted . . . at Cape Town from the first day of August to the 25 December 1826"; ibid 29: 94–95, "Return of Slaves Manumitted . . . in the Country Districts from the 1st day of August 1826 up to the latest period for which reports have been received" 27 December 1826; and two manumissions from the SO 17/1 Compensation Lists. I have previously published a joint article dealing with 1,075 Cape manumissions based on the data in the published Requesten. That set of data was lost in a move, and the entire task was repeated, this time with the addition of many more variables, such as wealth, age, and a more exact "marital status" of the owner. Much more research time was expended to obtain ages of the slaves. Linking these data to the data on the oceanic and domestic trade was in itself a useful exercise, since it transpired that manumitted slaves had rarely been on the domestic market. The data are satisfyingly complete from 1652 to 1795; missing from 1795 to 1808. One series of aggregated manumissions has been used to supplement the individual-level data, CAD SO 12/11: "Return of all manumissions since the 1st of January 1808 to the third of June, 1824 distinguishing each year and the sex of the persons manumitted." A second set of aggregated data, "Return of the number of both males and females, who have been emancipated . . . 26 April to July 1824," has lower figures; perhaps these were only adult slaves. I have interpolated average rates for the years between 1795 and 1806, where there are partial data or censuses, and also interpolated averages for the years 1829 to 1834, the very eve of emancipation. There are 1,751 coded cases, out of an estimated total of 4,200 Cape manumissions. The aggregated data have been used only in the rates (1652 to 1833) both general and sex- and age-specific. All other calculations using other variables have been drawn from the individual-level data.

slave were surrendered by the owner and the slave assumed a new — but at the Cape, unfortunately not full — legal and civic status and responsibility as a "free black." But manumission is better understood if approached less as a legal event — certainly not as a civil or religious rite — and more as a domestic process beginning and ending in the family. Inter- and intrafamilial relationships and considerations were far more important than all the Christian or legal precepts encouraging, allowing, or defining freedom for ex-slaves (see Figure 12-2).[2]

The Conditions of Manumission

The Cape slave regime was based on Roman Dutch law (South Africa is one of the few areas in which Roman Dutch law is *still* practiced). As Orlando Patterson has noted, Roman law influenced most of the slave holding systems of medieval and early modern Europe.[3] In Roman law, there were two broad categories of manumissions. First there was *manumisso censo*, in which the slave, after being manumitted, was registered on the census as a free citizen — at the Cape, as a burgher. At the Cape, as in ancient Rome, such manumissions were the rarest. Only a handful of manumission petitions out of 1,751 cases directly asked for a *manumisso censo*. The following request filed in August 1723 was made by a member of the slave's family, "that a certain slave born person, baptized Christiaan, procreated with a slave girl by the late Jacobus V . . . , late husband of the present wife of settler [black]smith Jan G . . . , and that therefore Burgher Councilors request that he may be enrolled as a burgher."[4] This type of manumission, bestowing burgher rights on mulatto children, was increasingly challenged as the political power of the burghers waxed and the power of the Company waned. One can see how, from the following petition filed in 1790, in the twilight of the Company's rule, desperate things had become for all free fathers who had married their slaves:

Jan Smok, burgher, more than 20 years ago married Johanna of the Cape, whom he had manumitted, after she had been baptized and confirmed. Various children were the fruits of this lawful marriage, who have been educated to the best of his means in the Christian Reformed religion, and in useful knowledge. In accordance with the requirements of the laws on the subject, he wishes to enroll his eldest son, now sixteen years old, in the list of burghers. For that purpose he obtained from the Cavalry captain, Johannes Munnik, a written order to the Burgher Secretary, Cajus Petrus Slotsboo, desiring that his said son should be enrolled . . . Slotsboo however had repeatedly refused to do so, pretending that he could not do so.

---

2 "The Freed Slave!" Courtesy of the Africana Museum. 61/1234–326 Slavery–1840.

3 Orlando Patterson, *Slavery and Social Death: A Comparative Study* (Cambridge, Mass.: Harvard University Press, 1982), p. 243.

4 Hendrik Carel Vos Leibbrandt, *Requesten (Memorials) 1715–1806* (Cape Town: South African Library, 1989), vol. 1, p. 57 (no. 64 of 1 August 1723/4).

Thereupon, the burgher messenger, Weesburg, called at the petitioner's house, and on behalf of the burgher infantry captain, Petrus Jesse Muller, summoned him to have his son enrolled in the fifth company, or the so-called "free Corps", in which . . . are to be enrolled, all youths, who although free born, have not been born in lawful wedlock. And as neither this son, nor any other of memorialist's children can be classed under this head . . . he believed that he would not be justified in obeying the order of Captain Muller . . . his children, being according to the laws, legitimate, belong to the body of burghers, and by no means to the free corps. But he will not occupy your precious time with the genealogical registers of those who

Figure 12–1. The freed slave, 1840.

are of humbler birth than his own children, and notwithstanding have been entrusted with burgher posts and duties.[5]

The second — and decidedly inferior — category of manumissions under Roman law entailed that the freed slave was not considered a full citizen or burgher, but a *libertus* or *liberta*, a freed person. At the Cape the *liberti* were termed *vrijzwarten*, free blacks. The Roman categories were syllogistically transformed in the Cape colonial setting into racial categories. Since all slaves were *ipso facto* black, freed slaves were termed free blacks even if descended from a European parent.[6]

The early Dutch manumission regulations initially were not framed in the elaborate Roman distinctions of *manumisso censo*, a *free* person versus a *freed* person, but in terms of cultural assimilation. At first the ability to understand, speak, and write Dutch headed the list of manumission desiderata. The test was administered, appropriately enough — considering the number of manumitted slave concubines — by the commissioner of marriage affairs.[7] To "animate" all slaves to learn Dutch, all slaves were forbidden from wearing hats until they had demonstrated their competence in the language. Similarly, only free persons were allowed to ride a horse.[8] Shoes, hats, and horses — symbols of the master class — were important props in the theater of subordination of all slaves in all the Dutch colonies. Subsequent legislation offered manumission as a reward, for example, for reporting arson or infanticide, or for acts of bravery, and in such cases, heathen status or linguistic shortcomings were overlooked.

Manumissions in the Lodge

Manumission regulations for the Lodge slaves stayed remarkably stable from 1685 until 1795, when the British acquired the Lodge slaves as part of their prize for conquest. The first restriction on manumission of Company-owned slaves was made in 1682, when the Company warned that their freed Lodge slaves, even old slaves who became impoverished, would be re-enslaved.[9] This threat was swept away three years later by the visiting patrician commissioner Adriaan van Reede tot Drakenstein. He set up more generous and exact — but still hard to meet —

---

5 Leibbrandt, *Requesten* (no 222. of 19 November 1790), vol. 3, 1159–1161.

6 This status could be contested either during the lifetime of the freeblack, or by his or her descendants. The process of "passing for white" was probably a continuous process from the seventeenth century, but was mostly initiated by fathers of European descent, although this declined after 1808. As indicated elsewhere (see p. 318) Cape women tended to marry *up* the racial hierarchy.

7 J. A. van der Chijs (comp.), *Nederlandsch-Indisch Plakkaatboek, 1602–1811* ('s-Gravenhage: M. Nijhoff, 1885), p. 575, "Van Dieman's Placcaat."

8 Van der Chijs, *Placcaat Boek*, vol. 2, 379, "Verbod voor slaven binnen Bat. op Een paard te zitten."

9 Van der Chijs, *Placcaat Boek*, vol. 1, 184, "Nopens die Vrijstelling van Kompanjieslawe."

conditions of manumission for all Company slaves. As has been noted, he urged that male and female imported slaves be freed after 30 years' service, but only those who "have worked hard and faithfully, who speak Dutch reasonably, who have taken confirmation in the Church *may* be freed with a specific resolution of the Political Council and buy their freedom at the price of 100 Florins, in small installments [*billicke termijne*] if need be." Such slaves also had to demonstrate, moreover, that they could earn their living. "Manumission," van Reede prophetically warned, "should be regarded as a favor, not a right."[10] Since slaves were imported to the Cape at an average age of 16, they could look forward to freedom only in old age, in their forties.

Creole slaves were to have the same rights when they reached the age of 40. Mulatto slaves were dealt with in a special category; male mulattos were to be freed at 25 years of age and female mulattos at 22. The Company required 100 florins recompense for such male slaves and 150 florins for women, who, preferably, should be bought by a Dutch employee who would manumit and marry her. The extra cost for women was based on the greater Company outlay for women's clothes over the years of employment (van Reede had seen to their wardrobes in detail).[11] Van Reede's conditions of freedom were framed along lines of age, racial descent, gender, and faithful service.

The chances of gaining freedom were directly related to social descent — slaves who were of mixed race, with some living relative of European descent, were the most likely to be freed. Considering the low survival rates of all imported Lodge slaves, the requirement of 30 years of service was impossible for most slaves to meet. Only three imported Lodge slaves ever obtained their freedom in this way (one from Madagascar, one from Sri Lanka, and one from Bengal).[12] The chances of an imported slave's satisfying Van Reede's conditions of 30 years of service were therefore minimal, less than .0005 percent.[13] Creole slaves stood a better, but by no means good, chance of freedom: although 4,213 slaves were born in the Lodge, only 103 locally born slaves ever obtained their freedom. Their probability of freedom was .005 percent. However, of the creole slaves who achieved freedom, almost a quarter (21.7 percent) were mulatto. Van Reede had favored mulatto slaves with the age requirements in his manumission regulations, but money still had to be found for their purchase — or an exchange slave had to be provided.

For a Lodge slave who did not directly satisfy the descent and age requirements for a Company manumission, a substitute slave could be provided. The

---

[10] Anna J. Böeseken (ed.), *Belangrike Kaapse Dokumente: Memoriën en Instructiën 1657–1699* (Cape Town: South African State Archives, 1967), vol. 1, 217.

[11] Böeseken, *Memoriën en Instructiën,* vol. 1, 206–207.

[12] Böeseken, *Memoriën en Instructiën,* "Instructie voor den Commandeur . . ." (16 July 1685), vol. 1, 206–207.

[13] Between 1652 and 1795 5,600 slaves were imported to the Lodge.

substitute would be meticulously inspected by the Company surgeons. In 1764 "Anna, daughter of Jacoba of the Cape, a slave in the lodge" wrote to the Council of Policy that "she has for some years served as Matron there and given satisfaction as far as she knows; she now wishes to be emancipated and offers in exchange for herself a male slave, named Cupido of Bengal (certificate of surgeon annexed, which mentions that Cupido is about 12 years old, healthy and strong)."[14] Money or an exchange slave *and* the fee required to post the bond were beyond most Lodge slaves' earning capacity. Each of 36 manumitted mulatto slaves in the Lodge managed to purchase him- or herself or another slave for their freedom. They must have been extraordinary individuals. Most of the other manumitted slaves required the help of a family member who was already out of the Lodge. For the few Lodge slaves who were manumitted with help from close family members, the parental connection was the most powerful (see Figure 12-2).[15]

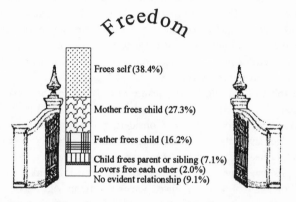

Figure 12–2. Relationship of manumitters to freed Lodge slaves, 1658 to 1795.

Some fathers would not own up to their liaisons with slaves, and therefore they did not help their children by slave mothers to gain their freedom, a fact of Cape life that van Reede's regulations were meant to address. Travelers' anecdotal evidence suggest that sexual activity between slave women and free men was extremely high in the Lodge, but it is impossible to establish the true incidence of miscegenation in the Lodge over the whole period.

First-generation Lodge slaves had a negligible chance of freedom because few survived, second-generation slaves had a slightly better chance, and mulatto slaves had the best chance. Women and children fared a lot better, and female children had a better chance for freedom than male children. Indeed, the possibility of freedom for male slaves as a whole was small. Mulatto women had the best chance,

---

[14] Leibbrandt, *Requesten* (no. 136 of 1764), vol. 1, 11.
[15] Shell, "Manucomb"; N = 108.

but only if their fathers were willing to step forward and acknowledge parentage. Altogether, only 108 imported, creole, and mulatto Company slaves were ever freed, fewer than one per year.

The Conditions of Manumission for Privately Owned Slaves

One would expect that the manumission process would be even more meticulously covered for those slaves who were privately owned, the majority of Cape slaves. Since each manumission changed the numerical proportion of free and unfree in the overall population, one would also expect that the settlers (who feared freed slaves) and the Church (which was obliged to look after indigent freed slaves) would have had an active role in the regulation of all private manumissions.

The Obsequium

Until 1731, the Cape was governed from Batavia and derived all its manumission directives from the early Statutes of India (1619).[16] Duties and deference from the manumitted slave and their kin to all members of the family who initiated or allowed the manumission were extremely important:

Those who are given their freedom out of slavery remain beholden, as well as their children and descendants, to show all honour, respect and reverence to their free lords and mistresses and indeed to all their [lords' and mistresses'] children and descendants.

And if any freed person is found who injures with word or deed or in any way, that person will be chained for life, or, according to circumstance, be rigorously punished.

In like manner the freed slave is beholden to their emancipators, their children and further descendants in the event of their becoming impoverished to support them [if necessary] by a monthly taxation of the justice.[17]

These duties of manumitted slaves to the families who emancipated them are nearly universal codes in all slave societies. (Such duties are termed the *obsequium* in Roman law. Orlando Patterson prefers the Arabic word *wala*.[18]) The Cape manumission requests reveal that such duties were sometimes expected but were not insisted upon. The texts of the requests reveal only one case so framed: Lijsje, freed in 1714 in the depths of one of the worst depressions, was "enjoined always to honor and respect the doers of this good deed."[19] Many slaves were required to

---

[16] Specifically, "Van Diemen's Placcaat" (1642) and also subsequent Batavian and local Cape statutes (plakkaaten); Van der Chijs, *Placcaat boek*, vol. 1, 572–576.

[17] Van der Chijs, "Van Diemen's Placcaat," vol. 1, 575.

[18] Patterson, *Slavery and Social Death*, 242.

[19] DO: "Transporten en Scheepenkennis," n.p., no. 245 (8 May 1714), "Moet altijd de vriende en Familie sal moeten erneeren en respecten . . . diese weldaad."

serve their masters or mistresses from periods ranging from a year to their owner's lifetime. One wonders about the quality of freedom in such cases, for instance, when Casper Schalker, a burgher, insisted that his slave, Thomas van Boegies, should be manumitted "on condition that he shall remain in his service until the death of memorialist."[20] Owners sometimes candidly admitted in their wording that such conditions implied an existence considerably short of freedom. One slave, Lena, was told that she would be "fully free" only after ten years' service to the widow Alders and her children.[21] However, most manumitted slaves (88 percent) had no service contract at all and were really free when manumitted. No court cases were ever instituted against a free black who had not performed his or her obligations. It is quite clear that most manumitted slaves left their owners' families behind to enjoy real freedom (see Figure 12-3).[22]

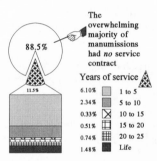

The overwhelming majority of manumissions had *no* service contract

88.5%

11.5%

Years of service

6.10%	1 to 5
2.34%	5 to 10
0.33%	10 to 15
0.51%	15 to 20
0.74%	20 to 25
1.48%	Life

Figure 12–3. Slaves' years of service after manumission, 1658 to 1828.

Religion and the Role of the Church

The close relationship that the Company Lodge had always had with the Dutch Reformed Church, fell away in 1795. Up to that point the Church was a prime actor in the manumission process, especially for the Lodge slaves. The role of the Cape Reformed Church in the manumission process was evangelical and charitable. On the one hand, it was the duty of every *predikant* and officer of the Church to exhort parishioners to instruct their slaves in the doctrines of Christianity and also to inform them that a baptized slave had certain qualified rights, such as not to be sold to heathens or Jews. There was also the delicately phrased expectation from the Synod of Dordt delegates that baptized (and, after 1770, confirmed) Christian

---

[20] Leibbrandt, *Requesten* (no. 115 of 1761), vol. 3, 1090.
[21] CAD CJ 3079 (28 June 1729), no. 92, folio 41.
[22] Shell, "Manucomb."

slaves should "enjoy equal rights of liberty with other Christians." However, this exception was never prevalent in the Cape, nor in any other Dutch colony.[23] Certain Cape historians have claimed that Christianity was a certain passport to freedom, but this was not the case. Clasina of Bengal, the single slave who brought suit against her owner claiming her freedom on grounds of baptism, lost her case decisively, much to relief of all nineteenth-century Reformed Cape slave owners.[24]

On the other hand, in its charitable aspect, the *Diaconij* (Church Council) of the Church had to provide the wherewithal if a freed slave, even an unbaptized freed slave, fell on hard times. It can be readily appreciated that the Church's evangelical and charitable aspects were in conflict. The more successful evangelical Christianity was, among the slaves, the more pressure would fall on the *Diaconij*'s poor fund if the slaves did not succeed (in a material sense) as freed persons. The Church complained to the Company about the inadequacy of the bond to be posted since freed slaves were turning to the church in times of need. The first mention of a bond for privately owned slaves bound for freedom was in 1708. The date is significant, for it fell only a few years after the Cape slaves enjoyed a numerical majority of the population and the patrician Van der Stel dynasty had been overthrown in the settler revolt.[25] After 1706, the free blacks no longer enjoyed the preferential protection they had under Van der Stel, who had baptized and freed many of his own slaves. It is entirely unsurprising that stricter restrictions on manumissions should therefore follow hard on the successful settler revolt. After 1708, owners intending to free slaves had to promise that the slave "would not become a burden to the poor fund for ten years."[26] This regulation was not strictly observed, however, and owners were reminded again in 1722. After that year, in addition to the bond, two guarantors were required for all manumission applications.[27]

In 1770 the Statutes of India were comprehensively revised and sent to the Cape. They specifically framed regulations for possible manumission if one parent was of European descent, a circumstance that had long been true for many Lodge slaves.[28] Similar regulations were reissued in 1777, with the understanding that

---

[23] This aspect is dealt with comprehensively in Chapter 11.

[24] Theal, *RCC*, "Letter from Sir John Cradock, to Lord Bathurst," 10: 4, 45–60;

[25] "De Statuten van Indië aan de Kaap . . . ," C. Spoelstra, *Bouwstoffen voor de Geschiedenis der Nederduitsch-Geref. Kerken in Zuid Afrika* (Amsterdam: Hollandsch-Afrikaansche Uitgewers-Maatscappij, 1906–1907, vol. 2, p. 607 (19 April 1708).

[26] Isobel Eirlys Edwards, *Towards Emancipation: A Study in South African Slavery* (Cardiff: University of Wales Press, 1942), p. 29. I have been unable to find the original document in *Resolutions* or in the *Placcaat Boek*; neither of these sources are complete transcriptions.

[27] Anna J. Böeseken et al. (eds.), *Suid-Afrikaanse Argriefstukke: Resolusies van die Politieke Raad* (Cape Town: Cape Times, 1957–1975; hereafter *Resolutions*), vol. 6, p. 208 (29 September 1722); Van der Chijs, *Plakkaat Boek*, vol. 2, p. 94.

[28] Theal, *RCC*, "Extracts from the Statutes of India, Chapter respecting slaves" Article 8, 9: 131–132.

the bond would now be 50 Rixdollars. Letters of freedom would not be issued before the *Diaconij* receipt for 50 Rixdollars was shown to the secretary of the Council of Policy.[29] On the other hand, they could be waived "under certain circumstances." Church and state thus worked hand in glove when it came to manumission. In the contest between the evangelical impulses of the Reformed tradition and the practical constraints of the poor fund, the poor fund won. Mentzel remarked in the 1780s that the Dutch Reformed Church was built from "surplus funds of the poor fund" so one may conclude that few freed slaves drew on the fund even though the bond kept being raised, ostensibly because of pressures on the poor fund from freed slaves.[30] Only in 1812 was the last ecclesiastical bar to freedom lifted. The Church, although nominally standing for the equality of all Christians, was primarily responsible for ever greater financial restrictions on manumissions and was also the direct beneficiary of thousands of Rixdollars from all Cape slaves, even Muslims, who sought their freedom.

Manumission as a Civil Right

In some slave societies, purchasing freedom was a public right. In Cuba and other areas of Spanish America, this right was called *coartación*. Under this system, accepted and formally codified by the Spanish crown in the eighteenth century, a slave had the right to demand that his or her appraised value be publicly declared by a court of law. The slave was allowed to pay that amount, in installments if need be.[31] Although some historians have suggested that Cape slaves always enjoyed a similar right if they satisfied certain conditions, in practice this applied only to Lodge slaves; the custom was not formalized at the Cape until 1826 in British Empire-wide legislation. It was eventually and very reluctantly instituted, with many provisos, despite the protests of many distraught Cape slave owners. The Reverend W. Wright, the abolitionist writer, noted in 1831: "When the 19th Ordinance was first published at the Cape, no part of it excited a greater outcry than the compulsory emancipation clause. The Burgher senate refused to proclaim the ordinance in the usual manner, and it required all the firmness of the Lieutenant Governor, General Bourke, to have the law carried into execution."[32]

---

[29] Spoelstra, *Bouwstoffen* (3 June 1777), vol. 2, 313; for a case of exceptional circumstances, see ibid. (1 December 1788), vol. 2, 334.

[30] Otto Friederich Mentzel, *A Complete and Authentic Geographical and Topographical Description . . .*, trans. G. V. Marais and J. Hoge, rev. ed. (Cape Town: Van Riebeeck Society, 1944), vol. 1, p. 122.

[31] David W. Cohen and Jack P. Greene (eds.), *Neither Slave nor Free* (Baltimore: Johns Hopkins University Press, 1972), pp. 85, 285.

[32] Ordinance 19, as quoted in William Wright, *Slavery at the Cape of Good Hope* (New York: Negro Universities Press, 1969 reprint), pages vi and 19.

This strikes one as a most important difference between slavery at the Cape and Luso-Iberian slavery. Because if manumission was *not* a public right at the Cape until 1826, the details of each manumission transaction lay in the domestic sphere, a matter of freedom to be worked out in detail between owner and slave. Up until 1826 the slave had no other recourse but to appeal to the most generous impulses of familial paternalism. Dependency then, always preceded and often followed freedom.[33]

Despite the increasing manumission bond, the very existence of the process of manumission suggests that slavery was not a closed system, that there was hope of escape from slavery. But the legal background, on its own, does not illuminate the practical process of manumission. The legislation dealing with manumission, just as in other slave regimes, was not an important guide to the process itself; indeed, most manumission laws were irrelevant to the process, as is revealed in the text of the actual manumission requests. Others have made this point before. Stuart Schwartz, an historian writing of seventeenth- and eighteenth-century Brazil, found that slave codes "provided virtually no guide whatsoever to the nature or reality of the Brazilian regime ... even the Brazilian municipal codes hardly mentioned manumission."[34] Legal codes, although they shed light on what the authorities *ideally* expected of owners and slaves, do not provide insights into the behavior of slave owners or explain slave manumissions.

The Company directors expected that the way the Company manumitted its own slaves in the Lodge would serve as an example to the colonists. This was not the case. As the free population of the colony became more and more diverse, the manumission regulations for Company slaves became less and less relevant for the slave population that was privately owned.

The Process of Manumission

The process of manumitting a single slave involved a minimum of two parties: the slave and the owner; the owner could be a person or an institution such as the Company or the Church. Eight percent of all manumissions were institutional. As manumission stipulations changed, individual manumissions were ratified by the Council of Policy, then by the Reformed Church, then, after 1795, by the local authorities. An example of the simplest type of individual manumission reads: "Johannes Henricus Blankenberg, junior merchant and secretary to the Orphan

---

[33] Robert C.-H. Shell, "Rangton of Bali: the Short Life and Material Possessions of a Cape Slave," *Kronos* 18 (1991): 1-6; see also *Kronos* 19 (1992): 161–199 for subsequent correspondence.

[34] Stuart Schwartz, "The Manumission of Slaves in Colonial Brazil: Bahia, 1684–1745," *Hispanic American Historical Review* 54 (November 1974): 610.

Chamber, wishes to manumit his slave girl, Lea of the Cape."[35] Sometimes the manumission transaction involved more than two parties, for apart from the slave and the owner, there was often a third person, whom I call a "manumitter," who purchased the slave from the owner for no other purpose than to free him or her. However, in most cases (61.5 percent) the owner was the manumitter as well.

The state had to be assured by either the manumitter or the owner that the manumitted slave would not become a burden on the Church poor fund. After 1708, two guarantors, usually relatives, were required for this. A compliant example of such a transaction reads: "Sara van Brakel, widow of the merchant and Dispenser, wishes to manumit her slave Damon of Bengal, offers as sureties herself and Christoffel Brand [her son]."[36] The manumission process increasingly came to resemble the baptism ceremony, which also required two witnesses. In the Cape slave society, manumission was a similar, civic rite of passage. Even for the manumission of a single slave, several other persons might be involved. Of all 1,751 manumissions analyzed here, however, most (51.6 percent) were part of family-related multiple manumissions (see Figure 12-4).[37]

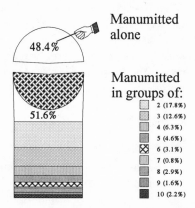

Figure 12–4. Distribution of slaves manumitted singly and in groups, 1652 to 1827.

The Crude Manumission Rate

Most slave societies had very low and, some have suggested, demographically insignificant rates of manumission. This was not the case at the Cape. The crude manumission rate, defined as the number of manumissions per 1,000 slaves per

---

[35] Leibbrandt, *Requesten* (no. 130 of 1768/70), vol. 1, 105.
[36] Leibbrandt, *Requesten* (no. 112 of 1767/8), vol. 1, 104.
[37] Shell, "Manucomb"; N = 1,751.

year, began in the seventeenth century at about five slaves per thousand per year and steadily declined until it was just above one-tenth of 1 percent of the total population in the years before the general emancipation of all slaves in 1834. However, this rate, small as it appears, had considerable demographic consequences, especially in the early period, from 1652 to 1708. The manumission rate also affected the census, as slaves were removed from the slave listings in one year and were listed as members of the free population in the next.

The crude Cape manumission rate fell below the high Brazilian manumission rates, as measured in different areas and periods by Stuart Schwartz, Mary Karasch, and Robert Wayne Selenes. The Cape manumission rate was higher than most anglophone Caribbean colonies, for example, the rate of Jamaica, as measured by Barry Higman. It was also higher than the very low rates of the antebellum South as revealed in the census of 1850. The Cape rate was, however, lower than those of other Dutch colonies of Suriname and Curaçao, as measured by Rosemary Brana-Shuta and W. E. Renkema. Suriname, long regarded as a brutal slave society, freed its slaves more readily than Curaçao, renowned for its moderate treatment of slaves. South Africa emerges as having the worst manumission record of all the Dutch colonies (see Figure 12-5).[38]

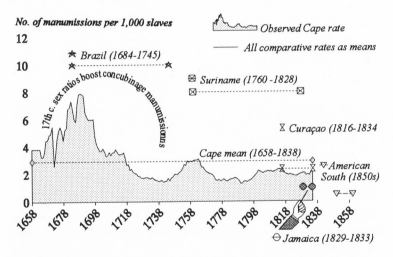

Figure 12–5. Comparative crude manumission rates, 1658 to 1858.

[38] Shell, "Manucomb" (sse page 676); Brazil: Stuart Schwartz, "The Manumission of Slaves in Colonial Brazil: Bahia, 1684–1745," *Hispanic American Historical Review* 54 (November 1974): 610; Suriname: Rosemary Brana-Shuta, "Approaching Freedom: The Manumission of Slaves in Suriname, 1760-1828," *Slavery and Abolition* 10 3 (December, 1989): 44-45; Curaçao: W. E. Renkema, *Het Curaçaose Plantagebedrijf in de negentiende eeuw* (Zutphen: Walburg Press, 1981), p. 120; American South: Robert Fogel and Stanley Engerman, *Time on the Cross.* 2 vols. (Boston: Brown and Company, 1975) 1: 150-1.

The Gendered Aspect of Manumission

The Cape findings show that the manumission process more often involved the freeing of female slaves rather than male slaves (see Figure 12-5).[39] This is especially astonishing since male slaves outnumbered female slaves in the population at risk (all enslaved persons) by six to one in some periods. Also, the manumission of female slaves, especially adult women and mothers, was a sacrifice from the slave owner's perspective, because all offspring of such slaves followed the mother into freedom. Young slaves, even a pregnant woman's child in utero, were considered free along with the mother. It is therefore not surprising that the proportion of female slaves manumitted fell off after 1808, when Cape slave owners were cut off from the oceanic slave trade. Slave women then became the main source of supply for all future slaves in the colony, and they were not freed as frequently (see Figures 12-6 and 12-7).[40]

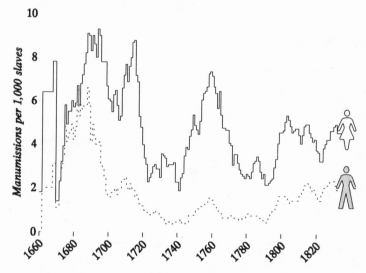

Figure 12–6. Manumission rates of adult female and male slaves, 1660 to 1830.

The early manumitted adult female slaves (1658 to 1713) were concubines (and often wives) of the numerous free bachelors at the Cape. Compared with the later, nineteenth-century female slaves, these early slaves (and their children) enjoyed greatly enhanced opportunities for freedom through their domestic connections and their conjugal liaisons with their owners. The first recorded manumission at the Cape was such an example: "Maria from Bengal, slave belonging to the sick-comforter Pieter van der Stael, sold into freedom to Jan Sacharias from

---

[39] Shell, "Manucomb."
[40] Shell, "Manucomb"; "Popucape."

Amsterdam on condition that she becomes his legal wife."[41] Jan Frederick Peensch approached the Council of Policy in 1787 for permission to free the slave Catherina of the Cape, who had been given to him by Pieter Hacker, the second in command, on condition that he marry her. Her six children came along with the gift, and Peensch promised to instruct the children, "whose father he is," and free them.[42]

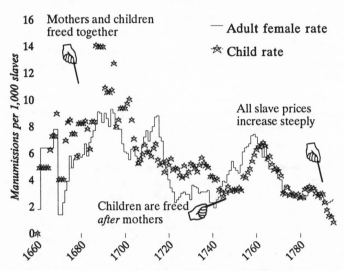

Figure 12–7. Manumission rates for women and children, 1658 to 1795.

From the start of the process, one of the ironies of manumission was clearly evident — only through the slave's most complete conjugal incorporation into the family was the greatest chance of civic freedom achieved. Most female slaves in the Cape up to 1834 were domestic servants and lodged within the owner's house. They were by far the closest slaves — in terms of physical propinquity, emotional ties, and domesticity — to the slave owners and their biological families. Up to 1808, these women often served as their nannies, or wet nurses.[43] Women slave owners, too, when they became independent through widowhood or divorce, had opportunities to free their most favored slaves, who were invariably female domestic slaves.

---

[41] Anna J. Böeseken, *Slaves and Free Blacks at the Cape, 1658–1700* (Cape Town: Tafelburg, 1977), p. 124.

[42] Leibbrandt, *Requesten* (no. 83 of 1787), vol. 3, 933.

[43] Mentzel, *Description*, vol. 1, 108, 122; this is more amply discussed in Chapter 10.

The Age Composition of Manumitted Slaves

One of the first objections scholars made to Frank Tannenbaum's use of manumission as an index of the openness of slave societies was that slave owners mostly manumitted old slaves who were past their productive years. Detractors of Tannenbaum argued that such manumissions were in fact cynical ejections of worn out slaves into penury — evidence not of the openness of the society, but rather of the callousness of a regime that would permit such patently fraudulent donations of liberty. Stewart Schwartz found, however, that in only 22 of the 1,176 Brazilian manumission *cartas* (2 percent) was the advanced age of the slave mentioned. At the Cape, up until 1795, manumission of old slaves was even more rare. Only 12 manumissions mention old slaves. Moreover, 9 of those slaves obtained their freedom not through their owner's callous action, but at the request of their own free family, who purchased them in order to free them. Three mothers-in-law obtained their freedom in this way.

Perhaps accusations about manumitting old slaves derive entirely from travelers. In his four volumes on the Cape slave society, Mentzel mentioned manumission three times. One mention was the following anecdote about the moving case of a 100-year-old slave:

The old slave was one of the first to be brought over to the Cape from Madagascar, in his younger days he had a daughter by a slave girl, who belonged to a wealthy burgher in the city. This daughter had saved about 24 Rixdollars with which she bought her father's freedom; *his owner gladly agreed,* as [the slave] was very old. The daughter then took her aged father with her [to the town] intending to care for him until his death, but he had hardly been with her for four weeks before time began to hang heavily on his hands and he returned to his former master. Since he was now a freeman, he hired himself as a shepherd at a wage of 12 Rixdollars a year, but he only lived a little while longer and so had to be buried by his former master.[44]

In 1764 one widow, herself aging, left one of her young male slaves, Corydon, to her newly freed old slave, Lea, "in order to earn a living for her." Once Lea died, Corydon was to be sold "according to his own choice," with the "purchase money to be distributed among those who had buried Lea."[45]

Relatively high numbers of children were manumitted in the last decade of the seventeenth century and the entire eighteenth century. In contrast, the early seventeenth-century material, which approximates the changing composition of the slave population, reflects a pattern in which adult and child slaves were manumitted in approximately the same proportions as they represented in the population at risk. The explanation for the relatively high proportion of adult manumissions in the early period was the manumission of concubines for marriage during the first 50 years, when there were few European women marriage partners. Thereafter,

---

[44] Mentzel, *Description,* vol. 3, 163 (emphasis added).
[45] Leibbrandt, *Requesten* (no. 44 of 1766), vol. 4, 1192.

the greater proportion of children in the manumitted group has a single explanation: slave families (that is, mothers and children) were manumitted in toto; children followed their mothers into freedom. In the later colonial period, the adult slave population was composed mainly of imported men who were rarely manumitted.

After 1808 it appears that greater percentages of both male and female slaves were manumitted when they were older. Why? With the supply of imported slaves cut off, all Cape owners were aware that the generous impulse of manumitting fertile slave women and their children could no longer be afforded. During this period, no more old slaves were actually manumitted than before; instead the emphasis should be placed on the dwindling practice of manumitting women and children. Thus, although the same proportion of old slaves was manumitted after 1808, they now comprised a larger proportion of all manumitted slaves. Two benchmark cases (Clasina of Bengal, 1809, and Steijntje of the Cape, 1807 to 1821) persuaded the settlers that they could turn down manumission requests made by women and children on grounds of baptism or miscegenation. These cases sealed the fate for female slaves and their offspring, cutting them off from manumission in the final era of Cape slavery (see Figure 12-8).[46]

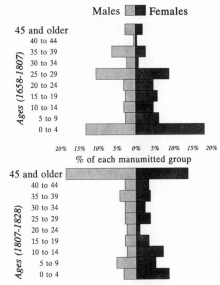

Figure 12–8. Population pyramids of manumitted slaves, before and after abolition.

One significant finding about Cape manumissions is that both young women and young men achieved freedom through manumission much more easily when the slave trade was active. This might also explain why Brazil had a high manumission rate in the nineteenth century, when the slave trade to that area was still active,

[46] Shell, "Manucomb."

while the American South had a low manumission rate after 1808, when most importation of slaves to that area had ceased. The link between the oceanic trade and high manumission rates, which Orlando Patterson has hinted at, was clear at the Cape. Almost a third of the manumissions were requested by patrician Cape Town slave owners, who were also involved in the oceanic slave trade. There are roughly three periods in the demographic history of manumission at the Cape: 1658 to 1685, which was characterized by manumission of a sexual partner and then marriage; 1686 to 1808, characterized by the practice of manumitting wet nurses and their children; and 1809 to 1834, characterized by the manumission of older slaves, male and female.

The Domicile of the Owner

Besides gender and descent, other factors affected Cape slaves' chances of being freed. A primary constraint on their freedom was the domicile of their owner.[47] Cape manumissions were overwhelmingly of urban slaves, whereas the bulk of the slave force after 1745 was rural. Although there is a large proportion of "unknowns" (15 percent), these include repatriating owners from Batavia who had no recoverable address. Such slaves were probably urban, albeit in Indonesia, since they had been servants in Jakarta. Moreover, some Cape rural owners sold their slaves to an urban person for the purpose of manumission. For this analysis such manumissions were conservatively coded as "rural," although urban manumitters initiated the process. For example, the "titular merchant" and magistrate of Swellendam exchanged his slave Hanna of the Cape to Cape Town-based Hendrik Looff, a German soldier who was a dispatch rider for the Company, shuttling between Swellendam and Cape Town. The rural magistrate insisted that another slave be given in exchange. (This is also the only recorded case of a private owner insisting on an exchange slave.) Looff, who had been wounded in a war and was thereby handicapped and also poor, duly provided a 12-year-old slave, Pieter of Mozambique. He married the emancipated Hanna in 1799.[48] Based on the data and the tenor of such individual cases as these, the probability of a rural slave's being freed appears to have been negligible. As the colony became more and more rural, the rate of manumission for the entire colony correspondingly decreased.

Why was manumission so overwhelmingly urban? This is a most complex question. Part of the explanation lies in the identity of the urban manumitting

---

[47] The *Requesten* do not always mention domicile. Each owner's address therefore had to be independently researched, most commonly with a link to a property transaction in the Deeds Office.

[48] Leibbrandt, *Requesten* (no. 163 of 1787), vol. 2, 722; J. Hoge, "Personalia of Germans at the Cape, 1652–1806," *Archives Year Book* 9 (1946): 246, s.v. "Looff."

owners. Most free blacks after 1706 decided to establish themselves in Cape Town, where there were more opportunities to make a living. In the port, they monopolized the barge and lighter traffic, fishing, candle making, and small retailing. From that humble economic base they manumitted the most slaves per capita of any group. The free blacks manumitted an astonishing 18 percent of all the manumitted slaves. Company employees stationed in the port were responsible for 30 percent of the manumissions; the Company itself manumitted 6.5 percent of all slaves from its urban Lodge. The burghers, who owned almost 93 percent of all slaves at the Cape by 1795, were responsible for only 33.8 percent of all manumissions, and these burghers were mostly of the patrician class, domiciled in the port (see Figure 12-9).[49]

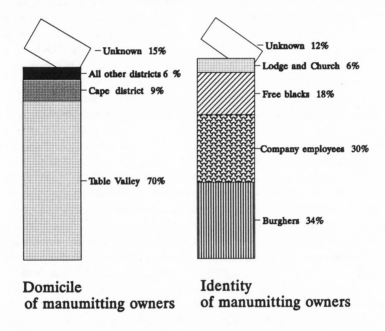

Domicile of manumitting owners

Identity of manumitting owners

Figure 12–9. Domicile and identity of manumitting owners, 1658 to 1830.

Wealth and Manumission

One might think that wealthy slave-owning families would be the most likely to free their slaves, since the manumission of a slave was a considerable financial sacrifice. In fact, this was true; the wealthiest colonists did manumit the most

---

[49] Shell, "Manucomb."

slaves.[50] Wealth is also highly correlated with age (age is the single best predictor of wealth even today); the average age of manumitting slave owners at the Cape was understandably high, 55 years. Many slaves were manumitted by testamentary disposition after their owners died. Such owners enjoyed their slaves' services until the very last moment. Since not all colonists made wills, there were some dramatic deathbed manumissions as the owners struggled to make their wishes concerning their slaves known to relatives who did not want to hear them. Jan Abel Beck, the son-in-law of Catherina Erasmus, the deceased widow of Roelof van de Burg, objected to the manumission of the creole slave nurse Jannetje of the Cape, and persuaded the heirs to place her on the inventory to be sold, instead of freeing her. Witnesses had to be called to swear that on the night of the widow's death she had called in sympathetic family members and her notarial agent, Johan Knockers, for no other purpose than to free Jannetje. The bedroom had been crowded with witnesses, one of whom had exclaimed when Knockers arrived: "Cousin, look! There is Monsieur Knockers." The agent went to her bedside and was told between coughs, "I am getting weak. [You are] to take care and put on paper that after [my] death, [my] slave Jannetje was to be manumitted."[51]

Heirs and relatives in a few cases felt cheated and challenged manumissions in court. Since there was only a slight presumption toward freedom, the courts did not routinely — or promptly — find in favor of such deathbed-manumitted slaves. Maria Pietersz wrote in her will in 1717, regarding the manumission of her slaves Abraham, Isaac, and Jacob, that each slave was to receive in addition to "complete freedom" considerable money when they came of age. The executor of her estate, Jan Rogier van Morselen, was to receive for his trouble in handling the estate a female slave named Venus van Bengal and a fishing seine. But "for some reason or another" Jan Rogier delayed the manumissions until his own death 22 years later.[52] The executors of Cape estates had to cope, after all, with the living.

Almost exactly one quarter (25.2 percent) of the manumitting owners successfully freed their slaves through testamentary manumission. The death of an owner also gave the survivors an opportunity to manumit slaves. Such was the case when Lucia of Batavia, the recent widow of the slave trader Domingo Rosa, petitioned the Council of Policy in 1780 to manumit her slave, Joseph of Batavia, who, she explained, was also "her brother."[53] When one considers the high

---

[50] The wealth variable was extremely carefully researched; it is more correctly seen as ranked rather than interval data. In the "poorest" category (value = 1) were people with no possessions or jobs. Recently freed slaves fell into this category, as did convicts, and convicted criminals. The "poor" category (value = 2) included people who had recently arrived in the colony or ex-slaves who had been free for some time. In the median-value group (5) were people with landed assets. The wealthiest owners (value = 9) were people who had estates worth more than 100,000 florins.

[51] Leibbrandt, *Requesten* (no. 108 of 31 July 1768/70), vol. 1, 424–425.

[52] Leibbrandt, *Requesten* (no. 82 of 1749), vol. 2, 633–634.

[53] Leibbrandt, *Requesten* (no. 78 of 18 November 1780), vol. 2, 694.

correlation between age and wealth, this is more than enough to account for the highly skewed wealth distribution among owners who manumitted their slaves (see Figure 12-10).[54]

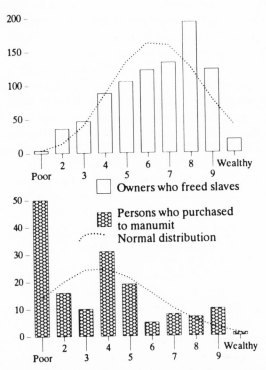

Figure 12–10. Wealth distribution of manumitting owners, 1658 to 1831.

The poorer groups were more highly represented among the manumitters, those who purchased slaves from another owner for the purpose of manumission. Some of these manumitters were so poor that they could not formalize the manumission through sureties and bonds, and the slaves — though technically bound for freedom — could easily find themselves back in a state of slavery. This happened in 1782 when the free black man Jephta of the Cape died intestate and in debt. Consequently, his wife and children, whom he had purchased "some years ago" from Maria Elisabeth Louw for the purpose of manumission, were to be sold as slaves by the Orphan Masters to defray his debt. Maria Louw, a widow and Jephta's former owner, generously paid the debts so that the astonished family could remain together in freedom.[55]

---

54 Shell, "Manucomb."
55 Leibbrandt, *Requesten* (no. 31 of 1782), vol. 2, 699.

Creole Slaves and Manumission

Imported or first-generation slaves had an extremely low chance of being manumitted. In contrast, creole or second-, third-, or fourth-generation slaves enjoyed greatly enhanced chances of manumission throughout the entire period of slavery at the Cape and mulatto slaves always enjoyed the highest probability of gaining freedom. There were several reasons for this pattern. First, all creole slaves spoke the same language as their owners and were therefore culturally closer to their owners. Second, many creole slaves had been born in the house of their owners, a fact of enormous sentimental importance in the paternalist way of thinking. A phrase that crops up repeatedly in the manumission requests is "*in zijn huijs gebore*" (born in his house). This carried little weight, however, in the rural, patriarchal households. Third, mulatto slaves were both somatically and often biologically closer to their owners. A number were the direct offspring of the colonists themselves. These were the true *famuli* — slaves *and* children of the family. Hence there was an element of descent involved in deciding who was to be freed. But such lineage slavery, in which the slave was fully incorporated into the family and thereby became free, did not predominate at the Cape. Only urban mulatto slaves stood a reasonable chance of manumission.

One interesting finding is that manumitting owners were predominantly (69.7 percent) first-generation colonists. Part of this population, of course, was first-generation free blacks, but even excluding them, immigrant colonists from Europe (especially from Germany) were much more likely to manumit than were second- or third-generation colonists. These immigrant manumitters were mostly German bachelors, and most were acquiring a bride by freeing their slave. Stephanus Beijer van Wurzburg, a soldier who claimed to have "built the Church organ at the Cape and looked after it for many years," manumitted Maria Amelia of the Cape and her children Stephanus and Cornelia. He married her four years later; the children were his own.[56] Whether such manumissions involved freedom or another type of bondage is not evident. The offspring of such manumissions did not always enjoy full civic equality. Understandably, as the rate of immigration slowed down, so, too, did this type of manumission (see Figure 12-11).[57]

---

[56] Leibbrandt, *Requesten* (no. 97 of 1754), vol. 1, 88; Hoge, "Personalia of Germans at the Cape," 30; C. Pama (comp.) and C. C. de Villiers (ed.), *Geslagregisters van die ou Kaapse Families* (Cape Town: Balkema, 1981), vol. 1, p. 43.

[57] Shell, "Manucomb"; N = 557.

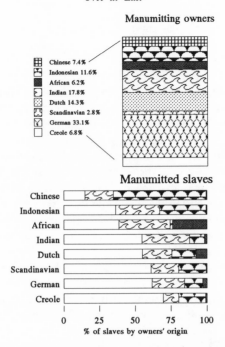

Figure 12–11. The somatic factor in who manumitted whom, 1658 to 1828.

The Promise of Freedom

Freed male slaves at the Cape began their freedom with a combination of formidable disadvantages. Among these were prejudice, poverty, the inability to obtain credit, and also the extreme difficulty of obtaining gainful employment in the Cape's oscillating and insecure economy. In the port, thousands of European Company employees were salaried and secure in their jobs but the Company was not an option for free blacks. The "poor whites" in the town, in particular, saw to it that free blacks were excluded from most occupations as early as 1727. Burgher councilors even forbade free blacks to sell such pathetic sundries as "toast and cakes" on the streets.[58] Excluded from agriculture by their inability to get credit, the freed male slaves were literally driven into the sea for employment: they were left with the precarious occupation of fishing the most dangerous waters of the South Atlantic, a part of the ocean that was (and is) a graveyard for ships of even the most experienced maritime nations. Although some freed slaves had to be helped by the poor fund of the Church, most found succor among the sympathetic free black Muslim community, many of whom owned slaves themselves and were regular manumitters. Considering the constraints against the freed slaves, the

[58] Leibbrandt, *Requesten* (no. 4 of 1727), vol. 1, 60–61.

cultural achievements of their community (which includes a sardonic sense of humour) were monumental.

The promise of freedom implicit in the existence of the process of manumission was from the outset of the Cape slave society contingent on the relationship between owner and slave in the household. Manumission in the public sphere — as a civil right — existed for only a few years (1831 to 1834). A Dutch visitor to the Cape in 1806, H. G. Nahuys van Burgst lamented this, interestingly, on racial grounds: "I have not yet spoken of those slaves who are blond and white and in this respect not inferior to the European complexion. Having already told you that in general the treatment of the slaves at the Cape is neither stern nor inhuman, I must alas! now declare, to the shame of the Capenaars, that I have gained the impression that the white slaves are dealt with too cruelly. In the Indies the most miserly, most inhuman resident would not dare to keep in slavery, however much he might desire it, any slave-child having but the semblance of blondness and by this causing surmise that it has a European or white father, but at the Cape the owner is so devoid of feeling that only very seldom does he grant his white domestic slaves their freedom. The child of a white slave-woman, born to a white European father is not only regarded as a slave, but there is not even a law in his favor compelling the colonist to let the European father have his child at a fair price."[59]

The Lodge, which reported European slaves as early as 1685, again served as a forerunner for the general slave population, by the eve of abolition, slave owners who fathered their slaves were leaving them in slavery. Manumission at the Cape is better regarded as a personalized and therefore domestic concession of freedom kept firmly in the private sphere, which over time, become more difficult to achieve for each slave. Despite all the legislation defining slaves' access to freedom, the process of manumission always began in the family. This was so whether manumission began in the waterfront shack of a free black fisherman who sought to free a member of his family, in the Cape Town cottage of a lonely German artisan bachelor who wanted a bride, or in a patrician house overlooking the Table Valley, as a grandiloquent deathbed gesture. Freedom was not a right conferred by the state, but a favor granted within the household (including the Lodge). It was a fact (shocking as it is) that the slave who stood the best chance of manumission was the slave whose owner was also his or her father. But whatever the relationship between the slaves and the ones who tried to gain freedom for them, the groundwork for manumission was always laid in the family.

---

[59] H. G. Nahuys van Burgst, *Adventures at the Cape of Good Hope in 1806* (Cape Town: Friends of the South African library, 1993), 82-3.

THIRTEEN

Conclusions
Slavery, the Authoritarian Cape Family
and Recursive Identities

SLAVERY, NOT THE FRONTIER and certainly not the process of industrialization, shaped South Africa. Whether those later processes made South Africa worse or better is an important but unanswered question. Slavery began in South Africa in an urban context in 1652 and was exported to the frontier by a process of resource alienation (land and surface water) and enforced labor acquisition. South African settlers developed a two-tiered system of slavery and serfdom that over time coalesced into what I have termed cadastral paternalism, in which rights to persons' labor were informally passed on to the next "free" generation when land was legally transferred. This system survived emancipation. Chattel slavery was always the preferred, but most expensive, system of labor for domestic and agricultural work. The second choice was the enserfment of autochthonous labor.

The way in which slaves and serfs were treated depended not so much on the cultural dispositions of Cape owners (Dutch, German, French, or English), but on the size of the owner's holding. The larger the holding, the more it took on a military style of management. Since there was only one large holding at the Cape (the Company Lodge), most slaves lived in small household distributions, but no one should infer that the Cape slave regime was mild because it was based on these small family holdings.

The family as metaphor and inspiration shaped the colonial society; the household was the crucible of social relations in South Africa. Nearly all social hierarchies were evolved there. The state, insofar as one can speak of such an institution at the Cape, had a limited role. For example, the Dutch East India Company did not force householders to purchase slaves or enserf the native people. The Company only set a dubious example. When the British imperial state manifested itself in 1795, it found itself aligned against a powerful, entrenched, patriarchal, atavistic, domestic order, which the original settlers had installed across the Cape landscape. As the settlers spread out through the colony, they created little "states in miniature." Their big households (the largest one

395

included one hundred individuals) were worlds to themselves. There, notions of family governance, slavery, and serfdom were elaborated and passed on to the next generation of settlers and slaves.

Climate and Slavery

The slave society that emerged at the Cape was quite different from the New World slave societies. A primary difference was climate. A previous generation of apologists once argued that the introduction of slavery in the New World was a consequence of epidemiological or climatic factors hostile to the European constitution. No one could ever make this argument for South Africa. The Cape's mild Mediterranean-style climate posed no problems for the European settlers. The population of European descent experienced one of the highest growth rates among colonial populations. Their family size exceeded the record-holding Hutterite family size of colonial America. The case of South Africa should, once and for all, prove that climate was not responsible for the introduction of slavery anywhere. Climate was only a feeble justification in the argot of slave apologetics.

Property and Personality within Slavery

What divided slavery from all other types of coerced labor, argued Moses Finley, the most influential historian of slavery in antiquity, was that the slave was considered in law as property.[1] Orlando Patterson, in his global analysis of slavery, sharply disagreed with Finley's notion. He maintained that the most significant aspect of slavery was the social domination of the slave's personality by the owner, a domination, I argue, best observed at the household level.[2] This is a particularly important definition, for by Patterson's standards twentieth-century South Africa is still a slave society, a point with which I will not quibble here. One of the most difficult philosophical problems in the analysis of slavery is that, at one and the same time, the slave was both personality and property. The two aspects were not mutually exclusive. The property relation belonged to the public and legal spheres, and manifested itself mainly when slaves changed hands, the social domination of personality belonged in the private sphere and is not necessarily confined to slavery. All slave societies have had the persistent and alluring axes of property and personality, which will always be attractive to scholars with a definitional purpose,

---

[1] Moses I. Finley, *International Encyclopedia of the Social Sciences* (New York: 1968), s.v. "Slavery."

[2] Orlando Patterson, *Slavery and Social Death: A Comparative Study* (Cambridge, Mass.: Harvard University Press, 1982).

although these axes were changing, often independently. They also differed widely from one society to another. Since the sociological aspects of personality and identity and the hegemonic aspects of legal systems have varied because of historical processes, reducing slavery to a monotonic definition (even in a single slave society) will always result in a frustrating conceptual kaleidoscope. All the historian can do is identify historical change around these axis'.

Slaves were indeed regarded as property at the Cape, and they themselves saw that they were property. At the Cape, some slaves used this precise legal relationship to exact revenge on their owners. Some desperate individuals, rather than murdering their owners for revenge, murdered their fellow slaves and then committed suicide. They were secure in their knowledge that the owner, bereft of slave property, would in all probability sink economically and certainly sink in status. In the Cape slave society, with its well-defined code of honor, itself a derivative of slavery, no revenge could be more exquisite.

The property relationship subtly changed and the rise of cadastral slavery, in which the slave was informally sold as part of the landed property, was one aspect of this change. The enserfment of the native people and their incorporation into the settler household also led to consequential changes in the overall slave system. As the slaves and serfs became more dependent on landowners, the question of their exact property status became moot. Both slaves and serfs became attached to the farm on which they had been born, not only by law (slaves) and custom (serfs), but also by multiple drug dependence (wine, tobacco, marijuana), indigence, deprivation of education, and, in the final resort, physical force. When the farm changed hands, slaves and serfs went along with the property. Cadastral slavery was never legally sanctioned, but rights to other persons', even "free" persons', labor were passed on informally every time a farm changed hands. Until the nineteenth century, there was no legal machinery to challenge the system.

Sex, Gender, and Slavery

Sex and gender are key analytical tools in the study of Cape slavery. Some female slaves and female serfs were simultaneously regarded as property and as potential wives. More than a thousand slaves became free mothers. Could not the property relation in slavery be considered a derivative of the owner's "possession" of his own family, a relationship apparent in Roman Dutch law? One Dutch word for slave, *lijfeigene* (literally, body-property), satisfactorily defined, at least from the viewpoint of the Cape slave owning class, what the slave meant to the Dutch colonial society.[3] This word had its analogue in the Hellenistic period, when the Greek

---

[3] The Dutch word *lijf* neatly bridges the distinction of one's life (the older meaning) and one's body (the modern meaning); s.v. *lijf* in Van Dale *Groot Woordenboek der*

word *soma* (body) also came to have the meaning of "slave."[4] In the Roman Dutch legal system, the free woman's minor status and the sanctioned usage of her body by men implied that she, too, shared some of the powerlessness and property status of the chattel slave and that perhaps that circumstance was the true legal antecedent to slavery. The distinction between a wife and a slave in the early Cape was by no means obvious.

The Hegelian View of Slavery

Must one agree with Hegel that only the owner held the power of life and death over the slave? The Hegelian view of the slave seems far too passive. Cape slaves held the power of life and death over themselves up to a point. They certainly held power over the lives of their comrade slaves and their owners, as the many slave suicides, slave-slave murders, slave-owner murders, rebellions, and "runnings amok" confirm. Many independent sources suggest that slaves took lives (including their own) rather more often than owners did. The system of slavery was thus too complicated to work under the simple Hegelian drive of the threat of death. The reaction of slaves to their condition required that other influences besides the owner's threats be brought to bear down on the slaves.

The Hegelian view, by concentrating only on the relationship of the owner over the slave, overlooks the role of slave resistance. External agencies such as the state and the Church, which were the only institutions powerful enough to intrude into the household, also have to be considered. In South Africa the state (such as it was), not the individual owner, was the only authority legally mandated to impose a death sentence on individuals, whether slave or free. Only gradually did slave owners acquire the right to punish their slaves themselves. While a few Cape slave owners did kill their slaves, they did not have the right to do so that the Roman *paterfamilias* did.

Settlers believed that the government should stay out of family governance, to avoid compromising the authority and honor of the patriarch. But slave owners always responded to the Cape society's social contract which served a whole range of purposes. Typical was the case of the nineteenth-century Cape slave owner who was so ashamed of being brought to court by a complaint of his slave that he sold all his land and slaves and "retired," even though the slave's complaint was found

---

Nederlandse Taal. That the word for slave does not appear in the earlier dictionaries suggests that it might have been a colonial neologism; see Verdam, *Middelnederlandsch Handwoordenboek*, and *Supplement.*

4 Moses I. Finley, "Was Greek Civilization Based on Slave Labour?" in Eugene Genovese (ed.), *The Slave Economies: Historical and Theoretical Perspectives* (New York: John Wiley, 1973), 1:21.

to be "spurious."[5] In early South Africa — and, one suspects, in all fledgling colonial societies — the family was virtually autonomous, and it resisted any intrusion by gradually constituting a colonial state that would not interfere with family governance but only buttress it. After 1795, however, the fledgling settler state in South Africa was challenged by an imperial state, which had its own overriding global interests. Paternalism, not unregulated patriarchy, was to be the new world order.

Rights of Slaves and the Social Contract

Rights belong to the public sphere. Generally rights do not emerge until there is a binding social contract, which is usually occasioned by civil war or colonial war. The South African settlers lost their wars, but even so, as a colonial society, they needed to create a new social contract or use metropolitan hand-me-downs. Nevertheless colonial South Africa perversely avoided a formal social contract as long as possible. In this view the early Cape settler was an agent of anarchy.

Slave-owning settlers tried to avoid any social contract that would deny them exclusive rights over family government. Generally, as the power and control of the Dutch East India Company waned, the rights of slaves diminished. While slaves never lost the right to complain, and while there was a "moral community" of slave owners, the Cape slave was at the mercy of the householder for a long period. Not surprisingly the few rights slaves had enjoyed, as embodied in Roman Dutch law, were degraded within the Cape slave society, until that most unlikely and dubious agent, the British Empire, brought a few uncertain and heavily filtered strands of the Enlightenment to the Cape and ultimately restored some of their rights and their freedom.

A slave may in one society have been forbidden to own land or movable property; in another forbidden to earn money or to marry, or prevented (surgically in the case of the eunuchs) from having offspring. But there does not seem to be a single set of rights that are denied all slaves, across the board.[6] Rights at the Cape came to be defined as slave owners' rights. These were rights over other people. When the first calls for settler republics were made in the eighteenth century, and then again in the nineteenth century, Samuel Johnson's magnificent irony was as applicable to them as it was for the Americans' slave holders' calls for liberty: "Is it

---

[5] W. W. Bird, *State of the Cape of Good Hope in 1822* (Cape Town: Struik, 1966 reprint), pp. 347–348.

[6] This may be compared to H. J. Nieboer's 1910 definition: "We may define a slave in the ordinary sense of the word, as a man who is the property of another, politically and socially at a lower level than the mass of the people, and performing compulsory labor." H. J. Nieboer, *Slavery as an Industrial System: Ethnological Researches* (New York: Burt Franklin, 1971), 5.

not strange that the greatest cries for freedom come from the drivers of negroes?" But even slave owner's rights involved a social contract and a rudimentary justice system, and once these were in place, they would become a platform for a more encompassing system. In South Africa, however, that process has taken hundreds of years.

Social Domination and Resistance

The implied total social control over slaves' lives, to which Patterson and other neo-Hegelians allude, was never manifest in the day-to-day running of the Cape slave household. When Manuel of Bengal an elderly Cape slave, who had been promised his freedom and then denied it, simply refused to be a slave any longer and made his owner's household intolerable with his "relentless insolence," neither his owner nor the Company authorities could do anything except lock him up. According to the neo-Hegelian view, such a reluctant slave should have been put to death for refusing to be a slave.[7] But such slaves were not killed because the social system could not have endured constant executions. Instead, owners devised a system of managing slaves that far surpassed Hegel's in its sophistication and psychological breadth. Most slaves were managed entirely within the family, and only exceptions were referred to the state, which was mandated to regulate and enforce the system of slavery.

The Mort Vivant View of Slaves

In Patterson's view, the slave was alienated from his own society and brought into another, physically still alive, but socially "dead." In Patterson's words, slavery "always originated (or was conceived of as having originated) as a substitute for death."[8] This *mort vivant* conception of slavery (slaves as the "living dead") is shared by Pierre Dockès in his study of medieval slavery. Since it has so many implications for the Cape slave society, the idea is worth exploring more fully.[9] Patterson and Dockès defer to one of the oldest justifications of slavery, that slaves were regarded as prisoners of war reprieved from death by merciful victors. The process was recognized in antiquity in the Romans' understanding of the Law of

---

[7] Richard Elphick and Robert C.-H. Shell, "Intergroup Relations: Khoikhoi, Slaves, Settlers, and Free Blacks," in R. Elphick and Herman Giliomee (eds.), *The Shaping of South African Society 1652–1820* (Middletown Conn.: Wesleyan University Press, 1989), p. 143.

[8] Patterson, *Slavery and Social Death*, 5.

[9] Pierre Dockès, *Medieval Slavery and Liberation* (Chicago: University of Chicago Press, 1982), pp. 4–5.

Nations (*Ius Gentium*). The conqueror had the right to sell his captives into slavery. By law, he also had the right to kill them. By making slaves of them, he spared their lives. Hence, the Latin word *servus* (servant) derived from the verb *servare* (to spare). In this view, the new owners (as representative of the victor state) were regarded as honorable because they had spared the life of the slave, while the slaves were pitied, but not despised, for the state into which they had fallen through no fault of their own.

This conception of slavery declined for two reasons. First, as soon as states started going to war solely to capture slaves, the victor/owner logically lost his "merciful" cachet. Slaves were no longer a by-product of wars, they were *the* products. However, although the *mort vivant* definition slowly lost currency, it could and did reemerge. Once the slave trade was suppressed at the Cape after 1808, the *mort vivant* justification for slavery quickly reemerged, as settlers turned to the native population. In the general imperial codification of Cape slave laws in the early nineteenth century, the most interesting Article Four stipulated that "Prisoners of war cannot be made slaves, even if they were *Caffres* or other barbarous nations living beyond the boundaries of this colony, such being contrary to the spirit of modern jurisprudence and the interests of the colony itself."[10] The law came into being for a reason. Colonial householders were turning to the native populations to acquire slaves and justifying their enslavement on the grounds of war. People at the Cape were never legally enslaved as prisoners of war, but native persons as early as 1731 did become prisoners in retaliation raids and were then folded into the enslaved or enserfed population.

The second reason for the overall decline of the *mort vivant* view of slaves was that the process of enslaving persons changed fundamentally over time. Most premodern colonial slave societies operating through the international slave market succeeded in recruiting third parties, sometimes new polities entirely dependent on the slave trade, to go to war on their behalf to obtain their slaves. So long as the oceanic slave trade was operating, all colonial slave owners were one step removed from the raw supply of slaves, as the Romans and Greeks had not been. Premodern slave societies could, in consequence, avoid having to confront and justify the brutal everyday acquisition and domestic incorporation of slaves. The formal process of enslavement and incorporation into the societies of antiquity had been an elaborate public ritual closely following on a war or a campaign. Returning Roman armies had marched in a public display with their thousands of slaves in tow. All premodern colonial societies were spared this incorporation spectacle by the relatively more discreet operations of the oceanic slave trade. It was a case of "out of sight, out of mind"; slaves were simply slaves, not spared prisoners

---

[10] George McCall Theal, *Records of the Cape Colony* (Cape Town: Struik, 1967; 9: 146, "Statement of the Laws of the Colony of the Cape of Good Hope Regarding Slavery" (16 March 1813).

of war. The mechanism of enslavement was not in the hands of the colonists; they knew little about the individual circumstances of enslavement. Indeed, most expressed outright disapproval of the slave trade; they could then pose as parental saviours of the unfortunate, orphaned slaves.

A new language for the slave trade emerged: in South Africa, slaves bought from the oceanic traders were thought of as being "saved" from savagery and heathendom by being brought into the Cape household and the Christian fold. This was doubly hypocritical, since imported slaves would probably never enter the Church, nor even be buried in a Christian graveyard, and certainly never in the family graveyard. That slaves arriving at the Cape were orphaned by the slave trade (only two slave families survived the Cape's middle passage), meant that the traumatized survivors were excellent candidates for purported inclusion into a slave-owning family. These orphans were then offered a partial life and partial identity in the family. That they had to learn a new language and a new way of life enhanced their childlike status, in the sense that children always have to be taught.

The *mort vivant* conception of slavery was merely a blunt instrument when one compares it with the remorseless and cynical reality of household slavery at the Cape, which was predicated on inclusion, the restoration of expectations and familial affect. This is a psychological terrain similar in some respects to that experienced by long-term kidnapping victims or hostages. Cape slaves were never regarded as socially dead, they were offered hope of a life. But that life began and ended in the owner's family.

Marginality and Slavery

Closely akin to the definition of the slave as an outsider, is all slaves' assumed "marginality"; both aspects may be addressed together. The term *marginality* was first used in French academic circles in 1908, to describe the temporary state after the slave was captured but before the slave was incorporated into the host society. In Arnold Van Gennep's original formulation, it was a sort of limbo state.[11] In 1934, H. Lévy-Bruhl used the concept. After Van Gennep's death in 1957, the work was translated into English and appeared in 1960 just as African history was starting to professionalize. Moses Finley introduced the concept into slavery circles in 1968. In 1972, according to the Suzanne Miers and Igor Kopytoff, the concept had become a permanent part of the secondary literature on African slavery.[12]

---

[11] The French word *marge* contains a figurative connotation of latitude, now lost in the leading sense of the modern translation. Arnold van Gennep, *The Rites of Passage* trans. Monika B. Vizedom and G. L. Cafee (Chicago: University of Chicago Press, 1960).

[12] Suzanne Meiers and Igor Kopytof (eds.), *Slavery in Africa: Historical and Anthropological Perspectives* (Madison: University of Wisconsin Press, 1977), p. 16, note 3.

From there marginality became a generalized—though ahistorical—description of the social status of all slaves. The concept is never questioned.

In a world in which the citizen is at the center of political life, for example in Aristotle's Greece, the slave represents the opposite pole: minimum participation in the *polis*. Slavery came to define the boundary of full (enfranchised) humanity. But the *metics* (foreign merchants and resident aliens) in Athens were also marginal in the same political sense that slaves were; metics, like slaves, enjoyed no civil rights. Nevertheless that fact does not reveal the interior condition of slaves relative to *metics*. One has to ask, marginal in relation to what?

In the South African case, the native people, slaves, and free blacks were fundamentally marginalized, though each in quite a different way. Many fables, cultural symbols, and even histories depend on different definitions of marginality. Marginality is a metaphor. In this work I have sought to specify, engender, and historicize marginality in relation to the dominant colonial social unit, the settler family, not in relation to political rights. Marginality was not simply a binary opposition, but it was a scalar concept. To the Cape owner, female slaves were not marginal humans on the periphery of the family, they were an integral part of that family. Male slaves were marginalized, but not to the same extent as Khoi serfs. And what would one say about the San people (the Bushmen)? Binary marginality cannot address the changing hierarchical and domestic nature of the Cape slave society. Marginality has to be seen as a scalar concept that can operate at every level, and it has to be historicized.

This book has traced how the European Christian paternalism of the seventeenth century was first infused into the colonial landscape by the settler family. That early paternalism was short-lived. The emerging colonial family helped create a clearly defined patriarchal order in the colonial setting by 1795, mainly achieved through the growth and extension of slavery and serfdom throughout the colony. The emergent and triumphant patriarchal order was then challenged, but not checked, by English metropolitan paternalism when the British occupied the Cape in 1795. Conflict between the entrenched domestic patriarchy and the paternalistic state is at the root of much of nineteenth-century South African history. The further households were from the agents of imperialism in the Cape slave society, the more likely they were to be based on patriarchal autonomy and unregulated atavistic domestic relations. Those far-flung patriarchal societies founded their own frontier republics as soon as they could. When legal slavery was effectively abolished in the Cape colony in 1838, the patriarchs left and the paternalists stayed. Fully 20 percent of the Europeans quit the colony to preserve their way of life.

Summary of Chapters

The ability to dispossess land and alienate water resources by horses and guns was at the heart of South Africa's colonial labor history. Land was so easy to acquire that every settler could acquire a farm. But no free person, whether settler or autochthon, wanted to work for someone else. So slaves were imported and the local Khoi were also enserfed.

There is a tendency in the comparative literature to deal with the slave trade as an end in itself. Philip Curtin's magisterial work on the Atlantic slave trade has had the unintended effect of reinforcing this trend: with a few exceptions slave trade studies have now become an end in themselves, focusing almost entirely on the important questions of numbers and mortality on the middle passage, but untethered from the societies they served.[13] Perhaps another example was set by the emphasis on studies of the antebellum American South, a society that did not depend on the oceanic slave trade after 1808 — so there was never a need to understand the slave trade of the world's most studied slave society. But most slave societies *were* dependent on their slave trades. In this book, the chapters on the slave trade and its effects show how the sex and age composition, and cultural origins of the imported slave population at the Cape shaped the slave-holding households in domestic, cultural, demographic, gender, and even emotional, terms.

The Cape slave trade demonstrates that African slaves were not universal among modern European slave societies. The origins of slaves at the Cape were due to happenstance, mercantile rivalries, and household demands. The Dutch *West* India Company forbade the Dutch *East* India Company from poaching on its slave preserves, Angola and the entire west coast of Africa. Because slave trading prospects on the east coast of Africa were poor and dominated by well-armed Muslim and Portuguese slavers in the seventeenth and early eighteenth century, the Lodge officials turned to Madagascar, and then the settlers and Company officials themselves (who came to own most of the slaves) turned mainly to the East, to the Indonesian and Indian possessions of the Dutch commercial empire. Consequently, female slaves from the Indian subcontinent and from the sprawling Indonesian Archipelago predominated in the Cape slave-holding households in the first century of occupation. Rarely were slave women and men in the same house from the same background. These early slave women were the progenitors of most of the creole slaves who were in the majority by about 1770. By the 1770s, however, most *imported* slaves were drawn from the east coast of Africa and Madagascar. At that point the Cape burghers could bypass the traditional inter-

---

[13] One notable exception is Daniel Littlefield, *Rice and Slaves: Ethnicity and the Slave Trade in Colonial South Carolina* (Baton Rouge: University of Louisiana Press, 1981).

locutors in the slave trade and buy slaves in bulk from French traders, who by then dominated trading in Madagascar and Mozambique. The injection of the resulting diversity of slave languages and cultures had significant implications for the creole culture that emerged at the Cape. A major characteristic of South African slavery was the widely differing and changing origins of Cape slaves.

The relative percentage of slaves within the households of the Cape colony was higher than in the contemporary colonies of the American South (with the exception of South Carolina), but much lower than in plantation slave societies such as Cuba, Barbados, the Leeward Islands, the Dutch Antilles, and Zanzibar. Most significant was the high proportion of adult male slaves at the Cape, as high as and sometimes higher than the greatly imbalanced Caribbean plantation slave societies, which are usually regarded as a benchmark for high sex ratios in slave societies. The Cape had slave distributions similar to those in colonial America and a slave sex composition similar to the Caribbean plantations before 1808. This sustained imbalance of the sexes at the Cape, at some points the highest of any recorded slave society, was a result of local householders' persistent preferences for adult male slaves. Until 1808, Cape slave owners found the inexpensive oceanic slave trade to the Cape to be the perfect source of forced labor. According to research on the seventeenth- and eighteenth- century Atlantic slave trade, the standard slave cargos from East Africa bound for the New World had a ratio of two male slaves to one female slave, never more, irrespective of the nationality of the carrier. One can only conclude, therefore, that the sustained high sex ratio of the slave population at the Cape was the result of local slave owners' preferences. By exercising this preference for male slaves, slave owners sacrificed the potential for male slaves to have an independent family life. Given the lack of female slaves, most male slaves were, in the sense of conjugal experience, outsiders. Even at emancipation in 1838, there were many elderly bachelor slaves. All imported slaves were orphans, individuals psychologically traumatized to be incorporated into what they had just lost, a family.

The highly imbalanced Cape slave population exhibited all the behavior sociologically associated with abnormally high sex ratios: violence, homosexual activity, drinking, and gambling. The settlers and officials simplistically attributed such behavior to the slaves' origins, a continuous justification for the slaves' inferior status. The origins of imported slaves explained everything for the slave owner. I call this pattern of associative thinking "naive anthropology." It was the forerunner of the racial attitudes common to the area. The highly imbalanced imported-slave sex ratio, combined with the wealthier slave owners' practice of incorporating the few female slaves into their home and household, as domestic workers, nannies, and wet nurses for their own children, resulted in a low absolute growth rate for the Cape slaves up to 1808.

Another reason for the early census pattern of low growth in the slave population was that a significant proportion of the few slave women were leaving the census slave population to become free. Such nanny or nurse slaves were generally manumitted, taking their children with them into freedom and into the free black community. In addition, some younger female slaves, once manumitted, married bachelor settlers and were even more fully incorporated into the settler society. Thus, combination with the disproportionate sex ratio, the partial or full domestic incorporation of slave women into the household as nurses and as wives presents itself as the best explanation for the demographic behavior of the slave population as recorded in the censuses.

One result of the low growth rate was that the Cape slave population was only gradually creolized. Creole slaves, whose sex ratio was absolutely normal, were always preferred to any imported slave. Not until the 1770 was were the majority of slaves locally born, or creole. As the household itself became a major source of slaves, the slave society changed in subtle ways. Creole slaves, because they lived longer and spoke the Cape patois, became the preferred slaves and lived out their lives in a paternalistic cocoon. Some remained in the same household in which they had been born.

Even after 1770, Cape slave owners were heavily dependent on the slave trade until its suppression in 1808. The rapid expansion of the colony deepened that dependence. Poorer, frontier-bound settlers, unable to buy the increasingly expensive slaves, turned to the native population for land and labor. These settlers seized the land, displaced the men into the interior, and took over the native women. This process began in 1723, was formalized in the 1770s, and greatly accelerated after 1808. The suppression of the oceanic slave trade makes 1808 possibly the most significant year in South Africa's colonial history. The suppression of slave imports exposed the native populations to the burgeoning population of labor-hungry settlers who were deprived of their traditional source of labor, the oceanic slave trade.

Analysis of the Cape's internal slave market clearly demonstrates the domestic incorporation of slave women, the marginalization of enslaved males, and the organization of the slave society on the family model. Once again, 1808 marks a clear watershed. On average, slaves imported before 1808 changed hands three times after they had been landed at the Cape: when they first arrived they were sold to a speculator, usually a Company official; then they were sold to a slave owner; and finally, when that owner died, they were sold to a new owner, usually a relative of the original head of household. The time between the first and the second transfer was short, a matter of months; the time between the second and final transfer was often most of the remaining life of the slave. The final change of ownership most often took the form of an inheritance. Most slaves stayed on the same property, their sale sometimes being registered along with the property in a cadastral transfer, a system akin to serfdom. Generally the percentage of all slaves sold at auction every year was low; slaves of a deceased owner were often reserved for other relatives. "Free" or casual labor was much more likely to be dislocated by dismissal at the time of such a property transfer.

Creole slaves, being born on the holding, or often "in the household," never went through the "arrival" sale and were even less likely to be sold to strangers outside the family. The creole slave family, despite its lack of legal standing, was increasingly respected by owners, who considered all creole slaves a part of the owners' family. By 1806 one traveler noted that it was considered a "matter of honor" never to sell a creole household slave.

After the suppression of the oceanic slave trade, all slaves became much more valuable, according to the law of supply and demand. In the era of rapid economic change and scarcity of slaves between 1808 and 1821, the percentage of slaves sold on the internal market increased; thereafter it decreased during a colony-wide depression (1823 to 1830). Considerable new evidence from the compensation lists, which were compiled with actuarial accuracy by British officials, shows that in this latter period relatively few slave families were broken up. When slave families were separated by sale, it was because of bankruptcies and sequestration proceedings. In proportion to the respective populations, fewer slave families were broken up during this period than before 1808. Over the long term, speculation in slaves at open auctions also declined. In short, slaves stayed in the owner's family. The intergenerational persistence of slaves in the owner's lineage was an important ingredient of Cape paternalism.

The implications of geographical dislocation as a result of slave sales changed as the colony expanded. After 1808, the colony expanded rapidly into the eastern part of the country, and geographical dislocation through the sale of slaves was more common. Also, many owners moved, taking their slaves with them. By 1834, fully one-sixth of all slaves, previously concentrated in the southwestern Cape, were in the newly settled Eastern districts. While the fear of sale had always been real to all slaves, when it did occur in the nineteenth century, it involved real geographical displacement and a sundering of every tie. The most frequently verbalized fear of Cape slaves was to be "sold upcountry."

From the geographical and slave-holding distributions of Cape slaves emerged the basis for labor control along the family model: paternalism in the urban regions, patriarchy in the frontier zones. With the single exception of the Lodge, there were no huge (1,000-slave) plantations as there were in the American South, Zanzibar, the Caribbean, and Brazil. The typical slave-holding household was small. Although the census returns show individual holdings of 100 slaves as early as 1730, such large holdings of slaves *always* belonged to owners who held several properties. The average rural slave holding was small compared with other contemporary slave societies, averaging between three slaves (in the eighteenth century) and five slaves (in the nineteenth century). Although the Dutch word for plantation (*plantagie*) was used even in the seventeenth century to describe Cape slave farms, only a handful of farms could boast more than 20 slaves. The average Cape *plantagie* was no more than a large household. The few large slave holdings belonged to the Cape gentry who represented 6 percent to 8 percent of all slave owners and who held title to most of the slaves, although some of the patriarchs' children would already have control of the slaves to which their fathers still held title. The ideal of the Cape patriarch was to provide for each of his children (sons and daughters) a property with the full — family — complement of slaves.

The second pattern evident in the Cape slave distributions was that the sex and age structure of the slave population fell into clearly perceived geographical patterns. The younger male slaves (capable of the heaviest manual labor) were at the core of the economy, in the towns, semiurban areas, and wherever intensive agriculture was practiced. Older male slaves were dispersed among the frontier regions, the areas of extensive agriculture, on "loan farms" or ranches where they worked as independent herders. Their age and experience were sufficient guarantees of their responsibility, and they led a sometimes unsupervised but still wholly dependent existence. Old age, poverty, and drug dependence were the final Cape guarantees of obedience. Most female slaves, irrespective of age, were housed with or near the wealthier colonists up until 1808, and they were almost universally based in or near the urban areas. All urban inventories that listed slaves included at least one female slave.

The urban and semiurban character of slavery of South Africa is surprising. The Dutch anthropologist H. J. Nieboer and the American historian Richard Wade have long argued that urban life and slavery were "incompatible." This was not the case at the Cape, where urban slavery, while posing challenging problems of control, never faltered, and in fact went from strength to strength in the nearly two centuries of slavery at the Cape. The Cape began as an urban slave society. Although by 1745 most slaves were living in the rural areas, the urban slave society continued to grow in absolute terms. In the 1820s, however, the proportion of slaves in the towns declined. This happened both because rural slave owners needed the slaves more than urban owners did and because a new generation of European immigrants gradually took over the slaves' work as artisans in the towns.

Historians have assumed that towns and cities, the loci of civilization and the source of modern commercial economies, could not have harbored sustained growth of slave populations. Yet, in well-studied ancient societies, such as those in Athens and Rome, slaves were an essential part of the polis, representing from 25 to 30 percent of the city's population. Other colonial societies besides the Cape, such as Brazil and the American South, also had urban slave cultures up until abolition, with as much as 25 percent of the slave force living in the cities. In this regard South African slavery was no different from other slave societies, except that there was, in the first century of occupation, an even higher proportion of urban slaves: nearly 50 percent of all slaves lived in the port town.

The most important distinction in the distribution of South African slaves was the type of holding the slaves were in: domestic service, agricultural, or industrial. Slave holdings revealed considerable stereotyping by phenotype, origin, creole status, and occupation. The Cape was similar to other New World slave societies in this one important aspect: settlers in colonial areas arrived with preconceived, very generalized, pre-Darwinian ideas about inferiority of people of non-European descent. In the Cape colonial domestic setting, slave owners came to rank slaves by origin *and* descent, and the degree to which these somatic factors were incorporated into the household and economy of the colony was surprising. The main evidence for this finding is compelling: it is the price slave owners were willing to pay for slaves of preferred origins, for creole slaves, and for slaves of European descent — what scholars of the domestic slave market have bluntly termed "ethnic premiums." Slaves were ranked (and priced) by the somatic factors of racial descent and also by origin, a system with muted resonance in all New World slave societies but elaborated most fully in South African households.

Descent and origin initially determined slaves' privileges, from type of occupation to possibilities for freedom. At the Cape, slaves from India and Indonesia were preferred for industrial tasks, African slaves for agricultural tasks, Indian and Indonesian slaves for service jobs, creole slaves and mulatto slaves for domestic and artisanal work. These stereotypes by origin and descent were arbitrary, and they changed according to the fluctuations in the slave trade and the extent of the creolization of the slave force. After 1770, when the South African slave force was creolizing and also being Africanized by new imports from East Africa, many of the purely perceived somatic distinctions based on origin changed. African slaves were moved into the service sector and onto the hinterland farms. Stereotyping by creole status and descent did not change, however; creole and mulatto slaves always cost more.

This evolving system of stereotyping by descent, creole status and origin at the household level is particularly important in the context of South African history. Several scholars have denied the importance (sometimes even the existence) of racial attitudes in the preindustrial period of South Africa, seeing it as a later phenomenon primarily linked to the introduction of "industrial capitalism." This was not so. The first outlines of racial and ethnic attitudes and colonial identities were deeply etched in the slave period.

If the individual patriarchal slave owner relied on a familial system of incorporation, the local patrician Dutch officials employed more draconian control measures with the slaves in the Dutch East India Company's Lodge, the largest single slave holding at the Cape. The Lodge was the statistical antithesis of the average slave-holding at the Cape. It was always the largest holding at the Cape, and it was organized along very different lines. Although there are no clear comparative analogues of this urban "plantation," the Lodge comes closest to what John Blassingame has termed the army model of slave management. Physical punishment within the Lodge was common. The Lodge was run internally, controlled by a military-like authority structure among the slaves. Free Europeans had only oversight, not direct control, over the Lodge. The Lodge management, like the colony as a whole, was based on descent, gender, and origin. After 1795 the Lodge, under the paternalistic vision of the British, became an old-age home for Company slaves.

The small average size of slave holdings at the Cape meant that the management of slaves was quite different from the more brutal system of whips and chains that the neo-abolitionist accounts of the Cape suggest. Cape slaves were whipped, but so, too, were all people at the Cape, that is, soldiers, sailors, and the native peoples. The colonial administration and society used corporal punishment as a sanction for all subsidiary sectors of the population. Slaves were protected by statute from being badly beaten, but they were more effectively protected by the self-interest of owners. Only "domestic chastisement" was allowed, that is, the same punishment that was meted out to wife and children (and in turn meted out by wife and children to slaves). This is not to say that chastisement of slaves was "mild" in a patriarchal setting. It must be remembered that although the British abolished physical torture in the first British occupation, the definition of domestic punishment for slaves was enlarged to allow for 25 lashes, which represented a triumph for the patriarchs over the more paternalistic British. There is every indication that Cape domestic life was brutal. Slave complaints of excessive maltreatment could be (and were) made to the Fiscal under the Dutch administration, and after 1817 to the Protector of Slaves, a British official. All slave corpses were inspected to see if there had been physical abuse. However, slave owners were always aware that their valuable slaves could be maimed or incapacitated by a severe beating.

The chains of domestic slavery at the Cape were principally psychological. Slaves were incorporated into a carefully organized domestic hegemony in which they were treated as permanent children. Slaves had certain carefully limited rights, but they remained minors unless freed, and even after manumission they were given only a certain proscribed freedom as free blacks. Free blacks could not work for the Company as burghers could; they were taxed, but were denied credit. After death, the estate of a freed slave belonged to his or her former owner. Even in death the ex-slave was regarded as a minor. Slaves resisted their fate in diverse ways, by suicide (which was rare), murder, rape, escape, running amok, and the ultimate Cape rebellion, arson.

The domestic control of all Cape slaves wavered between the army model for slaves at the Lodge and the few large holdings at the Cape, and a more nuanced, intimate, and highly gendered system of incorporation into the families of the owners of small holdings, a group that collectively came to own the majority of the Cape slave population. The exact choice of control along this army-family spectrum was made strictly according to the type and size of the holding. Since small holdings were much more common, I have suggested that familial incorporation, rather than the whip or other corporal punishment, best explains the management of most Cape slaves. Physical treatment of slaves depended entirely on the size of the holding.

The domestic and familial character of South African slavery changed and creolized the local vernacular architecture. The slave women were, until the nineteenth century, always housed in the owner's kitchen. Slave men were housed in separate slave quarters outside the main house, usually in a small hut, sometimes with a chimney. Fire was the main element affecting the Cape vernacular architecture. Arsonists were responsible for the "great fires" of the Cape, in Stellenbosch in 1710; in Cape Town in 1736 and again in 1798. The urban architecture rapidly took on a defensive aspect. Highly flammable pitched thatched roofs gave way to flat roofs on all official buildings by 1719. After 1736, flat roofs emerged on all rebuilt private houses. After 1798, no external shutters were allowed on urban buildings. Unadorned, plain, flat, squat, arsonproof dwellings emerged as the universal urban house style. Architecture was quite different on the isolated rural holding, where there was no great concentration of slaves as in the towns and villages. Rural architecture underwent a thorough transformation as symbolic hegemonic elements, such as the thatched roof and the central gable, became larger and more impressive, eventually dominating the rural landscape just as the fantastic *fazendas* (big houses) of Brazil, the *landhuizen* of Curaçao, the *haciendas* of the Yucatan, and the plantation houses of the antebellum South, dominated and came to symbolize their respective slave societies.

The family mode of management grew out of the Christian paternalism originally brought to the Cape by the seventeenth-century Dutch, German, and French settlers. In the colonial setting, however, the availability of land and the search for labor created conditions for a more independent and patriarchal mode of existence. This was accompanied by the establishment and elaboration of a Christian identity for Europeans as separate from the Muslim and "heathen" slaves and the godless Khoi. Dutch and German visitors to the Cape in the early nineteenth century did not recognize the Cape colonists as their fellow countrymen, describing their slave estates as "states in miniature" run in the "patriarchal mode." When the colony was occupied by the British in 1795, paternalism once again was infused into the colony. Many of the ensuing difficulties between the patriarchal Boers and the paternalist British may be squarely laid at the door of this conflict. Between 1795 and 1838, the public and private aspects of domestic arrangements were sharply contested.

At the heart of the familial incorporation of slaves was the slave woman. A significant difference between Cape slavery and other colonial slave societies was that slave women were kept within the owner's house, which also became their working and sleeping place. Nearly all Cape women slaves were domestic servants, but up until 1808 they also played important sociobiological roles in the slaveowning family. They were used in the home for embroidery, knitting, gardening, occasionally for brick making, and for agricultural labor at harvest time, but they were mainly valued for their adjunct biological duties, which had profound sexual and psychological implications for all in the orbit of the household. As the creolization of the slave force progressed and the proportion of slave women increased, they were used in the fields more often as well as the home. By the

1820s, Cape slave women were sometimes used as laborers, but they were still more greatly valued for their domestic roles and for the reproduction of future slaves. In short, an increasing range of work — childbearing, nurturing, and menial labor — fell on slave women. Unlike their counterparts in the American South, Cape slave women were almost universally excused from heavy field work and were securely embedded in the household. The close domestic propinquity of all slave women to their owners' families had important psychological and psycho-sexual ramifications.

In the seventeenth and eighteenth centuries, many free fathers had children by slave women in their household; most later manumitted their slave offspring. By the early nineteenth century, some Cape owners who fathered their own slaves sold them instead. As slaves became more expensive after 1808, property became more important than familial duty. The unusually imbalanced Cape sex ratios, the gender differentiation of tasks, and the incorporation of female slaves into the household all led to a slave society substantially different from other, New World slave societies. It resembles in many respects — in the incorporation of slave women into the household, in the manumission of mulatto children — African slave lineage systems.

The particular domestic configuration of Cape slavery — women inside the house, men outside — was advantageous to the slave owner in many ways. The domestic segregation of slaves by sex helped to undermine slave solidarity, for which there were few if any traditions of continuity. Whenever rebellion was being discussed in the male slave quarters, for example, the slave women were likely to alert the owner. That slaves at the Cape were not "allowed" to marry until 1823 further undermined slaves' opportunities for an independent family life. With no other options, female slaves were tied to, and therefore hopelessly identified with, the owner's family. Nonetheless, they had a far greater chance of escaping their bondage than did the male slaves. Slave women saw that their greatest chance of escape was through the settler family, whether this was through a nanny manumission or a concubinage manumission. But after 1808 and the end of the oceanic slave trade, this escape hatch started closing.

Reformed Christianity technically held a promise for all slaves of incorporation into the free community. The Synod of Dordt (1618–19), the last international synod of the Reformed tradition, had argued that slaves in Reformed households should be baptized and brought into Church membership and the Christian community, and some participants argued that "baptized slaves could never be sold." But this idealistic vision of baptism failed in all the colonies under the Reformed Church's ecclesiastical control, since the heads of household, not the church, made all decisions concerning baptism. In the Reformed tradition the head of household had more power over domestic religious life than in Catholic societies. Baptism belonged to the public sphere in Catholicism, but in the Reformed faith baptism was left in the private sphere, the individual household.

The net effect of the Synod of Dordt was to ensure that Christian slave owners did not baptize their slaves, nor indeed provide them with Christian instruction, for fear that Christian slaves would not be marketable. Most of the slaves baptized at the Cape were the Company's Lodge slaves, who were never sold, and only a handful of them ever acquired freedom. There was no Christian escape hatch for slaves at the Cape. Slave baptism rates declined in South Africa until 1838, and many urban male slaves and male free blacks turned to Islam instead. The Cape society that emerged after emancipation was deeply divided not only on grounds of status, gender, and race, but on grounds of religion as well.

For a Cape slave to be manumitted, he or she had to satisfy three conditions: demonstrate an ability to speak Dutch, provide a monetary guarantee to the Church fund against becoming a burden on the community, and show proof of baptism in the Reformed Church (Catholic baptism did not count). Freedom was never a right, only a favor to be granted. These requirements were stiffened over time. Although manumission rates in the seventeenth century were quite high, almost rivaling the high rates of Brazil, in the eighteenth century these rates became increasingly low when compared with other contemporary slave societies, and they continued to decline. With slave women far more likely to be manumitted than men, the adult manumitted population became predominantly female, but after 1808, when the slave trade ceased, the manumission of women slowed as well. The overall rate dropped to levels almost as low as the manumission rates in the American South, the slave society with the lowest recorded manumission rate.

The long-term decline in manumissions had several implications for the whole Cape society. First, the free black community remained small. Cape settlers never knew what it was like to have a large free black population in their midst, as their counterparts had in Brazilian towns and cities. Consequently the dominant class came to equate freedom with descent. Moreover, since many of the free black males were Muslims, an alternative free culture grew up alongside the settlers, one indifferent or hostile to the ostensibly Christian settlers ethos. The Cape slave society emerged on emancipation day not as an integrated, free Christian community, but as a society vertically segmented by religion and gender and horizontally stratified by color, class, and status.

Ironically, the small free black population, once freed, behaved in certain respects like their former masters. While they were shut out of agriculture because they could not obtain credit, and often nudged into poverty by the cost of their own manumission, many did come to own slaves and to treat them no differently than the settlers treated their slaves. Still, free black slave owners freed their slaves many times more frequently than their white counterparts. As one conservative historian wrote in the 1940s, their manumission record remains one of the "most beautiful pages" in the history of free blacks.

Overview

Until comparatively recently, South African historians have not devoted much attention to slavery or, indeed, to the entire social world of the seventeenth-, eighteenth-, and nineteenth-century Cape colony, which has remained the traditional haunt of antiquarian and settler scholarship. Most English-speaking historians who have ventured into this period have begun at the frontier and stayed there. The frontier was the perfect site for constructing heroic identities. The considerable distractions of that project facilitated the denial of slavery by subsequent historians. Knowledge of the geographical locations of settlers and slaves and the statistical distributions of slaves remove the props supporting such frontier-oriented history in colonial Cape history. In the first century of occupation, the frontier was simply too sparsely populated to have produced new social transformations of real significance. Economy and society orbited around the port of Cape Town and its immediate surroundings. This book is based on an alternative premise, namely that the important social contact was not across the frontier, but behind it. The evolution of attitudes and identities took place in the domestic setting between slave and master — the urban and rural households and all that went on inside them. Once these relationships were in place, they changed as the frontier loomed closer; expectations nurtured by a golden age of patriarchy were then played out in the frontier households. The frontier was the terminus, rather than the genesis, of social formation.

In the intimate domestic setting, the languages, religions, cultures, and attitudes of slaves and colonists meshed and changed in a reciprocal cultural exchange that was more important than the romantic frontier expeditions in charting the course of the South African *mentalités* in the seventeenth, eighteenth, and early nineteenth centuries. Exported to the frontier, these domestic attitudes and expectations were given new expression in the emerging relations with the native people. It was in the domestic setting that South Africans first knew and accommodated each other, in whatever sense they did. It was there that the children of slaves and serfs and masters grew up, inculcated the emergent order, elaborated it, refined it, and challenged it. It was there that the colony's attitudes based on descent were first articulated and received their bold and crude forms, and it was there that patrician, paternalist, and patriarchal orders emerged with their distinctly articulated regional systems of class, color, gender, religion, and privilege. Once begun in South Africa, slavery was difficult to stop. There is no evidence that slavery in South Africa was economically moribund, or secularly unstable, even though abolitionists sought to make that point. Only the energies of the world's most powerful empire could check its momentum. The truly frightening aspects of South African slavery were its efficiency, its near universal deployment, its convenience for owners, its long duration, and its suppression in the historical literature. The slave period, 1652 to 1838, was the true gestation period of South African culture.

Cape slavery had another legacy. Slavery brought different people together, not across the sights of a gun, as on the frontier, but in the setting of the home. Each slave was exposed to each owner and each settler to each slave on a very intimate footing. There was, in fact, a common reciprocal legacy, which might one day be considered more important than the unfair, but temporary and wholly worldly, advantages that the slave owners enjoyed through slavery. This legacy was the as yet unexamined creole culture of South Africa, with its new cuisine, its new architecture, its new music, its melodious, forthright, and poetic language, Afrikaans, first expressed in the Arabic script of the slaves' religion and written literature. The slave legacy also included the construction of the false identity of the Afrikaners, a term that etymologically denotes "locally born" and was in the early nineteenth century used for slaves born of European fathers and slave mothers. "Afrikaaner" should properly encompass all those who were born into Cape society, however universally unpopular that proposition may first appear.

Slave ancestors injected diversity and challenge into an oppressive settler culture, bending and finally changing it, creolizing it into a new culture. This was the product of their painful historical sojourn as members of the slave owners' households, a culture that neither descendants of slaves nor of owners in South Africa can yet bear to acknowledge. But it is toward this amalgam of human relationships, however difficult it may seem, that the historian must force readers to focus their thoughts. Another generation might find the trace elements, no matter how small, of a single domestic creole culture within the otherwise starkly stratified and bifurcated slave society of early South Africa.

On the first of January in 1838 (emancipation day), it rained with a steady drizzle. The Christians interpreted this as a sign of God's distress, almost one-fifth left the colony in disgust over the freeing of serfs (in 1828) and the slaves (in 1838) by the British Empire. The Muslims, who stayed, interpreted the rain as a sign of joy: they would later hold carnivals to celebrate that day. By 1838, the same year as the Battle of Blood River, South Africans in the Cape colony could not agree on what their sky was saying.

A *Chronology of Slavery and Serfdom at the Cape*

1602: Dutch East India Company established.

1609: First reports of slaves in Dutch Reformed households in the East Indies reach the Netherlands.

1619–

1621: Synod of Dordt delegates decide that baptized slaves should not be sold but should be treated as other Christians.

1642: Important edition of Statutes of India, Van Dieman's *placcaat* on slavery.

1652: Occupation of Cape Station by Dutch (April); Commander Van Riebeeck requests slaves (May).

1653: First slave arrives at the Cape.

1654: First Cape-based slave voyage to Madagascar, via Mauritius.

1658: Company soldiers are freed to become free burghers; secret voyage into Dahomey returns with 228 slaves; Portuguese slaver captured with 174 Angolan slaves, mainly children.

1687: First petition by burghers to open the slave trade to private enterprise.

1700: First *placcaat* restricting Eastern slaves being brought to the Cape (August 24).

1706: Burgher rebellion.

1713: Smallpox epidemic.

1717: Company directors decide that assisted European immigration should end.

1719: Petition by burghers to open up the slave trade to private enterprise.

1720: France occupies Mauritius, formerly the staging post for Cape slaving expeditions.

1721: Dutch establish a slaving post at Maputo (Lourenço Marques).

1732: Mutiny forces abandonment of Maputo post.

1742: Capitejn, a Christian ex-slave from Elmira, writes his dissertation on slavery and Christianity at Leiden University.

1745–

1746: Further petitions by burghers to open up the slave trade to private enterprise.

1753: Codification of slave law by Rijk Tulbagh, Cape Governor.

1755: Smallpox epidemic.

1767: Smallpox epidemic.

1767: Abolition of the importation of Asian male slaves.

1770: General re-codification of all law in the Statutes of India, including many articles affecting slaves.

1779: Petition by burghers to open the slave trade to private entrprise.

1784: Petition by burghers to open the slave trade to private enterprise; repeated *placcaat* for abolition of the importation of Asian male slaves.

1787: Repeated *placcaat* for abolition of the importation of Asian male slaves.

1791: Slave trade opened to private enterprise.

1795: First British occupation; torture abolished.

1802: The Cape colony reverts to the Netherlands, now Batavian Republic.

1807: Abolition of Slave Trade Act passed in Britain (March 25).

1808: Slave Trade Abolition Act enforced (March 1).

1813: Codification of Cape Slave Law by Fiscal Dennyson.

1823: Trinidad Order-in-Council affected slaves throughout the British empire.

1825: Royal Commission of Enquiry sits at the Cape, presents findings on Cape slavery.

1826: Slave owners revolt.

1828: Emancipation of the Lodge slaves and Khoi — "the Hottentot emancipation."

1833: Emancipation Decree passed in London.

1834–

1838: Four-year period of "apprenticeship" instituted.

1838: Emancipation becomes effective.

1910: Katie Jacobs, last creole slave, is interviewed.

Abbreviations

AR	Algemeine Rijksarchief
AYB	*Archives Year Book*
C	Dutch East India Company Records in CAD
CAD	Cape Archives Depot
CGHSB	Cape of Good Hope Savings Bank
CJ	Court of Justice
CO	Colonial Office (both CAD and PRO)
DO	Deeds Office
DNDT	Delft Nederlandsche Topografische Dienst
DRCA	Dutch Reformed Church Archives
DSAB	*Dictionary of South African Biography*
KA	Original VOC archival prefix
LJ	Leibbrandt's Journal (1699–1731)
LM	Leibbrandt's manuscripts in CAD
LR	Leibbrandt's Requesten (published)
M	Cape Archives Reference, Miscellaneous collections
MOOC	Master of Orphan Chamber, probate documents
NP	Notarial Protocols
OCF	Old Cape freeholds
OSF	Old Stellenbosch freeholds
PB	Placcaat Boeke
PRO	Public Record Office
QBSAL	*Quarterly Bulletin of the South African Library*
RCC	Theal, *Records of the Cape Colony*
SABP	South African Bound Pamphlets
SAL	South African Library
SO	Slave Office Papers
UB	Union Buildings
VC	Verbatim Copies series in CAD
VOC	Archival prefix for some Rijksarchief documents
VRS	Van Riebeeck Society

Glossary

Afrikaner (Africander)	*Creole slave of Malay and European descent; later, a person of "European" descent*
Aia (*Ayia*)	Nursemaid
Amok, Amuck	Solo, frenzied burst of violent revenge
Apprenticeship	Changing euphemism for bonded labor after 1808
Banditti, Bandiet	Convicts
Banneling	Political exile
Binnemoeders	Slave women appointed as overseers of slave women
Boer	Settler farmer
Buijtemoeders	Officials' wives who oversaw Company slave women
Burgher	Settler living in a town
Bushman	One of the San people
Cadastral slavery	A system whereby persons are sold along with land
Caffer	One of the Company slaves assigned to policing duties
Capon	A young male slave on the slave trade
Coartición	Cuban term for the process whereby slaves could purchase freedom
Creole	Locally born
Creolization	The process whereby a slave society becomes locally born
Fiscal	Company official second in command of colony *and* in charge of slaves' welfare
Free black	Nonindigene of insufficient European ancestry
Gulden (Guilder)	Dutch unit of currency
Halfslag (half-breed)	One of half-European descent, *not* a mixture of other groups
Heelslag (Full-breed)	One of non-European descent
Herrenvolk	The master class's race
Hottentots	The Khoikhoi
Knecht	Overseer, manservant
Malay	Slave from Indonesian Archipelago, sometimes Muslim
Mandoor	Slave overseer of other slaves
Mardijcker	Slave freed for defensive purposes
Matres	Female slave woman in charge of other slave women
Matronym	Part of name identifying mother
Mestiço	Half-breed
Minnemoer	Wet nurse
Monsterrollen	Garrison muster
Nuweling	Newly arrived slave

Officier jongen	Male slave officer
Onderbaas	Slave foreman
Ondermeesteress	Slave woman in charge of younger slave women
Oorlam	One who has been overseas or into the interior; experienced
Opgaaf	Colony muster and census
Palang	Heavy club carried by the Caffers
Patronym	Part of name identifying father
Patroon	Owner of the estate who had freed a slave
Prisoner-slaves	Convicts who lived as slaves
Prize negroes	Slaves captured on ships after 1808 and landed at the Cape
Rixdaalder (Rixdollar)	Unit of currency
Sambo	Locally born slave of mixed descent
Sjambok	Heavy, four-foot-long whip made of rhinoceros hide
Slameier	Muslim "Malay"
Stuiver	Subunit of currency
Toponym	Part of name identifying origin
Werf	Area around the main house

A Note on Terminology and Currency

MANY OF THE WORDS AND TERMS IN THIS BOOK, SUCH AS CAFFER and "half-breed" may seem offensive to some South African readers. No doubt many will be surprised to find that in this period the word *Afrikan[d]er* also meant mulatto or half-caste, and was applied to slaves *and* ex-slaves until the first Afrikaans language movement in the 1860s. It was only much later in the nineteenth century that "Afrikaner" came to be associated with its current meaning of Christian people of European descent, who style themselves "white." To avoid consternation I have used the word *mulatto,* for all such miscegenated Afrikaner slaves, grouping them under the broader "creole" category — that is, in the Spanish sense of *criolle,* "locally born." The descent rules at the Cape, from which these terms derive, were complex and are explained in the text. At the first occurrence of such words, I have put them in quotation marks, or in italics, but thereafter have used them as they were used in the period, freely. I have tried to avoid using Dutch, German, French, Malay, and Latin in the text, keeping the original words, in the case of pivotal translations, in notes. Some words will always defy translation, and in the preceding Glossary, I provide a short list of contextual definitions of such terms. Such words are also defined in the text and notes, and the still-curious reader is directed to the index.

During the Dutch period, the florin, guilder and rixdollar were the main currency denominations at the Cape.[1] According to Kristoff Glaman, the Dutch East India Company never succeeded in establishing a standard coin of the realm: bullion movement from West to East ensured that these currencies fluctuated widely depending on the area of their circulation.[2] When demonetized European coinage was sent to the East, the coinage was actually physically clipped. The Cape, being midway between East and West, dealt with both values. By 1658 there arose the terms "heavy" and "light" money: light (clipped) money which was fixed at 80 percent of its European heavy value. Officials were salaried in heavy money, but slave purchases from the East were often in light, sometimes called "Indian valuation." Moreover, many coins had different values simultaneously. The Company "unit of account" was, until 1658, the guilder, florin, or real, which had a theoretical equal value in both Holland and Batavia. This was changed, and the Rixdaalder (rixdollar) which replaced the florin or real as the unit of account, was fixed at 3 florins per rixdollar. This did not stay constant, but it is the best overall rate of exchange. I have used this rate of exchange for the thousands of slave sale prices. Spanish pieces of eight and realen were all roughly equivalent to a florin. One further quirk deserves mention: the payment of Cape property was invariably in florins until 1795.

---

[1] E. M. Shaw, "A History of Currency in South Africa," (Cape Town: South African Museum, Guide No. 5, 1956), pp. 1–14.

[2] Kristoff Glamann, *Dutch-Asiatic Trade: 1620–1740* (The Hague: Martinus Nijhoff, 1981), pp. 50–72.

There were various valuations of these denominations, even of "Cape" valuations. The basic unit of currency below the unit of the rixdollar was the stuiver, but apart from British pennies there was little metallic currency in circulation at the Cape. There were no real banks until the late eighteenth century. Because of the fluctuating value of the Rixdollar, gold and silver fled the country, as W. W. Bird, the chief comptroller of customs remarked in 1822: "The golden and silver age are forgotten by the inhabitants of the Cape, and are only remembered in Ovid's metamorphosis."[3] In the seventeenth century several other currencies were also accepted. To simplify, I have always converted all currencies to rixdollars, which survived well into the British periods (1795 to 1802 and 1806 to 1820), after which English pounds, shillings, and pence became the standard currency.

The basic unit of acreage was the morgen, which was about 2.25 acres. I have used the morgen throughout, since this measure also survived into the Batavian (1803–1806) and two British occupations (1795–1802; 1806–1815).

---

[3] W. W. Bird, *State of the Cape of Good Hope in 1822* (Cape Town: Struik, 1966 reprint), p. 39.

Appendices

RESEARCH FOR THIS BOOK was done using several data sets derived from archival sources. The methodological assumption is that the researcher can generate new historical knowledge from statistical variance and statistical significance. Individual cases drawn from the data set are used only to illustrate the findings generated by the data sets, but by establishing context and ambience they are still scientifically useful. When no systematic data were available for specific topics, I have freely, but skeptically, relied on anecdotal sources from travelers, officials, and diaries. With the exception of two data sets, no sampling was used. There are three basic kinds of data sets used in this study. The first type is data aggregated by year. An example is the table of slaves on pages 445–448 (drawn from "Popucape"); a combination of synchronic censuses, i.e. censuses or lists from one moment in time, for example, 1705; a diachronic prosopographies (see example Baptisms, Saledeed, and 1823sale). All the data sets are in *Lotus 1-2-3* format and in SPSS system files and are available on request from the author.

Data set name	Type[1]	Dates (Anno)[2]	Variable Quality[3]	No. var's[4]	No. of cases/years	Chapter Ref's	Archival groups[5]
1682opga	li	1680	n and a	14	168	5	AR KA 3994[6]
1693lodg	li	1693	n and a	7	369	6	VOC 4030, folios 359–367
1705mons	li	1705 (Jun)	li	4	542	1-5	AR
1705opga	ce	1706 (Dec)	n and a	4	513	1, 5	AR
1719opga	ce	1719 (May 1720)	n and a	26	800	5	AR VOC 4085
1762town	li	1762	n and a	12	266	5	CAD C 798
1823sale	li	1823–30	n and a	31	4,029	4	CAD
1833popp	ag	1833	n	3	NA	4,5	PRO CO 53/57
Baptisms	pr	1680–1731	n and a	45	1,124	11, 12	DRCA
Deedbook[7]	pr	1680–1731	n and a	30	2,047	All	DO; CAD; OSF; OCF
Fontaine[8]	li	1731	n and a	36	840	1, 5	AR (Rademacher)
Lodclock	ag	1656–1828	n	42	176 yrs	6	AR; CAD
Manucomb	pr	1658–1831	n and a	55	1,876	11, 12	CAD
Popucape	ag	1652–1835	n	260	176 yrs	All	AR; DO; DRCA; CAD; PRO
Saledeed	pr	1652–1782	n and a	45	4,107	4,5	DO; CAD

[1] Type of dataset: pr=prosopography; li=list; ce=census; ag=agregated data

[2] See discussion of Anno convention of dating censuses, p. 439.

[3] N=numeric, e.g. five slaves; A=alphanumeric, e.g. categorical data, e.g. "Malagasy" slave, or names, e.g. "Rangton."

[4] Variables are characteristics of individual cases, such as age (n) origin (a).

[5] See "List of Abbreviations," p. 419.

[6] Old numbering system.

[7] Privately published: Leonard Guelke, Robert Shell, comps., "The Deeds Book: The Cape Cadastral Calendar" (New Haven: Opgaaf Project, 1990), pp. 1–160.

[8] Privately published: Leonard Guelke, Robert Shell and Anthony Whyte, comps., "The De lla Fontaine Report" (New Haven: Opgaaf Project, 1990), pp. 1–148.

Appendix 2
The Records of the Slave Trade

Elimination of Creole Slaves from the Count
Several attempts have already been made to establish the geographic origins of the imported slaves, with quite different results. The first problem arises in establishing the origins of Cape slaves, all researchers have included the sizable "van der Kaap" (creole) population in their tabulations of origins. Since the rate of creolization (the percentage of Cape slaves who were locally born) changed quite independently of the slave trade, the inclusion of *any* creole slaves in *any* tabulation of origins confuses the exact breakdown of origins of imported slaves. Creolization, simply put, is a different process that had discrete demographic and cultural consequences within the household.[1]

Pars pro Toto (Part for the Whole)
The second major problem is that scholars have worked with tallies of one Cape slave population (there were three: burghers' slaves, officials' slaves, and the slave Lodge) and made assumptions about the others. We lack an overall estimate of the slave trade. The Lodge slave trade alone is well documented, since it was sanctioned and sponsored by the Company directors.[2] The slave Lodge was a discreet, small, and wholly atypical slave community whose numerical significance dwindled as the privately owned slave populations grew. By 1795 the privately owned slave force had grown to 60 times the

---

[1] See Appendix 3.

[2] Nevertheless there was much deviousness in the local record keeping. The accounting procedures are deeply flawed for every voyage: totals do not agree, and deliberate confusion is suspected. Some voyages are not mentioned, but did take place. The May 1679 voyage of the 1,000-ton *Oliphant*, one of the very largest ships in the Dutch fleet, is a case in point. According to the authors of *Dutch Asiatic Shipping*, the ship was "laid up in Batavia in 1665," but there was a voyage to Madagascar recorded in the *Brieven Overcomen*. However, the journal in the inventory is marked *uijtgenomen* ("taken out"); cf. AR: VOC 4014 (May 1679), folios 546, 719. Nor is the voyage mentioned in volume 2 of the heavily indexed *Resolutions*. The 1698 voyage of the Swaag is not mentioned in *Dutch Asiatic Shipping*, but it did bring slaves to the Cape; cf. Transporten T1697/8 (27 January 1698), n.p. Clear deceit is evident in the daily journal of 10 February 1711: "The Council decides to retain a vessel here until the commissioner's arrival . . . none have been imported since the time of Simon van der Stel," *LJ*, p. 245. No trip is recorded and yet we know from the Transporten that hundreds of slaves were imported from the time of Simon van der Stel. A "list of articles required for a slave trip to that Island [Madagascar]" in 1719 is mentioned in Leibbrandt *Requesten (Memorials) 1715–1806* (Cape Town: South African Library, 1989), vol. 5 index, p. 7371 [incorrect], but see *Requesten* (no. 59 of 18 July 1719), vol. 2, p. 737; however, there was no voyage mentioned in the carefully indexed and annotated *Resolutions*. One can be therefore be fairly certain that the documents concerning the Lodge slave trade are not as straightforward as they appear to be.

size of the slave Lodge; by 1826, the last recorded census of the Lodge, the Lodge population represented only .32 of 1 percent of all Cape slaves. The Lodge, in short, became an increasingly numerically insignificant part of the Cape slave population. Thanks to the work of James Armstrong and James Ravel, one may calculate the total number of slaves imported to the Lodge by tabulating origins and tallying purchases on all voyages.[3] Despite its numerical insignificance, the Lodge slave trade has dominated most discussion of the Cape slave trade. No one has ever made an estimate of the number of slaves imported by the officials, who were the main slave traders of the colony. A "100 percent surface chart" reveals the true proportions of the three populations (see Figure 5-10).

Underrepresentation

Underrepresentation is the third problem in analyzing the slave trade, and it concerns the bulk of the slave imports, the slave trade serving the individuals in the employ of the Company, and the free burgher and free black populations. Because of the multifaceted, illegal, and clandestine nature of most of this private Cape slave trade, these records are sometimes missing, often arcane, and always difficult to interpret. Perhaps for these reasons, no attempt, even in the roughest form, has ever been made to establish the number of slaves imported by these individuals at the Cape. The detailed though sometimes deliberately evasive and certainly incomplete slave transfers (1658 to 1732), probate records, annual censuses from 1658 through 1834, shipping movements, records of slave voyages themselves, and traveler's remarks do, however, allow for a preliminary, arithmetical reconstruction of the bulk of the slave trade. The techniques used here are familiar to historical demographers — namely, the techniques of stable population theory, first used by demographers for populations with inadequate data and quite suitable for historians.[4]

---

[3] Some of the Company slave voyages have been published: see the *Snuffelaar* (and *de Zeepost*) in E. C. Godée-Molsbergen (comp.), *Reizen in Zuid-Afrika* ('s-Gravenhage: Martinus Nijhoff, 1976), vol. 3, 220–257; the *De Brak* captained by Otto Lüder Hemmy, in A. Grandidier et al., *Collection des Ouvrages Anciens Concernant Madagascar* 6 (1913) — virtually impossible to obtain; the *De Brak* in Maurice Boucher, "The Voyage of a Cape Slaver in 1742," *Historia* 24, 1 (May 1979): 50–58; see also his fragment of a Danish Company voyage and the journal of a supercargo, in Boucher, "An Unexpected Visitor: Charles Barrington at the Cape," *South African Historical Journal* 13 (1981): 20–35; Robert Ross (ed.), "The Dutch on the Swahili Coast, 1776–78," part 1, *International Journal of African Historical Studies* 19, 2 (1986): 479–506; and part 2 Ibid. 19, 3 (1986): 305–358. The director of the South African Library, P. Westra, is busy with the voyage of the *Leidsman* in 1715 and it will appear shortly in the *QB South African Library*. Non-Company sources such as travelers' accounts, not being subject to the purview of the Company directors, provide invaluable commentary on the Lodge's archival sources.

[4] The main techniques are drawn from a handbook published by the United Nations, Department of Economic and Social Affairs: *The Concept of a Stable Population: Application to the Study of Populations of Countries with Incomplete Demographic Statistics* (New York: United Nations, 1968). This appendix draws its evidence from the level of individual slave sales (1658 to 1795), from slave voyages (1856 to 1822), from aggregated imports derived from the censuses (1656 to 1808), from the "compensation lists" for 1823 through 1829 (CAD SO 10/18), and

The Reconstitution of the Slaves Belonging to the Port Patriciate

An immediate problem to surmount is that the official census returns do not correlate with known individual slave trading voyages, nor do annual census increases correlate with the estimated totals of recorded slave trade imports, when controlled for natural reproduction, mortality, manumission, running away, and even migration of owners. In short, increases in the censuses are largely unexplained, at least by documented slave trading to the burghers. This problem is resolved, however, when one realizes that no Cape census ever accounted for Company officials' slaves and those belonging to a certain select group of wealthy, retired, urban burgher councilors, who obtained the privilege of staying off the burgher census rolls, but who were among the main actors in Cape slave trading. This group of slave owners, which has never been identified, I have termed the port's "patriciate."

There was, in short, a sizable Cape slave population, that was never systematically recorded nor mentioned in the secondary literature. Victor de Kock was probably most influential in obscuring the patriciate's slave population when he wrote: "Slaves at the Cape fell into two main classes: those belonging to the Dutch East India Company [the Lodge slaves] and those owned by individual officials, burghers and farmers."[5] A revised taxonomy of the Cape slave populations is the key to achieving a workable census of the Cape slave trade. The existence of the patriciate slave population is by no means speculative: we know of the slave population independently through the oceanic and domestic slave transfers up to 1795, through manumissions from 1658 to 1795, and through baptismal records from 1658 to 1795.[6] We also know of this slave population through Company officials' wills, auction (*vendu*) lists, and repatriations from 1658 through 1798, all of which indicate sizable households of slaves. Their aggregated slave holdings have been reconstituted from several independent sources, from slave

---

from a detailed estimate of the population made by British officials in August 1833 (PRO CO 53/57). The first class of records is the transfers, detailed records of individual slaves from 1658 through 1717. These slave transfers were, until recently, interfiled with the cadastral records of the Cape Town Municipal Deeds Office (DO), "Transporten en Schepenkennis" (1680 to 1715), and the overlapping and continuing series for 1717 to 1732 in CAD: "Obligatien, Schultbrieven" and "Misc. notarial documents," CJ 2914 to CJ 3081. Since some statements and all charts and graphs in this book are based on several thousand observations, I could scarcely footnote all; instead, an appendix reference in my dissertation is alluded to in the notes. See specifically the "sales appendix" for a full description of the compilation and coding of data. Robert C.-H. Shell, "Slavery at the Cape of Good Hope," Ph.D. dissertation, Yale University, 1986). After 1717 — the year of the decision to base the colony on slave labor — the individual transfer records start deteriorating until they disappear after 1732, in which year a new system of registering slaves came into being. Thereafter, slave traders and buyers only had a copy of the deed of sale. Very few of these private deeds of sale have survived in miscellaneous collections. There was no central registry of slaves from 1732 until 1817, the year of the establishment of the Slave Office. After 1732, therefore, the researcher is obliged to turn to the censuses, which begin in 1658 and run to 1793, start again in 1806 and run through to 1826.

[5] Victor de Kock, *Those in Bondage* (London: Allen & Unwin, 1950), p. 36.

[6] The latter also provide a guide to the number of creole slaves born in the households of the patriciate.

transfers for 1658 to 1732, and from specific registration events — for example, from the jump in slave enumerations in the 1706 through 1708 censuses. The unexplained surge in burgher holdings between 1706 and 1708 was a result of the plantation patriciate being recalled to the Netherlands and being forced to divest themselves of their slaves to the burghers. Another such event was a one-time slave corvée and registration of all company officials' slaves in 1762. The large jump in the Cape slave population between 1795 and 1798 is, in part, a result of resident Dutch East India Company officials, who were for the first time obliged, on oath, to give an account of their slave holdings to the new British administration. Adding the estimates of these patrician slaves to the slaves on the annual census allows one to estimate the total privately owned slave population much more accurately.

Patricians' slaves could be sold directly to the burghers or be bequeathed to burgher heirs (Company officials' offspring became burghers); in such cases the slaves would suddenly appear on the next year's census. Furthermore, in economically favorable times individual Company employees might leave the service (most often to marry a burgher's daughter); they and their slave returns would appear on the following year's census.[7] Once the Dutch East India Company stopped supporting the immigration of free people in 1717, those resigning from the Company and applying for burgher status represented the second greatest source of immigrants to the colony (the slave trade itself being the most important).[8] On the other hand, in hard times burghers sold their slaves to members of the patriciate, who always had substantially larger economic resources and salaries with which to weather rough periods; such slaves correspondingly "left" the census in the year following the sale.[9] Similarly, in hard times a few burghers would apply to be taken back into Company service, in which case their slaves would also disappear from the subsequent burgher census.

The significant but hitherto unexplained annual fluctuation of slaves on the exclusively burgher and free black census is, in the main, a registration artifact. Moreover, this fluctuation was not a random process but was correlated to both Cape maritime commercial cycles and economic conditions within the colony. This movement of slaves off and on the censuses — that is, slaves being traded and "moving" between the off-census patriciate and the enumerated burghers — continued until 1795, when Company officials ceased to be "officials" and became burghers. For the first time, the Dutch East India Company officials were not in charge of the record keeping of the colony, and they and their slaves were registered along with everybody else's. The year 1795 thus provides the last observation point for the patricians' slaves. The incoming British officials were never required to account for their slaves, and there is therefore something of a gap in their slave returns until 1838, which I have not reconstituted.

One way out of the dilemma posed by the nonregistration of the patricians' slaves is to add the new estimates of the patricians' slaves to the reliable burgher censuses and

---

[7] See Leibrandt's five-volume *Requesten,* which contains more than 1,000 such applications.

[8] Robert C.-H. Shell, "Immigration: The Forgotten Factor in South African Frontier Expansion," South African Research Project, New Haven, Conn., 1980.

[9] See Chapter 4 on the domestic trade.

from that new series of base numbers of slaves, calculate the slave trade to both populations by arithmetical means, controlling for both vital rates (fertility and mortality), for manumission, and for running away, data that have been independently collected. According to a visual observed matrix of this calculation showing formulae, approximately 1,770 calculations were solved simultaneously to retrodict the annual number of slaves imported, which came to 62,964 including the Lodge slaves, but excluding "prize negroes" and convicts.

Shortened Time Frames

A further problem is that no early researchers could have known how rapidly the slave trades to the Cape changed, both in magnitude and in geographical vectors. Their chosen periods of study — whether it was W. Blommaerts' 1652 to 1662 period, A. Böeseken's 1652 to 1700 span, my 1680 to 1731 dissertation period, H. P. Cruse's 1714 to 1795 period, J. L. M. Franken's 1672 to 1772 crime records, or even J. Armstrong's work on the entire Dutch period between 1652 and 1795 — resulted in assumptions that did not consider the total importation of all slaves from 1652 to 1808. In the early stages of research, how could anyone know that the second half of the seventeenth century, with its African slave majority, was a precursor of the nineteenth century? How could anyone guess that after 1795 and before 1808 more slaves would be imported to the Cape than at any other comparable period — and, moreover, from a wholly different direction? The estimates made by earlier researchers working with data from their chosen periods were valid only for those periods and not for the slave trade as a whole.

Sampling Errors

A problem with establishing origins has been inappropriate sampling. Franken, the Stellenbosch historian working in the 1930s, first tabulated slave origins using slave names mentioned in the voluminous crime records, assuming them to be representative of all slaves. He estimated that from 1672 to 1772, 63 percent of the imported slaves came from the Indonesian Archipelago.[10] However, since slaves mentioned in crime records were not a representative sample of all Cape slaves (rural crimes were underrepresented), little reliance should have been placed on Franken's work. Cruse, a Stellenbosch theologian, also worked on slave origins; he published his work shortly after World War II. He used only slave origins mentioned in published manumission requests between 1713 and 1795.[11] Just as Franken made assumptions about his crime records, so too did Cruse assume that his manumissions were a representative subset of all Cape slaves. This was also mistaken, but how could Cruse guess that Dutch-speaking slaves from the Eastern possessions managed to manumit themselves more easily than Africans, and especially Malagasy slaves? Moreover, since manumission was an urban process, the urban slaves, with their specific Eastern geographic origins, were

---

[10] J. L. M. Franken, "Vertolking aan die Kaap in Maleis en Portugees," *Huisgenoot* (18 June 1930), p. 41.

[11] H. P. Cruse, *Die Opheffing van die Kleurbevolking* (Stellenbosch: Die Christenstudentevereeniging van Suid Africa, 1947), pp. 267–268.

overrepresented in Cruse's tabulation. If one believed that Cruse's sample was sound, one would also have to believe that all slaves in the Lodge were born there, since lodge manumissions, with a handful of exceptions, were all for creole slaves. But more than 5,000 slaves were imported into the Lodge between 1652 and 1812. In short, manumitted slaves are not representative of any Cape slave population.[12] As it turned out, Cruse's calculations meshed with and therefore reinforced Franken's figures. Therefore later scholars, such as I. D. du Plessis, used Franken's and Cruse's figures in their popular works, from which they entered the historical consciousness of South Africa. Consequently most schoolchildren were traditionally taught that "a few Malay" slaves were brought to the Cape, although I. D. du Plessis simply added the "few."[13]

Frank Bradlow and Margaret Cairns, two South Africa-based historians, have made perhaps the most scientific and wide-ranging study. Both researchers were fully aware of the *changing* origins of the Cape slave force, and for the first time, probate documents and the slave registry from the Slave Office (1816 to 1824) were used for the entire period of Cape slavery. Bradlow and Cairns also used a larger sample size, drawn from a wider range of documents.[14] There were, however, built-in biases in their otherwise careful work. First, they considered "free blacks" synonymous with ex-slaves. The reason for this understandable but mistaken conflation is not obvious. All manumitted slaves did enter the "free black" community, but not all free blacks had been slaves, since at the Cape, many free blacks originated from the population of convicts and political exiles, all of whom came from Indonesia and other Eastern possessions, from Jaffnapatnam in Sri Lanka to Mocha on the Red Sea coast. When these exiles and convicts had served their time, they also entered the census's free black population and were confidently tabulated by Bradlow and Cairns as ex-slaves. However, they were not slaves and many of them simply left the colony after their sentences had been served.[15] Since the free blacks were a small group and the convicts and exiles sizable, the bias here was considerable. Assuming that free blacks were drawn from the slave population inflated their estimation of the Eastern component of all Cape slaves, since nearly all the exiles were Indonesian and nearly all convicts were Indo-Chinese, Indonesian, or Sri Lankan.[16]

---

[12] See Chapter 12 on manumission.

[13] I. D. du Plessis, *The Cape Malays,* 3rd ed. (Cape Town: Balkema, 1972), p. 3.

[14] Frank R. Bradlow and Margaret Cairns, *The Early Cape Muslims* (Cape Town: Balkema, 1978), pp. 80–106.

[15] Robert C.-H. Shell, "The Establishment and Spread of Islam . . . ," honors thesis, University of Cape Town, 1975, p. 21.

[16] I am aware that Hans Heese and Leon Hattingh have attacked this definition of free blacks. Their criticism has arisen, at least in part, because there was no real legal definition of free blacks in the Dutch East India Company period. Under the British administration this changed. A document detailing the legal status of free blacks before Ordinance 50 clearly *includes* the political exiles and convicts as "Free Blacks"; CAD M142 (6): "Laws relating to Freeblacks in the Colony of the Cape of Good Hope." Article One states clearly: "The class of people commonly called Freeblacks, has originated in this Colony partly from the manumissions of Slaves partly from the transportation of native Inhabitants of some of the East India Countries, removed to this Colony either as State-prisoners or as Convicts (*vide:* Interdiction of the 20 April 1779) and

Double Counting

Bradlow and Cairns also used manumission data, which are flawed as a source for slave origins on two counts. Since they incorporated slave transfers from the oceanic trade, their most important bias is double counting: all imported manumitted slaves had already been counted as slave imports in their lists recording ship-to-shore transactions of the slave trade. Since some manumitted slaves took on a new name (sometimes baptismal) at the time of manumission, I am convinced that such slaves were counted twice. For instance, "Ramtom van Matije" (a village in Bali) was imported in 1698, and in 1712 he was manumitted as "Rangton van Bali." The two records, housed in different archives, each with a different spelling for the same individual, would be counted as *two* individuals from the Indonesian Archipelago.[17] Of all events in a Cape slave's life, manumission was recorded with the most fidelity. More than fifteen hundred manumission requests are in published form; Bradlow and Cairns did not sample this class of documents, but instead counted them all. Manumissions therefore represent a sizable source of systemic error in the Bradlow-Cairns tabulations.

The same objection must also be leveled at their inclusion of imported slaves mentioned in domestic sales, since such slaves were also previously counted in ship-to-shore transactions. Also, there was no limit on the number of times a slave could be sold on the domestic market, which could therefore result in multiple counting of the same slave. Slaves imported from the Dutch possessions in Indonesia were invariably resold in Cape Town by Dutch officials wishing to make a quick profit; African and Malagasy slaves, on the other hand, were sold directly from ship to farm and were rarely resold. Indonesian slaves therefore appear more frequently in their tallies. Using Bradlow's and Cairn's system, a single slave could be imported, sold, sold again, and then manumitted, and be counted as four slaves. The thrust of their collaboration has, not surprisingly, tended to magnify the Eastern component of the origins of Cape slaves and therefore to confirm both Franken's and Cruse's research of a generation before, whose work they duly incorporated in one table, albeit with reservations.[18] Having said all this, the remainder of the Bradlow-Cairns collaboration is still more than useful. They brought to light the sizable number of slaves from the Indian subcontinent. Thanks to the explanatory notes, accurate tallying, and carefully stated assumptions behind each table, one can retrieve and rework much of their data on slave origins.[19]

---

finally also from the arrival of Indians and Chinese, who have been allowed for a time to reside in this Colony subject to removal at the pleasure of Government. The Freeblacks are thus originally foreigners, and as such distinguishable from the Hottentots and other Natives of this Colony." This definition of Free blacks is contested in Hans Heese, "Challenging Certain Aspects of Intergroup Relations in *The Shaping of South African Society, 1652–1840:* A Review Article," *Kronos* 17: 71–76, but see "A Reply to Hans Heese" and also Heese's riposte, *Kronos* 18 (1991).

[17] Robert C.-H. Shell, "Rangton of Bali: The Short Life and Personal Belongings of One Slave," *Kronos* 18 (1991): 1–6.

[18] Bradlow and Cairns, *The Early Cape Muslims,* p. 99, Table 7.

[19] However, all the biased data must be excised; all creole slaves must be cut from each remaining table; all "unknowns" must be dropped, a value that changes quite randomly in each class of documents. Leon Hattingh, the former head of the Historical Research Institute at the University of the Western Cape, has also counted the transfers, carefully rechecking and publish-

In strong contrast to Bradlow and Cairns, James Armstrong has tentatively targeted Madagascar as the main source for the privately owned Cape slaves up until 1795, his cutoff date. He has made only tentative estimates of "100–200 slaves per annum" for the bulk of the Cape slave trade; even in combination with the most generous rate of natural increase (which would result in a smaller slave trade), his estimates cannot account for the increase in the old or my revised "Anno" census returns (see page 445–448).[20] Moreover Armstrong has not made any discrete estimates of the slaves privately imported by the port's patriciate, Cape Town's most important slave traders, nor has he made any estimates beyond 1795, the period of heaviest trading.[21] James Armstrong has steadfastly held that the major source of Lodge slaves was Madagascar. His research, conducted over many years and in numerous archives in the Indian Ocean Basin, has concentrated on tabulating Company slave

---

ing verbatim copies of the primary material that Anna Böeseken and Margaret Cairns had earlier collected and published in 1975. His meticulously published material, up to 1679, insofar as it corrects the Böeseken data, has been incorporated in this volume. See J. L. Hattingh, "Kaapse Notariële Stukke Waarin Slawe van Vryburgers en Amptenare Vermeld Word," *Kronos* 14 (1988–9): 14–37; continued in the subsequent issue (pages are repeated in my copy, no doubt a printer's error). Hattingh, however, does not deal with the Lodge slaves imported by the Company.

[20] See the discussion on the revised *opgaaf* returns in Appendix 3. James Armstrong and Nigel Worden, "The Slaves, 1652–1834" in Richard Elphick and Herman Giliomee (eds.), *The Shaping of South African Society 1652–1820* rev. ed. (Middletown, Conn.: Wesleyan University Press, 1989), p. 120; Nigel Worden, another historian of Cape slavery, has concentrated on rural Cape slavery and has also made some tentative estimates of slave origins in the rural area of Stellenbosch (1722–1799) in one table, based on probate material, which in broad measure supports Franken and Cruse. However, the oceanic slave trade was conducted in the port city and his conclusions about that trade are therefore heavily inferential; also, he exclusively worked on burgher inventories, all officials' slaves' origins are missing. In addition, according to the census (*opgaaf*) returns, rural rates of creolization were quite different from urban, another source of bias in Worden's estimation of origins of imported slaves. There were, for instance more slave children per women in the Stellenbosch district. This is based on slave child-slave woman ratios by region in archival *opgaafs*, 1658 through 1834; a handy published summary (for every five years) is found in Coenraad Beyers, *Die Kaapse Patriotte* (*1779–1791*) (Cape Town: Juta, 1929), Bylaag (H): "Opgaaf rolle . . . Burghers, 1701–1793," pp. 240–249; and for annual totals, see Robert Ross et al., *The Economy of the Cape Colony in the Eighteenth Century* (Leiden: Intercontinenta, No. 7, 1987), "Appendices." Nigel Worden has, however, tabulated many thousands of cases from Stellenbosch inventories, valuable data which he has graciously shared and explained and I have reworked.

[21] His methodology is based on identifying and counting slave voyages. Since more than 10,000 ships visited the Cape in the Company period alone, it will be a long time before we know the result of this research, since there is no efficient way of identifying ships carrying slaves. Since the vast bulk of the Cape slave trade was conducted in a clandestine manner by Company officials and wealthy urban burghers building their private fortunes, and since the same people oversaw the archival sources detailing the oceanic trade in their primary state, records of the illegal trade are, not surprisingly, both sparse and extreme misleading. In the light of deliberate distortion by officials concerning the importation of privately owned slaves, the historian must make estimates that go beyond the preserved records, whose primary purpose, I argue, was to mislead the Company directors.

voyages, the only such work to use this painstaking approach. His austere research (almost every sentence is based on several archival sources) still points in the direction of Madagascar.[22] This source of slaves remained relatively constant, although Company imports in the first decade also came from the west coast of Africa, and between 1721 and 1730 from Delagoa Bay. Later, Company sponsored trade to the east coast of Africa resulted in most Lodge slaves originating from the African mainland.[23] A slim majority of all Lodge slaves *did* come from Madagascar in the period with which he deals, that is, up to 1795, but the Lodge survived another generation before all the slaves were released in 1828. Many more slaves from Mozambique were imported into the Lodge after 1795 and before 1826: for example, from "prize negro" ships (1795 to 1803) and even after 1808 slaves from the 1812 voyage of the *Restuardor* ended up in the Lodge. By 1826 the Lodge also included some prize negroes who were from Mozambique.[24] Mozambique and the east coast of Africa became the major source of Lodge slaves *after* 1786.

In the following passage Robert Ross summarizes the current lack of knowledge of the Cape slave trade:

[The Cape slaves] derived almost exclusively from five areas: the Indonesian Archipelago, Bengal, South India and Sri Lanka, Madagascar and the East African coast. They had been bought in the slave markets of Batavia, Chinsura, Cochin, Boina and Delegoa Bay or Mozambique island, brought there by an as-yet-little-understood network of traders including Bengali Banians, Buginese trader pirates, Chinese junk captains, Saklava king' Prazeros on the Zambezi. Portuguese officials in Delegoa Bay and south to Natal or [by] kidnappers in South India. From there they were sent to the Cape, very often in small numbers and semi-legally as the cargo of sailors and officials on the VOC ships, otherwise in more regularized, probably large French and Portuguese slaving ships which sold off a number of their generally sickly slaves on their way to the New World.[25]

How persistent the notion of the Asian origins of the imported Cape slave population proved to be is exemplified in a recent — and otherwise excellent — work on Cape slavery in which the author refutes an accurate nineteenth-century source on the African origins of Cape slaves in that period, with the quite erroneous assertion that "large numbers were, in fact, Asians." Not even a footnote was used to refute the original source, evidence of how ingrained the early assumptions still are in the current literature.[26]

---

[22] Armstrong and Worden, "The Slaves," 122–125.

[23] There were attempts by the Company to slave at Kilwa, Sofala, Zanzibar, and the Comores Islands later in the eighteenth century: Robert Ross (ed.), "The Dutch on the Swahili Coast, 1776–78," *International Journal of African Historical Studies* 19 2 (1986): 479–506; and part 2, ibid. 19 3 91986): 305–358.

[24] George McCall Theal, *Records of the Cape Colony* (Cape Town: Struik, 1967, hereafter *RCC*), 19: 264–268, "Return of Government Slaves."

[25] Robert Ross, *Cape of Torments* (London: Routledge and Kegan Paul, 1983), p. 13.

[26] Richard Watson, *The Slave Question* (Middletown, Conn.: Wesleyan University Press, 1990), p. 131.

New Methodology Used

In the light of conflicting estimates of both the proportions and origins of Cape slaves, how does one establish the origins of the Cape slave population? The approach used was to combine all the newly collected ship-to-shore transactions from 1656 to 1732[27] with later (1732 to 1799) random samples of probated slave owners' inventories, sources that all included the individual slaves' names and origins.[28] In addition, I have tabulated slaves' origins mentioned in surviving Cape Town domestic sales (eliminating any double counting) and blended them with the individual rural slaves' origins collected by Nigel Worden, Margaret Cairns, and other Cape historians. I have also tallied slaves' origins mentioned in Cape *vendus* and repatriations from 1658 through 1806, to obtain annual proportional estimates for the entire period.[29] All these quite independently collected data (for 1656 to 1824) were then weighted, lagged,[30] and multiplied by the independently calculated census estimates of the annual slave trade to chart the changing origins of the imported slave population. To these retrodicted annual totals, I have added the 5,100 Lodge slaves, data that James Armstrong has kindly provided.

Probate Records

The probate data are mainly taken from my own research (1652 through 1799) and from Nigel Worden's, Margaret Cairns's and Frank Bradlow's tabulations of rural inventories. Their data were adjusted to exclude "creole" and "unknown" components and also weighted from the relative regional proportions in the censuses to eliminate their rural bias. For the early nineteenth century I have exclusively relied on Margaret Cairns's tabulation of the slave registry returns from the second British occupation, both urban and rural, only pruning them of their "creole" and "unknown" components; both proportions changed independently of the operations of the slave trade.

Inventories

Disadvantages

Inventories are troublesome sources for the origins of slaves, since the probated slave was always passed on to another owner and could therefore conceivably be

---

[27] Because of the purposeful degradation of the record keeping of oceanic slave transfers after the inauguration of Jan de la Fontaine, a slave-trading governor, one cannot consult oceanic slave transfers after 1732. Cf. Leonard Guelke, Robert C.-H. Shell and Anthony Whyte (comps.), "The de la Fontaine Report" (New Haven, Conn.: Opgaaf Project, 1990), introduction.

[28] The latter two sets of 88 slaves provided by James Armstrong.

[29] Repatriation from South Africa was a random event, and therefore slave transfers resulting from repatriations provide a reliable guide to the origins of slaves. Since most repatriating owners were urban, these latter data, suitably weighted to their true proportion of the census, offset the considerable rural emphasis in the work of Cairns, Bradlow, and Worden. An early list of repatriating owners may be found in Guelke, Shell, and Whyte, "The de la Fontaine Report." A more comprehensive record of repatriating owners is in Leibbrandt, *Requesten,* passim.

[30] All probated material was lagged by 17.5 years, which was the difference between the mean age of imported slaves and the mean age of probated slaves. Cf. infra.

counted again in an heir's own inventory. Because half of the slaves in a typical will went to the younger generation, and since most slaves at the Cape suffered higher mortality than their owners, it is unlikely that many of those imported slaves survived through two generations of owners to be counted twice in consecutive generations of family wills. However, according to the Cape's partible inheritance scheme, the other half of the estate went to the deceased owner's spouse, whether male or female. It is therefore conceivable, but not very likely, that some probated slaves could be counted again when the inheriting spouse (or, for that matter, any laterally related heir) died. Since imported slaves from different regions had differing mortality rates, probate sampling could therefore also result in some minor double counting and undercounting.[31] For example, a typically long-lived Indonesian slave might survive through two owners, while a short-lived Malagasy slave might not live long enough to be probated.

The second drawback in using probated slaves' origins is that one can make few assumptions about exactly *when* an individual probated slave was imported. Since direct record links between a slave mentioned in a ship-to-shore transaction and the same slave recorded in a will or on a *vendu* list are virtually impossible to find because of changes of name (either baptismal changes or owner's preference), one is obliged to make an average estimate. For my calculations the average period between importation and the probate date was obtained by subtracting the average age of all slaves in ship-to-shore transactions from the average age of all probated noncreole slaves. I have somewhat glibly assumed that both averaged ages remained relatively constant throughout the period 1658 to 1808, on the basis that the age composition of imported slaves stayed relatively stable while there were no drastic changes in the life tables of Cape slave owners.[32] Thus, one can say with some confidence that probated slaves were imported, on average, 17.5 years before they were probated. This is a very useful figure, since it can be used to "lag" all probated slaves' origins to obtain a picture of the probable periods of importation for all imported slaves who were probated. Thus, to make an example of my assumption: I assume that Jephta of Bali, who was probated in the will of Jan Cornelissen in 1722, was *probably* imported in 1704. I rely here entirely on the law of large numbers.

Advantages
The advantages of using probate material far outweigh these considerable drawbacks and forced assumptions. First, wills, *vendu* lists, and inventories concern transferable property, and the compilers had a special interest in both their authenticity and accuracy. Second, inventories are the only source that reveal the origins of slaves

---

[31] See later section on mortality.

[32] The average age of 534 imported slaves in all probated sales — that is, sales in which either the Office of Sequestration, the Executors, the Orphan Chamber, or the Vendu Master were mentioned — was 37 years. In 1,170 ship-to-shore transactions, which recorded the exact age of the slave, the averaged age was 19.5 years. Many of the "unknowns" in the latter data were simply listed as "son" or "daughter" (children under 14) which suggest that if we knew the exact age of those children, a more accurate average would result in a longer period between importation and probate sale.

belonging to Company officials after 1731, after which time oceanic transfers recording their purchases were no longer maintained. A third attraction is that Cape probate material invariably provides information about both the locality and social status of the owner. Their final and compelling advantage lies in that they are also the only sources that systematically reveal the origins of *all* imported Cape slaves throughout the period, 1652 to 1833. They will assuredly provide the sources from which refinements of these estimates will emerge. David McCellan at the Cape Archives is busy coding the Notarial Protocols.

Appendix 3
The Slave Trade and Cape Demography

In the following analysis of the slave trade serving the patrician and burgher slave owners, I have made two estimates. The first, accepting the known low fertility-high mortality Cape data, retrodicts a large slave trade. The second, in deference to the possible inaccuracy or other inadequacies of the first model, is a hypothetical model based on high fertility and low mortality that retrodicts a smaller slave trade. The reason for stipulating two models is methodological conservatism. The data indicate that the Cape slave population increased at a faster rate than was possible by the most generous natural increase and by the currently accepted size of the slave trade to the Cape. This two-fold modeling procedure establishes a range of reality. Somewhere between the two estimates, one may reasonably be sure, lies the true picture of the slave trade. The two models may be expressed in the following single formula, in which the components may be substituted and the results subjected to sensitivity tests — for instance, testing against years for which the slave trade data are known, or simply testing and degrading the model until it fits or breaks down:

$$PI\,(ST + PL) = AISP + F + (D + M + R + E) \dots \dots \dots \dots 1$$

(where PI = predicted increase due to nonvital rates; ST = Oceanic Slave Trade; PL = Plagium (person-stealing, or enslaving of the authochthonous population); $AISP$ = annual increase in slave population; F = Fertility; D = Mortality; M = Manumission; R = Runaways; E = Emigration).

The equation was applied to each annual census (adjusted to include the slaves of the patriciate from 1658 through the end of 1807) to retrodict the annual increase that cannot be explained by the vital processes of fertility and mortality and the social processes of manumission, running away, and emigration. The result is the total unexplained increase, which, I argue, can only be due to two factors: the slave trade or plagium. It is not so much a model, divorced from reality, as it is an iterative arithmetical calculation using maximal and minimal vital limits on real observations of real populations.

The Cape Censuses and my "Anno" Convention

Since almost all of the calculations of the slave trade are based on the Cape censuses, a few words on these sources are needed. The reliability of the Cape censuses (*opgaafs*) has already been discussed elsewhere.[1] The *opgaaf* was an evolving document, that grew out of the *monsterrollen* (lists of the garrison) of the 1650s and 1660s, and by 1680 was one part militia muster, one part agricultural tax list, and one part demographic census. An import tax on slaves was levied in 1792, but landed slaves were not

---

[1] See Robert C.-H. Shell, Slavery at the Cape of Good Hope," Ph.D. dissertation, Yale University, 1986, vol. 2, appendix on the *opgaaf.*

taxed at the Cape until 1825. There is thus no reason to suspect inaccuracies in the census enumeration of slaves until the 1820s. Since the *Opgaaf* evolved most dramatically in the seventeeth century, it is natural that that period should be the most confusing in the document's history. Perhaps also for that reason there is no published series for that period. Scholars such as Coenraad Beyers and Robert Ross have resolutely concentrated their tabulations on the eighteenth century. Even in that period, when the *Opgaaf* had become a standard part of the administrative routine of the colony, quite sharp disagreement over dating occurs in the published versions of the *Sommaria,* or the totals from the *opgaafs.* This begins right at the outset of the eighteenth century. Beyers, for instance, dates his first *Opgaaf* on 1 January 1701, but it seems illogical to use that figure for describing anything in that year, since the figures clearly relate to the population events of 1700. From where does Beyers's date actually come? We know from other *opgaafs* that several dates appear on each *opgaaf,* relating to different stages in the production of the *opgaaf.* For instance, the *opgaaf* in VOC 4048 provides the first clue that something is wrong with Beyers's conventional dating. On folio 441 appears the note *"gecollationeert 20 March, 1703, genomen 31st December 1702."* Following that is the legend "Anno 1702" clearly implying that 1702 is the year referred to. This would imply that there was a considerable gap between the physically taking of the *Opgaaf* (shortly after the harvest), its collation, addition, final binding, and its dispatch to Holland — the copies in the Cape archives (VC series) are Theal's copies. This point may be made for all censuses in the eighteenth century and indeed for the nineteenth century as well. For example, CO 5968 has the following on its preprinted forms: "Date of Census . . . ," and then written in is: "April 1826 for 1825." In the "deaths" column is the legend, printed in italics *"during the last Year,"* (capitalized in the original), and then written in: "1825." At the top of the form is the printed title "POPULATION" and written next to it "for 1825." This is prima facie evidence that the dating conventions in the present interpretations are wrong. By the nineteenth century the sheer numbers of people involved must have necessitated a similar delay. Perhaps December was a busy time for the clerks who readied the document for the March shipment to the Chambers. Slaves sewed and bound all the large folios (they measured three feet by three and a half feet) in waterproof leather covers for their overseas shipment; this also took time.

Yet Robert Ross and Peter Van Duin in their work take VOC 4048 as representing the year 1703, using what I have termed a "literal" convention. There are understandably compelling reasons for them to do so. What else can they do, for example, with the *opgaaf* dated 23 January 1702, which I believe truly applies to "Anno 1701"? Changing their date-interpretation scheme would put them in contradiction with Beyers for 1701 — who, according to my "Anno" convention, interpreting by the assigned year, is also "off" by one year.

If one relied on archival "Letters Despatched" for these years, in which the *opgaaf Sommaria* are mentioned in March in the annual letter to Middelburg, one could also be guilty of misdating since all these letters' *opgaaf* totals apply to the previous year. Another compelling reason for redating these *opgaafs* is that otherwise there are no census figures for 1699. Did the turn of the century have something to do with this?

We do know that the English and Dutch calendars were not coordinated at the time. Did the VOC start afresh? For my analysis I have redated the eighteenth-century *opgaafs* according to the Anno convention, giving me both the *opgaaf* collation date and the assigned or Anno date, the real year. I have not done this for all censuses in the seventeenth century, since there was little lag time then between the taking of the census and its collation, the population having been much smaller.

Another approach to dating is to work with "benchmark years," years of which one is certain based on independent sources of demographic events. For example, all Cape historians are familiar with the smallpox epidemic of 1713, one can rightly assume that the *opgaaf* for that "anno" would be lower if it were taken in December 1713, which it was; Beyers has it right. Mentzel, by the way, for some reason used the census of 1710 for Anno 1713, which was not picked up by his editor. Robert Ross and Peter van Duin report a different census for their Anno 1713, namely 1714. The Ross and Van Duin compilation has an estimable advantage: they have an unbroken series. But is it right? The series I have used follow the Anno convention. I have independently collected *opgaafs* and their totals for most years. In missing years I have used an averaging technique, suitably adjusted.

From 1795 through 1806 the censuses are incomplete. The Company system probably broke down. We know they were taken, since both John Barrow and Robert Wilson used them, but only a few verbatim copy fragments from rural districts have survived. I have relied on these rural returns, averaging the previous census and the next to make rough estimates for those years. Between 1807 and 1816 the censuses were taken in the same way as before 1795. Generally they are regarded as being less reliable than the Dutch East India Company's enumerations, although no systematic work has yet appeared to substantiate this. A marginal comment by an unknown census enumerator substantiates this: "From the year 1808 the census only was taken in Cape Town and no return of the Cattle &c. made. From the Cape District the returns sent in were equally deficient until the year 1812 when a more regular system was introduced of taking the census."[2]

After 1816, two sets of slave censuses exist, the first a continuation of the census, and second the registration of all slaves by the Slave Office. The two sets are quite different and are biased in quite different ways. From the early 1820s slaves older than ten years of age were to be taxed at 1 pound, 10 shillings. The census was used as the basis for taxation.[3] Consequently, the Cape slave owner had every interest in providing lower census slave returns if he could get away with it. The slave registry had the opposite effect: an unregistered slave could legally claim freedom. There seemed to have been little cross-checking. As Bird, the comptroller of customs in 1820, noted: "The register of slaves exhibits a greater number than the official returns of taxes, as has been before intimated; probably runaway slaves are included in the register, and suppressed in the tax returns. The registry [of runaway slaves] is continued as the claim of property is retained."[4] I have used the lower, census returns for all these estimates, since I would

---

[2] CAD: CO 6135, n.p. (p. 4).

[3] George McCall Theal, *Records of the Cape Colony* (Cape Town: Struik, 1967), 28: 459–460 (Cape Town, John Thomas Bigge, 22 November 1826).

[4] W. W. Bird, *State of the Cape of Good Hope in 1822* (Cape Town: Struik, 1966 reprint), p. 355.

rather err on the conservative side. The registry returns may have included "place-holders," for potential "blackbirded" slaves (captured from the indigenous population); the only reliable aspect of the Slave Office records is the number of births per year.

Variables

Each component of the equation is explained in order of demographic impact.

Fertility

The number of live slave births per year were calculated from a wide range of sources. Underlying all calculations was the *General Fertility Rate,* i.e. the number of live births per 1,000 women aged 14 to 44. It may be represented by:

$$B/Pf15\text{-}44 \times 1000. \ldots\ldots\ldots\ldots\ldots\ldots\ldots.2^5$$

Since the Cape census divided females into two groups, i.e. girls below 14 and women over 14, the number of Cape census adult slave women was taken as being equivalent to the definitional cohort 15–44 years, although there is no way to know the upper end of the female age structure for the seventeenth and eighteenth centuries. To establish the *General Fertility Rate* for each year from 1658 to 1795, I used the number of slaves baptized per year divided by the number of adult lodge women × 1,000. Since all lodge slaves had to baptized within 8 days under supervision of a senior Company official, the baptisms represent a good estimate of live slave births. Since the lodge women were subject to excessive mortality, after epidemic years there were sometimes too few pregnant survivors in the following year to establish a credible general fertility rate (in several years there were no births whatsoever). In such years I did not hesitate to use an Averaged Lodge General Fertility Rate, using only non-catastrophic years. We also have the recorded number of live births for the years 1820 through figures collected by the slave registry office and subsequently investigated by Royal Commissioners. For 1833 I used the number of slaves under one year of age (live births in one year) divided by the exact definitional cohort of fecund women (14–44), since accurate data for that year allow these precise estimates.

I have substituted the Costa Rican fertility rate as the "high" version of fertility for the simple reason that it was the highest I could find. The Hutterite levels, the highest ever recorded, I considered inappropriate since I had used those in another context. Having established the general fertility rates for each year, the predicted number of live births was established by multiplying the two rates by the number of adult slave women. These two sets of data figures provide a "high/low" estimate of live births.

Mortality

I have created an annual series of numbers of death per thousand slaves from 1658 through 1834. "Real" mortality figures for known epidemic years, i.e. 1713 (Smallpox I), 1739–1741 ("measles and fevers", 1755 (Smallpox II), 1765 to April 1769 (Smallpox III), 1811 (Smallpox IV) were used instead of the multiplicand of rates, as special notice was taken of the exact number of deaths in these years by George McCall Theal and others.[6] The office of the registry of slaves provided sex specific mortality figures

---

[5] *Methods and Materials of Demography,* vol. 2, 472.

[6] 1755: 33 Free blacks, 581 slaves in July alone, 1109 slaves and free blacks died altogether from 1 May to 1 October; 1767: 145 free blacks, 251 slaves, mainly urban, George McCall Theal, *History of South Africa* (Cape Town: Struik, 1991), vol. 4, 115.

from 1820 through 1825,[7] figures which at least two nineteenth century authors, W. Wright and W. W. Bird, used as evidence of the "mildness of Cape slavery."[8] Since the slave office provided data about both male and female deaths, it is possible to use specific male and female death figures rather than multiplicands of the *Crude Death Rate* for these years. However, deaths for the registry office were not accurately recorded. Clifton Crais has pointed out the phenomenon of "zombie" slaves, autochthonous people who were enslaved and subsequently registered under a dead slave's name.[9] We have every reason to believe that deaths were not that promptly reported to the registry. Nevertheless, I have used those registry deaths at least as minimal mortality estimates for those years.

Predicted mortality estimates of the burgher and patrician slave populations in non-catastrophic years, i.e. years for which there was no detailed mortality data, were calculated from the adjusted and estimated censuses from 1652 through 1795 multiplied by the averaged *Crude Death Rate* of the lodge in non-catastrophic years.[10] Between 1719 and 1782, I have relied on the crude death rate of the lodge, the number of actual deaths were independently collected by Hans Jeese, James Armstrong and myself. For the years 1795 through 1806 I used the estimates of John Barrow, the English auditor-general at the Cape in the first British occupation, who consulted the now missing censuses between 1705 and 1802 and also collected crude mortality figures by counting slave burials, a technique he also used for the burgher population. His figures I accepted. Such burial information were obtained from the Fiscal's office. However, the Fiscal's records have not survived. Burial estimates might have resulted in his slave mortality estimates being too low, since slaves, especially those in rural areas were not buried properly at the Cape.[11] Between 1806 and 1819, I used averaged estimates of Barrow and slave registry returns from 1819 through 1825. From 1825 through 1834 I used the averaged deaths per annum from 1819 through 1825.

These calculations represent the high mortality model which results in a larger slave trade/plagium figure being generated. In order to establish a range of mortality I used the crude death rate of Costa Rica in 1961 to establish a "low" mortality range. This was then multiplied by the adjusted censuses from the beginning of the occupation to emancipation.

Manumission

Projections of the annual manumission rate were not needed since I had individual level data, the manumission figures themselves from 1658 to 1806, I have also added

---

[7] Theal, *RCC,* 28: 464

[8] Bird, *State of the Cape,* 69; William Wright, *Slavery at the Cape of Good Hope* (New York: Negro Universities Press, 1969 reprint) p. 72.

[9] Clifton Crais. "Slavery and Freedom along a Frontier: The Eastern Cape, South Africa, 1770–1838," *Slavery and Abolition* 11, 2 (September 1990): 190–210.

[10] The simplest and most common measure of mortality is the crude death rate. The crude death rate is defined as the number of deaths in a year per 1,000 of the midyear population — that is, $D/P \times 1,000$. See *Methods and Materials of Demography,* vol. 2, p. 394.

[11] John Barrow, *Travels to the Interior of Southern Africa,* 2nd Edition (London: T. Cadell, 1806), vol. 1, p. 51, his estimate for the Cape district was the crude death rate of 350 deaths for 11,891 slaves. He also suggested higher mortality for the rural regions, cf. 15.

published aggregated returns for male and female slaves from 1807 through 1823 and again have individual level data for the years 1823 through 1829. Throughout the period, the sex of the manumittee is specified. No rates were used, the actual numbers were simply substituted for "M" in the equation (1). Returns of manumission to the slave registry office were wholly unreliable for the same reason that deaths were under-reported and I have consequently used no registry data for manumission. The Dutch Reformed Church records also under reported the total number of manumissions. After 1713, manumissions went through a civil process, each slave being individually reviewed by the Council of Policy, only a fraction of all manumissions went through the ecclesiastical records.

Runaways

The runaway rate was established from the annual census and the numerical incidence of advertised runaways in probated and sequestration slave sales between 1658 and 1795 and from all domestic slaves between 1823 and 1829. Cape slave owners were confident enough of the recapture of their slaves to establish a price for runaway slaves. Two rates may be culled from such data. First, one can establish the *Crude Runaway Rate* which I have defined as the number of attempted runaways per 1,000 slaves, per year. Second the adjusted rate, which I have dubbed the *Getaway Rate* may be obtained by establishing the percentage of the price of a runaway slave of the price of a similar (sex, age and origin of the slave who did not run away in the same market. In other words, I accepted the buyers' price of a runaway as a reliable estimation of the probability of recapture. Thus, if the price of a runaway slave was 100 Rixdollars and the average price of a similar (age, sex, origin) stay-at-home slave was 200 Rixdollars, one may roughly conclude that the probability of recapture of that slave was 50 per cent. Thus, the crude rate may be adjusted to reveal the rate of runaway slaves who were successful, i.e. the getaway rate, the number of slaves per 1,000 who succeeded.

The runaway rates were sex specific. Male runaways were many times more common than females. Although female slaves did run away, there were insufficient to establish a rate for any period. The crude runaway rate in the nineteenth century was 1.32, which adjusted to a getaway rate of 1.3 slaves per thousand. I used averaged rates for the years in which there is no runaway data, a procedure patently in need of refinement. But data is wanting.

Outmigration

Slaves left the Cape in several ways. In the seventeenth century the Cape was a slave depot for the Gold mines at Sallida in the Indonesian archipelago. Up to 1795, slaves from the lodge and private burghers were given to transient officials who wanted companions for their wives, or needed wet nurses for their returning infant children. Throughout the period 1652 to 1834, slaves belonging to officials and burghers left on those occasions when officials were transferred to another posting in the East, or when burghers mi-grated. Also, throughout the period Cape Town traders sometimes sold slaves to outward bound Indiamen, which had suffered excessive crew mortality on the outward bound leg of their journey and needed replacements. Since the slave market in South Africa was expensive, such out-migration of slaves was negligible, far less of a loss than runaways.

Appendix 4: The Slaves

All these calculations, many admittedly based on heroic assumptions, resulted in the following table, which is used throughout this book.

The Cape slaves (Lodge slaves, VOC officials' slaves, and burghers' slaves combined).

ANNO	Men	Women	Boys	Girls
1652	1	NA	NA	NA
1653	NA	NA	NA	NA
1654	NA	NA	NA	NA
1655	NA	NA	NA	NA
1656	3	7	0	0
1657	28	22	20	19
1658	73	69	7	8
1659	60	64	7	14
1660	53	61	9	9
1661	44	53	9	15
1662	42	56	8	11
1663	53	55	13	16
1664	58	56	18	19
1665	61	56	20	22
1666	64	59	23	22
1667	100	66	27	27
1668	81	61	28	28
1669	84	63	32	31
1670	94	73	40	38
1671	103	80	42	43
1672	113	88	55	51
1673	149	102	64	61
1674	172	115	67	64
1675	194	125	71	68
1676	194	140	77	74
1677	230	147	82	78
1678	270	178	77	75
1679	276	195	82	80
1680	294	218	76	73
1681	297	224	74	71
1682	303	241	75	73
1683	316	259	71	68
1684	395	198	69	66
1685	234	244	68	58
1686	407	244	76	70
1687	503	253	84	61
1688	546	243	73	69
1689	568	256	78	70
1690	577	246	91	73

ANNO	Men	Women	Boys	Girls
1691	631	254	96	76
1692	642	250	94	81
1693	647	265	108	79
1694	672	292	100	76
1695	757	300	114	88
1696	772	316	116	93
1697	917	333	130	105
1698	964	349	111	98
1699	1,132	387	110	94
1700	1,224	388	116	108
1701	1,212	403	118	105
1702	1,270	407	129	104
1703	1,361	439	131	122
1704	1,401	437	128	117
1705	1,483	462	139	130
1706	1,540	483	135	136
1707	1,257	427	142	186
1708	1,616	504	169	190
1709	1,601	528	183	203
1710	1,570	546	193	212
1711	1,613	501	187	191
1712	1,889	536	208	176
1713	1,742	442	162	141
1714	1,859	484	173	145
1715	2,225	529	179	177
1716	2,328	565	187	170
1717	2,302	541	196	172
1718	2,328	562	195	176
1719	2,321	554	207	172
1720	2,349	568	195	187
1721	2,430	618	219	208
1722	2,686	679	215	220
1723	2,879	731	236	223
1724	3,204	796	259	226
1725	3,345	859	275	245
1726	3,512	911	310	260
1727	3,449	923	315	287
1728	3,420	953	322	302
1729	3,519	977	325	325
1730	3,746	1,023	346	323
1731	3,852	1.072	343	332
1732	3,901	1.073	389	370
1733	4,036	1.086	419	382
1734	4,362	1,109	418	396
1735	4,594	1,152	447	425
1736	4,730	1,132	467	418
1737	4,767	1,124	481	416
1738	4,699	1,124	465	450
1739	4,651	1,205	484	473

ANNO	Men	Women	Boys	Girls
1740	4,399	1,022	447	447
1741	5,024	1,247	457	435
1742	4,319	1,104	451	433
1743	4,043	1,088	486	430
1744	4,049	1,178	484	425
1745	4,011	1,208	534	429
1746	3,948	1,176	535	443
1747	3,984	1,178	521	454
1748	4,065	1,193	538	442
1749	4,277	1,221	556	466
1750	4,400	1,237	558	532
1751	4,564	1,296	566	441
1752	4,807	1,354	573	459
1753	4,962	1,404	627	454
1754	5,018	1,455	615	468
1755	4,628	1,288	465	385
1756	4,743	1,342	510	419
1757	4,707	1,318	537	415
1758	4,931	1,356	512	428
1759	5,119	1,384	537	440
1760	5,269	1,436	552	471
1761	5,470	1,476	531	434
1762	5,666	1,509	587	492
1763	5,972	1,625	651	501
1764	6,139	1,627	626	605
1765	6,289	1,681	664	546
1766	6,272	1,841	635	577
1767	6,374	1,759	656	576
1768	6,354	1,832	650	459
1769	6,398	1,859	613	511
1770	6,393	1,934	641	634
1771	6,790	2,004	667	622
1772	6,985	2,061	689	640
1773	6,980	2,128	712	661
1774	7,402	2,191	780	717
1775	7,553	2,289	800	746
1776	8,347	2,561	931	898
1777	8,369	2,498	939	886
1778	8,920	2,661	975	882
1779	8,830	2,654	980	890
1780	9,058	2,812	975	913
1781	8,654	2,827	993	879
1782	9,001	2,910	940	918
1783	9,625	3,020	994	1,002
1784	9,694	3,106	1,015	902
1785	9,983	3,208	1,158	840
1786	10,538	3,687	1,294	1,055
1787	10,249	3,449	1,096	976
1788	10,373	3,467	1,082	918

ANNO	Men	Women	Boys	Girls
1789	10,729	3,488	1,069	1,038
1790	11,027	3,803	1,186	1,139
1791	10,472	3,696	1,149	963
1792	10,419	3,960	1,274	1,087
1793	11,705	4,802	1,334	1,119
1794	12,951	5,652	1,397	1,259
1795	12,996	5,529	1,541	1,408
1796	13,399	5,893	1,638	1,512
1797	14,849	6,646	1,420	1,418
1798	14,765	6,598	1,708	1,650
1799	14,908	6,683	2,013	1,901
1800	15,051	6,768	2,318	2,153
1801	15,176	6,854	2,623	2,403
1802	15,259	6,974	2,575	2,339
1803	15,659	7,304	2,541	2,302
1804	15,802	7,485	2,327	2,114
1805	15,521	7,210	3,175	2,789
1806	15,713	7,194	3,846	3,409
1807	15,383	7,120	3,808	3,277
1808	17,364	8,587	2,052	1,840
1809	16,886	8,634	1,975	1,786
1810	16,903	8,682	2,143	1,920
1811	17,143	9,086	2,643	2,307
1812	16,197	8,616	2,770	2,566
1813	16,287	8,341	3,105	2,817
1814	16,683	8,103	3,197	3,318
1815	15,226	8,222	3,206	3,174
1816	15,221	8,270	3,529	3,386
1817	14,579	7,768	5,033	4,872
1818	14,447	7,663	5,207	4,917
1819	14,018	7,678	5,284	4,896
1820	13,855	7,681	5,334	5,080
1821	13,806	7,894	5,622	5,241
1822	13,578	7,926	5,733	5,436
1823	14,032	8,031	5,836	5,430
1824	12,732	7,935	5,763	5,436
1825	13,072	8,031	6,062	5,780
1826	13,055	8,055	6,173	5,933
1827	12,220	7,693	6,278	6,081
1828	11,898	7,753	6,507	6,413
1829	11,577	7,784	6,736	6,745
1830	12,155	7,814	6,792	6,822
1831	11,963	8,419	6,849	6,900
1832	11,678	8,108	7,135	7,309
1833	13,922	9,197	7,420	7,718
1834	12,374	9,037	7,206	7,661
1835	12,403	7,763	7,420	8,718

In 1835, the word "slaves" was crossed out and "apprentices" substituted.

The Archives

AN ABUNDANCE OF UNUSUAL PRIMARY SOURCES of all kinds endows the Cape with perhaps the richest documentation of any slave society, ancient or modern. Almost perfectly preserved annual censuses from 1658 through 1834, voluminous crime records (in duplicate), slave transfer records, petitions from settlers and free blacks, manumission requests, baptismal and cadastral registers, official weekly resolutions, a complete codification of all laws, a detailed daily fort journal, and a rich plethora of travelers' accounts all contribute to an embarrassment of riches for the historian. The challenge is to use these sources in a systematic way, without succumbing to a static sociology or an anecdotally driven overview. The sources are so rich and diverse that a multiplicity of interpretations of Cape slavery exist.[1]

This book is partly based on three major data collections. The first is from "the Opgaaf Project," which Leonard Guelke, a historical geographer, P. C. Lai, a computer scientist, and I have been working on for several years. This project involves linking the census householders and the cadastral records (including loan farms) to geographical coordinates at generational intervals; for a fuller description the "Opgaaf" appendix in Robert C.-H. Shell, "Slavery at the Cape of Good Hope," Ph.D. dissertation, Yale University, 1986. Some of the results of this project have been published elsewhere; see Leonard Guelke and Robert Shell, "An Early Colonial Landed Gentry: Land and Wealth in the Cape Colony 1682–1731," *Journal of Historical Geography* 9, 3 (1983): 265–286. The maps are drawn from the same project; see Leonard Guelke, "A Computer Approach to Mapping the *Opgaaf*: The Population of the Cape in 1731," *South African Journal of Photogrammetry, Remote Sensing and Cartography* 13, 4 (1983): 227–237. The second major data set is a collection of documents connected with Cape slavery, among which are the slave transfers. This collection involved the coding of 4,076 documents; see the "Sales" appendix in Shell, "Slavery at the Cape of Good Hope," vol. 2, page 297ff. for a description of this project. A further 4,039 slaves have been added from the nineteenth-century Slave Office compensation lists. A third data base of manumissions from the beginning of the colony to 1795, and some 300 slave manumissions from 1815 to 1831 provided the material for the manumission chapter.

The Hague

(AR VOC) prefixes in notes
Brieven Overcomen
Crime Records
Daily Fort Journals
Montsterrollen

---

[1] See the selected bibliography.

Opgaafs
Ships' Registers
Slave Voyages

The Cape Archives Depot

(CAD C. prefixes in notes)
Court of Justice
Obligatiën
Orphan Chamber
Slave Office
Vendu Rollen
Verbatim Copies

South African Library

SAL: Dessinian Collection, Item 983. "Een Korte beschrijving derselver Landen (Ansuanij en Madagascar) door Hendrik Frappe."
South African Bound Pamphlets

Documents Consulted in the Deeds Office, Cape Town

(DO prefix in notes)
DO: "Transporten en Schepenkennis"

Dutch Reformed Church Archives

(DRCA prefix in notes)
DRCA: Kaap Notule, Doop Registers GR1.

Union Buildings

(UB prefix in notes)
The following Requesten en Nominatien and Attestatiën records were in the process of being rebound in Pretoria when I consulted them; they therefore have two references. Since they have been in Pretoria for at least seven years, I thought it best to give both the "new" and the "old" acquisition numbers: UB C.225 (10 March 1718), folios 251–252; [C1079, 92–93].

Delft

(DNTD prefix in notes)
DNTD: Van der Graaf Collection. Stade, E. V. "Six pencil and wash drawings of the Cape Peninsula and surrounding districts during the first quarter of the 18th Century," M/1/983–987, and 989 (1710).

Public Record Office, United Kingdom

(PRO prefix in notes)
PRO (Chancery Lane): High Court of Admiralty HCA.29–285 [no date: 1701?],

"Defense of Captain William Kidd." Also see HCA.29–287 (15 May 1701), "Copy of warrant to the Keeper of Newgate to permit Cogi Babi Sultanam, Mr Persia and Mr Ongly to speak with Captain Kidd."
PRO (Kew): Colonial Office CO (1820 to 1833)

Cape of Good Hope Savings Bank

(CGHSB prefix in notes)
Early slave bank accounts

Select Bibliography

The Cape slave society is still a relatively obscure subject in both the South African and the comparative academic literatures. The work of James Armstrong (see page 460), Anna Böeseken, Margaret Cairns, Clifton Crais, Leon Hattingh, Ken Jordaan, John Edwin Mason, Jr., Mary Rayner, Robert Ross, and Nigel Worden has attracted new interest to aspects of this topic. In the following bibliography I have listed the works that have been most useful to me. I have annotated them where I felt the title of the work did not convey its real significance.

Bibliographies useful for Cape Slavery

Churms, B. V. "The Early Anti-Slavery Movement: Pamphlets in the S.A. Library." *Quarterly Bulletin of the South African Library* 39 (1984): 21–25.

Coolhaas, Willem Philippus. *A Critical Survey of Studies on Dutch Colonial History.* The Hague: Martinus Nijhoff, 1960.

Engels, Louise J. "Personal Accounts of the Cape of Good Hope written between 1652 and 1715." A bibliography approved by the University of London for the final part of the examination for the diploma in Librarianship.

Hampson, Ruth M. "Islam in South Africa: A Bibliography." School of Librarianship, University of Cape Town, 1964. A first-class and imaginative bibliography, it will remain the starting point for the study of Islam in South Africa.

Hopper, Mary Jane. *Slavery at the Cape.* School of Librarianship, University of Cape Town, 1964. Disappointing.

Mackenzie, Norman. "South African Travel Literature in the Seventeenth Century." *Archives Year Book* 18, 2 (1955): 1–112. One of two English bibliographic articles in the series on the period 1652 to 1795.

Mendelssohn, Sydney. *South African Bibliography.* 2 vols. London: Kegan Paul, 1910.

Miller, Joseph Calder. *Slavery: A Worldwide Bibliography, 1900–1982.* White Plains, N.Y.: Kraus International Publications, 1985. See also supplements in the journal entitled *Slavery and Abolition.*

Muller, C. F. J. et al. *South African History and Historians: A Bibliography.* Pretoria: University of South Africa Press, 1979.

Musiker, Reuben. *South African Bibliography.* London: Crosby Lockwood & Sons, 1970.

Saunders, Christopher, ed., with **Terri Straus,** comp. *Cape Town and the Cape Peninsula post–1806.* Center for African Studies, Occasional Papers 5, University of Cape Town, 1989. This is the best all-round bibliography for its period.

Schmidt, K. L. M. "Bibliography of Personal Accounts of the Cape of Good Hope in Printed Books, 1715–1850." School of Librarianship, University of Cape Town, 1955.

Scholtz, Philipus Lodewikus, et al. *Race Relations at the Cape of Good Hope, 1652–1795: A Select Bibliography.* Boston: G. K. Hall (for Institute for Historical Research, University of the Western Cape), 1981?

Schutte, G. J. *Nederlandse Publicaties Betreffende Zuid-Afrika, 1800–1899.* Cape Town: South African Library, 1989.

Smith, John David. *Black Slavery in the Americas.* Westport, Conn.: Greenwood Press, 1982. The most comprehensive bibliography on slavery in the United States.

Theal, George McCall. *Catalogue of Books and Pamphlets* . . . Cape Town: Maskew Miller, 1912.

Villiers, de David Willem. *Reisebeskrywings as Bronne vir die Kerkgeskiedskrywing van die Nederduitse Gereformeerde Kerk in Suid Afrika tot 1853.* Amsterdam: Vrije Universiteit te Amsterdam, 1959.

Westra, P. E. "The Abolition of Slavery at the Cape of Good Hope: Contemporary Publications and Manuscripts in the S.A. Library." *Quaarterly Bulletin of the South African Library* 39, 2 (1984): 58–66.

Published Documents and Travellers' Accounts mentioning Cape Slavery

Abā Ṭālib Ibn Muhammed Khān, Mirza Isfahani. *The Voyages of Mirza Abu Taleb Khan in Asia, Africa and Europe in the Years 1799, 1800, 1801, 1802 and 1803, Written by Himself in the Persian Language.* Trans. Charles Stewart. 2 vols. London: Longman, Hurst Rees and Orme, 1810. The writer (1752–1806?) was one of the few visitors to the Cape who was not from Europe. Unfortunately, the translator decided to cut some of the original: "The subjects so curtailed are: first the poetical effusions of the author, which in the original, occupy a number of pages. Secondly, the long list of his friends, at the principal places he visited" (preface, p. vii). This disclaimer does not appear in the subsequent 3-volume editions, although the "out-takes" were not put back. The writer was also a lively *habitué* of Lady Anne Barnard's (q.v.) soirées. An important and largely neglected source on the Cape free blacks and slaves circa 1800; cf. vol. 1, pp. 63–101.

Anon. *Almanak voor de Kaap de Goed Hoop voor Het Schrikkel-Jaar (MDCCCIV* [1804], also called *African Court Calendar* and later *Cape Town Street Directories.* Titles vary through the nineteenth century. Cape Town: Government Printers, 1804 onward. These useful little books, which started off as compilations of military personnel, grew in scope to list most of the "important" inhabitants of Cape Town and environs, their addresses, and occupations. The books served a commercial function, but they also have considerable value to the social historian, having a definite "who's who" component. Slaves are rarely listed, but most of the sizable free black population of Cape Town is listed. They have been partially reprinted by the South African Library, the only facility to own a complete set.

———. *Gleanings in Africa: Exhibiting a Faithful and Correct View* . . . London: James Cundee, 1806; reprint, New York: Negro Universities Press, 1969.

———. *Reyze van Het Oostindische Schip Barneveld.* 3rd ed. Dordrecht: Hendrik de Koning, 1764.

———. *The State of the Cape,* see Bird, W. W.

Barnard, Lady Anne. *The Letters of Lady Anne Barnard to Henry Dundas, from the Cape and Elsewhere, 1793–1803.* Ed. A. M. L. Robinson. Cape Town: Balkema, 1973.

Barrington, George. *A Voyage to Botany Bay, with a Description of the Country, Manners &c.* London: H. D. Symonds, 1794.

Barrow, John. *Travels into the Interior of Southern Africa, in Which Are Described the Character and the Condition of the Dutch Colonists . . .* 2nd ed. 2 vols. London: T. Cadell, 1806.

Bird, W. W. *State of the Cape of Good Hope in 1822.* London: John Murray, 1823; facsimile reprint, Cape Town: Struik, 1966. Written to inform visitors and prospective immigrants to South Africa, this work goes far beyond its stated purpose. There are details about every conceivable subject concerning the Cape, from the machinery of government to the social values of the Cape society. Many details of slaves. Sometimes attributed anonymously because of a scandal involving another Bird and the sale of government slaves to the public.

Böeseken, Anna J., ed. *Belangrike Kaapse Dokumente: Memoriën en Instructiën, 1657–1699.* 2 vols. Cape Town: South African State Archives, 1967.

Böeseken, Anna J., et al., eds. *Suid-Afrikaanse Argiefstukke: Resolusies van die Politieke Raad (1652–1732).* 8 vols. Cape Town: Cape Times, 1957–1975.

Bövingh, Johann Georg. *Kurze Nachrict von den Hottentotten . . .* Hamburg: Bey Casper Jahkel, 1714.

Bruijn, J. R., et al., eds. *Dutch-Asiatic Shipping in the 17th and 18th centuries.* The Hague: Martinus Nijhoff, 1979. These contain all details of Dutch East India Company ships passing the Cape; slaves are rarely mentioned.

Burchell, W. J. *Travels in the Interior of South Africa.* London: Longman, 1822–1824.

Buttner, J. D. *Accounts of the Cape, Brief Description of Natal, Journal Extracts on the East Indies.* Ed. G. S. Nienaber and R. Raven-Hart. Cape Town: Balkema, 1970.

Campbell, J. *Travels in the Interior of South Africa.* London: The Society, 1822.

Chavonnes, M.P. de. and **G. W. van Imhoff.** *The Reports of Chavonnes and his Council, and of Van Imhoff, on the Cape.* Cape Town: Van Riebeeck Society, 1918.

Chijs, van der J.A., comp. *Nederlandsch-Indisch Plakkaatboek, 1602–1811.* 's-Gravenhage: M. Nijhoff, 1885.

Dennyson, D. "Statement of the Laws of the Colony of the Cape of Good Hope Regarding Slavery." (16 March 1813) in George McCall Theal, *Records of the Cape Colony* (Cape Town: Struik, 1967), vol. 9, pp. 146–161.

Duff-Gordon, Lady Lucy. (Lucy Austin). *Letters from the Cape.* Oxford: Oxford University Press, 1927. Contains many reflections on interviews with ex-slaves and ex-slave owners.

Ewart, James. *James Ewart's Journal.* Cape Town: Struik, 1970. Unindexed, but useful.

Franken, J. L. M., ed. *Duminy Diaries.* Cape Town: Van Riebeeck Society, 1933. Contains account books of the day, detailing expenses of a slave owner.

Godée-Molsbergen, E. C. *Reizen in Zuid-Afrika in de Hollandse Tijd.* 4 vols. 's-Gravenhage: Martinus Nijhoff, 1916.

———. *South African History told in Pictures.* Amsterdam: S. L. van looy, 1913.

Government Publications. "Report from the select committee on aborigines (British settlements); with the official report and further evidence [minutes of evidence], Appendix and Index." *Imperial Blue Book.* 1837 number VII.425.

Hemmy, Gijsbert. *De Promontorio Bonae Spei, The Cape of Good Hope: A Latin Oration Delivered in the Hamburg Academy 10 April 1767.* Comp. K. D. White, G. S. Nienaber, and D. H. Varley. Cape Town: South African Public Library, 1959.

Hulshof, A., comp. "Compagnie's dienaren aan de Kaap in 1685." *Bijdragen en Mededelingen van Het Historisch Genootschap* 63 (1942): 347–369.

————, ed. "H. A. van Reede tot Drakenstein, Journal van zijn verblijf aan de Kaap." *Bijdragen en Mededelingen van Het Historisch Genootschap* 62 (1941): 1–245.

Jeffreys, Kathleen M. and **S. D. Naude,** eds. *Kaapse Plakkaatboek, 1652–1806.* 6 vols. Cape Town: Kaapse Argiefstukke, 1944–1949.

Kindersley, Mrs. *Letters from the Island of Teneriffe, Brazil, the Cape of Good Hope, and the East Indies.* London: J. Nourse, 1777.

Kolbe, Peter. *The Present State of the Cape of Good Hope: Containing the Natural History of the Cape . . .* 2 vols. London: Johnson Reprint Company, 1968; reprint of 1731 ed.

Legaut, François. *Travels and Adventures of François Leguat . . .* London: David Mortier, 1708.

Leibbrandt, Hendrik Carel Vos. *The Defense of Willem Adriaan van der Stel.* In Series *Precis of the Archives of the Cape of Good Hope.* Cape Town: W. A. Richards & Sons, Government Printers, 1897.

————. *Journal, 1699–1732.* In series *Precis of the Archives of the Cape of Good Hope.* Cape Town: W. A. Richards & Sons, Government Printers, 1896.

————. *Letters Despatched.* In series *Precis of the Archives of the Cape of Good Hope.* Cape Town: W. A. Richards & Sons, Government Printers, 1896.

————. *Requesten (Memorials) 1715–1806.* 5 vols. Cape Town: Cape Times, 1905; Cape Town: South African Library, 1989. The South African Library recently printed Leibbrandt's unfinished manuscripts CAD LM 16 and LM 17 as volumes 3 and 4, indexed these, and produced some further addenda in volume 5.

Lichtenstein, Henry. *Travels in Southern Africa.* 2 vols. Cape Town: Van Riebeeck Society, 1930.

Lockyer, Charles. *An Account of the Trade in India: Containing Rules for Good Government in Trade, Price Courants, and Table: With Descriptions of . . . the Cape of Good Hope, and St Helena . . .* London: Samuel Crouch, 1711. After traveling extensively in the East, Lockyer reached the Cape on his homeward voyage 22 May 1706, remaining there until July 12. His information on the Cape is refreshingly different from that of his contemporaries and therefore of great interest. He omits the customary topographical account; even the "Hotentots" are dealt with briefly. Instead he gives many interesting details concerning daily life, such as the cost of food and wine, the value in Rixdollars of other currencies, the strict control of the taverns and the sale of wine, and the monopoly system in regard to the retailing of meat. He speaks of the Company garden as being in a "declining" position, and describes such harbor facilities as there were for watering and unloading ships. Being primarily interested in trade, he gives details of goods to be bought and sold at the Cape, and their current prices.

Maxwell, John. "An Account of the Cape of Good Hope . . . in 1706 and 1707." *Philosophical Transactions of the Royal Society of London* 25, 310 (1708): 2423–2434.

Mayson, John Schofield. *The Malays of Cape Town.* Manchester: J. Galt, 1861;

reprint, Africana Connoisseurs Press, 1963. Although short, this work contains invaluable information about the slaves and free blacks, their origins, ways of life etc. The author interviewed many of the people he wrote about, so the book has a vivid and convincing tone absent from any travelers' accounts and contains material that could never be retrieved with other documents.

Mentzel, Otto Friederich. *A Complete and Authentic Geographical and Topographical Description of the Famous and all things considered Remarkable African Cape of Good Hope . . .* 3 vols. Trans. G. V. Marais and J. Hoge. Revised and edited with an introduction by H. J. Mandelbrote. Cape Town: Van Riebeeck Society, 1921, 1925, 1944; originally published Glogau: Christian Friederich Gunther, 1785–1787. Mentzel could lay claim to being the Herodotus of the early Cape. He used many original documents of the Dutch East India Company, some of which are now "lost," for example, the 1713 census. Mentzel also interviewed the colonists widely. He had no scientific background; consequently his work is full of people, not the flora, fauna, and astronomy that occupied his contemporaries. Many of his animadversions about the demography of the early Cape are open to question, but he approached all topics with scholarly zeal and vigor, correcting with Prussian precision his predecessors' errors. He traveled widely in the Cape and poked into all sorts of corners of Cape society, which practice gives his work a vivid tone absent from many of his contemporaries' work. According to James Armstrong, the original Glogau editions were very rare, which probably explains why Theal and Cory made so little use of Mentzel, rendering their versions of the early Cape immeasurably poorer. The Van Riebeeck Society publications in the 1920s and 1930s brought his work to a wider audience, but the editing, translation, and indexing of the four volumes could do with an overhaul, a task Vernon Forbes has already undertaken. No full biography of Mentzel exists.

_____. *Life at the Cape in Mid-Eighteenth Century, Being The Biography of Rudolf Siegfried Alleman, Captain of the Military Forces and Commander of the Castle in the Services of the Dutch India Company at the Cape of Good Hope.* Trans. Margaret Greenlees. Cape Town: Van Riebeeck Society, 1919; originally published in Glogau, 1784.

Moodie, Donald, comp. *The Record, or a Series of Official Papers Relative to the Condition and Treatment of the Native Tribes of South Africa.* Cape Town: Balkema, 1960. Surviving collection of the famous nineteenth-century series. Indexed.

Mossop, E. E. *Journals of the Expeditions of the Honorable Ensign Olof Bergh 1682 and 1683 and the Ensign Isaq Schrijver 1689.* Cape Town: Van Riebeeck Society, 1931.

Percival, Captain Robert. *An Account of the Cape of Good Hope.* London: Baldwin, 1804; reprint. New York: Negro Universities Press, 1969. Very biased against the Dutch, but has useful anecdotal information.

Philip, John. *Researches in South Africa.* 2 vols. London: James Duncan, 1828.

Pogson, Edward. "Impressions of Cape Town in 1834; Selected from the Diary of Edward Pogson by C. S. Hayter." *Cape Times Annual* (December 1931): 35–38.

Raven-Hart, R., comp. and ed. *Cape Good Hope, 1652–1702.* 2 vols. Cape Town: Balkema, 1971. A carefully annotated and meticulously indexed compilation of unusual late seventeenth-century sources on Cape history.

Riebeeck, van Jan Antonisz. *Daghregister gehouden by den oppercoopman, Jan*

Athonisz van Riebeeck. 3 vols. Ed. D. B. Bosman and H. B. Thom. Cape Town: Balkema, 1952–1957.

Schutte, G. J., ed. *Briefwisseling van Hendrik Swellengrebel Jr. oor Kaapse Sake, 1778–1792.* Cape Town: Van Riebeeck Society, 1982. Robert Ross (q.v.) and Peter van Duin (q.v.) have recently produced a work that sharply rebuts the "overproduction" thesis; however, they do not take into account the costs of the slave trade. Schutte's work shows that there *was* a problem with overproduction.

Schweister, Christopher, and **Christophorus Frikius Fryke.** *A Relation of Several Voyages Made into the East Indies . . . Done out of the Dutch.* London: D. Brown, 1700.

Semple, Robert. *Walks and Sketches at the Cape of Good Hope.* London: Baldwin, 1805; reprint of second ed. Cape Town: Balkema, 1968.

Simonsz, Cornelis Joan. "Opstel van Eenige Poincten, en ordres, getrocken . . ." (19 April 1708). In C. Graham Botha, ed. *Collecteana,* first series (Cape Town: Van Riebeeck Society, 1924), pp. 25–48. In 1702, Simonsz was appointed governor of Ceylon; on 24 February 1708 he returned to the Cape as a visiting commissioner. He immediately began an investigation of conditions there, his chief purpose being to determine to what extent the instructions left by H. A. van Reede in 1685 had been carried out. Simonsz deplored the ignorance of members of the Council of Justice, and instructed officials to follow only the Indian procedures. One of Simonsz's most important instructions was that the authorities should comply with the Statutes of India regarding slaves, especially the statute stipulating that a slave might be manumitted only when the owner could guarantee that he (the slave) would not become a vagrant within ten years. Decades later the Cape settlers, during the unrest of 1779, still praised his report. Simonsz was a well-trained jurist and translated the Tamil legal code, the *Tesawalami.*

Sparrman, Anders. *A Voyage to the Cape of Good Hope towards the Antarctic Polar Circle around the World and to the Country of the Hottentots and the Caffres from the year 1772–1776.* Ed. Vernon S. Forbes. 2 vols. Cape Town: Van Riebeeck Society Second Series, No. 7, 1977.

Spoelstra, C. *Bouwstoffen voor de Gerschiedenis der Nederduitsch-Geref. Kerken in Zuid Afrika.* 3 vols. Amsterdam: Hollandsch-Afrikaansche Uitgewers-Maatscappij, 1906–1907.

Stavorinus, J. S. *Voyages to the East Indies by the Late John Splinter Stavorinus, Esq., Rear-Admiral in the Service of the States General . . .* 3 vols. London: G. G. & J. Robinson, 1798.

Stel, van der Simon. "Insructie bij ons ondergesz. als afgaande, den Edele Heer Willem Adriaan van der Stel, Raad Extraords. van Nederlands India, als aankomenden Gouverneur onsen onvanger, mitsgaders den Raad, des Casteels de Goede Hoop . . ." (30 March 1699). In C. Graham Botha, ed. *Collecteana,* first series (Cape Town: Van Riebeeck Society, 1924): 11–24.

Tachard, Father Guy, in E. Strangman, ed. *Early French Callers at the Cape.* Cape Town: Juta, 1936.

Tas, Adam. *The Diary of Adam Tas.* Ed. Leo Fouché et al. Trans. J. Smuts. Cape Town: Van Riebeeck Society, 1969–1970. Only a fragment; the bulk of the diary is still missing. Essential reading, as few colonists of this period wrote anything, not to mention writing of slaves. See also Franken, Hudson, and Mentzel for other examples of this genre.

Theal, George McCall. *Records of the Cape Colony,* 36 vols. London: Government Printers, 1905.

Thunberg, Karl Peter. *Travels at the Cape of Good Hope, 1772–1775.* Cape Town: Van Riebeeck Society Second Series, No. 17, 1986.

Torance, Hugh. *Cape Town in 1823.* Glasgow: Maclehose, 1909. Mentions prize negroes, slave hiring, and "Malays." This short work is often ignored.

Valentijn, François. *Description of the Cape of Good Hope . . .* Ed. E. H. Raidt. Trans. R. Raven-Hart. 2 vols. Cape Town: Van Riebeeck Society, 1973; originally published Amsterdam, 1732.

Vos, Michiel Christiaan. *Merkwardige Verhaal.* Amsterdam: Noveker, 1867. Contains the colonial debate about whether slaves had souls.

Wilson, Robert. "Description of the Cape Colony in 1806." Unpublished manuscript. CAD: Verbatim Copies 58.

Ziegenbalgh, B. *Propagation of the Gospel.* London: Joseph Downing, Printer, 1718.

Secondary Works Mentioning Cape Slavery

Alphen, van J. G.. "Slawerny aan die Kaap: algemene afskaffing honderd Jaar gelede." *Huisgenoot* 19 (1934): 17ff.

Andaya, Leonard Y. *The Heritage of Arung Palakka: A History of South Sulawesi Celebes in the Seventeenth Century.* The Hague: Martinus Nijhoff, 1981.

Anon. "The Memorandum of the Historical and Aesthetic Aspects of the Old Supreme Court Building." Appendix C in "The Report of the Committee of Enquiry concerning the old Supreme Court Building, Cape Town and the Widening of Bureau Street." Pretoria: Government Printer, 1953–54. G.P.S. 11369–1953-4-48. Contains a short but useful history of the slave Lodge, using uncited archival material.

————. *Mr. C. van Vollenhoven's Verspreide Geschriften.* s'-Gravenhage: H. D. Tjeenk Willinck & Zoon, 1985.

————. "The Origin and Incidence of Miscegenation at the Cape during the Dutch East India Company's Regime, 1962–1795." *Race Relations Journal* 20 (1953): 23–27.

————. "Papers Relating to the Manumission of Steyntje & Her Children." Cape Town: George Greig, 1827.

————. "Sale of Slaves at the Cape of Good Hope." in *The Tourist, or Sketch Book of the Times* 1 15 (Monday, 17 December 1832): 122–123.

————. "Remarks on the Demoralizing Influence of Slavery by a Resident at the Cape of Good Hope." London: Bagster and Thomas, 1828. Published for the Society for the Mitigation and Gradual Abolition of Slavery throughout the British Dominions. I believe that this might have been written by Samuel Eusebius Hudson. This is a tenuous identification based on his style of anecdote and on the poem at the end of the piece, fragments of which are found in Hudson's essay on slavery (q.v.).

Arkin, M. "Agency and Island . . ." *Archives Year Book* (1965): 1.

————. "Supplies for Napoleon's Gaolers: John Company and the Cape — St. Helena Trade during the Captivity," *Archives Year Book* (1964): 1.

Armstrong, James C. "The Chinese at the Cape in the Dutch East India Period, 1652–1795." Mimeo, 12 May 1994.

————. "The Free Black Community at the Cape of Good Hope in the Seventeenth and Eighteenth Centuries." Mimeo of paper delivered at Duquesne University, Pittsburgh, November 1973.

————. "Madagascar and the Slave Trade in the Seventeenth Century." *Omaly Sy Anio* 17–20 (1983–84): 211–232. This excellent account could not have found a more obscure home. Available from Monsieur Le Directeur du Départment d'Histoire, E.E.S.-Lettres, B.P. 907 Antananarivo, Malagasy Republic.

————. "Malagasy Slave Names in the Seventeenth Century." Paper delivered at the University of Madagascar: Colloque d' Histoire Malgache, 13–18 April 1981, Mahajanga.

————. "Review of Ross' *The Economy of the Cape Colony in the Eighteenth Century*, Intercontinenta, 7 (Leiden: Center for the History of European Expansion, 1987)." In *The International Journal of African Historical Studies* 21, 4 (1988): 718–719.

————. "The Slaves, 1652–1795." In *The Shaping of South African Society, 1652–1820*. Ed. Richard Elphick and Herman Giliomee. Cape Town: Longman, 1979.

Arndt, E. H. D. *Banking and Currency Development in South Africa, 1652–1927.* Cape Town: Juta, 1928.

Bank, Andrew. "The Decline of Urban Slavery in Cape Town, 1806 to 1843." University of Cape Town, Centre for African Studies, 1991.

————. "Slavery in Cape Town, 1806 to 1834." Master's Thesis, History Department, University of Cape Town, 1991.

Beck, Roger Bearden. "The Legalization and Development of Trade on the Cape Frontier, 1817–1830." Ph.D. diss., University of Indiana, 1987. Little on slavery, but much new archival light shed on the frontier.

Beyers, Coenraad. *Die Kaapse Patriotte, 1779–1791.* Cape Town: Juta, 1929. Appendix H (pp. 240–249) contains the census details of Cape slaves, male and female, boys and girls, during the eighteenth century at five-year intervals; cf. Ross for a more detailed breakdown.

Blommaert, Willem. "Het invoeren van de slavernij aan de Kaap." *Archives Year Book* 1 (1938): 1–29. Willem Blommaert (1886–1934), a contemporary of Deherain's (q.v.), a Flemish historian, and one of Henri Pirenne's prize-winning students, died before he could complete his projected magnum opus on slavery at the Cape. His single extant scholarly contribution on the slave trade, posthumously edited by his colleague at Stellenbosch, H. Thom, appeared in the first volume of the *Archives Year Book*. Although Blommaert went beyond Deherain's work, which he cited, he still relied largely on published sources. Unfortunately this article, the first chapter of his projected work, deals only with the initial ten years of the slave trade to the Cape. According to a personal communication with Hermann Giliomee of the University of Cape Town, certain former students were planning to edit his unpublished manuscripts.

Blussé, Leonard. *Strange Company: Chinese Settlers, Metizo Women and the Dutch in VOC Batavia.* Providence, R.I.: Foris, 1988.

Blussé, Leonard, and **Femme Gaastra,** eds. *Companies and Trade: Essays on Overseas Trading Companies during the Ancien Regime.* Leiden: Leiden University Press, 1981. A modern comparative treatment of the rise and fall of the old companies.

Böeseken, Anna J. "Die Nederlandsche Commissarissen en die 18de Eeuse samelewing aan de Kaap." *Argiefjaarboek vir Suid Afrikaanse Geskiedenis* (1944): 1–253.

_____. "Die Verhouding tussen Blank en Nie-Blank in Suid Africa aan de hand van de vroegste Dokumente." *South African Historical Journal* 2 (November 1970): 3–18. An unusual and perceptive treatment of this difficult theme.

_____. "The First Fifteen Farmers in the Wagenmakersvalleij." In *Libraries and People: Essays offered to R. F. Immelman.* Ed. J. G. Kesting et al. Cape Town: Struik, 1970. The first fruits of a projected full-scale treatment of the farming community of this area; a few details of slaves.

_____. *Simon van der Stel en sy Kinders, 1658–1700.* Cape Town: Nasou, 1964. The premier biography of the largest slave trader in this period. Essential reading for the life and times of Cape folk.

_____. *Slaves and Free Blacks at the Cape, 1658–1700.* Cape Town: Tafelberg, 1977. Although the appendix of this work is heavily criticized by Leon Hattingh (q.v.) in a lead article in his own journal, (see *Kronos* 9 [1985]), these criticisms should not be taken as applying to her other substantial works of transcription for this period; her reputation for accuracy remains intact, as a sustained comparison with the original documents makes clear.

Böeseken, Anna J., with **Margaret Cairns.** *The Secluded Valley: Tulbagh: 't Land van Waveren, 1700–1804.* Cape Town: Perskor, 1989.

Boetzelaer, Baron van Asperen en Dubbeldam. *De Protestantsche Kerk in Nederlandsch-Indië.* The Hague: Nijhoff, 1947.

Boshoff, Anlen. "Slawe-orkeste en musiekinstrumente aan de Kaap." *Bulletin of the South African Cultural History Museum* 8 (1987): 49–55.

Bosman, Daniel Brink. *Oor die Ontstaan van Afrikaans.* 2nd ed. Amsterdam: Swets & Zeitlinger, 1928. One of the early works dismissing the creole and slave origins of Afrikaans.

_____, ed. *Briewe van Johanna Maria van Riebeeck . . .* Amsterdam: Die Skrywer, 1952.

Botha, C. Graham. *Collecteana.* First series. Cape Town: Van Riebeeck Society, 1924.

_____. *The Collected Works of C. Graham Botha, Volume One: General History and Social Life of the Cape of Good Hope.* Cape Town: Struik, 1962.

_____. *The Collected Works of C. Graham Botha, Volume two: History of Law, Medicine and Place Names in the Cape of Good Hope.* Cape Town: Struik, 1962.

_____. *The Collected Works of C. Graham Botha, Volume Three: Cape Archives and Records.* Cape Town: Struik, 1962.

_____. *The French Refugees at the Cape.* Cape Town: Struik, 1970. Original documents reproduced in appendixes are still useful; text has been overtaken by Maurice Boucher's more exhaustive work.

—————. *Place Names in the Cape Province.* Cape Town: Juta, 1926.

—————. *Social Life in the Cape Colony,* including *Social Customs in South Africa in the 18th Century.* Cape Town: Struik, 1973; reprint of 1926 edition. Botha relies heavily on Samuel E. Hudson (q.v.). Nevertheless, much information concerning a score of topics may be garnered from his works. The Cape's most prolific antiquarian.

Boucher, Maurice. "The Cape and Foreign Shipping, 1714–1723." *South African Historical Journal* 6 (1974): 3–29. Mention of slave-trading ships.

—————. "Dutch Commerce and Cape Trade in the mid-18th Century." *Kleio* 12 (1980): 14–17.

—————. "The Early Cape in New Perspective: Review Article." *Kleio* 12 (1980): 37–42.

—————. "Privateers at the Cape in 1744 and 1747." *Historia* 28, 2 (1983): 6–13.

—————. "An Unexpected Caller: Charles Barrington at the Cape in 1737." *South African Historical Journal* 13 (1981): 20–35.

—————. "The Voyage of a Cape Slaver in 1742." *Historia* 24 (May 1979): 50–58.

Bouws, J. "Slawemusiek in vergange se dae." *South African Musiekonderwyser* 90 (1976): 10–11.

Boxer, Charles Randolph. *The Dutch Seaborne Empire: 1600–1800.* New York: Knopf, 1965. Contains the celebrated essay on the Cape, "A Tavern of Two Seas," pp. 242–267. Boxer relies, in the main, on Anna J. Böeseken's work (q.v.).

Bradlow, Edna. "Emancipation and Race Relations at the Cape." *South African Historical Journal* 15 (1983): 10–33.

Bradlow, Frank. "Emancipation and Race Perceptions at the Cape." *South African Historical Journal* 15 (1983): 10–33.

—————. "Islam at the Cape of Good Hope." *South African Historical Journal* 13 (1981): 12–19. Relies on the work of R. Shell.

Bradlow, Frank R., and **Margaret Cairns.** *The Early Cape Muslims: A Study of Their Mosques, Genealogy and Origins.* Cape Town: Balkema, 1978. Part of a series of works rekindling interest in Islam and slaves at the Cape; has some interesting tables concerning slaves, and goes beyond the misleading subtitle.

Bruijn, J. R. "Between Batavia and the Cape: Shipping Patterns of the Dutch East India Company." *Journal of South East Asian Studies* 11 (1980): 251–265.

Bruijn, J. R., and **E. S. Van Eyck van Heslinga,** eds. *Muiterij: Oproer en bevechting op schepen van de VOC.* Haarlem: De Boer Maritiem, c. 1980.

Cairns, Margaret. "Appolonia of the Cape, 1716–1762." *Familia* 24 (1987): 85.

—————. "Armosyn Claasz of the Cape and Her Family." *Familia* 16 (1979): 84–99.

—————. "Elisabeth van Wijk, 1685–1720." *Familia* 12 (1975): 55.

—————. "Freeblack Landowners in the Southern Suburbs of the Cape Peninsula during the Eighteenth Century." *Kronos* 10 (1985): 23–48.

_____. "Gerringer and Bok." *Familia* 13 (1976): 27.

_____. "Gerrit Gerits van Oldenburg and Susanna van Mombaser." *Familia* 17 (1980): 49–56.

_____. "Goede Gift: Its Early History." *Simon's Town Historical Society Bulletin* 11 (July 1980): 63–68. An account of Anna Jacoba of the Cape, a slave woman.

_____. "Matthias Krugel: His Life and Family at the Cape, 1703–1731." *Familia* 14 (1977): 5–18.

_____. "The Murder of the Slave Joris at Simonsvlei." *Quarterly Bulletin of the South African Library* 38 (June 1984): 47–60.

_____. "The Notarial Protocol as a Source for Geneological History." *Familia* 10, 3 (1973): 61–62.

_____. "The Schröns, 1758–1841." *Familia* 20 (1983): 38–48, 53–56.

_____. "Slave Transfers, 1658–1795: A Preliminary Survey." *Kronos* 6 (1983): 5–20. A useful introduction to the topic and the archives of the Deeds Office, now superseded by Leon Hattingh's work (q.v.), but well worth consulting, as are all works by this authority on Cape history.

_____. "The Smuts Family Murders, 14 April, 1760." *Cabo* 2 (1980): 13–16.

_____. "Thomas James Campbell: A Problem of Identity." *Familia* 3, 23 (1986): 54–55, 62–65.

_____. "The Weigt Slaves of Wagenmakers Vallei and Their Emancipation." *Quarterly Bulletin of South African Library* 42 (June/July 1988): 145–150. Genealogical details of the emancipation and baptism of slaves belonging to the Weigt family, also mentioned by Lady Anne Barnard (q.v.).

_____. "Willem Stolts of the Cape, c. 1692–1750." *Familia* 16 (1979): 84–99.

Cock, Jacklyn. *Maids and Madams: A Study in the Politics of Exploitation.* Johannesburg: Ravan, 1980. Mentions connections to slavery.

Coetzee, C. G. "De Kompanjie se besetting van Delegoabaai." *Archives Year Book* 11, 2 (1948): 167–276. The major work on the Company's slave station in Maputo; details mainly the European presence there and the mutiny, but also contains details of slaves. Unindexed.

Cory, George Edward. "A Short History on Slavery at the Cape." South African Historical Society, CAD A 378, Volume D.

Crais, Clifton. "Slavery and Freedom along a Frontier: The Eastern Cape, South Africa, 1770–1838." *Slavery and Abolition* 11, 2 (September 1990): 190–210.

_____. *White Supremacy and Black Resistance in Pre-Industrial South Africa: The Making of the Colonial Order in the Eastern Cape.* Cambridge: Cambridge University Press, 1991.

Cruse, H. P. *Die Opheffing van die Kleurlingbevolking.* Stellenbosch: Die Christen-studentevereeniging van Suid Africa, 1947. One of the first works devoted to the history of the "colored people"; largely neglected, virtually unobtainable, but still useful on slaves and free blacks.

Cuthbertson, Gregory C. "The Impact of the Emancipation of Slaves on St. Andrews Scottish Church, 1838–1879." *Studies in the History of Cape Town* 3 (1980): 49–63.

Davids, Achmat. "The Afrikaans of the Cape Muslims from 1815 to 1915." Master's thesis, University of Natal, Durban, 1991.

Davids, Achmat. *The History of the Tana Baru.* Cape Town: The Committee for the Preservation of the Tana Baru, 1985.

Davids, Achmat. *The Mosques of the Bo-Kaap.* Athlone: The South African Institute of Arabic and Islamic Research, 1980.

Deherain, Pierre T. Henri. *Le Cap de Bonne-Esperance au XVII siecle.* Paris: Orstrom, 1909. The first scholar to address the Cape slave trade is virtually unknown to South African audiences. Pierre Henri Deherain (1867–1941), a French graduate of African history at the Sorbonne, wrote several articles on Cape slavery, including one on the Cape slave trade. These culminated in this book. Written in a lucid style and devoid of the parochial concerns of local historians, his work serves as a useful introduction to the topic. Deherain, however, never visited South Africa or Holland. Consequently, his research rests entirely on the published sources of the day, mainly the archival precis of H. C. V. Leibbrandt (q.v.).

_____. "L'esclavage au Cap de Bonne Esperance au XVIIe et XVIIIe Siecles." *Journal des Savants* (September 1907): 488–503.

_____. "La traite des esclaves a Madagascar au XVII siecle," *Nature* 32 (1904): 402 ff.

Dominicus, F. C. *Het Huiselik en Maatschappelik Leven van de Zuid-Afrikaner in de Eerste Helft der 18de Eeuw.* 's-Gravenhage: Martinus Nijhoff, 1919.

Dooling, Wayne. "Law and Community in a Slave Society: Stellenbosch District, c. 1760–1820," Master's thesis, University of Cape Town, 1991.

Duin, Peter van, with **Robert Ross.** "The Economy of the Cape Colony in the Eighteenth Century." Leiden: Intercontinenta, No. 7, 1987, pp. 1–166.

Edwards, Isobel Eirlys. *Toward Emancipation: A Study in South African Slavery.* Cardiff: University of Wales Press, 1942. Excellent bibliography on sources and still a useful study.

Elphick, Richard. "A Comparative History of White Supremacy." *Journal of Interdisciplinary History* 13, 3 (Winter 1983): 503–513. Review of George Fredrickson's work (q.v.).

_____. *Kraal and Castle: Khoikhoi and the Founding of South Africa.* New Haven, Conn.: Yale University Press, 1977. Among the most important works on South African history in the past 20 years, embodying North American scholarship, linguistic and quantitative analysis.

Elphick, Richard, and **Herman Giliomee,** eds. *The Shaping of South African Society, 1652–1820.* Cape Town: Longmans, 1979, revised ed., 1989

Elphick, Richard, and **Robert C.-H. Shell.** "Intergroup Relations: Khoikhoi, Settlers, Slaves and Free Blacks." In *The Shaping of South African Society, 1652–1820.* Ed. Richard Elphick and Herman Giliomee. Cape Town: Longmans, 1979; rev. ed. Middletown, Conn.: Wesleyan University Press, 1989, pp. 185–239. This book has also been translated into Afrikaans under the title, *Samelewing in Wording: Suid Afrika, 1652–1820.*

_____. "A Response to Hans Heese." *Kronos* 18 (1991): 67–71.

Fairbairn, John. "Five Papers on the Slave Question from the South African Commercial Advertiser." Cape Town: George Greig, 1831.

Filliot, J.M. *La Traite des Esclaves vers les Mascareignes au XVIIIe siécle.* Paris: Orstrom, 1974. A pioneering study of slave trading on the Indian Ocean. Useful for the Cape's Mauritian connection.

Franken, J. L. M. "'n Kaapse Huishoue in die 18de Eeu Uit Von Dessin se Briefboek en Memorial." *Archives Year Book* 1 (1940): 1–88. The scholar intrested in the life of a Cape Town slave trader will have to consult the original, but this condensed version provides some aspects of the everyday life of a Cape Town slave trader.

————. "Vertolking aan de Kaap in Maleis en Portugees." *Die Huisgenoot* (18 July 1930): 41–67.

Fredrickson, George M. *White Supremacy: A Comparative Study in American and South African History.* New York: Oxford University Press, 1981. Contains much material on the rise of racial slavery in South Africa, but see Elphick's review.

Gailey, Harry. "John Philip's Role in Hottentot Emancipation." *Journal of African History* 3 (1962): 419–433.

Gerber, Hilda. *Traditional Cookery of the Cape Malays.* Foreword by I. D. du Plessis. Amsterdam: Balkema, 1959. Contains a useful essay on slavery and Cape domestic cuisine by I. D. du Plessis.

Gerstner, Jonathan Neil. *The Thousand Generation Covenant: Dutch Reformed Covenant Theology and Group Identity in Colonial South Africa, 1652–1814.* Leiden: E. J. Brill, 1991.

Geyser, O. *Die Ou Hooggershofgebou.* Cape Town: Tafelberg, 1958. Contains some historical data on the old slave Lodge, for the most part unreferenced.

————. "Ou Hooggershofgebou in Kaapstad en sy vroeër inwoners." *Historia* 3 (June 1958): 83–88.

Giliomee, Herman. "Democracy and the Frontier: A Comparative Study of Bacon's Rebellion 1676 and the Graaf Reinet Rebellion 1795–1796." Paper delivered at Comparative Frontier Seminar, Yale University, Spring 1973.

Glamann, Kristoff. *Dutch-Asiatic Trade: 1620 to 1740.* 's-Gravenhage: Martinus Nijhoff, 1981. Best analysis of the sea trade around the Cape.

Godée-Molsbergen, E. C. "Hottentotten, slaven en blanken in compagniestijd in Zuid-Afrika." In *Handeling en medelingen van de Maatscappij der Nederlandsche Letterkunde te Leiden.* Leiden: E. J. Brill, 1912–13, pp. 102–118.

Godée-Molsbergen, E. C. and **Joh. Visscher.** *South African History: Pictorial Atlas.* Amsterdam: S. L. van Looy, 1913.

Gordon-Brown, A. *Pictorial Africana: A Survey of Old South African Paintings.* Cape Town: Balkema, 1975.

Grandidier, Alfred. *Collection des Ouvrages Anciens Concernant Madagascar.* Yale University, Sterling Memorial Library, Microfilm, B882. Cape slave voyage to Madagascar in French translation.

Greenstein, Lewis. "Slave and Citizen: The South African Case." *Race* 15 (1973): 25–45.

Greyling, J. C. *Die Vraagstuk van Slawenhandel en Slawerny in die Suid-Afrikaanse Republiek tot 1877.* Master's thesis, University of South Africa, 1943.

Guelke, Leonard. "The Anatomy of a Colonial Settler Population: Cape Colony 1657–1750." *The International Journal of African Historical Studies* 21, 3 (1988): 453–

473. First study using the family reconstitution techniques of the *Annales* school and the Cambridge Group.

————. "A Computer Approach to Mapping the *Opgaaf:* The Population of the Cape in 1731." *South African Journal of Photogrammetry, Remote Sensing and Cartography* 13, 4 (1983): 227–237. Contains maps and details of slave distributions.

————. "The Early European Settlement of South Africa." Ph.D. diss., University of Toronto, 1974.

————. "Frontier Settlement in Early Dutch South Africa." *Annals of the Association of American Geographers* 66, 1 (March 1976): 25–42.

————. "The White Settlers, 1652–1780." In *The Shaping of South African Society, 1652–1820.* Ed. Richard Elphick and Herman Giliomee. Cape Town: Longmans, 1979.

Guelke, Leonard, and **Robert C.-H. Shell.** "An Early Colonial Landed Gentry: Land and Wealth in the Cape Colony, 1682–1731." *Journal of Historical Geography* 9, 3 (1983): 265–286.

————. "Frontier Water Alienation and Khoikhoi Strategies of Survival, 1652–1780." *Journal of South African Studies* 18, 4 (December 1992): 1–22.

————, comps. "The Deeds Book: The Cape Cadastral Calendar." New Haven, Conn.: Opgaaf Project, 1990.

Guelke, Leonard, Robert C.-H. Shell, and **Anthony Whyte,** comps. "The de la Fontaine Report" New Haven, Conn.: Opgaaf Project, 1990.

Hall, Martin. "People in a Changing Landscape: Excavating Cape Town." Inaugural Lecture, University of Cape Town, 25 March 1992.

Halls, C. "Dutch Navigation off the East African Coast." *Tanzania Notes and Records* 67 (June 1967): 39–48.

Hancock, W. K. "Trek." *Economic History Review* 10, 3 (1957–58): 331–339.

Harries, Patrick. "Mozbiekers: The Immigration of an African Community to the Western Cape, 1876–1882." In Christopher Saunders, ed. *Studies in the History of Cape Town* 1 (1984): 153–164. Mention is made of Piet Retief's slaves.

Hattersley, Alan F. "Emancipation of Slaves at the Cape." *South African Quarterly Bulletin* 4, 2 (June 1922) 2–5.

————. "The Emancipation of Slaves at the Cape." *History* 8 (1923): 180–186.

————. "Slavery." *Standard Encyclopedia of South Africa*, vol. 9, pp. 658–660.

————. "Slavery at the Cape, 1652–1838." In *The Cambridge History of the British Empire,* vol. 8. Ed. Eric Walker. Cambridge: Cambridge University Press, 1963, pp. 266–76.

Hattingh, J. L. "A. J. Böeseken se addendum van Kaapse Slawe-verkooptransaksies: Foute en Regstellings." *Kronos* 9 (1984): 3–12.

————. "Beleid en praktyk: die doop van slawekinders en die sluit van gemengde verhoudings aan die Kaap voor 1720." *Kronos* 5 (1982): 25–42.

————. "Die Blanke nageslag van Louis van Bengale en Lijsbeth van die Kaap." *Kronos* 3 (1980): 5–51.

————. "Grondbesit in die Tafelvallei. Deel 1: Die Eksperiment: Vryswartes as Grondeienaars, 1652–1710." *Kronos* 10 (1985): 32–48.

_____. "Kaapse Notariële stukke waarin Slawe van Vryburgers en Amptenare vermeld word (1658–1730) — I." *Kronos* 14 (1988): 43–65.

_____. "Kaapse Notareële stukke waarin Slawe van Vryburgers en Amptenare vermeld word — II — Die Tweede Dekade 1671–1680." *Kronos* 15 (1989): 3–48.

_____. "Die Klagte oor goewerneur W. A. van der Stel se slawebesit-'n Beoordeling met Behulp van kwantitatiewe data." *Kronos* 7 (1983): 5–20.

_____. "Naamgewing aan Slawe, Vryswartes en ander Gekleurdes." *Kronos* 6 (1983): 5–20.

_____. "Slawevrystellings aan die Kaap, 1700–1720." *Kronos* 4 (1981): 24–37.

Heese, Hans Friedreich. *Groep sonder Grense: Die rol en status van de gemengde bevolking aan die Kaap, 1652–1795.* Bellville: Wes Kaaplandse Instituut vir Historiese Navorsing, 1984. Appendixes contain best researched lists of mixed marriages and miscegenating couples.

_____. "'n Huigelaar en sy slavin: Tryntjie se glas koringbier." *In De Kat* 10 (May 1986): 50–53.

_____. "Kriminele sake: Hofuitsprake aan die Kaap, 1700–1750." *Kronos* 12 (1987): 33–42.

_____. "Mortaliteit onder VOC Slawe, 1720–1782." *Kronos* 11 (1986): 7–14.

_____. "Slawegesinne in die W. Kaap, 1665–1795." *Kronos* 4 (1981): 38–48.

Hengherr, E. C. W. "Emancipation — and After: A Study of Cape Slavery and the Issues Arising from It, 1830–1843." Master's thesis, University of Cape Town, 1953. An early work, carefully researched; contains useful insights on the nature of slave urbanization.

Hoge, J. "Personalia of the Germans at the Cape, 1652–1806." *Archives Year Book* 9 (1946): 1–495.

Hoge, J. "Privaatskoolmeesters . . ." *Annals of the University of Stellenbosch* 19: 4–43.

Hopper, J. "Xhosa-Colonial Relations: 1770–1803." Ph.D. dissertation, Yale University, 1980.

Hughes, Kenneth. "Law, Religion and Bastardy: Some Thoughts on Illegitimacy in Comparative and Historical Perspective." Mimeo, 1991.

Hugo, A. M. "The Cape Vernacular." Inaugural lecture as Professor of Classics, 1971. Obtained from South African Library. No date, (1971?).

_____. "Familia [*sic*]" *Familia* 4, 5 (1967): 109–121.

Idenburg, P. J. *The Cape of Good Hope at the Turn of the Eighteenth Century.* Leiden: University Press, 1963.

Jordaan, Ken. "The Origins of the Afrikaners and Their Language, 1652–1720: A Study in Miscegenation and Creole." *Race* 15, 4 (1974): 461–495.

Kantor, Brian. "The Rixdollar and the Foreign Exchange" *South African Journal of Economics* (1970): 66–93.

Kent, Raymond K. *Early Kingdoms in Madagascar, 1500–1700.* New York: Holt, Rinehart and Winston, 1970.

King, M. "Slavery in South Africa." *Mentor* 34, 9 (1952): 3–4.

Kistner, W. "Anti-slavery Agitation against the Transvaal Republic, 1852–1868." *Archives Year Book* (1952): 195–278.

Kock, de Victor. *Those in Bondage: An Account of the Life of the Slave at the Cape in the Days of the Dutch East India Company.* London: Allen & Unwin, 1950. Victor de Kock's 1950 work is vitiated by an anecdotal approach, yet it is extremely useful because of the wide range of archival material he consulted but did not always cite.

Latsky, M. "Slawewetgewing aan die Kaap (1806–1834)." Master's thesis, University of Stellenbosch, 1943.

Leftwich, Adrian. "Colonialism and the Constitution of Cape Society under the Dutch East India Company." 2 vols. Ph.D. dissertation, University of York, 1976.

Legassick, Martin C. "The Frontier Tradition in South African Historiography." In Institute of Commonwealth Studies, *Collected Seminar Papers on the Societies of Southern Africa in the 19th and 20th Centuries* 12, 2 (London: 1970). Calls for an investigation of slavery and postindustrial labor relations.

―――――. "The Griqua, the Sotho-Tswana, and the Missionaries, 1780–1840: The Politics of a Frontier Zone." Ph.D. diss., University of California, Los Angeles, 1969.

Liebenberg, Barend Jacobus. "Die Vrystelling van die Slawe in die Kaap Kolonie en die Implikasies daarvan." Masters thesis, University of the Orange Free State, 1959.

Lima, de Suasso J. "Verslag der Gehoudene Byeenkomst en Juiste Aanteekingen der Redevoeringen by die gelegenheid Gedaan door de Advocaten Cloete, Brand, de Wet Faure, Hofmeyr en andere Heeren . . ." Cape Town: P. A. Brand, 1832.

Lückhoff, C. A. *Die Ou Hooggershofgebou: Die ingeligte openbare mening en die toekoms van die gebou.* Cape Town: Balkema, 1954.

MacCrone, Ian Douglas. "The Frontier Tradition and Race Attitudes in South Africa." *Race Relations Journal* 28, 3 (July–September 1961): 19–30.

―――――. *Race Attitudes in South Africa: Historical, Experimental and Psychological Studies.* Johannesburg: Witwatersrand University Press, 1957.

Malherbe, V. C. "Indentured and Unfree Labor in South Africa: Towards an Understanding." *South African Historical Journal* 24 (1991): 15–16.

Marais, Johannes Stephanus. *"The Cape Coloured People, 1652–1937.* Johannesburg: Witwatersrand University Press, 1968; first published 1939. Barely deals with the period 1652 to 1795, but still useful and insightful for slave related issues, mainly based on van Rensburg's thesis (q.v.).

Marais, Maria M. "Armesorg aan die Kaap onder die Kompanjie, 1652–1795." *Archives Year Book* 1 (1943): 1–72.

Mason, John Edwin, Jr. "Fit for Freedom: The Slaves. Slavery, and Emancipation in the Cape Colony, South Africa, 1806 to 1842." New Haven: Yale Ph. D., 1992.

―――――. "Hendrik Albertus and His Ex-slave Mey: A Drama in Three Acts." *Journal of African History* 31 (1990) 423–445.

―――――. "The Slaves, the Hotnots, and What Not: The World the Tourists Saw." Paper presented at South African Research Project seminar, Yale University, 17 April 1985.

―――――. "The Slaves and Their Protectors: Reforming Resistance in a Slave

Society, the Cape Colony, 1826–1834." *Journal of South African Studies* 17 (March 1991): 103–128.

Masselman, George. *The Cradle of Colonialism.* New Haven, Conn.: Yale University Press, 1963. An extremely readable and vivid history. An excellent introduction to the topic and to the historical background of the area from which many Cape slaves were drawn.

McKenzie, Kirsten. "Samuel Eusebius Hudson at the Cape of Good Hope, 1797–1807." Honors thesis, History Department, University of Cape Town, 1991.

Merwe, van der P. J. *Die Noordwaartse beweging van die Boere voor die Groot Trek, 1770–1842.* The Hague: W. P. van Stockum & Zoon, 1937.

_____. *Die Trekboer in die Geskiedenis van die Kaapkolonie 1657–1842.* Cape Town: Nasionale Pers Beperk, 1938.

_____. *Trek: studies oor die mobiliteit van die pioniersbevolking aan de Kaap.* Cape Town: Nasionale Pers, 1945.

Meulen, Jan van der. "Die Europäische Grundlage der kolonial Archtektur am Kap der Guten Hoffnung. Ph.D. diss., University of Marburg, 1962.

Miller, Thomas. *Considerations on the Exact Position of the Slave Question.* Cape Town: George Greig, 1831.

Mills, Wallace. "Cape Smoke: Alcohol Issues in the Cape Colony in the Nineteenth Century." *Contemporary Drug Problems* 12 (Summer 1985): 221–247.

Müller, A. L. "The Economics of Slave Labour at the Cape of Good Hope." *The South African Journal of Economics* 49, 1 (March 1981): 46–58. The only attempt to use econometric analysis on Cape slaves. The author lacks an adequate time series.

_____. "Slavery and the Development of South Africa." *The South African Journal of Economics* 49, 2 (June 1981): 153–165.

Neumark, S. D. *Economic Influences on the South African Frontier: 1652–1836.* Food Research Institute, Stanford University, Miscellaneous Publication No. 1, 1957. Entirely based on library research, this challenging book threw a spanner into the workings of South African historiography.

_____. "The Enemy Within: The Struggle for Ascendancy on the Cape Eastern Frontier, 1760–1799." Ph.D. diss., School of Oriental and African Studies, University of London, 1992.

_____. "The Labour Market of the Cape Colony, 1807–1828." In *Economy and Society in Pre-Industrial South Africa.* Ed. Shula Marks and Anthony Atmore. London: Longmans, 1980, pp. 171–207.

Newton-King, Susan, with **V. C. Malherbe.** *The Khoikhoi Rebellion in the Eastern Cape (1799–1803).* Centre for African Studies, University of Cape Town, 1981.

Nienaber, G. S. *Hottentots.* Pretoria, J.L. Schaik Beperk, 1963.

Nordholt, Henk Schulte. "Macht, Mense en Middelen: Patronen van Dynamiek in de Balische Politiek: 1700–1840." Ph.D. thesis, Vrije Universiteit van Amsterdam, 1980.

Oosterhoff, Jan. "Sodomy at Sea at the Cape of Good Hope during the Eighteenth Century," *Journal of Homosexuality* 16 1–2 (1988): 229–235.

Pama, C., comp., and **C. C. de Villiers.** *Geslagregisters van die ou Kaapse Families.* 2 vols. Cape Town: Balkema, 1981.

Pearse, G. E. *Eighteenth Century Architecture in South Africa.* Cape Town: Balkema, 1968.

Pederson, N. "Naval Heritage." *Commando* 5, 2 (1954): 27–29. About slave ships at the Cape. Contains details of slaving between 1795 and 1808; no citations, but based on archival work.

Pedro, K. J. "Die Doopbediening aan Slawe en Vryswartes in die Kaapse Kerk, 1802–1812." *Kronos* 9 (1984): 22–35.

Penn, Nigel. "The Frontier in the Western Cape." In *Papers in the Prehistory of the Western Cape.* Ed. John Parkington and Martin Hall. Oxford: BAR International Series 332, 1987, pp. 475–576.

Pieterse, D. J. "Beweerde slawehandel deur Boere: stelselmatige propaganda om [die] Republiek te ondermyn." *Huisgenoot* 20 (1936): 758–759.

Plessis, du J. *A History of Christian Missions in South Africa.* London: Longmans Green, 1911; reprinted 1961.

Plessis, du Izaak David. *The Cape Malays: History, Religion, Traditions, Folk Tales, the Malay Quarter.* 3rd ed. Cape Town: Balkema, 1972. Contains many anecdotes culled from oral interviews now no longer accessible.

Postma, Johannes Menne. *The Dutch in the Atlantic Slave Trade, 1600–1815.* Cambridge: Cambridge University Press, 1990.

Pretorius, C. "Verhaal van Anna Marais en die slaaf Claas van Bengalen." *Historia* 24 (March 1979): 42–49.

Ravell, James J. "The VOC Slave Trade between Cape Town and Madagascar, 1652–1795." Mimeo, Bilthoven, June 1979. Ravell, an independent researcher in Holland, has produced a useful chronicle of the trade from 1652 to 1795; however, his work remains in rough form and unpublished. Moreover, he has not yet obtained access to all the relevant archival material in the Deeds Office in Cape Town.

Rayner, Mary Isabel. "Wine and Slaves: The Failure of an Export Economy and the Ending of Slavery in the Cape Colony, South Africa, 1806–1834." Ph.D. diss., Duke University, 1986.

Rensburg, van A. Janse. "Die Toestand van die Slawe aan die Kaap, 1806–1834." Master's thesis, History Department, University of Cape Town, 1935. Forms the basis of J. S. Marais's commentary on slaves in this period (q.v.).

Richner, Jürg. "Cape Frontier Slavery: A Historical Overview of Southern African History, 1770–1843, with Particular Reference to the Enslaving of Indigenous People, Eastern Cape to Transorangia and Natal." Mimeo, 1991.

Robertson, H. M. "Some Doubts Concerning Early Land Tenure at the Cape." *South African Journal of Economics* 3 (1935): 158–172.

Rochlin, Samuel Abraham. "A Forgotten Name for the Cape Malays." *Bantu Studies* 8 (1934): 95–97.

Ross, Robert. *"Cape of Torments: Slavery and Resistance in South Africa.* London: Routledge and Kegan Paul, 1983. Although the author's views on the subject become colored by the crime records with which he almost exclusively deals, the book captures the atmosphere of the early Cape slave society admirably. The chapter on the Hanglip maroon community is particularly vivid.

_____. "The Changing Legal Position of the Khoisan in the Cape Colony." *African Perspectives* 2 (1979): 67–87.

_____. "The Dutch on the Swahili Coast, 1776–1778: Two Slaving Journals, Part I." *International Journal of African Historical Studies* 19, 2 (1986): 305–360.

_____. "The Dutch on the Swahili Coast, 1776–1778: Two Slaving Journals, Part II." *International Journal of African Historical Studies* 19, 3 (1986): 479–506.

_____. "The Last Years of the Slave Trade to the Cape Colony." *Slavery and Abolition* 9, 3 (December 1988): 209–219.

_____. "The Occupations of Slaves in Eighteenth Century Cape Town." *Studies in the History of Cape Town* 2 (1980): 1–14. A short but useful treatment of the topic.

_____. "Oppression, Sexuality and Slavery at the Cape of Good Hope." *Historical Reflections* 6 (1989) 421–433. A useful treatment of the topic.

_____. "The Rise of the Cape Gentry." *Journal of Southern African Studies* 9, 2 (April 1983): 194–217.

_____. "Smallpox at the Cape of Good Hope." In *African Historical Demography*. Edinburgh: Center of African Studies, 1977.

Ross, Robert, and **Peter van Duin.** *The Economy of the Cape Colony in the Eighteenth Century.* Leiden: Intercontinenta, No. 7, 1987, pp. 1–166. Contains little on slaves, despite being devoted to the demolition of the over production thesis; still useful for the tables.

Ryneveld, van W. S. "Replies to the Questions on the Importation, etc., of Slaves into the Colony; Proposed by His Excellency the Earl of Macartney, etc., etc." (29 November 1797). University of the Witwatersrand Library: Gubbins Collection. Sometimes cited as President of the Court of Justice, "Memorandum [on slavery]" (29 November 1797) Original ms. at Witwatersrand University, published by W.G.A. Mears, copy in Jagger Library. Cf. manuscript copy in CAD A 455 no. 33.

Saunders, Christopher C. "Between Slavery and Freedom: the Importation of Prize Negroes to the Cape in the Aftermath of Emancipation." *Kronos* 9 (1984): 36–43.

_____. "Liberated Africans in the Cape Colony in the First Half of the Nineteenth Century." *International Journal of African Historical Studies* 18 (1985): 223–39.

_____. "Nineteenth Century Farce: The Anglo-Portuguese Mixed Commission at the Cape of Good Hope." *Quarterly Bulletin of the South African Library* 37 (June 1983): 298–302.

Schoeman, Karel. "Slawe van die Kaap: 'n paar aantekinge." *Quarterly Bulletin of the South African Library* 39 (September 1984): 6–7.

Selms, van Adrianus. "Die Oudste Boek in Afrikaans: Isjmoeni se 'Bertroubare Woord'." *Hertzog Annale* (1952): 61–102.

Shaw, E. M. "A History of Currency in South Africa." Cape Town: South African Museum, Guide No. 5, 1956.

Shell, Robert C.-H. "The Tower of Babel? The Cape Trade (1658–1808):

Geographic Origins and Cultural Consequences within the Household." In Fred
Morton and Elizabeth Eldridge, eds., *Slaving on the Dutch Frontier.* Boulder: Westview,
1994.

————. "Dark Origins: 'Slaves and Free Blacks at the Cape, 1658–1700' by
Anna Böeseken." *Financial Mail* (February 1978): 432.

————. "De Meillon's People of Colour: Some Notes on Their Dress and
Occupations with Special Reference to *Cape Views and Costumes: Water-Colours by
H. C. de Meillon in the Brenthurst Collection* . . ." Johannesburg: The Brenthurst Press,
1978. Pamphlet, 16 pages.

————. "The Establishment and Spread of Islam at the Cape from the
Beginning of Company rule to 1838." Honors thesis, University of Cape Town, 1975.

————. "The Family and Slavery: The Cape Slave Society, 1680–1838." In
The Angry Divide. Ed. Mary Simons and Wilmot James. Cape Town: David Philip,
1989, pp. 20–39.

————. "A Family Matter: The Sale and Transfer of Human Beings at the
Cape, 1658 to 1830." *International Journal of African Historical Studies* 25, 2 (1992):
285–336.

————. "A Note on Autochthonous Slavery." *Quarterly Bulletin of the South
African Library* 43 (December 1988): 92–93.

————. "Rangton of Bali (1673–1720): Roots and Resurrection." *Kronos* 19
(November 1992): 167–199.

————. "Rangton of Bali: The Short Life and Material Possessions of a Cape
Slave." *Kronos* 18 (1991): 1–6.

————. "Religion, Civic Status and Slavery from Dordt to the Trek." *Kronos* 19
(November 1992): 28–63.

————. "Rites and Rebellion: Islamic Conversion at the Cape, 1808 to 1915."
In *Studies in the History of Cape Town*, vol. 5. Cape Town: University of Cape Town,
1984, pp. 1–46.

————. "S. E. Hudson on Funerals." *Quarterly Bulletin of the South African
Library* 44 (December 1989): 56–63.

————. "S.E. Hudson on Marriages and other Customs at the Cape." *Kronos*
15 (1989): 49–57.

————. "Slavery at the Cape of Good Hope: 1680–1731." 2 vols. Ph.D. diss.,
Yale University, 1986. Indexed.

————. "Tender Ties: The Women of the Cape Slave Society." Institute of
Commonwealth Studies: Collected Seminar Papers. *The Societies of Southern Africa* 17,
42 (1992): 1–34.

————. "Tooth Mutilation in the Early Cape." *Quarterly Bulletin of the South
African Library* 46 (September 1991): 39–40.

————, ed. "Katie Jacobs: An Early Oral History." *Quarterly Bulletin of the
South African Library* 3 46 (March 1992): 94–99.

————, ed. Samuel Hudson. "Auctions — their good and evil tendency." Parts
1 and 2. *Quarterly Bulletin of the South African Library* 39, 4 (June 1985): 147–151;
Quarterly Bulletin of the South African Library 40, 1 (September 1985): 12–18.

————, ed. " 'Slaves,' an Essay by Samuel Eusebius Hudson." *Kronos* 9 (1984):
44–70.

Spuy, van der Patricia. "Gender and Slavery: Towards a Feminist Revision." *South African Historical Journal* 25 (1991): 184–195. A suggestive review article of Caribbean slavery with some oblique comparative pointers for the Cape.

Stockenström, Eric. *Vrystelling van die Slawe.* Cape Town: Algemene Sending Kommissie van die Ned. Geref. Kerk in Suid Afrika, 1934. A centenary publication celebrating the emancipation.

Storrar, Patricia. "Count Gisbert Karel van Hogendorp and His Unfulfilled Dream." *Quarterly Bulletin of the South African Library* 44, 3 (March, 1990): 101.

Sutherland, Heather. "The Historiography of Slavery in Indonesia." Mimeo, Free University of Amsterdam, undated.

_____. "Mestizos as Middlemen? Ethnicity and Access in Colonial Macassar." Paper presented at the Dutch-Indonesian Historical Conference. Lange Vuursche, The Netherlands, 27–28 June 1980.

_____. "Slavery and the Slave Trade in Indonesia with Special Reference to Sulawesi, Problems and Perspectives." Mimeo, Free University of Amsterdam, undated.

Taylor, Jean Gelman. *The Social World of Batavia: European and Eurasian in Dutch Asia.* Madison: University of Wisconsin Press, 1983. A pioneering treatment that needs to be done for the Cape.

Theal, George McCall. *Chronicles of the Cape Commanders* ... Cape Town: W. A. Richards & Sons, 1882. Some of Theal's early work reprinted from colonial periodicals, containing some interesting maps and primary documents.

Theal, George McCall. *History of South Africa.* 11 vols. Cape Town: Struik, 1964.

Thompson, Leonard and **Howard Lamar,** eds. *The Frontier in History: North America and Southern Africa Compared.* New Haven, Conn.: Yale University Press, 1981.

Toit, du André. "No Chosen People: The Myth of the Calvinist Origins of Afrikaner Nationalism and Racial Ideology." *The American Historical Review* 88, 4 (October 1983): 920–952.

_____. "Captive to the Nationalist Paradigm." Mimeo, (no date).

_____. "Puritans in Africa?" Mimeo, 1981.

Toit, André du, and **H. Giliomee.** *Afrikaner Political Thought: Analysis and Documents, 1780–1850.* Cape Town: David Philip, 1983.

Toit, du, V. "1820 Settlers Had a Servant Problem." *1820* 26, 4 (1954): 17–21.

Trapido, Stanley. "Aspects in the Transition from Slavery to Serfdom: The South African Republic, 1842–1902." University of London: Institute of Commonwealth Studies Seminar Papers. *The Societies of Southern Africa in the 19th and 20th Centuries* 6 (1975): 24–31.

Trotter, A. P. *Old Cape Colony: A Chronicle of her Men and Houses from 1652 to 1806.* London: Archibald Constable, 1903.

Valkhoff, Marius. *New Light on Afrikaans and "Malayo-Portuguese.* Louvain: Peeters, 1972.

_____. *Studies in Portugal and Creole, with Special Reference to South Africa.* Johannesburg: Witwatersrand University Press, 1966.

Venter, P. J. "Die Inboek-stelsel: 'n Uitvloeisel van Slawerny in die Ou Dae." *Die Huisgenoot* (1 June 1934): 25, 59, 61.

_____. "Landdros en Heemrade (1682–1827)." *Archives Year Book* 2 (1940): 1–242. disappointing on slaves, but see previous entry.

Villiers, de Simon A. *Robben Island: Out of Reach, Out of Mind.* Cape Town: Struik, 1971. Eccentric treatment and insights, but useful for sources and photographs.

Visagie, G. G. *Regspleging en Reg aan die Kaap van 1652 to 1806, met 'n Bespreking van die Historiese Agtergrond.* Cape Town: Juta, 1969.

Walker, Eric A. *The Frontier Tradition in South Africa: A Lecture Delivered . . . at Rhodes House on the 5th March 1930.* Oxford: Oxford University Press, 1930.

Walt, A. van der J. H. *Die Ausdehnung der Kolonie am Kap der Guten Hoffnung 1770–1799.* Berlin: Emil Ebering, 1928.

Walton, James. *Homesteads and Villages of South Africa.* Pretoria: Van Schalk, 1952. The architecture of the slave society at the Cape is an untouched subject in the field of architectural history. The Cape literature bristles with the most lavish but invariably sentimental and disappointing "coffee table" treatments of Dutch home-steads. Walton is one of the few scholars to deal with the problem in an original and scientific way. He also discusses slave quarters and slave prices.

_____. *Old Cape Farmsteads.* Cape Town: Human and Rousseau, 1989,

_____. "The South African *Kapstijlhuis* and Some European Counterparts." *Restorica* 10 (December 1981): 2–8.

Watson, Richard L. "Religion and Antislavery at the Cape of Good Hope." In *Discovering the African Past.* Ed. Norman R. Bennet. Boston: Trustees of Boston University, 1987, pp. 95–107.

_____. "Slavery and Ideology: The South African Case." *International Journal of African Historical Studies* 20, 1 (1987): 27–43.

_____. *The Slave Question: Liberty and Property in South Africa.* Middletown, Conn.: Wesleyan University Press, 1990. The best contemporary treatment of Cape slavery and the property question.

Wet, de G. C. *Die Vryliede en Vryswartes in die Kaapse Nedersetting, 1657–1707.* Cape Town: Historiese Publikasie-Vereniging, 1981. A monumental and definitive work showing some methodological innovations. A few glimpses into the free black community.

Worden, Nigel Anthony. "Rural Slavery in the Western Districts of [the] Cape Colony during the eighteenth century." Ph.D. thesis, Cambridge University, April 1982.

Worden, Nigel Anthony. *Slavery in Dutch South Africa.* Cambridge: Cambridge University Press, 1985. An elegantly written synthesis of the topic of slavery in the Stellenbosch district. Although the author and I differ on many important aspects on Cape slavery — the ethnic division of labor, the development and extent of racial attitudes, the operations of the domestic slave market, existence of free knechts, the "family" and "army" modes of control, and so on — this has not stopped a fruitful cross-fertilization of ideas and sources.

_____. "Violence, Crime and Slavery on Cape Farmsteads in the Eighteenth Century." *Kronos* 5 (1982): 43–60.

Miers, Suzanne and **Kopytoff, Igor** (eds.). *Slavery in Africa: Historical and Anthropological Perspectives*. Madison: University of Wisconsin Press, 1977.

Miller, Joseph Calder. "Mortality in the Atlantic Slave Trade: Statistical Evidence on Causality" *Journal of Interdisciplinary History* 11, No. 3 (Winter 1981): 385–423.

Moller, Herbert. "Sex Compositions and Correlated Culture Patterns of Colonial America." *William and Mary Quarterly*. Second series 2 (1945): 113–153.

Morgan, Edmund S. *American Slavery, American Freedom*. New York: W. W. Norton, 1975.

————. *The Puritan Family: Religion and Domestic Relations in Seventeenth Century New England*. New York: Harper and Row, 1966.

Mousnier, Roland. *Social Hierarchies: 1450 to the present*. London: Croom Helm, 1973.

Mullin, Gerald W. *Flight and Rebellion: Slave Resistance in Eighteenth-Century Virginia*. London: Oxford University Press, 1972.

Nieboer, H.J. *Slavery as an Industrial System: Ethnological Researches*. New York: Burt Franklin, 1971 original edition,1910.

Palmer, Colin, *Human Cargoes: The British Slave Trade to Spanish America, 1700 to 1739*. Chicago: University of Illinois Press, 1981.

Patterson, Orlando. *Slavery and Social Death: A Comparative Study*. Cambridge: Harvard University Press, 1982.

Phillips, Ulrich Bonnel. *The Slave Economy of the Old South Selected Essays in Economic and Social History*. Edited with an introduction by Eugene D. Genovese, Baton Rouge: Louisiana State University Press, 1968. Reprint of original 1929 edition.

Prunty, Merle. "The Renaissance of the Southern Plantation." *Geographical Review* 45 (October 1955) (4): 470.

Price, Richard (ed.). *Maroon Societies: Rebel Slave Communities in the Americas*. New York: Anchor Books, 1973.

Raboteau, Albert J. *Slave Religion: The Invisible Institution in the Antebellum South*. Oxford: Oxford University Press, 1980.

Renkema, W. E. *Het Curaçaose Plantagebedriif in de negentiende eeuw*. Zutphen: Walburg Press, 1981.

Starobin, Robert S. *Industrial Slavery in the Old South*. Oxford University Press, 1975.

Tadman, Michael. *Speculators and Slaves: Masters, Traders, and Slaves in the Old South*. Madison: University of Wisconsin Press, 1989.

Tannenbaum, Frank. *Slave and Citizen: The Negro in the Americas*. New York: Alfred Knopf, 1946.

Thompson, Edgar T. "Virginia." in Edgar T. Thompson, (ed.). *Race: Individual and Collective Behaviour*. New York: Collier Macmillan, 1958.

Thompson, R. "Seventeenth Century English and Colonial Sex Ratios: A Postscript." *Population Studies* 1 28: 150ff.

Tietze, Christopher. "Reproduction Span and Rate of Reproduction Among Hutterite Women." *Fertility and Sterility*. 8 (January–February, 1957): 89–97.

Worden, Nigel Anthony, with **Candy Malherbe Comps.** *Always Working*. Pietermaritzburg: Shuter & Shooter, 1986. School text in pamphlet form.

Wright, William. *Slavery at the Cape of Good Hope*. London: John Rodwell, 1831; reprint, New York: Negro Universities Press, 1969.

Zyl, van der D. J. "Slaaf in die ekonomiese lewe van die Westlike distrikte van die Kaapkolonie, 1795–1834." *South African Historical Journal* 10 (1978): 3–25.

Works Cited in Comparative and Methodological Contexts

Bancroft, Frederick. *Slave Trading in the Old South*. New York: Frederick Ungar, 1959, original publication, 1931.

Berkener, Lutz K. "The Use and Misuse of Census Data for the Historical Analysis of Family Structure." *Journal of Interdisciplinary History* 4 (Spring, 1975): 721–738.

Berlin, Ira. *Slaves without Masters: The Free Negro in the Antebellum South* New York: Vintage, 1976.

Billings, Warren M. *The Old Dominion in the Seventeenth Century: A Documentary History of Virginia, 1606–1689*. Chapel Hill: University of North Carolina Press, 1975.

Blassingame, John W. *The Slave Community: Plantation Life in the Antebellum South*. New York: Oxford University Press, 1979.

Boserup, Ester. *The Conditions of Agricultural Growth: The Economics of Agrarian Growth*. New York: Aldine. 1965. The most important neo-Malthusian theorist of demography, with many implications for slave societies.

Boxer, Charles Randolph. *Race Relations in the Portuguese Colonial Empire, 1415–1825*. Oxford University Press, 1963.

Boxer, Charles Randolph. *The Golden Age of Brazil, 1695–1750* Berkeley: University of California Press, 1962.

Brana-Shuta, Rosemary. "Approaching Freedom: The Manumission of Slaves in Suriname, 1760–1828." *Slavery and Abolition* 10 3 (December, 1989): 66–93.

Calderhead, William L. "How extensive was the border state slave trade? A New Look" *Civil War History* 18 (March, 1972): 42–55.

Cohen, David W. and **Greene, Jack P.** (ed.). *Neither Slave nor Free: The Freedman of African Descent in the Slave Societies of the New World*. Baltimore: John Hopkins University Press, 1972.

Cooper, Frederick. "The Problem of Slavery in African Studies," *Journal of African History,* 20 1 (1979), 103–125.

Curtin, Philip D. *The Atlantic Slave Trade: A Census*. Madison: University of Wisconsin Press, 1969.

Davis, David Brion. *The Problem of Slavery in Western Culture*. New York: Cornell University Press, 1966.

Deburg, van William L. *The Slave Drivers: Black Agricultural Labor Supervisors in the Antebellum South*. Westport: Greenwood Press, 1979.

Diamond, Sigmund. "From Organization to Society: Virginia in the

Seventeenth Century." in Stanley N. Katz (ed.). *Colonial America: Essays in Politics and Social Development.* Boston: Little Brown and Company, 1971.

Dockès, Pierre. *Medieval Slavery and Liberation.* Chicago: Chicago University Press, 1982.

Domar, Evsey. "The Causes of Slavery or Serfdom: an Hypothesis." *Journal of Economic History.* 30 (1970): 18–32.

Dunn, Richard S. *Sugar and Slaves.* New York: Norton, 1972.

Eby, Cecil D. "Classical Names among Southern Negro Slaves." *American Speech.* 36 (May, 1961): 140–141.

Elkins, Stanley. *Slavery: A Problem in American Institutional and Intellectual Life.* Chicago: Chicago University Press, 1963.

Eltis, David. *Economic Growth and the Ending of the Slave Trade.* New York: Oxford University Press, 1987.

Engerman, Stanley L. and **Genovese, Eugene** (eds.). *Race and Slavery in the Western Hemisphere: Quantitative Studies.* New Jersey: Princeton University Press, 1975.

Finley, Moses I. *Economy and Society in Ancient Greece.* New York: Penguin, 1983.

Fogel, Robert and **Engerman, Stanley.** *Time on the Cross.* 2 vols. Boston: Brown and Company, 1975. Although heavily and (sometimes unfairly) criticized, *Time on the Cross* probably did more to stimulate studies in slavery and American history than most other works of the same period combined.

Freyre, Gilberto. *The Masters and the Slaves: A Study in the Development of Brazilian Civilization.* New York: Alfred Knopf, 1971.

Galenson, David W. *Traders, Planters and Slaves: Market Behavior in Early English America.* Cambridge: Cambridge University Press, 1986.

Gathorne-Hardy, Jonathan. *The Unnatural History of the Nanny.* New York: The Dial Press, 1973.

Gemery, Henry A. and **Hogendorn, Jan S.** (eds.). *The Uncommon Market: Essays in the Economic History of the Atlantic Slave Trade.* New York: Academic Press, 1979.

Gennep, van Arnold. *The Rites of Passage* trans. Monika B. Vizedom and G. L. Cafee Chicago: University of Chicago Press, 1960.

Genovese, Eugene D. (ed.). *The Slave Economies,* 2 Volumes. New York: John Wiley, 1973.

Genovese, Eugene D. and **Foner, Laura** (eds.). *Slavery in the New World: A Reader in Comparative History.* Englewood Cliffs, N.J.: Prentice Hall, 1969.

————. *Roll, Jordan, Roll: The World the Slaves Made.* New York: Vintage Books, 1976.

————. *In Red and Black: Marxian Explorations in Southern and Afro-American History.* Knoxville: The University of Tennessee Press, 1984, originally published 1968.

————. *From Rebellion to Revolution.* New York: Vintage, 1981.

Greven, Philip. *Four Generations . . . in Colonial Andover, Massachusetts.* Ithaca: Cornell University Press, 1970.

Gutman, Herbert and **Sutch, Richard.** "The Slave Family," in Paul A. David et

al. (eds.) *Reckoning with Slavery: A Critical Study in the Quantitative Histo[ry of] American Slavery.* New York: Oxford University Press, 1976.

Hajnal, John. "European Marriage Patterns in Perspective." in David V. G[lass] and David E. C. Eversly (eds.). *Population in History.* London: Arnold, 1965.

Heider, Fritz. *The Psychology of Interpersonal Relations.* New York: John Wil[ey &] Sons, 1958.

Hentig, van, Hans "The Sex Ratio: A Brief Discussion Based on the Un[ited] States Census Figures." *Social Forces.* 30 4 (May, 1952): 443–9.

Higginbotham, Leon A. *In the Matter of Color: Race and the American [Legal] Process.* Oxford University Press 1978.

Hoetink, Hermanus. *Slavery and Race Relations in the Americas: Compar[ative] Notes on their Nature and Nexus.* New York: Harper Torchbooks, 1973.

Hollingsworth, T. H. *Historical Demography.* Ithaca: Cornell University P[ress,] 1969.

Inkori J.E. (ed.). *Forced Migration: The Impact of the Export Slave Trade on Af[rican] Societies.* London: Hutchinson University Library, 1982.

Jordan, Winthrop D. *White over Black: American Attitudes towards the N[egro,] 1550–1880.* Penguin, 1969.

Klein, Herbert S. *The Middle Passage: Comparative Studies in the Atlantic [Slave] Trade.* Princeton: Princeton University Press, 1978.

Klein, Herbert S. "A Note on Mortality in the French Slave Trade in [the] Eighteenth Century." in Henry A. Gemery and Jan S. Hogendorn, *The Uncom[mon] Market, Essays in the Economic History of the Atlantic Slave Trade.* New York: Acad[emic] Press, 1979.

Kotlikoff, Laurence. "Towards A Quantitative Description of the New Orl[eans] Slave Market." Unpublished paper presented to the University of Chicago Works[hop] in History, 1975.

Ladurie, Le Roy Emmanuel. *Montaillou: Cathars and Catholics in a Fr[ench] Village, 1294–1324.* Penguin, 1980.

Laslett, Peter, (ed.). *Household and family in past time: Comparative studie[s.]* Cambridge: Cambridge University Press, 1972.

Lee, Richard B. "Lactation, Ovulation, Infanticide and Women's work: A St[udy] of Hunter-gatherer Population Regulation" in Mark Nathan Cohen, et al, *Bios[ocial] Mechanisms of Population Control* New Haven: Yale University Press, 1980, pp. 3[21–] 348.

Lovejoy, Paul. "Concubinage and the Status of Women Slaves in Early Colo[nial] Northern Nigeria." *Journal of African History* 29 (1988): 245–266.

Malthus, Thomas. *An Essay on the Principle of Population.* Anthony Flew (e[d.)] Pelican Classics, 1970 edition.

MacMullen, Ramsay. *Roman Social Relations, 50 B.C. to A.D. 284.* New Ha[ven:] Yale University Press, 1974.

McPherson, James M. *Ordeal by Fire: The Civil War and Reconstruction.* N[ew] York: Alfred A. Knopf, 1982.

Meillassoux, Claude. "Female Slavery," in Robertson and Klein (eds.), *Wo[men] and Slavery in Africa.* Madison: University of Wisconsin Press, 1983, 49–66.

Turner, Frederick Jackson. *The Frontier in American History,* with a foreword by Ray Allen Billington. New York: Holt, Rinehart and Winston, 1962.

Wade, Richard C. *Slavery in the Cities: The South 1820–1860.* Oxford University Press, 1972.

Weber, Max. *The Theory of Social and Economic Organization.* Translated by A.M. Henderson and Talcott Parsons. Oxford University Press, 1947.

Wiedemann, T.E.J. "Slavery" no. 19 in *Greece and Rome,* New Surveys in the Classics. Oxford: The Clarendon Press, 1987.

Wood, Peter H. *Black Majority: Negroes in South Carolina, from 1670 through the Stono Rebellion.* New York: Norton & Co., 1975.

Worden, Nigel Anthony, with **Candy Malherbe Comps.** *Always Working.* Pietermaritzburg: Shuter & Shooter, 1986. School text in pamphlet form.

Wright, William. *Slavery at the Cape of Good Hope.* London: John Rodwell, 1831; reprint, New York: Negro Universities Press, 1969.

Zyl, van der D. J. "Slaaf in die ekonomiese lewe van die Westlike distrikte van die Kaapkolonie, 1795–1834." *South African Historical Journal* 10 (1978): 3–25.

Works Cited in Comparative and Methodological Contexts

Bancroft, Frederick. *Slave Trading in the Old South.* New York: Frederick Ungar, 1959, original publication, 1931.

Berkener, Lutz K. "The Use and Misuse of Census Data for the Historical Analysis of Family Structure." *Journal of Interdisciplinary History* 4 (Spring, 1975): 721–738.

Berlin, Ira. *Slaves without Masters: The Free Negro in the Antebellum South* New York: Vintage, 1976.

Billings, Warren M. *The Old Dominion in the Seventeenth Century: A Documentary History of Virginia, 1606–1689.* Chapel Hill: University of North Carolina Press, 1975.

Blassingame, John W. *The Slave Community: Plantation Life in the Antebellum South.* New York: Oxford University Press, 1979.

Boserup, Ester. *The Conditions of Agricultural Growth: The Economics of Agrarian Growth.* New York: Aldine. 1965. The most important neo-Malthusian theorist of demography, with many implications for slave societies.

Boxer, Charles Randolph. *Race Relations in the Portuguese Colonial Empire, 1415–1825.* Oxford University Press, 1963.

Boxer, Charles Randolph. *The Golden Age of Brazil, 1695–1750* Berkeley: University of California Press, 1962.

Brana-Shuta, Rosemary. "Approaching Freedom: The Manumission of Slaves in Suriname, 1760–1828." *Slavery and Abolition* 10 3 (December, 1989): 66–93.

Calderhead, William L. "How extensive was the border state slave trade? A New Look" *Civil War History* 18 (March, 1972): 42–55.

Cohen, David W. and **Greene, Jack P.** (ed.). *Neither Slave nor Free: The Freedman of African Descent in the Slave Societies of the New World.* Baltimore: John Hopkins University Press, 1972.

Cooper, Frederick. "The Problem of Slavery in African Studies," *Journal of African History,* 20 1 (1979), 103–125.

Curtin, Philip D. *The Atlantic Slave Trade: A Census.* Madison: University of Wisconsin Press, 1969.

Davis, David Brion. *The Problem of Slavery in Western Culture.* New York: Cornell University Press, 1966.

Deburg, van William L. *The Slave Drivers: Black Agricultural Labor Supervisors in the Antebellum South.* Westport: Greenwood Press, 1979.

Diamond, Sigmund. "From Organization to Society: Virginia in the

Seventeenth Century." in Stanley N. Katz (ed.). *Colonial America: Essays in Politics and Social Development.* Boston: Little Brown and Company, 1971.

Dockès, Pierre. *Medieval Slavery and Liberation.* Chicago: Chicago University Press, 1982.

Domar, Evsey. "The Causes of Slavery or Serfdom: an Hypothesis." *Journal of Economic History.* 30 (1970): 18–32.

Dunn, Richard S. *Sugar and Slaves.* New York: Norton, 1972.

Eby, Cecil D. "Classical Names among Southern Negro Slaves." *American Speech.* 36 (May, 1961): 140–141.

Elkins, Stanley. *Slavery: A Problem in American Institutional and Intellectual Life.* Chicago: Chicago University Press, 1963.

Eltis, David. *Economic Growth and the Ending of the Slave Trade.* New York: Oxford University Press, 1987.

Engerman, Stanley L. and **Genovese, Eugene** (eds.). *Race and Slavery in the Western Hemisphere: Quantitative Studies.* New Jersey: Princeton University Press, 1975.

Finley, Moses I. *Economy and Society in Ancient Greece.* New York: Penguin, 1983.

Fogel, Robert and **Engerman, Stanley.** *Time on the Cross.* 2 vols. Boston: Brown and Company, 1975. Although heavily and (sometimes unfairly) criticized, *Time on the Cross* probably did more to stimulate studies in slavery and American history than most other works of the same period combined.

Freyre, Gilberto. *The Masters and the Slaves: A Study in the Development of Brazilian Civilization.* New York: Alfred Knopf, 1971.

Galenson, David W. *Traders, Planters and Slaves: Market Behavior in Early English America.* Cambridge: Cambridge University Press, 1986.

Gathorne-Hardy, Jonathan. *The Unnatural History of the Nanny.* New York: The Dial Press, 1973.

Gemery, Henry A. and **Hogendorn, Jan S.** (eds.). *The Uncommon Market: Essays in the Economic History of the Atlantic Slave Trade.* New York: Academic Press, 1979.

Gennep, van Arnold. *The Rites of Passage* trans. Monika B. Vizedom and G. L. Cafee Chicago: University of Chicago Press, 1960.

Genovese, Eugene D. (ed.). *The Slave Economies,* 2 Volumes. New York: John Wiley, 1973.

Genovese, Eugene D. and **Foner, Laura** (eds.). *Slavery in the New World: A Reader in Comparative History.* Englewood Cliffs, N.J.: Prentice Hall, 1969.

_____. *Roll, Jordan, Roll: The World the Slaves Made.* New York: Vintage Books, 1976.

_____. *In Red and Black: Marxian Explorations in Southern and Afro-American History.* Knoxville: The University of Tennessee Press, 1984, originally published 1968.

_____. *From Rebellion to Revolution.* New York: Vintage, 1981.

Greven, Philip. *Four Generations . . . in Colonial Andover, Massachusetts.* Ithaca: Cornell University Press, 1970.

Gutman, Herbert and **Sutch, Richard.** "The Slave Family," in Paul A. David et *al.* (eds.) *Reckoning with Slavery: A Critical Study in the Quantitative History of American Slavery.* New York: Oxford University Press, 1976.

Hajnal, John. "European Marriage Patterns in Perspective." in David V. Glass and David E. C. Eversly (eds.). *Population in History.* London: Arnold, 1965.

Heider, Fritz. *The Psychology of Interpersonal Relations.* New York: John Wiley & Sons, 1958.

Hentig, van, Hans "The Sex Ratio: A Brief Discussion Based on the United States Census Figures." *Social Forces.* 30 4 (May, 1952): 443–9.

Higginbotham, Leon A. *In the Matter of Color: Race and the American Legal Process.* Oxford University Press 1978.

Hoetink, Hermanus. *Slavery and Race Relations in the Americas:* Comparative *Notes on their Nature and Nexus.* New York: Harper Torchbooks, 1973.

Hollingsworth, T. H. *Historical Demography.* Ithaca: Cornell University Press, 1969.

Inkori J.E. (ed.). *Forced Migration: The Impact of the Export Slave Trade on African Societies.* London: Hutchinson University Library, 1982.

Jordan, Winthrop D. *White over Black: American Attitudes towards the Negro, 1550–1880.* Penguin, 1969.

Klein, Herbert S. *The Middle Passage: Comparative Studies in the Atlantic Slave Trade.* Princeton: Princeton University Press, 1978.

Klein, Herbert S. "A Note on Mortality in the French Slave Trade in the Eighteenth Century." in Henry A. Gemery and Jan S. Hogendorn, *The Uncommon Market, Essays in the Economic History of the Atlantic Slave Trade.* New York: Academic Press, 1979.

Kotlikoff, Laurence. "Towards A Quantitative Description of the New Orleans Slave Market." Unpublished paper presented to the University of Chicago Workshop in History, 1975.

Ladurie, Le Roy Emmanuel. *Montaillou: Cathars and Catholics in a French Village, 1294–1324.* Penguin, 1980.

Laslett, Peter, (ed.). *Household and family in past time: Comparative studies . . .* Cambridge: Cambridge University Press, 1972.

Lee, Richard B. "Lactation, Ovulation, Infanticide and Women's work: A Study of Hunter-gatherer Population Regulation" in Mark Nathan Cohen, et al, *Biosocial Mechanisms of Population Control* New Haven: Yale University Press, 1980, pp. 321–348.

Lovejoy, Paul. "Concubinage and the Status of Women Slaves in Early Colonial Northern Nigeria." *Journal of African History* 29 (1988): 245–266.

Malthus, Thomas. *An Essay on the Principle of Population.* Anthony Flew (ed.). Pelican Classics, 1970 edition.

MacMullen, Ramsay. *Roman Social Relations, 50 B.C. to A.D. 284.* New Haven: Yale University Press, 1974.

McPherson, James M. *Ordeal by Fire: The Civil War and Reconstruction.* New York: Alfred A. Knopf, 1982.

Meillassoux, Claude. "Female Slavery," in Robertson and Klein (eds.), *Women and Slavery in Africa.* Madison: University of Wisconsin Press, 1983, 49–66.

Miers, Suzanne and **Kopytoff, Igor** (eds.). *Slavery in Africa: Historical and Anthropological Perspectives.* Madison: University of Wisconsin Press, 1977.

Miller, Joseph Calder. "Mortality in the Atlantic Slave Trade: Statistical Evidence on Causality" *Journal of Interdisciplinary History* 11, No. 3 (Winter 1981): 385–423.

Moller, Herbert. "Sex Compositions and Correlated Culture Patterns of Colonial America." *William and Mary Quarterly.* Second series 2 (1945): 113–153.

Morgan, Edmund S. *American Slavery, American Freedom.* New York: W. W. Norton, 1975.

_____. *The Puritan Family: Religion and Domestic Relations in Seventeenth Century New England.* New York: Harper and Row, 1966.

Mousnier, Roland. *Social Hierarchies: 1450 to the present.* London: Croom Helm, 1973.

Mullin, Gerald W. *Flight and Rebellion: Slave Resistance in Eighteenth-Century Virginia.* London: Oxford University Press, 1972.

Nieboer, H.J. *Slavery as an Industrial System: Ethnological Researches.* New York: Burt Franklin, 1971 original edition,1910.

Palmer, Colin, *Human Cargoes: The British Slave Trade to Spanish America, 1700 to 1739.* Chicago: University of Illinois Press, 1981.

Patterson, Orlando. *Slavery and Social Death: A Comparative Study.* Cambridge: Harvard University Press, 1982.

Phillips, Ulrich Bonnel. *The Slave Economy of the Old South Selected Essays in Economic and Social History.* Edited with an introduction by Eugene D. Genovese, Baton Rouge: Louisiana State University Press, 1968. Reprint of original 1929 edition.

Prunty, Merle. "The Renaissance of the Southern Plantation." *Geographical Review* 45 (October 1955) (4): 470.

Price, Richard (ed.). *Maroon Societies: Rebel Slave Communities in the Americas.* New York: Anchor Books, 1973.

Raboteau, Albert J. *Slave Religion: The Invisible Institution in the Antebellum South.* Oxford: Oxford University Press, 1980.

Renkema, W. E. *Het Curaçaose Plantagebedriif in de negentiende eeuw.* Zutphen: Walburg Press, 1981.

Starobin, Robert S. *Industrial Slavery in the Old South.* Oxford University Press, 1975.

Tadman, Michael. *Speculators and Slaves: Masters, Traders, and Slaves in the Old South.* Madison: University of Wisconsin Press, 1989.

Tannenbaum, Frank. *Slave and Citizen: The Negro in the Americas.* New York: Alfred Knopf, 1946.

Thompson, Edgar T. "Virginia." in Edgar T. Thompson, (ed.). *Race: Individual and Collective Behaviour.* New York: Collier Macmillan, 1958.

Thompson, R. "Seventeenth Century English and Colonial Sex Ratios: A Postscript." *Population Studies* 1 28: 150ff.

Tietze, Christopher. "Reproduction Span and Rate of Reproduction Among Hutterite Women." *Fertility and Sterility.* 8 (January–February, 1957): 89–97.

Turner, Frederick Jackson. *The Frontier in American History,* with a foreword by Ray Allen Billington. New York: Holt, Rinehart and Winston, 1962.

Wade, Richard C. *Slavery in the Cities: The South 1820–1860.* Oxford University Press, 1972.

Weber, Max. *The Theory of Social and Economic Organization.* Translated by A.M. Henderson and Talcott Parsons. Oxford University Press, 1947.

Wiedemann, T.E.J. "Slavery" no. 19 in *Greece and Rome,* New Surveys in the Classics. Oxford: The Clarendon Press, 1987.

Wood, Peter H. *Black Majority: Negroes in South Carolina, from 1670 through the Stono Rebellion.* New York: Norton & Co., 1975.

Index

Aart, Theunis van (free knecht, 1731), 10

Abolition, of oceanic slave trade (1808) xxix; and age composition of slaves, 78; and bonded labor, 32; and creolization, 47–48, 58; and date of decree, xxx; and demography, xxxiv, 65, 124, 299; and manumission, 105, 384, 387; and the market for slaves, 89, 94; and orphans, 128; and prices of slaves, 122–123; and Prize Negroes, 146–147; and sex composition, 72, 73, 156; and slave families, 114–115; and stereotyping, 53; and urban proportion of slaves, 140. *See also* Oceanic slave trade

Abolitionists, xxxvi, 25, 101, 106, 108, 121, 130–132

Abortions, 312. *See also* Fertility

Abraham (slave, 1749), 390

Abyssinia, Cornelia van and Lijsbeth van (slaves, 1655), 42, 80

Adelaar, Jurian, 9

Adonis (slave, 1830), 257

Adriaanus, Lambert, 207

Adult naming patterns, 235

Afrikaans, 61–64, 227

Afrikaner, 56–57, 64. *See also* Identity

Age of slaves, 48; of combined slave populations, 78; in domestic market, 127; of Lodge, 77–78; range of, 84, 157; by region, 159

Albany (Eastern Cape), 36, 150, 157

Alders, Jan van Amsterdam (widow, 1720s), 378

Alkman, Cornelis Brust van (soldier, 1692), 253

Alleman, Rudolph, 269

Amenorrhea, 305

America (North): bartering of slaves, 108; concentration camps,183; conception of slavery, xxxiii; distribution of slaves, 151; division of slave labor, 159; domestic market for slaves, 86–87; indentured labor, 25; interracial marriages, 318; manumission, 383, 388; mulatto women, 57–58; overseers, 22; passes for urban slaves, 141–142; prices of slaves and stereotypes, 50; sex composition of slaves, 67–68, 73; slave distributions in, 135–136; slave traders, 106; slave women, 290

Amersvoort, 78–79

Amsterdam Classis, 338–339

Anabaptists, 340

Ancestry. *See* Descent

Andrews, Ethan Allen, 108

Andries (slave, 1721), 23

Andries (Lodge slave, 1693), 187

Andriesz, Pieter (knecht, 1692), 14

Anglo-Dutch War, 44–45

Angola, 249, 330, 404

Angola, Anthoni van (free black, 17th c.), 22

Angola, Anthony van (slave, 1671), 116

Anthropology, xxvi, 85; descent systems, 238

Apprenticeship system, 35, 144–145, 147, 148, 157, 364

Arab traders, 67, 189

Arabia, Achmet van (free black, 1824), 42

Architecture, 258, 261, 282

Armstrong, James Clyde, 5, 43, 67, 232, 428, 434

Arrack, 317

Arson, 248, 264–265, 272, 279

Artisans. *See* Occupations

Asiaam, Chinees (Lodge slave, 1693), 187

Aspeling, Eric (colonist), 360

Auctions: authenticity of records, 437; and notarial documents, 90, 429; in older districts, 148; of slaves, 49, 108, 109, 114, 160, 170; types of, 99

Ayliff, John, 34

Baaren slaves, xxxiv, 55, 81, 103, 169

Babijlonsche Tooren (farm), 59

Bachelors, 11, 18, 74, 217, 392

481